BaseBall america
DIRECTORY

CONNECT WITH US!

 **/USABaseball**

Join the more than 200,000 fans who like us on Facebook.

 **@USABaseball**

Over 50,000 people receive breaking news and special offers by following us on Twitter.

@USABaseball

Follow us on Instagram for a behind-the-scenes look at USA Baseball's events.

OUR PASTIME'S FUTURE

usabaseball.com

Baseball america
DIRECTORY

Editors
JOSH NORRIS, KEGAN LOWE

Assistant Editors
J.J. COOPER, MICHAEL LANANNA,
TEDDY CAHILL,
KYLE GLASER, BEN BADLER

Contributing
PAUL TRAP

Database & Application Development
BRENT LEWIS

Photo Editor
BRENDAN NOLAN

Design & Production
JAMES ALWORTH,
SARA HIATT MCDANIEL,
LINWOOD WEBB

Programming & Technical Development
BRENT LEWIS

Cover Photo
ED WOLFSTEIN

DISTRIBUTED BY SIMON & SCHUSTER ISBN-13: 978-1-932391-77-0

Baseball america
ESTABLISHED 1981
P.O. Box 12877, Durham, NC 27709 • Phone (919) 682-9635

EDITOR AND PUBLISHER B.J. Schecter *@bjschecter*
EXECUTIVE EDITORS J.J. Cooper *@jjcoop36*
Matt Eddy *@matteddyba*
DIRECTOR OF BUSINESS DEVELOPMENT Ben Leigh

EDITORIAL
ASSOCIATE EDITORS Kegan Lowe *@KeganLowe*
Josh Norris *@jnorris427*
SENIOR WRITER Ben Badler *@benbadler*
NATIONAL WRITERS Teddy Cahill *@tedcahill*
Carlos Collazo *@CarlosACollazo*
Kyle Glaser *@KyleAGlaser*
Michael Lananna *@mlananna*
SPECIAL CONTRIBUTOR Tim Newcomb *@tdnewcomb*

PRODUCTION
DESIGN & PRODUCTION DIRECTOR Sara Hiatt McDaniel
MULTIMEDIA MANAGER Linwood Webb
DESIGN ASSISTANT James Alworth

ADVERTISING
ADVERTISING DIRECTOR George Shelton
DIGITAL SALES MANAGER Larry Sarzyniak

BUSINESS
DIRECTOR OF OPERATIONS Hailey Carpenter
TECHNOLOGY MANAGER Brent Lewis
CUSTOMER SERVICE Jonathan Smith

STATISTICAL SERVICE
MAJOR LEAGUE BASEBALL ADVANCED MEDIA

BASEBALL AMERICA ENTERPRISES
CHAIRMAN & CEO Gary Green
PRESIDENT Larry Botel
GENERAL COUNSEL Matthew Pace
DIRECTOR OF MARKETING Amy Heart
INVESTOR RELATIONS Michele Balfour
DIRECTOR OF OPERATIONS Joan Disalvo
PARTNERS Jon Ashley
Stephen Alepa
Martie Cordaro
Brian Rothschild
Andrew Fox
Maurice Haroche
Dan Waldman
Sonny Kalsi
Glenn Isaacson
Robert Hernreich
Craig Amazeen
Peter Ruprecht
Beryl Snyder
Tom Steiglehner

3STEP
MANAGING PARTNER David Geaslen
CHIEF CONTENT OFFICER Jonathan Segal
CHIEF FINANCIAL OFFICER Sue Murphy
DIRECTOR OF DIGITAL CONTENT Tom Johnson
DIRECTOR OF OPERATIONS, DATABASE/VIDEO Brendan Nolan

Experience baseball history year-round
VISIT US IN COOPERSTOWN
and at
BASEBALLHALL.ORG

PRESERVING HISTORY. HONORING EXCELLENCE. CONNECTING GENERATIONS.

NATIONAL
★ ★ ★ ★ ★
BASEBALL
HALL OF FAME

TABLE OF CONTENTS

ED WOLFSTEIN

DAVID J. GRIFFIN/ICON SPORTSWIRE VIA GETTY IMAGES

WHAT'S NEW IN 2018

TRIPLE-A
Name Changes: Gwinnett Braves become Gwinnett Stripers

HIGH CLASS A
Name Changes: Tampa Yankees become Tampa Tarpons.

ROOKIE
Affiliation Changes: Greeneville (Appalachian) from Astros to Reds.
Affiliation Additions: Phillies adding a second Gulf Coast League team. Cubs, Giants, Indians adding a second Arizona League team.

BASEBALL... IT'S IN OUR DNA

LIVE LOOK-INS AND ANALYSIS ON MLB TONIGHT™
PLUS 5 LIVE GAMES EACH WEEK

MLB NETWORK™

OUR NATIONAL PASTIME
ALL THE TIME®

Map illustrations by Paul Trap

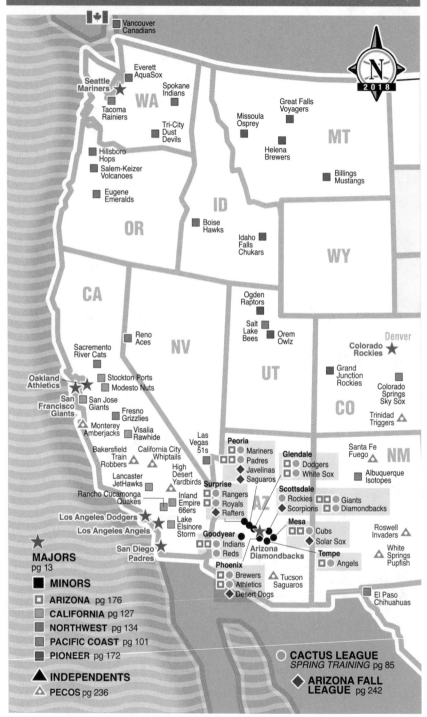

N 2018

Vancouver Canadians

Everett AquaSox

Seattle Mariners

Spokane Indians

WA

Tacoma Rainiers

Tri-City Dust Devils

Great Falls Voyagers

Missoula Osprey

MT

Hillsboro Hops

Salem-Keizer Volcanoes

Helena Brewers

Billings Mustangs

Eugene Emeralds

OR

ID

Boise Hawks

Idaho Falls Chukars

WY

CA

Reno Aces

Ogden Raptors

Denver

Sacramento River Cats

NV

Salt Lake Bees

Orem Owlz

Colorado Rockies

Oakland Athletics

Stockton Ports

Modesto Nuts

UT

Grand Junction Rockies

Colorado Springs Sky Sox

San Francisco Giants

San Jose Giants

Fresno Grizzlies

CO

Trinidad Triggers

Monterey Amberjacks

Visalia Rawhide

Las Vegas 51s

Peoria

Santa Fe Fuego

NM

Bakersfield Train Robbers

California City Whiptails

Mariners
Padres
Javelinas
Saguaros

Glendale

Dodgers
White Sox

Albuquerque Isotopes

Lancaster JetHawks

High Desert Yardbirds

Surprise

Scottsdale

Rockies
Scorpions

Giants
Diamondbacks

Rancho Cucamonga Quakes

Inland Empire 66ers

Rangers
Royals
Rafters

AZ

Roswell Invaders

Los Angeles Dodgers

Los Angeles Angels

Lake Elsinore Storm

Mesa

Cubs
Solar Sox

White Springs Pupfish

Goodyear

Indians
Reds

Arizona Diamondbacks

Tempe

Angels

San Diego Padres

Phoenix

Brewers
Athletics
Desert Dogs

Tucson Saguaros

El Paso Chihuahuas

MAJORS
pg 13

MINORS

☐ **ARIZONA** pg 176

☐ **CALIFORNIA** pg 127

☐ **NORTHWEST** pg 134

☐ **PACIFIC COAST** pg 101

☐ **PIONEER** pg 172

▲ **INDEPENDENTS**

△ **PECOS** pg 236

○ **CACTUS LEAGUE**
SPRING TRAINING pg 85

◆ **ARIZONA FALL**
LEAGUE pg 242

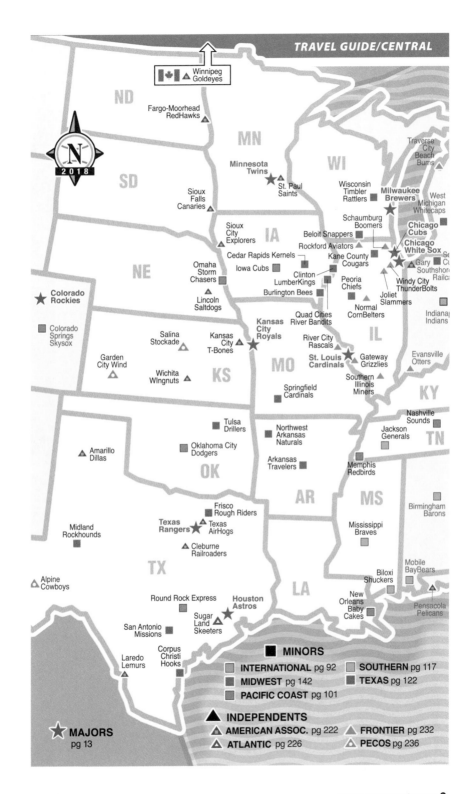

Winnipeg Goldeyes

ND

Fargo-Moorhead RedHawks

N 2018

SD

MN

Traverse City Beach Bums

WI

Minnesota Twins

St. Paul Saints

Wisconsin Timber Rattlers

Milwaukee Brewers

West Michigan Whitecaps

Sioux Falls Canaries

Schaumburg Boomers

Chicago Cubs

Sioux City Explorers

IA

Beloit Snappers

Rockford Aviators

Chicago White Sox

Gary Southshore Railca

Omaha Storm Chasers

Cedar Rapids Kernels

Iowa Cubs

Kane County Cougars

NE

Clinton LumberKings

Peoria Chiefs

Windy City ThunderBolts

Lincoln Saltdogs

Burlington Bees

Joliet Slammers

Colorado Rockies

Quad Cities River Bandits

Normal CornBelters

Indianap Indians

Colorado Springs Skysox

Kansas City Royals

Salina Stockade

Kansas City T-Bones

River City Rascals

IL

Garden City Wind

Wichita WIngnuts

KS

MO

St. Louis Cardinals

Gateway Grizzlies

Evansville Otters

Southern Illinois Miners

KY

Springfield Cardinals

Nashville Sounds

Tulsa Drillers

Northwest Arkansas Naturals

Jackson Generals

TN

Amarillo Dillas

Oklahoma City Dodgers

Arkansas Travelers

Memphis Redbirds

OK

AR

MS

Birmingham Barons

Frisco Rough Riders

Midland Rockhounds

Texas Rangers

Texas AirHogs

Mississippi Braves

Cleburne Railroaders

TX

Mobile BayBears

Alpine Cowboys

LA

Biloxi Shuckers

Round Rock Express

Houston Astros

New Orleans Baby Cakes

Pensacola Pelicans

San Antonio Missions

Sugar Land Skeeters

Laredo Lemurs

Corpus Christi Hooks

■ **MINORS**

□ **INTERNATIONAL** pg 92   □ **SOUTHERN** pg 117

■ **MIDWEST** pg 142   ■ **TEXAS** pg 122

■ **PACIFIC COAST** pg 101

▲ **INDEPENDENTS**

★ **MAJORS**
pg 13

▲ **AMERICAN ASSOC.** pg 222   △ **FRONTIER** pg 232

△ **ATLANTIC** pg 226   △ **PECOS** pg 236

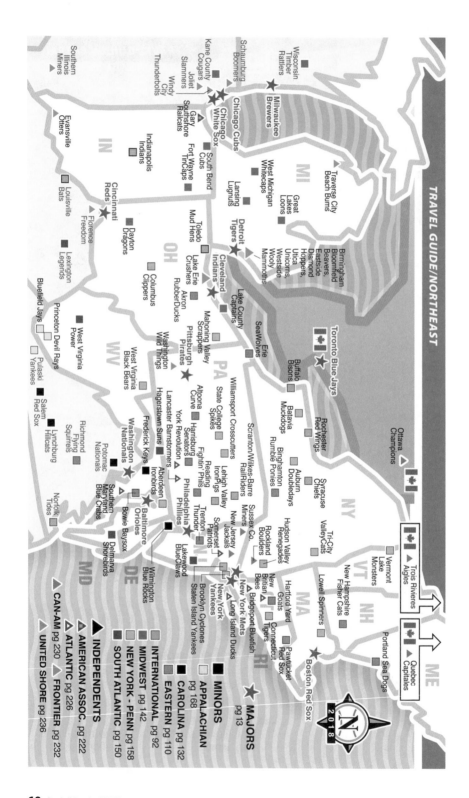

MAJORS pg 13

MINORS
INTERNATIONAL pg 92
EASTERN pg 110
CAROLINA pg 132
APPALACHIAN pg 168
SOUTH ATLANTIC pg 150
NEW YORK - PENN pg 158
MIDWEST pg 142

INDEPENDENTS
AMERICAN ASSOC. pg 222
ATLANTIC pg 226
FRONTIER pg 232
CAN-AM pg 230
UNITED SHORE pg 236

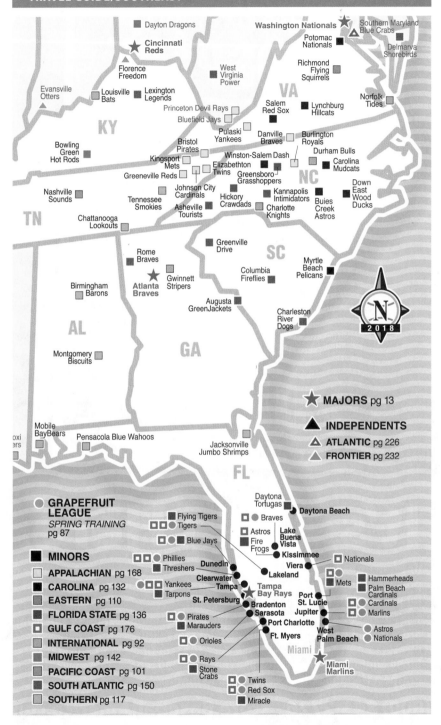

Dayton Dragons
Cincinnati Reds
Washington Nationals
Southern Maryland Blue Crabs
Potomac Nationals
Delmarva Shorebirds
Florence Freedom
West Virginia Power
Richmond Flying Squirrels
Evansville Otters
Louisville Bats
Lexington Legends
VA
Salem Red Sox
Lynchburg Hillcats
Norfolk Tides
Princeton Devil Rays
Bluefield Jays
KY
Pulaski Yankees
Danville Braves
Burlington Royals
Bowling Green Hot Rods
Bristol Pirates
Kingsport Mets
Winston-Salem Dash
Durham Bulls
Carolina Mudcats
Elizabethton Twins
Greeneville Reds
Greensboro Grasshoppers
NC
Down East Wood Ducks
Nashville Sounds
Johnson City Cardinals
Hickory Crawdads
Kannapolis Intimidators
Buies Creek Astros
Tennessee Smokies
Asheville Tourists
Charlotte Knights
TN
Chattanooga Lookouts
Greenville Drive
SC
Rome Braves
Myrtle Beach Pelicans
Birmingham Barons
Columbia Fireflies
Atlanta Braves
Gwinnett Stripers
Augusta GreenJackets
Charleston River Dogs
N 2018
AL
GA
Montgomery Biscuits

⭐ **MAJORS** pg 13

Mobile BayBears
oxi rs
Pensacola Blue Wahoos
Jacksonville Jumbo Shrimps
▲ **INDEPENDENTS**
△ **ATLANTIC** pg 226
▲ **FRONTIER** pg 232

FL

Daytona Tortugas
● **GRAPEFRUIT LEAGUE**
SPRING TRAINING pg 87
Daytona Beach
Flying Tigers
Braves
Tigers
Astros
Lake Buena Vista
Blue Jays
Fire Frogs
Kissimmee
Nationals
■ **MINORS**
Phillies
Viera
□ **APPALACHIAN** pg 168
Threshers
Dunedin
Hammerheads
■ **CAROLINA** pg 132
Yankees
Clearwater
Lakeland
Mets
Palm Beach Cardinals
□ **EASTERN** pg 110
Tarpons
Tampa
Tampa Bay Rays
Cardinals
□ **FLORIDA STATE** pg 136
St. Petersburg
Port St. Lucie
Marlins
■ **GULF COAST** pg 176
Pirates
Marauders
Bradenton
Sarasota
Jupiter
Astros
□ **INTERNATIONAL** pg 92
Orioles
Port Charlotte
Ft. Myers
West Palm Beach
Nationals
□ **MIDWEST** pg 142
Rays
■ **PACIFIC COAST** pg 101
Stone Crabs
Miami
□ **SOUTH ATLANTIC** pg 150
Twins
Miami Marlins
□ **SOUTHERN** pg 117
Red Sox
Miracle

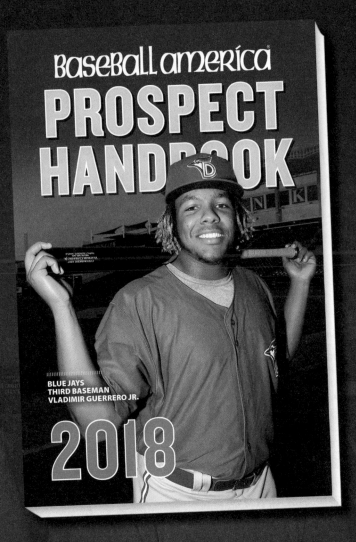

MAJOR
LEAGUES

MAJOR LEAGUE BASEBALL

Mailing Address: 245 Park Ave. New York, NY 10167.
Telephone: (212) 931-7800. **Website:** www.mlb.com.
Commissioner of Baseball: Rob Manfred.
Chief Communications Officer: Pat Courtney. **Chief Legal Officer:** Dan Halem. **Chief Operating Officer:** Tony Petitti. **Chief Financial Officer/Sr. Advisor:** Bob Starkey. **Chief Baseball Officer:** Joe Torre. **Executive Vice President, Commerce:** Noah Garden. **Executive Vice President, Strategy, Technology/Innovation:** Chris Marinak. **Executive Vice President, Product /Marketing:** Chris Park. **Chief Technology Officer:** Jason Gaedtke.

Rob Manfred

BASEBALL OPERATIONS

Senior VP, Baseball Operations: Kim Ng, Peter Woodfork. **Senior VP, Standards/Operations:** Joe Garagiola Jr. **Senior Director, Major League Operations:** Roy Krasik. **Senior Director, International Baseball Operations:** Chris Haydock. **Senior Director, Baseball Operations:** Jeff Pfeifer. **Senior Director, Major League Scouting Bureau:** Bill Bavasi. **Director, Minor League Operations:** Fred Seymour. **Senior Manager, Amateur Relations:** Chuck Fox. **Senior Manager, Latin American Game Development:** Joel Araujo. **Senior Manager, International Baseball Operations:** Giovanni Hernandez. **Manager, International Baseball Investigation & Compliance:** Melissa Bristol. **Coordinator, Umpire Operations:** Alejandro Bermudez. **Manager, International Baseball Operations:** Rebecca Seesel. **Manager, International Baseball Operations:** Shane Barclay. **Senior Coordinator, Major League Operations:** Gina Liento. **Senior Coordinator, On Field Operations:** Michael Sansarran. **Senior Coordinator, Baseball Operations:** Garrett Horan. **Senior Coordinator, Scouting Operations:** William Clements. **Pace of Game Analyst:** Chris Knettel. **Coordinator, International Baseball Operations:** Max Thomas. **Coordinator, International Baseball Operations:** Patrick Nathanson. **Executive Assistant, Baseball Operations:** Chris Romanello. **Senior Administrative Assistant:** Llubia Reyes-Bussey. **Senior Director, Umpire Operations:** Matt McKendry. **Senior Director, Instant Replay:** Justin Klemm. **Director, Major League Umpiring:** Randy Marsh. **Director, Umpiring Development:** Rich Rieker. **Director, Umpire Medical Services:** Mark Letendre. **Umpiring Supervisors:** Cris Jones, Tom Leppard, Chuck Meriwether, Ed Montague, Ed Rapuano, Charlie Reliford, Larry Young. **Manager, Instant Replay:** Jeffrey Moody. **Manager, Umpire Operations:** Raquel Wagner. **Senior Video Coordinator:** Freddie Hernandez. **Baseball Systems:** Nancy Crofts. Director, **Dominican Operations:** Rafael Perez. **Director, Arizona Fall League:** Steve Cobb.

COMMUNICATIONS

Telephone: (212) 931-7878. **Fax:** (212) 949-5654.
VP, Communications: John Blundell, Mike Teevan. **VP, Business Communications:** Matt Bourne. **Senior Director, Business Communications:** Steve Arocho, Ileana Peña. **Director, Communications:** Donald Muller. **Manager, Communications:** Lydia Devlin. **Specialist, Business Communications:** David Hochman. **Coordinator, Communications:** Yolyana Alvarez, Paul Koehler. **Coordinator, Business Communications:** Kerline Batista. **Executive Assistant, Communications:** Ginger Dillon. **Official Historian:** John Thorn.

AMERICAN LEAGUE

Year League Founded: 1901.
2018 Opening Date: March 29. **Closing Date:** Sept. 30.
Regular Season: 162 games.
Division Structure: East—Baltimore, Boston, New York, Tampa Bay, Toronto.
Central—Chicago, Cleveland, Detroit, Kansas City, Minnesota. **West**—Houston, Los Angeles, Oakland, Seattle, Texas.

Playoff Format: Two non-division winners with best records meet in one-game wildcard playoff. Wildcard winner and three division champions meet in two best-of-five Division Series. Winners meet in best-of-seven Championship Series.

All-Star Game: July 17, Nationals Park, Washington, D.C. (American League vs. National League).
Roster Limit: 25, through Aug. 31, when rosters expand to 40. **Brand of Baseball:** Rawlings.
Statistician: MLB Advanced Media, 75 Ninth Ave., 5th Floor, New York, NY 10011.

STADIUM INFORMATION

Team	Stadium	Dimensions			Capacity	2017 Att.
		LF	CF	RF		
Baltimore	Oriole Park at Camden Yards	333	410	318	45,971	2,028,424
Boston	Fenway Park	310	390	302	37,673	2,917,678
Chicago	Guaranteed Rate Field	330	400	335	40,615	1,629,470
Cleveland	Progressive Field	325	405	325	37,675	2,048,138
Detroit	Comerica Park	345	420	330	41,782	2,321,599
Houston	Minute Maid Park	315	435	326	40,976	2,306,623
Kansas City	Kauffman Stadium	330	410	330	37,903	2,220,370
Los Angeles	Angel Stadium	333	404	333	45,050	3,019,583
Minnesota	Target Field	339	404	328	39,504	2,051,279
New York	Yankee Stadium	318	408	314	50,291	3,146,966
Oakland	Oakland Coliseum	330	400	367	35,067	1,475,721
Seattle	Safeco Field	331	401	326	47,447	2,135,445
Tampa Bay	Tropicana Field	315	404	322	41,315	1,253,619
Texas	Globe Life Park in Arlington	332	400	325	48,114	2,507,760
Toronto	Rogers Centre	328	400	328	50,598	3,203,886

NATIONAL LEAGUE

Year League Founded: 1876.
2018 Opening Date: March 29. **Closing Date:** Sept. 30.
Regular Season: 162 games.
Division Structure: East—Atlanta, Miami, New York, Philadelphia, Washington.
Central—Chicago, Cincinnati, Milwaukee, Pittsburgh, St. Louis. **West**—Arizona, Colorado, Los Angeles, San Diego, San Francisco.

Playoff Format: Two non-division winners with best records meet in one-game wildcard playoff. Wildcard winner and three division champions meet in two best-of-five Division Series. Winners meet in best-of-seven Championship Series.

All-Star Game: July 17, Nationals Park, Washington, D.C. (American League vs. National League).
Roster Limit: 25, through Aug. 31 when rosters expand to 40. **Brand of Baseball:** Rawlings.
Statistician: MLB Advanced Media, 75 Ninth Ave., 5th Floor, New York, NY 10011.

STADIUM INFORMATION

Team	Stadium	Dimensions			Capacity	2017 Att.
		LF	CF	RF		
Arizona	Chase Field	330	407	334	49,033	2,134,375
Atlanta	SunTrust Park	335	400	325	41,500	2,505,252
Chicago	Wrigley Field	355	400	353	41,160	3,199,562
Cincinnati	Great American Ball Park	328	404	325	42,319	1,836,917
Colorado	Coors Field	347	415	350	50,499	2,602,524
Los Angeles	Dodger Stadium	330	395	330	56,000	3,765,856
Miami	Marlins Park	344	407	335	36,742	1,651,997
Milwaukee	Miller Park	344	400	345	41,900	2,558,722
New York	Citi Field	335	408	330	42,200	2,460,622
Philadelphia	Citizens Bank Park	329	401	330	43,647	1,905,354
Pittsburgh	PNC Park	325	399	320	38,496	1,919,447
St. Louis	Busch Stadium	336	400	335	46,681	3,447,937
San Diego	Petco Park	336	396	322	42,685	2,138,491
San Francisco	AT&T Park	339	399	309	41,503	3,303,652
Washington	Nationals Park	336	402	335	41,888	2,524,980

Arizona Diamondbacks

Office Address: Chase Field, 401 E. Jefferson St, Phoenix, AZ 85004.
Mailing Address: P.O. Box 2095, Phoenix, AZ 85001.
Telephone: (602) 462-6500. **Fax:** (602) 462-6599. **Website:** www.dbacks.com

OWNERSHIP
Managing General Partner: Ken Kendrick. **General Partners:** Mike Chipman, Jeff Royer.

BUSINESS OPERATIONS

President/CEO: Derrick Hall. **Executive Vice President, Business Operations/Chief Revenue Officer:** Cullen Maxey. **Executive Vice President/Chief Financial Officer:** Tom Harris. **Senior Advisor, President/CEO:** Luis Gonzalez. **Special Assistants, President/CEO:** Roland Hemond, Randy Johnson, J.J. Putz, Willie Bloomquist. **Special Advisor on Mexico, President/CEO:** Erubiel Durazo. **Executive Assistant, President/CEO:** Brooke Mitchell. **Executive Assistant, Managing General Partner & CFO:** Sandy Cox. **Executive Assistant, CRO:** Katy Bernham. **Executive Office Administrative Assistant:** Nicki Adair.

BROADCASTING
VP, Broadcasting: Scott Geyer. **Senior Director, Game Operations/DBTV Productions:** Rob Weinheimer.

Ken Kendrick

CORPORATE PARTNERSHIPS/MARKETING
VP, Corporate Partnerships: Judd Norris. **Senior Director, Corporate Partnership Services:** Kerri White. **VP, Marketing/Analytics:** Kenny Farrell. **Director, Marketing:** Rayme Lofgren. **Senior Manager, Hispanic Marketing:** Jerry Romo.

FINANCE/LEGAL
VP, Finance: Craig Bradley. **Director, Financial Management and Purchasing:** Jeff Jacobs. **Director, Accounting:** Jeffrey Barnes. **Senior VP and Chief Legal Officer:** Nona Lee. **Senior Counsel:** Caleb Jay.

COMMUNITY AFFAIRS
VP, Corporate/Community Impact: Debbie Castaldo. **Director, Community Events:** Robert Itzkowitz. **Senior Manager, Community/Foundation Operations:** Tara Trzinski. **Senior Manager, Community Initiatives/Partner Programs:** Dustin Payne.

COMMUNICATIONS/MEDIA RELATIONS
Senior VP, Content/Communications: Josh Rawitch. **Senior Director, Player/Media Relations:** Casey Wilcox. **Senior Manager, Player/Media Relations:** Patrick O'Connell. **Manager, Player/Media Relations:** Patrick Kurish. **Senior Manager, Corporate Communications:** Katie Krause.

SPECIAL PROJECTS/FAN EXPERIENCE
VP, Special Projects: Graham Rossini. **Director, Special Projects/Brand Development:** Matt Helmeid. **Director, Baseball Outreach/Development:** Jeff Rodin. **General Manager, Salt River Fields:** David Dunne.

2018 SCHEDULE
Standard Game Times: 6:40 p.m.; Sun. 1:10.

MARCH	8-9 . . . at Los Angeles (NL)	29-30 . . . . . San Francisco	13-14 . . . . .at Texas
29-31 . . . . .Colorado	10-13 . . . . . .Washington	**JULY**	16-19 . . . . . at San Diego
	14-16 . . . . . . .Milwaukee	1 . . . . San Francisco	21-22 . . . Los Angeles (AL)
APRIL	18-20 . . . at New York (NL)	2-4 . . . . St. Louis	24-26 . . . . Seattle
2-4 . . . . . Los Angeles (NL)	21-23 . . . . . at Milwaukee	5-8 . . . . San Diego	27-29 . . . at San Francisco
5-8 . . . . .at St. Louis	25-27 . . . . . . .at Oakland	10-12 . . . . . . at Colorado	30-31 . at Los Angeles (NL)
9-11 . . . at San Francisco	28-30 . . . . Cincinnati	13-15 . . . . . . at Atlanta	
13-15 . at Los Angeles (NL)		20-22 . . . . .Colorado	**SEPTEMBER**
17-19 . . . . San Francisco	**JUNE**	23-26 . . .at Chicago (NL)	1-2 . . at Los Angeles (NL)
20-22 . . . . . . San Diego	1-3 . . . . .Miami	27-29 . . . at San Diego	3-4 . . . . San Diego
24-26 . . . . at Philadelphia	4-6 . . . . . at San Francisco	30-31 . . . . Texas	6-9 . . . . Atlanta
27-29 . . . . at Washington	8-10 . . . . at Colorado		10-13 . . . . . at Colorado
30 . . . . . Los Angeles (NL)	11-13 . . . . Pittsburgh	**AUGUST**	14-16 . . . . . .at Houston
	14-17 . . . . .New York (NL)	2-5 . . . . . . San Francisco	17-19 . . . . . Chicago (NL)
MAY	18-19 . at Los Angeles (AL)	6-8 . . . . .Philadelphia	21-23 . . . . .Colorado
1-3 . . . . Los Angeles (NL)	21-24 . . . . at Pittsburgh	10-12 . . . . .at Cincinnati	24-26 . . . Los Angeles (NL)
4-6 . . . . Houston	25-28 . . . . at Miami		28-30 . . . . . at San Diego

GENERAL INFORMATION
Stadium (year opened): Chase Field (1998). **Home Dugout:** Third Base.
Team Colors: Sedona Red, Sonoran Sand and Black. **Playing Surface:** Grass.

TICKET SALES

Telephone: (602) 514-8400. **Fax:** (602) 462-4141. **Senior VP, Ticket Sales/Marketing:** John Fisher. **Senior Director, Ticket Sales:** Ryan Holmstedt. **Director, Ticket Operations:** Josh Simon. **Director, Business Analytics:** Brandon Buser. **Director, Season Ticket Sales/Inside Sales:** Mike Dellosa. **Director, Season Ticket Services:** Jamie Roberts.

BASEBALL OPERATIONS

Executive Vice President/General Manager: Mike Hazen. **Senior VP/Assistant GMs:** Jared Porter, Amiel Sawdaye. **VP, Latin Operations:** Junior Noboa. **Special Assistants to GM:** Burke Badenhop, Craig Shipley. **Director, Baseball Operations:** Sam Eaton. **Director, Research & Development:** Michael Fitzgerald. **Coordinator, Amateur Scouting & Baseball Administration:** Kristyn Pierce. **Assistant, Baseball Operations:** Chris Slivka. **Baseball Operations Fellow:** Alex Lorenzo. **Baseball Systems Lead Architect:** John Krazit. **Senior Baseball Systems Developer:** Deron Brown. **Mathematical Modeler, Baseball Analytics:** Cody Callahan. **Quantitative Researcher, Baseball Analytics:** Max Glick. **Baseball Analyst:** Max Phillips. **Pitching Strategist:** Dan Haren. **Hitting Strategist:** Robert Van Scoyoc.

Mike Hazen

MAJOR LEAGUE STAFF

Manager: Torey Lovullo. **Coaches: Bench**—Jerry Narron, **Pitching**—Mike Butcher, **Hitting**—Dave Magadan, **First Base**—Dave McKay, **Third Base**—Tony Perezchica, **Bullpen**—Mike Fetters, **Assistant Hitting Coach**—Tim Laker, **Quality Control/Catching**—Robby Hammock, **Major League**—Luis Urueta. **Bullpen Catcher**— Mark Reed, Humberto Quintero.

MEDICAL/TRAINING

Club Physician: Dr. Gary Waslewski. **Director, Sports Medicine & Performance:** Ken Crenshaw. **Head Trainer:** Ryan DiPanfilo. **Strength & Conditioning Coordinator:** Nate Shaw. **Assistant Strength & Conditioning Coordinator:** Matt Tenney. **Physical Therapist:** Ben Hagar.

PLAYER DEVELOPMENT

VP, Player Development: Mike Bell. **Assistant Director, Player Development:** Josh Barfield. **Senior Manager, Player Development:** Shawn Marette. **Assistant, Player Development:** Peter Bransfield. **Assistant, Latin American Baseball Operations:** Mariana Patraca. **Coordinators:** J.R. House (field/catching), Gil Velazquez (infield), Dan Carlson (pitching), Wellington Cepeda (short-season pitching), Chris Cron (hitting), Orlando Hudson (assistant), Rolando Arnedo (DSL coordinator), Kyle Torgerson (medical), Ryne Eubanks (assistant medical), Max Esposito (manual performance), Brad Arnsberg (rehab pitching), Vaughn Robinson (strength), Cory Swope (video), Jason Gallagher (assistant video), Bob Bensinger (complex). **Medical Administrator:** Jon Herzner. **Hillsboro Consultant:** Ben Petrick.

FARM SYSTEM

Class	Club (League)	Manager	Hitting Coach	Pitching Coach
Triple-A	Reno (PCL)	Greg Gross	Jason Camilli	Gil Heredia
Double-A	Jackson (SL)	Shelley Duncan	Vince Harrison	Doug Drabek
High A	Visalia (CAL)	Joe Mather	Franklin Stubbs	Jeff Bajenaru
Low A	Kane County (MWL)	Blake Lalli	Rick Short	Rich Sauveur
Short-season	Hillsboro (NWL)	Shawn Roof	Micah Franklin	Mike Parrott
Rookie	Missoula (PIO)	Mike Benjamin	Jose Amado	Shane Loux
Rookie	Diamondbacks (AZL)	Darrin Garner	Jonny Gomes	Manny Garcia

SCOUTING

Telephone: (602) 462-6500. **Fax:** (602) 462-6425.

Director, Amateur Scouting: Deric Ladnier. **Coordinator, Amateur Scouting:** Ian Rebhan. **Director, Pro Scouting:** Jason Parks. **Coordinator, Pro Scouting:** Cory Hahn. **Director, Latin American Scouting:** Cesar Geronimo. **Assistant Director, International Scouting:** Peter Wardell. **Director, Pacific Rim Operations:** Mack Hayashi. **Special Assistant, Pacific Rim Operations:** Jim Marshall. **National Crosscheckers:** Greg Lonigro (Connellsville, PA), James Merriweather III (Glendale, AZ). **National Pitching Supervisor:** Jeff Mousser (Gilbert, AZ). **National Junior College Supervisor:** Clark Crist (Phoenix, AZ). **Regional Supervisors:** Steve Connelly (Emerald Isle, NC), Frank Damas (Miami Lakes, FL), Steve McAllister (Chillicothe, IL), Doyle Wilson (Queen Creek, AZ). **Area Scouts:** Hudson Belinsky (Smyrna, GA), Nathan Birtwell (St. Louis, MO), Eric Cruz (Miami, FL), Orsino Hill (Elk Grove, CA), Kerry Jenkins (Nashville, TN), Jeremy Kehrt (Avon, IN), Hal Kurtzman (Lake Balboa, CA), Jeremiah Luster (Oceanside, CA), Rick Matsko (Davidsville, PA), Rusty Pendergrass (Missouri City, MO), Donnie Reynolds (Portland, OR), Mark Ross (Tucson,AZ), JR Salinas (Dallas, TX), Dennis Sheehan (Glasco, NY), George Swain (Wilmington, NC), Garry Templeton (San Marcos, CA), Jake Williams (Kansas City, MO), Luke Wrenn (Lakeland, FL). **Part-Time Scouts:** Doug Mathieson (Aldergrove, BC), Homer Newlin (Tallahassee, FL), Jerry Nyman (Stevensville, MT). **Major League Scouts:** Bill Bryk (Schererville, IN), Bill Gayton (San Diego, CA), Mike Piatnik (Winter Haven, FL). **Special Assignment Scouts:** Todd Greene (Alpharetta, GA), Alex Jacobs (Lakeland, FL), Mark Snipp (The Woodlands, TX), Tim Wilken (Dunedin, FL). **Professional Scouts:** Tucker Blair (Estero, FL), Mike Brown (Naples, FL), Chris Carminucci (Scottsdale, AZ), Bob Cummings (Oak Lawn, IL), Clay Daniel (Jacksonville, FL), Jeff Gardner (Costa Mesa, CA), Jack Goin (Eagan, MN), Drew Hedman (Phoenix, AZ), Brad Kelley (Scottsdale, AZ), Rob Leary (Melbourne, FL), TR Lewis (Marietta, GA), Tom Romenesko (Santee, CA), Scipio Spinks (Sugarland, TX). **Crosschecker, Latin America:** Francisco Cartaya (Collierville, TN), Luis Baez (Dominican Republic). **Supervisor, Venezuela:** Antonio Caballero. Coordinator, **Dominican Republic:** Omar Rogers. **International Scouts:** Jose Ortiz, Rafael Mateo, Ronald Rivas, Diego Bordas (Dominican Republic); Alfonzo Mora, Didimo Bracho, Kristians Pereira, David Chicarelli, Gregory Blanco (Venezuela); Luis Gonzalez Arteaga (Colombia); Jose Diaz Perez (Panama); Julio Sanchez (Ncaragua); Ray Padilla (Mexico); Kelvin Kondo (Brazil); Bradley Stuart (Curacao); Kyle Lee (Korea); TY Wei (Taiwan).

Atlanta Braves

Office Address: 755 Battery Avenue, SE Atlanta, GA 30339-3017.
Mailing Address: PO Box 723009, Atlanta, GA 31139-2704.
Telephone: (404) 522-7630. **Website:** www.braves.com.

OWNERSHIP
Operated/Owned By: Liberty Media. **Chairman/CEO:** Terry McGuirk. **Chairman Emeritus:** Bill Bartholomay. **Vice Chairman Emeritus:** John Schuerholz. **Senior Vice President:** Henry Aaron.

BUSINESS OPERATIONS
President, Development: Mike Plant. **Executive VP/Chief Legal Officer:** Greg Heller.

MARKETING/SALES
President, Business: Derek Schiller. **Senior VP, Marketing:** Adam Zimmerman. **Senior VP, Ticket Sales:** Paul Adams. **Senior VP, Corporate Sales & Premium Partnerships:** Jim Allen.

FINANCE
Senior VP/Chief Financial Officer: Unavailable.

Terry McGuirk

MEDIA RELATIONS/PUBLIC RELATIONS
Telephone: (404) 614-1556.
Senior Director, Media Relations: Brad Hainje. **Senior Manager, Media Relations:** Adrienne Midgley. **Senior Coordinator, Media Relations:** Jonathan Kerber. **Media Relations Coordinator:** Jared Burleyson. **Spanish Interpreter/Media Relations:** Franco García. **Senior Director, Public Relations:** Beth Marshall. **Public Relations Manager:** Unavailable.

STADIUM OPERATIONS
VP, Stadium Operations/Security: Unavailable. **Field Director:** Ed Mangan. **VP, Fan Experience:** Scott Cunningham. **PA Announcer:** Casey Motter. **Official Scorers:** Richard Musterer, Mike Stamus.

TICKETING
Telephone: (404) 577-9100. **Email:** ticketsales@braves.com.
VP, Ticket Operations: Anthony Esposito.

TRAVEL/CLUBHOUSE
Director of Team Travel: Jim Lovell. **Director, Equipment & Clubhouse Service:** John Holland.
Visiting Clubhouse Manager: Fred Stone.

2018 SCHEDULE
Standard Game Times: 7:35; Sat. 4:10; Sun. 1:35.

MARCH
29-31 . . . . . .Philadelphia

APRIL
2-4. . . . . Washington
6-8. . . . . . . at Colorado
9-11 . . . . . at Washington
13-15 . . . .at Chicago (NL)
16-18 . . . . .Philadelphia
19-22 . . . . .New York (NL)
23-26 . . . . .at Cincinnati
27-29 . . . . at Philadelphia

MAY
1-3. . . . . at New York (NL)
4-6. . . . . . . San Francisco
8-9. . . . . . . at Tampa Bay

10-13 . . . . at Miami
15-17 . . . . . Chicago (NL)
18-20 . . . . .Miami
21-23 . . . . at Philadelphia
25-27 . . . . . . .at Boston
28-30 . . . . .New York (NL)
31 . . . . Washington

JUNE
1-3. . . . . . . Washington
4-6. . . . . . at San Diego
8-10 . . at Los Angeles (NL)
12-13 . . . . .New York (NL)
14-17 . . . . . San Diego
19-20 . . . . . . at Toronto
22-24 . . . . Baltimore
25-27 . . . . Cincinnati

29-30 . . . . . .at St. Louis

JULY
1 . . . . .at St. Louis
2-4. . . . at New York (AL)
5-8. . . . . . . at Milwaukee
10-11 . . . . .Toronto
13-15 . . . . Arizona
20-22 . . . . at Washington
23-24 . . . . at Miami
26-29 . . . Los Angeles (NL)
30-31 . . . . .Miami

AUGUST
1 . . . . .Miami
2-5. . . . at New York (NL)
7-9. . . . . . at Washington
10-12 . . . . . .Milwaukee

13-15 . . . . .Miami
16-19 . . . . Colorado
20-22 . . . . at Pittsburgh
23-26 . . . . at Miami
28-29 . . . . . .Tampa Bay
31 . . . . Pittsburgh

SEPTEMBER
1-2. . . . . Pittsburgh
3-5. . . . . Boston
6-9. . . . . at Arizona
10-12 . . . at San Francisco
14-16 . . . . . Washington
17-19 . . . . . . St. Louis
20-23 . . . . .Philadelphia
25-27 . . at New York (NL)
28-30 . . . . at Philadelphia

GENERAL INFORMATION
Stadium (year opened):
SunTrust Park (2017).
Team Colors: Red, white and blue.

Home Dugout: First Base.
Playing Surface: Grass.

BASEBALL OPERATIONS

Telephone: (404) 522-7630. **Fax:** (404) 614-3308.

Executive Vice President/General Manager: Alex Anthopoulos. **Vice President of Baseball Operations/Assistant GM:** Perry Minasian. **Assistant GM/Research & Development:** Jason Paré. **Director of Major League Operations:** Alex Tamin. **Assistant Director, Pro Scouting/Analytics:** Matt Grabowski. **Manager, Baseball Video Operations:** Rob Smith. **Executive Assistants:** Chris Rice, Elizabeth Teran. **Assistant, Baseball Operations:** Danielle Monday. **Analyst, Baseball Operations:** Garrett Wilson. **Analyst, Major League Operations:** Noah Woodward. **Analysts, Research & Development:** Josh Malek, Scott Rapponotti, Michael Lord.

Alex Anthopoulos

MAJOR LEAGUE STAFF

Manager: Brian Snitker. **Coaches: Bench**—Walt Weiss, **Pitching**—Chuck Hernandez, **Hitting**—Kevin Seitzer, **Assistant Hitting Coach**—Jose Castro, **First Base**—Eric Young, **Third Base**—Ron Washington. **Bullpen Coach:** Marty Reed. **Bullpen Catcher:** Jose Yepez. **Catching Coach:** Sal Fasano.

MEDICAL/TRAINING

Director, Player Health/Head Trainer: George C. Poulis. **Director, Performance/Assistant Trainer:** Andrew Hauser. **Head Team Physician:** Dr. Gary M. Lourie. **Senior Advisor, Athletic Trainer:** Jeff Porter. **Assistant Trainer:** Mike Frostad. **Head Sports Performance Coach:** Bradford Scott. **Performance Therapist:** Jordan Wolf.

PLAYER DEVELOPMENT

Telephone: (404) 522-7630. **Fax:** (404) 614-1350.

Director, Player Development: Dom Chiti. **Assistant Director, Player Development:** Jonathan Schuerholz. **Manager, Minor League Administration:** Ron Knight. **Manager, Minor League Operations:** A.J. Scola. **Special Assistant to Pitching:** Dave Wallace. **Senior Advisors, Player Development:** Lee Elia, Carlos Chantres, Randy Ingle. **Field Coordinator:** Dave Trembley. **Pitching Coordinator:** Derrick Lewis. **Hitting Coordinator:** Mike Brumley. **Roving Coordinators:** Jeff Datz (catching), Adam Everett (infield), Joe Metz (medical), Nick Flynn (assistant medical), Mike Schofield (strength & conditioning), Chris Dayton (assistant strength & conditioning), Kyle Clements (video), John Shelby (outfield/baserunning). **Minor League Equipment Manager:** Jeff Pink. **Rehabilitation Coordinator:** Jesse Litsch.

FARM SYSTEM

Class	Club (League)	Manager	Hitting Coach	Pitching Coach
Triple-A	Gwinnett (IL)	Damon Berryhill	John Moses	Reid Cornelius
Double-A	Mississippi (SL)	Chris Maloney	Carlos Mendez	Dennis Lewallyn
High A	Florida (FSL)	Luis Salazar	Rene Tosoni	Mike Maroth
Low A	Rome (SAL)	Rocket Wheeler	Bobby Moore	Dan Meyer
Rookie	Danville (APP)	Barrett Kleinknecht	Barbaro Garbey	Kanekoa Texeira
Rookie	Braves (GCL)	Nestor Perez Jr.	Rick Albert	Elvin Nina
Rookie	Braves (DSL)	Jefferson Romero	Danny Santiesteban	Jose Rodriguez

SCOUTING

Telephone: (404) 522-7630. **Fax:** (404) 614-1350.

Special Assistants to Baseball Operations: Chipper Jones (Roswell, GA), Fred McGriff (Tampa, FL), Greg Walker (Pearson, GA), Andruw Jones (Duluth, GA). **Special Assignment Scout:** Billy Ryan. **Senior Advisor, Pro Scouting:** Tom Giordano. **Major League Scouts:** Dave Holliday (Bixby, OK), Matt Kinzer (Hammond, LA), Ron Marigny (Cypress, TX), Rick Ragazzo (Leona Valley, CA), Ted Simmons (Wildwood, MO), Terry R. Tripp (Harrisburg, IL), Rick Williams (Tampa, FL). **Professional Scouts:** Jason Dunn, Rod Gilbreath (Lilburn, GA), Devlin McConnell (Merion Station, PA), Trenton Mozes, Patrick Lowery (Silver Spring, MD), Alan Butts (Atlanta, GA). **Director, Scouting:** Brian Bridges. **Manager, Scouting Operations:** Dixie Keller. **Coordinator, Scouting:** Chris Lionetti. **Senior Advisor to Scouting:** Roy Clark (Marietta, GA), Tom Davis (Ripon, CA). **National Crosscheckers:** Tom Battista (Westlake Village, CA), Sean Rooney (Apex, NC), Deron Rombach (Arlington, TX). **Regional Crosscheckers: East**—Reed Dunn (Nashville, TN), **Midwest**—Terry C Tripp (Norris, IL). **Southern Supervisor:** Dustin Evans (Acworth,GA). **Area Scouts:** Kevin Barry (Kinmundy, IL), Billy Best (Holly Spings, NC), Hugh Buchanan (Snellville, GA), Justin Clark (Lakeland, FL), Dan Cox (Huntington Beach, CA), Nate Dion (Edmond, OK), Brett Evert (Salem, OR), Ralph Garr (Richmond, TX), Kevin Martin (Los Angeles, CA), Greg Morhardt (South Windsor, CT), Lou Sanchez (Miami, FL), Rick Sellers (Remus, MI), Darin Vaughan (Kingwood, TX), Ricky Wilson (Buckeye, AZ), Alan Sandberg (Ringwood, NJ), Smoke Laval (Reserve, LA), JD French (Kennett, MO). **Coordinator, Latin American Operations:** Jonathan Cruz. **Manager, Dominican Republic Administration & Operations:** Lothar Schott. **Administrative Assistant:** Ruth Peguero. **Coordinator:** Chris Roque (Central America). **International Scouts:** Carlos Garcia (Colombia), Daurys Nin (Dominican Republic).

Baltimore Orioles

Office Address: 333 W Camden St., Baltimore, MD 21201.
Telephone: (888) 848-BIRD. **Fax:** (410) 547-6272.
E-mail Address: birdmail@orioles.com. **Website:** www.orioles.com.

OWNERSHIP

Operated By: The Baltimore Orioles Limited Partnership Inc.
Chairman/CEO: Peter Angelos.

BUSINESS OPERATIONS

Executive Vice President: John Angelos. **Ownership Representative:** Louis Angelos.
VP/Special Liaison to Chairman: Lou Kousouris. **Director, Human Resources:** Lisa Tolson.
Director, Information Systems: James Kline.

Peter Angelos

FINANCE

Executive VP/CFO: Robert Ames. **VP, Finance:** Michael D. Hoppes, CPA.

PUBLIC RELATIONS/COMMUNICATIONS

Telephone: (410) 547-6150. **Fax:** (410) 547-6272.
VP, Communications/Marketing: Greg Bader. **Director, Public Relations:** Kristen Hudak.
Manager, Media Relations: Jim Misudek. **Coordinator, Public Relations:** Kailey Adams.
Coordinator, Digital Communications: Amanda Sarver. **Public Relations Assistant:** Adam
Esselman. **Public Relations Assistant:** Jackie Harig. **Director, Community Relations/
Promotions:** Kristen Schultz. **Director, Advertising:** Jason Snapkoski.

BALLPARK OPERATIONS

Director, Ballpark Operations: Kevin Cummings. **Head Groundskeeper:** Nicole Sherry. **PA Announcer:** Ryan
Wagner. **Official Scorers:** Jim Henneman, Marc Jacobson, Ryan Eigenbrode.

TICKETING

Telephone: (888) 848-BIRD. **Fax:** (410) 547-6270.
VP, Ticket Sales/Service Operations: Neil Aloise. **Director, Ticket Sales:** Mark Hromalik. **Director, Ticket
Operations/Fan Services:** Scott Rosier.

TRAVEL/CLUBHOUSE

Director, Team Travel: Kevin Buck.
Equipment Manager (Home): Chris Guth. **Equipment Manager (Road):** Fred Tyler.

2018 SCHEDULE

Standard Game Times: 7:05 p.m; Sun. 1:35

MARCH
29,31 . . . . Minnesota

APRIL
1 . . . . Minnesota
2-4 . . . . .at Houston
5-8 . . . . at New York (AL)
9-11 . . . . .Toronto
13-16 . . . . .at Boston
17-19 . . . . .at Detroit
20-23 . . . . Cleveland
24-26 . . . . . . .Tampa Bay
27-29 . . . . Detroit

MAY
1-3 . . . at Los Angeles (AL)
4-6 . . . . .at Oakland
8-10 . . . . Kansas City

11-13 . . . . . . .Tampa Bay
15-16 . . . . . .Philadelphia
18-20 . . . . .at Boston
21-24 . . . .at Chicago (AL)
25-27 . . . . . at Tampa Bay
28-30 . . . . .Washington
31 . . . . . . .New York (AL)

JUNE
1-3 . . . . . .New York (AL)
5-6 . . . . at New York (NL)
7-10 . . . . at Toronto
11-13 . . . . Boston
15-17 . . . . .Miami
19-21 . . . . at Washington
22-24 . . . . at Atlanta
25-28 . . . . Seattle

29-30 . . . Los Angeles (AL)

JULY
1 . . . . . . Los Angeles (AL)
3-4 . . . . . . at Philadelphia
5-8 . . . . . . at Minnesota
9-11 . . . . . .New York (AL)
13-15 . . . . Texas
20-22 . . . . at Toronto
23-25 . . . . Boston
26-29 . . . . . .Tampa Bay
31 . . . . . at New York (AL)

AUGUST
1 . . . . . . at New York (AL)
2-5 . . . . .at Texas
7-9 . . . . . . at Tampa Bay
10-12 . . . . Boston

14-15 . . . . .New York (NL)
17-19 . . . . . .at Cleveland
20-22 . . . . at Toronto
24-26 . . . . .New York (AL)
27-29 . . . . .Toronto
31 . . . . . . .at Kansas City

SEPTEMBER
1-2 . . . . . . .at Kansas City
3-5 . . . . .at Seattle
7-9 . . . . . . at Tampa Bay
11-13 . . . . Oakland
14-16 . . . . . Chicago (AL)
17-19 . . . . .Toronto
21-23 . . . at New York (AL)
24-26 . . . . .at Boston
27-30 . . . . Houston

GENERAL INFORMATION

Stadium (year opened): Oriole Park at
Camden Yards (1992).
Team Colors: Orange, black and white.

Home Dugout: First Base.
Playing Surface: Grass.

BASEBALL OPERATIONS

Telephone: (410) 547-6107. **Fax:** (410) 547-6271.

Executive Vice President, Baseball Operations: Dan Duquette.

Vice President, Baseball Operations: Brady Anderson. **Special Assistant to the EVP** of Baseball Operations: Lee Thomas. **Senior Advisor, Player Personnel:** Joe McIlvaine. **Director, Baseball Operations:** Tripp Norton. **Director, Professional Scouting/Special Projects:** Patrick Di Gregory. **Director, Team Travel:** Kevin Buck. **Coordinator, Video:** Mike Silverman. **Video Coaching/Advance Scouting Assistant:** Ben Sussman-Hyde. **Director, Pacific Rim Operations/Baseball Development:** Mike Snyder. **Director, Analytics & Major League Contracts :** Sarah Gelles. **Spanish Translator, Baseball Operations Assistant:** Ramon Alarcon.

Dan Duquette

MAJOR LEAGUE STAFF

Manager: Buck Showalter.

Coaches: Bench—John Russell, **Pitching**—Roger McDowell, **Hitting**—Scott Coolbaugh, **Assistant Hitting**—Howie Clark, **First Base**—Wayne Kirby, **Third Base**—Bobby Dickerson, **Bullpen**—Alan Mills, **Coach**—Einar Diaz.

MEDICAL/TRAINING

Head Athletic Trainer: Brian Ebel. **Assistant Athletic Trainer:** Mark Shires, Pat Wesley. **Assistant Athletic Trainer:** Chris Poole. **Strength and Conditioning Coach:** Joseph Hogarty. **Strength and Conditioning Coach:** Ryosuke Naito. **Team Physician/Medical Director:** Dr. William Goldiner. **Orthopedist:** Dr. Michael Jacobs. **Dentist:** Dr. Gus Livaditis. **Optometrist:** Dr. Elliott Myrowitz.

PLAYER DEVELOPMENT

Telephone: (410) 547-6120. **Fax:** (410) 547-6298.

Director, Minor League Operations: Kent Qualls. **Director, Player Development:** Brian Graham. **Director, Dominican Republic Baseball Operations:** Nelson Norman. **Director, Dominican Republic Academy:** Felipe Rojas Alou Jr. **Coordinator, Minor League Pitching:** John Wasdin. **Special Assignment Pitching Instructor:** Ramon Martinez. **Coordinator, Minor League Hitting:** Jeff Manto. **Manager, Minor League Administration:** Maria Arellano. **Assistant Director, Minor League & International Operations:** Cale Cox. **Administrator, Sarasota Operations:** Len Johnston. **Instructor, Special Assignment:** B.J. Surhoff. **Instructor, Special Assignment:** Mike Bordick. **Coordinator, Minor League Infield:** Dave Anderson. **Coordinator, Minor League Catching:** Don Werner. **Coordinator, Florida and Latin America Pitching:** Dave Schmidt. **Dominican Republic Field Coordinator:** Miguel Jabalera. **Coordinator, Pitching Rehabilitation:** Scott McGregor. **Minor League Medical Coordinator:** Dave Walker. **Latin American Medical Coordinator:** Manny Lopez. **Athletic Trainer, Pitching Performance:** Chris Correnti. **Coordinator, Sarasota Strength and Conditioning:** Ryan Driscoll. **Administrator, Dominican Republic Academy:** Jorge Perozo. **Minor League Equipment Manager:** Jake Parker. **Dominican Republic Equipment Manager:** Franklin Fajardo.

FARM SYSTEM

Class	Club (League)	Manager	Hitting Coach	Pitching Coach
Triple-A	Norfolk (IL)	Ron Johnson	Butch Davis	Mike Griffin
Double-A	Bowie (EL)	Gary Kendall	Keith Bodie	Kennie Steenstra
High A	Frederick (CL)	Ryan Minor	Kyle Moore	Blaine Beatty
Low A	Delmarva (SAL)	Buck Britton	Bobby Rose	Justin Lord
Short-season	Aberdeen (NYP)	Kevin Bradshaw	Tim Raines, Jr.	Mark Hendrickson
Rookie	Orioles (GCL)	Carlos Tosca	Milt May	Wilson Alvarez
Rookie	Orioles (DSL)	Elvis Morel	Ramon Caballo	Dionis Pascual

SCOUTING

Telephone: (410) 547-6212. **Fax:** 410-547-6928.

Director, Scouting: Gary Rajsich.

Special Assistant to the EVP, Scouting: Danny Haas. **Special Assistant to the EVP, Scouting:** Matt Haas. **Assistant Director, Scouting:** Brad Ciolek. **Administrator, Scouting:** Hendrik Herz. **Major League Scouts:** Dave Engle, Jim Howard, John Stockstill. **Professional Scouts:** Dave Machemer, Ron Schueler, Bill Wilkes.

International Scouts, Latin America: Joel Bradley, Calvin Maduro.

West Coast Supervisor: David Blume (Elk Grove, CA). **Lower Midwest Supervisor:** Jim Richardson (Marlow, OK). **Upper Midwest Supervisor:** Ernie Jacobs (Wichita, KS). **East Coast Supervisor:** Kirk Fredriksson (Gainesville, GA). **Mid-Atlantic Executive Scout:** Dean Albany (Baltimore, MD). **Area Scouts:** Kelvin Colon (Miami, FL), Adrian Dorsey (Nashville, TN), Thom Dreier (The Woodlands, TX), Dana Duquette (Boxborough, MA), Dan Durst (Rockford, IL), John Gillette (Gilbert, AZ), Ken Guthrie (Sanger, TX), David Jennings (Daphne, AL), Arthur McConnehead (Atlanta, GA), Rich Morales (Blacksburg, VA), Mark Ralston (Carlsbad, CA), Nathan Showalter (Baltimore, MD), Scott Thomas (Town & Country, MO), Brandon Verley (West Linn, OR), Scott Walter (Manhattan Beach, CA). **Special Assignment Scout:** Wayne Britton (Waynesboro, VA).

Boston Red Sox

Office Address: Fenway Park, 4 Yawkey Way, Boston, MA 02215.
Telephone: (617) 226-6000. **Fax:** (617) 226-6416. **Website:** www.redsox.com

OWNERSHIP

Principal Owner: John Henry. **Chairman:** Thomas C. Werner. **President/CEO:** Sam Kennedy. **President/CEO Emeritus:** Larry Lucchino.

BUSINESS OPERATIONS

EVP/FSG Corporate Strategy & General Counsel: Ed Weiss. **EVP/Business Affairs:** Jonathan Gilula. **EVP/Partnerships:** Troup Parkinson. **EVP/Chief Financial Officer:** Tim Zue. **SVP/Strategic Planning & Senior Counsel:** Dave Beeston.

BALLPARK OPERATIONS

VP/Ballpark Operations: Peter Nesbit. **VP/Fan Services & Entertainment:** Sarah McKenna. **VP/Florida Business Operations:** Katie Haas. **VP/Fenway Park Tours:** Marcita Thompson.

FINANCE/STRATEGY/ANALYTICS

VP/Finance: Ryan Oremus. **Financial Advisor to the President:** Jeff White.

Sam Kennedy

HUMAN RESOURCES/INFORMATION TECHNOLOGY

SVP/Human Resources: Amy Waryas. **VP/Information Technology:** Brian Shield.

LEGAL

SVP/Government Affairs & Special Counsel: David Friedman. **VP/Club Counsel:** Elaine Weddington Steward.

MARKETING/COMMUNICATIONS

SVP/Chief Marketing Officer: Adam Grossman. **VP/Marketing & Broadcasting:** Colin Burch. **Senior Director/Media Relations:** Kevin Gregg.

PARTNERSHIPS/CLIENT SERVICES

VP/Client Services: Marcell Bhangoo. **VP/Community, Alumni & Player Relations:** Pam Kenn.

TICKETING/SALES/EVENTS

SVP/Ticketing, Concerts, & Events: Ron Bumgarner. **SVP/Fenway Concerts & Entertainment:** Larry Cancro. **VP/Ticketing:** Richard Beaton. **VP/Ticketing Services & Operations:** Naomi Calder. **VP/Ticket Sales:** William Droste. **VP/Fenway Park Events:** Carrie Campbell.

RED SOX FOUNDATION

Honorary Chairman: Tim Wakefield. **Executive Director:** Rebekah Salwasser.

2018 SCHEDULE

Standard Game Times: 7:10 p.m.; Sun. 1:35

MARCH
29-31 . . . . . at Tampa Bay

APRIL
1 . . . . at Tampa Bay
2-3 . . . . at Miami
5-8 . . . . .Tampa Bay
10-12 . . . . .New York (AL)
13-16 . . . . . . Baltimore
17-19 . at Los Angeles (AL)
20-22 . . . . . . .at Oakland
24-26 . . . . . . at Toronto
27-29 . . . . . .Tampa Bay
30 . . . . Kansas City

MAY
1-2 . . . . Kansas City
3-6 . . . . .at Texas

8-10 . . . . at New York (AL)
11-13 . . . . . . .at Toronto
14-16 . . . . Oakland
18-20 . . . . . . Baltimore
22-24 . . . . . at Tampa Bay
25-27 . . . . Atlanta
28-30 . . . . .Toronto
31 . . . . .at Houston

JUNE
1-3 . . . . .at Houston
5-7 . . . . Detroit
8-10 . . . . . Chicago (AL)
11-13 . . . . . .at Baltimore
14-17 . . . . . . .at Seattle
19-21 . . . . . at Minnesota
22-24 . . . . Seattle

26-28 . . . Los Angeles (AL)
29-30 . . . at New York (AL)

JULY
1 . . . . . . at New York (AL)
2-4 . . . . . . at Washington
6-8 . . . . . .at Kansas City
9-11 . . . . Texas
12-15 . . . . .Toronto
20-22 . . . . .at Detroit
23-25 . . . . . .at Baltimore
26-29 . . . . . . .Minnesota
30-31 . . . . .Philadelphia

AUGUST
2-5 . . . . . . .New York (AL)
7-9 . . . . at Toronto
10-12 . . . . . .at Baltimore

14-15 . . . . at Philadelphia
17-19 . . . . . . .Tampa Bay
20-23 . . . . Cleveland
24-26 . . . . at Tampa Bay
28-29 . . . . .Miami
30-31 . . . .at Chicago (AL)

SEPTEMBER
1-2 . . . . . .at Chicago (AL)
3-5 . . . . at Atlanta
7-9 . . . . Houston
11-13 . . . . .Toronto
14-16 . . . . .New York (NL)
18-20 . . . at New York (AL)
21-23 . . . . . .at Cleveland
24-26 . . . . Baltimore
28-30 . . . . .New York (AL)

 GENERAL INFORMATION

Stadium (year opened): Fenway Park (1912).
Team Colors: Navy blue, red and white.

Home Dugout: First Base.
Playing Surface: Grass.

BASEBALL OPERATIONS

President, Baseball Operations: Dave Dombrowski. **SVP/Assistant GM:** Brian O'Halloran. **SVP/ Assistant GM:** Eddie Romero. **SVP/Player Personnel:** Allard Baird. **SVP/ Player Personnel:** Frank Wren. **VP/Special Asst. to the President of Baseball Operations:** Tony La Russa. **VP/Major and Minor League Operations:** Raquel Ferreira. **VP/Baseball Research & Development:** Zack Scott. **Senior Director, Team Travel:** Jack McCormick. **Assistant Director, Baseball Administration:** Mike Regan. **Director, Baseball Systems:** Mike Ganley. **Sr. Developers, Baseball Systems:** Eric Edvalson, Fred Hubert. **Sr. Analyst/Baseball Research & Development:** Greg Rybarczyk. **Analyst/Baseball Research & Development:** Joe McDonald, Spencer Bingol. **Assistant Director, Baseball Systems:** Ethan Faggett. **Executive Assistant:** Erin Cox. **Assistant, Baseball Operations:** Alex Gimenez. **Senior Advisor:** Bill James. **Special Assistants to GM:** Pedro Martinez, Jason Varitek.

Dave Dombrowski

MAJOR LEAGUE STAFF

Manager: Alex Cora. **Coaches: Bench**—Ron Roenicke, **Pitching**—Dana Levangie, **Assistant Pitching**—Brian Bannister, **Bullpen**—Craig Bjornson, **Hitting**—Tim Hyers, **Assistant Hitting**— Andy Barkett, **First Base**—Tom Goodwin, **Third Base**—Carlos Febles, **MLB**— Ramon Vazquez, **Bullpen Catchers**— Mani Martinez, Michael Brenly.

SPORTS MEDICINE SERVICE

Director, Sports Medicine Service/Head Athletic Trainer: Brad Pearson. **Medical Director:** Dr. Larry Ronan. **Head Team Orthopedist:** Dr. Peter Asnis. **Senior Physical Therapist/Clinical Specialist:** Jamie Creps. **Assistant Athletic Trainers:** Paul Buchheit, Masai Takahashi, Jon Jochim. **Head Strength & Conditioning Coach:** Kiyoshi Momose. **Coordinator of Athletic Performance/Major League Strength/Conditioning Coach:** Mike Roose. **Massage Therapists:** Russell Nua, Shinichiro Uchikubo. **Physical Therapist:** Adam Thomas.

PLAYER DEVELOPMENT

Vice President, Player Development: Ben Crockett. **Assistant Director, Player Development:** Brian Abraham. **Minor League Equipment Manager:** Mike Stelmach. **Minor League Clubhouse Assistant:** R.J. Warner. **Field Coordinator:** David Howard. **Latin American Pitching Coordinator/Rehab Coordinator:** Walter Miranda. **Latin American Pitching Adviser:** Goose Gregson. **Minor League Medical Coordinator:** Brandon Henry. **Minor League Strength/Conditioning Coordinator:** Edgar Barreto. **Latin Field Coordinator:** Jose Zapata. **Latin American Medical Pitching Development Analyst:** Dave Bush. **Coach/Interpreter:** Mickey Jiang. **Roving Instructors:** Andy Fox (infield), Chad Epperson (catching), Greg Norton (hitting), Ralph Treuel (pitching), Billy McMillon (outfield/baserunning).

FARM SYSTEM

Class	Club (League)	Manager	Hitting Coach	Pitching Coach	Position Coach
Triple-A	Pawtucket (IL)	Kevin Boles	Rich Gedman	Kevin Walker	Bruce Crabbe
Double-A	Portland (EL)	Darren Fenster	Nelson Paulino	Lance Carter	
Low A	Greenville (SAL)	Iggy Suarez	Wilton Veras	Bob Kipper	
Short-season Lowell (NYP)	Corey Wimberly	Nate Spears	Nick Green		
Rookie	Red Sox (GCL)	Tom Kotchman	Junior Zamora	Dick Such	
Rookie	Red Sox (DSL)	Aly Gonzalez	Carlos Adolfo	Oscar Lira	
Rookie	Red Sox (DSL)	Fernando Tatis	Ozzie Chavez	Humberto Sanchez	

SCOUTING

VP/Professional Scouting: Gus Quattlebaum. **VP/Amateur Scouting:** Michael Rikard. **VP/Player Personnel:** Jared Banner. **Assistant Director, Amateur Scouting:** Paul Toboni. **Assistant Director, International Scouting:** Adrian Lorenzo. **Assistant Director, Professional Scouting:** Harrison Slutsky. **Assistant, Player Personnel:** Marcus Cuellar. **Assistant, International Scouting:** James Kang. **Assistant, Amateur Scouting:** Devin Pearson. **Manager, Advance Scouting:** Steve Langone. **Advance Scouting Assistant:** JT Watkins. **Special Assignment Scouts:** Eddie Bane, Steve Peck, Brad Sloan. **Special Assistant, Player Personnel:** Mark Wasinger. **Global Crosschecker:** Paul Fryer. **Major League Scouts:** Jaymie Bane, Nate Field, Blair Henry, Tim Huff, Gary Hughes, Bob Hamelin, John Lombardo, Joe McDonald, Matt Mahoney, David Scrivines, Anthony Turco. **Crosscheckers:** John Booher (National), Fred Petersen (National Coordinator), Jim Robinson (National Coordinator), Quincy Boyd (National Coordinator), Dan Madsen (National Coordinator), Chris Mears (Pitching), Tom Kotchman (Florida). **Area Scouts:** Brandon Agamennone (Prospect, TX), Carl Moesche (Gresham, OR) Tim Collinsworth (Katy, TX), Lane Decker (Piedmont, OK), Raymond Fagnant (East Granby, CT), Todd Gold (Chicago, IL), Reed Gragnani (Henrico, VA) Stephen Hargett (Jacksonville, FL), Justin Horowitz (La Jolla, CA), Josh Labandeira, (Fresno, CA), Brian Moehler (Marietta, GA), Edgar Perez (Vega Baja, PR), Pat Portugal (Wake Forest, NC), John Pyle (Lexington, KY), Willie Romay (Miami Springs, FL), Adam Stern (Delaware, ON) Danny Watkins (Daphne, AL), Vaughn Williams (Gilbert, AZ), Jim Woodward (Claremont, CA). **Part Time Scouts:** JJ Altobelli, Rob English, Tim Martin, Jay Oliver, David Scrivines, Dick Sorkin, Terry Sullivan. **International Scouting, Global Scouting Supervisor:** Todd Claus. **Coordinator, Latin American Scouting:** Rolando Pino. **Coordinator, Pacific Rim Operations:** Brett Ward. **Special Assistant, International Operations:** Jesus Alou. **Assistant Director, Dominican Academy:** Javier Hernandez. **Assistant, Dominican Academy:** Martin Rodriguez. **Supervisor, Dominican Republic Scouting:** Manny Nanita. **Assistant Supervisor, Dominican Republic Scouting:** Jonathan Cruz. **Coordinator, Venezuela Scouting/Venezuela Scout:** Manny Padron. **International Scouts:** Domingo Brito (Dominican Republic), Alfredo Castellon (Colombia), Michel DeJesus (Dominican Republic), Angel Escobar (Venezuela), Aneko Knowles (Bahamas), Steve Fish (Australia), Cris Garibaldo (Panama), Ernesto Gomez (Venezuela), John Kim (Korea), Louie Lin (Taiwan), Wilder Lobo (Venezuela), Esau Medina (Dominican Republic), Rafael Mendoza (Nicaragua), Ramon Mora (Venezuela), Rafael Motooka (Brazil), Dennis Neuman (Aruba/Curacao), Alex Requena (Venezuela), Lenin Rodriguez (Venezuela), Rene Saggiadi (Europe), Darryn Smith (South Africa) **International Pro Scouts:** Shun Kakazu (Japan), Won Lee (Korea).

Chicago Cubs

Office Address: Wrigley Field, 1060 W. Addison St., Chicago, IL 60613.
Telephone: (773) 404-2827. **Website:** www.cubs.com.

OWNERSHIP
Chairman: Tom Ricketts. **Board of Directors:** Laura Ricketts, Pete Ricketts, Todd Ricketts and Tribune Company.

BUSINESS OPERATIONS

Tom Ricketts

President, Business Operations: Crane Kenney. **Vice President, Wrigley Field Restoration & Expansion:** Carl Rice. **Executive Assistant, Chairman:** Lorraine Switatly. **Executive Assistant, President Business Operations:** Michele Dietz. **Executive Assistant, Board & Stakeholder Relations:** Anne Lanctot. **Coordinator, Associate Events & Wellness:** Becky Rasor. **Chairman's Office Associate:** Robin Lestina-Cikanek.

BALLPARK/EVENT OPERATIONS
SVP, Strategy & Ballpark Operations: Alex Sugarman. **Assistant Director, Event Operations & Security:** Morgan Bucciferro. **Assistant Director, Guest Services:** Vanessa Brost. **Manager, Parking & Event Operations:** Ryan Mortensen. **Non-Baseball Event Manager:** Kate Osmer. **Coordinator, Ballpark Operations Payroll & Administration:** Kelly Bilbrey. **Event Operations Coordinator:** Maria Sapienza. **Major Event Coordinator:** Samantha Thrower. **Vice President, Facility & Supply Chain Operations:** Patrick Meenan. **Assistant Director, Grounds:** Roger Baird. **Assistant Director, Facilities:** Ryan Egan.

MARKETING/COMMUNICATIONS
Vice President, Marketing: Lauren Fritts. **Vice President, Commnications & Community Affairs:** Julian Green. **Director, Marketing & Fan Insights:** Kelly Linstroth. **Director, Communications:** Lindsay Bago. **Manager, Public Relations:** Alyson Cohen. **Assistant Director, Brand Development & Activation:** John Morrison. **Manager, Broadcast Relations:** Joe Rios.

LEGAL
Vice President, General Counsel: Bret Scharback. **Counsel:** Amy Timm. **Assistant Director, Chicago Cubs & Wrigley Field Archives:** Kristina Jarosik. **Legal Operations Specialist:** Patrick Schulte.

TICKET SALES/SALES & PARTNERSHIPS
Senior Vice President, Sales & Marketing: Colin Faulkner. **Vice President, Ticketing:** Cale Vennum. **Senior Director, Corporate Partnerships:** Allen Hermeling. **Assistant Director, Corporate Partnerships:** Alex Seyferth. **Manager, Corporate Partnership Sales Operations:** Kevin Kirkpatrick. **Senior Account Executive:** Ashley Facchini. **Senior Director, Ticket Sales:** Andy Blackburn. **Manager, Business Development:** Chris Weddige. **Manager, Group Ticket Sales:** Jason Tuton. **Account Executive, Premier Sales:** Diego Chahda, Jared Borlack, Steve Brauer, Gianna Siragusa. **Senior Business Development Executive, Ticket Sales & Hospitality:** Tom Fitzgerald, James Tuck.

2018 SCHEDULE
Standard Game Times: 7:05 p.m.; Sun. 1:20

MARCH		
29-31 . . . . at Miami		

APRIL
1 . . . . at Miami
2-3 . . . . .at Cincinnati
5-8 . . . . at Milwaukee
9-12 . . . . Pittsburgh
13-15 . . . . Atlanta
16-18 . . . . St. Louis
20-22 . . . . . at Colorado
24-25 . . . . . .at Cleveland
26-29 . . . . . .Milwaukee
30 . . . . Colorado

MAY
1-2 . . . . .Colorado
4-6 . . . . .at St. Louis

7-9 . . . . .Miami
11-13 . . . . . Chicago (AL)
15-17 . . . . . . at Atlanta
18-20 . . . . .at Cincinnati
22-23 . . . . . . Cleveland
25-27 . . . . . San Francisco
28-30 . . . . . at Pittsburgh
31 . . . . . at New York (NL)

JUNE
1-3 . . . . . at New York (NL)
5-7 . . . . .Philadelphia
8-10 . . . . Pittsburgh
11-13 . . . . . at Milwaukee
15-17 . . . . . . .at St. Louis
18-20 . . . Los Angeles (NL)
21-24 . . . . . .at Cincinnati

25-28 . at Los Angeles (NL)
29-30 . . . . . . Minnesota

JULY
1 . . . . Minnesota
3-4 . . . . Detroit
6-8 . . . . Cincinnati
9-11 . . . . at San Francisco
13-15 . . . . . at San Diego
19-22 . . . . . . St. Louis
23-26 . . . . .Arizona
27-29 . . . . . .at St. Louis
31 . . . . . . .at Pittsburgh

AUGUST
1 . . . . at Pittsburgh
2-5 . . . . San Diego
6-8 . . . . . .at Kansas City

10-12 . . . . . Washington
14-15 . . . . . .Milwaukee
16-19 . . . . at Pittsburgh
21-22 . . . . . .at Detroit
23-26 . . . . . . Cincinnati
27-29 . . . .New York (NL)
31 . . . . . at Philadelphia

SEPTEMBER
1-2 . . . . . at Philadelphia
3-5 . . . . . . at Milwaukee
6-9 . . . . . at Washington
10-12 . . . . . .Milwaukee
14-16 . . . . . . Cincinnati
17-19 . . . . . at Arizona
21-23 . . . .at Chicago (AL)
24-27 . . . . . . Pittsburgh
28-30 . . . . .St. Louis28-30

GENERAL INFORMATION

Stadium (year opened):
Wrigley Field (1914).
Team Colors: Royal blue, red and white.

Home Dugout: Third Base.
Playing Surface: Grass.

BASEBALL OPERATIONS

Telephone: (773) 404-2827. **Fax:** (773) 404-4147.
President, Baseball Operations: Theo Epstein. **Executive VP/General Manager:** Jed Hoyer. **Assistant GMs:** Randy Bush, Scott Haris. **Assistant GM, Strategic Initiatives:** Shiraz Rehman. **Director, Baseball Operations:** Jeff Greenberg. **Director, Research & Development:** Chris Moore. **Assistant Director, Minor League Operations:** Bobby Basham. **Senior Advisor:** Billy Williams. **Special Assistants, President/GM:** Kerry Wood, Jason Parks. **Director, Pro Scouting/Special Assistant, President/GM:** Kyle Evans. **Executive Assistant, President/GM:** Meghan Jones. **Traveling Secretary:** Vijay Tekchanadani. **Baseball Systems Architect:** Ryan Kruse. **Assistant Director, Research & Development:** Jeremy Greenhouse. **Analysts, Research & Development:** Sean Ahmed, Chris Jones, Bryan Cole. **Developer, Research & Development:** Albert Lyu. **Developer, Baseball Systems:** Rishi Chopra. **Assistant, Research & Development:** Garrett Chiado. **Coordinator, Baseball Operations:** Greg Davey. **Assistant, Baseball Ops.:** Alex Smith.

Theo Epstein

MAJOR LEAGUE STAFF

Manager: Joe Maddon. **Coaches: Bench**—Brandon Hyde, **Pitching**—Jim Hickey, **Hitting**—Chili Davis, **Assistant Hitting**—Andy Haines, **First Base**—Will Venable, **Third Base**—Brian Butterfield, **Catching**—Mike Borzello, **Bullpen**—Lester Strode. **Staff Assistants:** Franklin Font, Juan Cabreja. **Bullpen Catcher**— Chad Noble.

MEDICAL/TRAINING

Team Physician: Dr. Stephen Adams. **Team Orthopaedist:** Dr. Stephen Gryzio. **Orthopaedic Consultant:** Dr. Michael Schafer. **Director, Medical Administration:** Mark O'Neal. **Major League Athletic Trainer:** P.J. Mainville. **Major League Assistant Athletic Trainers:** Ed Halbur, Matt Johnson. **Strength & Conditioning Coordinator:** Tim Buss. **Major League Massage Therapist:** Laura Paluch.

MEDIA RELATIONS

Director, Media Relations: Peter Chase. **Assistant Director, Media Relations:** Jason Carr. **Coordinator, Media Relations:** Alex Wilcox.

PLAYER DEVELOPMENT

Telephone: (773) 404-4035. **Fax:** (773) 404-4147.
Senior Vice President, Player Development & Amateur Scouting: Jason McLeod. **Director, Player Development:** Jaron Madison. **Equipment Manager:** Dana Noeltner. **Manager, Mesa Administration:** Gil Passarella. **Major League Rehab Coordinator:** Jonathan Fierro. **Director, Mental Skills Program:** Josh Lifrak. **Latin America Coordinator, Mental Skills Program:** Rey Fuentes. **Mental Skills Program Coordinator:** Darnell McDonald. **Mental Skills Coordinator:** John Baker. **Minor League Coordinators:** Tim Cossins (field & catching), Jacob Cruz (hitting), Brendan Sagara (pitching), Tom Beyers (assistant hitting), Mike Mason, Steve Merriman (assistant pitching), Jeremy Farrell (infield), Doug Dascenzo (outfield & baserunning). **Latin America Field Coordinator:** Dave Keller. **Minor League Athletic Coordinator:** Chuck Baughman. **Minor League Strength & Conditioning Coordinator:** Doug Jarrow. **Minor League Rehab Pitching Coordinator:** Ron Villone.

FARM SYSTEM

Class	Club (League)	Manager	Hitting Coach	Pitching Coach
Triple-A	Iowa (PCL)	Marty Pevey	Desi Wilson	Rod Nichols
Double-A	Tennessee (SL)	Mark Johnson	Jesus Feliciano	Terry Clark
High A	Myrtle Beach (CL)	Buddy Bailey	Ty Wright	Anderson Tavarez
Low A	South Bend (MWL)	Jimmy Gonzalez	Ricardo Medina	Brian Lawrence
Short-season	Eugene (NWL)	Steve Lerud	Osmin Melendez	Armando Gabino
Rookie	Cubs (AZL)	Carmelo Martinez	Unavailable	Unavailable
Rookie	Cubs 1 (DSL)	Lance Rymel	Unavailable	Eduardo Villacis
Rookie	Cubs 2 (DSL)	Pedro Gonzalez	Unavailable	Jose Cueto

SCOUTING

Director, Professional Scouting/Special Assistant to the President/GM: Kyle Evans. **Assistant Director, Professional Scouting:** Andrew Bassett. **Special Assignment Scouts:** Jason Cooper (Kirkland, WA), Dave Klipstein (Keller, TX), Spike Lundberg (Murrietta, CA). **Special Assignment Scout/Supervisor, Pacific Rim Scouting:** Min Kyu Sung (Korea). **Major League Scouts:** Terry Kennedy (Chandler, AZ), Jake Ciarrachi (Chicago, IL), Joe Nelson (Jupiter, FL), Steve Boros (Kingwood, TX). **Pro Scouts:** Billy Blitzer (Brooklyn, NY), Matt Hahn (Tampa, FL), Nic Jackson (North Chesterfield, VA), Mark Kiefer (New Braunfels, TX), Kyle Phillips (Alpine, CA), Thad Weber (Friend, NE), Adam Wogan (Brooklyn, NY). **Part-Time Professional Scouts:** Robert Lofrano (Woodland Hills, CA), Mark Servais (La Crosse, WI). **Director, Amateur Scouting:** Matt Dorey (Portland, OR). **Assistant Director, Amateur Scouting:** Lukas McKnight (Libertyville, IL). **Assistant, Amateur Scouting:** Ella Cahill (Chicago, IL). **National Supervisors:** Sam Hughes (Atlanta, GA), Ron Tostenson (El Dorado Hills, CA). **Crosscheckers: Midwest/Northeast**—Tim Adkins (Huntington, WV), **Central**—Daniel Carte (Hurricane, WV), **West**—Shane Farrell (Chicago, IL), **Southeast**—Bobby Filotei (Mobile, AL). **Area Scouts:** Tom Clark (Lake City, FL), Chris Clemons (Robinson, TX), Trey Forkerway (Houston, TX), Edwards Guzman (Toa Baja, PR), Greg Hopkins (Camas, WA), Bobby Houston (Fallbrook, CA), John Koronka (Clermont, FL), Keith Lockhart (Dacula, GA), Alex Lontayo (Murrieta, CA), Alex McClure (Memphis, TN), Steve McFarland (Scottsdale, AZ), Tom Myers (Santa Barbara, CA), Ty Nichols (Broken Arrow, OK), John Pedrotty (Chicago, IL), Eric Servais (Minneapolis, MN), Matt Sherman (Kingston, MA), Billy Swoope (Norfolk, VA), Keronn Walker (Chicago, IL), Jacob Williams (Lexington, KY), Gabe Zappin (Walnut Creek, CA). **Director, International Scouting:** Louie Eljuana. **Director, International Pro Scouting:** Alex Suarez. **Assistant, International Scouting:** Kenny Socorro.

Chicago White Sox

Office Address: Guaranteed Rate Field, 333 W. 35th St., Chicago, IL 60616.
Telephone: (312) 674-1000. **Fax:** (312) 674-5116.
Website: whitesox.com, loswhitesox.com.

OWNERSHIP
Chairman: Jerry Reinsdorf.
Board of Directors: Robert Judelson, Judd Malkin, Allan Muchin, Jay Pinsky, Lee Stern, Burton Ury, Charles Walsh.
Special Assistant to Chairman: Dennis Gilbert. **Assistant to Chairman:** Barb Reincke. **Coordinator, Administration/
Investor Relations:** Katie Hermle.

Jerry Reinsdorf

BUSINESS OPERATIONS
Senior Executive Vice President: Howard Pizer. **Senior Director, Information Services:**
Don Brown. **Vice President, Human Resources:** Moira Foy. **Senior Coordinator, Human
Resources:** Leslie Gaggiano.

FINANCE
Senior VP, Administration/Finance: Tim Buzard. **VP, Finance:** Bill Waters. **Accounting
Manager:** Chris Taylor.

MARKETING/SALES
Senior VP, Sales/Marketing: Brooks Boyer. **Senior Director, Business Development/
Broadcasting:** Bob Grim. **Director, Game Presentation:** Cris Quintana. **Sr. Manager,
Scoreboard Operations/Production:** Jeff Szynal. **Sr. Manager, Game Operations:** Dan
Mielke. **Sr. Director, Corporate Partnerships Sales Development:** George McDoniel.
Sr. Director, Corporate Partnerships Activation: Gail Tucker. **Sr. Manager, Corporate
Partnerships Development:** Jeff Floerke. **Coordinators/Managers, Corporate Partnership Activation:** Adam
Delgado, Ashley Sorenson, Kat Claeys. **VP of Sales and Service:** Jim Willits. **Sr. Manager, Premium Seating Sales:** Rob
Boaz.

MEDIA RELATIONS/PUBLIC RELATIONS
Telephone: (312) 674-5300. **Fax:** (312) 674-5116.
Senior VP, Communications: Scott Reifert. **Senior Director, Media Relations:** Bob Beghtol. **Director, Public
Relations:** Sheena Quinn. **Assistant Director, Media Relations:** Ray Garcia. **Senior Coordinator, Public Relations:**
Julianne Bartosz. **Coordinators, Media Relations/Services:** Joe Roti, Hannah Sundwall. **VP, Community Relations/
Executive Director/CWS Charities:** Christine O'Reilly.
Director, Community Relations: Sarah Marten, Lindsey Jordan. **Manager, Youth Baseball Initiatives:** Anthony
Olivo. **Director, Digital Communications:** Brad Boron. **Director, Advertising/Design Services:** Gareth Breunlin.
Manager, Online Communications: Dakin Dugaw.

STADIUM OPERATIONS
Senior VP, Stadium Operations: Terry Savarise. **Senior Director, Park Operations:** Jonathan Vasquez.

2018 SCHEDULE
Standard Game Times: 7:15 p.m.; Sun. 1:10.

MARCH	8-9 . . . . Pittsburgh	29-30 . . . . .at Texas	13-15 . . . . . . .at Detroit
29-31 . . . . .at Kansas City	11-13 . . . .at Chicago (NL)		17-19 . . . . . . Kansas City
	15-16 . . . . . at Pittsburgh	**JULY**	21-22 . . . . . . Minnesota
APRIL	17-20 . . . . Texas	1 . . . . .at Texas	23-26 . . . . . . .at Detroit
1 . . . . . . .at Kansas City	21-24 . . . . Baltimore	2-4 . . . . .at Cincinnati	27-29 . . . at New York (AL)
2-4 . . . . at Toronto	25-27 . . . . . . .at Detroit	5-8 . . . . .at Houston	30-31 . . . . Boston
5-8 . . . . Detroit	28-30 . . . . . .at Cleveland	10-11 . . . . St. Louis	
9-11 . . . . . . .Tampa Bay		13-15 . . . . . . Kansas City	**SEPTEMBER**
12-15 . . . . . at Minnesota	**JUNE**	20-22 . . . . . . .at Seattle	1-2 . . . . Boston
16-18 . . . . . .at Oakland	1-3 . . . . .Milwaukee	23-26 . at Los Angeles (AL)	3-5 . . . . Detroit
20-22 . . . . Houston	5-7 . . . . at Minnesota	27-29 . . . . .Toronto	7-9 . . . . . Los Angeles (AL)
23-25 . . . . Seattle	8-10 . . . . .at Boston	31 . . . . Kansas City	10-12 . . . .at Kansas City
26-29 . . . . .at Kansas City	11-14 . . . . Cleveland		14-16 . . . . .at Baltimore
	15-17 . . . . Detroit	**AUGUST**	18-20 . . . . .at Cleveland
MAY	18-20 . . . . .at Cleveland	1-2 . . . . Kansas City	21-23 . . . . Chicago (NL)
1-2 . . . . .at St. Louis	21-24 . . . . Oakland	3-5 . . . . . . at Tampa Bay	24-26 . . . . Cleveland
3-6 . . . . Minnesota	26-28 . . . . . . Minnesota	6-8 . . . . . . .New York (AL)	28-30 . . . . . at Minnesota
		10-12 . . . . . . Cleveland	

GENERAL INFORMATION
Stadium (year opened):
Guaranteed Rate Field (1991).
Team Colors: Black, white and silver.

Home Dugout: Third Base.
Playing Surface: Grass.

Senior Director, Guest Services/Diamond Suite Operations: Julie Taylor. Head Groundskeeper: Roger Bossard. PA Announcer: Gene Honda. Official Scorers: Bob Rosenberg, Don Friske, Allan Spear.

TICKETING
Senior Director, Ticket Operations: Mike Mazza. Manager, Ticket Operations: Pete Catizone.

TRAVEL/CLUBHOUSE
Director, Team Travel: Ed Cassin.
Manager, White Sox Clubhouse: Rob Warren. Manager,Visiting Clubhouse: Jason Gilliam. Manager, Umpires Clubhouse: Joe McNamara Jr.

BASEBALL OPERATIONS

Rick Hahn

Executive Vice President: Ken Williams. Senior VP/General Manager: Rick Hahn. Assistant GM: Jeremy Haber. Special Assistants: Bill Scherrer, Dave Yoakum, Marco Paddy, Jim Thome, Jose Contreras. Major League Advance Scout: Bryan Little.
Executive Assistant to GM: Nancy Nesnidal. Senior Director, Baseball Operations: Dan Fabian. Director, Baseball Operations: Daniel Zien. Manager, Baseball Operations: Jeff Lachman. Coordinator Baseball Information: Devin Pickett. Director Baseball Analytics: Matt Koenig. Analyst, Baseball Operations: Emily Blady.

MAJOR LEAGUE STAFF
Manager: Rick Renteria
Coaches: Bench—Joe McEwing, Pitching—Don Cooper, Hitting—Todd Steverson, First Base—Daryl Boston, Third Base—Nick Capra, Bullpen—Curt Hasler, Assistant Hitting Coach—Greg Sparks, Manager of Cultural Development—Luis Sierra.

MEDICAL/TRAINING
Senior Team Physician: Dr. Nikhil Verma. Head Athletic Trainer: Herm Schneider. Assistant Athletic Trainer: Brian Ball. Director, Strength/Conditioning: Allen Thomas. Assistant Director, Strength/Conditioning: Ibrahim Rivera.

PLAYER DEVELOPMENT
Director, Player Development: Chris Getz. Senior Director, Minor League Operations: Grace Guerrero-Zwit. Senior Coordinator, Minor League Administration: Kathy Potoski. Senior Coordinator Latin American and Minor League Operations: Arturo Perez. PD Assistant/Video Coordinator: Rod Larson. Manager, Clubhouse/Equipment: Dan Flood. Field Coordinator: Doug Sisson. Director, Minor League Pitching Instruction: Kirk Champion. Hitting Coordinator: Mike Gellinger. Catching Coordinator: John Orton. Outfield/Baserunning Coordinator: Aaron Rowand. Infield Coordinator: Vance Law. Camp Coordinator: Tommy Thompson. Quality Control Coach: Everett Teaford. Leadership Development Coordinator: Ben Broussard. Assistant, Player Development: Rafael Santana. Pitching Assistant: J.R. Perdew. Rehab Pitching Coach: Brian Drahman. Education Coordinator: Erin Santana. Conditioning Coordinator: Dale Torborg. Minor League Medical/Rehabilitation Coordinator: Scott Takao. Physical Therapist: Derrick Garris. Latin/Cultural Development Coordinator: Anthony Santiago. Dominican Republic Academy Supervisor: Ever Magallanes.

FARM SYSTEM

Class	Club (League)	Manager	Hitting Coach	Pitching Coach
Triple-A	Charlotte (IL)	Mark Grudzielanek	Andy Tomberlin	Steve McCatty
Double-A	Birmingham (SL)	Julio Vinas	Cole Armstrong	Richard Dotson
High A	Winston-Salem (CL)	Omar Vizquel	Charlie Poe	Matt Zaleski
Low A	Kannapolis (SAL)	Justin Jirschele	Jamie Dismuke	Jose Bautista
Rookie	Great Falls (PIO)	Tim Esmay	Eric Richardson	John Ely
Rookie	White Sox (AZL)	Ryan Newman	Gary Ward	Felipe Lira
Rookie	White Sox (DSL)	Julio Valdez	Angel Gonzalez	Leo Hernandez

SCOUTING
Telephone: (312) 674-1000. Fax: (312) 674-5105.
Director, Amateur Scouting: Nick Hostetler (Hebron, KY).
Senior Advisor, Scouting Operations: Doug Laumann. National Crosscheckers: Nathan Durst (Sycamore, IL), Ed Pebley (Brigham City, UT), Mike Shirley (Anderson, IN). Regional Crosscheckers: East: Tim Bittner (Mechanicsville, PA), Midwest: Garrett Guest (Frankfort, IL), West-Derek Valenzuela (Temecula, CA), Southeast: Juan Alvarez (Miami, FL). Advisor to Baseball Department: Larry Monroe (Schaumburg, IL).
Area Scouts: Mike Baker (Santa Ana, CA), Kevin Burrell (Sharpsburg, GA), Robbie Cummings (Kansas City, MO), Ryan Dorsey (Dallas, TX) Abe Fernandez (Ft. Mill, SC), Mike Gagne (Portland, OR), Joel Grampietro (Revere, MA), Phil Gulley (Morehead, KY), Warren Hughes (Mobile, AL), JJ Lally (Denison, IA), George Kachigian (Coronado, CA), John Kazanas (Phoenix, AZ), Steve Nichols (Mount Dora, FL), Jose Ortega (Fort Lauderdale, FL), Noah St. Urbain (Stockton, CA), Adam Virchis (Modesto, CA), Chris Walker (Houston, TX), Justin Wechsler (Niles, MI), Kenny Williams, Jr. (Los Angeles, CA).
Pro Scouts: Bruce Benedict (Atlanta, GA), Joe Butler (Long Beach, CA), Toney Howell (Darien, IL) Chris Lein (Jacksonville, FL), Alan Regier (Gilbert, AZ), Daraka Shaheed (Vallejo, CA), Joe Siers (Wesley Chapel, FL), Keith Staab (College Station, TX), John Tumminia (Newburgh, NY), Bill Young (Scottsdale, AZ).
International Scouts: Amador Arias (Maracay, Venezuela), Marino DeLeon (Yamasa, Dominican Republic),Robinson Garces (Maracaibo, Venezuela), Tomas Herrera (Saltillo, Mexico), Reydel Hernandez (Puerto La Cruz, Venezuela), Ruddy Moreta, Supervisor Latin America (Santo Domingo, Dominican Republic), Miguel Peguero (Santo Domingo, Dominican Republic), Guillermo Peralta (Santiago, Dominican Republic), Omar Sanchez (Valencia, Venezuela), Fermin Ubri (Bani, Dominican Republic), Oliver Dominguez (Higuey, Dominican Republic).

Cincinnati Reds

Office Address: 100 Joe Nuxhall Way, Cincinnati, OH 45202.
Telephone: (513) 765-7000. **Fax:** (513) 765-7342.
Website: www.reds.com.

OWNERSHIP

Operated by: The Cincinnati Reds LLC. **President and Chief Executive Officer:** Robert H. Castellini. **Chairman:** W. Joseph Williams Jr. **Vice Chairman and Treasurer:** Thomas L. Williams. **Chief Operating Officer:** Phillip J. Castellini. **Executive Operations Manager:** Shellie Petrey. **President of Baseball Operations, General Manager:** Dick Williams. **Secretary and Treasurer:** Christopher L. Fister.

BUSINESS OPERATIONS

Senior Vice President, Business Operations: Karen Forgus. **Business Operations Assistant:** Teddy Siegel. **Business Operations, Assistant/Speakers Bureau:** Emily Mahle.

FINANCE/ADMINISTRATION

Sr. Vice President of Finance and CFO: Doug Healy. **Chief Legal Counsel:** James A. Marx. **Assistant to CFO/CLO:** Teena Schweier. **Vice President of Finance, Controller:** Bentley Viator. **Accounting Manager:** Jill Niemeyer. **Sr. Accountant:** Cathy Brakers. **Director, Financial Reporting/Payroll:** Leanna Weiss. **Payroll Accountant:** Ayanna Goddard.

SALES/TICKETING

VP, Ticketing & Business Development: Aaron Eisel. **Sr. Director, Ticket Sales & Service:** Mark Schueler. **Director, Season Sales & Retention:** Patrick Motague. **Manager, Sales/ Retention:** Shelley Volpenhein. **Season Sales Manager:** Chris Herrell. **Director, Premium Sales/Service:** Chris Bausano. **Premium Sales Manager:** Ryan Rizzo. **Sr. Director, Ticket Operations:** John O'Brien. **Manager of Ticket Partnerships:** Matthew Ollerdisse.

Bob Castellini

MEDIA RELATIONS

Vice President, Media Relations: Rob Butcher. **Director, Media Relations:** Larry Herms. **Director, Media Relations/Digital Content:** Jamie Ramsey.

COMMUNICATIONS/MARKETING

Vice President of Communications & Marketing: Ralph Mitchell. **Director of Digitial Media:** Lisa Braun. **Director of Marketing:** Audra Sordyl. **Director of Communications:** Jarrod Rollins. **Public Relations Manager:** Michael Anderson. **Promotional Purchasing/Broadcasting Admin.:** Lori Watt. **Communications Manager:** Brendan Hader. **Social Media Manager:** Chadwick Fischer. **Director of Creative Operations:** Jansen Dell. **Creative Services Manager:** Amy Calo. **Senior Designer:** Michael King. **Junior Graphic Designer:** Sara Treash.

COMMUNITY RELATIONS

Executive Director, Community Fund: Charley Frank. **Director, Community Relations:** Lindsey Dingeldein. **Diversity Relations Coordinator:** Natalya Herndon. **Director, Youth Academy & Sr. Outreach:** Jerome Wright.

2018 SCHEDULE

Standard Game Times: 7:10 p.m.; Sun. 1:10

MARCH		JULY	
MARCH	8-10 . . . . at New York (AL)	26-28 . . . Los Angeles (AL)	14-15 . . . . at Philadelphia
29-31 . . . . . at Tampa Bay	11-13 . . . . at Toronto	29-30 . . . at New York (AL)	17-19 . . . . . . .Tampa Bay
APRIL	14-16 . . . . Oakland	**JULY**	20-23 . . . . Cleveland
1 . . . . at Tampa Bay	18-20 . . . . Baltimore	1 . . . . . at New York (AL)	24-26 . . . . . at Tampa Bay
2-3 . . . . at Miami	22-24 . . . . . at Tampa Bay	2-4 . . . . . . at Washington	28-29 . . . . Miami
5-8 . . . . . . .Tampa Bay	25-27 . . . . Atlanta	6-8 . . . . . .at Kansas City	30-31 . . . .at Chicago (AL)
10-12 . . . .New York (AL)	28-30 . . . . .Toronto	9-11 . . . . Texas	**SEPTEMBER**
13-16 . . . . . . Baltimore	31 . . . . .at Houston	12-15 . . . . .Toronto	1-2 . . . . . .at Chicago (AL)
17-19 . at Los Angeles (AL)	**JUNE**	20-22 . . . . . . .at Detroit	3-5 . . . . at Atlanta
20-22 . . . . .at Oakland	1-3 . . . . .at Houston	23-25 . . . . . .at Baltimore	7-9 . . . . Houston
24-26 . . . . . . at Toronto	5-7 . . . . Detroit	26-29 . . . . . . Minnesota	11-13 . . . . .Toronto
27-29 . . . . . .Tampa Bay	8-10 . . . . . Chicago (AL)	30-31 . . . . . .Philadelphia	14-16 . . . . .New York (NL)
30 . . . . Kansas City	11-13 . . . . . .at Baltimore	**AUGUST**	18-20 . . . at New York (AL)
MAY	14-17 . . . . . .at Seattle	2-5 . . . . . . .New York (AL)	21-23 . . . . .at Cleveland
1-2 . . . . Kansas City	19-21 . . . . . at Minnesota	7-9 . . . . at Toronto	24-26 . . . . Baltimore
3-6 . . . . .at Texas	22-24 . . . . Seattle	10-12 . . . . . .at Baltimore	28-30 . . . . .New York (AL)

GENERAL INFORMATION

Stadium (year opened): Great American Ball Park (2003). **Team Colors:** Red, white and black.
Home Dugout: First Base.
Playing Surface: Grass.

BALLPARK OPERATIONS

Vice President, Ballpark Operations: Tim O'Connell. **Senior Director, Ballpark Operations:** Sean Brown. **Director, Ballpark Administration:** Colleen Rodenberg. **Security Manager:** Rebecca Vanderwaal. **Ballpark Operations Superintendent:** Bob Harrison. **Senior Manager, Guest/Event Operations:** Jan Koshover. **Ballpark Administrative Services Manager:** Jen Clemens. **Chief Engineer:** Roger Smith. **Assistant Chief Engineer:** Gary Goddard. **Head Groundskeeper:** Stephen Lord. **Assistant Head Groundskeeper:** Derrik Grubbs. **Grounds Supervisor:** Robbie Dworkin. **Public Safety Manager:** John Cordova.

BASEBALL OPERATIONS

Vice President, Assistant General Manager: Sam Grossman, Nick Krall. **Vice President, Senior Advisor to the GM:** Buddy Bell. **Senior Advisor to Baseball Operations:** Joe Morgan, Lou Piniella. **Senior Director, Interntational Operations:** Eric Lee. **Director, Sports Science Initiatives:** Charles Leddon. **Manager, Baseball Systems Development:** Brett Elkins. **Manager, Major League Video Operations:** Bo Thompson. **Manager, Baseball Analytics:** Michael Schatz. **Baseball Operations Analyst:** Mark Edwards, Pete Melgren. **Baseball Operations, Assistant & Spanish Translator:** Julio Morillo.

MEDICAL/TRAINING

Medical Director: Dr. Timothy Kremchek. **Assistant Medical Director:** Dr. Angel Velazquez. **Head Athletic Trainer:** Steve Baumann. **Assistant Athletic Trainers:** Jimmy Mattocks, Tomas Vera. **Stength & Conditioning Coordinator:** Sean Marohn.

Walt Jocketty

MAJOR LEAGUE STAFF

Manager: Bryan Price. **Coaches: Bench**—Jim Riggleman, **Hitting**—Don Long, **Pitching**— Mack Jenkins, **First Base**—Freddie Benavides, **Third Base**—Billy Hatcher, **Assistant Hitting**—Tony Jaramillo, **Assistant Pitching**—Ted Power, **Catching**—Mike Stefanski.

PLAYER DEVELOPMENT

Senior Director, Player Development: Jeff Graupe. **Special Assistant to GM, Player Performance:** Miguel Cairo, Eric Davis, Barry Larkin, Mario Soto. **Coordinator, Baseball Administration:** Melissa Hill. **Player Development Analyst:** Mark Heil. **Field Coordinator:** Bill Doran. **Hitting Coordinator:** Milt Thompson. **Pitching Coordinator:** Tony Fossas. **Latin American Field/Hitting Coordinator:** Joel Noboa. **Roving Outfield/Quality Control Instructor:** Darren Bragg. **Roving Outfield/Baserunner Instructor:** Delino DeShields. **Roving Catching Instructor:** Corky Miller. **Mental Skills Coach:** Frank Pfister. **Minor League Equipment Manager:** Jonathan Snyder. **Minor League Clubhouse Assistant:** John Bryk. **Minor League Video Coordinator:** Gary Hall.

FARM SYSTEM

Class	Club (League)	Manager	Hitting Coach	Pitching Coach
Triple-A	Louisville (IL)	Pat Kelly	Leon Durham	Jeff Fassero
Double-A	Pensacola (SL)	Jody Bell	Gookie Dawkins	Danny Darwin
High A	Daytona (FSL)	Ricky Gutierrez	Alex Pelaez	Tom Brown
Low A	Dayton (MWL)	Luis Bolivar	Daryle Ward	Seth Etherton
Rookie	Greeneville (APP)	Gookie Dawkins	Darryl Brinkley	Chad Cordero
Rookie	Billings (PIO)	Ray Martinez	Bryan LaHair	Derrin Ebert
Rookie	Reds (AZL)	Jose Nieves	Todd Takayoshi	Elmer Dessens
Rookie	Reds 1 (DSL)	Cristobal Rodriguez	E. Bens/L. Terrero	L. Andujar/L. Montano

SCOUTING

Assistant Director, Professional Scouting: Rob Coughlin. **Special Assistant to GM, Player Personnel:** Cam Bonifay, Shawn Pender, Terry Reynolds, Kevin Towers. **Special Assistant to the GM:** "J" Harrison, Marty Maier, John Morris, Jeff Schugel. **Professional Scout:** Gary Glover, Will Harford, Joe Jocketty, Bruce Manno, Mick Mattaliano, Jeff Morris, Steve Roadcap. **Manager, Pacfic RIm Scouting:** Rob Fidler. **Pacific Rim Scout:** Jamey Storvick. **Vice President Amateur Scouting:** Chris Buckley. **Assistant Director: Amateur Scouting:** Paul Pierson. **National Crosscheckers:** Jerry Flowers, Mark McKnight. **Regional Crosscheckers:** Bill Byckowski (East Coast, Canada), Rex De La Nuez (West Coast), Joe Katuska, Brad Meador (Midwest), Greg Zunino (Southeast). **Scouting Supervisors:** Charlie Aliano, Rich Bordi, Jeff Brookens, Sean Buckley, John Ceprini, Nick Christiani, Dan Cholowsky, Stephen Hunt, Rick Ingalls, Rick Jaques, Ben Jones, Mike Keenan, Mike Misuraca, Jim Moran, Hector Otero, John Poloni, Jonathan Reynolds, Paul Scott, Lee Seras, Andy Stack. **Scouts:** Larry Barton (Crestwood, KY), Jamie Bodaly (Langley, British Columbia, Canada), Ed Daub (Binghamton, NY), Jim Grief (Paducah, KY), Bill Killian (Stanwood, MI), Denny Negel (Cincinnati, OH), Lou Snipp (Humble, TX), Mike Steed (Beamsville, Ontario, Canada), Marlon Styes (Cincinnati, OH), Mike Wallace (Escondido, CA), Roger Weberg (Bemidji, MN). **Director, Interntaional Scouting:** Tony Arias. **Assistant Director, International Scouting:** Miguel Machado. **Director, Latin America Scouting:** Richard Jimenez. **International Crosschecker:** Bob Engel. **Coordinator, Dominican Republic:** Enmanuel Cartagena. **Coordinator, South America:** Richard Castro. **Coordinator, Carribbean/Mexican/Puerto Rico:** Hector Otero. **Supervisor, Dominican Republic:** Gary Peralta. **International Scouts:** Geronimo Blanco, Jose Valdelamar (Columbia), Edward Bens, Edgar Melo, Victor Nova, Carlos Pellerano, Felix Romero (Dominican Republic), Guillermo Armenta (Mexico), Anibal Reluz (Panama), Jean Paul Conde, Aguido Gonzalez, Victor Oramas, Ricardo Quintero (Venezuela).

Cleveland Indians

Office Address: Progressive Field, 2401 Ontario St., Cleveland, OH 44115.
Telephone: (216) 420-4200. **Fax:** (216) 420-4396.
Website: www.indians.com.

OWNERSHIP
Owner: Larry Dolan. **Chairman/Chief Executive Officer:** Paul Dolan. **Vice Chairman:** John Sherman.

BUSINESS OPERATIONS

President, Business Operations: Brian Barren. **Executive VP, Business:** Dennis Lehman.
Senior Vice President, Marketing/Strategy: Alex King. **Executive Administrative Assistant,
Ownership and Business Operations:** Dru Kosik.

CORPORATE PARTNERSHIPS/FINANCE
Senior Director, Corporate Partnership: Ted Baugh. **Director, Corporate Partnership
& Premium Hospitality:** Dom Polito. **Director, Premium Hospitality:** Ryan Robbins. **Senior
Sales Manager, Corporate Partnerships:** Bryan Hoffart. **Administrative Assistant:** Kim
Scott. **Senior VP, Finance/CFO:** Ken Stefanov. **VP/General Counsel:** Joe Znidarsic. **Vice
President, Finance:** Rich Dorffer. **Controller:** Erica Chambers. **Manager, Accounting:** Karen
Menzing. **Manager, Payroll Accounting/Services:** Mary Forkapa. **Concessions Accounting
Manager:** Diane Turner.

Larry Dolan

HUMAN RESOURCES
VP, Human Resources/Chief Diversity Officer: Sara Lehrke. **Director, Human Resources Operations:** Jennifer
Gibson. **Assistant Director, Talent Acquisition:** Mailynh Vu. **Manager, Talent Acquisition—Seasonal:** Valencia
Kimbrough. **Manager, Talent Development:** Nate Daymut. **Coordinator, Talent Development:** John Shand.
Coordinator, Benefits: Dori Jackson.

MARKETING
VP, Marketing/Brand Management: Nicole Schmidt. **Director, Brand Management:** Jason Wiedemann. **Manager,
Advertising/Promotions:** Anne Madzelan.

COMMUNICATIONS/BASEBALL INFORMATION
Telephone: (216) 420-4380. **Fax:** (216) 420-4430.
Senior VP, Public Affairs: Bob DiBiasio. **Senior Director, Communications:** Curtis Danburg. **Director, Baseball
Information:** Bart Swain. **Assistant Director, Baseball Information:** Court Berry-Tripp. **Major League Translator/
Family Relations Liaison:** Anna Bolton. **Team Photographer:** Dan Mendlik. **Coordinator, Communications and Team
Historian:** Jeremy Feador.

BALLPARK OPERATIONS
VP, Ballpark Operations: Jim Folk. **Senior Director, Ballpark Operations:** Jerry Crabb.

2018 SCHEDULE
Standard Game Times: 7:10 p.m.; Sun. 1:10.

MARCH	8-9 . . . . . . at Milwaukee	25-27 . . . . . . .at St. Louis	10-12 . . . .at Chicago (AL)
29-31 . . . . .at Seattle	11-13 . . . . . . Kansas City	29-30 . . . . . .at Oakland	13-15 . . . . . .at Cincinnati
	14-16 . . . . .at Detroit		17-19 . . . . Baltimore
APRIL	18-20 . . . . . .at Houston	**JULY**	20-23 . . . . .at Boston
1 . . . . .at Seattle	22-23 . . . .at Chicago (NL)	1 . . . . .at Oakland	24-26 . . . . .at Kansas City
2-4. . . at Los Angeles (AL)	24-27 . . . . Houston	2-4. . . . . . .at Kansas City	28-30 . . . . . . Minnesota
6-8. . . . . . . Kansas City	28-30 . . . . Chicago (AL)	6-8. . . . . Oakland	31 . . . . .Tampa Bay
9-12. . . . . Detroit	31 . . . . . . at Minnesota	9-11 . . . . Cincinnati	
13-15 . . . . .Toronto		12-15 . . . .New York (AL)	**SEPTEMBER**
17-18 . . . . at Minnesota	**JUNE**	20-22 . . . . .at Texas	1-2. . . . . . . .Tampa Bay
20-23 . . . . .at Baltimore	1-3. . . . . . at Minnesota	23-25 . . . . . . Pittsburgh	3-5. . . . . Kansas City
24-25 . . . . Chicago (NL)	5-6. . . . . . . .Milwaukee	27-29 . . . . . . .at Detroit	6-9. . . . . at Toronto
26-29 . . . . Seattle	8-10. . . . . . . .at Detroit	30-31 . . . . . at Minnesota	10-12 . . . . .at Tampa Bay
30 . . . . Texas	11-14 . . . .at Chicago (AL)		14-16 . . . . Detroit
	15-17 . . . . . . .Minnesota	**AUGUST**	18-20 . . . . . Chicago (AL)
MAY	18-20 . . . . Chicago (AL)	1 . . . . at Minnesota	21-23 . . . . Boston
1-2. . . . . Texas	22-24 . . . . Detroit	3-5. . . . Los Angeles (AL)	24-26 . . . .at Chicago (AL)
4-6. . . . . at New York (AL)		6-9. . . . . . . .Minnesota	27-30 . . . . .at Kansas City

GENERAL INFORMATION
Stadium (year opened):
Progressive Field (1994).
Team Colors: Navy blue, red and silver.

Home Dugout: Third Base.
Playing Surface: Grass.

Senior Director, Facility Operations: Seth Cooper. Head Groundskeeper: Brandon Koehnke. Director, Facility Maintenance: Ron Miller. Manager, Game Day Staff: Renee VanLaningham. Manager, Ballpark Operations: Steve Walters. Manager, Security: Omar Jufko. Director, Arizona Operations: Ryan Lantz.

TICKETING
Telephone: (216) 420-4487. Fax: (216) 420-4481. Ticket Services Manager: Shedrick Taylor. Manager, Ticket Operations: Seth Fuller. Ticket Services Coordinator: Paige Selle.

TEAM OPERATIONS/CLUBHOUSE
Director, Team Travel: Mike Seghi. Home Clubhouse Manager: Tony Amato. Assistant Home Clubhouse Manager: Brandon Biller. Director, Video Operations: Bob Chester.

BASEBALL OPERATIONS
President, Baseball Operations: Chris Antonetti. General Manager: Mike Chernoff. Assistant GMs: Matt Forman, Carter Hawkins. Vice President, Baseball Operations—Strategy/Administration: Brad Grant. Director, Baseball Operations: Eric Binder. Assistant Director, Baseball Operations: Alex Merberg. Senior Director, Baseball Research/Development: Sky Andrecheck. Assistant Director, Baseball Research/Development: Kevin Tenenbaum. Principal Data Scientist: Keith Woolner. Baseball Analyst: Max Marchi. Director, Baseball Administration: Wendy Hoppel. Executive Administrative Assistant: Marlene Lehky. Assistant, Baseball Operations: Sam Giller, Zach Morton.

Chris Antonetti

MAJOR LEAGUE STAFF
Manager: Terry Francona. Coaches: Bench—Brad Mills, Pitching—Carl Willis, Hitting—Ty Van Burkleo, First Base—Sandy Alomar Jr., Third Base—Mike Sarbaugh, Bullpen—Scott Atchison. Assistant Hitting Coach—Victor Rodriguez. Coach—Mark Budzinski, Brian Sweeney. Assistants, Major League Staff: Mike Barnett, Armando Camacaro, Ricky Pacione.

MEDICAL/TRAINING
Head Team Physician: Dr. Mark Schickendantz. Senior Director, Medical Services: Lonnie Soloff. Head Athletic Trainer: James Quinlan. Assistant Athletic Trainers: Jeff Desjardins, Michael Salazar.

PLAYER DEVELOPMENT
Director, Player Development: James Harris. Assistant Directors, Player Development: Matt Blake, Alex Eckelman. Administrative Assistant: Nilda Taffanelli. Advisors: Minnie Mendoza, Johnny Goryl, Tim Tolman. Special Assistants: Travis Hafner, Tim Belcher, Travis Fryman, Grady Sizemore, Dave Wallace, Robbie Thompson. Assistant Field Coordinator: Anthony Medrano. Coordinators: Ruben Niebla (pitching), John McDonald (defense), Ed Subel (strength/conditioning), Mark Allen (lower level pitching), Ken Knutson (pitching programs/rehab), Bruce Chen (cultural development), Andrew Pipkin (medical), Todd Kubacki (performance), Brian Miles (mental performance), Ryan Faer (Arizona Performance), Hasani Torres (Latin America Performance), Anna Bolton (Education and Language), Teddy Blackwell (Medical Administration).

FARM SYSTEM

Class	Club	Manager	Hitting Coach	Pitching Coach
Triple-A	Columbus (IL)	Chris Tremie	J.Narron/B. Magallanes	Steve Karsay
Double-A	Akron (EL)	Tony Mansolino	K. Howard/D. Malave	Rigo Beltran
High A	Lynchburg (CL)	Rouglas Odor	J. Toole/G. Fink	Tony Arnold
Low A	Lake County (MWL)	Luke Carlin	P. Lauritson/K. Hudson	Joe Torres
Short-season	Mahoning Valley (NYP)	Jim Pankovits	TBD/Omir Santos	Jason Blanton
Rookie	Indians (AZL)	Larry Day	J. Esposito/K. Correa	Joel Mangrum
Rookie	Indians (AZL)	Jerry Owens	J. Betances/M. Weiner	Owen Dew
Rookie	Indians (DSL)	Jose Mejia	Freddy Tiburicio	J. Sanchez/C. Jan
Rookie	Indians/Brewers (DSL)	Jose Mejia	M. Merganthaler/J. De La Cruz	

SCOUTING
Senior Director, Scouting Operations: John Mirabelli. Special Assistants to the GM: Steve Lubratich, Dave Malpass, Don Poplin. Vice President, Baseball Operations, Scouting/Administration: Brad Grant. Director, Amateur Scouting: Scott Barnsby. Senior Advisor, Amateur Scouting: Bo Hughes (Sherman Oaks, CA). Coordinator, Amateur Scouting: Clint Longenecker. Assistant, Amateur Scouting: Rob Cerfolio. National Crosschecker: Scott Meaney (Holly Springs, NC). Regional Crosscheckers: Kevin Cullen (Frisco, TX), Jon Heuerman (Chandler, AZ), Junie Melendez (Avon, OH), Mike Soper (Tampa, FL), Brad Tyler (Bishop, GA). Regional Crosscheckers: Jon Heuerman (Chandler, AZ), Kevin Cullen (Frisco, TX), Junie Melendez (Avon, OH), Mike Soper (Tampa, FL), Brad Tyler (Bishop, GA). Area Scouts: Steve Abney (Lawrence, KS), Chuck Bartlett (Starkville, MS), CT Bradford (Atlanta, GA), Mike Bradford (Raleigh, NC), David Compton (Cypress, CA), Aaron Etchison (Dexter, MI), Conor Glassey (Bothell, WA), Mike Kanen (Hoboken, NJ), Andrew Krause (Jacksonville, FL), Blaze Lambert (Burleson, TX), Pete Loizzo (Madison, WI), Don Lyle (Sacramento, CA), Bob Mayer (Somerset, PA), Carlos Muniz (San Pedro, CA), Ryan Perry (Phoenix, AZ), Steffan Segui (Tampa, FL), Kyle Van Hook (Brenham, TX). Part-Time Scouts: Matt Czechanski, Trent Friedrich, Bob Malkmus, Bill Schudlich, Adam Stahl, John Stott, Jose Trujillo. Director, Pro Scouting: Victor Wang. Pro Scouts: Mike Calitri (Tampa, FL), Doug Carpenter (North Palm Beach, FL), Chris Gale (Austin, TX), Trey Hendricks (Cleveland, OH), Dave Miller (Wilmington, NC), Brent Urcheck (Philadelphia, PA), Dan Budreika (Phoenix, AZ), Ethan Purser (Hiram, GA). Director, International Scouting: Paul Gillispie. Assistant Director, International Scouting: Jason Lynn. Assistant, International Scouting: Richard Conway. International Crosschecker: Koby Perez.

Colorado Rockies

Office Address: 2001 Blake St., Denver, CO 80205.
Telephone: (303) 292-0200. **Fax:** (303) 312-2116.
Website: www.coloradorockies.com.

OWNERSHIP
Operated by: Colorado Rockies Baseball Club Ltd. **Owner/General Partner:** Charles K. Monfort. **Owner/Chairman/Chief Executive Officer:** Richard L. Monfort. **Executive Assistant to the Owner/Chairman/Chief Executive Officer:** Terry Douglass.

BUSINESS OPERATIONS

Executive Vice President/Chief Operating Officer: Greg Feasel. **Assistant to Executive VP/Chief Operating Officer:** Kim Olson. **VP, Human Resources:** Elizabeth Stecklein.

FINANCE
Executive VP/CFO/General Counsel: Hal Roth. **General Counsel:** Brian Gaffney. **VP, Finance:** Michael Kent. **Senior Director, Purchasing:** Gary Lawrence. **Coordinator, Purchasing:** Gloria Giraldi. **Senior Director, Accounting:** Phil Emerson. **Accountants:** Joel Binfet, Laine Campbell. **Payroll Administrator:** Juli Daedelow.

SALES
VP, Corporate Partnerships: Walker Monfort. **Assistant to VP, Corporate Partnerships:** Nicole Ortiz. **Assistant Director, Corporate Partnerships:** Kari Anderson. **Senior Account Executive:** Nate VanderWal. **Account Executives:** Sam Porter, Chris Zumbrennen. **VP, Community/Retail Operations:** James P. Kellogg. **Sr. Director, Retail Operations:** Aaron Heinrich. **Sr. Director, In-Game Entertainment & Broadcasting:** Kent Krosbakken.

Richard Monfort

MARKETING/COMMUNICATIONS
Telephone: (303) 312-2325. **Fax:** (303) 312-2319.
VP, Marketing/Communications: Jill Campbell. **Supervisor, Advertising/Marketing:** Sarah Topf. **Assistant Director, Digital Media & Publications:** Julian Valentin. **Assistant, Social Media/Publications:** Lauren Jacaruso. **Coordinator, Communications/Marketing:** Erin Shneider. **Sr. Director, Communications:** Warren Miller. **Supervisor, Communications:** Cory Little. **Coordinators, Communications:** Nick Parson. **Assistant, Spanish Translator/Communications:** Abby Thayer.

BALLPARK OPERATIONS
VP, Ballpark Operations: Kevin Kahn. **Senior Director, Food Service Operations/Development:** Albert Valdes. **Senior Director, Guest Services:** Steven Burke. **Head Groundskeeper:** Mark Razum. **Assistant Head Groundskeeper:** Jon Larson. **Senior Director, Engineering/Facilities:** Allyson Gutierrez. **Director, Engineering:** Randy Carlill. **Director, Facilities:** Oly Olsen. **Senior Director, Information Systems:** Michael Bush. **Official Scorers:** Dave Einspahr, Dave Plati. **Public Address Announcer:** Reed Saunders.

2018 SCHEDULE
Standard Game Times: 6:40 p.m.; Sat. 6:10; Sun. 1:10.

MARCH
29-31 . . . . . at Tampa Bay

APRIL
2-5 . . . . . . at San Diego
6-8 . . . . Atlanta
9-11 . . . . San Diego
12-15 . . . at Washington
16-18 . . . . . at Pittsburgh
20-22 . . . . . Chicago (NL)
23-25 . . . . . San Diego
27-29 . . . . at Miami
30 . . . . . .at Chicago (NL)

MAY
1-2 . . . . . .at Chicago (NL)
4-6 . . . . . at New York (NL)
8-9 . . . . . Los Angeles (AL)

10-13 . . . . . . .Milwaukee
14-15 . . . . at San Diego
17-20 . . . at San Francisco
21-23 . at Los Angeles (NL)
25-27 . . . . . . Cincinnati
28-30 . . . . San Francisco

JUNE
1-3 . . . . . Los Angeles (NL)
5-7 . . . . .at Cincinnati
8-10 . . . . .Arizona
12-14 . . . . at Philadelphia
15-17 . . . . .at Texas
18-21 . . . . .New York (NL)
22-24 . . . . .Miami
26-28 . . . at San Francisco
29-30 . at Los Angeles (NL)

JULY
1 . . . . at Los Angeles (NL)
2-4 . . . . . . San Francisco
6-8 . . . . .at Seattle
10-12 . . . . .Arizona
13-15 . . . . Seattle
20-22 . . . . . . at Arizona
24-25 . . . . Houston
27-29 . . . . Oakland
30-31 . . . . .at St. Louis

AUGUST
1-2 . . . . .at St. Louis
3-5 . . . . . . at Milwaukee
6-8 . . . . Pittsburgh
9-12 . . . . . Los Angeles (NL)
14-15 . . . . . . .at Houston

16-19 . . . . at Atlanta
21-23 . . . . San Diego
24-26 . . . . St. Louis
27-28 . at Los Angeles (AL)
30-31 . . . . at San Diego

SEPTEMBER
1-2 . . . . at San Diego
3-5 . . . . . . San Francisco
7-9 . . . . .Los Angeles (NL)
10-13 . . . . .Arizona
14-16 . . . at San Francisco
17-19 . at Los Angeles (NL)
21-23 . . . . at Arizona
24-27 . . . . . .Philadelphia
28-30 . . . . . .Washington

GENERAL INFORMATION
Stadium (year opened): Coors Field (1995). **Playing Surface:** Grass.
Team Colors: Purple, black and silver.
Home Dugout: First Base.

TICKETING

Telephone: (303) 762-5437, (800) 388-7625. **Fax:** (303) 312-2115.
VP, Ticket Operations/Sales/Services: Sue Ann McClaren. **Senior Director, Ticket Services/Finance/Technology:** Kent Hakes. **Assistant Director, Ticket Operations:** Kevin Flood. **Senior Director, Season Tickets/Renewals/ Business Strategy:** Jeff Benner. **Assistant Director, Season Tickets:** Farrah Magee. **Senior Director, Groups/ Suites/Outbound Sales:** Matt Haddad. **Manager, Suites/Party Facilities:** Traci Abeyta. **Senior Account Executive, Outbound Sales:** Todd Thomas. **Supervisor, Inside Sales:** Justin Bennett.

TRAVEL/CLUBHOUSE

Director, Major League Operations: Paul Egins. **Manager, Major League Clubhouse:** Mike Pontarelli.

BASEBALL OPERATIONS

Senior VP/General Manager: Jeff Bridich. **Assistant to Senior VP/GM:** Adele Armagost. **Assistant GM, Baseball Operations/Assistant General Counsel:** Zack Rosenthal. **Assistant GM/Player Personnel:** Jon Weil. **Manager, Baseball Administration:** Domenic DiRicco. **Coordinator, Baseball Operations/Staff Counsel:** Matt Obernauer. **Manager, Baseball Research/Development:** Trevor Patch. **Baseball Data Architect:** Jamie Hollowell. **Special Assistant to the GM:** Danny Montgomery.

MAJOR LEAGUE STAFF

Manager: Bud Black. **Coaches: Bench**—Mike Redmond, **Pitching**—Steve Foster, **Hitting**—Duane Espy, **Assistant Hitting Coach**—Jeff Salazar, **Third Base**—Stu Cole, **First Base**—Tony Diaz, **Coach**—Ron Gideon, **Bullpen**—Darren Holmes, **Bullpen Catcher**—Aaron Munoz, **Director, Physical Performance**—Gabe Bauer, **Video**—Brian Jones.

Jeff Bridich

MEDICAL/TRAINING

Senior Director, Medical Operations/Special Projects: Tom Probst. **Medical Director:** Dr. Thomas Noonan. **Club Physicians:** Dr. Allen Schreiber, Dr. Douglas Wyland. **Head Trainer:** Keith Dugger. **Assistant Athletic Trainer:** Scott Gehret.

PLAYER DEVELOPMENT

Director, Pitching Operations: Mark Wiley. **Pitching Coordinator:** Doug Linton, Darryl Scott. **Catching Coordinator:** Mark Strittmatter. **Hitting and Bunting Coordinator:** Darin Everson. **Outfield and Baserunning Coordinator:** Anothony Sanders. **Rehab Coordinator:** Scott Murayama. **Assistant Rehab Coordinator:** Andy Stover. **Physical Performance Coordinator:** Trevor Swartz. **Mental Skills Coordinator:** Doug Chadwick. **Assistant Mental Skills Coordinator:** Unavailable. **Minor League Video Coordinator:** Jeff Nelson. **Supervisor, Cultural Development:** Josh Rosenthal. **Coordinator, Cultural Development:** Angel Amparo. **Latin America Field Coordinator:** Edison Lora. **Equipment Manager:** Ricky Dominguez.

FARM SYSTEM

Class	Club (League)	Manager	Hitting Coach	Pitching Coach
Triple-A	Albuquerque (PCL)	Glenallen Hill	Tim Doherty	Brandon Emanuel
Double-A	Hartford (EL)	Warren Schaeffer	Mark Brewer	Lee Stevens
High A	Lancaster (CAL)	Frank Gonzales	Unavailable	Dave Burba
Low A	Asheville (SAL)	Marv Foley	Norberto Martin	Ryan Kibler
Short-season	Boise (NWL)	Scott Little	Cesar Galvez	Bob Apodaca
Rookie	Grand Junction (PIO)	Unavailable	Jake Opitz	Doug Jones
Rookie	Rockies 1 (DSL)	Mauricio Gonzalez	Florentino Nunez	Eugenio Jose
Rookie	Rockies 2 (DSL)	Julio Campos	Michael Ramirez	Unavailable

SCOUTING

VP, Scouting: Bill Schmidt. **Senior Director, Scouting Operations:** Marc Gustafson. **Special Assistant, GM:** Danny Montgomery. **Assistant Scouting Director:** Damon Iannelli. **Special Assistant, Scouting:** Rick Mathews. **Assistant Director, Scouting Operations:** Sterling Monfort. **Assistant, Scouting/Baseball Operations:** Irma Castaneda. **Advance Scouts:** Chris Warren, Joe Little. **Special Assistant, Player Personnel:** Ty Coslow (Louisville, KY). **Major League Scouts:** Steve Fleming (Louisa, VA), Will George (Milford, DE), Jack Gillis (Sarasota, FL), Mark Germann (Denver, CO), Joe Housey (Hollywood, FL), Mike Paul (Tucson, AZ), John Corbin (Savannah, GA). **Professional Scout:** Doug Bernier (Littlejohn, CO). **National Crosscheckers:** Mike Ericson (Phoenix, AZ), Jay Matthews (Concord, NC). **Area Scouts:** Scott Alves (Phoenix, AZ), Brett Baldwin (Kansas City, MO), Julio Campos (Guaynabo, PR) John Cedarburg (Fort Myers, FL), Scott Corman (Lexington, KY), Jordan Czarniecki (Greenville, SC), Jeff Edwards (Fresno, TX), Sean Gamble (Atlanta, GA), Mike Garlatti (Edison, NJ), Matt Hattabaugh (Westminster, CA), Darin Holcomb (Woodland, CA), Jon Lukens (Dana Point, CA), Matt Pignataro (Seattle, WA), Jesse Retzlaff (Dallas, TX), Rafael Reyes (Miami, FL), Ed Santa (Powell, OH), Zack Zulli (Hammond, LA) **Part-Time Scouts:** Norm DeBriyn (Fayetteville, AR), Dave McQueen (Bossier City, LA), Greg Pullia (Plymouth, MA). **VP, International Scouting/Player Development:** Rolando Fernandez. **Supervisor, Venezuelan Scouting:** Orlando Medina. **International Scouts:** Phil Allen (Australia), Martin Cabrera (Dominican Republic), Carlos Gomez (Venezuela), Raul Gomez (International), Alving Mejias (International), Frank Roa (Dominican Republic), Jossher Suarez (Venezuela). **Part-Time International Scouts:** Rogers Figueroa (Colombia), Marius Loupadiere (Panama).

Detroit Tigers

Office Address: 2100 Woodward Ave, Detroit, MI 48201.
Telephone: (313) 471-2000. **Fax:** (313) 471-2138. **Website:** www.tigers.com

OWNERSHIP

Operated By: Detroit Tigers Inc. **President and CEO, Ilitch Holdings, Inc./Chairman and CEO, Detroit Tigers:** Christopher Ilitch. **Group President, Sports & Entertainment, Ilitch Holdings, Inc.:** Chris Granger.

BUSINESS OPERATIONS

Executive Vice President, Business Operations: Duane McLean. **Executive Assistant to Executive VP, Business Operations:** Peggy Thompson.

Chris Ilitch

FINANCE/ADMINISTRATION

VP, Finance/Administration/CFO: Stephen Quinn. **Senior Director, Finance:** Kelli Kollman. **Director, Purchasing/Supplier Diversity:** DeAndre Berry. **Accounting Manager/Treasury Analyst:** Sheila Robine. **Financial Analyst:** Kristin Jorgensen. **Accounts Payable Coordinator:** Debra Sword. **Accounts Receivable Coordinator:** Monica Basil. **Senior Director, Human Resources:** Karen Gruca. **Human Resources Coordinator:** Kelsey Shuck. **Internal Audit Manager:** Candice Lentz. **Payroll Administrator:** Mark Cebelak. **Payroll Coordinator:** Stephanie Jenkins. **Director, Authentics:** Marc Himelstein. **Authentics Coordinator:** Ashley Baughman. **Administrative/Accounting Assistant:** Tina Sidney.

PUBLIC/COMMUNITY AFFAIRS

VP, Community/Public Affairs: Elaine Lewis. **Director, Player Relations & Detroit Tigers Foundation:** Jordan Field. **Manager, Community Affairs:** Courtney Kaplan. **Detroit Tigers Foundation Coordinator:** Ashley Robinson. **Community Affairs Coordinator:** Michael Demand. **Administrative Assistant:** Donna Bernardo.

SALES/MARKETING

VP, Corporate Partnerships: Steve Harms. **Corporate Partnership Sales Directors:** Kurt Tiesman, John Wolski. **Corporate Partnership Sales Managers:** Soula Burns, Matt Stepnes. **Corporate Partnerships Account Executive:** Corey Thomas. **Partnership Services Manager:** Kaitlin Knutson. **Partnership Services Coordinators:** Jessica Langolf, Ellyn Yurgalite.

VP, Ticket/Suite Sales: Scot Pett. **Directory, Ticket Sales:** Steve Fox. **Director, Group Sales:** Dwain Lewis. **Assistant Director, Ticket Sales:** Jeff Lutz. **Director, Suite Sales/Service:** Rod Emmons. **Manager, Suite Sales/Service:** Dan Griesbaum. **Suite Sales/Services Account Manager:** Jeff Sanders. **Suite Sales/Services Coordinator:** Kelsey Decker.

VP, Marketing: Ellen Hill Zeringue. **Director, Marketing:** Ron Wade.

Graphic Designer: Courtney Foyt. **Digital/Social Media Specialist:** Mac Slavin. **Marketing/Promotions Administrative Coordinator:** Kelly Shaddock. **Manager, Promotions/Special Events:** Haley Kolff. **Promotions/Special Events Coordinators:** Erin Morris, Skylan Morris.

2018 SCHEDULE

Standard Game Times: 7:10 p.m.; Sun. 1:10.

MARCH
29-31 . . . . Pittsburgh

APRIL
1 . . . . Pittsburgh
2-4. . . . . Kansas City
5-8. . . . . .at Chicago (AL)
9-12 . . . . . .at Cleveland
13-15 . . . .New York (AL)
17-19 . . . . . . Baltimore
20-22 . . . . . Kansas City
24-26 . . . . . at Pittsburgh
27-29 . . . . .at Baltimore
30 . . . . .Tampa Bay

MAY
1-2. . . . . . . .Tampa Bay
3-6. . . . . .at Kansas City

7-9. . . . . .at Texas
11-13 . . . . Seattle
14-16 . . . . Cleveland
17-20 . . . . . . .at Seattle
21-23 . . . . . at Minnesota
25-27 . . . . . Chicago (AL)
28-31 . . . Los Angeles (AL)

JUNE
1-3. . . . . .Toronto
5-7. . . . . .at Boston
8-10 . . . . Cleveland
12-14 . . . . . . Minnesota
15-17 . . .at Chicago (AL)
19-20 . . . . .at Cincinnati
22-24 . . . . .at Cleveland
25-28 . . . . . . Oakland
29-30 . . . . . . at Toronto

JULY
1-2. . . . . . . at Toronto
3-4. . . . . .at Chicago (NL)
5-8. . . . . Texas
9-11 . . . . . at Tampa Bay
13-15 . . . . . .at Houston
20-22 . . . . Boston
23-25 . . . .at Kansas City
27-29 . . . . . . Cleveland
31 . . . . Cincinnati

AUGUST
1 . . . . Cincinnati
3-5. . . . . . . .at Oakland
6-8. . . at Los Angeles (AL)
10-12 . . . . . . Minnesota
13-15 . . . . Chicago (AL)
16-19 . . . . . at Minnesota

21-22 . . . . . Chicago (NL)
23-26 . . . . . Chicago (AL)
28-29 . . . .at Kansas City
30-31 . . . at New York (AL)

SEPTEMBER
1-2. . . . . at New York (AL)
3-5. . . . . .at Chicago (AL)
7-9. . . . . St. Louis
10-12 . . . . Houston
14-16 . . . . . .at Cleveland
17-19 . . . . . . Minnesota
20-23 . . . . . Kansas City
25-27 . . . . . at Minnesota
28-30 . . . . . at Milwaukee

GENERAL INFORMATION

Stadium (year opened):
Comerica Park (2000).
Team Colors: Navy blue, orange and white.

Home Dugout: Third Base.
Playing Surface: Grass.

MEDIA RELATIONS/COMMUNICATIONS

Telephone: (313) 471-2114. **Fax:** (313) 471-2138.

VP, Communications: Ron Colangelo. **Director, Baseball Media Relations:** Chad Crunk. **Coordinators, Media Relations:** Ben Fidelman, Bryan Loor-Almonte, Michele Wysocki. **Director, Broadcasting/In-Game Entertainment:** Stan Fracker.

BASEBALL OPERATIONS

Telephone: (313) 471-2000. **Fax:** (313) 471-2099.

Al Avila

Executive Vice President, Baseball Operations/General Manager: Al Avila. **Special Assistants to the GM:** Willie Horton, Al Kaline, Jim Leyland, Alan Trammell, Dick Egan, Mike Russell. **VP/Assistant GM:** David Chadd. **VP/Assistant GM/General Counsel:** John Westhoff. **VP, Player Personnel:** Scott Bream. **VP/Player Development:** Dave Littlefield. **Senior Director, Baseball Analytics/Operations:** Jay Sartori. **Director, Baseball Operations/Professional Scouting:** Sam Menzin. **Manager, Baseball Analytics:** Jim Logue. **Assistant Counsel, Baseball Operations:** Alan Avila. **Executive Assistant to the Executive Vice President, Baseball Operations/General Manager:** Marty Lyon. **Executive Assistant to the Assistant GM's:** Eileen Surma.

MAJOR LEAGUE STAFF

Manager: Ron Gardenhire. **Coaches: Pitching**—Chris Bosio, **Hitting** —Lloyd McClendon, **First Base**—Ramon Santiago, **Third Base**—Dave Clark, **Bullpen**—Rick Anderson, **Bench**—Steve Liddle, **Assistant Hitting**—Phil Clark.

MEDICAL/TRAINING

Senior Director, Medical Services: Kevin Rand. **Head Athletic Trainer:** Doug Teter. **Assistant Athletic Trainer:** Matt Rankin. **Physical Therapist:** Robbie Williams. **Strength/Conditioning Coach:** Chris Walter. **Assistant Strength/Conditioning Coach:** Yousef Zamat. **Team Physicians:** Dr. Michael Workings, Dr. Stephen Lemos, Dr. Louis Saco (Florida). **Coordinator, Medical Services:** Gwen Keating.

PLAYER DEVELOPMENT

VP, Player Development: Dave Littlefield. **Director, Minor League Operations:** Dan Lunetta. **Director, Player Development:** Dave Owen. **Director, Minor League/Scouting Administration:** Cheryl Evans. **Administrative Assistant, Minor League Operations:** Marilyn Acevedo. **Minor League Field Coordinator:** Bill Dancy. **Minor League Strength/Conditioning Coordinator:** Steve Chase. **Roving Instructors:** Bruce Fields (hitting), Scott Fletcher (hitting), A.J. Sager (pitching), Joe DePastino (catching), Jose Valentin (Infield), Gene Roof (outfield/baserunning), Jaime Garcia (assistant pitching), Brian Peterson (mental skills instructor), Josman Robles (Latin American performance coach).

FARM SYSTEM

Class	Club	Manager	Hitting Coach	Pitching Coach
Triple-A	Toledo(IL)	Doug Mientkiewicz	Brian Harper	Jeff Pico
Double-A	Erie(EL)	Andrew Graham	Mike Hessman	Willie Blair
High A	Lakeland(FSL)	Mike Rabelo	Tim Garland	Mark Johnson
Low A	West Michigan (MWL)	Lance Parrish	Mariano Duncan	Jorge Cordova
Short-season	Connecticut(NYP)	Gerald Laird	Rafael Martinez	Ace Adams
Rookie	Tigers West (GCL)	Gary Cathcart	Bill Springman	Mike Alvarez
Rookie	Tigers East (GCL)	Luis Lopez	Rafael Gil	Carlos Bohorquez
Rookie	DSL Tigers (DSL)	Ramon Zapata	Jose Ovalles	Jose Parra
Rookie	DSL Tigers 2 (DSL)	Jesus Garces	Marco Yepez	Luis Marte

SCOUTING

VP, Assistant General Manager: David Chadd. **VP, Player Personnel:** Scott Bream. **Director, Amateur Scouting:** Scott Pleis. **Assistant Director, Amateur/International Scouting:** Eric Nieto. **Amateur Scouting Video Coordinator:** Sam Nasci. **Amateur Scouting Interns:** Alex Tarandek, Joey Lothrop. **Amateur Scouting Video Intern:** Matt Zmuda. **Major League Scouts:** Ray Crone (Cedar Hill, TX), Jim Elliott (Winston-Salem, NC), Kevin Ellis (Katy, TX), Joe Ferrone (Grosse Pointe, MI), Randy Johnson (Valley Center, CA), Don Kelly (Mars, PA), Paul Mirocke (Tampa, FL), Yadalla Mufdi (Miami, FL), Jim Olander (Vail, AZ), Gary Pellant (Phoenix, AZ), Jim Rough (Ocala, FL), Bruce Tanner (New Castle, PA), **Senior Advisors:** Scott Reid (Phoenix, AZ), Murray Cook (Orlando, FL). **Special Assistants to the GM:** Dick Egan, Mike Russell. **National Crosscheckers:** Tim Hallgren (Cape Girardeau, MO), Steve Hinton (Mather, CA). **Regional Crosscheckers: East**—James Orr (Oviedo, FL), **Central**—Tim Grieve (New Braunfels, TX), **Midwest**—Mike Hankins (Greenwood, MO), **West**—Marti Wolever (Scottsdale, AZ). **Area Scouts:** Nate Avila (Pembroke Pines, FL), Bryson Barber (Atlanta, GA), Taylor Black (Raleigh, NC), Jim Bretz (South Windsor, CT), RJ Burgess (St. Petersburg, FL), Scott Cerny (Rocklin, CA), Dave Dangler (Camas, WA), Brad Fidler (Douglassville, PA), Justin Henry (Vicksburg, MS), Ryan Johnson (Wichita, KS), Jeff Kunkel (Ann Arbor, MI), Matt Lea (Austin, TX), Dave Lottsfeldt (Castle Rock, CO), Tim McWilliam (San Diego, CA), Steve Pack (San Marcos, CA), Mike Smith (Plano, TX), Harold Zonder (Louisville, KY). **Part-Time Scouts:** German Geigel (PR), Deryl Horton (MI), Mark Monahan (MI), Clyde Weir (MI). **Director, International Operations:** Tom Moore. Director, **Latin American Scouting:** Miguel Garcia. Director, **Latin American Player Development:** Manny Crespo. **International Operations Coordinator:** Rafael Gonzalez. **International Crosschecker:** Jeff Wetherby. **International Crosschecker:** Alejandro Rodriguez. Coordinator, **Pacific Rim:** Kevin Hooker. Director, **Dominican Republic Operations:** Ramon Perez. Director, **Dominican Academy/Cuban Specialist:** Oliver Arias. **Dominican Scouting Supervisor:** Aldo Perez. **Venezuelan Scouting Supervisor:** Jesus Mendoza. **Venezuelan Academy Administrator/Area Scout:** Oscar Garcia. **International Operations Intern:** Marcelo Parker and Cristian **Crespo. International Area Scouts:** Michael Hsieh (Taiwan), Ho-Kyun Im (Korea), Raul Leiva (Venezuela), Luis Molina (Panama), Delvis Pacheco (Venezuela), Rodolfo Penalo (Dominican Republic), Miguel Rodriguez (Dominican Republic), Carlos Santana (Dominican Republic), Yas Sato (Japan), Glenn Williams (Australia).

Houston Astros

Office Address: Minute Maid Park, Union Station, 501 Crawford, Suite 400, Houston, TX 77002.
Mailing Address: PO Box 288, Houston, TX 77001. **Telephone:** (713) 259-8000. **Fax:** (713) 259-8981.
Email Address: fanfeedback@astros.mlb.com. **Website:** www.astros.com.

OWNERSHIP
Owner/Chairman: Jim Crane.

BUSINESS OPERATIONS

President, Business Operations: Reid Ryan. **Executive Advisor:** Nolan Ryan. **Executive Assistant:** Eileen Colgin. **Senior VP, Business Operations:** Marcel Braithwaite. **Senior VP, Corporate Partnerships:** Matt Brand. **Senior VP, Community Relations/Executive Director, Astros Foundation:** Twila Carter. **Senior VP, Ticket Sales/Service:** Jason Howard. **Senior VP/General Counsel:** Giles Kibbe. **Senior VP, Marketing/Communications:** Anita Sehgal. **Chief Financial Officer:** Michael Slaughter. **VP, Tax:** Vito Ciminello. **VP, Communications:** Gene Dias. **VP, Strategy/Analytics:** Michael Dillon. **VP, Stadium Operations:** Bobby Forrest. **VP, Information Technology:** Chris Hanz. **VP, Foundation Development:** Marian Harper. **VP, Merchandising/Retail Operations:** Tom Jennings. **VP, Human Resources:** Vivian Mora. **VP, Finance:** Doug Seckel. **VP, Event Sales/Operations:** Stephanie Stegall. **VP, Marketing:** Jason Wooden. **Senior Director, Business Operations:** Dan O'Neill.

Jim Crane

COMMUNICATIONS/COMMUNITY RELATIONS
Senior Managers, Communications: Steve Grande, Dena Propis. **Coordinator, Communications:** Chris Peixoto. **Manager, Broadcasting:** Ginny Gotcher Grande. **Director, Astros Youth Academy:** Daryl Wade. **Manager, Astros Youth Academy:** Duane Stelly. **Coordinators, Community Relations/Astros Foundation:** Rachel Bubier, Andrew Remson. **Coordinator, Astros Youth Academy:** Megan Hays.

MARKETING/ANALYTICS
Senior Director, Marketing Operations and Insights: Craig Swaisgood. **Senior Director, Ballpark Entertainment:** Chris E. Garcia. **Senior Director, Business Strategy/Analytics:** Jay Verrill. **Director, Creative Services:** Chris David Garcia. **Senior Manager, Media Strategy/Marketing:** Ryan Smith. **Senior Managers, Marketing Entertainment:** Kyle Hamsher, Richard Tapia. **Senior Manager, Promotions/Events:** Brianna Carbonell. **Manager, Social Media:** Danny Farris.

CORPORATE PARTNERSHIPS
Senior Director, Corporate Partnerships: Creighton Kahoalii. **Senior Director, Corporate Partnerships/Special Event Sales:** Jeff Stewart. **Director, Sales/Corporate Sponsorships:** Keshia Henderson. **Sales Managers, Corporate Partnerships:** Enrique Cruz, Matt Richardson. **Senior Account Managers, Corporate Partnerships:** Melissa Hahn, Andrew Shipp. **Account Managers, Corporate Partnerships:** Chris Leahy, Everett Wolf.

2018 SCHEDULE
Standard Game Times: 7:10 p.m.; Sun. 1:10.

MARCH		
29-31 . . . . .at Texas		

APRIL
1 . . . . .at Texas
2-4 . . . . Baltimore
6-8 . . . . San Diego
9-11 . . . . . at Minnesota
13-15 . . . . Texas
16-19 . . . . .at Seattle
20-22 . . . .at Chicago (AL)
23-25 . . . Los Angeles (AL)
27-29 . . . . Oakland
30 . . . . . . New York (AL)

MAY
1-3 . . . . .New York (AL)
4-6 . . . . at Arizona

7-9 . . . . .at Oakland
11-13 . . . . Texas
14-16 . at Los Angeles (AL)
18-20 . . . . Cleveland
22-23 . . . . San Francisco
24-27 . . . . .at Cleveland
28-30 . . . at New York (AL)
31 . . . . Boston

JUNE
1-3 . . . . Boston
5-6 . . . . Seattle
7-10 . . . . .at Texas
12-14 . . . . . . .at Oakland
15-17 . . . .at Kansas City
18-20 . . . . . .Tampa Bay
22-24 . . . . Kansas City
25-27 . . . . .Toronto

28-30 . . . . . at Tampa Bay

JULY
1 . . . . at Tampa Bay
3-4 . . . . .at Texas
5-8 . . . . . . Chicago (AL)
9-12 . . . . Oakland
13-15 . . . . Detroit
20-22 . at Los Angeles (AL)
24-25 . . . . . . at Colorado
27-29 . . . . Texas
30-31 . . . . .at Seattle

AUGUST
1 . . . . .at Seattle
3-5 . . . at Los Angeles (NL)
6-7 . . . . . at San Francisco
9-12 . . . . Seattle

14-15 . . . . .Colorado
17-19 . . . . .at Oakland
20-22 . . . . .at Seattle
24-26 . at Los Angeles (AL)
27-29 . . . . Oakland
30-31 . . . Los Angeles (AL)

SEPTEMBER
1-2 . . . . . Los Angeles (AL)
3-5 . . . . .Minnesota
7-9 . . . . .at Boston
10-12 . . . . .at Detroit
14-16 . . . . Arizona
17-19 . . . . Seattle
21-23 . . . Los Angeles (AL)
24-26 . . . . at Toronto
27-30 . . . . . .at Baltimore

GENERAL INFORMATION
Stadium (year opened):
Minute Maid Park (2000).
Team Colors: Navy and orange.

Home Dugout: First Base.
Playing Surface: Grass.

STADIUM OPERATIONS
Senior Director, Stadium Operations: Thomas Bell. **Director, Audio/Visual:** Lowell Matheny. **Directors, Stadium Operations:** Dave McKenzie, Jonovon Rogers. **Director, Security/Parking:** Ben Williams. **Manager, Parking:** Gary Rowberry. **Manager, Engineering:** Michael Seighman. **Head Groundskeeper:** Izzy Hinojsa. **First Assistant Groundskeeper:** Chris Wolfe.

TICKETING
Senior Director, Ticket Sales: P.J. Keene. **Senior Director, Premium Sales/Service:** Clay Kowalski. **Director, Box Office Operations:** Bill Cannon. **Director, Season Ticket Service:** Jeff Close. **Director, Ticket Operations:** Mark Cole. **Director, Season Ticket Sales:** Andre Luck.

BASEBALL OPERATIONS

General Manager: Jeff Luhnow. **Assistant GM, Player Acquisition:** Mike Elias. **Special Assistant to the GM, Player Personnel:** Kevin Goldstein. **Special Assistant to the GM, Process Improvement:** Sig Mejdal. **Special Assistant to the GM, Baseball Operations:** Oz Ocampo. **Special Assistants:** Craig Biggio, Roger Clemens, Enos Cabell. **Senior Director, Baseball Operations, Research and Innovation:** Brandon Taubman. **Director, Research/Development:** Mike Fast. **Senior Technical Architect:** Ryan Hallahan. **Senior Developer, Research and Development:** Danny Friedheim. **Manager, Research and Development:** Colin Wyers. **Manager, Latin American Development/Operations:** Caridad Cabrera. **Senior Advisor, Latin American Development:** Julio Linares. **Manager, International Development/Operations:** Carlos Alfonso (Gilbert, AZ).

Jeff Luhnow

MAJOR LEAGUE STAFF
Manager: A.J. Hinch.
Coaches: Bench—Joe Espada, **Pitching**—Brent Strom, **Hitting**—Dave Hudgens, **Second Hitting**—Jeff Albert, **First Base**—Alex Cintron, **Third Base**—Gary Pettis, **Bullpen**—Doug White, **Bullpen Catcher**—Javier Bracamonte.

TEAM OPERATIONS/CLUBHOUSE
Senior Manager, Team Operations: Derek Vigoa. **Manager, Major League Advance Information:** Tom Koch-Weser. **Coordinator, Major League Advance Information:** Tommy Kawamura. **Coordinator, MLB Video/Advance Information:** Antonio Padilla. **Clubhouse Manager:** Carl Schneider. **Visiting Clubhouse Manager:** Steve Perry.

MEDICAL/TRAINING
Director, Sports Medicine/Performance: Bill Firkus. **Head Team Physician:** Dr. David Lintner. **Team Physicians:** Dr. Thomas Mehlhoff, Dr. James Muntz, Dr. Pat McCulloch. **Head Athletic Trainer:** Jeremiah Randall. **Assistant Athletic Trainer:** Scott Barringer. **Team Physical Therapist:** Matt Holland. **Massage Therapist:** Katsumi Oka. **Head Strength/Conditioning Coach:** Jacob Beiting. **Assistant Major League Strength/Conditioning Coach:** Trey Wiedman.

PLAYER DEVELOPMENT
Director, Player Development: Pete Putila. **Director, Player Development:** Armando Velasco. **Director, Florida Operations:** Jay Edmiston. **Supervisor, Education/Acculturation:** Doris Gonzalez. **Minor League Coordinators:** Josh Miller (pitching), Chris Holt (assistant pitching), Josh Bonifay (field), Mark Bailey (catching). **Complex Hitting Coach:** Ralph Dickenson. **Complex Pitching Coordinator:** Todd Naskedov. **Coordinator, Latin American Development:** Charlie Romero.

FARM SYSTEM

Class	Club	Manager	Hitting Coach	Pitching Coach
Triple-A	Fresno (PCL)	Rodney Linares	Darryl Robinson	Dyar Miller
Double-A	Corpus Christi (TL)	Omar Lopez	Troy Snitker	Bill Murphy
High A	Buies Creek (CAR)	Morgan Ensberg	Drew French	Ben Rosenthal
Low A	Quad Cities (SAL)	Mickey Storey	Graham Johnson	Dillon Lawson
Short-season	Tri-City (NYP)	Jason Bell	Jeremy Barnes	Erick Abreu
Rookie	Astros (GCL)	Wladimir Sutil	C. Cedeno/R. Rojas	Jose Rada
Rookie	Astros 1 (DSL)	Charlie Romero	Luis Mateo	Rick Aponte

SCOUTING
Asst. GM, Player Acquisition: Mike Elias. **Special Asst to the GM, Player Personnel:** Kevin Goldstein. **Special Asst to the GM, Baseball Operations:** Oz Ocampo. **Senior Scouting Advisor:** Charlie Gonzalez. **National Scouting Supervisor:** Kris Gross. **Domestic Crosscheckers:** Ralph Bratton (Austin, TX), Evan Brannon (St. Petersburg, FL), Brad Budzinski (Irvine, CA), Gavin Dickey (Atlanta, GA). **Domestic Scouts:** Travis Coleman (Birmingham, AL), Tim Costic (Los Angeles, CA), Ryan Leake (San Diego, CA), Bobby St. Pierre (Atlanta, GA), Jim Stevenson (Tulsa, OK), Aaron Tassano (Phoenix, AZ), Joey Sola (San Juan, PR). **Manager, Amateur Scouting Analysis:** Charles Cook. **Manager, Pro Scouting Analysis:** Matt Hogan. **Scouting Analysts:** Ronit Shah, Aaron DelGiudice, Will Sharp. **Manager, International Scouting:** Eve Rosenbaum. **Assistant Director, International Scouting:** Roman Ocumarez. **Supervisor, DR Scouting:** Alfredo Ulloa. **International Scouts/Venezuela:** Daniel Acuna, Enrique Brito, Jose Palacios. **Panama:** Carlos Gonzalez. **Dominican Republic/Nicaragua:** Leocadio Guevara. **Dominican Republic:** Jose Lima, Johan Maya, Francis Mojica. **Mexico:** Miguel Pintor.

VIDEO & TECHNOLOGY
Coordinator, International Technology: Hassan Wessin. **Tryout Technology Assistant:** Francisco Navarro. **Scouting Technology Assistant:** Carlos Vasquez. **Venezuela Camera Scout:** Carlos Freites. **Amateur Video Technicians:** Ryan Courville, Brandon Lowe.

Kansas City Royals

Office Address: One Royal Way, Kansas City, MO 64129.
Mailing Address: PO Box 419969, Kansas City, MO 64141.
Telephone: (816) 921-8000. **Fax:** (816) 924-0347. **Website:** www.royals.com.

OWNERSHIP

Operated By: Kansas City Royals Baseball Club, Inc. **Chairman/CEO:** David Glass. **President:** Dan Glass. **Board of Directors:** Ruth Glass, Don Glass, Dayna Martz, Julia Irene Kauffman. **Executive Assistant to the President:** Lora Woolever.

BUSINESS OPERATIONS

Senior Vice President, Business Operations: Kevin Uhlich. **Executive Administrative Assistant:** Cindy Hamilton. **Director, Royals Hall of Fame:** Curt Nelson. **Director, Authentic Merchandise Sales:** Justin Villarreal.

FINANCE/ADMINISTRATION

VP, Finance/Administration: David Laverentz. **Director, Finance:** Sydney Goodman. **Director, Human Resources:** Miriam Maiden. **Director, Renovation Accounting/Risk Management:** Patrick Fleischmann. **Director, Payroll:** Jodi Parsons. **Senior Director, Information Systems:** Brian Himstedt. **Senior Director, Ticket Operations:** Anthony Blue. **Director, Ticket Operations:** Chris Darr.

COMMUNICATIONS/BROADCASTING

VP, Communications/Broadcasting: Mike Swanson. **Assistant Director, Communications:** Mike Cummings. **Manager, Media Relations/Alumni:** Dina Blevins. **Coordinator, Communications/Broadcasting:** Nick Kappel.

David Glass

PUBLICITY/COMMUNITY RELATIONS

VP, Publicity: Toby Cook. **VP, Community Relations:** Ben Aken. **Director, Royals Charities:** Marie Dispenza. **Director, Community Outreach:** Betty Kaegel.

BALLPARK OPERATIONS

VP, Ballpark Operations/Development: TBA. **Senior Director, Groundskeeping/Landscaping:** Trevor Vance. **Senior Director, Stadium Engineering:** Todd Burrow. **Director, Ballpark Services:** Johnny Williams. **Director, Event Operations:** Isaac Riffel.

MARKETING/BUSINESS DEVELOPMENT

VP, Marketing/Business Development: Michael Bucek. **Senior Director, Event Presentation/Production:** Don Costante. **Director, Event Presentation/Production:** Steven Funke. **Director, Marketing/Advertising:** Brad Zollars. **Director, Digital/Social Media:** Erin Sleddens. **Senior Director, Corporate Partnerships/Broadcast Sales:** Jason Booker. **Senior Director, Client Services:** Michele Kammerer. **Senior Director, Sales/Service:** Steve Shiffman. **Director, Sales/Service:** Scott Wadsworth.

2018 SCHEDULE

Standard Game Times: 7:15 p.m.; Sun. 1:15.

MARCH		JULY	SEPTEMBER
29-31 . . . . . Chicago (AL)	8-10 . . . . . . .at Baltimore	29-30 . . . . .at Seattle	13-16 . . . . .Toronto
	11-13 . . . . . .at Cleveland		17-19 . . . .at Chicago (AL)
APRIL	14-16 . . . . . . .Tampa Bay	1 . . . . .at Seattle	20-23 . . . . . at Tampa Bay
1 . . . . Chicago (AL)	18-20 . . . . .New York (AL)	2-4 . . . . Cleveland	24-26 . . . . Cleveland
2-4 . . . . .at Detroit	21-23 . . . . . . .at St. Louis	6-8 . . . . Boston	28-29 . . . . Detroit
6-8 . . . . .at Cleveland	24-27 . . . . .at Texas	9-11 . . . . . . at Minnesota	31 . . . . Baltimore
9-11 . . . . Seattle	28-30 . . . . Minnesota	13-15 . . .at Chicago (AL)	
12-15 . . . Los Angeles (AL)		20-22 . . . . Minnesota	SEPTEMBER
16-18 . . . . . . at Toronto	JUNE	23-25 . . . . Detroit	1-2 . . . . Baltimore
20-22 . . . . . . .at Detroit	1-3 . . . . Oakland	26-29 . . . at New York (AL)	3-5 . . . . . . .at Cleveland
24-25 . . . . . . .Milwaukee	4-6 . . . at Los Angeles (AL)	31 . . . . . .at Chicago (AL)	7-9 . . . . . . at Minnesota
26-29 . . . . . Chicago (AL)	7-10 . . . . . . .at Oakland		10-12 . . . . Chicago (AL)
30 . . . . .at Boston	12-13 . . . . Cincinnati	AUGUST	13-16 . . . . . Minnesota
	15-17 . . . . Houston	1-2 . . . . .at Chicago (AL)	17-19 . . . . . at Pittsburgh
MAY	18-20 . . . . Texas	3-5 . . . . . . at Minnesota	20-23 . . . . . . .at Detroit
1-2 . . . . .at Boston	22-24 . . . . .at Houston	6-8 . . . . . . Chicago (NL)	25-26 . . . . .at Cincinnati
3-6 . . . . Detroit	26-27 . . . . . at Milwaukee	10-12 . . . . St. Louis	27-30 . . . . Cleveland

GENERAL INFORMATION

Stadium (year opened): Ewing M. Kauffman Stadium (1973). **Team Colors:** Royal blue and white.

Home Dugout: First Base. **Playing Surface:** Grass.

BASEBALL OPERATIONS

Telephone: (816) 921-8000. **Fax:** (816) 924-0347.
Senior VP, Baseball Operations/General Manager: Dayton Moore.
VP/Assistant GM, Player Personnel: J.J. Picollo. **VP/Assistant GM, Major League/
International Operations:** Rene Francisco. **VP/Assistant GM:** Scott Sharp. **Assistant GM,
Baseball Administration:** Jin Wong. **Assistant GM/Int'l Operations:** Albert Gonzalez. **Senior
Advisor to GM, Scouting/Player Development:** Mike Arbuckle. **Special Assistant to the
GM/Outfield, Bunting, Baserunning:** Rusty Kuntz. **Special Assistants to Baseball Ops:** Mike
Sweeney, Reggie Sanders. **Sr. Director, Baseball Ops/Administration:** Kyle Vena. **Sr. Director,
Quantitative Analysis/Player Personnel:** John Williams. **Sr. Director, Quantitative Analysis/
Amateur Scouting:** Daniel Mack. **Director, Baseball Admin./Quantitative Analysis:** Guy
Stevens. **Director, Behavioral Science:** Ryan Maid. **Director, Leadership Development:** Matt
Marasco. **Coordinator, Sports Science:** Austin Driggers. **Executive Asst to the GM:** Emily
Penning. **Baseball Operations Asst.:** Kevin Kuntz.

Dayton Moore

TRAVEL/CLUBHOUSE

Senior Director, Clubhouse Operations/Team Travel: Jeff Davenport. **Assistant Equipment Manager:** Patrick
Gorman. **Visiting Clubhouse Manager:** Chuck Hawke.

MAJOR LEAGUE STAFF

Manager: Ned Yost. **Coaches: Bench**—Dale Sveum, **Pitching**—Cal Eldred, **Hitting**—Terry Bradshaw, **First Base**—
Mitch Maier, **Third Base**—Mike Jirschele, **Bullpen**—Vance Wilson, **Quality Control/Catching**—Pedro Grifol. **Replay/
Advance Scouting Coordinator:** Bill Duplissea. **Bullpen Catcher:** Ryan Eigsti. **Special Assignment:** Jason Kendall.

MEDICAL/TRAINING

Team Physician: Dr. Vincent Key. **Head Athletic Trainer:** Nick Kenney. **Assistant Athletic Trainer:** Kyle Turner.
Strength/Conditioning: Ryan Stoneberg. **Assistant Strength/Conditioning, Latin America:** Luis Perez.

PLAYER DEVELOPMENT

VP/Assistant GM, Player Personnel: J.J. Picollo. **Director, Baseball Operations/Player Development & Scouting:**
Alec Zumwalt. **Assistant to Player Development/Video Coordinator:** Nick Relic. **Senior Coordinator:** Chino Cadahia.
Field Coordinator: Eddie Rodriguez. **Senior Pitching Advisor:** Bill Fischer. **Special Assistants, Player Development:**
John Wathan, Harry Spilman. **Coordinators:** Larry Carter (pitching), Jason Simontacchi (asst. pitching), Rafael Belliard
(infield), J.C. Boscan (catching), Carlos Reyes (pitching rehab), Chris DeLucia (medical), Tony Medina (Latin America
medical), Garrett Sherrill (strength/conditioning), Justin Hahn (rehab), Will Simon (equipment), Jeff Diskin (cultural
development), Monica Ramirez (ESL/Latin American Initiatives).

FARM SYSTEM

Class	Club (League)	Manager	Hitting Coach	Pitching Coach
Triple-A	Omaha (PCL)	Brian Poldberg	Brian Buchanan	Andy Hawkins
Double-A	Northwest Arkansas (TL)	Mike Rojas	Leon Roberts	Steve Luebber
High A	Wilmington (CL)	Darryl Kennedy	Abraham Nunez	Doug Henry
Low A	Lexington (SAL)	Scott Thorman	Jesus Azuaje	Mitch Stetter
Rookie	Idaho Falls (PIO)	Omar Ramirez	Damon Hollins	Jeff Suppan
Rookie	Burlington (APP)	Brooks Conrad	Nelson Liriano	Carlos Martinez
Rookie	Royals (AZL)	Tony Pena Jr.	A. David/R. Castro	Mark Davis
Rookie	Royals (DSL)	M. Bernard/R. Martinez	O. Joseph/W. Betemit	R. Feliz/J. Pimentel

SCOUTING

Telephone: (816) 921-8000. **Fax:** (816) 924-0347.
Senior Director, Pro Scouting/Assistant to the GM: Gene Watson. **Director, Scouting:** Lonnie Goldberg. **Assistant
Director, Scouting:** Dan Ontiveros. **Coordinator, Scouting Operations:** Jack Monahan. **Senior Advisors to the
GM:** Art Stewart, Donnie Williams. **Special Assistants to GM:** Louie Medina, Pat Jones, Mike Toomey, Mike Pazik, Jim
Fregosi, Jr., Tim Conroy, Gene Lamont. **Special Assignment Scouts:** Mitch Webster. **Professional Scouts:** Dennis
Cardoza (Munds Park, AZ), Mark Leavitt (DeLand, FL), Dave Oliver (Surprise, AZ), Mike Pazik (Bethesda, MD), Tony
Tijerina (Newark Valley, NY), Jon Williams (Imperial, MO). **Part-Time Professional Scout:** Rene Lachemann (Scottsdale,
AZ). **Advance Scout:** Cody Clark (Maumelle, AR) **National Supervisors:** Paul Gibson (Center Moriches, NY), Gregg
Kilby (Tampa, FL). **Regional Supervisors: Midwest**—Gregg Miller (Meeker, OK), **Southeast**—Sean Gibbs (Santa Rosa
Beach, FL), **West**—Gary Wilson (Sacramento, CA), **Northeast**—Keith Connolly (Fair Haven, NJ). **Area Supervisors:**
Rich Amaral (Huntington Beach, CA), Joe Barbera (Durham, NC), Jim Buckley (Tampa, FL), Travis Ezi (Gulfport, MS),
Casey Fahy (Mullica Hill, NJ), Jim Farr (Williamsburg, VA), Mike Farrell (Indianapolis, IN), Sean Gallagher (Cedar Park, TX),
Colin Gonzales (Dana Point, CA), Josh Hallgren (Walnut Creek, CA), Nick Hamilton (Atlanta, GA), Chad Lee (McKinney,
TX), Scott Melvin (Quincy, IL), Alex Mesa (Miami, FL), Ken Munoz (Scottsdale, AZ), Matt Price (Mission, KS), Joe Ross
(Kirkland, WA). **Special Assignment Scout:** Ralph Garr, Jr. (Houston, TX) **Part-Time Scouts:** Kirk Barclay (Wyoming,
ON), Eric Briggs (Bolivar, MO), Rick Clendenin (Clendenin, WV), Louis Collier (Chicago, IL), Corey Eckstein (Abbotsford,
BC), Will Howard (Columbus, GA), Jerry Lafferty (Kansas City, MO), Brittan Motley (Blue Springs, MO), Chad Raley (Baton
Rouge, LA), Johnny Ramos (Carolina, PR), Lloyd Simmons (Shawnee, OK). **Latin America Supervisor:** Orlando Estevez.
Assistant to International Operations: Daniel Guerrero. **International Scouts:** Luis Ortiz, Phil Dale (Australia), Neil
Burke (Australia), Jose Figuera (Venezuela), Edgarluis Fuentes (Venezuela), Alberto Garcia (Venezuela), Jose Gualdron
(Venezuela), Joelvis Gonzalez (Venezuela), Djionny Joubert (Curacao), Edson Kelly (Aruba), Juan Lopez (Nicaragua),
Nathan Miller (Taiwan), Rafael Miranda (Colombia), Fausto Morel (Dominican Republic), Ricardo Ortiz (Panama), Edis
Perez (Dominican Republic), Rafael Vasquez (Dominican Republic), Manabu Kuramochi (Tokyo, Japan).

Los Angeles Angels

Office Address: 2000 Gene Autry Way, Anaheim, CA 92806.
Mailing Address: 2000 Gene Autry Way, Anaheim, CA 92803.
Telephone: (714) 940-2000. **Fax:** (714) 940-2205.
Website: www.angels.com.

OWNERSHIP

Owner: Arte Moreno. **Chairman:** Dennis Kuhl. **President:** John Carpino.

BUSINESS OPERATIONS

Arte Moreno

Chief Financial Officer: Bill Beverage. **Senior Vice President, Finance/Administration:** Molly Jolly. **Director, Legal Affairs/Risk Management:** Alex Winsberg. **Associate Legal Counsel:** Jen Tedmori. **Controller:** Cris Lacoste. **Director, Finance:** Doug Mylowe. **Benefits Manager:** Cecilia Schneider. **Payroll Manager:** Lorelei Schlitz. **Accountants:** Kylie McManus, Jennifer Whynott. **Payroll Assistant:** Alison Kelso. **Accounts Payable Specialist:** Sarah Talamonte. **Financial Analyst:** Jennifer Jeanblanc. **Director, Human Resources:** Deborah Johnston. **Human Resources Generalist:** Mayra Castro. **Human Resources Coordinator:** Anthony Recinos. **Director, Information Services:** Al Castro. **Senior Network Engineer:** Neil Fariss. **Senior Desktop Support Analyst:** David Yun. **Technology Integration Specialist:** Paramjit Singh. **Network Administrator:** James Sheu.

CORPORATE SALES

VP, Sales: Neil Viserto. **Senior Director, Business Development:** Mike Fach. **Senior Corporate Account Executive:** Lesli Koontz, Rick Turner. **Corporate Account Executive:** Drew Zinser, Evan Harding. **Senior Manager, Partner Services:** Bobby Kowan. **Sponsorship Services Supervisor:** Erin Morey.

MARKETING/ENTERTAINMENT

Senior Manager, Ticket Marketing: Ryan Vance. **Marketing Manager:** Alex Tinyo, Vanessa Vega. **Graphic Designer:** Erin Goforth. **Social Media Coordinator:** Tara Nicodemo. **Marketing Events Coordinator:** Brianna Davoren. **Digital and Promotions Coordinator:** Hannah Stange. **Business Analyst:** Julius Evans. **Director, Entertainment/Production:** Peter Bull. **Entertainment Coordinator:** Samantha Andersen. **Team Photographer:** Blaine Ohigashi.

PUBLIC/MEDIA RELATIONS/COMMUNICATIONS

Telephone: (714) 940-2014. **Fax:** (714) 940-2205.
VP, Communications: Tim Mead. **Director, Communications:** Eric Kay. **Senior Manager, Communications:** Adam Chodzko. **Manager, Communications:** Matt Birch.

BALLPARK OPERATIONS/FACILITIES

Senior Director, Ballpark Operations: Brian Sanders. **Director, Ballpark Operations:** Sam Maida. **Senior Manager, Stadium Events/Operations:** Calvin Ching. **Guest Experience Manager:** Chris Warden.

2018 SCHEDULE

Standard Game Times: 7:07 p.m.; Sun. 12:37.

MARCH		
29-31 . . . . . . .at Oakland		

APRIL		
1 . . . . .at Oakland		
2-4. . . . . Cleveland		
6-8. . . . . Oakland		
9-11 . . . . .at Texas		
12-15 . . .at Kansas City		
17-19 . . . . Boston		
20-22 . . . San Francisco		
23-25 . . . . .at Houston		
27-29 . . . . .New York (AL)		

MAY		
1-3. . . . . Baltimore		
4-6. . . . . .at Seattle		
8-9. . . . . at Colorado		

10-13 . . . . . . .Minnesota
14-16 . . . . Houston
17-20 . . . . . .Tampa Bay
22-24 . . . . . . at Toronto
25-27 . . at New York (AL)
28-31 . . . . . . .at Detroit

JUNE
1-3 . . . . Texas
4-6. . . . . . . Kansas City
8-10 . . . . . at Minnesota
11-13 . . . . . .at Seattle
15-17 . . . . . .at Oakland
18-19 . . . . .Arizona
21-24 . . . . .Toronto
26-28 . . . . . .at Boston
29-30 . . . . . .at Baltimore

JULY		
1 . . . . .at Baltimore		
3-5. . . . . .at Seattle		
6-8. . . . . Los Angeles (NL)		
10-12 . . . . Seattle		
13-15 . at Los Angeles (NL)		
20-22 . . . . Houston		
23-26 . . . . . Chicago (AL)		
27-29 . . . . Seattle		
31 . . . . . at Tampa Bay		

AUGUST		
1-2. . . . . . . at Tampa Bay		
3-5. . . . . . . .at Cleveland		
6-8. . . . . Detroit		
10-12 . . . . Oakland		
13-15 . . . . . at San Diego		

16-19 . . . . .at Texas
21-22 . . . . at Arizona
24-26 . . . . Houston
27-28 . . . . .Colorado
30-31 . . . . . .at Houston

SEPTEMBER
1-2 . . . . .at Houston
3-5. . . . . .at Texas
7-9. . . . .at Chicago (AL)
10-12 . . . . Texas
13-16 . . . . Seattle
18-20 . . . . . .at Oakland
21-23 . . . . . .at Houston
24-26 . . . . Texas
28-30 . . . . Oakland

GENERAL INFORMATION

Stadium (year opened): Angel Stadium of Anaheim (1966). **Playing Surface:** Grass.
Team Colors: Red, dark red, blue and silver.
Home Dugout: Third Base.

Security Manager: Mark Macias. Director, Special Events: Courtney Wallace. Special Events Coordinator: Veronica Lee. Housekeeping Operations Manager: Nathan Bautista. Custodial Supervisors: Pedro Del Castillo, Ray Nells.

TICKETING
Director, Ticket Sales: Jim Panetta. Senior Manager, Ticket Operations: Sheila Brazelton. Manager, Ticket Office: Susan Weiss. Ticketing Supervisor: Armando Reyna. Director, Ticket Operations/Service: Tom DeTemple. Director, Premium Sales/Service: Kyle Haygood. Senior Business Development Account Executive: Jeff Leuenberger.

TRAVEL/CLUBHOUSE
Clubhouse Manager: Keith Tarter. Assistant Clubhouse Manager: Shane Demmitt. Visiting Clubhouse Manager: Brian "Bubba" Harkins. Senior Video Coordinator: Diego Lopez. Video Coordinator: Ruben Montano.

BASEBALL OPERATIONS

Billy Eppler

General Manager: Billy Eppler.
Assistant GMs: Jonathan Strangio, Steve Martone. Special Advisor: Bill Stoneman. Special Assistants to GM: Eric Chavez, Brad Ausmus. Director, Baseball Operations: Andrew Ball. Director, Analytics: Jonathan Luman. Coordinator, Baseball Administration: Adam Cali. Baseball Operations Assistants: Andrew Mack, Walter King. Assistant, Amateur Scouting: Aidan Donovan. Assistant, Pro and International Scouting: Nick Lampe.

MAJOR LEAGUE STAFF
Manager: Mike Scioscia. Coaches: Bench—Josh Paul, Pitching—Charles Nagy, Hitting—Eric Hinske, First Base—Alfredo Griffin, Third Base—Dino Ebel, Bullpen—Scott Radinsky, Bullpen Catcher—Tom Gregorio, Bullpen Catcher—Anel De Los Santos, Assistant Hitting—Paul Sorrento, Catching/Player Information—Steve Soliz.

MEDICAL/TRAINING
Team Physician: Dr. Craig Milhouse. Team Orthopedists: Dr. Steve Yoon, Dr. Ronald Kvitne, Dr. Brian Schulz. Director, Sport Science/Performance: Bernard Li. Head Athletic Trainer: Adam Nevala. Assistant Athletic Trainer: Rick Smith. Strength/Conditioning Coach: Lee Fiocchi. Assistant Strength/Conditioning Coach: Sean Johnson.

PLAYER DEVELOPMENT
Director, Minor League Operations: Mike LaCassa. Director, Player Development: Mike Gallego. Minor League Equipment Manager, Arizona: Brett Crane. Video Coordinator: Adam Hunt. Field Coordinator: Chad Tracy. Roving Instructors: Jeremy Reed (hitting), Shawn Wooten (assistant hitting), Matt Wise (pitching), Buddy Carlyle (assistant pitching), Jose Molina (catching), Bill Lachemann (catching/special assignment), Jon Nunnally (outfield/baserunning/bunting), Kernan Ronan (rehab pitching), Andrew Hawkins (rehab), David Newhan (infield), Bobby Knoop (special assignment infield), Geoff Hostetter (training coordinator), Ryan Crotin (strength/conditioning), Danny Escobar (rehab).

FARM SYSTEM

Class	Club	Manager	Hitting Coach	Pitching Coach
Triple-A	Salt Lake (PCL)	Keith Johnson	Donnie Ecker	Erik Bennett
Double-A	Mobile (SL)	Lou Marson	Lee Tinsley	Pat Rice
High A	Inland Empire (CAL)	Ryan Barba	Brian Betancourt	
Low A	Burlington (MWL)	Jack Howell	Matt Spring	Jonathan Van Eaton
Rookie	Orem (PIO)	David Stapleton,	D. Ortega/M. Del Campo	M. Wuertz/C. Seddon
Rookie	Angels (AZL)	Jack Santora	A. Gomez/R. Sebra	J. Cuevas/J. Oseguera
Rookie	Angels (DSL)	Hector De La Cruz	Raywilly Gomez	Jose Marte

SCOUTING
Director, Pro Scouting: Nate Horowitz. Major League/Special Assignment Scout: Ric Wilson (Gilbert, AZ). Professional Scouts: Jeff Cirillo (Medina, WA), Buck Coats (Lake Park, GA), Ben Francisco (Scottsdale, AZ), Phil Geisler (Mt Horeb, WI), Brendan Harris (Arlington, VA), Nick McCoy (Los Angeles, CA), Jim Miller (Valrico, FL), Jayson Nix (Lewisville, TX), Roman Rodriguez (Tampa, FL), Travis Ice (Lawrence, KS), Tim McIntosh (Golden Valley, MN), Andrew Schmidt (Anaheim, CA), Ken Stauffer (Katy, TX), Bobby Williams (Sarasota, FL). Director, Amateur Scouting: Matt Swanson. National Crosscheckers: Jeremy Schied (Temecula, CA), Jason Smith (Long Beach, CA), Steffan Wilson (Wayne, Pa). Regional Supervisors: East—Jason Baker (Lynchburg, VA), South—Brandon McArthur (Tampa, FL), Southeast—Nick Gorneault (Raleigh, NC), Northwest—Scott Richardson (Sacramento, CA), Southwest—Jayson Durocher (Phoenix, AZ). Hitting Crosschecker: Jason Ellison. Area Scouts: Don Archer (Canada), Jared Barnes (Baltimore, MD), John Burden (Fairfield, OH), Tim Corcoran (La Verne, CA), Christopher Cruz (Riverview, FL), Ben Diggins (Newport Beach, CA), Drew Dominguez (Chicago, IL), John Gracio (Mesa, AZ), Chad Hermansen (Henderson, NV), Steve Hernandez (Highland, CA), Todd Hogan (Dublin, GA), Ryan Leahy (Beverly, MA), Billy Lipari (Omaha, NE), Chris McAlpin (Moultrie, GA), Joel Murrie (Evergreen, CO), Ralph Reyes (Miami, FL), Omar Rodriguez (Puerto Rico), Brett Smith (Fullerton, CA), Brian Tripp (Walnut Creek, CA), Rudy Vasquez (San Antonio, TX), Rob Wilfong (San Dimas, CA), J.T. Zink (Hoover, AL). Director, International Scouting: Carlos Gomez. Assistant Director, International Scouting: Frankie Thon Jr (Doral, FL). International Scouting Supervisor: Marlon Urdaneta (Venezuela). International Scouts: Jochy Cabrera (Dominican Republic), Rusbell Cabrera (Dominican Republic), Lianmy Galan (Dominican Republic), Andres Garcia (Venezuela), Domingo Garcia (Dominican Republic), Ender Gonzalez (Venezuela), Raul Gonzalez (Panama), Francisco Tejeda (Dominican Republic). Director, International Scouting: Carlos Gomez. Assistant Director, International Scouting: Frankie Thon Jr (Doral, FL). International Scouting Supervisor: Marlon Urdaneta (Venezuela). International Scouts: Jochy Cabrera, Domingo Garcia, Franciso Tejeda (Dominican Republic), Andres Garcia, Ender Gonzalez, Carlos Ramirez (Venezuela), Raul Gonzalez (Panama).

Los Angeles Dodgers

Office Address: 1000 Vin Scully Ave., Los Angeles, CA 90012.
Telephone: (323) 224-1500. **Fax:** (323) 224-1269. **Website:** www.dodgers.com.

OWNERSHIP/EXECUTIVE OFFICE

Chairman: Mark Walter. **Partners:** Earvin 'Magic' Johnson, Peter Guber, Todd Boehly, Robert 'Bobby' Patton, Jr. **President/CEO:** Stan Kasten. **Special Advisors to Chairman:** Tommy Lasorda, Don Newcombe.

BUSINESS OPERATIONS

Executive Vice President: Bob Wolfe. **Executive VP/Chief Marketing Officer:** Lon Rosen.
CFO: Tucker Kain. **Senior VP/General Counsel:** Sam Fernandez. **Senior VP, Planning/Development:** Janet Marie Smith. **Senior VP, Corporate Partnerships:** Michael Wandell.
Sales/Partnership VP, Ticket Sales: David Siegel. **VP, Premium Sales/Services:** Antonio Morici. **Senior Director, Partnership Administration:** Jenny Oh. **Senior VP, Corporate Partnerships:** Greg Morrison. **Director, Season Sales:** David Kirkpatrick. **Director, Group Sales:** Afton Kurth. **Director, Partnership Sales Administration/Service:** Paige Kirkpatrick.

Mark Walter

FINANCE

VP, Finance: Eric Hernandez. **Director, Financial Planning/Analysis:** Gregory Buonaccorsi.
Director, Business Development/Analytics: Royce Cohen.

MARKETING/BROADCASTING

VP, Marketing/Broadcasting Communications: Erik Braverman. **Sr. Director, Advertising/Promotions:** Shelley Wagner. **Executive Producer, Production:** Greg Taylor. **Director, Graphic Design:** Ross Yoshida. **Sr. Director, Broadcast Engineering:** Tom Darin.

HUMAN RESOURCES/LEGAL

Senior Director, Human Resources: Leonor Romero. **Senior Counsel:** Chad Gunderson.

COMMUNICATIONS/COMMUNITY AFFAIRS

VP, External Affairs/Community Relations: Naomi Rodriguez. **Senior Director, Public Relations:** Joe Jareck.

INFORMATION TECHNOLOGY/STADIUM OPERATIONS/SECURITY/MERCHANDISE

VP, Information Technology: Ralph Esquibel. **Director, Technology Infrastructure:** Debra Jorgensen. **VP, Security/Guest Services:** Shahram Ariane. **Director, Facilities:** David Edford. **Assistant Director, Turf/Grounds:** Jordan Lorenz. **VP, Merchandise:** Allister Annear. **Director, Retail Operations:** Veronica Huerta.

TICKETING

Telephone: (323) 224-1471. **Fax:** (323) 224-2609.
VP, Ticket Development: Seth Bluman. **Director, Ticket Operations:** Aaron Dubner.

BASEBALL OPERATIONS

2018 SCHEDULE

Standard Game Times: 7:10 p.m.; Sun. 1:10

MARCH		
29-31 . . . . . San Francisco	8-9 . . . . Arizona	29-30 . . . . Colorado
APRIL	10-13 . . . . Cincinnati	**JULY**
1 . . . . San Francisco	15-17 . . . . at Miami	1 . . . . Colorado
2-4 . . . . at Arizona	18-20 . . . . at Washington	2-4 . . . . Pittsburgh
6-8 . . . . . at San Francisco	21-23 . . . . Colorado	6-8 . . . at Los Angeles (AL)
10-11 . . . . Oakland	25-27 . . . . . . San Diego	9-12 . . . . . at San Diego
13-15 . . . . Arizona	28-31 . . . . . .Philadelphia	13-15 . . . Los Angeles (AL)
16-18 . . . . at San Diego	**JUNE**	20-22 . . . . at Milwaukee
20-22 . . . . . . Washington	1-3 . . . . at Colorado	23-25 . . . . at Philadelphia
23-25 . . . . Miami	5-7 . . . . . . at Pittsburgh	26-29 . . . . at Atlanta
27-29 . . . at San Francisco	8-10 . . . . Atlanta	30-31 . . . . . . .Milwaukee
30 . . . . at Arizona	12-13 . . . . Texas	**AUGUST**
MAY	15-17 . . . . San Francisco	1-2 . . . . .Milwaukee
1-3 . . . . at Arizona	18-20 . . . .at Chicago (NL)	3-5 . . . . Houston
4-6 . . . . . . at San Diego	22-24 . . . at New York (NL)	7-8 . . . . .at Oakland
	25-28 . . . . . Chicago (NL)	9-12 . . . . . . at Colorado

SEPTEMBER
13-15 . . . . . San Francisco
17-19 . . . . . . .at Seattle
20-22 . . . . St. Louis
24-26 . . . . San Diego
28-29 . . . . .at Texas
30-31 . . . . .Arizona
1-2 . . . . .Arizona
3-5 . . . . . .New York (NL)
7-9 . . . . at Colorado
10-12 . . . .at Cincinnati
13-16 . . . . . . .at St. Louis
17-19 . . . . .Colorado
21-23 . . . . . . San Diego
24-26 . . . . at Arizona
28-30 . . . at San Francisco

GENERAL INFORMATION

Stadium (year opened): Dodger Stadium (1962).
Team Colors: Dodger blue and white.
Home Dugout: Third Base.
Playing Surface: Grass

Telephone: (323) 224-1500. **Fax:** (323) 224-1463.

President, Baseball Operations: Andrew Friedman. **General Manager:** Farhan Zaidi. **Senior VP, Baseball Operations:** Josh Byrnes. **Director, Baseball Administration:** Ellen Harrigan. **Director, Team Travel:** Scott Akasaki. **Director, Research & Development:** Doug Fearing. **Senior Advisor, Baseball Operations:** Gerry Hunsicker. **Special Assistants:** Pat Corrales, Raul Ibañez.

Farhan Zaidi

MAJOR LEAGUE STAFF

Manager: Dave Roberts. **Coaches: Bench**—Bob Geren, **Pitching**—Rick Honeycutt, **Hitting**—Turner Ward, **First Base**—George Lombard, **Third Base**—Chris Woodward, **Bullpen**—Mark Prior. **Assistant Hitting Coaches**—Brant Brown, Luis Ortiz. **Bullpen Catchers**—Fumi Ishibashi, Steve Cilladi. **Major League Video Coordinator:** John Pratt. **Game Planning/Communications Coach:** Danny Lehmann.

Medical/Training Director of Player Health: Ron Porterfield. **Head Athletic Trainer:** Neil Rampe. **Assistant Athletic Trainer:** Nate Lucero. **Assistant Athletic Trainer:** Thomas Albert. **Strength & Conditioning Coach:** Brandon McDaniel. **Assistant Strength & Conditioning Coach:** Travis Smith. **Physical Therapist:** Johnathan Erb. **Assistant Athletic Trainer/Soft Tissue Specialist:** Yosuke Nakajima.

PLAYER DEVELOPMENT

Telephone: (323) 224-1500. **Fax:** (323) 224-1359.

Director, Player Development: Brandon Gomes. **Senior Advisor to Player Development:** Charlie Hough. **Field Coordinator:** Clayton McCullough. **Coordinators:** Don Alexander (pitching logistics), Tarrik Brock (outfield/ baserunning), Chris Fetter (pitching integration), Paco Figueroa (hitting), Travis Barbary (catching), Shaun Larkin (skills development), Kremlin Martinez (assistant pitching), Ryan Sienko (assistant catching), Aaron Bates (assistant hitting). **Special Assistant, Infield:** Jose Vizcaino. **Instructor:** Maury Wills. **Rehab Coordinator:** Greg Sabat.

CAMPO LOS PALMAS

Latin American Pitching Coordinator: Kremlin Martinez. **Latin American Defensive Coordinator:** Pedro Mega. **Latin American Field Coordinator:** Carson Vitale. **Latin American Hitting Coordinator:** Humberto Miranda.

CAMELBACK RANCH

Senior Manager, Player Development: Matt McGrath. **Manager, Baseball Operations-Glendale:** Juan Rodriguez.

FARM SYSTEM

Class	Club (League)	Manager	Hitting Coach	Pitching Coach
Triple-A	Oklahoma City (PCL)	Bill Haselman	Adam Melhuse	Bill Simas
Double-A	Tulsa (TL)	Scott Hennessey	Terrmel Sledge	Dave Borkowski
High A	Rancho Cucamonga (CAL)	Drew Saylor	Justin Viele	Connor McGuiness
Low A	Great Lakes (MWL)	John Shoemaker	Jair Fernandez	Bobby Cuellar
Rookie	Ogden (PIO)	Jeremy Rodriguez	Dustin Kelly	Dean Stiles
Rookie	Dodgers (AZL)	Mark Kertenian	Jarek Cunningham	Luis Meza
Rookie	Dodgers (DSL)	K. Collado/A. Chubb	Sergio Mendez	R. Giron/R. Troncoso

SCOUTING

VP, Amateur/International Scouting: David Finley. **Director, Amateur Scouting:** Billy Gasparino. **National Crosschecker:** John Green. **National Crosschecker:** Brian Stephenson. **Advisor, Amateur Scouting:** Gib Bodet. **North East Regional Crosschecker:** Jon Adkins. **South East Regional Crosschecker:** Alan Matthews. **Midwest Regional Crosschecker:** Rob St. Julien. **Special Advisor, Amateur Scouting:** Paul Cogan. **Scouting Coordinator:** Zach Fitzpatrick. **Part-Time Scout:** Mike Diaz, Luis Faccio. **Coordinator, Video Scouting:** Matthew Doppelt. **Area Scouts:** Garrett Ball (GA, AL), Clint Bowers (Southern TX), Adrian Casanova (Southern FL, Puerto Rico), Brian Compton (AZ, UT, CO, NM), Bobby Darwin (Inner City Los Angeles Specialist), Stephen Head (NE, KS, IA, MO), Henry Jones (ID, OR, AK, HI, WA), Heath Holliday (North Texas: TX, OK, AR), Lon Joyce (NC, SC), Tom Kunis (Northern CA, Northern NV), Marty Lamb (IN, KY, OH, TN), Benny Latino (LA, MS, AL, Western FL), Trey Magnuson (MT, ND, WY, SD, MN , WI, IL, MI,), Brent Mayne (Southern CA), Dennis Moeller (Central and Southern CA), Paul Murphy (Northeast: ME, VT, NH, MA, RI, CT, NY, NJ, DE) Jonah Rosenthal (Western PA, MD, DE, WV, VA, DC), Wes Sargent (North Florida). **Director, Player Personnel:** Galen Carr. **Director, Baseball Development/Scouting:** Alex Slater. **Professional Scouts:** Peter Bergeron, Greg Booker, DJ Carrasco, Franco Frias, Scott Groot, Bill Latham, Vance Lovelace, Jeff McAvoy, Tydus Meadows, Steve Pope, Tim Schmidt, Matt Smith, Chris Stasio, Phillip Stringer, Les Walrond. **Pro Scouting Coordinator:** Dan Kolodin. **VP, International Scouting:** Ismael Cruz. **Senior Scouting Advisor, Dominican Republic:** Ralph Avila. **International Crosscheckers:** Roman Barinas, Brian Parker. **Director, Pacific Rim:** Jon Deeble. **Coordinator, International Scouting:** Javier Camps. **Latin American Scouting Supervisor:** Luis Marquez. **Venezuela & Central America Supervisor:** Clifford Nuitter. **Special Assignment Scout, Latin America:** Mike Tosar. **Video Coordinator:** Tibaldo Hernandez. **International Scouts:** Jose Briceno, Jean Castro, Leon Canelon, Cristian Guzman, Oswaldo Villalobos, Paul Brazon, Rafael Arcila (Venezuela), Mike Brito, Andres Simancas, Juvenal Soto (Mexico), Rolando Chirino (Curacao), Cary Broder (Pacific Rim), Johnathan Genao, Elvio Jimenez, Manelik Pimentel, Felvin Veloz, Laiky Uribe, Dunior Zerpa (Dominican Republic), Miguel Orozco (Columbia), Nestor Perez (Europe), Yogo Suzuk (Japan), Andre Park (Korea).

Miami Marlins

Office Address: Marlins Park, 501 Marlins Way, Miami, FL 33125
Telephone: (305) 480-1300. **Fax:** (305) 480-3012.
Website: www.marlins.com.

OWNERSHIP
Chairman & Principal Owner: Bruce Sherman.

BUSINESS OPERATIONS
Chief Executive Officer: Derek Jeter. **Senior Vice President, Strategy & Development:** Adam Jones. **Senior Vice President/Chief of Staff:** Caroline O'Connor. **Executive Assistant to CEO:** Nicolette Lawrence. **Coordinator, Chief of Staff:** Karen De Leon.

ADMINISTRATION
VP, Human Resources: Ana Hernandez. **Manager, Human Resources:** Giselle Lopez. **Coordinator, Human Resources:** Alex Vigil, Kaitlyn Stoltzenberg. **Director, Risk Management:** Fred Espinoza. **Coordinator, Risk Management:** Claudia Avila.

FINANCE
Executive Vice President & Chief Financial Officer: Michel Bussiere. **Senior Vice President, Finance:** Susan Jaison. **Administrator, Payroll:** Carolina Calderon. **Coordinator, Payroll:** Edgar Perez. **Director, Accounting:** Michael Mullane. **Supervisor, Accounts Payable:** Anthony Paneque. **Senior Staff Accountant:** John Cantalupo. **Coordinator, Accounts Payable:** Brian Weeks. **Coordinator, Accounting:** David Villa.

Derek Jeter

MARKETING
Sr. Director, Strategy/Engagment: Alex Buznego. **Director, Events/Promotions:** Juan Martinez. **Director, Marketing:** Sara Kamber. **Manager, Marketing:** Melisa Ramos. **Manager, Marketing Ops.:** Boris Menier. **Manager, Events/Promotions:** Sergio Xiques. **Supervisor, Promotions:** Rafael Capdevila. **Manager, Digitial Marketing:** Joseph Cervone. **Coordinator, Marketing:** Karry Pomes. **Coordinator, Entertainment/Promotions:** Lauren Licamara.

LEGAL
Senior Counsel: Ashwin Krishnan. **Associate Counsel:** Stephanie Galvin. **Executive Assistant, Legal:** Sade Diaz.

SALES/TICKETING
Vice President, Sales and Service: Ryan Bertschman. **Director, Suites:** Truscott Miller. **Manager, Inside Sales:** David Campbell. **Senior Account Executive, Suites:** Chema Sanchez. **Account Executive, Suites:** Greg Lynch. **Senior Account Executive, Business Development:** Daniel Saucier. **Senior Inside Sales Representative:** Jairo Acevedo, William Noel III, Isaac Paladino. **Coordinator, Sales & Service:** Patty Lora. **Director, Ticket Operations:** Mardi Dilger.

COMMUNICATIONS/MEDIA RELATIONS
Senior VP, Communications/Outreach: Jason Latimer. **Director, Publications/Baseball Information:** Marty

2018 SCHEDULE
Standard Game Times: 7:10 p.m.; Sun. 1:10

MARCH		
29-31 . . . . . Chicago (NL)	7-9 . . . . . at Chicago (NL)	29-30 . . . . New York (NL)
	10-13 . . . . Atlanta	
APRIL	15-17 . . . Los Angeles (NL)	**JULY**
1 . . . . Chicago (NL)	18-20 . . . . at Atlanta	1 . . . . New York (NL)
2-3 . . . . Boston	21-23 . . . at New York (NL)	2-4 . . . . Tampa Bay
5-8 . . . . at Philadelphia	25-27 . . . . . . Washington	5-8 . . . . . at Washington
9-11 . . . . . New York (NL)	28-31 . . . . . at San Diego	9-11 . . . . Milwaukee
13-15 . . . . . . Pittsburgh		13-15 . . . . . Philadelphia
16-17 . . at New York (AL)	**JUNE**	20-22 . . . . at Tampa Bay
19-22 . . . . at Milwaukee	1-3 . . . . at Arizona	23-24 . . . . Atlanta
23-25 . at Los Angeles (NL)	5-7 . . . . .at St. Louis	26-29 . . . . . . Washington
27-29 . . . . Colorado	8-10 . . . . San Diego	30-31 . . . . . . at Atlanta
30 . . . . Philadelphia	11-14 . . . . . San Francisco	
	15-17 . . . . . at Baltimore	**AUGUST**
MAY	18-20 . . at San Francisco	1 . . . . at Atlanta
1-2 . . . . Philadelphia	22-24 . . . . . at Colorado	2-5 . . . . at Philadelphia
4-6 . . . . at Cincinnati	25-28 . . . . Arizona	6-8 . . . . St. Louis
		10-12 . . . . New York (NL)

13-15 . . . . . . at Atlanta
17-19 . . . . at Washington
21-22 . . . . New York (AL)
23-26 . . . . Atlanta
28-29 . . . . at Boston
31 . . . . Toronto
SEPTEMBER
1-2 . . . . Toronto
3-5 . . . . Philadelphia
7-9 . . . . . at Pittsburgh
10-13 . . at New York (NL)
14-16 . . . at Philadelphia
17-18 . . . . . Washington
20-23 . . . . . Cincinnati
24-26 . . . . at Washington
28-30 . . . at New York (NL)

GENERAL INFORMATION
Stadium (year opened): Marlins Park (2012).   **Playing Surface:** Grass.
Team Colors: Red-Orange, Yellow, Blue, Black, White.
Home Dugout: Third Base.

Sewell. **Manager, Baseball Information:** Joe Vieira. **Manager, Communications:** Jon Erik Alvarez. **Coordinator, Communications:** Maria Armella. **Director, Broadcasting:** Emmanuel Munoz. **Manager, Broadcasting:** Kyle Sielaff. **Senior Director, Community Outreach:** Angela Smith. **Manager, Community Outreach & Marlins Ayudan:** Nicholas Crimarco. **Coordinator, Community Outreach Initiatives:** Natalie Martinez. **Coordinator, Youth Baseball:** Jason Ramos. **VP/Executive Director, Marlins Foundation:** Alfredo Mesa. **Director, Marlins Foundation:** Alan Alvarez. **Manager, Foundation & Initiatives:** Sarah Garcia.

TRAVEL/CLUBHOUSE
Director, Team Travel: Manny Colon. **Equipment Manager:** John Silverman. **Visiting Clubhouse Manager:** Rock Hughes. **Assistant Clubhouse Manager:** MIchael Diaz.

BASEBALL OPERATIONS

Telephone: (305) 480-1300. **Fax:** (305) 480-3032.
President, Baseball Operations: Michael Hill. **Assistant General Manager:** Brian Chattin.
Baseball Operations Advisor: D.J. Svihlik. **Director, Player Personnel:** Dan Greenlee.
Director, Team Travel: Manny Colon. **Major League Video Coordinator:** Joseph Nero.
Executive Assistant to President of Baseball Operations: Amanda Guevara.

MAJOR LEAGUE STAFF
Manager: Don Mattingly.
Pitching Coach: Juan Nieves. **Hitting Coach:** Mike Pagliarulo. **Assistant Hitting Coach:** Frank Menechino. **Bench Coach:** Tim Wallach. **First Base/Infield Coach:** Perry Hill. **Third Base Coach:** Fredi Gonzalez. **Bullpen Coordinator:** Robert Flippo. **Administrative Coach:** Ed Lucas. **Catching Coach:** Brian Schneider. **Outfield/Baserunning Coach:** Lorenzo Bundy.

Michael Hill

MEDICAL/TRAINING
Medical Director: Dr. Lee Kaplan. **Head Athletic Trainer:** Dusin Luepker. **Strength & Conditioning Coach:** Ty Hill. **Athletic Trainers:** Mike Kozak, Gene Basham. **Equipment Manager, Home Clubhouse:** John Silverman. **Visting Clubhouse Manager:** Michael Rock Hughes.

PLAYER DEVELOPMENT
Vice President, Player Development & Scouting: Gary Denbo. **Director, Player Development:** Dick Scott. **Assistant Director, Player Development:** Brett West. **Manager, Player Development & Scouting:** Geoff Degroot. **Coordinator, Player Development & International Operations:** Hector Crespo. **Minor League Video Coordinator:** Joseph Lisewski. **Sports Psychologist:** Robert Seifer, Ph. D. **Intern, Player Development:** Luis Dorante. **Pitching Coordinator:** Chris Michalak. **Assistant Pitching Coordinator:** Brendan Sagara. **Infield Coordinator:** Jorge Hernandez. **Outfield & Baserunning Coordinator:** Quinton McCracken. **Catching Coordinator:** Paul Phillips. **Minor League Strength & Conditioning Coordinator:** Kevin Barr. **Athletic Training Coordinator:** Brian Bobier. **Minor League Rehab Coordinator:** Steve Carlin. **Video Coordinator:** Joseph Lisewski. **Latin America Field Coordinator:** Julio Bruno. **Latin America Advisor:** Miguel Bonilla. **Minor League Clubhouse/Equipment Coordinator:** Mark Brown.

FARM SYSTEM
Class	Club (League)	Manager	Hitting Coach	Pitching Coach
Triple-A	New Orleans (PCL)	Arnie Beyeler	Tommy Gregg	Jeremy Powell
Double-A	Jacksonville (SL)	Randy Ready	Kevin Witt	Storm Davis
High A	Jupiter (FSL)	Kevin Randel	Danny Santin	Unavailable
Low A	Greensboro (SAL)	Todd Pratt	Frank Moore	Mark DiFelice
Short-season	Batavia (NYP)	Mike Jacobs	Jesus Merchan	Jason Erickson
Rookie	Marlins (GCL)	John Pachot	Rigoberto Silverio	Manny Olivera
Rookie	Marlins (DSL)	Ray Nunez	Rony Peralta	Jose Duran/Freddery Arias

SCOUTING
VP, Scouting: Stan Meek. **Assistant Director, Amateur Scouting:** Michael Youngberg. **Assistant, Amateur Scouting:** Josh Kapiloff. **Director, Pro Scouting:** Jim Cuthbert. **Assistant, Pro Scouting:** Preston Higbe, Alexandria Rigoli. **Special Assignment Scout:** Willie Fraser (Hopewell Junction, NY), Dominic Viola (Holly Springs, NC), Aaron Sele (Laguna Nigel, CA). **Major League Scout:** Paul Ricciarini (Pittsfield, MA), Kevin Bootay (Elk Grove, CA). **Professional Scouts:** Pierre Arsenault (Pierrefonds, QC), Matt Gaski (Tempe, AZ), Phil Rossi (Jessup, PA), Clint Robinson (Cave Springs, AR), Tony Russo (Montgomery, IL), David Espinosa (Miami, FL). **National Crosschecker:** David Crowson (College Station, TX), Eric Valent (Wyomissing, PA). **Regional Supervisors: Southeast**—Mike Cadahia (Miami, FL), **Northeast**—Steve Payne (Barrington, RI). **Central**—Steve Taylor (Shawnee, OK). **West**—Scott Goldby (Yuba City, CA), **Canada**—Steve Payne (Barrington, RI). **Area Scouts:** Eric Brock (Indianapolis, IN), Christian Castorri (Dacula, GA), Robby Corsaro (Victorville, CA), Donovan O'Dowd (Delray Beach, FL), Alex Smith (Abingdon, MD), John Hughes (Walnut Creek, CA), Brian Kraft (Bixby, OK), Adrian Puig (Miami, FL), Blake Newsome (Florence, SC), Tim McDonnell (Westminster, CA), Bob Oldis (Iowa City, Iowa), Gabe Sandy (Damascus, OR), Scott Stanley (Peoria, AZ), Ryan Wardinsky (The Woodlands, TX), Mark Willoughby (Hammond, LA), Nick Zumsande (Fairfax, IA). **Director, International Operations:** Fernando Seguignol. **Coordinator, Player Development & International Operations:** Hector Crespo. **International Crosschecker:** Carmen Carcone. **Assistant, International Operations:** Jacob Jola. **Coordinator, Latin America Operations:** Miguel Bonilla. **Latin America Field Coordinator:** Julio Bruno. **Supervisor, Dominican Republic:** Sandy Nin. **Scout, Dominican Republic:** Hugo Aguero, Domingo Ortega, Aneury Osoria, Felix Munoz. **Supervisor, Venezuela:** Wilmer Castillo. **Scout, Venezuela:** Robin Ordonez. **Scout, Panama:** Luis Cordoba. **Scout, Colombia:** Alvaro Julio.

Milwaukee Brewers

Office Address: Miller Park, One Brewers Way, Milwaukee, WI 53214.
Telephone: (414) 902-4400. **Fax:** (414) 902-4053. **Website:** www.brewers.com.

OWNERSHIP
Operated By: Milwaukee Brewers Baseball Club.
Chairman/Principal Owner: Mark Attanasio.

BUSINESS OPERATIONS
Chief Operating Officer: Rick Schlesinger. **Senior Vice President, Communications & Affiliate Operations:** Tyler Barnes. **Senior Vice President, Stadium Operations:** Steve Ethier. **Senior Vice President, Marketing & Fan Strategy:** Teddy Werner. **General Counsel & Senior Vice President, Administration:** Marti Wronski. **Executive Assistant, Ownership Group:** Samantha Ernest. **Executive Assistant, General Manager:** Nichole Kinateder. **Executive Assistant, Paralegal:** Kate Rock. **Executive Assistant:** Adela Reeve.

Mark Attanasio

FINANCE/ACCOUNTING
VP, Finance/Accounting: Jamie Norton. **Accounting Director:** Vicki Wise. **Senior Manager, Payroll:** Vickie Nikoley. **Financial Analysts:** Cory Loppnow, Jackie Bauer, Mike Anheuser. **Staff Accountant:** Samantha Berg. **Accounts Payable Specialist:** Taikana Bentley. **Payroll Clerk:** Rita Flores. **Director, Human Resources:** Brenda Best.

MARKETING/BUSINESS STRATEGY
VP, Strategy & Analytics: Mike Schwartz. **Senior Director, Marketing:** Kathy Schwab. **Director, Creative Design & Strategy:** Jeff Harding. **Director, Marketing/Brand Strategy:** Evan Entler. **Senior Manager, Consumer Insights & Strategy:** Maria Grossberg. **Senior Manager, Data Science:** Keith Rush. **Senior Manager, Multicultural Marketing:** Thad McGrew. **Senior Manager, Strategy/Analytics:** Maxwell Stejskal. **Coordinator, Business Intelligence:** Danny Henken. **Coordinator, Marketing:** Teryn Bordwell. **Coordinator, Marketing/Promotions:** Brittany Luznicky.

MEDIA RELATIONS/PUBLICATIONS:
Senior Director, Media Relations: Mike Vassallo. **Director, New Media:** Caitlin Moyer. **Senior Manager, Media Relations:** Ken Spindler. **Manager, Media Relations:** Zach Weber. **Spanish Translator/Media Relations Assistant:** Carlos Brizuela. **Coordinator, Communications/Mini-Marathon:** Bryn Winter. **Coordinator, New Media:** Aaron Oberley. **Coordinator, New Media Video:** Giavonna Heath. **Publications Assistant:** Robbin Barnes.

STADIUM OPERATIONS
Vice President, Stadium Operations: Bob Hallas. **General Manager, Performance Clean:** Scott Knusta. **Senior Director, Security:** Randy Olewinski. **Director, Event Services:** Matt Lehmann. **Director, Grounds:** Michael Boettcher. **Manager, Event Services:** Scott Quade. **Manager, Grounds:** Zak Peterson. **Manager, Landscape:** Josh Ruplinger. **Manager, Warehouse:** John Weyer.

2018 SCHEDULE
Standard Game Times: 7:10 p.m.; Sun. 1:10.

MARCH		JULY	
29-31 . . . . . at San Diego	10-13 . . . . . . at Colorado	1 . . . . .at Cincinnati	17-19 . . . . . . .at St. Louis
APRIL	14-16 . . . . at Arizona	2-4 . . . . .Minnesota	20-22 . . . . Cincinnati
2-4 . . . . St. Louis	18-20 . . . . at Minnesota	5-8 . . . . Atlanta	24-26 . . . . Pittsburgh
5-8 . . . . Chicago (NL)	21-23 . . . . .Arizona	9-11 . . . . at Miami	28-30 . . . .at Cincinnati
9-11 . . . . .at St. Louis	24-27 . . . . .New York (NL)	12-15 . . . . . at Pittsburgh	31 . . . . . . at Washington
13-15 . . at New York (NL)	28-30 . . . . St. Louis	20-22 . . . Los Angeles (NL)	**SEPTEMBER**
16-18 . . . . . . Cincinnati	**JUNE**	23-25 . . . . . . Washington	1-2 . . . . . . at Washington
19-22 . . . . .Miami	1-3 . . . . .at Chicago (AL)	26-29 . . . at San Francisco	3-5 . . . . Chicago (NL)
24-25 . . . .at Kansas City	5-6 . . . . .at Cleveland	30-31 . at Los Angeles (NL)	7-9 . . . . . . San Francisco
26-29 . . . .at Chicago (NL)	8-10 . . . . . at Philadelphia	**AUGUST**	10-12 . . . .at Chicago (NL)
30 . . . . .at Cincinnati	11-13 . . . . . Chicago (NL)	1-2 . . . at Los Angeles (NL)	14-16 . . . . Pittsburgh
MAY	15-17 . . . . .Philadelphia	3-5 . . . . .Colorado	17-19 . . . . Cincinnati
1-2 . . . . . . .at Cincinnati	18-20 . . . . . at Pittsburgh	7-9 . . . . San Diego	21-23 . . . . . at Pittsburgh
4-6 . . . . Pittsburgh	21-24 . . . . St. Louis	10-12 . . . . . . at Atlanta	24-26 . . . . . . .at St. Louis
8-9 . . . . Cleveland	26-27 . . . . . Kansas City	14-15 . . . .at Chicago (NL)	28-30 . . . . Detroit
	28-30 . . . . . .at Cincinnati		

GENERAL INFORMATION
Stadium (year opened):
Miller Park (2001).
Team Colors: Navy blue, gold and white.

Home Dugout: First Base.
Playing Surface: Grass.

TICKETING
Telephone: (414) 902-4000. **Fax:** (414) 902-4056.

Vice President, Ticket Sales: Jim Bathey. **Senior Director, Ticket Sales:** Billy Friess. **Senior Director, Ticket Services & Technology:** Jessica Brown. **Director, Group Ticket Sales:** Chris Kimball. **Director, Inside Sales:** Jason Fry. **Director, Suite Sales:** Chris Rothwell. **Director, Suite Services:** Kristin Miller.

BASEBALL OPERATIONS
Telephone: (414) 902-4400. **Fax:** (414) 902-4515.

General Manager: David Stearns. **VP/Assistant GM:** Matt Arnold. **Senior Advisor:** Doug Melvin. **VP, Baseball Projects:** Gord Ash. **Vice President, Player Personnel:** Karl Mueller. **Special Assistant, General Manager/Pro Scouting/Player Personnel:** Dick Groch. **Special Assistant, Baseball Strategy:** Shawn Hoffman. **Director, Baseball Operations:** Matt Kleine. **Director, Baseball Research & Development:** Dan Turkenkopf. **Manager, Baseball Research & Quantitative Analysis:** Nick Davis. **Manager, Video Operations:** Matt Keris. **Senior Developer, Baseball Systems:** Jerry Thomas. **Senior Analyst, Baseball Research & Development:** Andrew Fox. **Analyst, Baseball Research & Development:** Ethan Bein. **Senior Administrator, Baseball Operations:** Barb Stark.

David Stearns

MAJOR LEAGUE STAFF
Manager: Craig Counsell. **Coaches: Bench**—Pat Murphy, **Pitching**—Derek Johnson, **Hitting**—Darnell Coles, **First Base**—Carlos Subero, **Third Base**—Ed Sedar, **Bullpen**—Lee Tunnell. **Coach**—Jason Lane. **Bullpen Catchers:** Marcus Hanel, Robinson Diaz.

MEDICAL/TRAINING
Director, Medical Operations: Roger Caplinger. **Head Team Physician:** Dr. William Raasch. **Team Physicians:** Dr. Mark Niedfeldt, Dr. Craig Young. **Director, Psychological Services:** Matt Krug, Ph.D. **Head Athletic Trainer:** Dan Wright. **Assistant Athletic Trainers:** Rafael Freitas, Dave Yeager. **Manager, Integrative Sports Performance:** Bryson Nakamura. **Rehabilitation Strength & Conditioning Specialist:** Tim Gifford. **Strength & Conditioning Specialist:** Josh Seligman. **Strength & Conditioning Assistant:** Jason Meredith. **Coordinator, Integrative Sports Performance:** Sara Goodrum. **EAP Provider, Sports Psychology Professional:** Blake Pindyck.

PLAYER DEVELOPMENT
Farm Director: Tom Flanagan. **Assistant Farm Director:** Eduardo Brizuela. **Assistant Director, Roving Outfield & Baserunning Coordinator:** Tony Diggs. **Senior Manager, Baseball Administration:** Mark Mueller. **Hitting Coordinator:** Kenny Graham. **Field Coordinator & Catching Instructor:** Charlie Greene. **Roving Infield Coordinator:** Bob Miscik. **Athletic Training Coordinator:** Frank Neville. **Pitching Coordinator:** Rick Tomlin. **Assistant Pitching Coordinator:** Mark Dewey. **Maryvale Clubhouse Manager:** Travis Voss.

FARM SYSTEM

Class	Club (League)	Manager	Coach	Pitching Coach
Triple-A	Colorado Springs (PCL)	Rick Sweet	Al LeBoeuf/Ned Yost	Fred Dabney
Double-A	Biloxi (SL)	Mike Guerrero	S. Guerrero/C. Caufield	Chris Hook
High A	Brevard County (FSL)	Joe Ayrault	D. Joppie/E. Maysonet	David Chavarria
Low A	Wisconsin (MWL)	Matt Erickson	Hainley Statia	Steve Cline
Rookie	Helena (PIO)	Nestor Corredor	Liu Rodriguez	Mark Dewey/Rolando Valles
Rookie	Brewers (AZL)	Rafael Neda	Brenton Del Chiaro	Nat Ballenberg
Rookie	Brewers (DSL)	Victor Estevez	L. De Los Santos/J. Pena	Jesus Hernandez

SCOUTING
Telephone: (414) 902-4400. **Fax:** (414) 902-4059.

VP, Scouting: Ray Montgomery. **Senior Advisor, Scouting:** Marv Thompson. **Special Advisor, Scouting:** Zack Minasian. **Special Assignment Scout:** Scott Campbell. **Director, Amateur Scouting:** Tod Johnson. **Director, International Scouting:** Mike Groopman. **Assistant Director, Amateur Scouting:** Tim McIlvaine. **Manager, Advance Scouting:** Brian Powalish. **Assistant, Scouting Operations:** Oscar Garcia. **Coordinator, Advance Scouting:** Walker McKinven. **Coordinator, Scouting Operations:** Andrew Percival. **Developmental Scout:** Adam Hayes. **Supervisor, Pro Scouting:** Bryan Gale, Taylor Green. **Pro Scouting Crosschecker:** Mike Berger, Ben McDonough, Ryan Thompson, Derek Watson. **Professional Scouts:** Larry Aaron (Fayetteville, GA), Jeff Bianchi (Lancaster, PA), Joey Prebynski (Phoenix), Pete Vuckovich Jr. (Myrtle Beach, SC). **Pro/Amateur Scouts:** Pete Orr (Newmarket, Ontario), Ross Pruitt (Jupiter, FL). **Pro/International Scouts:** Bryan Bullington (Mokena, IL), Eduardo Sanchez (Dominican Republic). **National Supervisors, Amateur Scouting:** Doug Reynolds, Steve Riha, Jim Rooney. **Regional Supervisors, Amateur Scouting:** Josh Belovsky, Dan Nellum, Corey Rodriguez, Brian Stankey, Mike Serbalik. **Area Scouts:** Drew Anderson (IA, KS, MN, MO, ND, NE, SD), Ty Blankmeyer (NY, NJ, New England), Mike Burns (Central FL), James Fisher (DC, DE, MD, PA, VA, Eastern WV), Taylor Frederick (NC, SC), Joe Graham (Northern CA), KJ Hendricks (Northern TX), Dan Huston (Central CA), Harvey Kuenn Jr. (IL, IN, MI, WI), Lazaro Lianes (South FL, Puerto Rico), Mark Muzzi (AR, Northwestern LA, OK, Northern TX), Scott Nichols (AL, Eastern LA, MS, Western FL), Wynn Pelzer (Southern CA), Jeff Scholzen (AZ, CO, NM, NV, UT, WY), Jeff Simpson (KY, OH, TN, Western WV), Craig Smajstrla (Southern TX, Southwestern LA), Steve Smith (GA, Northern FL), Area Scout (AK, HI, ID, MT, OR, WA, Western Canada). **Senior Advisor, International Scouting:** Manny Batista. **Latin America Crosschecker:** Luis Perez. **Venezuela Scout Supervisor/Player Development Advisor:** Fernando Veracierto. **Central America Supervisor:** Jairo Castillo. **International Scouts:** Elvis Cruz, Julio De La Cruz, Jose Morales, Rodolfo Rosario (Dominican Republic), Reinaldo Hidalgo, Jose Rodriguez, Edgar Suarez (Venezuela). **Latin America Video Scouts:** Diego Flores, Jean Carlos Reynoso.

Minnesota Twins

Office Address: Target Field, 1 Twins Way, Minneapolis, MN 55403.
Telephone: (612) 659-3400. **Fax:** 612-659-4025. **Website:** www. twinsbaseball.com.

OWNERSHIP

Operated By: The Minnesota Twins. **Executive Chair:** Jim Pohlad. **Executive Board:** Jim Pohlad, Bob Pohlad, Bill Pohlad, Dave St. Peter.

BUSINESS OPERATIONS

President/Chief Executive Officer, Minnesota Twins: Dave St. Peter. **Executive Vice President/Chief Business Officer, Business Development:** Laura Day. **Executive VP/Chief Administrative Officer/CFO:** Kip Elliott. **Director, Ballpark Development/Planning:** Dan Starkey.

HUMAN RESOURCES/FINANCE/TECHNOLOGY

Sr. Director, Human Resources: Leticia Silva. **Director, Payroll:** Lori Beasley. **Human Resources Generalist:** Holly Corbin. **Coordinator, Payroll/Benefits:** Alison Lemke. **Coordinator, Human Resources:** Maria Salazar.

MARKETING

Senior Director, Marketing/Content: Chris Iles. **Director, Twins Productions:** Sam Henschen. **Creative Director:** Rodd Isberto. **Senior Manager, Advertising:** Will Delaney. **Manager, Digital Content:** Brea Hinegardner. **Manager, Video:** Jim Diehl. **Manager, Marketing/Promotions:** Mitch Retelny. **Manager, Marketing/Communications:** Beth Vail Palm.

Jim Pohlad

CORPORATE PARTNERSHIPS

Senior Director, Corporate Partnership: Jeff Jurgella. **Managers, Corporate Partnerships:** Doug Beck, Karen Cleary, Chad Jackson. **Director, Partnership Strategy/Development:** Jordan Woodcroft. **Manager, Broadcast Traffic/Administration:** Amy Johnson. **Specialist, Partner Activation:** Brittany Kennedy. **Project Manager:** Joe Morin.

COMMUNICATIONS

Telephone: (612) 659-3471. **Fax:** (612) 659-4029.
Senior Director, Communications: Dustin Morse. **Senior Manager, Communications:** Mitch Hestad. **Manager, Communications/Publications:** Mike Kennedy. **Coordinator, Communications:** Cori Frankenberg.

COMMUNITY RELATIONS

Senior Director, Community Affairs: Bryan Donaldson. **Senior Manager, Community Relations:** Stephanie Johnson. **Manager, Community Programs:** Josh Ortiz. **Senior Coordinator, Community Relations:** Sondra Ciesielski.

TICKETING/EVENTS

Telephone: 1-800-33-TWINS. **Fax:** (612) 659-4030.

2018 SCHEDULE

Standard Game Times: 7:10 p.m.; Sun 1:10.

MARCH		
29-31 . . . . . .at Baltimore		

APRIL		
1 . . . . at Baltimore		
2-4. . . . . . . at Pittsburgh		
5-8. . . . . Seattle		
9-11 . . . . Houston		
12-15 . . . . . Chicago (AL)		
17-18 . . . . Cleveland		
20-22 . . . at Tampa Bay		
23-26 . . . at New York (AL)		
27-29 . . . . Cincinnati		

MAY		
1-2. . . . . .Toronto		
3-6. . . . . .at Chicago (AL)		
7-8. . . . . .at St. Louis		

10-13 . at Los Angeles (AL)	
15-16 . . . . St. Louis	
18-20 . . . . . . .Milwaukee	
21-23 . . . . Detroit	
25-27 . . . . .at Seattle	
28-30 . . . . .at Kansas City	
31 . . . . Cleveland	

JUNE		
1-3. . . . . Cleveland		
5-7. . . . . . . Chicago (AL)		
8-10 . . . . Los Angeles (AL)		
12-14 . . . . .at Detroit		
15-17 . . . . . .at Cleveland		
19-21 . . . . Boston		
22-24 . . . . Texas		
26-28 . . . .at Chicago (AL)		

29-30 . . . .at Chicago (NL)	

JULY		
1 . . . . . . .at Chicago (NL)		
2-4. . . . . . at Milwaukee		
5-8. . . . . Baltimore		
9-11 . . . . . . Kansas City		
12-15 . . . . . .Tampa Bay		
20-22 . . . .at Kansas City		
23-25 . . . . . . at Toronto		
26-29 . . . . . .at Boston		
30-31 . . . . Cleveland		

AUGUST		
1 . . . . Cleveland		
3-5. . . . . . . Kansas City		
6-9. . . . . . . .at Cleveland		
10-12 . . . . .at Detroit		

14-15 . . . . . . Pittsburgh	
16-19 . . . . Detroit	
21-22 . . . .at Chicago (AL)	
23-26 . . . . Oakland	
28-30 . . . . .at Cleveland	
31 . . . . .at Texas	

SEPTEMBER		
1-2. . . . . .at Texas		
3-5. . . . . . . .at Houston		
7-9. . . . . Kansas City		
10-12 . . . .New York (AL)		
13-16 . . . . .at Kansas City		
17-19 . . . . . . .at Detroit		
21-23 . . . . . .at Oakland		
25-27 . . . . Detroit		
28-30 . . . . . Chicago (AL)		

GENERAL INFORMATION

Stadium (year opened): Target Field (2010). **Playing Surface:** Grass.
Team Colors: Red, navy blue and white.
Home Dugout: First Base.

Senior Director, Box Office: Mike Stiles. Manager, Box Office: Ashley Geldert. Manager, Call Center: Mark Engstrom. Supervisor, Box Office: Colleen Seeker. Coordinator, Call Center Operations: Chris Frogge. Coordinator, Ticket Operations/Special Events: Kelton Splett. Coordinator, Ticket Operations: Colin Sheehan.

BALLPARK OPERATIONS
Senior Vice President, Operations: Matt Hoy.
Senior Director, Ballpark Operations: Dave Horsman. Manager, Ballpark Operations: Jase Miller. Senior Director, Facilities: Gary Glawe. Senior Director, Guest Experience: Patrick Forsland. Sr. Manager, Guest Services: Katie Rock. Head Groundskeeper: Larry DiVito. Manager, Grounds: Al Kuehner. Manager, Event Security: Scott Larson. Coordinator, Office Services: Josh Fallin. Ballpark Operations Assistant: Chelsey Falzone. Manager, Retail Sales/Authentics: Venika Streeter. Assistant, Front Office: Tina Flowers.

BASEBALL OPERATIONS

Derek Falvey

Executive VP/Chief Baseball Officer: Derek Falvey.
Senior VP/General Manager: Thad Levine. VP, Player Personnel: Mike Radcliff. VP/Assistant GM: Rob Antony. Director, Minor League Operations: Jeremy Zoll. Special Assistant to the GM: Tom Kelly. Special Assistants: Michael Cuddyer, LaTroy Hawkins, Torii Hunter.
Analyst, Baseball Research: Zane MacPhee. Director, Team Travel: Mike Herman. Baseball Operations Assistant: Ezra Wise. Developers, Baseball Systems: Jerad Parish, Nick Rogers. Manager, Baseball Systems: Jeremy Raadt.

MAJOR LEAGUE STAFF
Manager: Paul Molitor. Coaches: Bench—Derek Shelton, Pitching—Garvin Alston, Hitting—James Rowson, Major League Coach—Jeff Pickler, First Base—Jeff Smith, Third Base—Gene Glynn, Bullpen—Eddie Guardado, Assistant Hitting—Rudy Hernandez. Equipment Manager: Rod McCormick, Assistant Home Clubhouse Manager: Tim Burke. Visitors Clubhouse: Marcus McKenzie. Director, Major League Video: Sean Harlin. Bullpen Catcher—Nate Dammann.

MEDICAL/TRAINING
Director, Medical Services: Dr. John Steubs. Club Physicians: Dr. Vijay Eyunni, Dr. Tom Jetzer, Dr. Jon Hallberg, Dr. Diane Dahm, Dr. Amy Beacom, Dr. Pearce McCarty, Dr. Rick Aberman. Head Trainer: Tony Leo. Assistant Trainers: Masamichi Abe, Mat Biancuzzo. Strength/Conditioning Coach: Perry Castellano.

PLAYER DEVELOPMENT
Telephone: (612) 659-3480. Fax: (612) 659-4026.
Director, Minor League Operations: Jeremy Zoll. Senior Manager, Minor League Administration: Kate Townley. Manager, Minor League Administration: Brian Maloney. Assistant, Florida/International Operations: Rafael Yanez. Assistant, Florida Operations: Victor Gonzalez. Minor League Coordinators: Edgar Varela (field), Rick Eckstein (hitting), Sam Perlozzo (infield/baserunning), Mike Quade (outfield), Tanner Swanson (catching), Pete Maki (pitching) Erik Beiser (strength/conditioning), Jose Marzan (Latin America), Chad Jackson (rehab), David Jeffrey (video).

FARM SYSTEM

Class	Club (League)	Manager	Coach	Pitching Coach
Triple-A	Rochester (IL)	Joel Skinner	Chad Allen	Stu Cliburn
Double-A	Chattanooga (SL)	Tommy Watkins	Javier Valentin	Ivan Arteaga
High A	Fort Myers (FSL)	Ramon Borrego	Steve Singleton	Henry Bonilla
Low A	Cedar Rapids (MWL)	Toby Gardenhire	Brian Dinkelman	Cibney Bello
Rookie	Elizabethton (APP)	Ray Smith	Jeff Reed	Luis Ramirez
Rookie	Twins (GCL)	Dan Ramsay	M. Borgschulte/L. Rodriguez	V. Vasquez/F. Jagoda
Rookie	Twins (DSL)	Robbie Robinson	Carlos Hernandez	M. Santana/C.Hernandez

SCOUTING
Director, Scouting: Sean Johnson.
Coordinator, Pro Scouting: Assistant Scouting Director: Tim O'Neil, Vern Followell. Senior Advisors, Scouting: Deron Johnson, Larry Corrigan. Senior Manager, Scouting/International Administration: Amanda Daley. Coordinator, Amateur Scouting: Brit Minder. Scouting Supervisors: Southeast— Billy Corrigan. West Coast— Elliott Strankman, East Coast— Mark Quimuyog, Midwest Supervisor: Mike Ruth. Area Scouts: Andrew Ayers (AZ, CO, NM, UT, WY, So. NV), Joe Bisenius (IA, MN, NE, ND, SD, WI) Kyle Blackwell (WA, OR, ID, MT, AK), Trevor Brown (TX, No. LA), Walt Burrows (Canada), J.R. DiMercurio (AR, KS, MO, OK), Brett Dowdy (FL), Derrick Dunbar (KY, MS, TN), Justin (Mid-Atlantic), John Leavitt (HI, CA), Seth Moir (CA), Jeff Pohl (MI, IN, IL), Jack Powell (GA, AL), Michael Quesada (NV, CA), Freddie Thon (FL, PR), Nick Venuto (OH, WV, PA, NY), Matt Williams (NC, SC, VA), Greg Runser (TX, LA), John Wilson (CT, NJ, NY, MA, VA, MD, VT, RI, ME, NH, DE, DC) Junior College Scout: Ty Dawson. Professional Scouts: Ken Compton. Special Assignment Scout: Earl Frishman. Pro Scouts: Bob Hegman, John Manuel, Bill Mele, Bill Milos, Keith Stohr, Earl Winn, Wesley Wright. Scouts: Glenn Godwin, Mike Larson. International Scouts Coordinator, Latin American Scouting: Fred Guerrero. Dominican Republic: Luis Lajara, Manuel Luciano, Eury Luis, Eduardo Soriano. Coordinator, Venezuela Scouting: Jose Leon. Venezuela: Marlon Nava, Oswaldo Troconis. Pacific Rim: David Kim. Part-Time Scouts: Hector Barrios (Panama), John Cortese (Italy), Kenny Su (Taiwan), Koji Takahashi (Japan), Lester Victoria (Curacao) Juan Padilla, Franklin Parra, Pablo Torres (Venezuela).

New York Mets

Office Address: Citi Field, 126th Street, Flushing, NY 11368.
Telephone: (718) 507-6387. **Fax:** (718) 507-6395.
Website:www.mets.com. **Twitter:** @mets.

OWNERSHIP

Operated By: Sterling Mets LP. **Chairman/Chief Executive Officer:** Fred Wilpon. **President:** Saul B. Katz. **Chief Operating Officer:** Jeff Wilpon.

BUSINESS OPERATIONS

Executive VP/Chief Revenue Officer: Lou DePaoli. **Executive Director, Business Intelligence/Analytics:** John Morris.

LEGAL/HUMAN RESOURCES

Executive VP/Chief Legal Officer: David Cohen. **VP/Deputy General Counsel:** Neal Kaplan. **Senior Counsel:** James Denniston. **Senior Counsel:** Jessica Villanella. **VP, Human Resources:** Holly Lindvall.

FINANCE

CFO: Mark Peskin. **VP, Controller:** Len Labita. **VP, Financial Planning & Analysis:** Peter Woll. **Assistant Controller/Director:** John Ventimiglia.

Fred Wilpon

MARKETING/COMMUNICATIONS/SALES

Senior VP, Marketing/Communications: David Newman. **Executive Producer, Entertainment Marketing/Productions:** Joe DeVito. **Executive Director, Entertainment Marketing/Productions:** Tim Gunkel. **Executive Director, Marketing:** Mark Fine. **Executive Director, Broadcasting/Special Events:** Lorraine Hamilton.

MEDIA RELATIONS

Telephone: (718) 565-4330. **Fax:** (718) 639-3619.
VP, Media Relations: Jay Horwitz. **Executive Director, Communications:** Harold Kaufman. **Director, Media Relations:** Ethan Wilson.

TICKETING

Telephone: (718) 507-8499. **Fax:** (718) 507-6369.
VP, Ticket Sales/Services: Chris Zaber. **Senior Director, Group Sales:** Wade Graf. **Senior Director, New Business Development:** Kenny Koperda. **Senior Director, Season Ticket Account Services:** Jamie Ozure. **Senior Director, Ticket Operations:** Jarett Parver.

VENUE SERVICES/OPERATIONS/TECHNOLOGY

Senior VP, Venue Services/Operations: Mike Landeen. **VP, Metropolitan Hospitality:** Heather Collamore. VP,

2018 SCHEDULE

Standard Game Times: 7:10 p.m.; Sun. 1:10.

MARCH		
29-31 . . . . St. Louis	11-13 . . . . at Philadelphia	JULY
APRIL	15-16 . . . . .Toronto	1 . . . . at Miami
1 . . . . St. Louis	18-20 . . . . .Arizona	3-4. . . . . at Toronto
2-4. . . . . . . .Philadelphia	21-23 . . . . .Miami	6-8. . . . . . . .Tampa Bay
5-8. . . . . at Washington	24-27 . . . . . at Milwaukee	9-11 . . . . . . .Philadelphia
9-11 . . . . at Miami	28-30 . . . . at Atlanta	12-15 . . . . . . Washington
13-15 . . . . . . .Milwaukee	31 . . . . .'. . Chicago (NL)	20-22 . . . at New York (AL)
16-18 . . . . . Washington	**JUNE**	23-25 . . . . San Diego
19-22 . . . . . at Atlanta	1-3. . . . . . Chicago (NL)	26-29 . . . . at Pittsburgh
24-26 . . . . . .at St. Louis	5-6. . . . . Baltimore	31 . . . . . . at Washington
27-29 . . . . . at San Diego	8-10 . . . .New York (AL)	**AUGUST**
MAY	12-13 . . . . . at Atlanta	1 . . . . at Washington
1-3. . . . . Atlanta	14-17 . . . . at Arizona	2-5. . . . . Atlanta
4-6. . . . . .Colorado	18-21 . . . . . at Colorado	6-8. . . . . Cincinnati
7-9. . . . . . .at Cincinnati	22-24 . . .Los Angeles (NL)	10-12 . . . . at Miami
	25-27 . . . . . . Pittsburgh	14-15 . . . . . at Baltimore
	29-30 . . . . at Miami	

16-19 . . . . at Philadelphia
20-23 . . . . . San Francisco
24-26 . . . . . . Washington
27-29 . . .at Chicago (NL)
31 . . . . . at San Francisco
SEPTEMBER
1-2. . . . . at San Francisco
3-5. . . at Los Angeles (NL)
7-9. . . . . . . .Philadelphia
10-13 . . . . .Miami
14-16 . . . . .at Boston
17-19 . . . . at Philadelphia
20-23 . . . . at Washington
25-27 . . . . Atlanta
28-30 . . . . .Miami

GENERAL INFORMATION

Stadium (year opened):
Citi Field (2009).
Team Colors: Blue and orange.

Home Dugout: First Base.
Playing Surface: Grass.

Ballpark Operations: Sue Lucchi. VP, Technology & Corporate Procurement: Tom Festa. VP, Guest Experience/ Venue Services: Chris Brown. Executive Director, Venue Services: Paul Schwartz. Executive Director, Building Operations: Peter Cassano. Senior Director, Ballpark Operations: Michael Dohnert.

TRAVEL/CLUBHOUSE
Clubhouse Manager: Kevin Kierst. Assistant Clubhouse Manager: Dave Berni. Visiting Clubhouse Manager: Tony Carullo. Director, Team Travel: Brian Small.

BASEBALL OPERATIONS

Sandy Alderson

Telephone: (718) 803-4013, (718) 565-4339. Fax: (718) 507-6391.
General Manager: Sandy Alderson. Senior VP/Assistant GM: John Ricco. Special Assistant to GM: J.P. Ricciardi. Special Assistant to GM: Omar Minaya. Special Assistant to GM: Terry Collins. Manager, Baseball Administration: June Napoli. Director, Baseball Research/Development: T.J. Barra. Senior Coordinator, Baseball Systems Development: Joe Lefkowitz. Coordinator, Baseball Operations: Jeffrey Lebow. Coordinator, Advance Scouting/Video Replay: Jim Kelly. Director, Player Relations/Programs/Community Engagement: Donovan Mitchell. Director, Team Travel: Brian Small. Manager, Video Operations: Joseph Scarola. Coordinator, Video Operations: Sean Haggans.

MAJOR LEAGUE STAFF
Manager: Mickey Callaway. Coaches: Bench—Gary DiSarcina, Pitching—Dave Eiland, Hitting—Pat Roessler, Assistant Hitting—Tom Slater, First Base—Ruben Amaro Jr., Third Base—Glenn Sherlock, Bullpen—Ricky Bones.

MEDICAL/TRAINING
Medical Director: Dr. David Altchek. Physician: Dr. Struan Coleman. Director of Performance & Sports Science: Jim Cavallini. Head Athletic Trainer: Brian Chicklo. Assistant Athletic Trainer: Joseph Golia. Strength & Conditioning Coordinator: Dustin Clarke. Physical Therapist: John Zajac.

PLAYER DEVELOPMENT
Telephone: (718) 565-4302. Fax: (718) 205-7920.
Director, Player Development: Ian Levin. Minor League Field Coordinator: Kevin Morgan. Director, Minor League Operations: Ronny Reyes. Director, Latin American Operations: Juan Henderson. International Field Coordinator: Rafael Landestoy. Assistant Director, Player Development: Nick Francona. Coordinators: Jennifer Wolf (minor league/international operations), Colin Schwarz (minor league information), Lamar Johnson (hitting), Ryan Ellis (hitting performance), Ron Romanick (pitching), Phil Regan (assistant pitching), Bob Natal (catching coordinator), Benny Distefano (outfield), Tim Teufel (infield), Jon Debus (rehab pitching), Matt Hunter (medical), Dave Pearson (physical therapist), Jon Cioffi (strength/conditioning). Equipment/Operations Manager: John Mullin.

FARM SYSTEM

Class	Club	Manager	Hitting Coach	Pitching Coach
Triple-A	Las Vegas (PCL)	Tony DeFrancesco	Joel Chimelis	Glenn Abbott
Double-A	Binghamton (EL)	Luis Rojas	Val Pascucci	Frank Viola
High A	St. Lucie (FSL)	Chad Kreuter	Joel Fuentes	Marc Valdes
Low A	Savannah (SAL)	Pedro Lopez	Ender Chavez	Jonathan Hurst
Short-season	Brooklyn (NYP)	Edgardo Alfonzo	Marlon Anderson	Royce Ring
Rookie	Kingsport (APP)	Sean Ratliff	Delwyn Young	Josue Matos
Rookie	Mets (GCL)	Jose Carreno	Rafael Fernandez	Ariel Prieto
Rookie	Mets 1 (DSL)	Manny Martinez	Leo Hernandez	Francis Martinez
Rookie	Mets 2 (DSL)	Yucarybert De La Cruz	Gilbert Gomez	B. Marte/R. Roque

SCOUTING
Telephone: (718) 565-4311. Fax: (718) 205-7920.
VP, Amateur/International Scouting: Tommy Tanous. Director, Amateur Scouting: Marc Tramuta. Coordinator, Amateur Scouting: Bryan Hayes. National Crosschecker: Doug Thurman. Pitching Supervisor, National: John Hendricks (Clemmons, NC). Global Crosschecker: Steve Barningham (Land O'Lakes, FL). Regional Supervisors: National Crosschecker/Southeast Supervisor—Mike Ledna, West—Drew Toussaint, Northeast—Marlin McPhail, Midwest—Mac Seibert. Area Supervisors: Cesar Aranguren (Miami, FL), Nathan Beuster (St. Charles, MO), Jet Butler (Brandon, MS), Daniel Coles (Raleigh, NC), Ray Corbett (College Station, TX), Jarrett England (Murfreesboro,TN), Chris Hervey (Ann Arbor, MI), Tyler Holmes (Roseville, CA), Tommy Jackson (Birmingham, AL), John Kosclak (Milton, MA), Claude Pelletier (St. Lazare, Quebec), Jim Reeves (Camas, WA), Brian Reid (Gilbert, AZ), Justin Schwartz (Beverly Hills, CA), Max Semler (Allen, TX), Jim Thompson (Philadelphia, PA), Jon Updike (Apopka, FL), Evan Wise (Fullerton, CA). Senior Director, Pro Scouting: Jim D'Aloia. Assistant Director, Professional Scouting: Bryn Alderson. Professional Scouts: Mack Babitt (Richmond, CA), Conor Brooks (Plymouth, MA), Thomas Clark (Shrewsbury, MA), Tim Fortugno (Elk Grove, CA), David Keller (Houston, TX), Joseph Kowal (Yardley, PA), Ash Lawson (Athens, TN), Shaun McNamara(Worcester, MA), Art Pontarelli (Lincoln, RI), Roy Smith (Chicago, IL), Rudy Terrasas (Santa Fe, TX). Senior Director, International Scouting: Chris Becerra. International Supervisors: Gerardo Cabrera (Coordinator, Latin American Scouting), Hector Rincones (Coordinator, Latin American Scouting), Harold Herrera (Coordinator, Latin American Scouting). Supervisor, Venezuela: Ismael Perez. International Scouts: Marciano Alvarez, Kelvin Dominguez, Fernando Encarnacion, Miguel Vasquez (Dominican Republic), Gabriel Low, Fred Mazuca (Mexico), Robert Espejo, Nestor Moreno, Carlos Perez, Andres Nunez (Venezuela), Bon Kim (Asia).

New York Yankees

Office Address: Yankee Stadium, One East 161st St., Bronx, NY 10451.
Telephone: (718) 293-4300.
Website: www.yankees.com, www.yankeesbeisbol.com. **Twitter:** @Yankees, @YankeesPR, @LosYankees, @LosYankeesPR.

OWNERSHIP

Managing General Partner/Co-Chairperson: Harold Z. (Hal) Steinbrenner. **General Partner/Co-Chairperson:** Henry G. Steinbrenner. **General Partner/Vice Chairperson:** Jennifer Steinbrenner Swindal. **General Partner/Vice Chairperson:** Jessica Steinbrenner. **Vice Chairperson:** Joan Steinbrenner.

BUSINESS OPERATIONS

Harold Steinbrenner

President: Randy Levine, Esq.
Chief Operating Officer/General Counsel: Lonn A. Trost, Esq.
Senior VP, Strategic Ventures: Marty Greenspun. **Senior VP, Chief Security Officer:** Sonny Hight. **Senior VP, Yankee Global Enterprises/Chief Financial Officer:** Anthony Bruno. **Senior VP, Corporate/Community Relations:** Brian E. Smith. **Senior VP, Corporate Sales/Sponsorship:** Michael J. Tusiani. **Senior VP, Marketing:** Deborah Tymon. **Senior VP, Stadium Operations:** Doug Behar. **VP/Chief Financial Officer, Accounting:** Robert B. Brown. **Deputy General Counsel/VP, Legal Affairs:** Alan Chang. **Chief Financial Officer/Senior VP, Financial Operations:** Scott M. Krug. **VP, Chief Information Officer:** Mike Lane.

COMMUNICATIONS/MEDIA RELATIONS

Telephone: (718) 579-4460. **Fax:** (718) 293-8414.
Vice President, Communications/Media Relations: Jason Zillo. **Director, Baseball Information/Public Communications:** Michael Margolis. **Assistant Director, Baseball Information:** Lauren Moran. **Manager, Media Services:** Alexandra Trochanowski. **Sr. Coordinator, Communications/Media Relations:** Rob Morse. **Coordinator, Communications/Media Relations:** Kaitlyn Brennan. **Administrative Assistant, Communications/Media Relations:** Germania-Dolores Hernandez. **Bilingual Media Relations Coodinator:** Marlon Abreu. **Japanese Media Advisor:** Yoshiki Sato.

TICKET OPERATIONS

Telephone: (718) 293-6000.
VP, Ticket Sales/Service/Operations: Kevin Dart.

BASEBALL OPERATIONS

Senior VP/General Manager: Brian Cashman.
Senior VP/Assistant GM: Jean Afterman, Esq. **VP, Assistant GM:** Michael Fishman. **VP, Baseball Operations:** Tim Naehring. **Special Advisors:** Reggie Jackson, Hideki Matsui, Nick Swisher.
Director, Team Travel & Player Services: Ben Tuliebitz. **Director, Quantitative Analysis:** David Grabiner.

2018 SCHEDULE

Standard Game Times: 7:05 p.m.; Sat.-Sun. 1:05.

MARCH		JULY	SEPTEMBER
29-31 . . . . . . at Toronto	8-10 . . . . Boston	25-27 . . . . at Philadelphia	9-12 . . . . Texas
	11-13 . . . . Oakland	29-30 . . . . Boston	14-16 . . . . . . Tampa Bay
APRIL	15-16 . . . . at Washington	**JULY**	17-19 . . . . Toronto
1 . . . . at Toronto	18-20 . . . . at Kansas City	1 . . . . Boston	21-22 . . . . at Miami
2-4 . . . . Tampa Bay	21-23 . . . . at Texas	2-4 . . . . Atlanta	24-26 . . . . at Baltimore
5-8 . . . . Baltimore	25-27 . . . Los Angeles (AL)	6-8 . . . . at Toronto	27-29 . . . . Chicago (AL)
10-12 . . . . . . at Boston	28-30 . . . . Houston	9-11 . . . . . . at Baltimore	30-31 . . . . Detroit
13-15 . . . . . . at Detroit	31 . . . . at Baltimore	12-15 . . . . . at Cleveland	
16-17 . . . . Miami		20-22 . . . . New York (NL)	**SEPTEMBER**
19-22 . . . . Toronto	**JUNE**	23-25 . . . . at Tampa Bay	1-2 . . . . Detroit
23-26 . . . . . Minnesota	1-3 . . . . at Baltimore	26-29 . . . . Kansas City	3-5 . . . . at Oakland
27-29 at Los Angeles (AL)	5-6 . . . . at Toronto	31 . . . . Baltimore	7-9 . . . . at Seattle
30 . . . . at Houston	8-10 . . . at New York (NL)		10-12 . . . at Minnesota
	12-13 . . . . . Washington	**AUGUST**	14-16 . . . . Toronto
MAY	14-17 . . . . . Tampa Bay	1 . . . . Baltimore	18-20 . . . . Boston
1-3 . . . . at Houston	19-21 . . . . Seattle	2-5 . . . . at Boston	21-23 . . . . . Baltimore
4-6 . . . . Cleveland	22-24 . . . . at Tampa Bay	6-8 . . . . at Chicago (AL)	24-27 . . . . at Tampa Bay
			28-30 . . . . . . at Boston

GENERAL INFORMATION

Stadium (year opened):
Yankee Stadium (2009).
Team Colors: Navy blue and white.

Home Dugout: First Base.
Playing Surface: Grass.

Director, Baseball Operations: Matt Ferry. **Coordinator, Baseball Operations:** Stephen Swindal, Jr. **Major League Systems Architect:** Brian Nicosia. **Senior Web Developer:** Nick Eby. **Senior iOS Developer:** Michael Traverso. **Special Assignment Scout:** Jim Hendry. **Analysts, Quantitative Analysis:** Theodore Feder, Justin Sims, Sam Waters. **Database Engineer, Baseball Operations:** Jesse Bradford. **Nutritional Consultant:** Cynthia Sass. **Director, Mental Conditioning:** Chad Bohling.

MAJOR LEAGUE STAFF

Manager: Aaron Boone.
Coaches: Bench— Josh Bard, **Pitching**—Larry Rothschild, **Hitting**—Alan Cockrell, **Assistant Hitting**—Marcus Thames, **Assistant Hitting**—P.J. Pilittere, **First Base**—Reggie Willits, **Third Base**—Phil Nevin, **Bullpen**—Mike Harkey, **Bullpen Catcher**—Radley Haddad.

Brian Cashman

MEDICAL/TRAINING

Team Physician, New York: Dr. Christopher Ahmad.
Head Team Internist: Paul Lee, M.D., M.P.H. **Team Internist:** William Turner, M.D. **Senior Advisor, Orthopedics:** Stuart Hershon, M.D. **Head Athletic Trainer:** Steve Donohue. **Physical Therapist/Assistant Athletic Trainer:** Michael Schuk. **Assistant Athletic Trainer:** Tim Lentych. **Massage Therapist:** Doug Cecil. **Director, Strength/Conditioning:** Matthew Krause.

PLAYER DEVELOPMENT

Senior Director, Player Development: Kevin Reese.
Director, Performance Science: John Kremer. **Director, Player Development:** Eric Schmitt. **Director, Minor League Operations:** Hadi Raad. **Enterprise Solutions Engineer:** Rob Owens. **Field Coordinator:** Jody Reed. **Coordinator, Instruction:** Pat McMahon. **Hitting Coordinators:** Greg Colbrunn, Edwar Gonzalez. **Pitching Coordinator (upper level):** Scott Aldred. **Pitching Coordinator (lower level):** Danny Borrell. **Catching Coordinator:** J.D. Closser. **Rehab Pitching Instructor:** Greg Pavlick. **Rehab Position Player Instructor:** Tony Franklin. **Player Development Consultants:** Marc Bombard, Tino Martinez, Orlando Hernandez. **Video Coordinator, Player Development:** Tyler DeClerck. **Manager, International Operations:** Vic Roldan.
Medical Coordinator, Preventative Programs: Mike Wickland. **Medical Coordinator:** Mark Littlefield. **Strength/ Conditioning Coordinator:** Rigo Febles. **Assistant Strength/Conditioning Coordinator:** Mike Kicia.

FARM SYSTEM

Class	Club (League)	Manager	Hitting Coach	Pitching Coach
Triple-A	Scranton/WB (IL)	Al Pedrique	Phil Plantier	Tommy Phelps
Double-A	Trenton (EL)	Jay Bell	Ty Hawkins	Tim Norton
High A	Tampa (FSL)	Pat Osborn	Eric Duncan	Jose Rosado
Low A	Charleston (SAL)	Julio Mosquera	Scott Seabol	Justin Pope
Short-season	Staten Island (NYP)	Lino Diaz	Ken Joyce	Travis Phelps
Rookie	Pulaski (APP)	Nick Ortiz	Francisco Leandro	Gerardo Casadiego
Rookie	Yankees I (GCL)	David Adams	Rich Arena	Gabe Luckert
Rookie	Yankees II (GCL)	TBA	T. Blaser/K. Mahoney	Elvys Quezada
Rookie	Yankees I (DSL)	Conabo Cosme	Rainiero Coa	Gabriel Tatis

SCOUTING

Telephone: (813) 875-7569. **Fax:** (813) 873-2302.
VP, Amateur Scouting: Damon Oppenheimer.
Assistant Director, Amateur Scouting: Ben McIntyre. **Director, Professional Scouting:** Dan Giese. **National Crosscheckers:** Brian Barber, Tim Kelly, Steve Kmetko, Jeff Patterson. **Pitching Analyst, Amateur Scouting:** Scott Lovekamp. **Hitting Analyst, Amateur Scouting:** Jeff Deardorff. **Analyst, Amateur Scouting:** Scott Benecke. **Draft Medical Coordinator:** Justin Sharpe. **Video Coordinator, Amateur Scouting:** Mitch Colahan. **Video Manager, Amateur Scouting:** Tristam Osgood, Bryce Harman.
Professional Scouts: Joe Caro, Kendall Carter, Matt Daley, Jay Darnell, Brandon Duckworth, Bill Emslie, Abe Flores, Kevin Hart, Shawn Hill, Aaron Holbert, Cory Melvin, Pat Murtaugh, JT Stotts, Alex Sunderland, Dennis Twombley, Aron Weston, Tom Wilson.
Area Scouts: Troy Afenir, Tim Alexander, Denis Boucher, Andy Campbell, Bobby DeJardin, Mike Gibbons, Billy Godwin, Matt Hyde, David Keith, Steve Lemke, Mike Leuzinger, Carlos Marti, Ronnie Merrill, Darryl Monroe, Bill Pintard, Cesar Presbott, Matt Ranson, Brian Rhees, Tyler Robertson, Mike Thurman, Mike Wagner.
Director, International Player Development: Vic Roidan. **Director, International Scouting:** Donny Rowland. **Director, Dominican Republic Operations:** Mario Garza. **Director, Latin Baseball Academy:** Joel Lithgow. **International Hitting Instructor:** Edwin Beard. **International Pitching Instructor:** Gabriel Tatis. **Video Coordinator, International Operations:** Taylor Emanuels.
International Crosschecker/Coordinator, Int'l Scouting/Pacific Rim: Steve Wilson. **Crosschecker, International Scouting:** Dennis Woody. **Scouting Coordinator, Dominican Republic:** Raymon Sanchez. **Crosscheckers, Latin America:** Miguel Benitez, Victor Mata, Juan Rosario. **International Crosschecker:** Ricardo Finol. **Assistant, International Scouting:** Yunior Tabares. **Supervisor, Venezuela:** Jose Gavidia. **Dominican Republic Scouts:** Esteban Castillo, Raul Gonzalez, Arturo Pena, Juan Piron, Jose Ravelo, Jose Sabino. **Venezuela Scouts:** Alan Atacho, Darwin Bracho, Roney Calderon, Cesar Suarez, Jesus Taico, Luis Tinoco. **Mexico Scouts:** Lee Sigman. **International Scouts:** Rudy Gomez, Chi Lee (South Korea), Carlos Levy (Panama), Edgar Rodriguez (Nicaragua), Borman Landaeta, Luis Sierra (Colombia), John Wadsworth (Australia), Troy Williams (Europe).

Oakland Athletics

Office Address: 7000 Coliseum Way, Oakland, CA 94621.
Telephone: (510) 638-4900. **Fax:** (510) 562-1633. **Website:** www.oaklandathletics.com.

OWNERSHIP

Managing Partner/Board Member: John Fisher. **Chariman Emeritus:** Lew Wolff. **Board Members:** Sandy Dean, Bill Gurtin, Keith Wolff.

BUSINESS OPERATIONS

President: David Kaval. **Executive Assistant:** Carolyn Jones. **General Counsel:** Neil Kraetsch. **Assistant General Counsels:** Ryan Horning, D'Lonra Ellis.

FINANCE/ADMINISTRATION

David Kaval

VP, Finance: Paul Wong. **Senior Director, Finance:** Kasey Jarcik. **Director, Finance:** John Anki. **Payroll Manager:** Rose Dancil. **Senior Accountant, Accounts Payable:** Isabelle Mahaffey. **Accounting Manager:** Nick Cukar. **Senior Accounts:** Danna Mouat, Casey Quirke. **Director, Human Resources:** Andre Chambers. **Human Resources Manager:** Elizabeth Espinoza. **Human Resources Assistant:** Katie Strehlow. **Director, Information Technology:** Nathan Hayes. **Senior Manager, IT:** David Frieberg. **Desktop Administrator:** Chris Jio.

SALES/MARKETING

VP, Sales/Marketing: Troy Smith. **Coordinator, Marketing:** Elizabeth Staub. **Director, Marketing:** Travis LoDolce. **Marketing Manager:** Laiken Whitters. **Creative Services Manager:** Mike Ono. **Team Photographer:** Michael Zagaris. **Senior Manager, Ballpark Events:** Heather Rajeski.

PUBLIC RELATIONS/COMMUNICATIONS

VP, Communications/Community: Catherine Aker. **Baseball Information Manager:** Mike Selleck. **Media Relations/Broadcasting Coordinator:** Mark Ling. **Director, Alumni/Family Relations:** Detra Paige. **Senior Coordinator, Alumni/Family Relations:** Melissa Guzman. **Senior Director, Engineering/Multimedia Services:** David Don. **Public Address Announcer:** Dick Callahan.

STADIUM OPERATIONS

VP, Stadium Operations: David Rinetti. **Senior Director, Stadium Operations:** Paul La Veau. **Senior Manager, Stadium Operations Events:** Kristy Ledbetter. **Stadium Services Manager:** Randy Duran. **Guest Services Manager:** Elisabeth Aydelotte. **Stadium Operations Manager:** Matt Van Norton. **Stadium Operations Coordinator:** Jason Silva. **Head Groundskeeper:** Clay Wood.

TICKET SALES/OPERATIONS/SERVICES

Director, Ticket Operations: David Adame. **Senior Director, Service/Retention:** Josh Ziegenbusch. **Ticket Services Manager:** Victoria Hill. **Premium Services Manager:** Matt Langseth. **Premium Services Coordinator:** Katie Grubbs. **Ticket Operations Manager:** Austin Redman. **Box Office Coordinator:** Patricia Heagy.

2018 SCHEDULE

Standard Game Times: 7:05 p.m.; Sun. 1:05.

MARCH
29-31 . . . Los Angeles (AL)

APRIL
1 . . . . . . Los Angeles (AL)
2-5 . . . . Texas
6-8 . . at Los Angeles (AL)
10-11 . at Los Angeles (NL)
13-15 . . . . .at Seattle
16-18 . . . . . Chicago (AL)
20-22 . . . . Boston
23-25 . . . . .at Texas
27-29 . . . . . .at Houston

MAY
1-3 . . . . .at Seattle
4-6 . . . . Baltimore
7-9 . . . . Houston

11-13 . . . at New York (AL)
14-16 . . . . .at Boston
17-20 . . . . . . at Toronto
22-24 . . . . Seattle
25-27 . . . . Arizona
28-31 . . . . .Tampa Bay

JUNE
1-3 . . . . . .at Kansas City
5-6 . . . . .at Texas
7-10 . . . . . Kansas City
12-14 . . . . Houston
15-17 . . . Los Angeles (AL)
19-20 . . . . . at San Diego
21-24 . . . at Chicago (AL)
25-28 . . . . at Detroit
29-30 . . . . Cleveland

JULY
1 . . . . Cleveland
3-4 . . . . San Diego
6-8 . . . . . . .at Cleveland
9-12 . . . . . . .at Houston
13-15 . . . at San Francisco
20-22 . . . . . San Francisco
23-26 . . . . .at Texas
27-29 . . . . . at Colorado
30-31 . . . . .Toronto

AUGUST
1 . . . . .Toronto
3-5 . . . . Detroit
7-8 . . . . . Los Angeles (NL)
10-12 . at Los Angeles (AL)
13-15 . . . . Seattle
17-19 . . . . Houston

20-22 . . . . Texas
23-26 . . . . . at Minnesota
27-29 . . . . . .at Houston
30-31 . . . . .Seattle)

SEPTEMBER
1-2 . . . . Seattle
3-5 . . . . . .New York (AL)
7-9 . . . . Texas
11-13 . . . . . .at Baltimore
14-16 . . . at Tampa Bay
18-20 . . . Los Angeles (AL)
21-23 . . . . . . .Minnesota
24-26 . . . . .at Seattle
28-30 . at Los Angeles (AL)

GENERAL INFORMATION

Stadium (year opened):
O.co Coliseum (1968).
Team Colors: Kelly green and gold.

Home Dugout: Third Base.
Playing Surface: Grass.

TRAVEL/CLUBHOUSE

Director, Team Travel: Mickey Morabito. **Equipment Manager:** Steve Vucinich. **Visiting Clubhouse Manager:** Mike Thalblum. **Assistant Equipment Manager:** Brian Davis. **Umpire/Clubhouse Assistant:** Matt Weiss. **Arizona Clubhouse Manager:** James Gibson. **Arizona Assistant Clubhouse Managers:** Thomas Miller, Chad Yaconetti.

BASEBALL OPERATIONS

Executive Vice President, Baseball Operations: Billy Beane.

General Manager: David Forst. **Assistant GM:** Dan Kantrovitz. **Assistant GM, Pro Scouting & Player Personnel:** Dan Feinstein. **Assistant GM/Director, Player Personnel:** Billy Owens. **Director, Baseball Systems:** Rob Naberhaus. **Special Assistants to GM:** Grady Fuson, Chris Pittaro. **Executive Assistant:** Betty Shinoda. **Director, Baseball Administration:** Pamela Pitts. **Video Coordinator:** Adam Rhoden. **Special Assistant to Baseball Operations:** Scott Hatteberg. **Research Scientist:** David Jackson-Hanen. **Baseball Operations Analyst:** Pike Goldschmidt. **Baseball Operations Analyst:** Ben Lowry.

Billy Beane

MAJOR LEAGUE STAFF

Manager: Bob Melvin.

Coaches: Bench—Ryan Christenson; **Pitching**— Scott Emerson; **Batting**—Darren Bush; **First Base**—Al Pedrique; **Third Base**—Matt Williams; **Bullpen**—Marcus Jensen; **Assistant Hitting Coach**— Mike Aldrete; **Quality Control Coach**—Mark Kotsay; **Bullpen Catcher**—Phil Pohl; **Bullpen Catcher**—Jeremy Dowdy.

MEDICAL/TRAINING

Head Athletic Trainer: Nick Paparesta. **Assistant Athletic Trainers:** Jeff Collins, Brian Schulman. **Strength/Conditioning Coach:** Josh Cuffe. **Asst. Strength/Conditioning Coach:** Terence Brannic. **Major League Massage Therapist:** Ozzie Lyles. **Team Physicians:** Dr. Allan Pont, Dr. Elliott Schwartz. **Team Orthopedist:** Dr. Jon Dickinson. **Associate Team Orthopedist:** Dr. Will Workman. **Arizona Team Physicians:** Dr. Fred Dicke, Dr. Doug Freedberg.

PLAYER DEVELOPMENT

Telephone: (510) 638-4900. **Fax:** (510) 563-2376.

Director, Player Development: Keith Lieppman. **Director, Minor League Operations:** Zak Basch. **Coordinator, Player Development:** Nancy Moriuchi. **Coordinator, Minor League Merchandise & Equipment:** Thomas Miller. **Senior Facility Manager (AZ):** James Gibson. **Clubhouse Manager (AZ):** Chad Yaconetti. **Minor League Roving Instructors:** Juan Navarrete (infield), Steve Scarsone (infield), Gil Patterson (pitching), Jim Eppard (hitting). **Minor League Medical Coordinator:** Nate Brooks. **Coordinator, Medical Services:** Larry Davis. **Latin American Medical Coordinator:** Javier Alvidrez. **Minor League Strength/Conditioning Coordinator:** A.J. Seeliger. **Minor League Assistant Strength/Conditioning Coordinator:** Matt Rutledge. **Latin America Strength/Conditioning Coordinator:** J.D. Howell. **Minor League Coordinator of Instruction:** Ed Sprague. **Special Instructor, Pitching/Rehabilitation:** Craig Lefferts. **Minor League Instructor:** Hiram Bocachica. **Minor League Rehabilitation Coordinator:** Travis Tims. **Manager, Minor League Technology & Development:** Ed Gitlick.

FARM SYSTEM

Class	Club (League)	Manager	Coach	Pitching Coach
Triple-A	Nashville (PCL)	Fran Riordan	Eric Martins	Rick Rodriguez
Double-A	Midland (TL)	Scott Steinmann	Tommy Everidge	Steve Connelly
High A	Stockton (CAL)	Rick Magnante	Brian McArn	Corey Bryan
Low A	Beloit (MWL)	Webster Garrison	Juan Dilone	Don Schulze
Short-season	Vermont (NYP)	Aaron Nieckula	Lloyd Turner	Carlos Chavez
Rookie	Athletics (AZL)	Eddie Menchaca	Ruben Escalera	Gabriel Ozuna
Rookie	Athletics (DSL)	Carlos Casimiro	Rahdames Mota	David Brito

SCOUTING

Director, Scouting: Eric Kubota (Rocklin, CA). **Assistant Director, Scouting:** Michael Holmes (Winston Salem, NC). **Scouting Coordinator:** Haley Alvarez (San Francisco, CA). **Scouting Assistant:** Greg Ledford (Oakland, CA). **West Coast Supervisor:** Scott Kidd (Folsom, CA). **Midwest Supervisor:** Mark Adair (University City, MO). **Midwest Supervisor:** Armann Brown (Austin, TX). **East Coast Supervisor:** Marc Sauer (Tampa, FL). **Pro Scouts:** Jeff Bittiger (Saylorsburg, PA), Grant Brittain (Hickory, NC), Dan Freed (Lexington, IL), Trevor Ryan (San Jose, CA), Will Schock (Oakland, CA), Tom Thomas (Phoenix, AZ), Mike Ziegler (Orlando, FL). **Area Scouts:** Anthony Aliotti (Los Angeles, CA), Anthony Aloisi (Nashville, TN), Neil Avent (Charlotte, NC), Jim Coffman (Portland, OR), Steve Cohen (Spring, TX), Craig Conklin (Malibu, CA), Scott Cousins (Scottsdale, AZ), Ruben Escalera (Carolina, PR), Tripp Faulk (Richmond, VA), Julio Franco (Weston, FL), Matt Higginson (Grimsby, ON), Derek Lee (Frankfort, IL), Kevin Mello (El Cerrito, CA), Kelcey Mucker (Baton Rouge, LA), Chris Reilly (Rockwall, TX), Trevor Schaffer (Belleair, FL), Al Skorupa (Overland Park, KS), Rich Sparks (Macomb, MI), Jemel Spearman (Cumming, GA), Dillon Tung (Los Angeles, CA), Ron Vaughn (Windsor, CT).

Special Assistant to Professional and International Scouting: Steve Sharpe (Prairie Village, KS). **Director, Latin American Operations:** Raymond Abreu (Santo Domingo, DR). **International Scouts:** Yendri Bachelor (Dominican Republic), Ruben Barradas (Venezuela), Dan Betreen (Australia), Juan Carlos De La Cruz (Dominican Republic), Angel Eusebio (Dominican Republic), Andri Garcia (Venezuela), Adam Hislop (Taiwan), Lewis Kim (South Korea), Wilfredo Magallanes (Dominican Republic), Juan Mosquera (Panama/Nicaragua), Tito Quintero (Colombia), Amaurys Reyes (Dominican Republic), Toshiyuki Tomizuka (Japan), Daniel Tovar (Venezuela), Oswaldo Troconis (Venezuela), Juan Villanueva (Venezuela).

Philadelphia Phillies

Office Address: Citizens Bank Park, One Citizens Bank Way, Philadelphia, PA 19148.
Telephone: (215) 463-6000. **Website:** www.phillies.com.

OWNERSHIP

Operated By: The Phillies. **President:** Andy MacPhail. **Chairman:** David Montgomery. **Chairman Emeritus:** Bill Giles.

BUSINESS OPERATIONS

VP/General Counsel: Rick Strouse. **VP, Human Resources/Customer Services:** Kathy Killian.
Director, Ballpark Enterprises/Business Development: Joe Giles.
Director, Human Resources/Benefits: JoAnn Marano.

BALLPARK OPERATIONS

Executive VP: David Buck. **Director, Operations/Facility:** Mike DiMuzio. **Director,
Operations/Events:** Eric Tobin. **Director, Operations/Security:** Sal DeAngelis. **Director, Field
Operations:** Mike Boekholder. **Director, Landscaping & Site Work Operations:** Pam Hall. **PA
Announcer:** Dan Baker. **Official Scorers:** Mark Gola, Mike Maconi, Dick Shute.

COMMUNICATIONS

Telephone: (215) 463-6000. **Fax:** (215) 389-3050
VP, Communications: Bonnie Clark. **Director, Baseball Communications:** Greg Casterioto.

David Montgomery

FINANCE

Sr. VP/CFO: John Nickolas. **Director, Payroll Services:** Karen Wright. **Director, Business
Intelligence:** Josh Barbieri. **Director, Finance:** John Fetsick. **Director, Finance:** Shannon Snellman.

BROADCAST/VIDEO SERVICES

Director, Broadcasting/Video Services: Mark DiNardo. **Director, Video Production:** Dan Stephenson. **Director,
Video Coaching Services:** Kevin Camiscioli. **Chief Technical Engineer:** Dave Abramson.

MARKETING/PROMOTIONS

VP, Marketing Programs/Events: Kurt Funk. **VP, Marketing/New Media:** Michael Harris. **Manager, Client Services/
Alumni Relations:** Debbie Nocito. **Director, Corporate Partnerships:** Rob MacPherson. **Director, Advertising Sales:**
Brian Mahoney. **Director, Corporate Sales:** Scott Nickle. **Director, Marketing Services/Events:** James Trout. **Director,
Entertainment:** Chris Long.

SALES/TICKETS

Telephone: (215) 463-1000. **Fax:** (215) 463-9878.
Sr. VP, Sales/Ticket Operations/Projects: John Weber. **Director, Ticket Technology/Development:** Chris Pohl.
Director, Sales: Derek Schuster. **Director, Suite Sales/Client Services:** Kevin Beale. **Director, Group Sales:** Vanessa
Mapson. **Director, Ticket Services/Intern Program:** Phil Feather. **Director, Season Ticket Services:** Mike Holdren.
Director, Premium Sales/Services: Matt Kessler. **Director, Ticket Operations:** Ken Duffy. **Sales/Services:** Matt Kessler.

2018 SCHEDULE

Standard Game Times: 7:05 p.m.; Sun. 1:35

MARCH
29-31 . . . . at Atlanta

APRIL
2-4. . . . . at New York (NL)
5-8. . . . . Miami
9-11 . . . . Cincinnati
13-15 . . . . . at Tampa Bay
16-18 . . . . at Atlanta
19-22 . . . . Pittsburgh
24-26 . . . . Arizona
27-29 . . . . Atlanta
30 . . . . at Miami

MAY
1-2. . . . . at Miami
4-6. . . . . . at Washington

7-10 . . . . . . San Francisco
11-13 . . . . .New York (NL)
15-16 . . . . . .at Baltimore
17-20 . . . . . .at St. Louis
21-23 . . . . Atlanta
25-27 . . . . .Toronto
28-31 . at Los Angeles (NL)

JUNE
1-3. . . . . at San Francisco
5-7. . . . . .at Chicago (NL)
8-10 . . . . . . .Milwaukee
12-14 . . . . . . .Colorado
15-17 . . . . at Milwaukee
18-20 . . . . St. Louis
22-24 . . . . at Washington
25-27 . . . . .New York (AL)

28-30 . . . . . .Washington

JULY
1 . . . . .Washington
3-4. . . . . Baltimore
6-8. . . . . . at Pittsburgh
9-11 . . . at New York (NL)
13-15 . . . . at Miami
20-22 . . . . San Diego
23-25 . . . Los Angeles (NL)
26-29 . . . .at Cincinnati
30-31 . . . . .at Boston

AUGUST
2-5. . . . . .Miami
6-8. . . . . at Arizona
10-12 . . . . . at San Diego

14-15 . . . . Boston
16-19 . . . . .New York (NL)
21-23 . . . . at Washington
24-26 . . . . at Toronto
27-29 . . . . . .Washington
31 . . . . Chicago (NL)

SEPTEMBER
1-2. . . . . . . Chicago (NL)
3-5. . . . . at Miami
7-9. . . . at New York (NL)
10-12 . . . . . . Washington
14-16 . . . . .Miami
17-19 . . . . .New York (NL)
20-23 . . . . at Atlanta
24-27 . . . . . at Colorado
28-30 . . . . Atlanta

GENERAL INFORMATION

Stadium (year opened):
Citizens Bank Park (2004).
Team Colors: Red, white and blue.

Home Dugout: First Base.
Playing Surface: Natural Grass.

TRAVEL/CLUBHOUSE

Manager, Visiting Clubhouse: Kevin Steinhour. **Manager, Clubhouse Services:** Phil Sheridan. **Manager, Equipment/Umpire Services:** Dan O'Rourke. **Coordinator, Team Travel:** Jameson Hall.

BASEBALL OPERATIONS

VP/General Manager: Matt Klentak. **Assistant GM:** Bryan Minniti. **Assistant GM:** Scott Proefrock. **Assistant GM:** Ned Rice. **Senior Advisors to the President/GM:** Pat Gillick. **Senior Advisors, GM:** Larry Bowa, Charlie Manuel. **Special Assistants, GM:** Bart Braun, Pete Mackanin, Jorge Velandia. **Director, International Scouting:** Sal Agostinelli. **Director, Amateur Scouting:** Johnny Almaraz. **Director, Baseball Operations:** Scott Freedman. **Director, Baseball Research & Development:** Andy Galdi. **Director, Amateur Scouting Administration:** Rob Holiday. **Director, Player Development:** Joe Jordan. Director, **Minor League Operations:** Lee McDaniel. **Director, Professional Scouting:** Mike Ondo.

Matt Klentak

MAJOR LEAGUE STAFF

Manager: Gabe Kapler. **Coaches: Bench**—Rob Thomson, **Pitching**—Rick Kranitz, **Hitting**—John Mallee, **First Base**—Jose Flores, **Third Base**—Dusty Wathan, **Assistant Pitching**—Chris Young, **Bullpen**—Jim Gott, Bullpen Catcher/**Receiving**—Craig Driver, Bullpen Catcher/**Catching**—Bob Stumpo. Manager, **Advance Scouting:** Mike Calitri. **Major League Player Information Coordinator:** Sam Fuld.

MEDICAL/TRAINING

Director, Medical Services: Dr. Michael Ciccotti. **Head Athletic Trainer:** Scott Sheridan. **Assistant Athletic Trainers:** Shawn Fcasni, Chris Mudd. **Major League Strength & Conditioning Coach:** Paul Fournier. **Assistant Strength & Conditioning Coach:** Dong Lien.

PLAYER DEVELOPMENT

Director, Player Development: Joe Jordan. **Director, Minor League Operations:** Lee McDaniel. **Special Assistant, Player Development:** Steve Noworyta. **Director, Florida Operations/GM, Clearwater Threshers:** John Timberlake. Assistant Director, **Minor League Operations/Florida:** Joe Cynar. **Assistant Director, International Operations:** Ray Robles. **Field Coordinator:** Doug Mansolino. **Outfield Coordinator:** Andy Abad. **Assistant Field Coordinator/ Hitting:** Andy Tracy. **Assistant Hitting:** Frank Cacciatore. **Pitching Coordinator:** Rafael Chaves. **Baserunning Coordinator:** Rob Ducey. **Roving Pitching Coach:** Carlos Arroyo. **Infield Coordinator:** Chris Truby. **Catching Coordinator:** Ernie Whitt. **Minor League Player Information Coordinator:** Ben Werthan. **Minor League Video Coordinator:** Josh Lipman.

FARM SYSTEM

Class	Club (League)	Manager	Hitting Coach	Pitching Coach
Triple-A	Lehigh Valley (IL)	Gary Jones	Sal Rende	Dave Lundquist
Double-A	Reading (EL)	Greg Legg	Kevin Riggs	Steve Schrenk
High A	Clearwater (FSL)	Shawn Williams	John Mizerock	Aaron Fultz
Low A	Lakewood (SAL)	Marty Malloy	Tyler Henson	Brad Bergesen
Short-season	Williamsport (NYP)	Pat Borders	Christian Marrero	Hector Berrios
Rookie	Phillies (GCL)	Roly deArmas	Rafael DeLima	Hector Mercado
Rookie	Phillies-1 (DSL)	Nelson Prada	Chris Heintz	Matt Hockenberry
Rookie	Phillies-2 (DSL)	Orlando Munoz	Homy Ovalles	Les Straker

SCOUTING

Director, Amateur Scouting: Johnny Almaraz. **Director, Amateur Scouting Administration:** Rob Holiday. **Assistant Director, Scouting:** Greg Schilz (Washington, DC). **National Scouting Coordinator:** Bill Moore (Alta Loma, CA). **Regional Supervisors:** Darrell Conner (West/Riverside, CA), Buddy Hernandez (Southeast/Winter Garden, FL), Brad Holland (Southwest/Gilbert, AZ), Gene Schall (Midwest/Harleysville, PA), Stewart Smothers (Mid-Atlantic/ Northeast/ Springfield, VA). **Area Scouts:** Alex Agostino (Quebec), Connor Betbeze (Philadelphia, PA), Shane Bowers (La Verne, CA), Will Brunson (New Braunfels, TX), Joey Davis (Rocklin, CA), Chris Duffy (Glendale, AZ), Mike Garcia (Moreno Valley, CA), Aaron Jersild (Alpharetta, GA), Brian Kohlscheen (Norman, OK), Kellan McKeon (Elon, NC), Timi Moni (Nashville, TN), Justin Morgenstern (Chicago, IL), Justin Munson (Kansas City, MO), Demerius Pittman (Corona, CA), Luis Raffan (Miami, FL), Hilton Richardson (Kirkland, WA), Mike Stauffer (Brandon, MS), Jeff Zona Jr. (Clermont, FL). **Director, International Scouting:** Sal Agostinelli (Kings Park, NY). **Coordinator, International Scouting:** Greg McMillin (Philadelphia, PA). **International Coordinator:** Jesús Méndez. **Latin American Coordinator:** Carlos Salas. **International Scouts:** Rafael Alvarez (Venezuela), Roberto Aquino (Dominican Republic), Oneri Fleita (Mexico), Ubaldo Heredia (Latin America), Howard Norsetter (Pacific Rim), Norman Anciani (Panama), Alvaro Blanco (Colombia), Alex Choi (South Korea), Derrick Chung (International Pro Scout), Juan Feliciano de Castro (Dominican Republic), Franklin Felida (Dominican Republic), Luis García (Dominican Republic), Charlie Gastelum (Mexico), Gene Grimaldi (Antilles), Andrés Hiraldo (Dominican Republic), Dargello Lodowica (Curacao), William Mota (Venezuela), Isao O'Jimi (Japan), Romulo Oliveros (Venezuela), Bernardo Pérez (Dominican Republic), Philip Riccobono (Korea), Claudio Scerrato, Ebert Velásquez, Youngster Wang. **Special Assignment Scouts:** Craig Colbert, Howie Freiling, Dave Hollins, Charley Kerfeld, Mike Koplove, Terry Ryan, Dan Wright. **Director, Professional Scouting:** Mike Ondo. **Professional Scouts:** Erick Dalton, Todd Donovan, Jeff Harris (Chico, CA), Steve Jongewaard (West Chester, OH), Gordon Lakey (Barker, TX), Jesse Levis (Fort Washington, PA), Jon Mercurio (Coraopolis, PA), Roy Tanner (Palatka, FL).

Pittsburgh Pirates

Office Address: PNC Park at North Shore, 115 Federal St., Pittsburgh, PA, 15212.
Mailing Address: PO Box 7000, Pittsburgh, PA 15212.
Telephone: (412) 323-5000. **Fax:** (412) 325-4412. **Website:** www.pirates.com. **Twitter:** @Pirates.

OWNERSHIP
Chairman of the Board: Robert Nutting.
Board of Directors: Donald Beaver, Eric Mauck, G. Ogden Nutting, Robert Nutting, William Nutting, Duane Wittman.

BUSINESS OPERATIONS
President: Frank Coonelly. **Executive Vice President & Chief Financial Officer:** Jim Plake.
Senior VP, Business Affairs/General Counsel: Bryan Stroh.

COMMUNICATIONS
VP, Communications/Broadcasting: Brian Warecki. **Director, Baseball Communications:**
Jim Trdinich. **Director, Broadcasting:** Marc Garda. **Director, Media Relations:** Dan Hart.
Manager, Business Communications/Social Media: Terry Rodgers.

COMMUNITY RELATIONS
Senior VP, Community/Public Affairs: Patty Paytas. **Director, Community Relations:**
Michelle Capobianco. **Manager, Youth Baseball Initiatives:** Chris Ganter. **Manager, Pirates
Charities:** Jackie Hunter.

Frank Coonelly

MARKETING
Senior Vice President, Revenue: Brian Colbert. **Senior Director, Marketing/Special
Events:** Brian Chiera. **Director, Alumni Affairs/Promotions/Licensing:** Joe Billetdeaux. **Director, Advertising/
Creative Services:** Kiley Cauvel. **Director, Special Events/Game Presentation:** Christine Serkoch. **Director, PNC Park
Events:** Ann Elder. **Manager, Advertising/Digital Marketing:** Haley Artayet. **Manager, Special Events:** Jason Koval.
Manager, Promotions/Licensing/Authentics: Megan Vizzini. **Manager, Game Presentation:** Matt Zidik.

CORPORATE SPONSORSHIPS
VP, Corporate Partnerships: Aaron Cohn. **Manager, Corporate Partnerships:** Chris Stevens. **Manager, Client
Services:** Brittany Ryce.

STADIUM OPERATIONS
Executive VP/General Manager, PNC Park/Facilities: Dennis DaPra. **Senior Director, Ballpark Operations:**
Chris Hunter. **Senior Director, Florida Operations:** Jeff Podobnik. **Director, Field Operations:** Matt Brown. **Director,
Guest Experience:** Chuck Miller. **Manager, Cleaning Operations:** Sissy Burkhart. **Manager, Ballpark Operations:** J.J.
McGraw. **Manager, Security/Service Operations:** Mark Weaver.

2018 SCHEDULE
Standard Game Times: 7:05 p.m.; Sun. 1:35.

MARCH			
29,31 . . . . .at Detroit	8-9. . . . . .at Chicago (AL)	25-27 . . . at New York (NL)	9-12 . . . . at San Francisco
	11-13 . . . . . San Francisco	29-30 . . . . . at San Diego	14-15 . . . . . at Minnesota
APRIL	15-16 . . . . . Chicago (AL)		16-19 . . . . Chicago (NL)
1 . . . . .at Detroit	17-20 . . . . San Diego	**JULY**	20-22 . . . . Atlanta
2,4 . . . . Minnesota	22-24 . . . . .at Cincinnati	1 . . . . at San Diego	24-26 . . . . at Milwaukee
5-8 . . . . Cincinnati	25-27 . . . . St. Louis	2-4. . . at Los Angeles (NL)	28-30 . . . . . . at St. Louis
9-12 . . . . .at Chicago (NL)	28-30 . . . . Chicago (NL)	6-8. . . . . . .Philadelphia	31 . . . . at Atlanta
13-15 . . . . . . at Miami	31 . . . . .at St. Louis	9-11 . . . . . . Washington	
16-18 . . . . . . .Colorado		12-15 . . . . . .Milwaukee	**SEPTEMBER**
19-22 . . . at Philadelphia	**JUNE**	20-22 . . . . .at Cincinnati	1-2. . . . . at Atlanta
24-26 . . . . . Detroit	1-3. . . . . . . .at St. Louis	23-25 . . . . .at Cleveland	3-5. . . . . Cincinnati
27-29 . . . . St. Louis	5-7. . . .Los Angeles (NL)	26-29 . . . .New York (NL)	7-9. . . . . .Miami
30 . . . . . at Washington	8-10 . . . . .at Chicago (NL)	31 . . . . Chicago (NL)	10-12 . . . . . . at St. Louis
	11-13 . . . . at Arizona		14-16 . . . . at Milwaukee
MAY	15-17 . . . . . . Cincinnati	**AUGUST**	17-19 . . . . . Kansas City
1-3. . . . . at Washington	18-20 . . . . .Milwaukee	1 . . . . Chicago (NL)	21-23 . . . . . .Milwaukee
4-6. . . . . . at Milwaukee	21-24 . . . . Arizona	3-5. . . . . St. Louis	24-27 . . . .at Chicago (NL)
		6-8. . . . . . . at Colorado	28-30 . . . . .at Cincinnati

GENERAL INFORMATION
Stadium (year opened): **Home Dugout:** Third Base.
PNC Park (2001). **Playing Surface:** Grass.
Team Colors: Black and gold.

BASEBALL OPERATIONS

Executive VP/General Manager: Neal Huntington. **VP, Assistant General Manager:** Kyle Stark. **Assistant GM:** Kevan Graves. **Special Assistants to GM:** Ron Hopkins, Sean McNally, Matt Ruebel, Jax Robertson, Greg Smith, Doug Strange. **Director, Baseball Operations:** Will Lawton. **Baseball Operations Assistant:** Trey Rose. **Special Assistants to Baseball Operations:** Jamey Carroll, Scott Elarton, Grady Little, Kevin Young. **Senior Advisor, Baseball Operations:** Nick Leyva. **Director, Personnel:** Dr. Chris Johnson. **Senior Director, Baseball Informatics:** Dan Fox. **Major League Quantitative Analyst:** Bob Cook. **Analyst, Baseball Informatics:** Andrew Gibson. **Quantitative Analysts:** Joe Douglas, Justin Newman. **Data Architect:** Josh Smith. **Developer, Baseball Informatics:** Brian Hulick. **Director, Cultural Initiatives:** Hector Morales. **Special Assistant to GM/Cultural Initiatives:** Mike Gonzalez. **Video Coordinator:** Kevin Roach. **Video Advance Scout:** Joe Hultzen.

Neal Huntington

MAJOR LEAGUE STAFF

Manager: Clint Hurdle. **Coaches: Bench**—Tom Prince, **Coach**—Dave Jauss, **Pitching**—Ray Searage, **Assistant Pitching**—Justin Meccage, **Hitting**—Jeff Branson, **Assistant Hitting**—Jeff Livesey, **First Base**—Kimera Bartee, **Third Base**—Joey Cora, **Bullpen**—Euclides Rojas. **Bullpen Catchers:** Herberto Andrade, Jordan Comadena.

MEDICAL/TRAINING

Medical Director: Dr. Patrick DeMeo. **Team Physicians:** Dr. Darren Frank, Dr. Dennis Phillips, Dr. Michael Scarpone, Dr. Robert Schilken, Dr. Edward Snell. **Director of Sports Medicine:** Todd Tomczyk. **Head Major League Athletic Trainer:** Brian Housand. **Assistant Major League Athletic Trainer:** Ben Potenziano. **Major League Strength/Conditioning Coach:** Jim Malone. **Physical Therapist:** Kevin "Otis" Fitzgerald. **Sports Science Coordinator:** Brendon Huttmann.

PLAYER DEVELOPMENT

Sr Director, Minor League Operations: Larry Broadway. **Assistant Director, Minor League Operations:** Brian Selman. **Coordinator, Minor League Operations:** TJ Large. **Senior Field Coordinator:** Brad Fischer. **Assistant Field Coordinator:** Bobby Scales. **Coordinator of Instruction:** Dave Turgeon. **Senior Pitching Coordinator:** Scott Mitchell. **Assistant Pitching Coordinator:** Tom Filer. **Latin American Pitching Coordinator:** Amaury Telemaco. **Infield Coordinator:** Gary Green. **Hitting Coordinator:** Larry Sutton. **Minor League Video Coordinator:** Ryan Gaynor. **Minor League Equipment Manager:** Pat Hagerty. **Medical Services Coordinator:** Carl Randolph. **Senior Coordinator, Rehab/Athlete Development:** AJ Patrick. **Strength & Conditioning Coordinator:** Joe Hughes. **Director, Mental Conditioning:** Bernie Holliday. **Mental Conditioning Coordinator:** Tyson Holt. **EAP/Coordinator, Personal/Professional Development:** Jon Hammermeister. **Nutritionist:** Allison Mauer. **Senior Advisor, Latin American Operations:** Luis Silverio. **Senior Advisor, Player Development:** Woody Huyke, Mike Lum. **Latin American Field Coordinator:** Mendy Lopez. **Senior Advisor, Dominican Summer League:** Cecilio Beltre. **Education Coordinator:** Mayu Fielding.

FARM SYSTEM

Class	Club (League)	Manager	Hitting Coach	Pitching Coach
Triple-A	Indianapolis (IL)	Brian Esposito	Ryan Long	Stan Kyles
Double-A	Altoona (EL)	Michael Ryan	Keoni De Renne	Bryan Hickerson
High A	Bradenton (FSL)	Gera Alvarez	Butch Wynegar	Matt Ford
Low A	West Virginia (SAL)	Wyatt Toregas	Chris Peterson	Joel Hanrahan
Short-season	West Virginia (NYP)	Kieran Mattison	Jonathan Prieto	Tom Filer
Rookie	Bristol (APP)	Miguel Perez	Austin McClune	Joey Seaver
Rookie	Pirates (GCL)	Dave Turgeon	Kory DeHaan	Drew Benes
Rookie	Pirates (DSL)	Gavi Nivar	Luis Natera	D. Urbina/D. Sanchez

SCOUTING

Fax: (412) 325-4414.

Senior Director, Amateur Scouting: Joe Delli Carri. **Assistant Director, Amateur Scouting:** Mike Mangan. **Coordinator, Amateur Scouting:** Matt Skirving. **National Supervisors:** Jack Bowen (Bethel Park, PA), Jimmy Lester (Columbus, GA). **Regional Supervisors:** Jesse Flores (Sacramento, CA), Trevor Haley (Temperance, MI), Sean Heffernan (Florence, SC). **Area Supervisors:** Rick Allen (Moorpark, CA), Matt Bimeal (Olathe, KS), Adam Bourassa (Cincinnati, OH), Eddie Charles (Auburn, NY), Phil Huttmann, (McKinney, TX), Jerry Jordan (Kingsport, TN), Wayne Mathis (Cuero, TX), Darren Mazeroski (Panama City Beach, FL), Tim Osborne (Woodstock, GA), Nick Presto (Palm Beach Gardens, FL), Dan Radcliff (Palmyra, VA), Mike Sansoe (Fairfield, CA), Brian Tracy (Yorba Linda, CA), Derrick Van Dusen (Phoenix, AZ), Anthony Wycklendt (Oak Creek, WI). **Part-Time Scout:** Enrique Hernandez (Puerto Rico). **Director, Pro Scouting:** Steve Williams. **Major League Scouts:** Mike Basso, Ricky Bennett, Jim Dedrick, Bob Minor. **Pro Scouts:** Carlos Berroa, Rodney Henderson, Andrew Lorraine, Alvin Rittman, Everett Russell, Gary Varsho. **Scouting Assistants:** John Birkbeck, Matt Taylor. **Director, International Scouting:** Junior Vizcaino. **Regional Supervisor/Assistant Director, International Scouting:** Max Kwan. **Coordinator of International Operations:** Matt Benedict. **Administrator, Dominican Republic:** Emmanuel Gomez. **International Supervisors:** Emilio Carrasquel (Venezuela); Raul Lopez (Mexico); Tony Harris (International/Australia); Fu-Chun Chiang (Far East); Tom Gillespie (Europe/Africa). **International Scouts:** Victor Santana, Esteban Alvarez, Cristino Valdez, Emmanuel Gomez, Daury Nin (Dominican Republic); Jessie Niana, Pedro Avila, Omar Gonzalez (Venezuela); Roberto Saucedo, Luis Borges (Mexico); Eugene Helder (Aruba); Orlando Covo, Robinson Ortega, Cristobal Santoya, Jose Mosquera (Columbia); Mark Van Zanten (Curacao); Jesus Morelli (Nicaragua); Jose Pineda (Panama); Oleg Boyko, Christian Dresel, Martjin Nijhoff (Europe).

St. Louis Cardinals

Office Address: 700 Clark Street, St. Louis MO 63102.
Telephone: (314) 345-9600. **Fax:** (314) 345-9523. **Website:** www.cardinals.com.

OWNERSHIP

Operated By: St. Louis Cardinals, LLC. **Chairman/Chief Executive Officer:** William DeWitt, Jr. **President:** Bill DeWitt III. **Senior Administrative Assistant to Chairman:** Grace Kell. **Senior Administrative Assistant to President:** Julie Laningham. **Sr. VP & General Counsel:** Mike Whittle.

BUSINESS OPERATIONS

FINANCE

Fax: (314) 345-9520.
Senior VP/Chief Financial Officer: Brad Wood. **Director, Finance:** Rex Carter. **Director, Human Resources:** Ann Seeney. **VP, Event Services/Merchandising:** Vicki Bryant.

MARKETING/SALES/COMMUNITY RELATIONS

Fax: (314) 345-9529.
Senior VP, Sales/Marketing: Dan Farrell. **Administrative Assistant, VP, Sales/Marketing:** Gail Ruhling. **VP, Corporate Marketing/Stadium Entertainment:** Thane Van Breusegen. **Director, Scoreboard Operations/Fan Entertainment/Senior Executive:** Tony Simokaitis. **Director, Publications:** Steve Zesch. **VP, Community Relations/Executive Director, Cardinals Care:** Michael Hall. **Administrative Assistant:** Bonnie Parres.

Bill DeWitt III

COMMUNICATIONS

Fax: (314) 345-9530.
VP, Communications: Ron Watermon. **Director, Communications:** Brian Bartow. **Supervisor of Baseball Communications:** Michael Whitty. **Coordinator of Baseball Information and Media Services:** Chris Tunno. **PA Announcer:** John Ulett. **Official Scorers:** Gary Muller, Jeff Durbin, Mike Smith.

STADIUM OPERATIONS

Fax: (314) 345-9535.
VP, Stadium Operations: Matt Gifford. **VP, Facility Planning & Engineering:** Joe Abernathy. **Administrative Assistant:** Hope Baker. **Director, Security:** Philip Melcher. **Director Facility/Security/Stadium Operations:** Hosei Maruyama. **Head Groundskeeper:** Bill Findley.

TICKETING

Fax: (314) 345-9522.
VP, Ticket Sales/Service: Joe Strohm. **Director, Ticket Sales/Marketing:** Martin Coco. **Director, Ticket Sales/Services:** Rob Fasoldt.

2018 SCHEDULE

Standard Game Times: 7:15 p.m.; Sun. 1:15.

MARCH			
29-31 . . . at New York (NL)	10-13 . . . . . at San Diego	29-30 . . . . Atlanta	13-16 . . . . . Washington
	15-16 . . . . . at Minnesota		17-19 . . . . . . Milwaukee
APRIL	17-20 . . . . . Philadelphia	**JULY**	20-22 . at Los Angeles (NL)
1 . . . . . at New York (NL)	21-23 . . . . . Kansas City	1 . . . . Atlanta	24-26 . . . . . . at Colorado
2-4 . . . . . . at Milwaukee	25-27 . . . . . at Pittsburgh	2-4 . . . . at Arizona	28-30 . . . . Pittsburgh
5-8 . . . . Arizona	28-30 . . . . . at Milwaukee	5-8 . . . . at San Francisco	31 . . . . Cincinnati
9-11 . . . . Milwaukee	31 . . . . Pittsburgh	10-11 . . . .at Chicago (AL)	
12-15 . . . . . at Cincinnati		13-15 . . . . . . Cincinnati	**SEPTEMBER**
16-18 . . . at Chicago (NL)	**JUNE**	19-22 . . . at Chicago (NL)	1-2 . . . . Cincinnati
20-22 . . . . . Cincinnati	1-3 . . . . Pittsburgh	23-25 . . . at Cincinnati	3-5 . . . . . at Washington
24-26 . . . . New York (NL)	5-7 . . . . Miami	27-29 . . . Chicago (NL)	7-9 . . . . at Detroit
27-29 . . . . at Pittsburgh	8-10 . . . . . at Cincinnati	30-31 . . . . . . Colorado	10-12 . . . . . . Pittsburgh
	11-13 . . . . . San Diego		13-16 . . . Los Angeles (NL)
MAY	15-17 . . . . Chicago (NL)	**AUGUST**	17-19 . . . . . . at Atlanta
1-2 . . . . . Chicago (AL)	18-20 . . at Philadelphia	1-2 . . . . Colorado	21-23 . . . San Francisco
4-6 . . . . . Chicago (NL)	21-24 . . . . at Milwaukee	3-5 . . . . at Pittsburgh	24-26 . . . . . . Milwaukee
7-8 . . . . Minnesota	25-27 . . . . . Cleveland	6-8 . . . . at Miami	28-30 . . . at Chicago (NL)
		10-12 . . . at Kansas City	

GENERAL INFORMATION

Stadium (year opened): Busch Stadium (2006). **Team Colors:** Red and white.

Home Dugout: First Base. **Playing Surface:** Grass.

TRAVEL/CLUBHOUSE
Fax: (314) 345-9523.
Traveling Secretary: C.J. Cherre. **Equipment Managers:** Ernie Moore, Mark Walsh. **Visiting Clubhouse Manager:** Rip Rowan. **Video Coordinator:** Chad Blair.

BASEBALL OPERATIONS

President of Baseball Operations: John Mozeliak. **Vice President & General Manager:** Michael Girsch. **Senior Executive Assistant to the President of Baseball Operations:** Linda Brauer. **Assistant General Manager:** Moises Rodriguez. **Senior Special Assistant to GM:** Bob Gebhard, Mike Jorgensen, Red Schoendienst. **Special Assistant to GM:** Ryan Franklin, Willie McGee. **Special Assistant to GM, Player Procurement:** Matt Slater. **Director, Major League Administration:** Judy Carpenter-Barada. **Director, Baseball Administration:** John Vuch. **Director, Baseball Development:** Dane Sorensen. **Director, Baseball Analytics and Systems:** Jeremy Cohen. **Manager, Player Communications:** Melody Yount. **Manager, Baseball Systems:** Patrick Casanta. **Baseball Development Analysts:** Kevin Seats, Brian Seyfert. **Baseball Operations Analyst:** Emily Wiebe. **Application Developer:** Jennifer Long.

John Mozeliak

MAJOR LEAGUE STAFF
Telephone: (314) 345-9600. **Manager:** Mike Matheny. **Coaches: Bench**—Mike Shildt. **Pitching**—Mike Maddux. **Hitting**—John Mabry. **Assistant Hitting Instructor**—Bill Mueller. **First Base**—Oliver Marmol. **Third Base**—Jose Oquendo. **Bullpen**—Bryan Eversgerd. **Coach:** Willie McGee. **Bullpen Catchers**—Jamie Pogue, Kleininger Teran.

MEDICAL/TRAINING
Head Orthopedic Surgeon: Dr. George Paletta. **Team Physician/Minor League Liaison:** Brian Mahaffey. **Head Trainer:** Adam Olsen. **Assistant Trainers:** Jeremy Clipperton, Chris Conroy. **Strength & Conditioning Coach:** Pete Prinzi. **Performance Physical Therapist:** Jason Shutt. **Physical Therapist:** Thomas Knox. **Director, Performance:** Robert Butler.

PLAYER DEVELOPMENT
Director, Player Development: Gary LaRocque. **Administrator Minor League Operations:** Tony Ferreira. **Pitching Specialist:** Chris Carpenter. **Minor League Field Coordinator:** Mark DeJohn. **Assistant Minor League Field Coordinator:** Ron Warner. **Coordinators:** Jose Leger (Latin America Field & Academy Development), TIm Leveque (pitching), Luis Aguyao (infield), George Greer (offensive strategist), Randy Niemann (pitching), Steve Turco (roving), Ryan Ludwick (hitting), Jason Isringhausen (pitching), Barry Weinberg (medical advisor), Matt Leonard (rehab coordinator), Keith Joynt (medical, player development), Jose Alvarez (assistant rehab, coordinator), Paul Davis (manager, pitching analytics), Frank D'Aversa (assistant minor league rehab), Aaron Rhodes (strength & conditioning). **Minor League Equipment Manager:** Dave Vondarhaar.

FARM SYSTEM

Class	Club (League)	Manager	Hitting Coach	Pitching Coach
Triple-A	Memphis (PCL)	Stubby Clapp	Mark Budaska	Dernier Orozco
Double-A	Springfield (TL)	Johnny Rodriguez	Jobel Jimenez	Darwin Marrero
High A	Palm Beach (FSL)	Dann Bilardello	Brandon Allen	Will Ohman
Low A	Peoria (MWL)	Chris Swauger	Russ Chambliss	Cale Johnson
Short-season	State College (NYP)	Joe Kruzel	Roger LaFrancois	Adrian Martin
Rookie	Johnson City (APP)	Roberto Espinoza	Cody Gabella	Rick Harig
Rookie	Cardinals (GCL)	Steve Turco	Jose Leon	Giovanni Carrara
Rookie	Cardinals (DSL)	John Matos	Nabo Martinez	Unavailable

SCOUTING
Fax: (314) 345-9519. **Director, Scouting:** Randy Flores. **Manager, Pro Scouting:** Jared Odom. **Manager, Scouting Analytics:** Matt Bayer. **Amateur Scouting Coordinator/Analyst:** Tyler Hadzinsky. **Special Assistant to Amateur Scouting:** Mike Roberts. **Special Advisor to the Scouting Director:** Jamal Strong. **Professional Scouts:** Patrick Elkins (Catonsville, MD), Brian Hopkins (Holly Springs, NC), Jeff Ishii (Chino, CA), Mike Jorgensen (Fenton, MO), Marty Keough (Scottsdale, AZ), Aaron Klinic (Scottsdale, AZ), Deric McKamey (Cincinnati, OH), Ricky Meinhold (St. Petersburg, FL), Joe Rigoli (Parsippany, NJ), Kerry Robinson (Ballwin, MO). **National Crosscheckers:** Aaron Looper (Shawnee, OK), Sean Moran (Doylestown, PA). **Regional Crosscheckers:** Dominic "Ty" Boyles (Dallas, TX), Aaron Krawiec (Gilbert, AZ), Zach Mortimer (Sacramento, CA), Kevin Saucier (Pensacola, FL). **Area Scouts:** Jabari Barnett (Kingwood, TX), Clint Brown (Tuscaloosa, AL), Jason Bryans (Windsor, Ontario), TC Calhoun (Stanley, NC), Mike Dibiase (Tampa, FL), Mike Garciaparra (Manhattan Beach, CA), Dirk Kinney (Olathe, KS), Tom Lipari (Tulsa, OK), Jim Negrych (Phoenixville, PA), Charles Peterson (Columbia, SC), Stacey Pettis (Brentwood, CA), Juan Ramos (Carolina, PR), Chris Rodriguez (Vancouver, WA), Mauricio Rubio (Portland, OR), Nathan Sopena (Cary, IL), Brock Ungricht (San Diego, CA). **Part-Time Scouts:** Jim Foster (St. Louis, MO), Karl Sakuda (Honolulu, HI). **Director, International Operations & Administration:** Luis Morales. **Coordinator, International Operations:** Joseph Quezada. **Scouting Supervisor, Dominican Republic:** Angel Ovalles. **Administrator, Dominican Republic Operations:** Aaron Rodriguez. **Senior International Crosschecker:** Joe Almaraz (San Antonio, TX). **Latin American Crosschecker:** Damaso Espino. **Dominican Republic, Scouting Supervisor:** Angel Ovalles. **Venezuela Scouting Supervisor:** Jose Gonzalez Maestre. **International Scouts:** Jean Carlos Alvarez, Raymi Dicent, Braly Guzman, Alix Martinez (Dominican Republic), Jose Gonzalez Maestre, Estuar Ruiz, Jhohan Acevedo, Adel Granadillo, Estuar Ruiz (Venezuela), Ramon Garcia (Mexico), Carlos Balcazar (Colombia).

San Diego Padres

Office Address: Petco Park, 100 Park Blvd, San Diego, CA 92101.
Mailing Address: PO Box 122000, San Diego, CA 92112. **Telephone:** (619) 795-5000.
E-mail address: comments@padres.com. **Website:** www.padres.com. **Twitter:** @padres.
Facebook: www.facebook.com/padres. **Instagram:** www.instagram.com/padres

OWNERSHIP
Operated By: Padres LP. **Managing Partner:** Peter Seidler. **Executive Chairman:** Ron Fowler. **Chief Operating Officer:** Erik Greupner. **Special Advisor to the Executive Chariman:** Bill Johnston.

BUSINESS OPERATIONS
Executive VP, Business Administration/General Counsel: Erik Greupner. **VP, Strategy/Innovation:** Ryan Gustafson. **Senior VP, Chief Financial Officer:** Ronda Sedillo. **Vice President, Information Technology:** Ray Chan. **Sr. Director, Human Resources:** Sara Greenspan. **Director, Accounting:** Chris James.

LEGAL
Senior Vice President/General Counsel: Caroline Perry. **Associate General Counsel/Baseball Operations Compliance Officer:** Stephanie Wilka.

COMMUNITY RELATIONS/MILITARY AFFAIRS
Telephone: (619) 795-5265. **Fax:** (619) 795-5266. **Senior VP, Community/Military Affairs:** Tom Seidler. **Military Affairs Advisor:** J.J. Quinn. **Director, Public Affairs:** Diana Puetz.

ENTERTAINMENT/MARKETING/COMMUNICATIONS/CREATIVE SERVICES
Sr. VP/Chief Marketing Officer: Wayne Partello. **Director, Communications:** Craig Hughner. **Director, Content:** Nicky Patriarca. **Director, Entertainment/Production:** Erik Meyer. **Director, Marketing/Brand Activation:** Katie Jackson. **Director, Production:** Brendan Nieto.

BALLPARK OPERATIONS/HOSPITALITY
VP, Ballpark Operations/GM, Petco Park: Mark Guglielmo. **VP/Chief Hospitality Officer:** Scott Marshall. **Senior Director, Ballpark Operations:** Nick Capo. **Senior Director, Security:** Len Davey. **Director, Event Operations:** Ken Kawachi. **Director, Field Operations:** Matt Balough. **Director, Guest Services:** Kameron Durham. **Official Scorers:** Jack Murray, Bill Zavestoski.

TICKETING
Telephone: (619) 795-5500. **Fax:** (619) 795-5034. **VP, Corporate Partnerships:** Sergio Del Prado. **VP, Ticket Sales:** Eric McKenzie. **Director, Group Tickets/Hospitality:** Curt Waugh. **Director, Membership Services:** Sindi Edelstein. **Director, Partnership Services:** Eddie Quinn. **Director, Ticket Operations:** Jim Kiersnowski. **Director, Petco Parks Events:** Kristie Ewing, Allie Asuncion.

Ron Fowler

2018 SCHEDULE
Standard Game Times: 7:10 p.m.; Sat. 5:40; Sun. 1:40

MARCH
29-31 . . . . . . .Milwaukee

APRIL
2-5. . . . . .Colorado
6-8. . . . . .at Houston
9-11 . . . . . . at Colorado
12-15 . . . . San Francisco
16-18 . . . Los Angeles (NL)
20-22 . . . . at Arizona
23-25 . . . . . at Colorado
27-29 . . . .New York (NL)
30 . . . . . at San Francisco

MAY
1-2. . . . . at San Francisco
4-6. . . . .Los Angeles (NL)

7-9 . . . . .Washington
10-13 . . . . St. Louis
14-15 . . . . .Colorado
17-20 . . . . at Pittsburgh
21-23 . . . at Washington
25-27 . at Los Angeles (NL)
28-31 . . . . .Miami

JUNE
1-3. . . . . Cincinnati
4-6. . . . . Atlanta
8-10 . . . . at Miami
11-13 . . . . . .at St. Louis
14-17 . . . . . . at Atlanta
19-20 . . . . Oakland
21-24 . . at San Francisco
25-27 . . . . .at Texas

29-30 . . . . . . Pittsburgh

JULY
1 . . . . Pittsburgh
3-4. . . . . . . .at Oakland
5-8. . . . . at Arizona
9-12 . . . .Los Angeles (NL)
13-15 . . . . Chicago (NL)
20-22 . . . at Philadelphia
23-25 . . .at New York (NL)
27-29 . . . . .Arizona
30-31 . . . San Francisco

AUGUST
2-5. . . . . .at Chicago (NL)
7-9. . . . . . . at Milwaukee
10-12 . . . . . .Philadelphia

13-15 . . . Los Angeles (AL)
16-19 . . . . Arizona
21-23 . . . . . at Colorado
24-26 . at Los Angeles (NL)
28-29 . . . . Seattle
30-31 . . . . .Colorado

SEPTEMBER
1-2. . . . . .Colorado
3-4. . . . . at Arizona
6-9. . . . . . . .at Cincinnati
11-12 . . . . .at Seattle
14-16 . . . . Texas
17-19 . . . . San Francisco
21-23 . at Los Angeles (NL)
24-26 . . . at San Francisco
28-30 . . . . Arizona

GENERAL INFORMATION
Stadium (year opened):
Petco Park (2004).
Team Colors: Padres Blue and White

Home Dugout: First Base.
Playing Surface: Grass.

TRAVEL/CLUBHOUSE
Director, Player & Staff Services: T.J. Lasita. **Manager, Equipment & Clubhouse:** Spencer Dallin. **Assistant Equipment Manager/Umpire Room Attendant:** Tony Petricca. **Visiting Clubhouse Manager:** David Bacharach.

BASEBALL OPERATIONS
Telephone: (619) 795-5077. **Fax:** (619) 795-5361. **Executive VP/General Manager:** A.J. Preller. **VP/Assistant GM:** Fred Uhlman Jr. **VP, Scouting Operations:** Don Welke. **Assistant GM:** Josh Stein. **Senior Advisor to GM/Director, Player Personnel:** Logan White. **Director, Player Health and Performance:** Don Tricker. **Director, Baseball Operations:** Nick Ennis. **Director, Baseball Information Systems:** Matt Klotsche. **Senior Advisor, Baseball Operations:** Trevor Hoffman. **Special Assistant to the GM:** James Keller. **Special Assistant to the GM, Scouting:** David Post. **Special Assistant, Baseball Operations:** Mark Loretta. **Special Assistant, Player Development:** Moises Alou. **Architect, Baseball Systems:** Wells Oliver. **Senior Analyst:** Dave Cameron. **Analyst, Research & Development:** Tristan Sandler. **Manager, Major League Advance Scouting/Video Ops:** Patrick Coghlan. **Coordinator, Major League Translation/Baseball Ops:** David Longley. **Coordinator, Amateur Scouting & Baseball Ops:** Layne Gross. **Coordinator, Scouting/Player Development Video:** Ethan Dixon. **Executive Assistant:** Michaelene Courtis.

A.J. Preller

MAJOR LEAGUE STAFF
Manager: Andy Green. **Bench Coach:** Mark McGwire. **Pitching Coach:** Darren Balsley. **Hitting Coach:** Matt Stairs. **First Base:** Skip Schumaker. **Third Base:** Glenn Hoffman. **Bullpen:** Doug Bochtler. **Coordinator:** Keith Werman.

MEDICAL/TRAINING
Club Physician: UC San Diego Health—Dr. Catherine Robertson, Dr. Kenneth Taylor. **Head Athletic Trainer:** Mark Rogow. **Assistant Athletic Trainers:** Paul Navarro, Will Sinon. **Strength & Conditioning Coach:** Brett McCabe. **Assistant Strength & Conditioning Coach:** Scott Cline.

PLAYER DEVELOPMENT
Telephone: (619) 795-5343. **Fax:** (619) 795-5036. **Director, Player Development:** Sam Geaney. **Assistant Director, Player Development:** Ben Sestanovich. **Special Assignment Advisor, Assistant Field Coordinator:** Steve Lyons. **Manager, Minor League Adminstration/Peoria Operations:** Todd Stephenson. **Manager, International Operations:** Cesar Rizik. **Manager, Minor League Equipment & Clubhouse:** Zach Nelson. **Director, Professional Development:** Jason Amoroso. **Roving Instructors:** Ryley Westman (Coordinator, Instruction), Kevin Hooper (Infield Coordinator), Tony Tarasco (High Performance and OF/Baserunning Coordinator), Gorman Heimueller (Roving Pitching Instructor), Eric Junge (Minor League Pitching Instructor), Oscar Bernard (Minor League Hitting Instructor), Dave Bingham (Instructor, Player Development), Seiichiro Nakagaki (Director, Applied Sports Sciences), Ben Fritz (Coordinator, AZ/Rehab) Ben Fraser (Minor League ATC Coordinator), Joseph Tarantino (Medical Adminstration Coordinator), John Biggar, Tanner Fields (Minor League Physical Therapists), Dan Byrne (Strength & Conditioning Coordinator), Eric Wood (Assistant Strength & Conditioning), Vincente Cafaro (Latin America Player Development).

FARM SYSTEM

Class	Farm Club (League)	Manager	Hitting Coach	Pitching Coach
Triple-A	El Paso (PCL)	Rod Barajas	Morgan Burkhart	Bronswell Patrick
Double-A	San Antonio (TL)	Philip Wellman	Raul Padron	Jimmy Jones
High A	Lake Elsinore (CAL)	Edwin Rodriguez	Doug Banks	Pete Zamora
Low A	Fort Wayne (MWL)	Anthony Contreras	Jonathan Mathews	Burt Hooton
Short-season	Tri-City (NWL)	Aaron Levin	Oscar Salazar	Giancarlo Alvarado
Rookie	Padres1 (AZL)	Vinny Lopez	Pat O'Sullivan	Leo Rosales
Rookie	Padres2 (AZL)	Unavailable	Raul Gonzalez	Unavailable
Rookie	Padres (DSL)	Miguel Del Castillo	E. Rincon/J. Pozo	N. Cruz/J. Quezada

SCOUTING
Director, Amateur Scouting: Mark Conner. **Director, Professional Scouting:** Pete DeYoung. **Director, International Scouting/Field Coordinator:** Chris Kemp. **Director, Pacific Rim Operations:** Acey Kohrogi. **Assistant Director, Amateur Scouting:** Kurt Kemp. **Coordinator, Amateur Scouting:** Sam Ray. **National Crosscheckers:** Chip Lawrence. **Supervisors:** Yancy Ayres, Josh Emmerick, Chris Kelly, Andrew Salvo. **Amateur Scouts:** Stephen Baker (Pensacola, FL), Justin Baughman (Portland, OR), Nick Brannon (Huntersville, NC), Eddie Ciafardini (San Diego, CA), Brian Cruz (Pembroke Pines, FL), Kevin Ham (Katy, TX), Troy Hoerner (Greenville, MI), Dustin Johnson (Alexandria, VA), Jake Koenig (Hartford, CT), Nick Long (Lake Forest, CA), Matt Maloney (Granville, OH), John Martin (Tampa, FL), Steve Moritz (Kennesaw, GA), James Parker (Phoenix, AZ), Tim Reynolds (Livermore, CA), Matt Schaffner (Dallas, TX), Jeff Stevens (Manhattan Beach, CA), Tyler Stubblefield (Canton, GA), **Part-Time Scouts:** Willie Ronda (Las Lomas Rio Piedras, PR), Murray Zuk (Souris, Manitoba). **Pro Scouting Crosschecker:** Mike Juhl (Charlotte, NC). **Professional Scouts:** Keith Boeck (Phoenix, AZ), Chris Bourjos (Scottsdale, AZ), Spencer Graham (Gresham, OR), Tim Holt (Allen, TX), Mark Merila (Minneapolis, MN), Dominic Scavone (Palm Harbor, FL), Duane Shaffer (Goodyear, AZ), Tyler Tufts (Macedonia, OH), Mike Venafro (Fort Myers, FL), Cory Wade (Zionsville, IN). **International Scouting Supervisor:** Trevor Schumm. **International Crosschecker/Mexico Supervisor:** Bill McLaughlin. **Coordinator, Latin American Scouting:** Felix Feliz. **Supervisor, Venezuela:** Vfrain Linares. **Supervisor, Dominican Republic:** Alvin Duran. **International & Part-Time Scouts:** Antonio Alejos, Manuel Martin, Victor Magdaleno, Luis Prieto (Venezuela), Andres Cabadias (Columbia), Milton Croes (Aruba), Emenejildo Diaz, Jonatthan Feliz, Martin Jose, Ysrael Rojas, Jose Salado (Dominican Republic), Po-Hsuan Keng (Taiwan), Ricardo Montenegro (Panama), Hoon NamGung (South Korea), Takashi Saito (Japan), Damian Shanahan (Australia).

San Francisco Giants

Office Address: AT&T Park, 24 Willie Mays Plaza, San Francisco, CA 94107.
Telephone: (415) 972-2000. **Fax:** (415) 947-2800. **Website:** sfgiants.com, sfgigantes.com.

OWNERSHIP
Operated by: San Francisco Baseball Associates L.P.

BUSINESS OPERATIONS
President/Chief Executive Officer: Laurence M. Baer. **Special Assistants:** Will Clark, Willie Mays. **Senior Advisor:** Willie McCovey.

Laurence M. Baer

FINANCE/LEGAL/INFORMATION TECHNOLOGY
Executive VP/General Counsel: Jack F. Bair. **VP/General Counsel:** Amy Tovar. **Senior VP/Chief Financial Officer:** Lisa Pantages. **Senior VP/CIO/Chairman, San Jose Giants:** Bill Schlough. **VP, Information Technology:** Ken Logan. **VP, Finance:** Matt Causey.

ADMINISTRATION
Executive VP, Administration: Alfonso Felder. **Senior VP, Operations/Facilities:** Jorge Costa. **VP, Ballpark Operations:** Gene Telucci. **VP, Guest Services:** Rick Mears. **Senior VP/Chief People Officer:** Leilani Gayles. **Senior VP, Giants Enterprises:** Stephen Revetria. **Senior VP, Event Strategy & Services:** Sara Grauf.

COMMUNICATIONS
Telephone: (415) 972-2445. **Fax:** (415) 947-2800.
Executive VP, Communications/Senior Advisor to the CEO: Staci Slaughter. **VP, Public Affairs/Community Relations:** Shana Daum. **Executive Director, Giants Community Fund:** Sue Petersen. **Senior Director, Broadcast Communications & Media Operations:** Maria Jacinto. **Senior Director, Media Relations:** Matt Chisholm. **Senior Manager, Hispanic Communications & Marketing:** Erwin Higueros. **Media Relations Manager:** Liam Connolly. **Media Relations Coordinator:** Megan Brown.

BUSINESS OPERATIONS
Executive VP, Business Operations: Mario Alioto. **Senior VP, Partnerships/Business Development:** Jason Pearl. **VP, Partnership Sales & Business Development:** Brenden Mallette. **VP, Retail Operations:** Dave Martinez. **VP, Marketing/Advertising:** Danny Dann. **VP, SFG Productions:** Paul Hodges. **VP, Brand Development/Digital Media:** Bryan Srabian. **VP, CreativeServices/Visual Identity:** Nancy Donati. **PA Announcer:** Renel Brooks-Moon.

TICKETING
Telephone: (415) 972-2000. **Fax:** (415) 972-2500.
Senior VP, Ticket Sales/Services: Russ Stanley. **VP, Ticket Sales/Premium Seating:** Jeff Tucker. **VP, Ticket Operations & Services:** Steve Fanelli. **VP, Strategic Revenue Services:** Jerry Drobny. **VP, Client Retention/Sales Strategy:** Rocky Koplik.

2018 SCHEDULE
Standard Game Times: 7:15 p.m.; Sun. 1:05

MARCH
29-31 . at Los Angeles (NL)

APRIL
1 . . . . at Los Angeles (NL)
3-4 . . . . Seattle
6-8 . . . . . Los Angeles (NL)
9-11 . . . . Arizona
12-15 . . . . at San Diego
17-19 . . . . . . at Arizona
20-22 . at Los Angeles (AL)
23-25 . . . . . Washington
27-29 . . Los Angeles (NL)
30 . . . . San Diego

MAY
1-2 . . . . San Diego

4-6 . . . . at Atlanta
7-10 . . . . . at Philadelphia
11-13 . . . . at Pittsburgh
14-16 . . . . Cincinnati
17-20 . . . . Colorado
22-23 . . . .at Houston
25-27 . . . .at Chicago (NL)
28-30 . . . . . at Colorado

JUNE
1-3 . . . . Philadelphia
4-6 . . . . Arizona
8-10 . . . . . at Washington
11-14 . . . . at Miami
15-17 . at Los Angeles (NL)
18-20 . . . . .Miami
21-24 . . . . San Diego

26-28 . . . . Colorado
29-30 . . . . . . .at Arizona)

JULY
1 . . . . at Arizona
2-4 . . . . at Colorado
5-8 . . . . St. Louis
9-11 . . . . . Chicago (NL)
13-15 . . . . Oakland
20-22 . . . .at Oakland
24-25 . . . . . . .at Seattle
26-29 . . . . .Milwaukee
30-31 . . . . at San Diego

AUGUST
2-5 . . . . at Arizona
6-7 . . . . Houston
9-12 . . . . Pittsburgh

13-15 . at Los Angeles (NL)
17-19 . . . . .at Cincinnati
20-23 . . . at New York (NL)
24-26 . . . . Texas
27-29 . . . . Arizona
31 . . . . . . .New York (NL)

SEPTEMBER
1-2 . . . . . .New York (NL)
3-5 . . . . at Colorado
7-9 . . . . . . at Milwaukee
10-12 . . . . Atlanta
14-16 . . . . Colorado
17-19 . . . . . at San Diego
21-23 . . . . .at St. Louis
24-26 . . . . San Diego
28-30 . . . Los Angeles (NL)

GENERAL INFORMATION
Stadium (year opened): AT&T Park (2000).   **Playing Surface:** Grass.
Team Colors: Black, orange and cream.
Home Dugout: Third Base.

BASEBALL OPERATIONS

Telephone: (415) 972-1922. **Fax:** (415) 947-2929.

Executive VP, Baseball Operations: Brian R. Sabean. **Senior VP/General Manager:** Bobby Evans. **Senior VP/Assistant GM, Player Personnel/Senior Advisor to the GM:** Dick Tidrow. **VP/Assistant GM:** Jeremy Shelley. **VP/Assistant GM, Scouting/International Operations:** John Barr. **VP, Baseball Operations:** Yeshayah Goldfarb. **Special Assistants to GM:** Felipe Alou, Jack Hiatt, Randy Winn. **Director of Baseball Personnel Admin:** Clara Ho. **Executive Assistant to Baseball Operations/Administration:** Karen Sweeney.

Brian Sabean

MAJOR LEAGUE STAFF

Manager: Bruce Bochy. **Coaches: Bench**—Hensley Meulens. **Pitching**—Curt Young. **Hitting**—Alonzo Powell/Rick Schu. **First Base**—Jose Alguacil, **Third Base**—Ron Wotus. **Bullpen**—Matt Herges. **Major League Staff/Video Replay Analyst:** Shawon Dunston, Taira Uematsu. **BP Pitcher/Video Replay Analyst:** Chad Chop. **Manager, Pro Video Systems:** Yo Miyamoto. **Assistant, Pro Video Systems:** Patrick Yount.

MEDICAL/TRAINING

Team Physicians: Dr. Anthony Saglimbeni, Dr. Robert Murray, Dr. Ken Akizuki, Dr. Tim McAdams. **Senior Director of Athletic Training:** Dave Groeschner. **Head Athletic Trainer:** Anthony Reyes. **Assistant Athletic Trainer:** Eric Ortega. **Physical Therapist:** Tony Reale. **Strength and Conditioning Coach:** Carl Kochan. **Assistant Strength and Conditioning Coach/Sports Science Coordinator:** Saul Martinez. **Massage Therapist:** Haro Ogawa. **Coordinator, Medical Administration:** Chrissy Yuen. **Mental Performance Coach:** Bob Tewksbury. **Director of Employee Assistance Program and Organizational Health:** Mike Mombrea.

PLAYER DEVELOPMENT

Vice President, Player Development: David Bell. **Assistant Director, Player Development:** Alan Zinter (offense), Kyle Haines, Matt Buschmann, Geoff Head, Eric Flemming. **Coordinator, Minor League Pitching:** Julio Rael. **Coordinator, Minor League Hitting:** David Hansen. **Coordinator, Fundamentals:** Tom Trebelhorn. **Infield Coordinator:** Alvaro Espinoza. **Outfield and Baserunning Coordinator:** Vince Coleman. **Catching Coordinator:** Billy Hayes. **Manager, Arizona Baseball Operations:** Gabe Alvarez. **Coordinator, Education/Cultural Development:** Laura Nunez. **Analyst, Player Development:** Michael Gries. **Special Assistant, Player Development:** Joe Amalfitano, Gene Clines. **Director, Arizona Field Operations:** Josh Warstler.

FARM SYSTEM

Class	Farm Club (League)	Manager	Hitting Coach	Pitching Coach
Triple-A	Sacramento (PCL)	Dave Brundage	Damon Minor	Steve Kline
Double-A	Richmond (EL)	Willie Harris	Francisco Morales	Glenn Dishman
High A	San Jose (CAL)	Lipso Nava	Wilfredo Romero	Matt Yourkin
Low A	Augusta (SAL)	Jolbert Cabrera	Thomas Neal	Clayton Rapada
Short-season	Salem-Keizer (NWL)	Hector Borg	Jake Fox	Dwight Bernard
Rookie	Giants 1 (AZL)	Carlos Valderrama	Travis Ishikawa	M. Rodriguez/Lee Smith
Rookie	Giants 2 (AZL)	Billy Horton	Doug Clark	Mike Couchee
Rookie	Giants (DSL)	Jose Montilla	C. Chenworth/J. Parra	M. Aguasvivas/O. Matos

SCOUTING

Telephone: (415) 972-2360. **Fax:** (415) 947-2929. **Assistant Director, Pro & Amateur Scouting:** Adam Nieting. **Asst. Baseball Ops Admin.:** Mike Navolio. **Senior Advisors, Pro Scouting:** Lee Elder, Joe Lefebvre, Matt Nerland, Darren Wittcke. **Advance Scouts:** Steve Balboni (Berkeley Heights, NJ), Keith Champion (Ballwin, MO). **Major League Scouts:** Joe Bochy (Plant City, FL), Brian Johnson (Detroit, MI), Michael Kendall (Rancho Palos Verde, CA), Jalal Leach (Sacramento, CA), Bob Mariano (Fountain Hills, AZ), Glenn Tufts (Bridgewater, MA), Paul Turco Jr (Chicago, IL), Tom Zimmer (Seminole, FL). **Special Assistant to Scouting:** Ellis Burks. **Pro Scout:** Tim Rock (Orlando, FL). **Senior Advisors, Amateur Scouting:** Ed Creech (Moultrie, GA), John Flannery (Liberty Hill, TX). **Part Time:** Doug Mapson (Chandler, AZ). **National Pitching Coordinator:** Daniel Murray (Prairie Village, KS). **National Pitching Crosschecker:** Bert Bradley (Mattoon, IL). **National Crosscheckers:** John Castleberry (High Point, NC), Joe Strain (Englewood, CO). **Supervisors: Northeast**—Arnold Brathwaite (Linthicum Heights, MD). **Midwest**—Andrew Jefferson (St.Louis, MO). **Southeast**—Mike Metcalf (Sarasota, FL). **West**— Matt Woodward (Camas, WA). **Area Scouts: Northeast**—Ray Callari (Cote Saint Luc, Quebec), Kevin Christman (Noblesville, IN), John DiCarlo (Glenwood, NJ), Mark O'Sullivan (Haverhill, MA), Donnie Suttles (Marion, NC). **Southeast**—Jose Alou (Boynton Beach, FL), Jim Gabella (Deltona, FL), Luke Murton (McDonough, GA), Jeff Wood (Birmingham, AL). **Midwest**—Todd Coryell (Plainfield, IL), James Mouton (Missouri City, TX), Jared Schlehuber (Tulsa, OK), Todd Thomas (Dallas, TX). **West**—Brad Cameron (Los Alamitos, CA), Larry Casian (Salem, OR), Chuck Fick (Newbury Park, CA), Chuck Hensley Jr. (Mesa, AZ), Keith Snider (Stockton, CA). **Senior Consultants, Part-Time Scouts:** Jorge Posada Sr. (Rio Piedras, PR). **International Scouting, Director of Operations:** Joe Salermo. **International Crosschecker:** Charlie Sullivan. **Latin American Crosschecker:** Junior Roman. **Director, Dominican Republic Operations:** Pablo Peguero. **Scouting Supervisor, Venezuela:** Ciro Villalobos. **Assistant Director, DR Operations/Latin America Crosschecker:** Felix Peguero. **Dominican Republic Crosschecker:** Jesus Stephens. **International Scouts:** Abner Abreu, Jonathan Bautista, Gabriel Elias, Luis Polonia Jr. (Dominican Republic), Jonathan Arraiz, Edgar Fernandez, Juan Marquez, Oscar Montero, Neriel Morillo, Robert Moron, Ciro Villalobos Jr. (Venezuela), Jim Patterson (Australia), Daniel Mavarez (Colombia), Quincy Martina (Curacao/Bonaire/Aruba), Jeff Kusumoto (Japan), Luis Pena Ortiz, Ernesto Cantu (Mexico), Sandy Moreno (Nicaragua), Rogelio Castillo (Panama). **Dominican Republic Facility Manager:** Francis Mieses. **International Baseball Operations Administrator:** Joan Cuevas. **Clubhouse Manager, Dominican Republic:** Victor Aquino. **Dominican Republic English Instructor:** Georgia Feliz. **DR Video Coordinator & Technology Administrator:** Edgar Ferreira.

Seattle Mariners

Office Address: 1250 First Ave. South, Seattle, WA 98134.
Mailing Address: PO Box 4100, Seattle, WA 98194.
Telephone: (206) 346-4000. **Fax:** (206) 346-4400. **Website:** www.mariners.com.

OWNERSHIP

Board of Directors: John Stanton (Chairman), John Ellis, Buck Ferguson, Chris Larson, Howard Lincoln, Jeff Raikes, Frank Shrontz.
President/Chief Executive Officer: Kevin Mather. **Senior Vice President & Special Advisor to the Chairman and CEO:** Randy Adamack.

BUSINESS OPERATIONS

John Stanton

FINANCE

Executive Vice President and Chief Financial Officer: Tim Kornegay. **Vice President, Finance:** Greg Massey. **Director, Internal Audit Operations:** Connie McKay. **Vice President, Human Resources:** Lisa Winsby.

LEGAL & GOVERNMENTAL AFFAIRS/ COMMUNITY RELATIONS

Executive Vice President and General Counsel: Fred Rivera. **Deputy General Counsel:** Melissa Robertson. **VP, Corporate Business & Community Relations:** Joe Chard. **Senior Director, Community Relations:** Gina Hasson.

SALES

Senior Vice President, Sales: Frances Traisman. **Senior Director, Corporate Business:** Ingrid Russell-Narcisse. **Senior Director, Ticket Sales:** Cory Carbary. **Director, Group Business Development:** Bob Hellinger.

MARKETING/COMMUNICATIONS

Telephone: (206) 346-4000. **Fax:** (206) 346-4400.
Senior VP, Marketing/Communications: Kevin Martinez. **Vice President, Communications:** Tim Hevly. **Senior Director, Public Information:** Rebecca Hale. **Senior Manager, Baseball Information:** Kelly Munro. **Coordinator, Baseball Information:** Ryan Hueter. **Senior Director, Mariners Productions:** Ben Mertens. **Senior Director, Marketing:** Gregg Greene. **Director, Marketing:** Mandy Lincoln. **Director, Graphic Design:** Carl Morton.

TICKETING

Telephone: (206) 346-4001. **Fax:** (206) 346-4100.
Senior Director, Ticketing & Parking Operations: Malcolm Rogel. **Director, Ticket Services:** Jennifer Sweigert.

STADIUM OPERATIONS

Senior Vice President, Ballpark Events & Operations: Trevor Gooby. **Senior Director, Engineering/Maintenance:** Ryan van Maarth. **Senior Director, Event Sales:** Alisia Anderson.

2018 SCHEDULE

Standard Game Times: 7:10 p.m.; Sun. 1:10.

MARCH		JULY	
29-31 . . . . Cleveland	11-13 . . . . .at Detroit	1 . . . . Kansas City	17-19 . . . Los Angeles (NL)
APRIL	15-16 . . . . Texas	3-5 . . . . Los Angeles (AL)	20-22 . . . . Houston
1 . . . . Cleveland	17-20 . . . . Detroit	6-8 . . . . Colorado	24-26 . . . . . . at Arizona
3-4 . . . . . at San Francisco	22-24 . . . . .at Oakland	10-12 . at Los Angeles (AL)	28-29 . . . . at San Diego
5-8 . . . . . . at Minnesota	25-27 . . . . . . Minnesota	13-15 . . . . . at Colorado	30-31 . . . . . . .at Oakland
9-11 . . . . . .at Kansas City	28-31 . . . . Texas	20-22 . . . . Chicago (AL)	**SEPTEMBER**
13-15 . . . . Oakland	**JUNE**	24-25 . . . San Francisco	1-2 . . . . .at Oakland
16-19 . . . . Houston	1-3 . . . . .Tampa Bay	27-29 . at Los Angeles (AL)	3-5 . . . . Baltimore
20-22 . . . . .at Texas	5-6 . . . . . . .at Houston	30-31 . . . . Houston	7-9 . . . . . .New York (AL)
23-25 . . . .at Chicago (AL)	7-10 . . . . . at Tampa Bay	**AUGUST**	11-12 . . . . . . San Diego
26-29 . . . . .at Cleveland	11-13 . . . Los Angeles (AL)	1 . . . . Houston	13-16 . at Los Angeles (AL)
MAY	14-17 . . . . Boston	2-5 . . . . .Toronto	17-19 . . . . . .at Houston
1-3 . . . . Oakland	19-21 . . . at New York (AL)	6-8 . . . . .at Texas	21-23 . . . . . . .at Texas
4-6 . . . . . Los Angeles (AL)	22-24 . . . . . . .at Boston	9-12 . . . . . . .at Houston	24-26 . . . . Oakland
8-10 . . . . at Toronto	25-28 . . . . . .at Baltimore	13-15 . . . . . .at Oakland	27-30 . . . . Texas
	29-30 . . . . . . Kansas City		

GENERAL INFORMATION

Stadium (year opened): Safeco Field (1999).   **Home Dugout:** First Base.
Team Colors: Northwest green,   **Playing Surface:** Grass.
silver and navy blue.

Director, Ballpark Event Operations: Michael Hilburn. VP, Information Services: Dave Curry. Director, Information Systems: Oliver Roy. Director, Database/Applications: Justin Stolmeier. Senior Director, Procurement: Norma Cantu. Head Groundskeeper: Bob Christofferson. Assistant Head Groundskeepers: Tim Wilson, Leo Liebert. PA Announcer: Tom Hutyler. Official Scorer: Eric Radovich.

MERCHANDISING
Senior Director, Retail Operations: Julie McGillivray. Director, Retail Merchandising: Renee Steyh. Director, Retail Stores: Mary Beeman.

TRAVEL/CLUBHOUSE
Director, Major League Operations: Jack Mosimann. Clubhouse Manager: Ryan Stiles. Visiting Clubhouse Manager: Jeff Bopp. Video Coordinator: Jimmy Hartley. Assistant Video Coordinator: Craig Manning.

BASEBALL OPERATIONS
Executive VP/General Manager: Jerry Dipoto.
VP, Assistant GM: Jeff Kingston. Special Assistants to the GM: Joe Bohringer, Roger Hansen, Tom McNamara. Director, Baseball Operations: Justin Hollander.

Jerry Dipoto

MAJOR LEAGUE STAFF
Manager: Scott Servais. Bench—Manny Acta. Pitching—Mel Stottlemyre, Jr. Hitting—Edgar Martinez. First Base—Chris Prieto. Third Base—Scott Brosius. Bullpen—Mike Hampton. Assistant Coach—Jim Brower. Bullpen — Brian Delunas.

MEDICAL/TRAINING
Director, High Performance: Dr. Lorena Martin. Medical Director: Ed Khalfayan. Club Physician: Mitch Storey. Head Trainer: Rick Griffin. Assistant Trainers: Rob Nodine, Matt Toth, Yoshi Nakazawa. Strength/Conditioning: James Clifford.

PLAYER DEVELOPMENT
Telephone: (206) 346-4316. Fax: (206) 346-4300.
Director, Player Development: Andy McKay. Coordinator, Player Development: James Roche. Administrator, Player Development: Jan Plein. Coordinator, Organization Instruction: Mike Micucci. Field Coordinator: Carson Vitale. Special Assistant Coordinator: Alvin Davis. Special Assistant, Player Development: Dan Wilson. Hitting Coordinator: Hugh Quattlebaum. Pitching Coordinator: Oscar Marin. Special Assistant, Player Development: Pete Harnisch. Organizational Pitching Development/Rehab Coach: Brad Mills. Organization Pitching Coach: Cody Buckel. Assistant Hitting/Catching Coordinator: Tony Arnerich. Performance Specialist Coordinator: Rob Fumagalli. Coordinator, Professional Development: Leslie Manning. Mental Skills Coach: David Franco.

FARM SYSTEM

Class	Club (League)	Manager	Coach	Pitching Coach
Triple-A	Tacoma (PCL)	Pat Listach	David Berg	Lance Painter
Double-A	Arkansas (TL)	Daren Brown	R. Howell/J. VanOstrand	Ethan Katz
High A	Modesto (CAL)	Mitch Canham	Joe Thurston	Pete Woodworth
Low A	Clinton (MWL)	Denny Hocking	Jose Umbria	Doug Mathis
Short-season	Everett (NWL)	Jose Moreno	Eric Farris	D. Acevedo/M. Hernandez
Rookie	Peoria (AZL)	Zac Livingston	TBD	Yoel Monzon
Rookie	Mariners (DSL)	Cesar Nicolas	David Flores	J. Amancio/A. Leichman

SCOUTING
VP, Scouting: Tom Allison. Director, Amateur Scouting: Scott Hunter. Player Personnel Coordinators: West & Southeast —Brendan Domaracki. Central & Northeast —Jason Karegeannes. Amateur Scouting Coordinator: Tim Stanton. Special Assistants to Scouting: Mark Lummus (Godley, TX), Bill Masse (Manchester, CT), Woody Woodward (Palm Coast, FL).
Major League Scouts: Justin Germano (San Diego, CA), John Hester (Scottsdale, AZ), Greg Hunter (Seattle, WA), Bobby Korecky (Estero, FL), Jason Lefkowitz (Pleasantville, NY), Lee MacPhail (Shaker Heights, OH), Nick Manno (Columbia Station, OH), Howard McCullough (Greenville, NC) John McMichen (Cincinnati, OH), Chris Pelekoudas (Mesa, AZ), Andy Pratt (Peoria, AZ).
Territorial Supervisors: West—Taylor Cameron (Long Beach, CA), Northeast—Devitt Moore (Bryn Mawr, PA), Southeast—Jesse Kapellusch (Cooper City, FL). Area Supervisors: Jordan Bley (Pittsburg, CA), Tyrus Bowman (Dallas, TX), Ben Collman (German Valley, IL), Dan Holcomb (Birmingham, AL), Ryan Holmes (Moorpark, CA), Tyler Holub (Durham, NC), Amanda Hopkins (Phoenix, AZ), Jackson Laumann (Florence, KY), Rob Mummau (Palm Harbor, FL), Brian Nichols (Taunton, MA), Gary Patchett (Wildomar, CA), Alex Ross (Kirkland, WA), Dan Rovetto (Davie, FL), Rafael Santo Domingo (San Juan, PR), Taylor Terrasas (Slidell, LA), Ross Vecchio (Canonsburg, PA), Austin Wates (Austin, TX), John Wiedenbauer (Johns Creek, GA).
Director, International: Tim Kissner (Kirkland, WA). International Cross-Checker: Tom Shafer (Chicago, IL), Supervisor, Dominican Republic: Eddy Toledo (Sato Domingo, DR). Coordinator, Special Projects: Ted Heid (Peoria, AZ). Administrative Director, Dominican Operations: Martin Valerio (Santo Domingo, Dominican Republic). Coordinator, Venezuelan Operations: David Brito (Valencia, Venezuela).
International Scouts: Tristan Loetzsch (Australia), Manabu Noto (Saitama, Japan).

Tampa Bay Rays

Office Address: Tropicana Field, One Tropicana Drive, St. Petersburg, FL 33705.
Telephone: (727) 825-3137. **Fax:** (727) 825-3111.

OWNERSHIP

Principal Owner: Stuart Sternberg

BUSINESS OPERATIONS

Presidents: Brian Auld, Matt Silverman
Chief Business Officer: Jeff Cogen. **Chief Development Officer:** Melanie Lenz. **Senior Vice President, Administration/General Counsel:** John Higgins. **VP/Chief Financial Officer:** Rob Gagliardi. **VP, Operations/Facilities:** Rick Nafe. **VP, Information Technology:** Juan Ramirez. **VP, Corporate Partnerships:** Brian Richeson. **VP, Ticket Sales and Service:** Jeff Tanzer. **VP, Human Resources and Organizational Engagement:** Jennifer Lyn Tran. **VP, Strategy and Development:** William Walsh. **VP, Marketing and Creative Services:** Eric Weisberg. **VP, Employee and Community Development:** Bill Wiener, Jr.

FINANCE

Senior Director, Controller: Patrick Smith. **Director, Financial Planning and Analysis:** Jason Gray.

Stuart Sternberg

MARKETING/COMMUNITY RELATIONS

Senior Director, Marketing/Creative Services: Eric Weisberg. **Senior Director, Public Affairs:** Rafaela Amador Fink. **Director, Marketing:** Amy Miller. **Director, Creative:** Warren Hypes. **Executive Director, Rays Baseball Foundation:** Stephen Thomas.

COMMUNICATIONS/BROADCASTING

Senior Director, Communications: Dave Haller . **Senior Director, Broadcasting:** Larry McCabe.

TICKET SALES

Phone: (888) FAN-RAYS. **Director, Ticket Sales:** Dan Newhart. **Director, Ticket Services and Technology:** Matt Fitzpatrick. **Director, Season Ticket Services:** Josh Muirhead. **Director, Ticket Operations:** Robert Bennett. **Assistant Director, Ticket Operations:** Ken Mallory

STADIUM OPERATIONS

Senior Director, Game Operations and Security: Jim Previtera. **Senior Director, Guest Relations:** Cass Halpin. **Director, Stadium Operations:** Chris Raineri. **Head Groundskeeper:** Dan Moeller. **Travel/Clubhouse:** Chris Westmoreland. **Manager, Home Clubhouse:** Ryan Denlinger. **Manager, Visitor Clubhouse:** Guy Gallagher. **Video Coordinator:** Chris Fernandez

---

2018 SCHEDULE

Standard Game Times: 7:10 p.m.; Sun. 1:10.

MARCH		JULY	
MARCH	8-9 . . . . Atlanta	28-30 . . . . Houston	14-16 . . . at New York (AL)
29-31 . . . . Boston	11-13 . . . . . .at Baltimore	**JULY**	17-19 . . . . .at Boston
APRIL	14-16 . . . . .at Kansas City	1 . . . . Houston	20-23 . . . . . . Kansas City
1 . . . . Boston	17-20 . at Los Angeles (AL)	2-4 . . . . at Miami	24-26 . . . . Boston
2-4 . . . . . at New York (AL)	22-24 . . . . Boston	6-8 . . . . . at New York (NL)	28-29 . . . . at Atlanta
5-8 . . . . .at Boston	25-27 . . . . Baltimore	9-11 . . . . Detroit	31 . . . . .at Cleveland
9-11 . . . .at Chicago (AL)	28-31 . . . . . . .at Oakland	12-15 . . . . . at Minnesota	**SEPTEMBER**
13-15 . . . . .Philadelphia	**JUNE**	20-22 . . . . .Miami	1-2 . . . . .at Cleveland
16-18 . . . . Texas	1-3 . . . . .at Seattle	23-25 . . . .New York (AL)	3-5 . . . . at Toronto
20-22 . . . . . . Minnesota	5-6 . . . . . at Washington	26-29 . . . . .at Baltimore	7-9 . . . . Baltimore
24-26 . . . . .at Baltimore	7-10 . . . . Seattle	31 . . . . . Los Angeles (AL)	10-12 . . . . Cleveland
27-29 . . . . .at Boston	11-13 . . . . .Toronto	**AUGUST**	14-16 . . . . Oakland
30 . . . . .at Detroit	14-17 . . at New York (AL)	1-2 . . . . . Los Angeles (AL)	17-19 . . . . .at Texas
MAY	18-20 . . . . . .at Houston	3-5 . . . . . . Chicago (AL)	20-23 . . . . at Toronto
1-2 . . . . .at Detroit	22-24 . . . . .New York (AL)	7-9 . . . . Baltimore	24-27 . . . . .New York (AL)
4-6 . . . . .Toronto	25-26 . . . . . . Washington	10-12 . . . . . . at Toronto	28-30 . . . . .Toronto

---

GENERAL INFORMATION

Stadium (year opened): Tropicana Field (1998). **Playing Surface:** AstroTurf
Team Colors: Dark blue, light blue, yellow. Game Day Grass 3D-60 H.
Home Dugout: First Base.

BASEBALL OPERATIONS

President, Baseball Operations: Matt Silverman.
Senior VP, Baseball Operations: Chaim Bloom. **Senior VP Baseball Operations/GM:** Erik Neander. **VP, Baseball Operations:** James Click. **Director, Baseball Operations:** Graham Tyler. **Administrator, Baseball Operations:** Sandy Dengler. **Special Assistant to the GM:** Bobby Heck. **Special Assistant, Baseball Operations:** Tom Foley. **Director, Baseball Systems:** Brian Plexico. **Director, Baseball Development:** Peter Bendix. **Developers, Baseball Systems:** Ryan Kelley, Nick Siefken. **Analytics Developer, Baseball Systems:** Michael Vanger. **Director, Analytics:** Jonathan Erlichman. **Director, Pitching Research/Development:** Joshua Kalk. **Assistant, Major League Operations:** Jeremy Sowers.

Erik Neander

SKIP MILOS

MAJOR LEAGUE STAFF
Manager: Kevin Cash.
Coaches: Bench—Charlie Montoyo, **Pitching**—Kyle Snyder, **Hitting**—Chad Mottola, **First Base**—Ozzie Timmons, **Third Base**—Matt Quatraro, **Bullpen**—Stan Boroski, **Coach**— Rocco Baldelli.

MEDICAL/TRAINING
Medical Director: Dr. James Andrews. **Medical Team Physician:** TBA. **Orthopedic Team Physician:** Dr. Koco Eaton. **Head Athletic ML Medical Coordinator:** Paul Harker. **Trainer:** Joe Benge. **Assistant Athletic Trainers:** Mark Vinson, Mike Sandoval. **Strength/Conditioning Coach:** Trung Cao. **Strength/Conditioning Assistant:** Joe Greany.

PLAYER DEVELOPMENT
Telephone: (727) 825-3267. **Fax:** (727) 825-3493.
Director, Minor League Operations: Mitch Lukevics.
Assistant, Minor League Operations: Jeff McLerran. **Assistant, International/Minor League Operations:** George Pappas. **Administrator, International/Minor League Operations:** Giovanna Rodriguez. **Field Coordinators:** Jim Hoff, Bill Evers, Michael Johns. **Minor League Coordinators:** Skeeter Barnes (outfield/baserunning), Hector Torres (infield), Dick Bosman (pitching), Dewey Robinson (pitching), Jorge Moncada (pitching), Charlie Haeger (pitching), Steve Livesey (hitting), Steve Henderson (hitting), Paul Hoover (catching), Aaron Scott (medical), Joe Benge (medical), Joel Smith (rehabilitation), Chris Tomashoff (Latin American medical), Jairo De La Rosa (Latin American cultural), Patrick Trainor (strength/conditioning), Lance Green (mental skills), James Schwabach (mental skills).

FARM SYSTEM

Class	Club (League)	Manager	Hitting Coach	Pitching Coach
Triple-A	Durham (IL)	Jared Sandberg	D. DeMent/B. Johnson	Rick Knapp
Double-A	Montgomery (SL)	Brady Williams	J. Nelson/G. Redus	R.C. Lichtenstein
High A	Charlotte (FSL)	Jim Morrison	J. Szekely/G. Melendez	Steve Watson
Low A	Bowling Green (MWL)	Reinaldo Ruiz	M. Castillo/J. Owens	Brian Reith
Short-season	Hudson Valley (NYP)	Craig Albernaz	A. Freire/R. Valenzuela	Jose Gonzalez
Rookie	Princeton (APP)	Danny Sheaffer	W. Rincones/B.Butera	Jim Paduch
Rookie Rays	(GCL)	Tomas Francisco	R.Guerrero/S. Smedley	M. DeMerritt/ A.Bastardo
Rookie Rays 1	(DSL)	Julio Zorrilla	Omar Luna	Roberto Yil
Rookie Rays 2	(DSL)	Esteban Gonzalez	Ivan Ochoa	L. Urena/L. Romero

SCOUTING
Director, Pro Scouting: Kevin Ibach (Geneva, IL). **Coordinator, Pro Scouting:** Ryan Bristow. **Director, Amateur Scouting:** Rob Metzler. **Senior Advisor, Scouting/Baseball Operations:** R.J. Harrison (Phoenix, AZ). **Assistant, Amateur Scouting:** Jeff Johnson. **Administrator, Amateur Scouting:** Samantha Bireley. **Special Assignment Scouts:** Mike Juhl (Indian Trail, NC), Fred Repke (Carson City, NV). **Professional/International Crosschecker:** Mike Brown (Chandler, AZ), **Professional Scouting Crosschecker:** Jason Cole (Austin, TX) **Major League Scout:** Bob Cluck (San Diego, CA). **Pro Scouts:** Michael Brown (Chandler, AZ), Ken Califano (Aberdeen, MD), Jason Cole (Austin, TX), Max Cohen (New York, NY), JD Elliby (Mansfield, TX) Jason Grey (Mesa, AZ),Brian Keegan (Matthews, NC), Ken Kravec (Sarasota, FL), Mike Langill (Gilbert, AZ), Dave Myers (Seattle, WA), Tyler Chamberlain-Simon (Tampa, FL), Jeff Stewart (Normal, IL), Tyler Stohr (Jacksonville, FL). **National Crosschecker:** Chuck Ricci (Williamsburg, VA). **Midwest Regional Supervisor:** Jeff Cornell (Lee's Summitt, MO). **Northeastern Regional Supervisor:** Brian Hickman (Fort Mill, SC). **Southeastern Regional Supervisor:** Kevin Elfering (Wesley Chapel, FL). **Western Regional Supervisor:** Jake Wilson (Ramona, CA). **Pitching Crosschecker:** Ryan Henderson (Phoenix, AZ). **Scout Supervisors:** Tim Alexander (Jamesville, NY), Matt Alison (Lenexa, KS), Steve Ames (Nashville, TN), James Bonnici (Auburn Hills, MI), Zach Clark (Pennington, NJ), Tom Couston (St. Petersburg, FL), Rickey Drexler (New Iberia, LA), Brett Foley (Trinity, FL), Jonathan Hall (Dallas, TX), David Hamlett (Phoenix, AZ), Joe Hastings (Charlotte, NC), Ryan Henderson (Gilbert, AZ), Milt Hill (Cumming, GA), Alan Hull (Redwood City, CA), Jaime Jones (Poway, CA), Paul Kirsch (Wilsonville, OR), Pat Murphy (Marble Falls, TX), Victor Rodriguez (Miramar, FL), Greg Whitworth (Huntington Beach, CA), Lou Wieben (Little Ferry, NJ). **Part-Time Area Scouts:** Jose Hernandez (Miami, FL), Gil Martinez (San Juan, PR), Graig Merritt (Pitts Meadow, Canada), Casey Onaga (Honolulu, HI), Jack Sharp (Dallas, TX), Donald Turley (Spring, TX). **Director, International Scouting:** Carlos Rodriguez (Tampa, FL). Assistant **Director, International Operations:** Patrick Walters (Tampa, FL). **International Crosschecker:** Steve Miller (Tampa, FL). **Director, South American Operations:** Ronnie Blanco. **Consultant, International Operations:** John Gilmore. **Consultant, Pacific Rim Operations:** Jay Shindo. **Scouting Supervisor, Colombia:** Angel Contreras. **Scouting Supervisor, Mexico:** Eddie Diaz. **Scouting Supervisor, Dominican Republic:** Danny Santana. **Scouting Supervisor, Venezuela:** Marlon Roche. **International Scouts:** Nilson Antigua, Jose Gomez, Remmy Hernandez, Matias Laureano, Victor Torres (Dominican Republic), William Bergolla, Juan Francisco Castillo, Federico Hernandez, Carlos Leon, Edward Rojas (Venezuela), Tiago Campos, Adriano De Souza (Brazil), Carlos Herazo (Latin America), Keith Hsu (Taiwan), Chairon Isenia (Curacao), Joe Park (Korea), Tateki Uchibori (Japan), Jiri Vitt (Czech Republic), Gustavo Zapata (Panama).

Texas Rangers

Office Address: 1000 Ballpark Way, Arlington, TX 76011. **Mailing Address:** P.O. Box 90111, Arlington, TX 76011. **Telephone:** (817) 273-5222. **Fax:** (817) 273-5110. **Website:** www.texasrangers.com. **Twitter:** @Rangers.

OWNERSHIP

Co-Chairman and Managing Partner: Ray C. Davis. **Co-Chairman:** Bob R. Simpson. **Chairrman, Ownership Committee:** Neil Leibman.

BUSINESS OPERATIONS

Executive VP, Business Operations: Rob Matwick. **Executive Vice President, Chief Marketing & Revenue Officer:** Joe Januszewski. **Executive VP/CFO:** Kellie Fischer. **Executive VP/General Counsel:** Katie Pothier. **Executive VP, Communications:** John Blake. **Executive VP, Entertainment/Productions:** Chuck Morgan. **Executive Assistant to Co-Chairman:** Keli West. **Executive Assistant to Business Operations/Finance:** Gabrielle Stokes. **Executive Assistant to CRMO/Legal:** Briana O'Neill. **Manager, Ownership Concierge Services:** Amy Beam.

FINANCE/ACCOUNTING

VP/Controller: Starr Gulledge.

HUMAN RESOURCES/LEGAL/INFORMATION TECHNOLOGY

Ray Davis

Senior VP, Human Resources/Risk Management: Terry Turner. **Corporate Counsel:** Ilana Miller. **Director, Human Resources:** Mercedes Riley. **VP, Information Technology:** Mike Bullock. **Assistant VP, Customer Service:** Donnie Pordash.

PROJECT DEVELOPMENT

Senior VP, Project Development: Jack Hill. **Project Accountant:** Kelley Walker.

COMMUNICATIONS/COMMUNITY RELATIONS

VP, Broadcasting/Communications: Angie Swint. **Assistant VP, Player/Alumni Relations:** Taunee Taylor. **Senior Director, Media Relations:** Rich Rice. **Director, Social Media:** Kaylan Eastepp. **Manager, Photography:** Kelly Gavin. **Manager, Media Relations:** Brian SanFilippo. **Manager, Communications:** Madison Pelletier. **Coordinator, Communications:** Kate Munson. **Coordinator, Player Relations:** Stephanie Gentile. **Coordinator, Social Media:** Kyle Smith. **VP, Community Outreach/Executive Director, Foundation:** Karin Morris. **Director, Youth Baseball and Youth Academy Programs:** Juan Leonel Garciga.

FACILITIES/RETAIL/EVENTS

Senior VP, Operations & Events: Sean Decker. **VP, Events:** Mark Neifeld. **Senior Director, Maintenance:** Mike Call. **Senior Director, Facility Operations:** Duane Arber. **Director, Major League Grounds:** Dennis Klein. **Director, Complex Grounds:** Steve Ballard. **Director, Retail:** George Dunn. **Director, Tours & Experiences:** Lindsey Hopper. **Director, Sales:** Jared Schrom. **Director, Event Operations:** Pedro Soto, Jr.

2018 SCHEDULE

Standard Game Times: 7:05 p.m.; Sun. 2:05.

MARCH	7-9 . . . . Detroit	29-30 . . . . . Chicago (AL)	16-19 . . . Los Angeles (AL)
29-31 . . . . Houston	11-13 . . . . . . .at Houston	**JULY**	20-22 . . . . . . .at Oakland
APRIL	15-16 . . . . .at Seattle	1 . . . . Chicago (AL)	24-26 . . . at San Francisco
1 . . . . Houston	17-20 . . . .at Chicago (AL)	3-4 . . . . Houston	28-29 . . . Los Angeles (NL)
2-5 . . . . .at Oakland	21-23 . . . .New York (AL)	5-8 . . . . .at Detroit	31 . . . . Minnesota
6-8 . . . . .Toronto	24-27 . . . . . Kansas City	9-11 . . . . .at Boston	**SEPTEMBER**
9-11 . . . . Los Angeles (AL)	28-31 . . . . .at Seattle	13-15 . . . . . .at Baltimore	1-2 . . . . .Minnesota
13-15 . . . . . . .at Houston		20-22 . . . . Cleveland	3-5 . . . . . Los Angeles (AL)
16-18 . . . . . at Tampa Bay	**JUNE**	23-26 . . . . Oakland	7-9 . . . . .at Oakland
20-22 . . . . Seattle	1-3 . . . at Los Angeles (AL)	27-29 . . . . . .at Houston	10-12 . at Los Angeles (AL)
23-25 . . . . Oakland	5-6 . . . . Oakland	30-31 . . . . at Arizona	14-16 . . . . . at San Diego
27-29 . . . . . . at Toronto	7-10 . . . . Houston		17-19 . . . . .Tampa Bay
30 . . . . . . .at Cleveland	12-13 . at Los Angeles (NL)	**AUGUST**	21-23 . . . . Seattle
	15-17 . . . . . . .Colorado	2-5 . . . . Baltimore	24-26 . at Los Angeles (AL)
MAY	18-20 . . . .at Kansas City	6-8 . . . . Seattle	27-30 . . . . .at Seattle
1-2 . . . . .at Cleveland	22-24 . . . . . at Minnesota	9-12 . . . . at New York (AL)	
3-6 . . . . Boston	25-27 . . . . . . San Diego	13-14 . . . . .Arizona	

 ## GENERAL INFORMATION

Stadium (year opened):   **Home Dugout:** First Base.
Globe Life Park in Arlington (1994). **Playing Surface:** Grass.
Team Colors: Royal blue and red.

MARKETING/GAME PRESENTATION

VP, Marketing: Becky Kimbro. **Director, Advertising/Marketing:** Sarah Opgenorth. **Senior Director, Game Entertainment/Productions:** Chris DeRuyscher.

BASEBALL OPERATIONS

Telephone: (817) 273-5222. **Fax:** (817) 273-5285.
President, Baseball Operations/General Manager: Jon Daniels.
Executive Assistant to President, Baseball Operations/GM: Joda Parent.
Special Assistants to the GM: Darren Oliver, Ivan Rodriguez, Michael Young, Colby Lewis, Mark Connor. **Director, Baseball Operations:** Matt Vinnola. **Director, Pitching Research/Development:** Todd Walther. **Director, Advance Scouting:** Adam Lewkowicz. **Director, Baseball Analytics:** Todd Slavinsky. **Senior Analyst, Baseball Operations:** Ryan Murray. **Senior Developer Baseball Systems:** Kim Eskew. Database Developer, Micah Outlaw. **Analyst, Baseball Operations:** Andrew Koo.

MAJOR LEAGUE STAFF

Manager: Jeff Banister.
Coaches: Bench—Don Wakamatsu. **Pitching**—Doug Brocail. **Hitting**—Anthony Iapoce. **First Base**—Steve Buechele. **Third Base**—Tony Beasley. **Assistant Pitching Coach**—Dan Warthen. **Bullpen**— Hector Ortiz. **Assistant Hitting Coach**—Justin Mashore.

MEDICAL/TRAINING

Senior Director, Medical Operations/Sports Science: Jamie Reed. **Team Physician:** Dr. Keith Meister. **Team Internist:** Dr. David Hunter. **Spine Consultant:** Dr. Andrew Dossett. **Head Trainer:** Kevin Harmon. **Assistant Trainer:** Matt Lucero. **Physical Therapist:** Regan Wong. **Director, Strength/Conditioning:** Jose Vazquez. **Team Nutritionist:** Stephanie Fernandes.

Jon Daniels

PLAYER DEVELOPMENT

Telephone: (817) 436-5999. **Fax:** (817) 273-5285.
Assistant General Manager: Jayce Tingler. **Director, Peak Performance:** Josiah Igono. **Assistant Director Player Development:** Paul Kruger. **Assistant, Player Development:** Casey Fox. **Field Coordinator:** Corey Ragsdale. **Pitching Coordinator:** Danny Clark. **Coordinators:** Josue Perez (hitting), Dwayne Murphy (assistant hitting/outfield), Damon Mashore (baserunning), Chris Briones (catching), Jeff Andrews (assistant pitching), Keith Comstock (rehab pitching), Kenny Holmberg (infield), Napoleon Pichardo (strength/conditioning), Eric McMahon (assistant strength/conditioning), Jason Roberts (medical), Sean Fields (rehab), Chris Olson (assistant medical/rehab). **Coordinator, Arizona Operations:** Stosh Hoover. **Minor League Equipment Manager:** Chris Ackerman.

FARM SYSTEM

Class	Club (League)	Manager	Coach	Pitching Coach
Triple-A	Round Rock (PCL)	Jason Wood	H. Johnson/G. Petralli	Brian Shouse
Double-A	Frisco (TL)	Joe Mikulik	Jason Hart	Greg Hibbard
High A	Down East (CL)	Spike Owen	K. Hook/C. Maldonado	Steve Mintz
Low A	Hickory (SAL)	Matt Hagen	C. Lambin/T. Thomas	Jose Jaimes
Short-season	Spokane (NWL)	Kenny Holmberg	Jared Goedert	Jono Armold
Rookie	Rangers (AZL)	Matt Siegel	S. Manriquez/J. Moore/G. Rodriguez	H. Lugo/C. Egelston
Rookie	Rangers (DSL)	Carlos Cardoza	S. Adriana/A. Infante/R. De La Rosa/L. Encarnacion	J. Delgado/G. Blanco

SCOUTING

Assistant GM Pro Scouting, Research/Development/Pacific Rim Operations: Josh Boyd. **Assistant GM, Major League Operations/International Scouting:** Mike Daly. **Assistant GM, Player Development:** Jayce Tingler. **Senior Director, Amateur Scouting:** Kip Fagg. **Manager, Amateur Scouting:** Ben Baroody. **Special Assistant to the GM:** James Keller (Sacramento, CA). **National Crosscheckers:** Clarence Johns (Atlanta, GA), Jake Krug (Flower Mound, TX). **West Coast Crosschecker:** Casey Harvie (Lake Stevens, WA). **Midwest Crosschecker:** Randy Taylor (Katy, TX). **Eastern Crosschecker:** Ryan Coe (Acworth, GA). **Southeast Crosschecker:** Brian Williams (Cincinnati, OH). **Area Scouts:** Josh Simpson (Chandler, AZ), Brett Campbell (Orlando, FL), Roger Coryell (Ypsilanti, MI), Bobby Crook (Fort Worth, TX), Steve Flores (Temecula, CA), Brian Matthews (Mount Joy, PA), Todd Guggiana (Long Beach, CA), Jay Heafner (Charlotte, NC), Bob Laurie (Plano, TX), Gary McGraw (Gaston, OR), Michael Medici (Danville, IN), Butch Metzger (Sacramento, CA), Brian Morrison (Birmingham, AL), Takeshi Sakurayama (Manchester, CT), Dustin Smith (Olathe, KS), Cliff Terracuso (Jupiter, FL), Derrick Tucker (Kennesaw, GA). **Part-Time Scouts:** Chris Collias (Oak Park, MI), Rick Schroeder (Phoenix, AZ). **Assistant, Pro Scouting:** Mike Parnell. **Special Assistants:** Mike Anderson (Austin, TX), Scot Engler (Montgomery, IL), Scott Littlefield (Long Beach, CA), Greg Smith (Gettysburg, PA). **Pro Scouts:** Russ Ardolina (Rockville, MD), Jay Eddings (Tulsa, OK), Mike Grouse (Lubbock,TX), Brian Sikorski (Fraser, MI), Jonathan George (Pittsburgh, PA), Donzell McDonald (Chandler, AZ), Elliott Blair (Argyle, TX), Vinny Rottino (Milwaukee, WI). **Director, International Scouting:** Rafic Saab. **Assistant, International Scouting:** Hamilton Wise. **International Crosschecker:** Trey Hendricks. **Supervisor, Dominican Republic:** Willy Espinal. **Supervisor, Venezuela:** Jhonny Gomez. **Dominican Program Coordinator/Dominican Area Scout:** Danilo Troncoso. **Latin America Crosschecker:** Chu Halabi.

International Scouts: Jose Fernandez (Florida). Rafael Belen (Dominican Republic), Moises de la Mota (Dominican Republic), Carlos Gonzalez (Venezuela), Juan Salazar (Venezuela), Carlos Plaza (Venezuela), Carlos Barrios (Venezuela), Rafael Cedeno (Panama), Eduardo Thomas (Panama), Hamilton Sarabia (Colombia), Manuel Velez (Mexico). **Video Scout, Dominican Republic:** Michael Acevedo. **Assistant, International Operations:** Jose Vargas. **DR Complex Administrator:** Marlenis Alejo. **Director, Pacific Rim Operations:** Joe Furukawa (Japan). **Manager, Pacific Rim:** Hajime Watabe (Japan). **International Scout:** Daniel Chang (Taiwan).

Toronto Blue Jays

Office/Mailing Address: 1 Blue Jays Way, Suite 3200, Toronto, Ontario M5V 1J1.
Telephone: (416) 341-1000. **Fax:** (416) 341-1245. **Website:** www.bluejays.com.

OWNERSHIP

Operated by: Toronto Blue Jays Baseball Club. **Principal Owner:** Rogers Communications Inc. Chairman, **Toronto Blue Jays:** Edward Rogers. **Vice Chairman, Rogers Communications Inc.:** Phil Lind. **President and CEO, Rogers Communication:** Joe Natale. **President, Media Business Unit:** Rick Brace. **Chief Financial Officer, Rogers Communication:** Tony Staffieri.

BUSINESS OPERATIONS

President and CEO: Mark A. Shapiro. **President Emeritus:** Paul Beeston. **Executive Vice President, Baseball Operations and General Manager:** Ross Atkins. **Executive Vice President, Business Operations:** Andrew Miller. **Executive Assistant to the President and CEO:** Gail Ricci.

FINANCE/ADMINISTRATION

Senior Director, Finance: Lynda Kolody. **Director, Blue Jays Payroll:** Brenda Dimmer. Manager, **Revenue Reporting:** Josh Hoffman. **Financial Business Manager:** Leslie Galant-Gardiner. **Financial Analyst:** Dylan Hewko. **Financial Analyst:** Melissa Paterson. **Senior Payroll Administrator:** Marichu Estrella. **Senior Manager, Blue Jays Payroll:** Sharon Dykstra.

MARKETING/COMMUNITY RELATIONS

Mark Shapiro

Vice President, Marketing: Marnie Starkman. **Director, Marketing:** Kristy-Leigh Boone. **Director, Creative Services & Marketing Management:** Sherry Oosterhuis. **Director, Game Entertainment:** Matthew Shelton.

BASEBALL MEDIA

Vice President, Communications: Sebastian Gatica. **Vice President, Communications:** Jay Stenhouse. **Manager, Fan Engagement:** Jessica Beard.

STADIUM OPERATIONS/SECURITY

Vice President, Stadium Operations and Security: Mario Coutinho. **Manager, Game Operations:** Karyn Gottschalk. **Control Room Guard:** Desmond Buchanan. **Control Room Guard:** Althea Hussey. **Control Room Guard:** Bojan Fogl. **Control Room Operator:** Kyle Rutherford. **Security Guard:** Ryan Cobham. **Security Guard:** Christopher Adams. **Security Guard:** Juris Batraks. **Security Guard:** Randall Harris. **Security Guard:** Tom Puckrin.

TICKET OPERATIONS

Director, Ticket Operations: Justin Hay. **Director, Ticket Sales & Operations:** Eric Cowell. **Director, Ticket Executive & Promoter Ticketing:** Sheila Stella. **Manager, Ticket Sales and Services:** John Santana. **Manager, Box Office:** Christina Dodge. **Manager, Assistant Box Office:** Rachel De Sousa. **Coordinator, Ticket Operations:** Richard Chautems. **Coordinator, Ticket Sales & Service:** Cassandra Brunshaw. **Coordinator, Executive & Promoter Ticketing:**

2018 SCHEDULE

Standard Game Times: 7:07 p.m.; Sat/Sun: 1:07

MARCH	8-10 . . . . Seattle	29-30 . . . . Detroit	13-16 . . . . .at Kansas City
29-31 . . . . .New York (AL)	11-13 . . . . Boston	**JULY**	17-19 . . . at New York (AL)
APRIL	15-16 . . . at New York (NL)	1-2 . . . . Detroit	20-22 . . . . Baltimore
1 . . . . New York (AL)	17-20 . . . . Oakland	3-4 . . . . . .New York (NL)	24-26 . . . . . .Philadelphia
2-4 . . . . . . Chicago (AL)	22-24 . . . Los Angeles (AL)	6-8 . . . . . .New York (AL)	27-29 . . . . . .at Baltimore
6-8 . . . . .at Texas	25-27 . . . . at Philadelphia	10-11 . . . . at Atlanta	31 . . . . at Miami
9-11 . . . . . .at Baltimore	28-30 . . . . .at Boston	12-15 . . . . . . .at Boston	**SEPTEMBER**
13-15 . . . . .at Cleveland	**JUNE**	20-22 . . . . Baltimore	1-2 . . . . at Miami
16-18 . . . . . . Kansas City	1-3 . . . . .at Detroit	23-25 . . . . . . Minnesota	3-5 . . . . .Tampa Bay
19-22 . . . at New York (AL)	5-6 . . . . . .New York (AL)	27-29 . . . .at Chicago (AL)	6-9 . . . . Cleveland
24-26 . . . . Boston	7-10 . . . . Baltimore	30-31 . . . . . .at Oakland	11-13 . . . . .at Boston
27-29 . . . . Texas	11-13 . . . . . at Tampa Bay	**AUGUST**	14-16 . . at New York (AL)
30 . . . . at Minnesota	15-17 . . . . . Washington	1 . . . . .at Oakland	17-19 . . . . . .at Baltimore
MAY	19-20 . . . . Atlanta	2-5 . . . . .at Seattle	20-23 . . . . . . .Tampa Bay
1-2 . . . . . . at Minnesota	21-24 . at Los Angeles (AL)	7-9 . . . . Boston	24-26 . . . . Houston
4-6 . . . . . . at Tampa Bay	25-27 . . . . . .at Houston	10-12 . . . . . .Tampa Bay	28-30 . . . . . at Tampa Bay

GENERAL INFORMATION

Stadium (year opened): Rogers Centre (1989).
Team Colors: Blue and white.

Home Dugout: Third Base.
Playing Surface: AstroTurf 3D Xtreme.

Sonia Privato. **System Administrator:** Richard Overend. **Specialist, Ticket Support:** Chrsitian Taylor. **Account Executive:** Mike Skrobacky. **Account Executive:** Alex Husarewych. **Account Executive:** Jeff Gale. **Account Executive:** Jonathan Bagnell. **Account Executive:** Glenn Jackson. **Inside Ticket Sales Representative:** Ryan McMorrow.

TRAVEL/CLUBHOUSE
Director, Team Travel/Clubhouse Operations: Mike Shaw. **Senior Manger, Visiting Clubhouse:** Kevin Malloy. **Clubhouse Manager:** Scott Blin. **Clubhouse Manager, Equipment:** Mustafa Hassan. **Equipment Manager:** Jeff Ross.

BASEBALL OPERATIONS

Executive Vice President, Baseball Operations/General Manager: Ross Atkins. **Senior Vice President, Baseball Operations and Assistant GM:** Tony LaCava. **Vice President, Baseball Operations:** Ben Cherington. **Assistant GM:** Joe Sheehan. **Assistant GM:** Andrew Tinnish. **Director of Team Travel & Clubhouse Ops:** Mike Shaw. **Director of Scouting:** Steve Sanders. **Director of Scouting:** Mike Murov. **Sr. Manager, Major League Admin:** Heather Connolly. **Manager, Analytics:** Sanjay Choudhury. **Executive Assistant to GM:** Anna Coppola. **Major League Chef:** Nigel Baston. **Coordinator, Baseball Research:** Jeremy Reesor. **Professional Crosschecker:** Kevin Briand. **Professional Crosschecker:** Jon Lalonde. **Visiting Clubhouse, Sr. Manger:** Kevin Malloy. **Clubhouse Manager:** Scott Blin. **Clubhouse Manager, Equipment:** Mustafa Hassan. **Equipment Manager:** Jeff Ross. **Special Assistant to the Organization:** Roberto Alomar, Sandy Alomar Jr., Tim Raines, Carlos Delgado, Pat Hentgen, Paul Quantrill.

Ross Atkins

MAJOR LEAGUE STAFF
Manager: John Gibbons. **Coaches: Bench**—DeMarlo Hale, **Pitching**—Pete Walker, **Hitting**—Brook Jacoby,
First Base—Tim Leiper, **Third Base**—Luis Rivera, **Bullpen**—Dane Johnson, **Quality Control**—Mike Mordecai. **Bullpen Catchers:** Alex Andreopoulos, Jason Phillips.

HIGH PERFORMANCE/MEDICAL STAFF
Director of High Performance: Angus Mugford. **Assistant Director of High Performance:** Clive Brewer. **Head Athletic Trainer, Major League:** Nikki Huffman. **Head Strength and Conditioning:** Donovan Santas. **Head of Mental Performance:** Paddy Steinfort. **Head of Nutrition:** Stephanie Wilson. **Assistant Strength and Conditioning Coordinator, Major League:** Scott Weberg. **Fueling Coordinator:** Antonio Castillo. **ATC/Transaction Coordinator:** Jeff Stevenson.

PLAYER DEVELOPMENT
Telephone: (727) 734-8007. **Fax:** (727) 734-8162.
Director, Player Development: Gil Kim. Director, **Minor League Operations:** Charlie Wilson. **Field Coordinator:** Eric Wedge. **Pitching Coordinator:** Jeff Ware. **Hitting Coordinator:** Guillermo Martinez. **Senior Pitching Advisor:** Rick Langford. **Rehab Pitching Coach:** Darold Knowles. **Catching Coordinator:** Ken Huckaby. **Infield Coordinator:** Danny Solano. **Latin America Player Advisor:** Omar Malave. **Equipment Coordinator:** Billy Wardlow. **Coordinator, Latin America Operations:** Blake Bentley. **Coordinator, Minor League Operations:** Michael Nielsen. **Player Development Assistant:** Megan Evans. **Player Development Assistant:** Joe Sclafani. **Administrative Assistant:** Kim Marsh.

FARM SYSTEM

Class	Club (League)	Manager	Hitting Coach	Pitching Coach	Position Coach
Triple-A	Buffalo (IL)	Bobby Meacham	Corey Hart	Bob Stanley	Devon White
Double-A	New Hampshire (EL)	John Schneider	Hunter Mense	Vince Horsman	Andy Fermin
High A	Dunedin (FSL)	Casey Candaele	Donnie Murphy	Mark Riggins	Michel Abreu
Low A	Lansing (MWL)	Cesar Martin	Matt Young	Antonio Caceres	Dave Pano
Short-season	Vancouver (NWL)	Dallas McPherson	Aaron Mathews	Jim Czajkowski	
Rookie	Bluefield (APP)	Dennis Holmberg	Carlos Villalobos	Adam Bernero	Chris Schaeffer
Rookie	Blue Jays (GCL)	Luis Hurtado	Paul Elliott	Rafael Lazo	George Carroll
Rookie	Blue Jays (DSL)	John Tamargo Jr.	Julio Germosen	Yoel Hernandez	Jose Mateo

SCOUTING
Director, Professional Scouting: Ryan Mittleman. **Director, Amateur Scouting:** Steve Sanders. **Manager, Amateur and International Scouting:** Harry Einbinder. **Coordinator, Professional Scouting:** David Haynes. **Coordinator, Amateur Scouting:** Kory Lafreniere. **Assistant, International Scouting:** Julio Ramirez. **Special Assignment Scouts:** Russ Bove, Dean Decillis. **Major League Scout/Pacific Rim Operations:** Dan Evans. **Major League Scouts:** Jim Beattie, Sal Butera, Jon Lalonde, Chuck LaMar, Jim Skaalen. **Professional Scouts:** Matt Anderson, Kevin Briand, Jon Bunnell, Kimball Crossley, Kevin Fox, Jeremy Gordon, Bryan Lambe, Brad Matthews Jr., David May Jr. **Scout:** Mitch Leeds. **National Supervisor:** Blake Crosby. **Regional Crosscheckers:** C.J. Ebarb Jr., Tim Rooney, Paul Tinnell, Jamie Lehman. **Area Scouts:** Joey Aversa Jr. (Fountain Valley, CA), Coulson Barbiche (Milford, OH), Jason Beverlin (Charlotte, NC), Matt Bishoff (Tampa, FL), Dallas Black (Springdale, AR), Darold Brown (Phoenix, AZ), Ryan Fox (Yakima, WA), Pete Holmes (Boston, MA), Matthew Huck (Chicago, IL), Brian Johnston (Austin, TX), Randy Kramer (Aptos, CA), Jim Lentine (San Clemente, CA), Nate Murrie (Bowling Green, KY), Don Norris (Hoover, AL), Matt O'Brien (Clermont, FL), Wes Penick (Clive, IA), Bud Smith (Lakewood, CA), Mike Tidick (Statesboro, GA), Gerald Turner (Euless, TX), Doug Witt (Brooklyn, MD). **Scout:** Brandon Bishoff. **Canadian Scouts:** Adam Arnold (London, ON), Jay Lapp (London, ON), Jasmin Roy (Longueuil, QC). **Director, Latin American Operations:** Sandy Rosario. **Dominican Scouting Supervisor:** Lorenzo Perez. **Venezuelan Scouting Supervisor:** Jose Contreras. **Mexican Scouting Supervisor:** Aaron Acosta. **International Scout:** Henry Sandoval. Santo Domingo, **DR:** Alexis de la Cruz. Santo Domingo, **DR:** Luciano del Rosario. Santo Domingo, **DR:** Fausto Espinosa. Cartagena, **COL:** Enrique Falcon. Mao, **DR:** Johan Gomez. Barquisimeto, **VZ:** Miguel Leal. Maracaibo, **VZ :** Alirio Ledezma. San Pedro de Macoris, **DR:** Luis Natera. Aragua, **VZ:** Francisco Plasencia. Santo Domingo, **DR:** Eric Ramirez. Managua, **NIC:** Daniel Sotelo. Colon, **PA:** Alex Zapata.

Washington Nationals

Office Address: 1500 South Capitol Street SE, Washington, DC 20003.
Telephone: (202) 640-7000. **Fax:** (202) 547-0025.
Website: www.nationals.com.

OWNERSHIP

Managing Principal Owner: Theodore N. Lerner. **Principal Owners:** Annette M. Lerner, Mark D. Lerner, Judy Lenkin Lerner, Edward L. Cohen, Debra Lerner Cohen, Robert K. Tanenbaum, Marla Lerner Tanenbaum.

BUSINESS OPERATIONS

Chief Operating Officer, Lerner Sports: Alan Gottlieb. **Chief Revenue/Marketing Officer:** Valerie Camillo. **Chief Financial Officer:** Lori Creasy. **Senior Vice President:** Elise Holman.

BALLPARK ENTERPRISES

Executive Director, Ballpark Enterprises: Emily Dunham. **Senior Manager, Event Sales:** Kathryn Sutton. **Event Sales Manager:** Kristin Blaser. **Coordinator, Ballpark Enterprises:** Heather Lamb.

LEGAL

Senior VP/General Counsel, Baseball/Business Operations: Damon Jones. **Deputy General Counsel:** Betsy Philpott. **Coordinator, Legal:** Gwendolyn Lockamn.

Ted Lerner

HUMAN RESOURCES

VP, Human Resources: Alexa Herndon. **Director, Benefits:** Stephanie Giroux. **Manager, Employee Relations:** Siobhan Francis. **Manager, Recruiting:** Tara Haney.

COMMUNICATIONS

VP, Communications: Jennifer Giglio. **Executive Director, Communications:** Elizabeth Alexander. **Director, Communications:** Kyle Brostowitz. **Manager, Communications:** Carly Rolfe. **Coordinator, Communications:** Christopher Browne.

COMMUNITY RELATIONS

VP, Community Engagement: Gregory McCarthy. **Executive Director, Player & Community Relations:** Shawn Bertani. **Senior Manager, Community Relations:** Collin Lever, Nicole Murray.

MARKETING/BROADCASTING

VP, Brand Marketing: Kristine Friend. **Senior Director, Marketing & Advertising:** Chauncey McCall. **VP, Broadcasting/Game Presentation:** Jacqueline Coleman. **Senior Manager, Promotions & Events:** Kelly Trimble.

TICKETING/SALES

VP, Ticket Sales & Service: Ryan Bringger. **Senior Director, Ticket Sales:** Joseph Dellwo. **Senior Manager, Group Sales:** Tom Breslin. **Director, Premium Sales/Service:** Kai Murray. **Vice President, Ticket Operations & Sales Optimization:** Andrew Bragman. **Director, Ticket Operations:** Tyler Hubbard.

2018 SCHEDULE

Standard Game Times: 7:05 p.m.; Sun. 1:35

MARCH	7-9 . . . . . . at San Diego	25-26 . . . . . at Tampa Bay
29-31 . . . . . .at Cincinnati	10-13 . . . . at Arizona	28-30 . . . . at Philadelphia
	15-16 . . . . .New York (AL)	
APRIL	18-20 . . . Los Angeles (NL)	**JULY**
1 . . . . .at Cincinnati	21-23 . . . . San Diego	1 . . . . . . at Philadelphia
2-4. . . . . at Atlanta	25-27 . . . . at Miami	2-4. . . . . Boston
5-8 . . . . . .New York (NL)	28-30 . . . . . .at Baltimore	5-8. . . . . .Miami
9-11 . . . . Atlanta	31 . . . . at Atlanta	9-11 . . . . . . at Pittsburgh
12-15 . . . . . . .Colorado		12-15 . . . at New York (NL)
16-18 . . . at New York (NL)	**JUNE**	20-22 . . . . Atlanta
20-22 . at Los Angeles (NL)	1-3. . . . . at Atlanta	23-25 . . . at Milwaukee
23-25 . . . at San Francisco	5-6. . . . . .Tampa Bay	26-29 . . . . at Miami
27-29 . . . . Arizona	8-10 . . . . . San Francisco	31 . . . . . .New York (NL)
30 . . . . Pittsburgh	12-13 . . at New York (AL)	
	15-17 . . . . . . at Toronto	**AUGUST**
MAY	19-21 . . . . . . Baltimore	1 . . . . . . .New York (NL)
1-3. . . . . Pittsburgh	22-24 . . . . .Philadelphia	2-5. . . . . Cincinnati
4-6. . . . . . .Philadelphia		7-9. . . . . Atlanta
		10-12 . . .at Chicago (NL)
		13-16 . . . . . . .at St. Louis
		17-19 . . . . .Miami
		21-23 . . . . .Philadelphia
		24-26 . . . at New York (NL)
		27-29 . . . . at Philadelphia
		31 . . . . .Milwaukee
		SEPTEMBER
		1-2. . . . . .Milwaukee
		3-5. . . . . St. Louis
		6-9. . . . . . . Chicago (NL)
		10-12 . . at Philadelphia
		14-16 . . . . . . at Atlanta
		17-18 . . . . . . at Miami
		20-23 . . . .New York (NL)
		24-26 . . . . . . .Miami
		28-30 . . . . . at Colorado

GENERAL INFORMATION

Stadium (year opened):
Nationals Park (2008).
Team Colors: Red, white and blue.

Home Dugout: First Base.
Playing Surface: Grass.

BUSINESS STRATEGY & ANALYTICS

Senior VP, Consumer Revenue: Mike Shane. **Executive Director, Strategy:** Mike Carney.

BALLPARK OPERATIONS

Senior VP, Ballpark Operations: Frank Gambino. **VP, Ballpark Operations:** Jonathan Stahl. **Coordinator, Ballpark Operations:** Kathryn Phillips. **Director, Field Operations:** John Turnour. **Director, Guest Experience:** Maurice Ruffin. **Senior Director, Event Operations:** Lisa Marie Czop. **Director, Facilities:** Mark Carlson.

BASEBALL OPERATIONS

General Manager/President, Baseball Operations: Mike Rizzo. **Assistant GM/VP, Baseball Operations:** Bob Miller. **Assistant GM/VP, Player Personnel:** Doug Harris. **Assistant GM/VP, Scouting Operations:** Kris Kline. **Assistant GM/VP, Finance:** Ted Towne. **VP, Clubhouse Operations/Team Travel:** Rob McDonald. **Senior Advisor, GM:** Phillip Rizzo. **Special Assistant, Major League Administration:** Harolyn Cardozo. **Director, Baseball Operations:** Michael DeBartolo. **Analysts, Baseball Operations:** James Badas, Christopher Rosenbaum. **Coordinator, Baseball Operations:** John Wulf. **Baseball Operations Video Coordinator:** James Goodwin. **Director, Baseball Research & Development:** Samuel Mondry-Cohen. **Senior Analyst, Baseball Research & Development:** Lee Mendelowitz. **Assistant, Clubhouse/Team Travel:** Ryan Wiebe.

MAJOR LEAGUE STAFF

Manager: Dave Martinez. **Coaches: Bench**—Chip Hale, **Pitching**—Derek Lilliquist, **Hitting**—Kevin Long, **First Base**—Tim Bogar, **Third Base**—Bob Henley, **Bullpen**—Henry Blanco. **Assistant Hitting Coach:** Joe Dillon.

Mike Rizzo

MEDICAL/TRAINING

Executive Director, Medical Services: Harvey Sharman. **Lead Team Physician:** Dr. Robin West. **Chairman, Medical Services Advisory Board:** Dr. Keith Pyne. **Director, Mental Conditioning:** Mark Campbell. **Director, Athletic Training:** Paul Lessard. **Head Athletic Trainer:** Dale Gilbert. **Athletic Trainer:** Greg Barajas. **Athletic Training Assistant:** John Hsu. **Team Physician/Internis:** Dr. Dennis Cullen. **Team Physician, Florida:** Dr. Bruce Thomas. **Team Chiropractor:** Dr. Hirad Bagy. **Director of Visual Performance:** Dr. Keith Smithson.

PLAYER DEVELOPMENT

Vice President, Senior Advisor to the General Manager: Bob Boone. **Director, Player Development:** Mark Scialabba. **Director, Minor League Operations:** Ryan Thomas. **Senior Advisor, Player Development:** Spin Williams. **Coordinators:** Billy Gardner (roving), Tommy Shields, Jeff Garber (field), Troy Gingrich (hitting), Paul Menhart (pitching), Gary Thurman (outfield/baserunning), Michael Barrett (catching), Mark Grater (rehab pitching), Jonathan Kotredes (medical & rehab), Tony Rogowski (strength & conditioning). **Manager, Minor League Operations:** J.J. Esteves. **Administrator, Minor League Operations:** Dianne Wiebe. **Strength & Conditioning Coach:** Matt Eiden. **Assistant Major League Strength Coach:** Brett Henry.

FARM SYSTEM

Class	Club	Manager	Hitting Coach	Pitching Coach
Triple-A	Syracuse (IL)	Billy Gardner Jr.	Brian Daubach	Bob Milacki
Double-A	Harrisburg (EL)	Matt LeCroy	Brian Rupp	Michael Tejera
High A	Potomac (CL)	Tripp Keister	Luis Ordaz	Sam Narron
Low A	Hagerstown (SAL)	Patrick Anderson	Amaury Garcia	TIm Redding
Short-season	Auburn (NYP)	Jerad Head	Mark Harris	Franklin Bravo
Rookie	Nationals (GCL)	Mario Lisson	J. Mejia/L. Jeronimo	Larry Pardo
Rookie	Nationals (DSL)	Sandy Martinez	Jose Herrera	Pablo Frias

SCOUTING

Assistant GM/VP, Player Personnel: Doug Harris. **Assistant GM/VP, Scouting Operations:** Kris Kline. **Assistant Director of Amateur Scouting:** Mark Baca. **Director, Scouting Operations:** Eddie Longosz. **Manager, Advance Scouting:** Jonathan Tosches. **Coordinator, Advance Scouting:** Greg Ferguson. **Major League Advance Scout:** Chris Rosenbaum. **Major League Professional Scout:** Colin Sebean. **National Crosschecker:** Fred Costello, Jimmy Gonzales. **Area Supervisors:** Ray Blanco (S. FL), Justin Bloxom (IN, IL, MI, MN, WI), Bryan Byrne (N. CA, NV), Brian Cleary (KY, OH, TN, WV), Paul Faulk (NC, SC), Ben Gallo (S. CA, HI), Ed Gustafson (AR, LA, N, TX, OK), Brandon Larson (IA, KS, MO, ND, NE, SD), Steve Leavitt (C. CA, S. CA), John Malzone (CT, MA, ME, NH, NJ, NY, PA, RI, VT), Alan Marr (C. FL, N. FL), Alex Morales (C. FL, N. FL), Bobby Myrick (DC, MD, VA, DE), Scott Ramsay (ID, MT, OR, WA, WY, Canada), Mitch Sokol (AZ, CO, El Paso, Las Vegas, NM, UT), Tyler Willt (S. TX). **Independent League Coordinator/Area Supervisor:** Eric Robinson. **Director, Player Procurement:** Kasey McKeon. **Director, Scouting Operations:** Eddie Longosz. **Special Assistants to the GM:** Steve Arnieri, Chuck Cottier, Mike Cubbage, Michael Daughtry, Dan Jennings, Ron Rizzi, Jay Robertson, Bob Schaefer, Peter Vuckovich, De Jon Watson. **Vice President, Interntaional Operations:** Johnny DiPuglia. **Administrator, DSL Academy/Area Scout:** Alex Rodriguez (Puerto Rico). **Coordinator, Venezuela:** German Robles. **Assistant, Interntional Scouting:** Taisuke Sato. **Interntional Crosscheckers:** Fausto Severino, Modesto Ulloa (Latin America). **International Area Scouts:** Eduardo Cabrera (Colobmia), David Leer (Curacao and Aruba), Pablo Arias, Virgilio De Leon, Carlos Ulloa, Riki Vasquez (Dominican Republic), Miguel Ruiz (Panama), Salvador Donadelli, Juan Indriago, Ronald Morillo, Juan Munoz, Oscar Alvarado (Venezuela).

MEDIA INFORMATION

LOCAL MEDIA INFORMATION

AMERICAN LEAGUE

BALTIMORE ORIOLES
Radio Announcers: Joe Angel, Ben McDonald. **Flagship Station:** WJZ-FM 105.7 The Fan.
TV Announcers: Mike Bordick, Rick Dempsey, Jim Hunter, Jim Palmer, Gary Thorne. **Flagship Station:** Mid-Atlantic Sports Network (MASN).

BOSTON RED SOX
Radio Announcers: Joe Castiglione, Tim Neverett. **Flagship Station:** WEEI (93.7 FM/850 AM).
TV Announcers: Dave O'Brien, Jerry Remy. **Flagship Station:** New England Sports Network (regional cable).

CHICAGO WHITE SOX
Radio Announcers: Ed Farmer, Darrin Jackson, Chris Rongey (pre/post). **Flagship Station:** WLS-AM 890.
TV Announcers: Ken Harrelson, Steve Stone, Jason Benetti. **Flagship Stations:** WGN TV-9, WPWR-TV, Comcast SportsNet Chicago (regional cable).

CLEVELAND INDIANS
Radio Announcers: Tom Hamilton, Jim Rosenhaus. **Flagship Station:** WTAM 1100-AM.
TV Announcers: Rick Manning, Matt Underwood, Andre Knott, Jensen Lewis, Al Pawlowski (Pre/post). **Flagship Station:** SportsTime Ohio.

DETROIT TIGERS
Radio Announcers: Dan Dickerson, Jim Price. **Flagship Station:** WXYT 97.1 FM and AM 1270.
TV Announcers: Mario Impemba, Rod Allen, Kirk Gibson, Craig Monroe, John Keating. **Flagship Station:** FOX Sports Detroit (regional cable).

HOUSTON ASTROS
Radio Announcers: Steve Sparks, Robert Ford. **Spanish:** Alex Trevino, Francisco Romero. **Flagship Stations:** KBME 790-AM, KLAT 1010-AM (Spanish).
TV Announcers: Todd Kalas, Geoff Blum. **Flagship Station:** ROOT Sports Houston.

KANSAS CITY ROYALS
Radio Announcers: Denny Matthews, Steve Physioc, Steve Stewart. **Kansas City Affiliate:** KCSP 610-AM.
TV Announcers: Ryan Lefebvre, Rex Hudler, Joel Goldberg, Jeff Montgomery (pre-game). **Flagship Station:** FOX Sports Kansas City.

LOS ANGELES ANGELS
Radio Announcers: Terry Smith, Mark Langston. **Flagship Station:** AM 830, 1330 KWKW (Spanish).
TV Announcers: Victor Rojas, Mark Gubicza. **Spanish TV Announcers:** Jose Tolentino, Jose Mota, Amaury Pi-Gonzalez. **Flagship TV Station:** Fox Sports West (regional cable).

MINNESOTA TWINS
Radio Announcers: Cory Provus, Dan Gladden. **Radio Network Studio Host:** Kris Atteberry. **Radio Engineer:** Kyle Hammer. Spanish Radio **Play-by-Play:** Alfonso Fernandez. **Spanish Radio Analyst:** Tony Oliva. **Flagship Station:** 1500 ESPN.
TV Announcers: Bert Blyleven, Dick Bremer, Roy Smalley, Jack Morris. **Flagship Station:** Fox Sports North.

NEW YORK YANKEES
Radio Announcers: John Sterling, Suzyn Waldman. **Flagship Station:** WFAN 660-AM, WADO 1280-AM. **Spanish Radio Announcers:** Francisco Rivera, Rickie Ricardo.
TV Announcers: David Cone, Jack Curry, John Flaherty, Michael Kay, Al Leiter, Bob Lorenz, Meredith Marakovits, Paul O'Neill, Ken Singleton. **Flagship Station:** YES Network (Yankees Entertainment & Sports).

OAKLAND ATHLETICS
Radio Announcers: Vince Cotroneo, Ken Korach. **Flagship Station:** KGMZ 95.7 The Game, FM.
TV Announcers: Ray Fosse, Glen Kuiper. **Flagship Stations:** Comcast SportsNet California.

SEATTLE MARINERS
Radio Announcers: Rick Rizzs, Aaron Goldsmith. **Flagship Station:** 710 ESPN Seattle (KIRO-AM 710).
TV Announcers: Mike Blowers, Dave Sims. **Flagship Station:** ROOT Sports Northwest.

TAMPA BAY RAYS
Radio Announcers: Andy Freed, Dave Wills. **Flagship Station:** WDAE 620 AM/95.3 FM Tampa/St. Petersburg **TV Announcers:** Brian Anderson, Dewayne Staats. **Flagship Station:** FOX Sports Sun.

TEXAS RANGERS
Radio Announcers: Eric Nadel, Matt Hicks, Jared Sandler; Spanish-Eleno Ornelas, Jose Guzman. **Flagship Station:** 105.3 The FAN FM, KFLC 1270 AM (Spanish).
TV Announcers: Dave Raymond, Tom Grieve, C.J. Nitkowski, Emily Jones. **Flagship Station:** FOX Sports Southwest (regional cable).

TORONTO BLUE JAYS
Radio Announcers: Jerry Howarth, Joe Siddal, Mike Wilner. **Flagship Station:** SportsNet Radio Fan 590-AM.
TV Announcers: Buck Martinez, Pat Tabler, Dan Shulman. **Flagship Station:** Rogers Sportsnet.

NATIONAL LEAGUE

ARIZONA DIAMONDBACKS
Radio Announcers: Greg Schulte, Tom Candiotti, Mike Ferrin, Rodrigo Lopez (Spanish), Oscar Soria (Spanish), Richard Saenz (Spanish). **Flagship Stations:** Arizona Sports 98.7 FM.
TV Announcers: Steve Berthiaume, Bob Brenly. **Flagship Stations:** FOX Sports Arizona (regional cable).

ATLANTA BRAVES
Radio Announcers: Jim Powell, Don Sutton. **Flagship Stations:** WCNN-AM 680, The Fan (93.7 FM), WYAY-FM (106.7).
TV Announcers: Chip Caray, Joe Simpson, Tom Glavine. **Flagship Stations:** FOX Sports South/Southeast (regional cable).

CHICAGO CUBS
Radio Announcers: Pat Hughes, Ron Coomer. **Flagship Station:** 670 The Score.
TV Announcers: Len Kasper, Jim Deshaies. **Flagship Stations:** CSN Chicago (regional cable), ABC7 Chicago, WGN-TV (OTAs).

CINCINNATI REDS
Radio Announcers: Marty Brennaman, Thom Brennaman, Jeff Brantley, Jim Kelch, Chris Welsh, Doug Flynn. **Flagship Station:** WLW 700-AM.
TV Announcers: Chris Welsh, Jeff Brantley, George Grande. **Flagship Station:** Fox Sports Ohio (regional cable).

COLORADO ROCKIES
Radio Announcers: Jack Corrigan, Jerry Schemmel. **Flagship Station:** KOA 850-AM & 94.1 FM.
TV Announcers: Drew Goodman, Jeff Huson, Ryan Spilborghs.

LOS ANGELES DODGERS
Radio Announcers: Rick Monday, Charley Steiner. **Spanish:** Jaime Jarrín, Jorge Jarrin. **Flagship Stations:** AM570 Fox Sports LA, KTNQ 1020-AM (Spanish).
TV Announcers: Joe Davis, Orel Hershiser, Nomar Garciaparra, Alanna Rizzo, John Hartung, Jerry Hairston, Jr. **Spanish:** Pepe Yniguez, Fernando Valenzuela, Manny Mota. **Flagship Stations:** SportsNet LA (regional cable).

MIAMI MARLINS
Radio Announcers: Dave Van Horne, Glenn Geffner. **Flagship Stations:** WINZ 940-AM, WAQI 710-AM (Spanish).
Spanish Radio Announcers: Felo Ramirez, Yiky Quintana. **Flagship Stations:** FSN Florida (regional cable).

MILWAUKEE BREWERS
Radio Announcers: Bob Uecker, Jeff Levering, Lane Grindle. **Flagship Station:** WTMJ 620-AM.
TV Announcers: Brian Anderson, Bill Schroeder, Matt Lepay. **Flagship Station:** Fox Sports Wisconsin.

NEW YORK METS
Radio Announcers: Howie Rose, Josh Lewin and Wayne Randazzo. **Flagship Station:** WOR 710-AM.
TV Announcers: Gary Cohen, Keith Hernandez, Ron Darling, Steve Gelbs, Nelson Figueroa. **Flagship Stations:** Sports Net New York (regional cable), PIX11-TV.

PHILADELPHIA PHILLIES
Radio Announcers: Scott Franzke, Larry Andersen, Jim Jackson. **Flagship Station:** SportsRadio 94WIP (94.1 FM).
TV Announcers: Tom McCarthy, Ben Davis, John Kruk, Gregg Murphy, Mike Schmidt. **Flagship Stations:** CSNPhilly, NBC 10.

PITTSBURGH PIRATES
Radio Announcers: Joe Block, Steve Blass, Greg Brown, Bob Walk, John Wehner. **Flagship Station:** Sports Radio 93.7 FM The Fan.
TV Announcers: Joe Block, Steve Blass, Greg Brown, Bob Walk, John Wehner. **Flagship Station:** ROOT SPORTS (regional cable).

ST. LOUIS CARDINALS
Radio Announcers: Mike Shannon, John Rooney, Ricky Horton. **Flagship Station:** KMOX 1120 AM.
TV Announcers: Jim Edmonds, Ricky Horton, Al Hrabosky, Tim McCarver, Dan McLaughlin, John Claiborne. **Flagship Station:** Fox Sports Midwest.

SAN DIEGO PADRES
Radio Announcers: Ted Leitner and Jesse Agler. **Flagship Stations:** Entercom FM 949.
TV Announcers: Don Orsillo, Mark Grant. **Flagship Station:** Fox Sports San Diego. **Spanish Announcers:** Eduardo Ortega, Carlos Hernandez on XEMO-860-AM.

SAN FRANCISCO GIANTS
Radio Announcers: Mike Krukow, Duane Kuiper, Jon Miller, Dave Flemming.
Spanish: Tito Fuentes, Edwin Higueros. **Flagship Station:** KNBR 680-AM (English); ESPN Deportes-860AM (Spanish).
TV Announcers: CSN Bay Area—Mike Krukow, Duane Kuiper; **KNTV-NBC 11**—Jon Miller, Mike Krukow. **Flagship Stations:** KNTV-NBC 11, CSN Bay Area (regional cable).

WASHINGTON NATIONALS
Radio Announcers: Charlie Slowes, Dave Jageler. **Flagship Station:** WJFK 106.7 FM.
TV Announcers: Bob Carpenter, FP Santangelo, Dan Kolko. **Flagship Station:** Mid-Atlantic Sports Network (MASN).

NATIONAL MEDIA INFORMATION

BASEBALL STATISTICS

ELIAS SPORTS BUREAU INC. NATIONAL MEDIA BASEBALL STATISTICS

Official Major League Statistician Mailing Address: 500 Fifth Ave., Suite 2140, New York, NY 10110. **Telephone:** (212) 869-1530. **Fax:** (212) 354-0980. **Website:** www.esb.com.

President: Seymour Siwoff.

Executive Vice President: Steve Hirdt. **Vice President:** Chris Thorn.

MLB ADVANCED MEDIA

Official Minor League Statistician Mailing Address: 75 Ninth Ave., New York, NY 10011. **Telephone:** (212) 485-3444. **Fax:** (212) 485-3456. **Website:** MiLB.com.

Director, Stats: Chris Lentine. **Senior Manager, Stats:** Shawn Geraghty.

Senior Stats Supervisors: Jason Rigatti, Ian Schwartz. **Stats Supervisors:** Lawrence Fischer, Jake Fox, Dominic French, Kelvin Lee.

MILB.COM OFFICIAL WEBSITE OF MINOR LEAGUE BASEBALL

Mailing Address: 75 Ninth Ave, New York, NY 10011. **Telephone:** (212) 485-3444. **Fax:** (212) 485-3456. **Website:** MiLB.com.

Director, Minor League Club Initiatives: Nathan Blackmon. **Managing Producer, MiLB.com:** Brendon Desrochers.

STATS LLC

Mailing Address: 203 N. LaSalle St. Chicago, IL, 60601. **Telephone:** (847) 583-2100. **Fax:** (847) 470-9140. **Website:** www.stats.com. **Email:** sales@stats.com. **Twitter:** @STATSBiznews; @STATS_MLB. **CEO:** Ken Fuchs. **Chief Operating Officer:** Robert Schur. **EVP, Global Sales & Marketing:** Greg Kirkorsky. **SVP, Products:** Jim Corelis. **VP, Marketing:** Kirsten Porter. **Associate Vice President, Data Operations:** Allan Spear. **Manager, Baseball Operations:** Jeff Chernow

GENERAL INFORMATION

SCOUTING

MAJOR LEAGUE BASEBALL SCOUTING BUREAU
Mailing Address: 245 Park Avenue, 34th Floor, New York, NY 10167
Year Founded: 1974.
Senior Director: Bill Bavasi. **Director:** Bob Fontaine.
Scouting Coordinators: William Clements, Diego Delgado.
Scouts: Tom Burns (Harrisburg, PA); Dan Dixon (Temecula, CA); Rusty Gerhardt (New London, TX); Chris Heidt (Rockford, IL); Harry Shelton (Ocoee, FL); Robin Wallace (MA); Ila Borders (Portland, OR).
Video Scouts: Leon De Winter (Phoenix, AZ); Ryan Lakey (Dallas, TX); Mark Nader (Orlando, FL); Christie Wood (Raleigh, NC).
Latin America Scouts: Henry Gonzalez (DR—Latin America Supervisor); Julio Cordido (VZ Coordinator); Christian Reyes (DR Coordinator); Michael Cruz (Video—DR); Eduardo Perez (DR); Wilson Peralta (DR); Abraham Despradel (DR).

PROFESSIONAL BASEBALL SCOUTS FOUNDATION
Mailing Address: 3914 Corte Cancion, Thousand Oaks, CA 91360. **Telephone:** (818) 224-3906 / **Fax** (805) 378-7126. **Email:** cindy.pbsf@yahoo.com. **Website:** www.pbsfonline.com.
Chairman: Dennis J. Gilbert. **Executive Director:** Cindy Picerni. **Board of Directors:** Bill "Chief" Gayton, Pat Gillick, Derrick Hall, Roland Hemond, Gary Hughes, Jeff Idelson, Dan Jennings, JJ Lally, Tommy Lasorda, Frank Marcos, Roberta Mazur, Bob Nightengale, Damon Oppenheimer, Jared Porter, Tracy Ringolsby, John Scotti, Dale Sutherland, Dave Yoakum.

SCOUT OF THE YEAR FOUNDATION
Mailing Address: P.O. Box 211585, West Palm Beach, FL 33421. **Telephone:** (561) 798-5897, (561) 818-4329. **E-mail Address:** bertmazur@aol.com.
President: Roberta Mazur. **Vice President:** Tracy Ringolsby. **Treasurer:** Ron Mazur II. **Board of Advisers:** Pat Gillick, Roland Hemond, Gary Hughes, Tommy Lasorda. **Scout of the Year Program Advisory Board:** Tony DeMacio, Joe Klein, Roland Hemond, Gary Hughes, Dan Jennings, Linda Pereira.

UMPIRES

JIM EVANS ACADEMY
Mailing Address: 200 South Wilcox St., #508, Castle Rock, CO 80104. **Telephone:** (303) 290-7411. **E-mail Address:** jim@umpireacademy.com. **Website:** www.umpireacademy.com.
Operator: Jim Evans.

MINOR LEAGUE BASEBALL UMPIRE TRAINING ACADEMY
Mailing Address: P.O. Box A, St. Petersburg, FL, 33731-1950. **Telephone:** (877) 799-UMPS. **Fax:** (727) 456-1745. **Email:** info@MiLBUmpireAcademy.com. **Website:** www.MiLBUmpireAcademy.com
Director: Dusty Dellinger. **Chief of Instruction:** Mike Felt. **Curriculum Coordinator:** Larry Reveal. **Lead Rules Instructor:** Jorge Bauza. **Lead Field Instructor:** Darren Spagnardi. **Lead Cage Instructor:** Tyler Funneman. **Classroom Instructor:** Brian Sinclair. **Field Instructor:** Jay Pierce. **Medical Coordinator:** Mark Stubblefield. **Administrator:** Andy Shultz.

MINOR LEAGUE BASEBALL UMPIRE DEVELOPMENT
Street Address: 9550 16th Street North, St Petersburg, FL 33716. **Mailing Address:** P.O. Box A, St. Petersburg, FL 33731-1950. **Telephone:** (727) 822-6937. **Fax:** (727) 821-5819.
President/CEO: Pat O'Conner. **Secretary/VP, Legal Affairs/General Counsel:** D. Scott Poley. **Director, Umpire Development:** Dusty Dellinger. **Chief, Instruction/Umpire Development Evaluator:** Mike Felt. **Field Evaluators/Instructors:** Jorge Bauza, Tyler Funneman, Larry Reveal, Darren Spagnardi, Brian Sinclair and Mark Lollo. **Medical Coordinator:** Mark Stubblefield. **Special Assistant, Umpire Development:** Lillian Patterson.

WENDELSTEDT UMPIRE SCHOOL
Mailing Address: P.O. Box 1079 Albion, MI, 49224. **Telephone:** 800-818-1690. **Fax:** 888-881-9801. **Email Address:** admin@umpireschool.com. **Website:** www.umpireschool.com.

WORLD UMPIRES ASSOCIATION
Year Founded: 2000.
President: Joe West. **Vice President:** Fieldin Culbreth. **Secretary/Treasurer:** Jim Reynolds. **Governing Board:** Dan Bellino, Dan Iassogna, Jeff Kellogg, Bill Miller, Tim Timmons, Bill Welke. **Labor Counsel:** TBA. **Administrator:** Phil Janssen.

TRAINERS

PROFESSIONAL BASEBALL ATHLETIC TRAINERS SOCIETY
Mailing Address: 1201 Peachtree St., 400 Colony Square, Suite 1750, Atlanta, GA 30361. **Telephone:** (404) 875-4000, ext. 1. **Fax:** (404) 892-8560. **E-mail Address:** rmallernee@mallernee-branch.com or sam@theromanogroup.com. **Website:** www.pbats.com
Year Founded: 1983
President: Mark O'Neal (Chicago Cubs). **Secretary:** Ron Porterfield (Tampa Bay Rays). **Treasurer:** Tom Probst

(Colorado Rockies). **American League Head Athletic Trainer Representative:** Nick Kenney (Kansas City Royals). **American League Assistant Athletic Trainer Representative:** Brian Ball. (Chicago White Sox). **National League Head Athletic Trainer Representative:** Keith Dugger (Colorado Rockies). **National League Assistant Athletic Trainer Representative:** Ben Potenziano (Pittsburgh Pirates). **Immediate Past President:** Richie Bancells (Baltimore Orioles). **General Counsel:** Rollin Mallernee II. **Communications and Public Relations:** Neil Romano.

MUSEUMS

BABE RUTH BIRTHPLACE
Office Address: 216 Emory St., Baltimore, MD 21230. **Telephone:** (410) 727-1539. **Fax:** (410) 727-1652. **E-mail Address:** info@baberuthmuseum.org. **Website:** www.baberuthmuseum.org.
Year Founded: 1973.
Executive Director: Shawn Herne. **Director Emeritus:** Mike Gibbons. **Communications:** Cathy Zaorski.
Fall/Winter Hours: Museum open Tuesday-Sunday, 10 a.m. to 5 p.m. **Closed:** New Year's Day, Thanksgiving and Christmas. **Spring/Summer Hours:** Museum open Monday-Sunday, 10 a.m. to 5 p.m. Open until 7 on Oriole Night Game Days

CANADIAN BASEBALL HALL OF FAME AND MUSEUM
Museum Address: 386 Church St. South, St. Marys, Ontario N4X 1C2. **Mailing Address:** P.O. Box 1838, St. Marys, Ontario N4X 1C2. **Telephone:** (519) 284-1838. **Fax:** (519) 284-1234. **E-mail Address:** baseball@baseballhalloffame.ca. **Website:** www.baseballhalloffame.ca.
Year Founded: 1983.
Director Operations: Scott Crawford.
Hours: May (weekends only) Saturday 10:30-4:00; Sunday noon-4:00. **June 1-Aug. 31:** Monday-Saturday, 10:30-4:00; Sunday, noon-4:00. **Sept. 1-Oct. 8:** Thursday-Saturday 10:30-4:00; Sunday noon-4:00.

FIELD OF DREAMS MOVIE SITE
Address: 28995 Lansing Rd., Dyersville, IA, 52040. **Mailing Address:** PO Box 300 Dyersville, IA 52040. **Telephone:** (563) 875-8404; (888) 875-8404. **Fax:** (888-519-2254). **E-mail Address:** info@fodmoviesite.com. **Website:** www.fodmoviesite.com.
Year Founded: 1989.
Gift Shop Office/Business Manager: Betty Boeckenstedt. **Hours:** April-November, 9 a.m.-6 p.m.

WORLD OF LITTLE LEAGUE: PETER J. MCGOVERN MUSEUM AND OFFICIAL STORE
Office Address: 525 US 15, South Williamsport, PA 17702. **Mailing Address:** P.O. Box 3485, Williamsport, PA 17701. **Telephone:** (570) 326-3607. **Fax:** (570) 326-2267. **E-mail Address:** museum@littleleague.org. **Website:** www. LittleLeagueMuseum.org. **Facebook:** LittleLeagueMuseum
Year Founded: 1982.
Vice President/Executive Director: Lance Van Auken. **Director, Public Programming/Outreach:** Janice Ogurcak. **Curator:** Adam Thompson.
Museum Hours: Open 9 a.m. to 5 p.m., Monday-Sunday. **Closed:** Easter, Thanksgiving, Dec. 24, 25, 31 and New Year's Day

LOUISVILLE SLUGGER MUSEUM AND FACTORY
Office Address: 800 W. Main St., Louisville, KY 40202. **Telephone:** (502) 588-7228, (877) 775-8443. **Fax:** (502) 585-1179. **Website:** www.sluggermuseum.com.
Year Founded: 1996.
Executive Director: Anne Jewell.
Museum Hours: Jan. 1-June 30/Aug. 10-Dec. 31: Mon-Sat 9 a.m.-5 p.m., Sun. 11 a.m.-5 p.m.; **July 1-Aug. 9:** Sun-Thurs 9 a.m.-6 p.m., Fri-Sat 9 a.m.-8 p.m. **Closed:** Thanksgiving/Christmas Day.

NATIONAL BASEBALL HALL OF FAME AND MUSEUM
Address: 25 Main St., Cooperstown, NY 13326. **Telephone:** (888) 425-5633, (607) 547-7200. **Fax:** (607) 547-2044. **E-mail Address:** info@baseballhall.org. **Website:** www.baseballhall.org.
Year Founded: 1939.
Chairman: Jane Forbes Clark. **Vice Chairman:** Joe Morgan. **President:** Jeff Idelson.
Museum Hours: Open daily, year-round, closed only Thanksgiving, Christmas and New Year's Day. 9 a.m.-5 p.m. Summer hours, 9 a.m.-9 p.m. (Memorial Day weekend through the day before Labor Day.)
2015 Hall of Fame Induction Weekend: July 28-31, Cooperstown, NY.

NEGRO LEAGUES BASEBALL MUSEUM
Mailing Address: 1616 E. 18th St., Kansas City, MO 64108. **Telephone:** (816) 221-1920. **Fax:** (816) 221-8424. **E-mail Address:** bkendrick@nlbm.com. **Website:** www.nlbm.com.
Year Founded: 1990.
President: Bob Kendrick. **Executive Director Emeritus:** Don Motley.
Museum Hours: Tues.-Sat. 9 a.m.-6 p.m.; Sun. noon-6 p.m.

RESEARCH

SOCIETY FOR AMERICAN BASEBALL RESEARCH
Mailing Address: Cronkite School at ASU, 555 N Central Ave., #416 , Phoenix, AZ 85004. **Website:** www.sabr.org.
Year Founded: 1971.
President: Vince Gennaro. **Vice President:** Leslie Heaphy. **Secretary:** Todd Lebowitz. **Treasurer:** F.X. Flinn. **Directors:** Bill Nowlin, Ty Waterman, Chris Dial, Emily Hawks. **CEO:** Marc Appleman. **Director of Editorial Content:** Jacob Pomrenke.

ALUMNI ASSOCIATIONS

MAJOR LEAGUE BASEBALL PLAYERS ALUMNI ASSOCIATION
Mailing Address: 1631 Mesa Ave., Copper Building, Suite D, Colorado Springs, CO 80906. **Telephone:** (719) 477-1870. **Fax:** (719) 477-1875. **E-mail Address:** postoffice@mlbpaa.com. **Website:** www.baseballalumni.com. **Facebook:** facebook.com/majorleaguebaseballplayersalumniassociation. **Twitter:** @MLBPAA.
Chief Executive Officer: Dan Foster (dan@mlbpaa.com). **Chief Operating Officer:** Geoffrey Hixson (geoff@mlbpaa.com). **Vice President, Operations:** Mike Groll (mikeg@mlbpaa.com). **Director, Communications:** Nikki Warner (nikki @mlbpaa.com). **Director, Membership:** Kate Hutchinson (Kate@mlbpaa.com). **Director, Memorabilia:** Greg Thomas (greg@mlbpaa.com). **Database Administrator:** Chris Burkeen (cburkeen@mlbpaa.com)

MAJOR LEAGUE ALUMNI MARKETING
Chief Executive Officer: Dan Foster (dan@mlbpaa.com). **Chief Operating Officer:** Geoffrey Hixson (geoff@mlbpaa.com). **Vice President, Legends Entertainment Group:** Chris Torgusen (chris@mlbpaa.com). **Vice President of Operations:** Mike Groll (mikeg@mlbpaa.com). **Marketing Coordinator, Legends Entertainment Group:** Ryan Thomas (rthomas@mlbpaa.com). **Director of New Business Development:** Pete Kelly (pete@mlbpaa.com). **Sales Manager:** Amy Wagner (Amy@mlbpaa.com).

MINOR LEAGUE BASEBALL ALUMNI ASSOCIATION
Mailing Address: P.O. Box A, St. Petersburg, FL 33731-1950. **Telephone:** (727) 822-6937. **Fax:** (727) 821-5819. **E-Mail Address:** alumni@MiLB.com. **Website:** www.milb.com.

BASEBALL ASSISTANCE TEAM (B.A.T.)
Mailing Address: 245 Park Ave., 31st Floor, New York, NY 10167. **Telephone:** (212) 931-7822, **Fax:** (212) 949-5433. **Website:** www.baseballassistanceteam.com.
Year Founded: 1986.
To Make a Donation: (866) 605-4594.
President: Randy Winn. **Vice President:** Bob Watson. **Board of Directors:** Sal Bando, Dick Freeman, Steve Garvey, Luis Gonzalez, Raul Ibanez, Adam Jones, Mark Letendre, Diane Margolin, Buck Martinez, Alan Nahmias, Christine O'Reilly, Staci Slaughter, Gary Thorne, Bob Watson, Greg Wilcox, Randy Winn. **Director:** Erik Nilsen. **Secretary:** Thomas Ostertag. **Treasurer:** Scott Stamp. **Advisor:** Laurel Prieb. **Consultant:** Sam McDowell. **Consultant:** Tim McDowell. **Consultant:** Dr. Genoveva Javier. **Consultant:** Benny Ayala. **Operations:** Vladimir Cruz, Michelle Fucich.

ASSOCIATION OF PROFESSIONAL BALL PLAYERS OF AMERICA
Address: 101 S. Kraemer Blvd., Suite 112 Placentia, CA 92870. **Phone:** 714-528-2012. **Fax:** 714-528-2037. **Website:** www.apbpa.org. **E-mail:** ballplayersassn@aol.com
President: Jim Rantz. **1st Vice President:** Del Crandall. **2nd Vice President:** Marti Wolever. **Secretary-Treasurer:** Dick Beverage. **Directors:** Dusty Baker, Tony LaRussa, Bobby Grich, Brooks Robinson, Ryne Sandberg, Tom Lasorda Wes Parker, Cal Ripken Jr., Nolan Ryan, Mike Scioscia. **Advisory Council:** Jay Johnstone, Tal Smith, Chuck Stevens. **Membership Services Manager:** Patty Joost (patty@apbpa.org)

MINISTRY

BASEBALL CHAPEL
Mailing Address: P.O. Box 10102, Largo FL 33773. **Telephone:** (610) 999-3600. **E-mail Address:** office@baseballchapel.org. **Website:** www.baseballchapel.org.
Year Founded: 1973.
President: Vince Nauss. **Hispanic Ministry:** Cali Magallanes, Gio Llerena. **Ministry Operations:** Rob Crose, Steve Sisco. **Board of Directors:** Don Christensen, Greg Groh, Dave Howard, Vince Nauss, Walt Wiley.

CATHOLIC ATHLETES FOR CHRIST
Mailing Address: 3703 Cameron Mills Road, Alexandria, VA 22305. **Telephone:** (703) 239-3070. **E-mail Address:** info@catholicathletesforchrist.org. **Website:** www.catholicathletesforchrist.org.
Year Founded: 2006.
President: Ray McKenna. **MLB Ministry Coordinator:** Kevin O'Malley. **MLB Athlete Advisory Board Members:** Mike Sweeney (Chairman), Jeff Suppan (Vice Chairman), Sal Bando, Tom Carroll, David Eckstein, Tyler Flowers, Terry Kennedy, Jack McKeon, Darrell Miller, Mike Piazza, Vinny Rottino, Craig Stammen, Trevor Williams.

TRADE/EMPLOYMENT

BASEBALL WINTER MEETINGS
Mailing Address: P.O. Box A, St. Petersburg, FL 33731. **Telephone:** (727) 822-6937. **Fax:** (727) 821-5819. **E-Mail Address:** BaseballWinterMeetings@milb.com. **Website:** www.baseballwintermeetings.com.
2018 Convention: Dec. 9-13, Mandalay Bay Hotel, Las Vegas, NV.

BASEBALL TRADE SHOW
Mailing Address: P.O. Box A, St. Petersburg, FL 33731-1950. **Telephone:** (866) 926-6452. **Fax:** (727) 683-9865. **E-Mail Address:** TradeShow@MiLB.com. **Website:** www.BaseballTradeShow.com. **Contact:** Noreen Brantner, Sr. Asst. Director, Exhibition Services & Sponsorships.
2018 Convention: Dec. 9-13, Mandalay Bay Hotel, Las Vegas, NV.

PROFESSIONAL BASEBALL EMPLOYMENT OPPORTUNITIES
Mailing Address: P.O. Box A, St. Petersburg, FL 33731-1950. **Telephone:** 866-WE-R-PBEO. **Fax:** 727-821-5819. **Website:** www.PBEO.com. **Email:** info@PBEO.com. **Contact:** Mark Labban, Manager, Business Development.

BASEBALL CARD MANUFACTURERS

PANINI AMERICA INC.
Mailing Address: Panini America, 5325 FAA Blvd., Suite 100, Irving TX 75061. **Telephone:** (817) 662-5300, (800) 852-8833. **Website:** www.paniniamerica.net. **Email:** RM_Marketing@paniniamerica.net. **Marketing Manager:** Scott Prusha.

GRANDSTAND CARDS
Mailing Address: 23007 Ventura Blvd.,, Woodland Hills, CA 91364. **Telephone:** (818) 992-5642. **Fax:** (818) 348-9122. **E-mail Address:** gscards1@pacbell.net.

TOPPS
Mailing Address: One Whitehall St., New York, NY 10004. **Telephone:** (212) 376-0300. **Fax:** (212) 376-0573. **Website:** www.topps.com.

UPPER DECK
Mailing Address: 5830 El Camino Real, Carlsbad, CA 92008. **Telephone:** (800) 873-7332. **Fax:** (760) 929-3142. **E-mail Address:** qa@upperdeck.com. **Website:** www.upperdeck.com.

REVIVING BASEBALL IN INNER CITIES
Mailing Address: 245 Park Avenue 30th Fl, New York, NY 10167
Telephone: (212) 931-7800. **Fax:** (212) 949-5695
Year Founded: 1989
Senior Vice President, Youth Programs: Tony Reagins (Tony.Reagins@mlb.com). **Vice President, Youth Programs:** David James (David.James@mlb.com). **E-mail-** rbi@mlb.com. **Website:** www.mlb.com/rbi

MLB YOUTH ACADEMIES

CINCINNATI REDS YOUTH ACADEMY
Director: Jerome Wright
Asst. Director: Jeremy Hamilton
Mailing Address: 2026 E. Seymour Avenue. Cincinnati , OH 45327
Phone Number: 513-765-5000

COMPTON YOUTH ACADEMY
Vice President: Darrell Miller
Mailing Address: 901 East Artesia Blvd. Compton, CA

HOUSTON ASTROS YOUTH ACADEMY
Director: Daryl Wade
Mailing Address: 2801 South Victory Drive. Houston, TX 77088

KANSAS CITY ROYALS URBAN YOUTH ACADEMY
Director: Darwin Pennye
Email: Darwin.Pennye@royals.com

NEW ORLEANS YOUTH ACADEMY
Director: Eddie Anthony Davis III
Mailing Address: 6403 Press Drive. New Orleans, LA 70126
Phone Number: 504-282-0443

PHILADELPHIA YOUTH ACADEMY
Director: Jon Joaquin
Phone Number: 215-218-5634
Director: Rob Holiday
Phone Number: 215-218-5204

PUERTO RICO BASEBALL ACADEMY AND HIGH SCHOOL

Director: Luis Cintron
Phone Number: 787-712-0700
Lucy Batista: Headmaster
Phone Number: 787-531-1768

TEXAS RANGERS YOUTH ACADEMY

Director: Karin Morris
Mailing Address: 3500 Goldman Street. Dallas, TX 75212
Phone Number: 817-273-5297

WASHINGTON NATIONALS YOUTH ACADEMY

Executive Director: Tal Alter
Mailing Address: 3675 Ely Place SE. Washington, DC 20019
Phone Number: 202-827-8960

SPRING TRAINING

CACTUS LEAGUE

For spring training schedules, see page 216

ARIZONA DIAMONDBACKS

MAJOR LEAGUE
Complex Address: Salt River Fields at Talking Stick, 7555 North Pima Road, Scottsdale, AZ 85256. **Telephone:** (480) 270-5000. **Seating Capacity:** 11,000 (7,000 fixed seats, 4,000 lawn seats). **Location:** From Loop-101, use exit 44 (Indian Bend Road) and proceed west for approximately one-half mile; turn right at Pima Road to travel north and proceed one-quarter mile; three entrances to Salt River Fields will be available on the right-hand side.

MINOR LEAGUE
Complex Address: Same as major league club.

CHICAGO CUBS

MAJOR LEAGUE
Complex Address: Sloan Park, 2330 West Rio Salado Parkway, Mesa, AZ 85201. **Telephone:** (480) 668-0500. **Seating Capacity:** 15,000. **Location:** on the land of the former Riverview Golf Course, bordered by the 101 and 202 interchange in Mesa.

MINOR LEAGUE
Complex Address: 2510 W. Rio Salado Parkway, Mesa, AZ 85201. **Telephone:** (480) 668-0500

CHICAGO WHITE SOX

MAJOR LEAGUE
Complex Address: Camelback Ranch-Glendale, 10710 West Camelback Road, Phoenix, AZ 85037. **Telephone:** (623) 302-5000. **Seating Capacity:** 13,000. **Hotel Address:** Residence Inn Phoenix Glendale Sports and Entertainment District, 7350 N Zanjero Blvd, Glendale, AZ 85305, **Telephone:** (623) 772-8900. **Hotel Address:** Renaissance Glendale Hotel & Spa, 9495 W Coyotes Blvd, Glendale, AZ 85305. **Telephone:** 629-937-3700.

MINOR LEAGUE
Complex/Hotel Address: Same as major league club.

CINCINNATI REDS

MAJOR LEAGUE
Complex Address: Cincinnati Reds Player Development Complex, 3125 S Wood Blvd, Goodyear, AZ 85338. **Telephone:** (623) 932-6590. **Ballpark Address:** Goodyear Ballpark, 1933 S Ballpark Way, Goodyear, AZ 85338. **Telephone:** (623) 882-3120. **Hotel Address:** Marriott Residence Inn, 7350 N Zanjero Blvd, Glendale, AZ 85305. **Telephone:** (623) 772-8900. **Fax:** (623) 772-8905.

MINOR LEAGUE
Complex/Hotel Address: Same as major league club.

CLEVELAND INDIANS

MAJOR LEAGUE
Complex Address: Cleveland Indians Player Development Complex 2601 S Wood Blvd, Goodyear, AZ 85338; Goodyear Ballpark 1933 S Ballpark Way, Goodyear, AZ 85338. **Telephone:** (623) 882-3120. **Location: From Downtown Phoenix/East Valley:** West on I-10 to Exit 127, Bullard Avenue and proceed south (left off exit), Bullard Avenue turns into West Lower Buckeye Road. Turn left onto Wood Blvd. **Hotel Address:** (Media) Hampton Inn and Suites, 2000 N Litchfield Rd, Goodyear, AZ 85395. **Telephone:** (623) 536-1313. **Hotel Address:** Holiday Inn Express, 1313 N Litchfield Rd, Goodyear, AZ 85395. **Telephone:** (623) 535-1313. **Hotel Address:** TownePlace Suites, 13971 West Celebrate Life Way, Goodyear, AZ 85338. **Telephone:** (623) 535-5009. **Hotel Address:** Residence Inn by Marriott, 2020 N Litchfield Rd, Goodyear, AZ 85395. **Telephone:** (623) 866-1313.

MINOR LEAGUE
Complex Address: Same as major league club.

COLORADO ROCKIES

MAJOR LEAGUE
Complex Address: Salt River Fields at Talking Stick, 7555 North Pima Rd, Scottsdale, AZ 85258. **Telephone:** (480) 270-5800. **Seating Capacity:** 11,000 (7,000 fixed seats, 4,000 lawn seats). **Location:** From Loop-101, use exit 44 (Indian Bend Road Talking Stick Way) and proceed west for approximately one-half mile; turn right at Pima Road to travel north and proceed one-quarter mile; three entrances to Salt River Fields will be available on the right-hand side. **Visiting Team Hotel:** The Scottsdale Plaza Resort, 7200 North Scottsdale Road, Scottsdale, AZ 85253. **Telephone:** (480) 948-5000. **Fax:** (480) 951-5100.

MINOR LEAGUE
Complex/Hotel Address: Same as major league club.

KANSAS CITY ROYALS

MAJOR LEAGUE
Complex Address: Surprise Stadium, 15850 North Bullard Ave, Surprise, AZ 85374. **Telephone:** (623) 222-2000. **Seating Capacity:** 10,700. **Location:** I-10 West to Route 101 North, 101 North to Bell Road, left on Bell for five miles, stadium on left. **Hotel Address:** Wigwam Resort, 300 East Wigwam Blvd, Litchfield Park, Arizona 85340. **Telephone:** (623) 935-3811.

MINOR LEAGUE
Complex Address: Same as major league club. **Hotel Address:** Comfort Hotel and Suites, 13337 W Grand Ave, Surprise, AZ 85374. **Telephone:** (623) 583-3500.

LOS ANGELES ANGELS

MAJOR LEAGUE
Complex Address: Tempe Diablo Stadium, 2200 West Alameda Drive, Tempe, AZ 85282. **Telephone:** (480) 858-7500. **Fax:** (480) 438-7583. **Seating Capacity:** 9,558. **Location:** I-10 to exit 153B (48th Street), south one mile on 48th Street to Alameda Drive, left on Alameda.

MINOR LEAGUE
Complex Address: Tempe Diablo Minor League Complex, 2225 W Westcourt Way, Tempe, AZ 85282. **Telephone:** (480) 858-7558.

LOS ANGELES DODGERS

MAJOR LEAGUE

Complex Address: Camelback Ranch, 10710 West Camelback Rd, Phoenix, AZ 85037. **Seating Capacity:** 13,000, plus standing room. **Location:** I-10 or I-17 to Loop 101 West or North, Take Exit 5, Camelback Road West to ballpark. **Telephone:** (623) 302-5000. **Hotel:** Unavailable.

MINOR LEAGUE

Complex/Hotel Address: Same as major league club.

MILWAUKEE BREWERS

MAJOR LEAGUE

Complex Address: Maryvale Baseball Park, 3600 N 51st Ave, Phoenix, AZ 85031. **Telephone:** (623) 245-5555. **Seating Capacity:** 9,000. **Location:** I-10 to 51st Ave, north on 51st Ave. **Hotel Address:** Unavailable.

MINOR LEAGUE

Complex Address: Maryvale Baseball Complex, 3805 N 53rd Ave, Phoenix, AZ 85031. **Telephone:** (623) 245-5600. **Hotel Address:** Unavailable.

OAKLAND ATHLETICS

MAJOR LEAGUE

Complex Address: Hohokam Stadium, 1235 North Center Street, Mesa, AZ 85201. **Telephone:** 480-907-5489. **Seating Capacity:** 10,000.

MINOR LEAGUE

Complex Address: Fitch Park, 160 East 6th Place, Mesa, AZ 85201. **Telephone:** 480-387-5800. **Hotel Address:** Unavailable.

SAN DIEGO PADRES

MAJOR LEAGUE

Complex Address: Peoria Sports Complex, 8131 West Paradise Lane, Peoria, AZ 85382. **Telephone:** (619) 795-5720. **Fax:** (623) 486-7154. **Seating Capacity:** 12,000. **Location:** I-17 to Bell Road exit, west on Bell to 83rd Ave. **Hotel Address:** La Quinta Inn & Suites (623) 487-1900, 16321 N 83rd Avenue, Peoria, AZ 85382.

MINOR LEAGUE

Complex/Hotel: Country Inn and Suites (623) 879-9000, 20221 N 29th Avenue, Phoenix, AZ 85027.

SAN FRANCISCO GIANTS

MAJOR LEAGUE

Complex Address: Scottsdale Stadium, 7408 East Osborn Rd, Scottsdale, AZ 85251. **Telephone:** (480) 990-7972. **Fax:** (480) 990-2643. **Seating Capacity:** 11,500. **Location:** Scottsdale Road to Osborne Road, east on Osborne for a 1/2 mile. **Hotel Address:** Hilton Garden Inn Scottsdale Old Town, 7324 East Indian School Rd, Scottsdale, AZ 85251. **Telephone:** (480) 481-0400.

MINOR LEAGUE

Complex Address: Giants Minor League Complex 8045 E Camelback Road, Scottsdale, AZ 85251. **Telephone:** (480) 990-0052. **Fax:** (480) 990-2349.

SEATTLE MARINERS

MAJOR LEAGUE

Complex Address: Seattle Mariners, 15707 North 83rd Street, Peoria, AZ 85382. **Telephone:** (623) 776-4800. **Seating Capacity:** 12,339. **Location:** Hwy 101 to Bell Road exit, east on Bell to 83rd Ave, south on 83rd Ave. **Hotel Address:** La Quinta Inn & Suites, 16321 N 83rd Ave, Peoria, AZ 85382. **Telephone:** (623) 487-1900.

MINOR LEAGUE

Complex Address: Peoria Sports Complex (1993), 15707 N 83rd Ave, Peoria, AZ 85382. **Telephone:** (623) 776-4800. **Fax:** (623) 776-4828. **Hotel Address:** Hampton Inn, 8408 W Paradise Lane, Peoria, AZ 85382. **Telephone:** (623) 486-9918.

TEXAS RANGERS

MAJOR LEAGUE

Complex Address: Surprise Stadium, 15754 North Bullard Ave, Surprise, AZ 85374. **Telephone:** (623) 266-8100. **Seating Capacity:** 10,714. **Location:** I-10 West to Route 101 North, 101 North to Bell Road, left at Bell for seven miles, stadium on left. **Hotel Address:** Residence Inn Surprise, 16418 N Bullard Ave, Surprise, AZ 85374. **Telephone:** (623) 249-6333.

MINOR LEAGUE

Complex Address: Same as major league club. **Hotel Address:** Holiday Inn Express and Suites Surprise, 16549 North Bullard Ave, Surprise AZ 85374. **Telephone:** (800) 939-4249.

GRAPEFRUIT LEAGUE

For spring training schedules, see page 216

ATLANTA BRAVES

MAJOR LEAGUE

Stadium Address: Champion Stadium at ESPN Wide World of Sports Complex, 700 S Victory Way, Kissimmee, FL 34747. **Telephone:** (407) 939-1500. **Seating Capacity:** 9,500. **Location:** I-4 to exit 25B (Highway 192 West), follow signs to Magic Kingdom/Wide World of Sports Complex, right on Victory Way. **Hotel Address:** World Center Marriott, World Center Drive, Orlando, FL 32821. **Telephone:** (407) 239-4200.

MINOR LEAGUE

Complex Address: Same as major league club. **Telephone:** (407) 939-2232. **Fax:** (407) 939-2225. **Hotel Address:** Marriot Village at Lake Buena Vista, 8623 Vineland Ave, Orlando, FL 32821. **Telephone:** (407) 938-9001.

BALTIMORE ORIOLES

MAJOR LEAGUE

Complex Address: Ed Smith Stadium, 2700 12th Street, Sarasota, FL 34237. **Telephone:** (941) 893-6300. **Fax:** (941) 893-6377. **Seating Capacity:** 7,500. **Location:** I-75 to exit 210, West on Fruitville Road, right on Tuttle Avenue.

MINOR LEAGUE

Complex Address: Buck O'Neil Baseball Complex at Twin Lakes Park, 6700 Clark Rd, Sarasota, FL 34241. **Telephone:** (941) 923-1996.

BOSTON RED SOX

MAJOR LEAGUE

Complex Address: JetBlue Park at Fenway South, 11500 Fenway South Drive, Fort Myers, FL 33913. **Telephone:** (239) 334-4700. **Directions: From the North:** Take I-75 South to Exit 131 (Daniels Parkway); Make a left off the exit and go east for approximately two miles; JetBlue Park will be on your left. **From the South:** Take I-75 North to Exit 131 (Daniels Parkway); Make a right off exit and go east for approximately two miles; JetBlue Park will be on your left.

MINOR LEAGUE

Complex/Hotel Address: Fenway South, 11500 Fenway South Drive, Fort Myers, FL 33913.

DETROIT TIGERS

MAJOR LEAGUE

Complex Address: Joker Marchant Stadium, 2301 Lakeland Hills Blvd, Lakeland, FL 33805. **Telephone:** (863) 686-8075. **Seating Capacity:** 9,568. **Location:** I-4 to exit 33 (Lakeland Hills Boulevard).

MINOR LEAGUE

Complex Address: Tigertown, 2125 N Lake Ave, Lakeland, FL 33805. **Telephone:** (863) 686-8075.

HOUSTON ASTROS

MAJOR LEAGUE

Complex Address: The Ballpark of the Palm Beaches, 5444 Haverhill Road, West Palm Beach, FL 33407. **Telephone:** (844) 676-2017. **Seating Capacity:** 7,838. **Location:** Exit Florida's Turnpike onto Okeechobee Blvd. Proceed east to Haverhill Road turning left onto Haverhill Road. On game days, all vehicles may park in one of two grass parking areas. Proceed toward the stadium for disabled parking or drop-off. The North entrance on Haverhill Road will be right-out only. **Hotel Address:** Unavailable.

MINOR LEAGUE

Complex Information: Same as major league club. **Hotel Address:** Unavailable.

MIAMI MARLINS

MAJOR LEAGUE

Complex Address: Roger Dean Stadium, 4751 Main Street, Jupiter, FL 33458. **Telephone:** (561) 775-1818. **Telephone:** (561) 799-1346. **Seating Capacity:** 7,000. **Location:** I-95 to exit 83, east on Donald Ross Road for one mile to Central Blvd, left at light, follow Central Boulevard to circle and take Main Street to Roger Dean Stadium. **Hotel Address:** Palm Beach Gardens Marriott, 4000 RCA Boulevard, Palm Beach Gardens, FL 33410. **Telephone:** (561) 622-8888. **Fax:** (561) 622-0052.

MINOR LEAGUE

Complex/Hotel Address: Same as major league club.

MINNESOTA TWINS

MAJOR LEAGUE

Complex Address: Centurylink Sports Complex/Hammond Stadium, 14100 Six Mile Cypress Parkway, Fort Myers, FL 33912. **Telephone:** (239) 533-7610. **Seating Capacity:** 8,100. **Location:** Exit 21 off I-75, west on Daniels Parkway, left on Six Mile Cypress Parkway. **Hotel Address:** Four Points by Sheraton, 13600 Treeline Avenue South, Ft. Myers, FL 33913. **Telephone:** (800) 338-9467.

MINOR LEAGUE

Complex/Hotel Address: Same as major league club.

NEW YORK METS

MAJOR LEAGUE

Complex Address: Tradition Field, 525 NW Peacock Blvd, Port St. Lucie, FL 34986. **Telephone:** (772) 871-2100. **Seating Capacity:** 7,000. **Location:** Exit 121C (St Lucie West Blvd) off I-95, east 1/4 mile, left onto NW Peacock. **Hotel Address:** Hilton Hotel, 8542 Commerce Centre Drive, Port St. Lucie, FL 34986. **Telephone:** (772) 871-6850.

MINOR LEAGUE

Complex Address: Same as major league club. **Hotel Address:** Main Stay Suites, 8501 Champions Way, Port St. Lucie, FL 34986. **Telephone:** (772) 460-8882.

NEW YORK YANKEES

MAJOR LEAGUE
Complex Address: George M. Steinbrenner Field, One Steinbrenner Drive, Tampa, FL 33614. **Telephone:** (813) 875-7753. **Hotel:** Unavailable.

MINOR LEAGUE
Complex Address: Yankees Player Development/ Scouting Complex, 3102 N Himes Ave, Tampa, FL 33607. **Telephone:** (813) 875-7569. **Hotel:** Unavailable.

PHILADELPHIA PHILLIES

MAJOR LEAGUE
Complex Address: Spectrum Field, 601 N Old Coachman Road, Clearwater, FL 33765. **Telephone:** (727) 467-4457. **Fax:** (727) 712-4498. **Seating Capacity:** 8,500. **Location:** Route 60 West, right on Old Coachman Road, ballpark on right after Drew Street. **Hotel Address:** Holiday Inn Express, 2580 Gulf to Bay Blvd, Clearwater, FL 33765. **Telephone:** (727) 797-6300. **Hotel Address:** La Quinta Inn, 21338 US 19 North, Clearwater, FL 33765. **Telephone:** (727) 799-1565.

MINOR LEAGUE
Complex Address: Carpenter Complex, 651 N Old Coachman Rd, Clearwater, FL 33765. **Telephone:** (727) 799-0503. **Fax:** (727) 726-1793. **Hotel Addresses:** Hampton Inn, 21030 US Highway 19 North, Clearwater, FL 34625. **Telephone:** (727) 797-8173. **Hotel Address:** Econolodge, 21252 US Hwy 19, Clearwater, FL 34625. **Telephone:** (727) 799-1569.

PITTSBURGH PIRATES

MAJOR LEAGUE
Stadium Address: 17th Ave West and Ninth Street West, Bradenton, FL 34205. **Seating Capacity:** 8,500. **Location:** US 41 to 17th Ave, west to 9th Street. **Telephone:** (941) 747-3031. **Fax:** (941) 747-9549.

MINOR LEAGUE
Complex: Pirate City, 1701 27th St E, Bradenton, FL 34208.

ST. LOUIS CARDINALS

MAJOR LEAGUE
Complex Address: Roger Dean Stadium, 4751 Main Street, Jupiter, FL 33458. **Telephone:** (561) 775-1818. **Fax:** (561) 799-1380. **Seating Capacity:** 7,000. **Location:** I-95 to exit 58, east on Donald Ross Road for 1/4 mile. **Hotel Address:** Embassy Suites, 4350 PGA Blvd, Palm Beach Gardens, FL 33410. **Telephone:** (561) 622-1000.

MINOR LEAGUE
Complex: Same as major league club. **Hotel:** Double Tree Palm Beach Gardens. **Telephone:** (561) 622-2260.

TAMPA BAY RAYS

MAJOR LEAGUE
Stadium Address: Charlotte Sports Park, 2300 El Jobean Road, Port Charlotte, FL 33948. **Telephone:** (941) 206-4487. **Seating Capacity:** 6,823 (5,028 fixed seats). **Location:** I-75 to US-17 to US-41, turn left onto El Jobean Rd. **Hotel Address:** None.

MINOR LEAGUE
Complex: Same as major league club.

TORONTO BLUE JAYS

MAJOR LEAGUE
Stadium Address: Florida Auto Exchange Stadium, 373 Douglas Ave, Dunedin, FL 34698. **Telephone:** (727) 733-9302. **Seating Capacity:** 5,509. **Location:** US 19 North to Sunset Point; west on Sunset Point to Douglas Avenue; north on Douglas to Stadium; ballpark is on the southeast corner of Douglas and Beltrees.

MINOR LEAGUE
Complex Address: Bobby Mattick Training Center at Englebert Complex, 1700 Solon Ave, Dunedin, FL 34698. **Telephone:** (727) 734-8007. **Hotel Address:** Clarion Inn & Suites, 20967 US Highway 19 North Clearwater, FL 33765. **Telephone:** (727) 799-1181.

WASHINGTON NATIONALS

MAJOR LEAGUE
Stadium Address: The Ballpark of the Palm Beaches, 5444 N. Haverhill Road, West Palm Beach, FL 33407. **Telephone:** (844) 676-2017.

MINOR LEAGUE
Complex: Same as major league club.

ULTIMATE CADDY *VIII*

"It ain't just a cup holder anymore!"

BAG HOOK

CUP HOLDER

PHONE HOLDER

ADVERTISING MEDIUM

It's all about customer convenience!

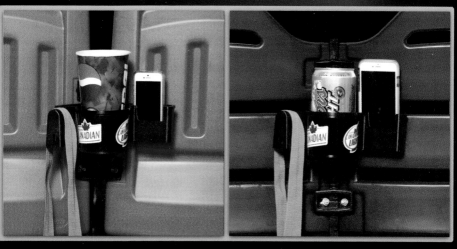

Thank You!!
"Finally Convenience Where You Need it!"
RESTROOM CADDY

Airport Gift Shop
Beverages
Books
Snacks

Cup Holder
Bag Hook
Phone Holder

Optional
Ad Panel
Easily
Changeable

Cosmetic Frame

Load Capacity 60+ Pounds

You're Welcome!!
Mounts Anywhere - Any Color!

For Samples Contact

CADDY PRODUCTS, INC.

www.caddyproducts.com   (800) 845-0591   info@caddyproducts.com

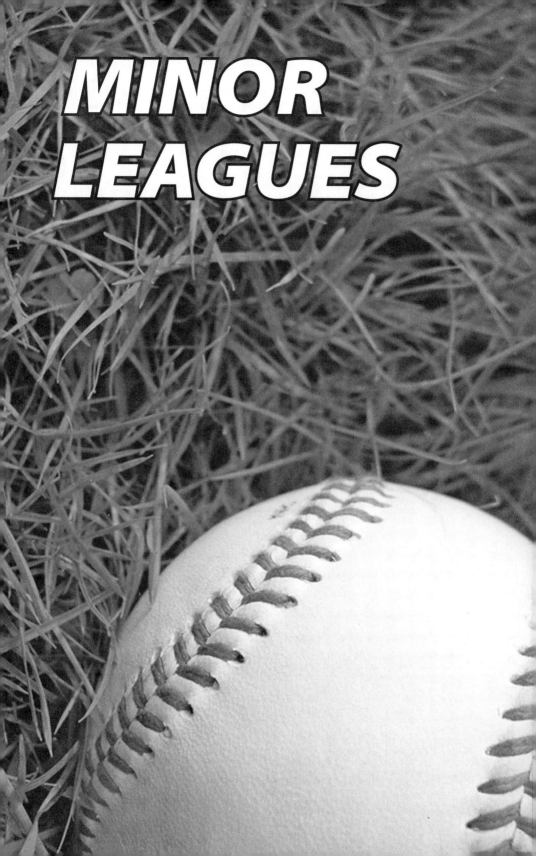

MINOR
LEAGUES

MINOR LEAGUE BASEBALL

THE NATIONAL ASSOCIATION OF PROFESSIONAL BASEBALL LEAGUES

MINOR LEAGUE BASEBALL ™

Street Address: 9550 16th St. North, St. Petersburg, FL 33716. **Mailing Address:** PO Box A, St. Petersburg, FL 33731-1950. **Telephone:** (727) 822-6937. **Fax:** (727) 821-5819. **Fax/Marketing:** (727) 894-4227. **Fax/Licensing:** (727) 825-3785. **President & CEO:** Pat O'Conner

Vice President: Stan Brand. **Chief Operating Officer:** Brian Earle. **Chief Marketing & Commercial Officer:** David Wright. **Chief Financial Officer:** Sean Brown. **Sr. VP, Legal Affairs & General Counsel:** D. Scott Poley. **Senior VP, Digital Strategy & Business Development:** Katie Davison. **Special Counsel:** George Yund. **VP, Baseball & Business Operations:** Tim Brunswick. **VP, Marketing Strategy & Research:** Kurt Hunzeker. **Sr. Executive Advisor to the President:** Dan O'Brien Jr. **Assistant to the President:** Bill Smith. **Sr. Dir., Communications:** Jeff Lantz. **Dir., Information Technology:** Rob Colamarino. **Dir., Licensing:** Sandie Hebert. **Dir., Special Events:** Stefanie Loncarich. **Dir., Security/Facility Ops.:** Earnell Lucas. **Dir., Diversity & Inclusion:** Vince Pierson. **Asst. Dir., Licensing:** Carrie Adams. **Asst. Dir., Baseball & Business Operations:** Andy Shultz. **Deputy General Counsel:** Robert Fountain. **Controller:** James Dispanet. **Asst. Dir., Community Engagement:** Courtney Nehls. **Asst. Dir., Corporate Communications:** Mary Marandi. **Asst. Dir., Partnership Marketing:** Heather Raburn. **Sr. Accountant:** Michelle Heystek. **Sr. Mgr., Marketing Strategy & Research:** Cory Bernstine. **Mgr., Human Resources:** Tara Thornton. **Sr. Mgr., Brand Development:** Ryan Foose. **Mgr., Baseball Ops./Exec. Asst. To President:** Mary Wooters. **Mgr., Special Events & Programming:** Mark Labban. **Mgr., Business Development & Media:** Curtis Walker. **Mgr., Partnership Marketing:** William Kent Jr. **Contract Mgr./Legal Asst.:** Jeannette Machicote. **Mgr., Partnership Marketing:** Scott Ester. **Mgr., Trade Show Services:** Eileen Sahin-Murphy. **Mgr., Business Development & Media:** Zack Stone. **Assoc. Counsel:** Shannon Finucane. **Coord., Social Media Marketing:** Brad Friedman. **Coord., Enterprise Marketing:** Meghan Madson. **Coord., Trademarks & Intellectual Properties:** Melissa Giesler-Hassell. **Coord., Ecommerce & Merchandising:** Christopher Walker. **Coord., Special Events:** Paige Hegedus. **Coord., Events & Partnerships:** Jessica Nori. **Analytics Specialist:** Belicia Montgomery. **Production Designer:** Vincent Pettofrezzo. **Receptionist:** Kim Bradbury.

Pat O'Conner

AFFILIATED MEMBERS/COUNCIL OF LEAGUE PRESIDENTS

Triple-A

League	President	Telephone	Fax Number
International	Randy Mobley	(614) 791-9300	(614) 791-9009
Mexican	Javier Salinas	TBA	TBA
Pacific Coast	Branch Rickey	(512) 310-2900	(512) 310-8300

Double-A

League	President	Telephone	Fax Number
Eastern	Joe McEacharn	(207) 761-2700	(207) 761-7064
Southern	Lori Webb	(770) 321-0400	(770) 321-0037
Texas	Tim Purpura	(682) 316-4100	(682) 316-4100

High Class A

League	President	Telephone	Fax Number
California	Charlie Blaney	(805) 985-8585	(805) 985-8580
Carolina	Geoff Lassiter	(336) 691-9030	(336) 464-2737
Florida State	Ken Carson	(727) 224-8244	(386) 252-7495

Low Class A

League	President	Telephone	Fax Number
Midwest	Dick Nussbaum	(574) 231-3000	(574) 231-3000
South Atlantic	Eric Krupa	(727) 538-4270	(727) 499-6853

Short-Season

League	President	Telephone	Fax Number
New York-Penn	Ben Hayes	(727) 289-7112	(727) 683-9691
Northwest	Mike Ellis	(406) 541-9301	(406) 543-9463

Rookie Advanced

League	President	Telephone	Fax Number
Appalachian	Lee Landers	(704) 252-2656	Unavailable
Pioneer	Jim McCurdy	(509) 456-7615	(509) 456-0136

Rookie

League	President	Telephone	Fax Number
Arizona	Bob Richmond	(208) 429-1511	(208) 429-1525
Dominican Summer	Orlando Diaz	(809) 532-3619	(809) 532-3619
Gulf Coast	Operated by MiLB	(727) 456-1734	(727) 821-5819

NATIONAL ASSOCIATION BOARD OF TRUSTEES

TRIPLE-A
At-large: Ken Young (Norfolk). **International League:** Ken Schnacke, Chairman (Columbus). **Pacific Coast League:** Sam Bernabe (Iowa). **Mexican League:** Gerardo Benavides Pape (Monclova).

DOUBLE-A
Eastern League: Joe Finley (Trenton). **Southern League:** Stan Logan, Secretary (Birmingham). **Texas League:** Matt Gifford (Springfield).

CLASS A
California League: Tom Volpe (Stockton). **Carolina League:** Chuck Greenberg (Myrtle Beach). **Florida State League:** Ron Myers (Lakeland).
Midwest League: Tom Dickson (Lansing). **South Atlantic League:** Chip Moore (Rome).

SHORT-SEASON
New York-Penn League: Marv Goldklang, Vice Chairman (Hudson Valley). **Northwest League:** Bobby Brett (Spokane).

ROOKIE
Appalachian League: Mitch Lukevics (Princeton). **Pioneer League:** Dave Elmore, (Idaho Falls). **Gulf Coast League:** Reid Ryan (Astros).

PROFESSIONAL BASEBALL UMPIRE CORP.
President & CEO: Pat O'Conner.
Secretary/Sr. VP, Legal Affairs & General Counsel: D. Scott Poley.
VP, Baseball/Business Operations: Tim Brunswick. **Director, MiLB Umpire Development:** Dusty Dellinger. **Mgr., Umpire Technology:** Tom Honec. **Mgr., Umpire Development:** Jess Schneider. **Chief of Instruction:** Mike Felt.
Field Evaluators/Instructors: Jorge Bauza, Tyler Funneman, Jay Pierce, Larry Reveal, Brian Sinclair, Darren Spagnardi.

GENERAL INFORMATION

Medical Coordinator: Mark Stubblefield.
VP, Baseball/Business Operations: Tim Brunswick. **Director, MiLB Umpire Development:** Dusty Dellinger. **Chief of Instruction:** Mike Felt. **Field Evaluators/Instructors:** Jorge Bauza, Tyler Funneman, Mark Lollo, Larry Reveal, Brian Sinclair, Darren Spagnardi. **Video Technician:** Tom Honec. **Medical Coordinator:** Mark Stubblefield. **Special Assistant:** Lillian Patterson.

		Regular Season			All-Star Games	
	Teams	Games	Opening Day	Closing Day	Date	Host
International	14	140	April 5	Sept. 3	* July 11	Columbus
Pacific Coast	16	140	April 5	Sept. 3	* July 11	Columbus
Eastern	12	140	April 5	Sept. 3	July 11	Trenton
Southern	10	140	April 5	Sept. 3	June 19	Birmingham
Texas	8	140	April 5	Sept. 3	June 26	Midland
California	8	140	April 5	Sept. 3	June 19	Lancaster
Carolina	10	140	April 5	Sept. 3	June 19	Carolina
Florida State	12	140	April 5	Sept. 2	June 16	Tampa
Midwest	16	140	April 5	Sept. 3	June 21	Lansing
South Atlantic	14	140	April 5	Sept. 3	June 21	Greensboro
New York-Penn	14	76	June 15	Sept. 3	Aug. 14	State College
Northwest	8	76	June 15	Sept. 3	^ Aug. 7	Grand Junction
Appalachian	10	68	June 19	Aug. 29	None	
Pioneer	8	76	June 15	Sept. 6	^ Aug. 7	Grand Junction
Arizona	15	56	June 18	Aug. 27	None	
Gulf Coast	18	56	June 18	Aug. 25	None	

*Triple-A All-Star Game. ^Northwest League vs. Pioneer League.

INTERNATIONAL LEAGUE

Address: 55 South High St., Suite 202, Dublin, Ohio 43017.
Telephone: (614) 791-9300. **Fax:** (614) 791-9009.
E-Mail Address: office@ilbaseball.com. **Website:** www.ilbaseball.com.

Years League Active: 1884.
President/Treasurer: Randy Mobley.
Vice President: Ken Young. **League Administrator:** Chris Sprague. **Corporate Secretary:** Max Schumacher.
Directors: Don Beaver (Charlotte); Jeff Wilpon (Syracuse); Joe Finley (Lehigh Valley); Mike Birling (Durham); Erik Ibsen (Toledo); North Johnson (Gwinnett); Stuart Katzoff (Louisville); Bob Rich Jr. (Buffalo); Joe Gregory (Norfolk); Josh Olerud (Scranton/Wilkes-Barre); Ken Schnacke (Columbus); Bruce Schumacher (Indianapolis); Naomi Silver (Rochester); Mike Tamburro (Pawtucket). **Office Manager:** Gretchen Addison.
Division Structure: North—Buffalo, Lehigh Valley, Pawtucket, Rochester, Scranton/Wilkes-Barre, Syracuse. **West**—Columbus, Indianapolis, Louisville, Toledo. **South**—Charlotte, Durham, Gwinnett, Norfolk.
Regular Season: 140 games. **2018 Opening Date:** April 5. **Closing Date:** Sept 3.
All-Star Game: July 11 at Columbus (IL vs Pacific Coast League).

Randy Mobley

Playoff Format: South winner meets West winner in best of five series; wild card (non-division winner with best winning percentage) meets North winner in best of five series. Winners meet in best-of-five series for Governors' Cup championship.
Triple-A Championship Game: Sept. 18 at Columbus (IL vs Pacific Coast League).
Roster Limit: 25. **Player Eligibility:** No restrictions.
Official Baseball: Rawlings ROM-INT.
Umpires: Ryan Additon (Davie, FL); Erich Bacchus (Germantown, MD); Adam Beck (Winter Springs, FL); John Bacon (Sherrodsville, OH); Sean Barber (Lakeland, FL); Jeff Carnahan (Crystal River, FL); Ryan Clark (McDonough, GA); Eric Gillam (Roscoe, IL); Scott Costello (Barrie, Canada); Christopher Graham (Newmarket, Canada); Nic Lentz (Holland, MI); Shane Livensparger (Jacksonville Beach, FL); Brennan Miller (Woodbridge, VA); Daniel Merzel (Hopkinton, MA); Brian Peterson (Wilmington, DE); Roberto Ortiz (Orlando, FL); Charlie Ramos (Grand Rapids, MI); Jeremie Rehak (Monroesville, PA); Jeremy Riggs (Suffolk, VA); Chris Segal (Burke, VA); Nate Tomlinson (Ogdensburg, WI); Alex Tosi (Lake Villa, IL); Jansen Visconti (Latrobe, PA); Chad Whitson (Dublin, OH); Ryan Wills (Williamsburg, VA); Mike Wiseman (White Lake, MI).

STADIUM INFORMATION

Club	Stadium	Opened	LF	CF	RF	Capacity	2017 Att.
Buffalo	Coca-Cola Field	1988	325	404	325	18,025	526,574
Charlotte	BB&T Ballpark	2015	325	400	315	10,002	628,526
Columbus	Huntington Park	2009	325	400	318	10,100	616,059
Durham	Durham Bulls Athletic Park	1995	305	400	327	10,000	547,841
Gwinnett	Coolray Field	2009	335	400	335	10,427	210,075
Indianapolis	Victory Field	1996	320	402	320	14,500	641,141
Lehigh Valley	Coca-Cola Park	2008	336	400	325	10,000	555,146
Louisville	Louisville Slugger Field	2000	325	400	340	13,131	467,024
Norfolk	Harbor Park	1993	333	400	318	12,067	359,263
Pawtucket	McCoy Stadium	1946	325	400	325	10,031	409,960
Rochester	Frontier Field	1997	335	402	325	10,840	445,581
Scranton/WB	PNC Field	2013	330	408	330	10,000	439,412
Syracuse	NBT Bank Stadium	1997	330	400	330	11,671	292,054
Toledo	Fifth Third Field	2002	320	408	315	10,300	533,014

Dimensions

BUFFALO BISONS

Address: Coca-Cola Field, One James D. Griffin Plaza, Buffalo, NY 14203.
Telephone: (716) 846-2000. **Fax:** (716) 852-6530.
E-Mail Address: info@bisons.com. **Website:** www.bisons.com.
Affiliation (first year): Toronto Blue Jays (2013). **Years in League:** 1886-90, 1912-70, 1998-

OWNERSHIP/MANAGEMENT

Operated By: Rich Products Corp.
Principal Owner/President: Robert Rich Jr. **President, Rich Entertainment Group:** Melinda Rich. **Vice President/Chief Operating Officer, Rich Entertainment Group:** Joseph Segarra. **President, Rich Baseball Operations:** Jon Dandes.
VP/General Manager: Mike Buczkowski. **VP/Secretary:** William Gisel. **Corporate Counsel:** Jill Bond, William Grieshober. **VP/Operations & Finance:** Kevin Parkinson. **VP/Food Service Operations:** Robert Free. **Assistant General**

Manager: Anthony Sprague. **Director, Stadium Operations:** Tom Sciarrino. **Senior Accountants:** Chas Fiscella. **Accountants:** Amy Delaney, Tori Dwyer. **Director, Ticket Operations:** Mike Poreda. **Director, Marketing & Public Relations:** Brad Bisbing. **Graphic Design:** Michele Lange. **Director, Corporate Sales:** Jim Harrington. **Group Sales Manager:** Geoff Lundquist. **Entertainment/Promotions Manager:** Mike Simoncelli. **Sales Coordinators:** Rachel Osucha. **Account Executives:** Mark Gordon, Nick Iacona, Kim Milleville, Burt Mirti, Shaun O'Lay. **Manager, Merchandise:** Victoria Rebmann. **Social Media & Sponsorship Coordinator:** Bethany Sickler. **Manager, Office Services:** Margaret Russo. **Executive Assistant:** Tina Lesher. **Community Relations:** Gail Hodges. **General Manager, Food Service Operations:** Sean Regan. **Food Service Operations Supervisor:** Curt Anderson. **Head Groundskeeper:** Chad Laurie. **Chief Engineer:** Pat Chella. **Home Clubhouse/Baseball Operations Coordinator:** Scott Lesher. **Visiting Clubhouse Manager:** Steve Morris.

FIELD STAFF
Manager: Bobby Meacham. **Hitting Coach:** Corey Hart. **Pitching Coach:** Bob Stanley. **Coach:** Devon White. **Athletic Trainer:** Bob Tarpey. **Strength/Conditioning Coach:** Brian Pike.

GAME INFORMATION
Radio Announcers: Ben Wagner, Duke McGuire. **No. of Games Broadcast:** 140. **Flagship Station:** ESPN 1520. **PA Announcer:** Jerry Reo, Tom Burns. **Official Scorers:** Kevin Lester, Jon Dare. **Stadium Name:** Coca-Cola Field. **Location:** From north, take I-190 to Elm Street exit, left onto Swan Street; From east, take I-190 West to exit 51 (Route 33) to end, exit at Oak Street, right onto Swan Street; From west, take I-190 East, exit 53 to I-90 North, exit at Elm Street, left onto Swan Street. **Standard Game Times:** 7:05 pm, Sun 1:05. **Ticket Price Range:** $9-15.
Visiting Club Hotel: Adams Mark, 120 Church St, Buffalo, NY 14202. **Telephone:** (716) 845-5100.

CHARLOTTE KNIGHTS

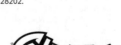

Address: BB&T Ballpark, 324 S. Mint St., Charlotte, NC 28202.
Telephone: (704) 274-8300. **Fax:** 704-274-8330.
E-Mail Address: knights@charlotteknights.com. **Website:** www.charlotteknights.com.
Affiliation (first year): Chicago White Sox (1999). **Years in League:** 1993-

OWNERSHIP/MANAGEMENT
Operated by: Knights Baseball, LLC.
Principal Owners: Don Beaver, Bill Allen.
Chief Operating Officer: Dan Rajkowski. **General Manager:** Rob Egan. **Director, Special Projects:** Julie Clark. **VP, Marketing:** Mark Smith. **VP, Sales:** Chuck Arnold. **VP, Communications:** Tommy Viola. **VP, Entertainment:** David Ruckman. **VP, Stadium Operations:** Tom Gorter. **Business Manager:** Michael Sanger. **Director, Ticket Sales/ Operations:** Matt Millward. **Director, Broadcasting/Team Travel:** Matt Swierad. **Director, Community Relations:** Cassidy MacQuarrie. **Director, Video Production:** Kyle Guertin. **Director, Season Membership Sales:** Brett Butler. **Director, Group Ticket Sales:** Samantha Davis. **Business Development Executives:** Mark Dacko, Shea Maple. **Client Services Manager:** Patrick Lally. **Creative Director:** Bill Walker. **Manager, Stadium Operations:** Nick Braun. **Merchandise Manager:** Ryan Petrere. **Promotions Manager:** Courtney Wright. **Entertainment Specialist:** Brittany Egan. **Sr. Ticket Sales Account Executives:** Yogi Brewington, Kevin Hughes. **Ticket Sales Account Executives:** Otto Loor, Ethan Samarel. **Inside Sales Manager:** David Woodard. **Ticket Operations Manager:** Jonathan English. **Ticket Membership Sales Associate:** Daniel Straney. **Ticket Sales Service Representatives:** Amanda Bullard, Dylan Evans. **Premium Services Manager:** Nicole Dietrich. **Business/Community Relations Coordinator:** Megan Smithers. **Head Groundskeeper:** Matt Parrott. **Assistant Groundskeeper:** Keith Salmon. **Director, Special Events:** Chelsea Herre. **Special Events Coordinator:** Nicole Copsis. **Inside Sales Representatives:** Erik Drew, Ryan Lank, Jacklen McManus, Jeffrey Reisner. **Front Desk Receptionist:** Maddy Craft

FIELD STAFF
Manager: Mark Grudzielanek. **Pitching Coach:** Steve McCatty. **Hitting Coach:** Andy Tomberlin. **Coach:** Garey Ingram. **Trainer:** James Kruk. **Conditioning:** Shawn Powell.

GAME INFORMATION
Radio Announcers: Matt Swierad, Mike Pacheco. **No. of Games Broadcast:** 140. **Flagship Station:** ESPN 730 AM. **PA Announcer:** Ken Conrad. **Official Scorers:** Jerry Bowers, Dave Friedman, Jack Frost, Mychal Frost, Richard Walker. **Stadium Name:** BB&T Ballpark. **Location:** Exit 10 off Interstate 77. **Ticket Price Range:** $8-$21.
Visiting Club Hotel: Doubletree by Hilton Charlotte, 895 W. Trade St., Charlotte, NC 28202.

COLUMBUS CLIPPERS

Address: 330 Huntington Park Lane, Columbus, OH 43215.
Telephone: (614) 462-5250. **Fax:** (614) 462-3271. **Tickets:** (614) 462-2757.=
E-Mail Address: info@clippersbaseball.com. **Website:** www.clippersbaseball.com.
Affiliation (first year): Cleveland Indians (2009). **Years in League:** 1955-70, 1977-

OWNERSHIP/MANAGEMENT
General Manager: Ken Schnacke. **Director, Merchandising:** Krista Oberlander. **Director, Marketing/Sales:** Mark

Galuska. **Director, Communications/Media:** Joe Santry.

Assistant Director, Sales, Special Events/Birthday Parties: Travis Allard. **Director, Game Operations/Creative Services:** Yoshi Ando. **Director, Ballpark Operations:** Steve Dalin. **Assistant Director, Ticket Sales:** Kevin Daniels. **Ballpark Superintendent:** Gary Delozier. **Support Services:** Marvin Dill. **Administration Assistant Marketing:** Michael Eckstein. **Administration Assistant, Ticket Sales:** Jacob Fleming. **Assistant Director, Group Sales:** Robert Freese. **Home Clubhouse Manager:** Tanner Graham. **Assistant Director, Group Sales/Little League Programs:** Cedric Hatton. **Executive Assistant to the President/GM:** Ashley Held. **Director, Group Sales:** Ben Keller. **Director, Promotions/In-Game Entertainment:** Steve Kuilder. **Assistant Director, Ticket Operations:** Eddie Langhenry. **Assistant Director, Broadcasting:** Scott Leo. **Maintenance Supervisor:** Curt Marcum. **Director, Sponsorship Relations:** Joyce Martin. **Director, Multimedia/Telecast:** Larry Mitchell. **Assistant Office Manager:** Beth Morris. **Assistant Director, Sales:** Jonathan Nye. **Assistant Director, Marketing/School Programs/Kids Club:** Emily Poynter. **Director, Finance/Administration:** Ashley Ramirez. **Assistant Director, Ballpark Operations:** Tom Rinto. **Visiting Clubhouse Manager:** Colin Shaub. **Director, Event Planning:** Micki Shier. **Assistant Director, Media Relations/Statistics:** Anthony Slosser. **Assistant Director, Event Planning/Catering/Suites:** Amanda Smithey. **Assistant GM:** Mark Warren. **Assistant Director, Multimedia/Telecast:** Pat Welch. **Assistant Director, Business Operations:** Shelby White. **Assistant Director, Merchandising:** Schuyler Wright. **Director, Ticket Operations:** Scott Ziegler. **Head Groundskeeper:** Wes Ganobcik. **Director, Multimedia:** Ryan Mitchell. **Director, Social Media/Website:** Matt Leininger. **GM, Levy Food/Beverage:** Jeff Roberts.

FIELD STAFF

Field Manager: Chris Tremie. **Pitching Coach:** Steve Karsay. **Hitting Coach:** Johnny Narron. **Bench Coach:** Bobby Magallanes. **Trainer:** Chad Wolfe. **Strength/Conditioning Coach:** Scott Nealon.

GAME INFORMATION

Radio Announcers: Ryan Mitchell, Scott Leo. **No of Games Broadcast:** 144. **Flagship Station:** WMNI 920 AM/easy 95.1 FM.

PA Announcer: Matt Leininger. **Official Scorer:** Jim Habermehl, Ray Thomas, Ty Debevoise and Paul Pennell.

Stadium Name: Huntington Park. **Location: From North:** South on I-71 to I-670 west, exit at Neil Avenue, turn left at intersection onto Neil Avenue. **From south:** North on I-71, exit at Front Street (#100A); turn left at intersection onto Front Street, turn left onto Nationwide Blvd. **From East:** West on I-70, exit at Fourth Street, continue on Fulton Street to Front Street, turn right onto Front Street, turn left onto Nationwide Blvd. **From West:** East on I-70, exit at Fourth Street, continue on Fulton Street to Front Street, turn right onto Front Street, turn left onto Nationwide Blvd. **Ticket Price Range:** $4-20.

Visiting Club Hotel: Crowne Plaza, 33 East Nationwide Blvd, Columbus, OH 43215. **Telephone:** (877) 348-2424. **Visiting Club Hotel:** Drury Hotels Columbus Convention Center, 88 East Nationwide Blvd, Columbus, OH 43215. **Telephone:** (614) 221-7008. **Visiting Club Hotel:** Hyatt Regency Downtown, 350 North High Street, Columbus, OH 43215. **Telephone:** (614) 463-1234. **Visiting Club Hotel:** Holiday Inn Downtown Capitol Square, 175 East Town Street, Columbus OH 43215, Telephone (614) 242-3908.

DURHAM BULLS

Office Address: 409 Blackwell St., Durham, NC 27701. **Mailing Address:** PO Box 507, Durham, NC 27702

Telephone: (919) **687-6500 Fax:** (919) 687-6560
Website: durhambulls.com. **Twitter:** @DurhamBulls
Affiliation (first year): Tampa Bay Rays (1998). **Years in League:** 1998-

OWNERSHIP/MANAGEMENT

Operated by: Capitol Broadcasting Company, Inc.

President/CEO: Jimmy Goodmon. **Vice President:** Mike Birling. **Assistant General Manager, Sales:** Chip Allen. **Assistant General Manager, Operations:** Scott Strickland. **Business Manager:** Rhonda Carlile. **Accounting Supervisor:** Theresa Stocking. **Staff Accountant:** Alicia McMillen. **Receptionist:** Caitlynn Walker. **Director of Corporate Partnerships:** Nick Bavin. **Manager of Corporate Partnerships:** Morgan Weber. **Sponsorship Account Executive:** Andrew Ferrier, Edward Richards. **Sponsorship Coordinator:** Ashley Crabtree. **Head Groundskeeper:** Cameron Brendle. **Operations Manager:** Cortlund Beneke, Roger Rose. **Head Groundskeeper, Durham Athletic Park:** Joe Stumpo. **Director, Special Events:** LaTosha Smith. **Director of Marketing/Communications:** Matt Sutor. **Promotions Director:** Faith Inman. **Radio/TV Broadcaster:** Patrick Kinas. **Mascot/Community Relations Coordinator:** Nico Tennant. **Media Relations Coordinator:** Jeff Bowe. **Director of Merchandising/Team Travel:** Bryan Wilson. **Merchandising Assistant:** Ashley Adams. **Director of Ticketing:** Peter Wallace. **Director of Ticket Sales:** Brian Simorka. **Box Office Manager:** Daniel Nobles. **Senior Corporate Account Executive:** Chris Jones. **Corporate Account Executive:** Izzy Piedmonte, Ben Trachtman. **Senior Account Executive, Group Sales:** Cassie Fowler. **Group Sales Account Executive:** Max Gagnon, Karlee Tanel. **Ticket Sales Representative:** Jalen Burks, Courtney Fowler, Victor Jones, TJ Mixson. **Director of Food and Beverage:** Dave Levey. **Executive Chef:** Curtis Wong. **Concessions Manager:** Todd Feneley. **Hospitality & Catering Manager:** Matt Messner.

FIELD STAFF

Manager: Jared Sandberg. **Pitching Coach:** Rick Knapp. **Coach:** Dan DeMent, Ben Johnson. **Athletic Trainer:** Scott Thurston. **Strength & Conditioning Coach:** Bryan King.

GAME INFORMATION
Broadcasters: Patrick Kinas, Scott Pose. **No. of Games Broadcast:** 140. **Flagship Station:** 96.5 FM and 99.3 FM. **PA Announcer:** Tony Riggsbee. **Official Scorer:** Brent Belvin.
Stadium Name: Durham Bulls Athletic Park. **Location:** From Raleigh, I-40 West to Highway 147 North, exit 12B to Willard, two blocks on Willard to stadium; From I-85, Gregson Street exit to downtown, left on Chapel Hill Street, right on Mangum Street. **Standard Game Times:** 7:05 pm, Sat. 6:35 pm, Sun. 5:05 pm. **Ticket Price Range:** $7-14.
Visiting Club Hotel: Hilton Durham Near Duke University; 3800 Hillsborough Road, Durham, NC 27705. **Telephone:** (919) 383-8033.

GWINNETT STRIPERS

Office Address: 2500 Buford Drive, Lawrenceville, GA 30043.
Mailing Address: P.O. Box 490310, Lawrenceville, GA 30049.
Telephone: (678) 277-0300. **Fax:** (678) 277-0338.
E-Mail Address: stripersinfo@braves.com. **Website:** www.gostripers.com.
Affiliation (first year): Atlanta Braves (1966). **Years in League:** 1884, 1915-17, 1954-64, 1966-

OWNERSHIP/MANAGEMENT
Vice President & General Manager: North Johnson. **Assistant GM:** Shari Massengill. **Office Manager:** Tyra Williams. **Corporate Partnerships Account Representative:** Gabe Rendon. **Ticket Sales Manager:** Jerry Pennington. **Account Executives:** Marc Flick, Ryan Logan, Dylan Powers, Katie Soraghan. **Ticket Operations Coordinator:** Elizabeth Brooks. **Media Relations Manager:** Dave Lezotte. **Social Media Coordinator:** Anastasia Hamilton. **Community Relations and Promotions Coordinator:** Chryssi Attig. **Creative Services Coordinator:** Nick Gosen. **Director, Stadium Operations:** Ryan Stoltenberg. **Stadium Operations Coordinator:** Rick Fultz. **Facilities Engineer:** Gary Hoopaugh. **Sports Turf Manager:** McClain Murphy. **Team Store Merchandise Coordinator:** Leah Benton. **Clubhouse Manager:** Nick Dixon.

FIELD STAFF
Manager: Damon Berryhill. **Pitching Coach:** Reid Cornelius. **Hitting Coach:** John Moses.

GAME INFORMATION
Radio Announcer: Tony Schiavone.
No. of Games Broadcast: 140. **Flagship Station:** 97.7 FM.
PA Announcer: Kevin Kraus. **Official Scorers:** Guy Curtright, Jack Woodard, Phil Engel, Stan Awtrey. **Stadium Name:** Coolray Field.
Location: I-85 (at Exit 115, State Road 20 West) and I-985 (at Exit 4); follow signs to park. **Ticket Price Range:** $8-40.
Visiting Club Hotels: Courtyard by Marriott Buford/Mall of Georgia, 1405 Mall of Georgia Boulevard, Buford, GA 30519. **Telephone:** (678) 745-3380. Fairfield Inn & Suites Atlanta Buford/Mall of Georgia, 1355 Mall of Georgia Boulevard, Buford, GA 30519. **Telephone:** (678) 714-0248.

INDIANAPOLIS INDIANS

Address: 501 W. Maryland Street, Indianapolis, IN 46225.
Telephone: (317) 269-3542. **Fax:** (317) 269-3541.
E-Mail Address: Indians@IndyIndians.com. **Website:** www.indyindians.com.
Affiliation (first year): Pittsburgh Pirates (2005). **Years in League:** 1963, 1998-

OWNERSHIP/MANAGEMENT
Operated By: Indians Inc.
Chairman of the Board/Chief Executive Officer: Bruce Schumacher. **President & General Manager:** Randy Lewandowski. **Senior Vice President, Community Affairs:** Cal Burleson. **Chairman Emeritus:** Max Schumacher. **Assistant General Manager, Corporate Sales/Marketing:** Joel Zawacki. **Assistant General Manager, Tickets/Operations:** Matt Guay. **Director, Communications:** Charlie Henry. **Baseball Communications Manager:** Cheyne Reiter. **Community Relations Manager:** Emily Hitchcock. **Telecast/Production Manager:** Scott Templin. **Telecast/Production Assistant:** Alex Leachman. **Voice of the Indians:** Howard Kellman. **Broadcaster:** Andrew Kappes. **Director, Corporate Sales:** Christina Toler. **Corporate Sales Account Executives:** Shelby Barrett, Nathan Butler. **Partnership Activation Manager:** Kylie Kinder. **Partnership Activation Coordinator:** Hayden Barnack. **Director, Creative Services:** Adam Pintar. **Graphic Designer:** Jessica Davis. **Director, Marketing/Promotions:** Kim Stoebick. **Director, Merchandise:** Mark Schumacher. **Merchandise Manager:** Katarina Burns. **Director, Field Operations:** Joey Stevenson. **Field Operations Manager:** Adam Basinger. **Senior Director, Business Operations:** Brad Morris. **Business Operations Coordinator:** Sarah McKinney. **Guest Relations Coordinator:** Cara Carrion. **Senior Director, Facilities:** Tim Hughes. **Senior Facilities Manager:** Allan Danehy. **Director, Stadium Operations:** Andrew Jackson. **Stadium Operations Coordinator:** Eddie Acheson. **Operations Support:** Ricky Floyd, Sandra Reaves. **Home Clubhouse Manager:** Bob Martin. **Visiting Clubhouse Manager:** Jeremy Martin. **Director of Tickets, Sales/Services:** Chad Bohm. **Director, Tickets, Premium Services/Events:** Kerry Vick. **Senior Ticket Services Manager & Internship Coordinator:** Bryan Spisak. **Senior Ticket Sales Account Executives:** Ryan Barrett, Jonathan Howard, Garrett Rosh. **Ticket Sales Account Executives:** Noelle Cook, Ty Eaton, Rebecca Spitzig.

FIELD STAFF
    Manager: Brian Esposito. **Hitting Coach:** Ryan Long. **Pitching Coach:** Stan Kyles. **Assistant Coach:** Greg Picart. **Athletic Trainer:** Dru Scott. **Strength & Conditioning Coach:** Alan Burr.

GAME INFORMATION
    Radio Announcers: Howard Kellman, Andrew Kappes. **Flagship Station:** Fox Sports 97.5 FM/1260 AM.
    PA Announcer: David Pygman. **Official Scorers:** Ed Holdaway, Bill McAfee, Kim Rogers, Kit Stetzel, Jeff Williams. **Stadium Name:** Victory Field. **Location:** I-70 to West Street exit, north on West Street to ballpark; I-65 to Martin Luther King and West Street exit, south on West Street to ballpark. **Standard Game Times:** 7:05 pm; 1:35 (Wed/Sun.); 7:15 (Fri.). **Ticket Price Range:** $11-17. **Visiting Club Hotel:** Holiday Inn Indy Downtown, 515 S. West Street, Indianapolis, IN 46225. **Telephone:** (317) 631-9000.

LEHIGH VALLEY IRONPIGS

    Address: 1050 IronPigs Way, Allentown, PA 18109.
    Telephone: (610) 841-7447. **Fax:** (610) 841-1509.
    E-Mail Address: info@ironpigsbaseball.com. **Website:** www.ironpigsbaseball.com.
    Affiliation (first year): Philadelphia Phillies (2008). **Years in League:** 2008-

OWNERSHIP/MANAGEMENT
    Ownership: LV Baseball LP;
    President & General Manager: Kurt Landes; Vice President, **Marketing & Entertainment:** Lindsey Knupp; **Vice President, Ticket Sales:** Brian DeAngelis; **Media Relations & Broadcasting:** Matt Provence; **Media/Broadcast Assistant:** Pat McCarthy; Director, **Digital Media & Communications:** Chris Dunham; **Director, Multimedia Design & Entertainment:** Rob Sternberg; **Manager, Multimedia Design & Entertainment:** Matt Cech; **Executive Director, IronPigs Charities:** Diane Donaher; **Manager, Community Relations:** Jeffrey Draluck; **Director, Concessions:** Alex Rivera; **Senior Manager, Concessions:** Brock Hartranft; **Director, Events & Catering:** Allison Valentine; **Manager, Catering &Hospitality:** Steve Agosti; **Executive Chef:** Jerry Rogers; **Director, Corporate Partnerships:** Tom Bendetti; **Managers, Marketing Services:** Dean Hirschberg, Mike Holley; **Administrative Assistant:** Pat Golden; **Director, Field Operations:** Ryan Hills; **Director, Stadium Operations:** Jason Kiesel; **Managers, Stadium Operations:** Justin Kulhamer; **Director, Finance:** Denise Ahner; **Senior Manager, Finance:** Michelle Perl; **Director, Managers, Corporate Partnerships:** Matt Jacobs, Pete Kandianis, Nick Wilder; **Manager, Promotions & Entertainment:** Zach Betkowski; **Director, Guest Experience:** Brad Ludwig; **Director, Group Sales:** Ryan Hines; **Managers, Group Sales:** Derek Tellinghuisen; **Account Executives, Groups:** Chad Mazepa, Billy Misiti; **Senior Manager, Ticket Sales:** Erik Hoffman; **Manager, Ticket Operations:** Brittany Balonis; **Manager, Ticket Operations & Analytics:** Andrew Lupo; **Manager, Premium Sales:** Adam Puskar; **Account Executives, Tickets:** Nick DiChristofaro, Mike Moneta; **Director, Merchandise:** TBD

FIELD STAFF
    Manager: Gary Jones. **Hitting Coach:** Sal Rende. **Pitching Coach:** David Lundquist. **Assistant Coach: Wes Helms Trainers:** Jon May. **Strength/Conditioning:** Ricky White.

GAME INFORMATION
    Radio Announcers: Matt Provence, Pat McCarthy. **No. of Games Broadcast:** 144. **Flagship Radio Station:** ESPN 1160/1240/1320 AM. **Television Station:** TV2. **Television Announcers:** Mike Zambelli, Steve Degler, Matt Provence, Doug Heater. **No. of Games Televised:** 71 (all home games).
    PA Announcer: Jim Walck. **Official Scorers:** Mike Falk, Jack Logic, David Sheriff, Dick Shute.
    Stadium Name: Coca-Cola Park. **Location:** Take US 22 to exit for Airport Road South, head south, make right on American Parkway, left into stadium. **Standard Game Times:** 7:05 pm, Sat. 6:35, Sun. 1:35.

LOUISVILLE BATS

    Address: 401 E Main St, Louisville, KY 40202.
    Telephone: (502) 212-2287. **Fax:** (502) 515-2255.
    E-Mail Address: info@batsbaseball.com. **Website:** www.batsbaseball.com.
    Affiliation (first year): Cincinnati Reds (2000). **Years in League:** 1998-

OWNERSHIP/MANAGEMENT
    Chairman: Stuart and Jerry Katzoff (MC Sports).
    Board of Directors: Dan Ulmer Jr., Edward Glasscock, Gary Ulmer, Kenny Huber, Steve Trager, Michael Brown. **President/CEO:** Gary Ulmer. **Senior Vice President:** Greg Galiette. **Vice President, Stadium Operations/Technology:** Scott Shoemaker. **Vice President, Business Operations:** James Breeding. **Controller:** Michele Anderson. **Accounting Assistant:** Becky Reeves. **Director, Media/Public Relations:** Alex Mayer. **Director, Broadcasting:** Nick Curran. **Director, Baseball Operations:** Josh Hargreaves. **Director, Online Media/Design:** Tony Brown. **Director, Business Development:** Bryan McBride. **Director, Business Operations:** Kyle Reh. **Director, Corporate Suites:** Malcolm Jollie. **Assistant Director, Ticket Operations:** Andrew Siers. **Senior Account Executive:** Hal Norwood. **Corporate Marketing Manager:** Michael Harmon. **Corporate Marketing Manager:** Kristen Stonicher. **Corporate Marketing Manager:** David Barry. **Director of Entertainment:** Casey Rusnak. **Corporate Sales Manager:** Shelby Harding. **Manager, Team Store/**

Merchandise: Kat Steponovich. **Manager/Coordinator, Stadium Operations:** Nathan Renfrow. **Head Clubhouse Manager:** Derrick Jewell. **Visiting Clubhouse Manager:** Ryan Dammeyer. **Head Groundskeeper:** Tom Nielsen. **Assistant Groundskeeper:** Bobby Estienne. **Club Physicians:** Walter Badenhausen, M.D.; John A. Lach, Jr., M.D. **Club Dentist:** Pat Carroll, D.M.D. **Chaplains:** Bob Bailey, Jose Castillo.

FIELD STAFF

Manager: Pat Kelly. **Pitching Coach:** Jeff Fassero. **Hitting Coach:** Leon Durham. **Bench Coach:** Dick Schofield. **Trainer:** Steve Gober. **Strength/Conditioning Coach:** Cole Durham.

GAME INFORMATION

Radio Announcers: Nick Curran. **No. of Games Broadcast:** 142. **Flagship Station:** WKRD 790-AM. **PA Announcer:** Charles Gazaway. **Official Scorer:** Neil Rohrer. **Organist:** Bob Ramsey. **Stadium Name:** Louisville Slugger Field. **Location:** I-64 and I-71 to I-65 South/North to Brook Street exit, right on Market Street, left on Jackson Street; stadium on Main Street between Jackson and Preston. **Ticket Price Range:** $8-18. **Visiting Club Hotel:** Galt House Hotel, 140 North Fourth Street, Louisville, KY 40202. **Telephone:** (502) 589-5200.

NORFOLK TIDES

Address: 150 Park Ave, Norfolk, VA 23510.
Telephone: (757) 622-2222. **Fax:** (757) 624-9090.
E-Mail Address: receptionist@norfolktides.com. **Website:** www.norfolktides.com.
Affiliation (first year): Baltimore Orioles (2007). **Years in League:** 1969-

OWNERSHIP/MANAGEMENT

Operated By: Tides Baseball Club Inc.
President: Ken Young. **General Manager:** Joe Gregory.
Assistant GM: Ben Giancola. **Director, Media Relations:** Ian Locke. **Director, Community Relations:** Heather McKeating. **Director, Ticket Operations:** Gretchen Todd. **Director, Group Sales:** John Muszkewycz. **Director, Premium Services:** Stephanie Hierstein. **Director, Stadium Operations:** Mike Zeman. **Business Manager:** Dawn Coutts. **Director, Business Development/Gameday Experience:** Mike Watkins. **Corporate Sponsorships/Promotions:** Jonathan Mensink, John Rogerson. **Manager, Merchandising:** AnnMarie Piddisi Ambler. **Assistant Director, Stadium Operations:** Mike Cardwell. **Assistant to Director, Tickets:** Sze Fong. **Administrative Assistant:** Lisa Blocker. **Event Staff Manager:** Joanna Wauhop.
Head Groundskeeper: Kenny Magner. **Assistant Groundskeeper:** Justin Hall. **Home Clubhouse Manager:** Kevin Casey. **Visiting Clubhouse Manager:** Jack Brenner. **Media Relations Assistant:** Shawn Largent. **Community Relations Assistant:** Markel Smith. **Group Sales Representatives:** Emily Plowman, Chip Woytowitz. **Box Office Assistant:** Conner Peloquin. **Merchandise Assistant:** Blair Bridges.

FIELD STAFF

Manager: Ron Johnson. **Hitting Coach:** NA. **Pitching Coach:** Mike Griffin. **Field Coach:** Jose Hernandez. **Athletic Trainer:** Chris Poole. **Strength/Conditioning Coach:** Trevor Howell.

GAME INFORMATION

Radio Announcers: Pete Michaud, Jeff McCarragher. **No. of Games Broadcast:** 140. **Flagship Station:** ESPN 94.1 FM.
PA Announcer: Jack Ankerson. **Official Scorers:** Mike Holtzclaw, Jim Hodges. **Stadium Name:** Harbor Park. **Location:** Exit 9, 11A or 11B off I-264, adjacent to the Elizabeth River in downtown Norfolk. **Standard Game Times:** 6:35 pm during weekdays in April & May, 7:05 pm, Sun 1:05 pm (first half of season); 4:05 pm (second half of season). **Ticket Price Range:** $10-15. **Visiting Club Hotel:** Sheraton Waterside, 777 Waterside Dr, Norfolk, VA 23510. **Telephone:** (757) 622-6664.

PAWTUCKET RED SOX

Office Address: One Ben Mondor Way, Pawtucket, RI 02860.
Mailing Address: PO Box 2365, Pawtucket, RI 02861.
Telephone: (401) 724-7300. **Fax:** (401) 724-2140.
E-Mail Address: info@pawsox.com. **Website:** www.pawsox.com.
Affiliation (first year): Boston Red Sox (1973). **Years in League:** 1973-

OWNERSHIP/MANAGEMENT

Operated by: Pawtucket Red Sox Baseball Club, Inc.
Chairman: Larry Lucchino. **Vice Chairman:** Mike Tamburro. **Senior Vice President/General Manager:** Dan Rea. **Treasurer:** Jeff White. **VP, Sales/Sponsorship:** Michael Gwynn. **VP, Communications and Community Relations:** Bill Wanless. **VP, Sales:** Rob Crain. **VP/Chief Financial Officer:** Joseph Goldberg. **VP/Club Counsel:** Kim Miner. **VP Operations/Warehouse Operations:** Dave Johnson. **Director, Merchandising:** Brooke Coderre. **Senior Director, Media Creation:** Kevin Galligan. **Senior Director, Fan Services:** Rick Medeiros. **Senior Director, Ticket Sales:** Matt Harper. **Special Assistant to Chairman:** Bart Harvey. **Special Assistant to President:** Jackie Dempsey. **Special Assistant to President/GM:** Joseph Bradlee. **Manager, McCoy Events:** Grace Eng. **Manager, Accounting/Data Analytics:** Matt Levin. **Director, Ticket Operations:** Sam Sousa. **Account Executives:** Mike Lyons, Chris Murphy,

Ben Proctore, Jim Cain, Jack Verducci, Anthony Cahill, John Basler. **Field Superintendant:** Matt McKinnon. **Director, Clubhouse Operations:** Carl Goodreau. **Executive Chef:** Rob Gemma.

FIELD STAFF

Manager: Kevin Boles. **Hitting Coach:** Rich Gedman. **Pitching Coach:** Kevin Walker. **Coach:** Bruce Crabbe. **Trainer:** Eric Velazquez. **Strength/Conditioning Coach:** Kirby Retzer.

GAME INFORMATION

Radio Announcers: Josh Maurer, Will Flemming. **No. of Games Broadcast:** 140. **Flagship Station:** WHJJ 920-AM. **PA Announcers:** Ben DeCastro, Scott Fraser. **Official Scorer:** Bruce Guindon.

Stadium Name: McCoy Stadium. **Location:** From north, 95 South to exit 2A in Massachusetts (Newport Ave); follow Newport Ave for 2 miles, right on Columbus Ave, follow one mile, stadium on right; From south, 95 North to exit 28 (School Street); right at bottom of exit ramp, through two sets of lights, left onto Pond Street, right on Columbus Ave, stadium entrance on left; From west (Worcester); 295 North to 95 South and follow directions from north; From east (Fall River); 195 West to 95 North and follow directions from south. **Standard Game Times:** 7 pm, Sat. 6, Sun 1. **Ticket Price Range:** $5-11. **Visiting Club Hotel:** Hampton Inn Pawtucket, 2 George St, Pawtucket, RI 02860. **Telephone:** (401) 723-6700.

ROCHESTER RED WINGS

Address: One Morrie Silver Way, Rochester, NY 14608.
Telephone: (585) 454-1001. **Fax:** (585) 454-1056.
E-Mail: info@redwingsbaseball.com. **Website:** RedWingsBaseball.com.
Affiliation (first year): Minnesota Twins (2003). **Years in League:** 1885-89, 1891-92, 1895-present

OWNERSHIP/MANAGEMENT

Operated by: Rochester Community Baseball, Inc.
President/CEO/COO: Naomi Silver.
Chairman: Gary Larder. **General Manager:** Dan Mason. **Assistant GM:** Will Rumbold. **Controller:** Michelle Schiefer. **Director, Human Resources:** Paula LoVerde. **Ticket Office Mgr. & Business Coordinator:** Dave Welker. **Manager, Operations:** Marcia DeHond. **Director, Communications:** Nate Rowan. **Director, Corporate Development:** Nick Sciarratta. **Manager, Social Media & Promotions:** Tim Doohan. **Director, Group Sales:** Bob Craig. **Group Sales & Tickets Reps:** Kevin Lute & Mike Ewing. **Senior Director, Sales:** Matt Cipro. **Director, Ticket Operations:** Rob Dermody. **Assistant Director, Ticket Operations:** Eric Friedman. **Director, Game Day Operations:** Travis Sick. **Director, Video Production:** Matt Miller. **Director, Merchandising:** Casey Sanders. **Merchandising Assistant:** Kathy Bills. **Head Groundskeeper:** Gene P Buonomo. **Assistant Groundskeeper:** Geno Buonomo. **Office Mgr. & Community Relations Coordinator:** Gini Darden. **GM, Food/Beverage:** Jeff Dodge. **Business Manager, Food/Beverage:** Dave Bills. **Manager, Concessions:** Jeff DeSantis. **Director, Catering:** Courtney Trawitz. **Sales Manager, Catering:** Steve Gonzalez. **Executive Chef:** Ryan Donalty. **Manager, Warehouse:** Tyler Klobusicky.

FIELD STAFF

Manager: Joel Skinner. **Hitting Coach:** Chad Allen. **Pitching Coach:** Stu Cliburn. **Trainer:** Chris Johnson. **Strength Coach:** Tyler Burks. **Bullpen Coach:** Mike McCarthy.

GAME INFORMATION

Radio Announcer: Josh Whetzel. **No. of Games Broadcast:** 140. **Flagship Stations:** WHTK 1280-AM.

PA Announcers: Kevin Spears, Rocky Perrotta. **Official Scorers:** Warren Kozireski, Brendan Harrington, Craig Bodensteiner. **Stadium Name:** Frontier Field. **Location:** I-490 East to exit 12 (Brown/Broad Street) and follow signs; I-490 West to exit 14 (Plymouth Ave) and follow signs. **Standard Game Times:** 7:05 pm, Sun 1:35. **Ticket Price Range:** $8-12. **Visiting Club Hotel:** Holiday Inn Rochester Downtown, 70 State St, Rochester, NY 14608. **Telephone:** (585) 546-3450.

SCRANTON/WILKES-BARRE RAILRIDERS

Address: 235 Montage Mountain Rd., Moosic, PA 18507.
Telephone: (570) 969-2255. **Fax:** (570) 963-6564.
E-Mail Address: info@swbrailriders.com.
Website: www.swbrailriders.com.
Affiliation (first year): New York Yankees (2007). **Years in League:** 1989-

OWNERSHIP/MANAGEMENT

Owned by: SWB Yankees, LLC. **Operated by:** SWB Yankees, LLC.
Team President/General Manager: Josh Olerud. **Chief Financial Officer/Financial Controller:** Scott A'Hara. **VP,**

Assistant General Manager: Katie Beekman. **VP, Ticket Sales:** Robert McLane. **Sr. Director, Ticket Operations:** Felicia Adamus. **Director, Marketing:** Megan Jones. **Sr. Director, Corporate Services & Design:** Kristina Knight. **Director, Media Relations/Broadcasting:** Adam Marco. **Director, Community Relations:** Jordan Maydole. **Sr. Director, Marketing/Entertainment:** Barry Snyder. **Director, Baseball & Business Operations:** William Steiner. **Director, Video Production:** Victor Sweet. **Corporate Sales Manager:** Jim Tunison. **Corporate Partnership Executive:** Kerry Meyers. **Corporate Sales Executive:** Russ Canzler. **Sr. Corporate Services Manager:** Noelle Richard. **Corporate Service Managers:** Allie Bowen, Kat Sokirka. **Fan Services Manager:** Nick Sharpe. **Sr. Inside Sales Manager:** Kelly Cusick. **Inside Sales Representatives:** Brian O'Shaughnessy, Joe Yudichak. **Corporate Ticket Sales Executives:** Nick Bolka, Ricky Goykin, Jeff Smolens, Joe Tucciarone. **Group Sales Manager:** Mike Harvey. **Group Sales Coordinator:** Tim Duggan. **Group Sales Coordinator/RailRiders University Manager:** Robby Judge. **Media Relations Manager/Broadcaster:** Adam Giardino. **Manager, Foundation & Finance:** Amy Miller. **Manager, Ticket Operations:** Stephanie Puckett. **Director, Field Operations:** Steve Horne. **Operations Manager/Asst. Groundskeeper:** Paul Tumavitch. **Director, Ballpark Operations:** Joe Villano.

FIELD STAFF

Manager: Bobby Mitchell. **Hitting Coach:** Phil Plantier. **Pitching Coach:** Tommy Phelps. **Defensive Coach:** Travis Chapman. **Bullpen Coach:** Doug Davis. **Athletic Trainer:** Darren London. **Clubhouse Manager:** Mike Macciocco.

GAME INFORMATION

Radio Announcers: Adam Marco, Adam Giardino. **No. of Games Broadcast:** 140. **Flagship Stations:** 1340 WYCK-AM, 1400 WICK-AM, 1440 WCDL-AM. **Television Announcer:** Adam Marco. **No. of Games Broadcast:** TBA. **Flagship Station:** TBA. **PA Announcers:** TBA. **Official Scorers:** Dave Lauriha, John Errico, Armand Rosamilia, Kevin Southard. **Stadium Name:** PNC Field. **Location:** Exit 182 off Interstate 81; stadium is on Montage Mountain Road. **Standard Game Times:** 6:35 pm (April/May) 7:05 pm (June-August); Sun. 1:05 pm. **Ticket Price Range:** $10-$16. **Visiting Club Hotel:** Hilton Scranton & Conference Center. **Telephone:** (570) 343-3000.

SYRACUSE CHIEFS

Address: One Tex Simone Drive, Syracuse, NY 13208.
Telephone: (315) 474-7833. **Fax:** (315) 474-2658.
E-Mail Address: baseball@syracusechiefs.com. **Website:** www.syracusechiefs.com.
Affiliation (first year): Washington Nationals (2009). **Years in League:** 1885-89, 1891-92, 1894-1901, 1918 1920-27, 1934-55, 1961-

OWNERSHIP/MANAGEMENT

Operated by: NY Mets.
General Manager: Jason Smorol. **Director, Sales/Marketing:** Kathleen McCormick. **Director, Finance:** Frank Santoro. **Director, Group Sales:** Arnold Malloy. **Director, Broadcasting/Public Relations:** Kevin Brown. **Director, Ticket Sales:** Will Commisso. **Director, Multimedia Production:** Anthony Cianchetta. **Manager, Corporate Sales:** Julie Cardinali. **Manager, Luxury Suites/Guest Relations:** Bill Ryan. **Director, Community Relations/Social Media:** Kyle Fussner/Danny Tripodi. **Head Groundskeeper:** John Stewart.

FIELD STAFF

Manager: Billy Gardner Jr. **Hitting Coach:** Brian Daubach. **Pitching Coach:** Bob Milacki. **Trainer:** Jeff Allred. **Strength Coordinator:** Mike Warren.

GAME INFORMATION

Radio Announcers: Eric Gallanty. **No. of Games Broadcast:** 142. **Flagship Station:** The Score 1260 AM. **PA Announcers:** Nick Aversa. **Official Scorer:** Dom Leo.
Stadium Name: NBT Bank Stadium. **Location:** New York State Thruway to exit 36 (I-81 South); to 7th North Street exit, left on 7th North, right on Hiawatha Boulevard. **Standard Game Times:** 7:05 pm, Sun. 1:05 pm. **Ticket Price Range:** $6-14. **Visiting Club Hotel:** Embassy Suites @ Destiny USA

TOLEDO MUD HENS

Address: 406 Washington St., Toledo, OH 43604.
Telephone: (419) 725-4367. **Fax:** (419) 725-4368.
E-Mail Address: mudhens@mudhens.com. **Website:** www.mudhens.com.
Affiliation (first year): Detroit Tigers (1987). **Years in League:** 1889, 1965-

OWNERSHIP/MANAGEMENT

Operated By: Toledo Mud Hens Baseball Club, Inc.
Chairman of the Board: Michael Miller. **Vice President:** David Huey. **Secretary/Treasurer:** Charles Bracken. **President/CEO:** Joseph Napoli.
GM/Executive Vice President: Erik Ibsen. **President, Chief Marketing Officer:** Kim McBroom. **CFO:** Brian Leverenz. **Accounting:** Sheri Kelly, Shelly Solis. **Assistant Controller:** Tom Mitchell.
Director, Events/Entertainment: Michael Keedy. **Communications/Media Director:** Andi Roman. **Director, Ticket**

Sales/Services: Thomas Townley. **Director Food & Beverage:** Chris Shannon.

Gameday Operations Manager: Greg Setola. **Director Corporate Partnerships:** Ed Sintic. **Corporate Sales Consultant:** Rob Rice.

Game Plan Consultants: Phil Bargardi, PJ Carr, John Dotson, Becky Fitts, Adam Haman, David Sims. **Group Sales Manager:** Kyle Moll. **Group Consultant:** Laura Heinz, Rita Natter, Brian Wilson. **Ticket Services Team:** Troy Hammersmith, Haley Dennis, Samantha Hoot.

Box Office Manager: Jennifer Hill. **Manager, Digital Communications:** Nathan Steinmetz. **Game Plan Advisor:** Colleen Rerucha. **Special Events Coordinator:** Emily Croll. **Director, Game Day Coordinator:** Tyler Clark, CJ O'Leary. **Director Media Services:** Greg Tye. **Creative Director:** Dan Royer. **Graphic Design Assistants:** Will Melon, Alex Dartt, **Director, Merchandise & Licensing:** Craig Katz. **Manager, Swamp Shop:** Adam Stone. **Manager, Office Manager:** Carol Hamilton. **Executive Assistants:** Beth Loy, Brenda Murphy, Pam Miranda. **Turf Manager:** Jake Tyler. **Clubhouse Manager:** Joe Sarkisian. **Team Historian:** John Husman.

FIELD STAFF

Manager: Doug Mientkiewicz. **Hitting:** Brian Harper. **Pitching Coach:** Jeff Pico. **Third Base Coach:** Basilio Cabrera. **Trainer:** Chris McDonald.

GAME INFORMATION

Radio Announcer: Jim Weber. **No. of Games Broadcast:** 140. **Flagship Station:** WCWA 1230-AM. **TV Announcers:** Jim Weber, Matt Melzak. **No. of Games Broadcast:** 70 (all home games). **TV Flagship:** Buckeye Cable Sports Network (BCSN).

PA Announcer: Mason. **Official Scorers:** Jeff Businger, Ron Kleinfelter, John Malkoski Jr., John Malkoski Sr., Lee Schuh, Jason Parkins.

Stadium Name: Fifth Third Field. **Location:** From Ohio Turnpike 80/90, exit 54 (4A) to I-75 North, follow I-75 North to exit 201-B, left onto Erie Street, right onto Washington Street; From Detroit, I-75 South to exit 202-A, right onto Washington Street; From Dayton, I-75 North to exit 201-B, left onto Erie Street, right on Washington Street; From Ann Arbor, Route 23 South to I-475 East, I-475 east to I-75 South, I-75 South to exit 202-A, right onto Washington Street. **Ticket Price Range:** $12.

Visiting Club Hotel: Park Inn, 101 North Summit, Toledo, OH 43604. **Telephone:** (419) 241-3000.

PACIFIC COAST LEAGUE

PACIFIC COAST LEAGUE

Address: One Chisholm Trail, Suite 4200, Round Rock, Texas 78681.
Telephone: (512) 310-2900. **Fax:** (512) 310-8300.
E-Mail Address: office@pclbaseball.com. **Website:** www.pclbaseball.com.
President: Branch B. Rickey.
Vice President: Don Logan (Las Vegas).
Directors: John Traub (Albuquerque), Dave Elmore (Colorado Springs), Josh Hunt (El Paso), Chris Cummings (Fresno), Sam Bernabe (Iowa), Don Logan (Las Vegas), Peter B. Freund (Memphis), Frank Ward (Nashville), Lou Schwechheimer (New Orleans), Gary Green (Omaha), Larry Freedman (Oklahoma City), Eric Edelstein (Reno), Chris Almendarez (Round Rock), Jeff Savage (Sacramento), Marc Amicone (Salt Lake), Aaron Artman (Tacoma).
Director, Business: Melanie Fiore. **Vice President, Baseball Operations:** Dwight Hall.
Public Relations & Operations Assistant: Matt Grilli.
Division Structure: American Conference—Northern: Colorado Springs, Iowa, Oklahoma City, Omaha. **Southern:** Memphis, Nashville, New Orleans, Round Rock. **Pacific Conference—Northern:** Fresno, Reno, Sacramento, Tacoma. **Southern:** Albuquerque, El Paso, Las Vegas, Salt Lake.
Regular Season: 140 games. **2018 Opening Date:** April 5. **Closing Date:** Sept 3.
All-Star Game: July 11 at Columbus (PCL vs International League).

Branch Rickey

Playoff Format: Pacific Conference/Northern winner meets Southern winner, and American Conference/Northern winner meets Southern winner in best-of-five semifinal series. Winners meet in best-of-five series for league championship.
Triple-A Championship Game: Sept 18 at Columbus (PCL vs International League).
Roster Limit: 25. **Player Eligibility Rule:** No restrictions; **Brand of Baseball:** Rawlings ROM.
Umpires: David Arrieta (Maracaibo, Zulia, Venezuela), Ryan Blakney (Glendale, AZ), John Bostwick (Moorpark, CA), Mike Cascioppo (Escondido, CA), Nestor Ceja (Arleta, CA), Paul Clemons (Oxford, KS), Matt Czajak (Flower Mound, TX), Ramon De Jesus (Santo Domingo, Dominican Republic), Derek Eaton (Tracy, CA), Travis Eggert (Pine, AZ), Blake Felix (Fort Worth, TX), Bryan Fields (Phoenix, AZ), Clayton Hamm (Spicewood, TX), Javerro January (Southaven, MS), John Libka (Port Huron, MI), Nick Mahrley (Phoenix, AZ), Ben May (Milwaukee, WI), Lee Meyers (Madera, CA), Clay Park (Georgetown, TX), Garrett Patterson (Scottsdale, AZ), Sean Ryan (Waunakee, WI), Jason Starkovich (Greeley, CO), Brett Terry (Portland, OR), Junior Valentine (Maryville, TN), Clint Vondrak (Reno, NV), Tom Woodring (Las Vegas, NV), Alex Ziegler (Metairie, LA).

STADIUM INFORMATION

Club	Stadium	Opened	LF	CF	RF	Capacity	2017 Att.
Albuquerque	Isotopes Park	2003	340	400	340	13,500	542,502
Colorado Springs	Security Service Field	1998	350	410	350	8,500	265,095
El Paso	Southwest University Park	2014	322	406	322	8,018	544,668
Fresno	Chukchansi Park	2002	324	400	335	12,500	428,341
Iowa	Principal Park	1992	335	400	335	11,000	535,660
Las Vegas	Cashman Field	1983	328	433	328	11,500	359,059
Memphis	AutoZone Park	2000	319	400	322	10,000	350,007
Nashville	First Tennessee Park	2015	330	405	310	10,000	593,679
New Orleans	Shrine on Airline	1997	325	400	325	10,000	349,883
Oklahoma City	Chickasaw Bricktown Ballpark	1998	325	400	325	9,000	444,224
Omaha	Werner Park	2011	310	402	315	9,023	358,777
Reno	Aces Ballpark	2009	339	410	340	9,100	347,502
Round Rock	Dell Diamond	2000	330	405	325	8,722	610,681
Sacramento	Raley Field	2000	330	403	325	14,014	562,237
Salt Lake	Smith's Ballpark	1994	345	420	315	14,511	483,202
Tacoma	Cheney Stadium	1960	325	425	325	6,500	374,951

ALBUQUERQUE ISOTOPES

Address: 1601 Avenida Cesar Chavez SE, Albuquerque, NM 87106
Telephone: (505) 924-2255. **Fax:** (505) 242-8899.
E-Mail Address: info@abqisotopes.com. **Website:** www.abqisotopes.com.
Affiliation (first year): Colorado Rockies (2015). **Years in League:** 1972-2000, 2003-

OWNERSHIP/MANAGEMENT

President: Ken Young. **Vice President/Secretary/Treasurer:** Emmett Hammond. **VP/GM:** John Traub. **VP, Corporate Development:** Nick LoBue. **Assistant GM, Business Operations:** Chrissy Baines. **Assistant GM, Sales/Marketing:** Adam Beggs. **Director, Public Relations:** Kevin Collins. **Director, Retail Operations:** Kara Hayes. **Director, Stadium Operations:** Bobby Atencio. **Director, Accounting/Human Resources:** Cynthia DiFrancesco. **Box Office/Administration Manager:** Mark Otero.

Community Relations Manager: Michelle Montoya. Marketing/Promotions Manager: Dylan Storm. Game Production Manager: Kris Shepard. Suite Relations Manager: Paul Hartenberger. Travel Coordinator/Home Clubhouse Manager: Ryan Maxwell. Season Tickets/Group Sales Manager: Jason Buchta. Ticket Sales Executives: Alex Clark, Terry Clark, Aaron Robinson, CJ Scroger, Malcolm Smith. Graphic Designer: Alvin Garcia. Public Relations Assistant: Andrew Cockrum. Front Office Assistant: Margaret Harris. Retail Operations Assistant: Michael Malgieri. Stadium Operations Assistant: Tony Troyer. Head Groundskeeper: Clint Belau. Assistant Groundskeeper: Ryan Coleman. GM, Spectra Food & Hospitality: Patrick Queeney. Assistant GM, Spectra Food & Hospitality: Nick Korth. Suites and Catering Manager: Sylvia Carter. Head Chef: Ryan Curry. Spectra Office Manager: Angela Goniea.

FIELD STAFF

Manager: Glenallen Hill. Hitting Coach: Tim Doherty. Pitching Coach: Brandon Emanuel. Athletic Trainer: Heath Townsend. Physical Performance Coach: Marcus Lefton

GAME INFORMATION

Radio Announcer: Josh Suchon. No. of Games Broadcast: 140. Flagship Station: KNML 610-AM. PA Announcer: Francina Walker. Official Scorers: Gary Herron, Brent Carey, John Miller, Frank Mercogliano.

Stadium Name: Isotopes Park. Location: From I-25, exit east on Avenida Cesar Chavez SE to University Boulevard; From I-40, exit south on University Boulevard SE to Avenida Cesar Chavez. Standard Game Times: 6:35 pm / 7:05 pm. Sun 1:35/6:05 pm. Ticket Price Range: $8-$27.

Visiting Club Hotel: Sheraton Albuquerque Airport Hotel, 2910 Yale Blvd SE, Albuquerque, NM 87106. Telephone: (505) 843-7000.

COLORADO SPRINGS SKY SOX

Address: 4385 Tutt Blvd., Colorado Springs, CO 80922.
Telephone: (719) 597-1449. Fax: (719) 597-2491.
E-Mail address: info@skysox.com. Website: www.skysox.com.
Affiliation (first year): Milwaukee Brewers (2015). Years in League: 1988-Present.

OWNERSHIP/MANAGEMENT

Operated By: Colorado Springs Sky Sox Inc.

Principal Owner: David Elmore. President/General Manager: Tony Ensor. Director, Public Relations: Shane Philipps. Assistant GM/Senior Director, Corporate Sales: Chris Phillips. Senior Director, Ticketing/Merchandise: Trent Hale. Senior Director, Group Sales: Keith Hodges. Director, Broadcasting: Dan Karcher. Director, Accounting: Ben Knowles. Director, Production and Promotions: Abby Kappel. Director, Marketing: Kyle Fritzke. Vice President, Field Operations: Steve DeLeon. Manager, Community Relations: Sierra Todd. Manager, Stadium Operations: Eric Martin. Assistant Director, Group Sales: Dustin True. Manager, Group Sales: Jonathan Basil. Manager, Box Office: Trent Hale. Event Manager: Brien Smith. GM, Diamond Creations: Don Giuliano. Executive Chef: Chris Evans. Home Clubhouse Manager: Cole Filosa. Visiting Clubhouse Manager: Steve Martin.

FIELD STAFF

Manager: Rick Sweet. Coaches: Ned Yost IV, David Joppie. Pitching Coach: Fred Dabney.

GAME INFORMATION

Radio Announcer: Dan Karcher. No. of Games Broadcast: 140. Flagship Station: Xtra Sports 1300. PA Announcer: Josh Howe. Official Scorer: Marty Grantz, Rich Wastler.

Stadium Name: Security Service Field. Location: I-25 South to Woodmen Road exit, east on Woodmen to Powers Blvd., right on Powers to Barnes Road. Standard Game Times: 6:40 pm, Sat. 6:00, Sun. 1:30. Ticket Price Range: $5-15. Visiting Club Hotel: Hilton Garden Inn, 1810 Briargate Parkway, Colorado Springs, CO 80920. Telephone: (719) 598-6866.

EL PASO CHIHUAHUAS

Address: 1 Ballpark Plaza, El Paso, TX 79901.
Telephone: (915) 533-2273. Fax: (915) 242-2031.
E-Mail Address: info@epchihuahuas.com. Website: www.epchihuahuas.com.
Affiliation (first year): San Diego Padres (2014). Years in League: 2014-

OWNERSHIP/MANAGEMENT

Owner/Chairman of the Board: Paul Foster. Owner/CEO/Vice Chairman: Josh Hunt. Owners: Alejandra de la Vega Foster, Woody Hunt.

President: Alan Ledford. Vice President/General Manager: Brad Taylor.

Director, Finance & Administration: Pamela De La O. Accounting Manager: Heather Hagerty. Accounting Assistant: Pamela Nieto.

Director, Corporate Partnerships: Becky Lee. Manager, Corporate Partnerships & Suite Services: Judge Scott. Corporate Partnerships Activation Specialist: Alex O'Connor. Account Executive, Corporate Partnerships: Ryan Knox.

Director, Ticket Sales & Service: Nick Seckerson. Manager, Season Seat Sales: Primo Martinez. Senior Specialist, Hospitality & Military Sales: Monica Castillo. Manager, Ticket Operations & Analytics: Ross Rotwein. Manager,

Group Sales: Brittany Morgan. **Group Sales Operations Specialist:** Killian Valleiu. **Account Executives, Ticket Sales:** Patrick Burns, Corey Cerrone, Alex Lakinske, Jay Morris, Austin Weber. **Account Executives, Group Sales:** Matt Heiligenberg, George Pinon, Janine Quiroz. **Ticket Operations Assistant:** Ruben Armendariz. **Ticket Sales Assistant:** Eduardo Cabrera
 Director, Marketing & Communications: Angela Olivas. **Manager, Video & Digital Production:** Juan Gutierrez. **Manager, Broadcast & Media Relations:** Tim Hagerty. **Manager, Promotions & Community Relations:** Andy Imfeld. **Mascot & Entertainment Supervisor:** Grant Gorham. **Production & Social Media Coordinator:** Gage Freeman. **Community Relations & Promotions Coordinator:** Kate Lewis.
 Director, Guest Services & Baseball Operations: Lizette Espinosa. **Director, Ballpark Operations:** Douglas Galeano. **Manager, Facilities & Operations:** Will Forney. **Manager Grounds, Head Groundskeeper:** Travis Howard. **Assistant Groundskeeper:** Tony Tafoya. **Baseball Operations Assistant & Facilities Supervisor:** Michael Raymundo. **Guest Services & Operations Supervisor:** Evan Ruiz. **Manager, Retail & Merchandise Operations:** Denise Richardson.

FIELD STAFF
 Manager: Rod Barajas. **Hitting Coach:** Morgan Burkhart. **Pitching Coach:** Bronswell Patrick. **Coach:** Lance Burkhart. **Trainers:** Nathan Stewart, Dan Turner.

GAME INFORMATION
 Radio Announcer: Tim Hagerty. **No. of Games Broadcast:** 140. **Flagship Station:** ESPN 600 AM El Paso. **PA Announcer:** Larry Berg. **Official Scorer:** Bernie Ricono. **Stadium Name:** Southwest University Park. **Standard Game Times:** 7:05, Sun 1:05. **Ticket Price Range:** $5-10.50. **Visiting Club Hotel:** Hilton Garden Inn.

FRESNO GRIZZLIES

Address: 1800 Tulare St, Fresno, CA 93721.
Telephone: (559) 320-4487. **Fax:** (559) 264-0795.
E-Mail Address: info@fresnogrizzlies.com. **Website:** www.FresnoGrizzlies.com.
Affiliation (first year): Houston Astros (2015). **Years in League:** 1998-

OWNERSHIP/MANAGEMENT
 Operated By: Fresno Baseball Club, LLC.
 General Manager/Executive Vice President: Derek Franks. **Director, Marketing:** Sam Hansen. **Director, Ticket Sales:** Andrew Milios. **Director, Stadium Maintenance:** Harvey Kawasaki. **Community Fund Director:** Whitney Campbell. **Director, Corporate Sales:** Jason Hannold. **Director, Partnership Marketing:** Andrew Melrose. **Ticket Sales Manager:** Cody Holden. **Account Executive:** Kyle Selna. **Account Executive:** Brandon Aurecchione. **Entertainment Manager:** Ray Ortiz. **Media Relations Manager:** Paul Braverman. **Marketing Manager:** Andy Inman. **Graphic Designer:** Dorian Castro. **Inside Sales Manager:** Andrew Hacnik. **Stadium Maintenance Manager:** Ira Calvin. **Merchandise Manager:** Lalonnie Calderon. **Assistant Merchandise Manager:** Chris Calderon. **Ballpark Development Manager:** Jon Stockton. **Assistant Ticket Sales Manager:** Eric Moreno. **Finance Manager:** Monica DeLacerda. **Entertainment/Mascot Coordinator:** Troy Simeon. **Ticket Sales Assistant:** Angie Cazares. **Partnership Activation Coordinator:** Belinda Gonzalez-Diaz. **Administrative Assistant:** Yanet Richardson. **Head Groundskeeper:** David Jacinto.

FIELD STAFF
 Manager: Rodney Linares. **Hitting Coach:** Darryl Robinson. **Pitching Coach:** Dyar Miller. **Trainer:** Lee Meyer. **Strength & Conditioning:** Taylor Rhodes. **Development Coach:** Ray Hernandez.

GAME INFORMATION
 Radio Announcer: Doug Greenwald. **No. of Games Broadcast:** 140. **Flagship Radio Station:** 1430 AM KYNO.
 Stadium Name: Chukchansi Park. **Location:** 1800 Tulare St, Fresno, CA 93721. **Directions:** From 99 North, take Fresno Street exit, left on Fresno Street. From 99 South, take Fresno Street exit, left on Fresno Street, right on Broadway to H Street. From 41 North, take Van Ness exit toward Fresno, left on Van Ness, left on Inyo or Tulare, stadium is straight ahead. From 41 South, take Tulare exit, stadium is located at Tulare and H Streets, or take Van Ness exit, right on Van Ness, left on Inyo or Tulare, stadium is straight ahead. **Ticket Price Range:** $10-19.
 Visiting Club Hotel: Doubletree Downtown Fresno, 2233 Ventura St. Fresno, CA 93721. **Telephone:** (559)-268-1000.

IOWA CUBS

Address: One Line Drive, Des Moines IA 50309.
Telephone: (515) 243-6111. **Fax:** (515) 243-5152.
Website: www.iowacubs.com.
Affiliation (first year): Chicago Cubs (1981). **Years in League:** 1969-

OWNERSHIP/MANAGEMENT
 Operated By: Raccoon Baseball Inc.
 Chairman/Principal Owner: Michael Gartner. **Executive Vice President:** Michael Giudicessi. **President/General Manager:** Sam Bernabe. **Shareholder:** Mike C. Gartner. **VP/Assistant GM:** Randy Wehofer. **VP/CFO:** Sue Tollefson.

Director, Media Relations: Shelby Cravens. **Director, Video and Multimedia Arts:** Justin Walters. **Director, Ticket Operations:** Clayton Grandquist. **VP/Director, Luxury Suites:** Brent Conkel. **VP/Stadium Operations:** Jeff Tilley. **Manager, Stadium Operations:** Nic Peters, Andrew Quillin, Dustin Halderson. **Corporate Relations:** Red Hollis, Eric Hammes, Sarah Engbretson, Jason Gellis, John Rodgers. **VP/Head Groundskeeper:** Chris Schlosser. **Assistant Groundskeeper:** Chase Manning. **Director, Merchandise:** Lisa Hufford. **Manager, Merchandise:** Abby Meirick. **Accounting:** Lori Auten, Jill Vento. **Director, Information Technology:** Ryan Clutter. **Landscape Coordinator:** Shari Kramer.

FIELD STAFF
Manager: Marty Pevey. **Hitting Coaches:** Desi Wilson, Chris Valaika. **Pitching Coach:** Rod Nichols. **Athletic Trainers:** Ed Halbur, Mike McNulty. **Strength/Conditioning:** Ryan Clausen.

GAME INFORMATION
Radio Announcers: Alex Cohen, Deene Ehlis. **No. of Games Broadcast:** 140. **Flagship Station:** AM 940 KPSZ.
PA Announcers: Aaron Johnson, Mark Pierce, Corey Coon, Rick Stageman, Joe Hammen. **Official Scorers:** Doug Howard, Michael Pecina, James Hilchen, Steve Mohr. **Stadium Name:** Principal Park. **Location:** I-80 or I-35 to I-235, to Third Street exit, south on Third Street, left on Line Drive. **Standard Game Times:** 7:08 pm, Sun. 1:08. **Ticket Price Range:** $5-16. **Visiting Hotel:** Hampton Inn and Suites Downtown, 120 SW Water Street, Des Moines IA 50309. **Telephone:** (515) 244-1650.

LAS VEGAS 51S

Address: 850 Las Vegas Blvd North, Las Vegas, NV 89101.
Telephone: (702) 943-7200. **Fax:** (702) 943-7214.
E-Mail Address: info@lv51.com. **Website:** www.lv51.com.
Affiliation (first year): New York Mets (2013). **Years in League:** 1983 - present (35 years)

OWNERSHIP/MANAGEMENT
Operated By: Summerlin Las Vegas Baseball Club LLC.
President/COO: Don Logan. **General Manager/Vice President, Sales/Marketing:** Chuck Johnson. **VP, Operations/Security:** Nick Fitzenreider. **Vice President, Ticket Sales:** Erik Eisenberg. **VP of Community Relations & Customer Experience:** Melissa Harkavy. **Director, Ticket Operations:** Siobhan Steiermann. **Director, Sponsorships:** James Jensen. **Controller:** Scott Montes. **Staff Accountant:** Felicity Khan. **Director, Broadcasting:** Russ Langer. **Social Media Strategist/Brand Manager:** Ashley Seda. **Business Development:** Larry Brown. **Media Relations Director:** Jim Gemma. **Ticket Operations Assistant:** Michelle Taggart. **Administrative Assistants:** Jan Dillard, Esther Lopez. **Account Executives, Ticket Sales:** Bryan Frey, TJ Thedinga. **Retail Operations Manager:** Jason Weber. **Operations Manager:** Chip Vespe. **Travel Coordinator & Clubhouse Manager:** Steve Dwyer.

FIELD STAFF
Manager: Tony DeFrancesco. **Hitting Coach:** Joel Chimelis. **Pitching Coach:** Glenn Abbott. **Bullpen Coach:** Jeremy Accardo. **Athletic Trainer:** Grant Hufford. **Assistant Athletic Trainer:** Kiyoshi Tada. **Strength/Conditioning Coach:** Josh Fields.

GAME INFORMATION
Radio Announcer: Russ Langer. **No. of Games Broadcast:** 140. **Flagship Station:** NBC Sports AM 920 'The Game'.
PA Announcer: Dick Calvert. **Official Scorer:** Peter Legner.
Stadium Name: Cashman Field. **Location:** I-15 to US 95 exit (downtown), east to Las Vegas Boulevard North exit, one-half mile north to stadium. **Standard Game Time:** 7:05 pm. **Ticket Price Range:** $12-17.
Visiting Club Hotel: Golden Nugget Hotel & Casino, 129 Fremont Street, Las Vegas, NV 89101. **Telephone:** (702) 385-7111.

MEMPHIS REDBIRDS

Office Address: 198 Union, Memphis, TN 38103. **Stadium Address:** 200 Union Ave, Memphis, TN 38103.
Telephone: (901) 721-6000. **Fax:** (901) 328-1102.
Website: www.memphisredbirds.com.
Affiliation (first year): St. Louis Cardinals (1998). **Years in League:** 1998-

OWNERSHIP/MANAGEMENT
Ownership: Peter B. Freund.
President/General Manager: Craig Unger. **Senior Director, Corporate Sales & Marketing:** Mike Voutsinas. **Senior Director, Operations:** Mark Anderson. **Director, Media and Public Relations:** Michael Schroeder. **Manager, Group Sales:** Lisa Peterson. **Manager, Ticket Operations:** Gian D'Amico. **Manager, Digital Media:** Peter Fleischer. **Graphic Designer:** Martheus Wade. **After Effects/Video Editor:** Dilland Wavra. **Accounting Manager:** Cindy Neal. **Office Manager:** Jackie Likens. **Groundskeeper:** Ben Young. **Assistant Groundskeeper:** Brian Bowe. **Facilities Manager:** Spencer Shields.

FIELD STAFF

Manager: Stubby Clapp. **Hitting Coach:** Mark Budaska. **Pitching Coach:** Dernier Orozco. **Trainer:** Matt Corvo.

GAME INFORMATION

Radio Announcer: Steve Selby. **No. of Games Broadcast:** 140. **Flagship Station:** WHBQ 560-AM. **PA Announcer:** TBA. **Official Scorer:** J.J. Guinozzo, Eric Opperman.
Stadium Name: AutoZone Park. **Location:** North on I-240, exit at Union Avenue West, one and half miles to park. **Standard Game Times:** 7:05, Sat. 6:35, Sun 2:05. **Ticket Price Range:** $9-23.
Visiting Club Hotel: Sleep Inn at Court Square, 40 N Front, Memphis, TN 38103. **Telephone:** (901) 522-9700.

NASHVILLE SOUNDS

Address: 19 Junior Gilliam Way, Nashville, TN 37219.
Telephone: (615) 690-HITS. **Fax:** (615) 256-5684.
E-Mail address: info@nashvillesounds.com. **Website:** www.nashvillesounds.com.
Affiliation (first year): Oakland Athletics (2015). **Years in League:** 1998-

OWNERSHIP/MANAGEMENT

Operated By: MFP Baseball. **Owners:** Frank Ward, Masahiro Honzawa.
GM/Chief Operating Officer: Adam Nuse. **VP, Operations:** Doug Scopel. **VP, Fan Relations:** Amy Schoch. **VP, Sales:** Bryan Mayhood. **Director, Finance:** Barb Walker. **Director, Ticket Operations:** Cooper Fazio. **Director, Activation:** Danielle Gaw. **Director, Media Relations:** Chad Seely. **Director, Marketing:** Alex Wassel. **Director, Entertainment:** Mary Hegley. **Director, Retail:** Katie Ward. **Director, Advertising:** Ryan Madar. **Director, Broadcasting:** Jeff Hem. **Director, Corporate Sales:** Chris Freeman. **Director, Stadium Operations:** Jeremy Wells. **Director, Video and Digital Production:** Erik Sharpnack. **Business Development:** Kevin Soto, Taylor Fisher. **Accounting Manager:** Halie Montgomery. **Merchandise Manager:** Wade Becker. **Community Relations Manager:** Destiny Whitmore. **Ticket Operations Manager:** CJ Berthelsen. **Stadium Operations Manger:** Austin Brunk. **Assistant Stadium Operations Manager:** Caleb Yorks. **Account Executive, Ticket Sales:** Mandy Valentine, Mahalie Shorrock, Sierra Siegel, Harrison Hunter. **Ticket Operations Coordinator:** Irving Alvarez. **Membership Services Coordinator:** Kyle Graves. **Promotions and Activation Coordinator:** Shannyn Wong. **Guest Relations/Season Ticket Activation Associate:** Allie Guido. **Mascot Coordinator:** Buddy Yelton. **Creative Assistant:** RV Oliver. **Community Relations Seasonal Associate:** Allie Doheny. **Head Groundskeeper:** Thomas Trotter. **Assistant Groundskeeper:** Shay Adams. **Clubhouse & Equipment Manager:** Matt Gallant. **Team Photographer:** Mike Strasinger.

FIELD STAFF

Manager: Fran Riordan. **Hitting Coach:** Eric Martins. **Pitching Coach:** Rick Rodriguez. **Trainer:** Brad LaRosa. **Strength/Conditioning Coach:** Henry Torres.

GAME INFORMATION

Radio Announcer: Jeff Hem. **No. of Games Broadcast:** 140. **Flagship Station:** ALT 97.5 FM
PA Announcer: Eric Berner. **Official Scorers:** Eric Jones, Kyle Parkinson, Cody Bush.
Stadium Name: First Tennessee Park. **Location:** I-65 to exit 85 (Rosa L Parks Blvd) and head south; Turn left on Jefferson St, then turn right onto 5th Ave North, then turn left on Jackson St. **Standard Game Times:** 7:05, Sat 6:35, 7:05 pm, Sun 2:05 (April-June 19), 6:35 (June 26-August 14). **Ticket Price Range:** $9-35. **Visiting Club Hotel:** Millennium Maxwell House, 2025 Rosa L Parks Blvd, Nashville, TN, 37228.

NEW ORLEANS BABY CAKES

Address: 6000 Airline Dr, Metairie, LA 70003.
Telephone: (504) 734-5155. **Fax:** (504) 734-5118.
E-Mail Address: TBA. **Website:** www.cakesbaseball.com.
Affiliation (first year): Miami Marlins (2009). **Years in League:** 1998-

OWNERSHIP/MANAGEMENT

Principal Owner/President: Lou Schwechheimer. **Co-Owner:** Don Beaver. **Chief Operating Officer:** Matt White **Senior Vice President/General Manager:** Augusto "Cookie" Rojas. **General Counsel:** Walter Leger. **Assistant General Manager, Fan Experience:** Bob Moullette. **Director, Broadcasting/Team Travel:** Tim Grubbs. **Director, Public Relations:** Dave Sachs. **Director, Community Relations:** Rachel Whitley. **Director, Stadium Operations:** Craig Schaffer. **Director, Ticket Operations:** Alex Rankin. **Director, Clubhouse:** Brett Herbert. **Group Sales Manager:** Trevor Johnson. **Group Sales:** Kyle Hamer, Margaret Schleismann, Patrick Vath. **Corporate Sales Executives:** Kyle Guille, Kristin Rojas. **Game Day Operations:** Alex Knudsen. **Head Groundskeeper:** Scott Blanchette. **Administrative Assistant:** Susan Radkovich.

FIELD STAFF

Manager: Arnie Beyeler. **Hitting Coach:** Tommy Gregg. **Pitching Coach:** Jeremy Powell. **Defensive Coach:** Robert Rodriguez. **Athletic Trainer:** Greg Harrel. **Strength & Conditioning:** Robert Reichert. **Video Assistant:** Alex Burritt.

GAME INFORMATION

Radio Announcers: Tim Grubbs, Ron Swoboda. **No. of Games Broadcast:** 140. **Flagship Station:** 1280 AM.

PA Announcer: Manny Pepis. **Official Scorer:** Brandon Scardigli.

Stadium Name: Shrine on Airline. **Location:** I-10 West toward Baton Rouge, exit at Clearview Pkwy (exit 226) and continues south, right on Airline Drive (US 61 North) for 1 mile, stadium on left; From airport, take Airline Drive (US 61) east for 4 miles, stadium on right. **Standard Game Times:** 7 pm, Sat. 6, Sun. 1. **Ticket Price Range:** $5-13. **Visiting Club Hotel:** Crowne Plaza New Orleans Airport, 2829 Williams Blvd, Kenner, LA 70062. **Telephone:** (504) 467-5611.

OKLAHOMA CITY DODGERS

Address: 2 S Mickey Mantle Dr., Oklahoma City, OK 73104.
Telephone: (405) 218-1000. **Fax:** (405) 218-1001.
E-Mail Address: info@okcdodgers.com. **Website:** www.okcdodgers.com.
Affiliation (first year): Los Angeles Dodgers (2015). **Years in League:** 1963-1968, 1998-

OWNERSHIP/MANAGEMENT

Operated By: MB OKC LLC. **Principal Owner:** Mandalay Baseball
President/General Manager: Michael Byrnes. **Senior Vice President:** Jenna Byrnes. **Vice President, Ticket Sales:** Kyle Daugherty. **Vice President, Corporate Partnerships:** Scott Sterling. **Senior Director, Operations:** Mitch Stubenhofer. **Director, Finance/Accounting:** Jon Shaw. **Director, Ticket Sales:** Kyle Logan. **Director, Ticket Operations:** Russell Durrant. **Director, Partner Services:** Ben Beecken. **Director, Facility Operations:** Harlan Budde. **Director, Communications/Broadcasting:** Alex Freedman. **Creative Director:** Nate Newby. **Director, Food Service Operations:** Al Splisbury. **Managing Director, OKC Dodgers Baseball Foundation:** Jennifer Van Tuyl. **Communications Coordinator:** Lisa Johnson. **Baseball Operations Manager:** Josh Ingram. **Retail Operations Manager:** Otilia Mares. **Office Manager:** Travis Hunter. **Head Groundskeeper:** Monte McCoy. **Clubhouse Manager:** T.J. Leonard.

FIELD STAFF

Manager: Bill Haselman. **Hitting Coach:** Adam Melhuse. **Pitching Coach:** Bill Simas. **Coach:** Luis Matos. **Athletic Trainer:** Jason Kirkman. **Strength/Conditioning Coach:** Tyler Norton.

GAME INFORMATION

Radio Announcer: Alex Freedman. **No. of Games Broadcast:** 144. **Station:** KGHM-AM 1340 (www.1340thegame. com).

PA Announcer: Jared Gallagher. **Official Scorers:** Jim Byers, Mark Heusman, Rich Tortorelli.

Stadium Name: Chickasaw Bricktown Ballpark. **Location:** Bricktown area in downtown Oklahoma City, near interchange of I-235 and I-40, off I-235 take Sheridan exit to Bricktown; off I-40 take Shields exit, north to Bricktown. **Standard Game Times:** 7:05 pm, Sun 2:05 (April-May), 6:05 (June-Aug). **Ticket Price Range:** $9-25.

Visiting Club Hotel: Courtyard Oklahoma City Downtown, 2 West Reno Ave., Oklahoma City, OK 73102. **Telephone:** (405) 232-2290.

OMAHA STORM CHASERS

Address: Werner Park, 12356 Ballpark Way, Papillion, NE 68046.
Administrative Office Phone: (402) 734-2550. **Ticket Office Phone:** (402) 738-5100. **Fax:** (402) 734-7166. **E-mail Address:** info@omahastormchasers.com. **Website:** www.omahastormchasers. com. **Affiliation (first year):** Kansas City Royals (1969). **Years in League:** 1998-

OWNERSHIP/MANAGEMENT

Operated By: Alliance Baseball Managing Partners. **Owners:** Gary Green, Larry Botel, Eric Foss, Brian Callaghan, Stephen Alepa, Peter Huff.
CEO: Gary Green. **President/General Manager:** Martie Cordaro. **Assistant GM:** Laurie Schlender. **Assistant GM, Operations:** Andrea Bedore. **Assistant GM, Sales:** Sean Olson. **Driector, Human Resources/Administration:** Keri Feyerherm. **Director, Broadcasting:** Mark Nasser. **Director, Business Development:** Dave Endress. **Director, Grounds:** Noah Diercks. **Director, Marketing/Communications:** Kaci Long. **Ballpark Operations Manager:** Matt Owen. **Community Relations Manager:** Becki Frishman. **Head Senior Corporate Account Manager:** Jason Kinney. **Client Services Manager:** Cody Stewart. **Creative Services Manager:** Coeli Danella. **Event Presentation/Marketing Manager:** Cody Allen. **Mascot/Theme Night Manager:** Nick Sandberg. **Media Operations Manager:** Andrew Green. **Ticket Operations Manager:** Anna Del Castillo. **Group Ticket Sales Executives:** Caleb Dieckmann, Michael Herman, Cody Smoot. **Group Sales Executive, Military Relations:** Cory Livingston. **Marketing/Promotions Coordinator:** Andrew Asbury. **Special Events/Community Relations Coordinator:** Kathleen Ezell. **Broadcast Assistant:** Donny Baarns. **Multicultural Marketing Lead:** Jhonnathan Omaña. **Sales Assistant:** Sara Howard. **Ticket Operations Assistant:** Kendall Hendrix. **Front Office Assistant:** Donna Kostal.

FIELD STAFF

Manager: Brian Poldberg. **Hitting Coach:** Brian Buchanan. **Pitching Coach:** Andy Hawkins. **Athletic Trainer:** Dave Iannicca. **Strength Coach:** Phil Falco.

GAME INFORMATION

Radio Announcers: Mark Nasser, Donny Baarns. **No. of Games Broadcast:** 140. **Flagship Station:** KZOT-AM 1180.

PA Announcer: Craig Evans. **Official Scorers:** Frank Adkisson, Ryan White.
Stadium Name: Werner Park. **Location:** Highway 370, just east of I-80 (exit 439). **Standard Game Times:** 6:35 pm (April-May), 7:05 (June-Sept), Fri./Sat. 7:05, Sun. 2:05.
Visiting Club Hotel: Courtyard Omaha La Vista, 12560 Westport Parkway, La Vista, NE 68128. **Telephone:** (402) 339-4900. **Fax:** (402) 339-4901.

RENO ACES

Address: 250 Evans Ave, Reno, NV 89501.
Telephone: (775) 334-4700. **Fax:** (775) 334-4701.
Website: www.renoaces.com.
Affiliation (first year): Arizona Diamondbacks (2009). **Years in League:** 2009-

OWNERSHIP/MANAGEMENT

President: Eric Edelstein.
Chief Financial Officer: Chris Gelfuso. **Chief Operating Officer:** Chris Holland. **Chief Revenue Officer:** Samantha Hicks. **Director, Ticket Sales:** Alyssa Reilly. **Merchandise Manager:** Andre Moyce. **Director, Marketing:** Audrey Hill. **VP, Business Development:** Brian Moss. **Visiting Clubhouse Manager:** Bubba Hearn. **Assistant Groundskeeper:** Corey Diaz. **Sr. Director, Corporate Partnership:** Doug Raftery. **Assistant Groundskeeper:** Drew Tice. **Sales Communications Manager:** Jackson Gaskins. **Senior Accountant:** Jamie Smith. **Creative Manager:** Jared Longland. **Outside Sales Manager:** Jeff Turner. **Sales Academy Manager:** Jillian Stoker. **Director, Field Operations:** Joe Hill. **Ballpark Operations & Safety Manager:** Justin Kilburn. **Ticket Operations Coordinator:** Liz Bell. **Ballpark Operations/Technology Manager:** Max Martin. **Corporate Partnerships Coordinator:** Max Simpson. **Human Resources Manager/Senior Accountant:** Melinda Jessee. **Facilities Manager:** Miguel Paredes. **Ticket Operations Supervisor:** Nick Yardley. **Jr. Accountant:** Rebecca Reyes. **Corporate Partnerships Services Manager:** Regan Hahesy. **Director, Broadcasting:** Ryan Radtke. **Director, Ticket Operations:** Sarah Bliss. **Fan Experience Manager:** Sarah Neumann. **Special Events Manager:** Sean Smock. **Sales & Analytics Coordinator:** Shane Kocick. **Production & Entertainment Manager:** Shaun Tatz. **Marketing Manager:** Vince Ruffino. **Account Executive, Corporate Partnerships:** Max Margulies. **Sales Academy Executives:** Thomas Beckley, Aaron Lightcap, Henry Fassinger. **Account Executives, Aces:** Clara Eickhoff, Alex Strathearn. **Account Executives, Group Sales:** Ross Melen, Miles Hendrick. **Account Executive, Outside Sales:** Aaron Harmon, Denis O'Grady.

FIELD STAFF

Manager: Greg Gross. **Hitting Coach:** Jason Camilli. **Pitching Coach:** Gil Heredia. **Coach:** Mike Lansing. **Athletic Trainer:** Paul Porter. **Strength & Conditioning Coach:** Steven Candelaria.

GAME INFORMATION

Radio Announcer: Ryan Radtke. **No. of Games Broadcast:** 142. **Flagship Station:** Fox Sports 630 AM.
PA Announcers: Cory Smith, Chris Payne. **Official Scorers:** Derek Neff, Nick Saccomanno, Katie Rihn, Gregg Zive.
Stadium Name: Greater Nevada Field. **Location: From north, south and east:** I-80 West, Exit 14 (Wells Ave.), left on Wells, right at Kuenzli St., field on right; From West, I-80 East to Exit 13 (Virginia St.), right on Virginia, left on Second, field on left. **Standard Game Times:** 7:05 p.m., 6:35 p.m., 1:05 p.m. **Ticket Price Range:** $8-35.

ROUND ROCK EXPRESS

Address: 3400 East Palm Valley Blvd, Round Rock, TX 78665.
Telephone: (512) 255-2255. **Fax:** (512) 255-1558.
E-Mail Address: info@rrexpress.com. **Website:** www.roundrockexpress.com.
Affiliation (first year): Texas Rangers (2011). **Year in League:** 2005-

OWNERSHIP/MANAGEMENT

Operated By: Ryan Sanders Baseball, LP. **Principal Owners:** Nolan Ryan, Don Sanders. **Owners:** Reese Ryan, Reid Ryan, Brad Sanders, Bret Sanders, Eddie Maloney.
CEO, Ryan Sanders Baseball: Reese Ryan. **Chief Operating Officer, Ryan Sanders Baseball:** JJ Gottsch. **Executive Assistant, Ryan Sanders Baseball:** Debbie Bowman. **Administrative Assistant, Ryan Sanders Baseball:** Jacqueline Bowman.
President: Chris Almendarez. **General Manager:** Tim Jackson. **Advisor to President/GM:** Dave Fendrick. **Senior Vice President, Marketing:** Laura Fragoso. **VP, Corporate Sales:** Henry Green. **VP, Ticket Sales:** Gary Franke. **VP, Administration/Accounting:** Debbie Coughlin. **VP, Communications/PR:** Jill Cacic. **Senior Director, United Heritage Center:** Scott Allen. **Senior Director, Ticket Operations:** Ross Scott. **Director, Broadcasting:** Mike Capps. **Director, Ballpark Entertainment:** Steve Richards. **Director, Community Relations and Special Events:** Elisa Fogle. **Director, Retail Operations:** Joe Belger. **Director, Stadium Maintenance:** Aurelio Martinez. **Director, Stadium Operations:** Gene Kropff. **Director, Ticket Sales:** Stuart Scally. **Creative Marketing Coordinator:** Julia Essington. **Grassroots Marketing Coordinator:** Casey Schnautz. **Client Services:** Zach Pustka. **IT Director:** Sam Isham. **Communications Coordinator:** Andrew Felts
Season Memberships and Suite Services Coordinator: Aschley Eschenburg. **Senior Account Executive:** Alyssa Coggins. **Account Executives:** Oscar Rodriguez, Lucas Allison, David Kirk, Chaniel Nelson. **Head Groundskeeper:** Garrett Reddehase. **Grounds Keeper:** Nick Rozdilski. **Clubhouse Manager:** Kenny Bufton. **Maintenance Staff:** Ofelia

Gonzalez. **Electrician/HVAC Maintenance Staff:** Leslie Hitt. **Office Manager:** Wendy Abrahamsen.

FIELD STAFF
    Manager: Jason Wood. **Hitting Coach:** Howard Johnson. **Pitching Coach:** Brian Shouse. **Coach:** Geno Petralli. **Trainer:** Carlos Olivas. **Strength Coach:** Eric McMahon.

GAME INFORMATION
    Radio Announcers: Mike Capps. **No. of Games Broadcast:** 140. **Flagship Station:** The Zone 1300 AM. **PA Announcer:** Glen Norman. **Official Scorer:** Tommy Tate.
    Stadium Name: Dell Diamond. **Location:** US Highway 79, 3.5 miles east of Interstate 35 (exit 253) or 1.5 miles west of Texas Tollway 130. **Standard Game Times:** 7:05 pm, 6:05, 1:05. **Ticket Price Range:** $7-$30.
    Visiting Club Hotel: Hilton Garden Inn, 2310 North IH-35, Round Rock, TX 78681. **Telephone:** (512) 341-8200.

SACRAMENTO RIVER CATS

    Address: 400 Ballpark Drive, West Sacramento, CA 95691
    Telephone: (916) 376-4700. **Fax:** (916) 376-4710.
    E-Mail Address: reception@rivercats.com. **Website:** www.rivercats.com
    Affiliation (first year): San Francisco Giants (2015). **Years in League:** 1903, 1909-11, 1918-60, 1974-76, 2000-

OWNERSHIP/MANAGEMENT
    Majority Owner/CEO: Susan Savage. **President:** Jeff Savage.
    General Manager: Chip Maxson. **Senior Manager, Human Resources:** Shani Crosby. **Vice President, Finance:** Maddie Strika. **Accounting Coordinator:** Calvin Nguyen. **Executive Assistant:** Shari Koepplin. **Receptionist:** Courtney Cino. **Vice President, Partner Services:** Greg Coletti. **Director, Business Development:** Andrew Dean. **Manager, Partnership Services:** Kim Bare. **Manager, Key Accounts:** Ellese Dias. **Director, Marketing:** Emily Williams. **Manager, Communications & Baseball Operations:** Daniel Emmons. **Coordinator, Multimedia/Graphic Design:** Mike Villarreal. **Coordinator, Creative Services:** Aaron Davis. **Coordinator, Marketing:** Kriselle Pons. **Coordinator, Digital Marketing:** Sasha Margulies. **Mascot Coordinator:** Stephen Webster. **Vice President, Ticket Sales & Membership Services:** Adam English. **Director, Ticket Operations:** Joe Carlucci. **Senior Manager, Ticket Sales:** Joey Van Cleave. **Manager, Corporate Sales:** John Watts. **Senior Account Executive, Corporate Sales:** Jack Barbour. **Account Executives, Corporate Sales:** Andrew Chibani, Troy Loparco, Sean Piper, Kelly Wilga. **Senior Account Executives, Group Sales:** Garrett Backhaus, Jeff Goldsmith, Alexis Stevens. **Account Executives, Group Events:** Erika Busch, James Collins, Cole Johnson, Daniel Mason. **Account Executives, Inside Sales:** Peyton Burnham, Austin Kromminga, Justin Wiley. **Manager, Membership and Suite Services:** Hayley Fernandez. **Membership Experience Specialists:** Kyle Strom, Christine Visitacion, Calee Williams. **Merchandise Manager:** Rose Holland. **Assistant Merchandise Manager:** Erin Kilby. **Coordinator, Website/Research:** Brent Savage. **Director, Stadium Operations:** Brett Myers. **Manager, Events/Entertainment:** Brittney Nizuk. **Coordinator, Events/Entertainment:** Vicky Wilhelm. **Head Groundskeeper:** Chris Shastid. **Facility Supervisor:** Anthony Hernandez. **Facility Operations:** Mike Correa. **Grounds Coordinator:** Marcello Clamar. **Landscaper:** Rafael Quiroz. **General Manager, Food/Beverage:** Corey Brandt. **Executive Chef:** Tim Benham. **Concessions Manager:** Sean Gerkensmeyer. **Premium Manager:** Jacob Leithner.

FIELD STAFF
    Manager: Dave Brundage. **Hitting Coach:** Damon Minor. **Pitching Coach:** Steve Kline. **Fundamentals Coach:** Nestor Rojas. **Athletic Trainer:** David Getsoff. **Strength and Conditioning Coach:** Andy King. **Bullpen Catcher and Team Administrator:** Travis Higgs.

GAME INFORMATION
    Radio Broadcaster: Johnny Doskow. **No. of Games Broadcast:** 140. **PA Announcer:** TBD. **Official Scorers:** Mark Honbo, Doug Kelly, Brian Berger.
    Stadium Name: Raley Field. **Location:** I-5 to Business-80 West, exit at Jefferson Boulevard. **Standard Game Time:** 7:05 pm. **Ticket Price Range:** $10-$70. **Visiting Club Hotel:** Holiday Inn Capitol Plaza.

SALT LAKE BEES

    Address: 77 W 1300 South, Salt Lake City, UT 84115.
    Telephone: (801) 325-2337. **Fax:** (801) 485-6818.
    E-Mail Address: info@slbees.com. **Website:** www.slbees.com.
    Affiliation (first year): Los Angeles Angels (2001). **Years in League:** 1915-25, 1958-65, 1970-84, 1994-.

OWNERSHIP/MANAGEMENT
    Operated by: Larry H. Miller Baseball Inc.
    Principal Owner: Gail Miller. **President, Miller Sports & Entertainment:** Steve Starks. **President, Miller Management Corporation:** Clark Whitworth. **President, Vivint Smart Home Arena:** Jim Olson. **Chief Revenue Officer:** Don Stirling. **Chief Customer Officer:** Craig Sanders. **Chief Financial Officer:** John Larson. **President/General**

Manager: Marc Amicone. **Assistant GM:** Bryan Kinneberg. **Senior VP, Corporate Partnerships:** Chris Baum. **Senior VP, Communications:** Frank Zang. **General Counsel:** Sam Harkness. **Senior VP, Corporate Partnerships:** Chris Baum. **VP of Corporate Partnerships:** Ted Roberts. **Director, Broadcasting:** Steve Klauke. **Director, Ticket Sales:** Brad Jacoway. **Director, Corporate Partnerships:** Kim Brown. **Director, Marketing:** Brady Brown. **Director, Ticket Operations:** Derrek DeGraaff. **Communications Manager:** Kraig Williams. **Game Operations and Marketing Manager:** Nikki Sim. **Youth Programs Coordinator:** Nate Martinez. **Clubhouse Manager:** Eli Rice. **Head Groundskeeper:** Brian Soukup.

Marketing & Promotions Manager: Brady Brown. **VP, Food Services:** Mark Stedman. **Director, Food Services:** Dave Dalton. **Youth Programs Coordinator:** Nate Martinez. **Clubhouse Manager:** Eli Rice. **Head Groundskeeper:** Brian Soukup.

FIELD STAFF
Manager: Keith Johnson. **Hitting Coach:** Unavailable. **Pitching Coach:** Erik Bennett. **Trainer:** Brian Reinker.

GAME INFORMATION
Radio Announcer: Steve Klauke. **No. of Games Broadcast:** 140. **Flagship Station:** 1280 AM.
PA Announcer: Jeff Reeves. **Official Scorers:** Howard Nakagama, Jeff Cluff, Brooke Frederickson
Stadium Name: Smith's Ballpark. **Location:** I-15 North/South to 1300 South exit, east to ballpark at West Temple.
Standard Game Times: 6:35 (April-May), 7:05 (June-Sept). **Ticket Price Range:** $10-24.

TACOMA RAINIERS

Address: 2502 South Tyler St, Tacoma, WA 98405.
Telephone: (253) 752-7707. **Fax:** (253) 752-7135.
Website: www.tacomarainiers.com.
Affiliation (first year): Seattle Mariners (1995). **Years in League:** 1960-Present

OWNERSHIP/MANAGEMENT
Owners: The Baseball Club of Tacoma.
President: Aaron Artman. **CFO:** Brian Coombe. **Vice President, Sales:** Shane Santman. **Director, Administration/ Asst. to the President:** Patti Stacy. **Senior Director, Ticket Sales:** Tim O'Hollaren. **Director, Business Development:** Ben Nelson. **Director, Ticket Operations:** Adam Dolezal. **Director, Baseball Operations and Merchandise:** Ashley Schutt. **Director, Ballpark Operations:** Nick Cherniske. **Director, Partner Development:** Julia Falvey. **Director, Group Sales and Event Marketing:** Caitlin Calnan. **Creative Director:** Casey Catherwood. **Vice President, Marketing:** Megan Mead. **Graphic Designer:** Kelsey Fausko. **Manager, Media and Communications:** Brett Gleason. **Manager, Stadium Operation:** Isaiah Dowdell. **Managers, Partner Services:** Hayley Adams, Taryn Duncan, Yvette Yzaguirre. **Manager, Ticket Operations:** Mandi Forbeck. **Manager, Group Sales:** Chris Aubertin. **Manager, Box Office:** Necia Borba. **Manager, Corporate Sales:** Ryan Bucciarelli, Kevin Drugge, Greg McCall, Stetson Olson, Tyler Olsson, Zach Smith. **Coordinator, Group Events:** Richard Feltenberger, Brooke Lunsford, Maddie Miller, Hayley Tamagni. **Coordinator, Technical:** Anthony Phinney. **Head Groundskeeper:** Michael Huie. **Financial Analyst:** Jack Kelly. **Coordinator, Front Desk/Reception:** Allie Brown. **Home Clubhouse Manager:** Shane Hickenbottom.

FIELD STAFF
Manager: Pat Listach. **Hitting Coach:** Dave Berg. **Pitching Coach:** Lance Painter. **Trainers:** TBA. **Performance Specialist:** TBA.

GAME INFORMATION
Radio Broadcaster: Mike Curto.
No. of Games Broadcast: 140/140. **Flagship Station:** KHHO 850-AM. **PA Announcer:** Randy McNair. **Official Scorers:** Kevin Kalal, Gary Brooks, Michael Jessee, Jon Gilbert. **Stadium Name:** Cheney Stadium.
Location: From I-5, take exit 132 (Highway 16 West) for 1.2 miles to 19th Street East exit, merge right onto 19th Street, right onto Clay Huntington Way and follow into parking lot of ballpark. **Standard Game Times:** 7:05, Sun. 1:35. **Ticket Price Range:** $7.50-$25.50. **Visiting Club Hotel:** Hotel Murano, 1320 Broadway Plaza, Tacoma, WA 98402. **Telephone:** (253) 238-8000.

EASTERN LEAGUE

Address: 30 Danforth St, Suite 208, Portland, ME 04101.
Telephone: (207) 761-2700. **Fax:** (207) 761-7064.
E-Mail Address: elpb@easternleague.com. **Website:** www.easternleague.com.
Years League Active: 1923-
President/Treasurer: Joe McEacharn.
Vice President/Secretary: Charlie Eshbach. **VP:** Chuck Domino. **Assistant to President:**
Bill Rosario. **Directors:** Fernando Aguirre (Erie), Ken Babby (Akron), Art Solomon (New
Hampshire), Mark Butler (Harrisburg), Lou DiBella (Richmond), Geoff Iacuessa (Portland), Joe
Finley (Trenton), John Hughes (Binghamton), Bob Lozinak (Altoona), Brian Shallcross (Bowie),
Josh Solomon (Hartford), Craig Stein (Reading).
Division Structure: Eastern—Binghamton, Hartford, New Hampshire, Portland, Reading,
Trenton. **Western**—Akron, Altoona, Bowie, Erie, Harrisburg, Richmond.
Regular Season: 140 games. **2018 Opening Date:** April 5. **Closing Date:** Sept 3.
All-Star Game: July 11 at Trenton.
Playoff Format: Top two teams in each division meet in best-of-five series. Winners meet in
best-of-five series for league championship.
Roster Limit: 25. **Player Eligibility Rule:** No restrictions.
Brand of Baseball: Rawlings.

Joe McEacharn

Umpires: Derek Gonzales (Mesa, AZ), Rich Grassa (Lindenhurst, NY), Aaron Higgins (Elk
Grove, CA), Justin Houser (Mattawan, MI), Ben Levin (Cincinnati, OH), John Mang (Youngstown, OH), Christopher
Marco (Waterdown, Ontario), Takahito Matsuda (Seiyo, Japan), Jacob Metz (Edmonds, WA), Richard Riley (Alexandria,
VA), Thomas Roche (Hamden, CT), Randy Rosenberg (Arlington, VA), Michael Savakinas (Fairborn, OH), Chris Scott
(Davidsonville, MD), Sean Shafer-Markle (Grand Rapids, MI), Patrick Sharshel (Castle Pines, CO), Derek Thomas (Cape
Coral, FL), JC Velez-Morales (San Juan, Puerto Rico).

STADIUM INFORMATION

Club	Stadium	Opened	LF	CF	RF	Capacity	2017 Att.
Akron	Canal Park	1997	331	400	337	7,630	343,351
Altoona	Peoples Natural Gas Field	1999	325	405	325	7,210	294,486
Binghamton	NYSEG Stadium	1992	330	400	330	6,012	190,765
Bowie	Prince George's Stadium	1994	309	405	309	10,000	234,789
Erie	UPMC Park	1995	317	400	328	6,000	214,394
Harrisburg	Metro Bank Park	1987	325	400	325	6,300	262,872
Hartford	Dunkin' Donuts Park*	2018	325	400	325	6,146	395,196
New Hampshire	Northeast Delta Dental Stadium	2005	326	400	306	6,500	284,108
Portland	Hadlock Field	1994	315	400	330	7,368	356,153
Reading	FirstEnergy Stadium	1951	330	400	330	9,000	411,698
Richmond	The Diamond	1985	330	402	330	9,560	386,185
Trenton	Arm & Hammer Park	1994	330	407	330	6,150	349,013

Dimensions

AKRON RUBBERDUCKS

Address: 300 S Main St, Akron, OH 44308.
Telephone: (330) 253-5151. **Fax:** (330) 253-3300.
E-Mail Address: information@akronrubberducks.com.
Website: www.akronrubberducks.com.
Affiliation (first year): Cleveland Indians (1989). **Years in League:** 1989-

OWNERSHIP/MANAGEMENT

Operated By: Fast Forward Sports Group / Akron Baseball, LLC. **Principal Owner/CEO:** Ken Babby.
President: Jim Pfander. **CFO:** Shawn Carlson. **General Manager/COO:** Jim Pfander. **Assistant GM:** Scott Riley.
Controller: Leslie Wenzlawsh. **Financial Assistant:** TBD. **Coordinator, Promotions:** Sara Varela. **Director, Public/
Media Relations:** Adam Liberman. **Director, Broadcasting/Baseball Information:** Dave Wilson. **Manager,
Merchandise:** Jeff Campano. **Coordinator, Creative Services:** Zach Aaron. **Director, Stadium Operations:** Adam
Horner. **Head Groundskeeper:** Chris Walsh. **Assistant Groundskeeper:** James Petrella. **Assistant Director, Ballpark
Operations:** James Parsons. **Director, Food/Beverage:** Brian Manning. **Assistant Director, Food/Beverage:** Bob
Demyan. **Director, Premium Experience:** Sam Dankoff. **Executive Chef:** James Phillips. **Office Manager:** Missy Dies.
Manager, Community Relations: Alex Hawks. **Director, Ticket Operations:** Brian Flenner. **Director, Ticket Sales:** Jody
Sellers. **Senior Group Sales Manager:** Mitch Cromes. **Ticket Sales Executives:** Roy Jacobs, Ryan Jones, Dom DeMarco,
Thyran Nowden, Kyle Hixenbaugh, Joe Mayancsik, Rik Segal. **Director, Corporate Partnerships:** David Bordonaro.
Manager, Corporate Partnerships: Juli Donlen. **Graphic Designer:** Scott Watkins. **Director, Player Facilities:** Shad
Gross.

FIELD STAFF

Manager: Tony Mansolino. **Hitting Coach:** Kevin Howard. **Pitching Coach:** Rigo Beltran. **Bench Coach:** TBD. **Trainer:** Jeremy Heller.

GAME INFORMATION

Radio Announcers: Jim Clark, Dave Wilson. **No. of Games Broadcast:** 140. **Flagship Station:** Fox Sports Radio 1350-AM. **PA Announcer:** DJ Nivens. **Official Scorer:** Chuck Murr.

Stadium Name: Canal Park. **Location:** From I-76 East or I-77 South, exit onto Route 59 East, exit at Exchange/Cedar, right onto Cedar, left at Main Street; From I-76 West or I-77 North, exit at Main Street/Downtown, follow exit onto Broadway Street, left onto Exchange Street, right at Main Street. **Standard Game Time:** 6:35 (April-May); 7:05 pm (June-Sept), Sun 2:05. **Ticket Price Range:** $5-11. **Visiting Club Hotel:** Fairfield Inn & Suites by Marriott Akron Fairlawn. **Telephone:** (330) 665-0641.

ALTOONA CURVE

Address: Peoples Natural Gas Field, 1000 Park Avenue, Altoona, PA 16602
Telephone: (814) 943-5400. **Fax:** (814) 942-9132
E-Mail Address: frontoffice@altoonacurve.com. **Website:** www.altoonacurve.com
Affiliation (first year): Pittsburgh Pirates (1999). **Years in League:** 1999-

OWNERSHIP/MANAGEMENT

Operated By: Lozinak Professional Baseball.

Managing Members: Bob and Joan Lozinak. **COO:** David Lozinak. **CFO:** Mike Lozinak. **General Manager:** Derek Martin. **Senior Advisor:** Sal Baglieri. **Director of Finance:** Mary Lamb. **Administrative Assistant:** Donna Harpster. **Director of Communications & Broadcasting:** Trey Wilson. **Communications & Broadcasting Assistant:** Garret Mansfield. **Director of Ticketing:** Nathan Bowen. **Box Office Manager:** Jess Knott. **Ticket Account Manager:** Ed Moffett. **Ticket Account Manager:** Joel Fox. **Director of Corporate Partnerships:** Corey Homan. **Director of Business Development:** Adam Erikson. **Manager of Partnership Services:** Jade Giantini. **Director of Community Relations:** Emily Rosencrants. **Director of Ballpark Operations:** Doug Mattern. **Head Groundskeeper:** Chris Mason. **Director of Concessions:** Glenn McComas.

Assistant Director of Concessions: Michelle Anna. **Director of Entertainment and Branding:** Isaiah Arpino. **Director of Creative Services:** David Gallagher. **Director of Marketing, Promotions & Special Events:** Mike Kessling. **Director of Merchandise:** Michelle Gravert.

FIELD STAFF

Manager: Michael Ryan. **Hitting Coach:** Keoni De Renne. **Pitching Coach:** Bryan Hickerson. **Trainer:** Justin Ahrens. **Strength/Conditioning:** Joe Schlesinger.

GAME INFORMATION

Radio Announcers: Trey Wilson, Nathan Bowen, Garret Mansfield. **No. of Games Broadcast:** 140. **Flagship Station:** 1240 AM, WRTA. **PA Announcer:** Rich DeLeo. **Official Scorers:** Ted Beam, Dick Wagner. **Stadium Name:** Peoples Natural Gas Field. **Location:** Located just off the Frankstown Road Exit off I-99. **Standard Game Times:** 7 p.m., 6 p.m. (April-May); Sat. 6 p.m.; Sun 1 p.m., 6 p.m. **Ticket Price Range:** $5-12. **Visiting Club Hotel:** Altoona Grand Hotel.

BINGHAMTON RUMBLE PONIES

Office Address: 211 Henry St., Binghamton, NY 13901.
Mailing Address: PO Box 598, Binghamton, NY 13902.
Telephone: (607) 722-3866. **Fax:** (607) 723-7779.
E-Mail Address: info@bingrp.com. **Website:** www.bingrp.com.
Affiliation (first year): New York Mets (1992). **Years in League:** 1923-37, 1940-63, 1966-68, 1992-

OWNERSHIP/MANAGEMENT

President: John Hughes. **Managing Director & Assistant General Manager:** John Bayne. **Director of Broadcasting & Media Relations:** Tim Heiman. **Director of Marketing and Promotions:** Eddie Saunders. **Director of Stadium Operations:** Richard Tylicki. **Interim Director of Stadium Operations:** Tim Thorick. **Director of Video Production:** Jonathan Beck. **Director of Community Relations & Box Office Manager:** Branden Kimble. **Director of Creative Services:** Sabrina Warren. **Director of Food and Beverage:** Bill Koehler. **Sports Turf Manager:** Tyler Spry. **Sales Manager:** Steve Poploski. **Senior Account Executive:** Seth Distler. **Account Executive:** Tony Rogers.

FIELD STAFF

Manager: Luis Rojas. **Hitting Coach:** Valentino Pascucci. **Pitching Coach:** Frank Viola. **Bench Coach:** Luis Rivera.

GAME INFORMATION

Radio Announcer: Tim Heiman. **No. of Games Broadcast:** 140. **Flagship Station:** WNBF 1290-AM. **PA Announcer:** Frank Perney.

Official Scorer: Matt Ferraro. **Stadium Name:** NYSEG Stadium. **Location:** I-81 to exit 4S (Binghamton), Route 11 exit to Henry Street. **Standard Game Times:** 6:35, 7:05 (Fri-Sat), 1:05 (Day Games). **Ticket Price Range:** $7 - $14. **Visiting Club Hotel:** Holiday Inn Downtown

BOWIE BAYSOX

Address: Prince George's Stadium, 4101 NE Crain Hwy, Bowie, MD 20716.
Telephone: (301) 805-6000. **Fax:** (301) 464-4911.
E-Mail Address: info@baysox.com. **Website:** www.baysox.com.
Affiliation (first year): Baltimore Orioles (1993). **Years in League:** 1993-

OWNERSHIP/MANAGEMENT

Owned By: Maryland Baseball Holding LLC.
President: Ken Young. **General Manager:** Brian Shallcross. **Assistant GM:** Phil Wrye. **Director, Ticket Operations:** Charlene Fewer. **Director, Sponsorships:** Matt McLaughlin. **Assistant Director, Ticket Operations:** Sam Colein. **Promotions Manager:** Chris Rogers. **Communications Manager:** Joe Fitzhenry. **Sponsorship Account Manager/Director of Broadcasting:** Adam Pohl. **Group Events Managers:** Stephen Clark, Scott Rupp. **Box Office Manager:** Landon Ferrell. **Director, Video Production:** Mitchell Block. **Facility Manager & Head Groundskeeper:** Stephen King, Jr. **Facility Manager & Assistant Groundskeeper:** Marcus VonHertensberg. **Director, Gameday Personnel:** Darlene Mingioli. **Clubhouse Manager:** Dallas Darling. **Bookkeeper:** Carol Terwilliger.

FIELD STAFF

Manager: Gary Kendall. **Hitting Coach:** TBA. **Pitching Coach:** Kennie Steenstra. **Bench Coach:** TBA. **Athletic Trainer:** Brian Guzman. **Strength & Conditioning Coach:** Patrick Armstrong.

GAME INFORMATION

Radio Announcer: Adam Pohl/Joe Fitzhenry. **No. of Games Broadcast:** 140. **Flagship Station:** www.1430wnav.com. **PA Announcer:** Adrienne Roberson. **Official Scorers:** Ted Black, Dan Gretz, Jason Lee. **Stadium Name:** Prince George's Stadium. **Location:** 1/4 mile south of US 50/Route 301 Interchange in Bowie. **Standard Game Times:** Mon-Thu, Sat. 6:35 pm, Fri 7:05 pm, Sun 1:35 pm. **Ticket Price Range:** $7-17. **Visiting Club Hotel:** Crowne Plaza Annapolis, 173 Jennifer Rd, Annapolis, MD 21401. **Telephone:** (410) 266-3131.

ERIE SEAWOLVES

Address: 110 E 10th St, Erie, PA 16501.
Telephone: (814) 456-1300. **Fax:** (814) 456-7520.
E-Mail Address: seawolves@seawolves.com. **Website:** www.seawolves.com.
Affiliation (first year): Detroit Tigers (2001). **Years in League:** 1999-

OWNERSHIP/MANAGEMENT

Principal Owners: At Bat Group, LLC.
CEO: Fernando Aguirre. **President:** Greg Coleman. **Assistant GM, Communications:** Greg Gania. **Assistant GM, Sales:** Mark Pirrello. **Director, Accounting/Finance:** Amy McArdle. **Director, Operation:** Chris McDonald. **Director, Entertainment:** Nathan Brecht. **Director, Ticket Sales:** Brendan O'Neill. **Account Executive:** Dan Jones. **Community Engagement Manager:** Hunter Horenstein. **Director, Merchandise:** Justin Cartor. **Director, Food/Beverage:** Will Cleis. **Ticket Operations Manager:** Tom Barnes. **Concessions Supervisor:** Jake Badach. **Executive Chef:** Ed Coleman.

FIELD STAFF

Manager: Andrew Graham. **Hitting Coach:** Mike Hessman. **Pitching Coach:** Willie Blair. **Coach:** Santiago Garrido. **Trainer:** T.J. Obergefell. **Strength/Conditioning Coach:** Jeff Mathers.

GAME INFORMATION

Radio Announcer: Greg Gania. **No. of Games Broadcast:** 140. **Flagship Station:** Fox Sports Radio WFNN 1330-AM. **PA Announcer:** Bob Shreve. **Official Scorer:** Les Caldwell. **Stadium Name:** UPMC Park. **Location:** US 79 North to East 12th Street exit, left on State Street, right on 10th Street. **Standard Game Times:** 6:05 p.m. (April-May, Sept.), Sun 1:35 p.m. **Ticket Price Range:** $9-15. **Visiting Club Hotel:** Clarion Lake Erie, 2800 West 8th St., Erie, PA 16505. **Telephone:** (814) 833-1116.

HARRISBURG SENATORS

Office Address: FNB Field, City Island, Harrisburg, PA 17101.
Mailing Address: PO Box 15757, Harrisburg, PA 17105. **Telephone:** (717) 231-4444. **Fax:** (717) 231-4445.
E-Mail address: information@senatorsbaseball.com. **Website:** www.senatorsbaseball.com.
Affiliation (first year): Washington Nationals (2005). **Years in League:** 1924-35, 1987-

OWNERSHIP/MANAGEMENT

Principal Owner: Mark Butler.
President: Kevin Kulp. **General Manager:** Randy Whitaker. **Assistant General Manager/Ticket Sales Manager:** Jon Boles. **Accounting Manager:** Donna Demczak. **Accounting Assistant:** Izzy Carter. **Senior Corporate Sales**

Executive: Todd Matthews. **Corporate Sales Executive:** Joseph Quinn. **Director, Group Sales:** Jessica Moyer. **Account Executives:** Brenton Bender, Sage Berry, Kevin Hickey. **Group Sales Account Executives:** Jeff Bell and Tyler Lyles. **Sales Service Coordinator:** Josh Bleyer. **Group Sales Interns:** Jason Croft and Kyle Kondracki. **Box Office Manager:** Matt McGrady. **Box Office Intern:** TBD. **Director, Merchandise:** Ann Marie Naumes. **Director of Stadium Operations:** Tim Foreman. **Head Groundskeeper:** Brandon Forsburg. **Stadium Operations and Groundskeeping intern:** Tyler Rivera. **Director of Public Relations & Broadcaster:** Terry Byrom. **Broadcasting and Media Assistant:** Gregory Wong.

Director, Marketing: Ashley Grotte. **Community Relations Coordinator:** JK McKay. **Marketing/Community Relations Intern:** Annie Choiniere. **Director of Game Entertainment:** Scott Ciaccia. **Game Entertainment Coordinator:** Sami Lesniak.

FIELD STAFF
Manager: Matt LeCroy. **Coach:** Brian Rupp. **Pitching Coach:** Michael Tejera. **Trainer:** T.D. Swinford. **Strength Coach:** R.J. Guyer.

GAME INFORMATION
Radio Announcers: Terry Byrom & Greg Wong. **No. of Games Broadcast:** Home-70 Road-70 Internet only at senatorsbaseball.com. **PA Announcer:** TBD. **Official Scorers:** Andy Linker and Mick Reinhard. **Stadium Name:** FNB Field. **Location:** I-83, exit 23 (Second Street) to Market Street, bridge to City Island. **Ticket Price Range:** $9-35. **Visiting Club Hotel:** Holiday Inn Harrisburg East, 815 S. Eisenhower Blvd, Middletown, Pa. 17057. **Telephone:** (717) 939-1600. **Visiting Team Workout Facility:** Planet Fitness, 480 Port View Dr., Harrisburg, Pa. 17111. **Telephone:** (717) 558-9821.

HARTFORD YARD GOATS

Address: Dunkin' Donuts Park, 1214 Main Street, Hartford CT 06103
Telephone: (860) **246-4628 Fax:** (860) 247-4628
E-Mail Address: info@yardgoatsbaseball.com. **Website:** www.YardGoatsBaseball.com
Affiliation (first year): Colorado Rockies (2015). **Years in League:** 2015-

OWNERSHIP/MANAGEMENT
President: Tim Restall. **General Manager:** Mike Abramson. **Assistant General Manager, Sales:** Josh Montinieri. **Assistant General Manager, Operations:** Dean Zappalorti. **Director, Broadcasting & Media Relations:** Jeff Dooley. **Executive Director of Business Development:** Steve Given. **Director of Event Services:** Conor Geary. **Special Events Coordinator:** Mellaney Castro. **Director of Security:** John Netkovick. **Director, Game Day Operations:** Shaun O'Brien. **Assistant, Director of Operations:** Narjay Hinds. **Operations Assistant:** Jimmy Bruno. **Director, Community Partnerships:** Tiffany Young. **Controller:** Jim Bonfiglio. **Human Resources Manager:** Shannon White. **Client & Team Relations Manager:** Amanda Goldsmith. **Promotions and Creative Services Manager:** Caroline Jette. **Game Production Manager:** Mike Doyle. **Marketing Manager:** Jacqueline Crockwell. **Merchandise Manager:** AJ Massaro. **Box Office Manager:** Sage Vigliarolo. **Ticket Sales Manager:** Steve Mekkelsen. **Ticket Sales Account Executive:** Matt DiBona. **Ticket Sales Account Executive:** Shawn Perry. **Ticket Sales Account Executive:** Tom Baxter. **Ticket Sales Account Executive:** Travis Mistretta. **Ticket Sales Account Executive:** Anna Franzreb. **Ticket Sales Account Executive:** Kyle Abad. **Ticket Sales Account Executive:** Tacara Robinson. **Sports Turf Manager:** Kyle Calhoon. **Assistant Sports Turf Manager:** J. Matthew Picard. **Administrative Assistant:** Brisely Tifa. **Professional Sports Catering: Assistant Director of Operations:** Stew Silvis. **Senior Concession Manager:** Zack Hermayer. **Executive Chef:** Chris Micci. **Premium Manager:** Denise Picard.

FIELD STAFF
Manager: Warren Schaeffer. **Hitting Coach:** Lee Stevens. **Pitching Coach:** Mark Brewer. **Trainer:** Hoshito Mizutani.

GAME INFORMATION
Radio Announcers: Jeff Dooley, Dan Lovallo. **No. of Games Broadcast:** 140. **Flagship Station:** News Radio 1410. **PA Announcer:** John Sheatsley. **Official Scorer:** Jim Keener.

Stadium Name: Dunkin' Donuts Park. **Directions: From the West:** Take 84 East to Exit 50 (Main Street). Take Exit 50 toward Main St. Use the left lane to merge onto Chapel St S. Turn left onto Trumbull St. Use the middle lane to turn left onto Main St. **From the East:** Take 84 West to Exit 50 (US-44 W/Morgan Street). Follow I-91 S/Main St. Take a slight right onto Main St. **From the North:** Take 91 South to Exit 32A - 32B (Trumbull St). Turn left onto Market St. Turn right onto Morgan St. Take a slight right onto Main St. **From the South:** Take 91 North to Exit 32A - 32B (Market St). Use the left lane to take Exit 32A-32B for Trumbull St. Use the middle lane to turn left onto Market St. Turn right onto Morgan St. Take a slight right onto Main St. **Ticket Price Range:** $6-22. **Visiting Club Hotel:** Holiday Inn Express, 2553 Berlin Turnpike, Newington, CT 06111. (860) 372-4000.

NEW HAMPSHIRE
FISHER CATS

Address: 1 Line Dr, Manchester, NH 03101.

Telephone: (603) 641-2005. **Fax:** (603) 641-2055.
E-Mail Address: info@nhfishercats.com. **Website:** www.nhfishercats.com.
Affiliation (first year): Toronto Blue Jays (2004). **Years in League:** 2004-

OWNERSHIP/MANAGEMENT

Operated By: DSF Sports. **Owner:** Art Solomon.
President: Mike Ramshaw. **General Manager:** Jim Flavin. **Deputy General Manager:** Jenna Raizes. **VP, Sales:** Jeff Tagliaferro
VP, Stadium Operations: Tim Hough. **Executive Director, Finance and Human Resources:** Debbie Morin.
Executive Director, Sales: Erik Lesniak. **Director, Hospitality and Special Events:** Stephanie Fournier. **Sports Turf Manager:** Christo Wallace. **Director, Ticket Sales:** Matt Freeman. **Box Office Manager:** Tara Leeth. **Merchandise Manager:** Jake Moore. **Broadcasting and Media Relations Manager:** Tyler Murray. **Production Manager:** Evan O'Brien. **Facility Operations Manager:** D.J. Peer. **Corporate Sales Manager:** Tom Devarenne. **Marketing and Promotions Manager:** Sarah Lenau. **Corporate Sales and Promotions Coordinator:** Andrew Marais. **Ticket Sales Account Executives:** Colin Cyr, John Evans, Xavier Rentz. Professional Sports Catering, Director, **Food & Beverage:** Jesse DaSilva.

FIELD STAFF

Manager: John Schneider. **Hitting Coach:** Hunter Mense. **Pitching Coach:** Vince Horsman. **Athletic Trainer:** Drew MacDonald. **Strength/Conditioning:** Ryan Maedel.

GAME INFORMATION

Radio Announcers: Tyler Murray, Bob Lipman, Tyler Zickel, Charlie Sherman. **No. of Games Broadcast:** 140.
Flagship Station: WGIR 610-AM. **PA Announcer:** Ben Altsher. **Official Scorers:** Chick Smith, Lenny Parker. **Stadium Name:** Northeast Delta Dental Stadium. **Location:** From I-93 North, take I-293 North to exit 5 (Granite Street), right on Granite Street, right on South Commercial Street, right on Line Drive. **Ticket Price Range:** $12.
Visiting Club Hotel: Country Inn & Suites, 250 South River Rd., Bedford, N.H. 03110. **Telephone:** (603) 666-4600.

PORTLAND SEA DOGS

Office Address: 271 Park Ave, Portland, ME 04102. **Mailing Address:** PO Box 636, Portland, ME 04104.
Telephone: (207) 874-9300. **Fax:** (207) 780-0317.
E-Mail address: seadogs@seadogs.com. **Website:** www.seadogs.com.
Affiliation (first year): Boston Red Sox (2003). **Years in League:** 1994-

OWNERSHIP/MANAGEMENT

Operated By: Portland, Maine Baseball, Inc.
Chairman: Bill Burke. **Treasurer:** Sally McNamara. **President:** Charles Eshbach. **Executive Vice President/ General Manager:** Geoff Iacuessa. **Senior VP:** John Kameisha. **VP, Financial Affairs/Game Operations:** Jim Heffley. **Vice President/Communications & Fan Experience:** Chris Cameron. **Assistant General Manager/Sales:** Dennis Meehan. **Director, Corporate Sales:** Justin Phillips. **Account Manager-Sales:** John Muzzy. **Ticket Office Manager:** Bryan Pahigian. **Assistant Ticket Office Manager:** Allison Casiles. **Director, Creative Services:** Ted Seavey. **Mascot Coordinator:** Tim Jorn. **Director, Media Relations & Broadcasting:** Mike Antonellis. **Director, Food Services:** Mike Scorza. **Assistant Director, Food Services:** Greg Moyes. **Ticket Office Coordinator:** Alan Barker, Samantha Fletcher. **Clubhouse Managers:** Mike Coziahr, Mike McHugh. **Head Groundskeeper:** Jason Cooke.

FIELD STAFF

Manager: Darren Fenster. **Hitting Coach:** Lee May Jr. **Pitching Coach:** Paul Abbott. **Athletic Trainer:** Scott Gallon. **Strength & Conditioning Coach:** Chris Messina.

GAME INFORMATION

Radio Announcer: Mike Antonellis. **No. of Games Broadcast:** 140. **Flagship Station:** WPEI 95.9 FM. **PA Announcer:** Paul Coughlin. **Official Scorer:** Thom Hinton. **Stadium Name:** Hadlock Field. **Location:** From South, I-295 to exit 5, merge onto Congress Street, left at St John Street, merge right onto Park Ave; From North, I-295 to exit 6A, right onto Park Ave. **Ticket Price Range:** $6-11.
Visiting Club Hotel: Fireside Inn & Suites, 81 Riverside St., Portland, ME 04103. **Telephone:** (207) 774-5601.

READING FIGHTIN PHILS

Office Address: Route 61 South/1900 Centre Ave, Reading, PA 19605. **Mailing Address:** PO Box 15050, Reading, PA 19612.
Telephone: (610) 370-2255. **Fax:** (610) 373-5868.
E-Mail Address: info@fightins.com. **Website:** www.fightins.com.
Affiliation (first year): Philadelphia Phillies (1967). **Years in League:** 1933-35, 1952-61, 1963-65, 1967-

OWNERSHIP/MANAGEMENT

Operated By: E&J Baseball Club, Inc. **Principal Owner:** Reading Baseball LP. **Managing Partner:** Craig Stein.

General Manager: Scott Hunsicker. **Exec. Director, Sales:** Joe Bialek. **Exec. Director, Operations:** Matt Hoffmaster. **Exec. Director, Baseball Operations & Merchandise:** Kevin Sklenarik. **Exec. Director, Tickets:** Mike Becker. **Exec. Director, Community & Fan Development:** Mike Robinson. **Exec. Director, Business Development:** Anthony Pignetti. **Controller:** Kris Haver. **Head Groundskeeper:** Dan Douglas.

Chief Director, Promotions: Todd Hunsicker. **Director, Marketing & Exec. Director, Baseballtown Charities:** Tonya Petrunak. **Video Director:** Andy Kauffman. **Director, Food & Beverage:** Travis Hart. **Office Manager:** Deneen Giesen. **Director, Groups:** Jon Nally. **Director, Public Relations/Media Relations & Radio Broadcaster:** Mike Ventola. **Director, Client Fulfillment/Clubhouse Operations:** Andrew Nelson. **Director, Extra Events:** Stephen Thomas.

Director, Graphic Arts/Merchandise: Ryan Springborn. **Asst. Director, Groups:** Brian Wells. **Asst. Director, Operations:** Jarred Smeltz. **Asst. Director, Food & Beverage:** Nick Crosby.

FIELD STAFF

Manager: Greg Legg. **Hitting Coach:** Kevin Riggs. **Pitching Coach:** Steve Schrenk. **Assistant Coach:** Rico Brogna.

GAME INFORMATION

Radio Announcer: Mike Ventola. **No. of Games Broadcast:** 140. **Flagship Station:** 610 AM Sports
Official Scorers: Paul Jones, Brian Kopetsky, Josh Leiboff, Dick Shute.
Stadium Name: FirstEnergy Stadium. **Location:** From east, take Pennsylvania Turnpike West to Morgantown exit, to 176 North, to 422 West, to Route 12 East, to Route 61 South exit; From west, take 422 East to Route 12 East, to Route 61 South exit; From north, take 222 South to Route 12 exit, to Route 61 South exit; From south, take 222 North to 422 West, to Route 12 East exit at Route 61 South. **Standard Game Times:** 7:05 pm, 6:35 (April-May), Sun. 2:05. **Ticket Price Range:** $5-11.
Visiting Club Hotel: Crowne Plaza Reading Hotel 1741 Papermill Road, Wyomissing, PA 19610. **Telephone:** (610) 376-3811.

RICHMOND FLYING SQUIRRELS

Address: 3001 N Boulevard, Richmond, VA 23230.
Telephone: (804) 359-3866. **Fax:** (804) 359-1373.
E-Mail Address: info@squirrelsbaseball.com. **Website:** www.squirrelsbaseball.com.
Affiliation: San Francisco Giants (2009). **Years in League:** 2009-

OWNERSHIP/MANAGEMENT

Operated By: Navigators Baseball LP. **President/Managing Partner:** Lou DiBella.
CEO: Chuck Domino. **Vice President/COO:** Todd "Parney" Parnell.
General Manager: Ben Rothrock. **Controller:** Faith Casey-Harriss. **Executive Director, Tickets:** Patrick Flower. **Director, Business Development:** Marty Steele. **Director of Broadcasting, Communications & Marketing:** Jay Burnham. **Executive Director, Community Outreach:** Megan Angstadt. **Director, Group Sales:** Camp Peery. **Assistant Director, Group Sales:** Chris Walker. **Group Sales Executives:** Garrett Erwin, Caroline Phipps. **Corporate Sales Executive:** Mike Caddell. **Director, Food/Beverage:** Josh Barban. **Executive Director, Field Operations:** Steve Ruckman. **Director, Stadium Operations:** Evan Smith.

FIELD STAFF

Manager: Willie Harris. **Hitting Coach:** Francisco Morales. **Pitching Coach:** Glenn Dishman. **Special Assistant:** Gene Clines. **Bullpen Coach:** Eliezer Zambrano. **Athletic Trainer:** Hiro Sato. **Strength Coach:** Jonathan Medici.

GAME INFORMATION

Radio Announcers: Jay Burnham, Sam Ravech. **No. of Games Broadcast:** 140. **Flagship Station:** Fox Sports Richmond WRNL-AM.
PA Announcer: Anthony Opperman. **Official Scorer:** Scott Day.
Stadium Name: The Diamond. **Location:** Right off I-64 at the Boulevard exit. **Standard Game Times:** 7:05 pm, Sat. 6:35, Sun. 5:05. **Ticket Price Range:** $7-12.
Visiting Club Hotel: Comfort Suites at Virginia Center Commons, 10601 Telegraph Road, Glen Allen, VA. **Telephone:** (804) 262-2000.

TRENTON THUNDER

Address: One Thunder Road, Trenton, NJ 08611.
Telephone: (609) 394-3300. **Fax:** (609) 394-9666.
E-Mail address: fun@trentonthunder.com. **Website:** www.trentonthunder.com.
Affiliation (first year): New York Yankees (2003). **Years in League:** 1994-Present

OWNERSHIP/MANAGEMENT

Operated By: Garden State Baseball, LLP.
General Manager/COO: Jeff Hurley. **Senior VP, Corporate Sales/Partnerships:** Eric Lipsman. **VP Ticket Sales:** John Fierko. **VP, Marketing/Sponsorship:** Lydia Rios. **Director, Merchandising:** Joe Pappalardo. **Director, Food/Beverage:** Kelly Kromer. **Director, Creative Services:** Dee Lugo. **Director, Corporate/Community Affairs:** Vince Marcucci. **Director, Group Sales:** Jon Bodnar. **Head Groundskeeper:** Jason Smith. **Controller:** Trevor Hain. **Broadcast and Public Relations Manager:** Jon Mozes. **Manager, Baseball & Stadium Operations:** Bryan Rock. **Manager, Web**

MINOR LEAGUES

/Creative Services: Dylan DeSimine. **Manager, Box Office:** Sean O'Brien. **Manager, Special Events:** Chuck Keller. **Managers, Group Sales:** Jack Rymal, Michael Heyer. **Group Sales Account Executives:** Matt Hillman, Brian Davis, Kevin Brady. **Ticket Sales Account Executive:** Bernadette Marco, Freddy Strebeck, Tommy Kay, Teddy Smallwood. **Database Manager:** Jackie Mott. **Chef:** Corey Anderson. **Office Manager:** Lauren Cox.
   Bat Dog: Rookie

FIELD STAFF

   Manager: Jay Bell. **Hitting Coach:** Ty Hawkins. **Pitching Coach:** Tim Norton. **Bullpen Coach:** Luis Dorante. **Defensive Coach:** Raul Dominguez. **Trainer:** Jimmy Downam. **Strength/Conditioning Coach:** Anthony Velazquez.

GAME INFORMATION

   Radio Announcers: Jon Mozes. **No. of Games Broadcast:** 140. **Flagship Station:** 920 AM The Jersey – Fox Sports Radio. **PA Announcer:** Kevin Scholla, Ryan Shute. **Official Scorers:** Jay Dunn, Greg Zak, Greg Zak Sr. **Stadium Name:** ARM & HAMMER Park. **Location:** From I-95, take Route 1 North to Route 29 South, stadium entrance just before tunnel; From NJ Turnpike, take Exit 7A and follow I-195 West, Road will become Route 29, Follow through tunnel and ballpark is on left. **Standard Game Times:** Monday-Friday 10: 30, 11:00, 12:00, 7:00. Sat. 5:00, 7:00. Sun 1:00, 5:00. **Ticket Price Range:** $11-13.

SOUTHERN LEAGUE

Telephone: (770) 321-0400. **Fax:** (770) 321-0037. **E-Mail Address:** office@southernleague.com. **Website:** www.southernleague.com.
Years League Active: 1964-

President: Lori Webb.
Vice President: Steve DeSalvo. **Directors:** Hunter Reed (Biloxi), Jonathan Nelson (Birmingham), Jason Freier (Chattanooga), Reese Smith (Jackson), Ken Babby (Jacksonville), Steve DeSalvo (Mississippi), Ralph Nelson (Mobile), Todd Parnell (Montgomery), Jonathan Griffith (Pensacola), Doug Kirchhofer (Tennessee).
Director, Media Relations: Michael Guzman
Division Structure: North—Birmingham, Chattanooga, Jackson, Montgomery, Tennessee. **South**—Biloxi, Jacksonville, Mississippi, Mobile, Pensacola.
Regular Season: 140 games (split schedule). **2018 Opening Date:** April 5. **Closing Date:** Sept. 3.
All-Star Game: June 19 in Birmingham, AL.
Playoff Format: First-half division winners meet second-half division winners in best-of-five series. Winners meet in best of five series for league championship.
Roster Limit: 25. **Player Eligibility Rule:** No restrictions.
Brand of Baseball: Rawlings.
Umpires: Unavailable.

Lori Webb

STADIUM INFORMATION

Club	Stadium	Opened	Dimensions LF	CF	RF	Capacity	2017 Att.
Biloxi	MGM Park	2015	335	400	335	6,000	167,151
Birmingham	Regions Field	2013	320	400	325	8,500	391,725
Chattanooga	AT&T Field	2000	325	400	330	6,362	209,948
Jackson	The Ballpark at Jackson	1998	310	395	320	6,000	120,695
Jacksonville	Baseball Grounds of Jacksonville	2003	321	420	317	11,000	325,743
Mississippi	Trustmark Park	2005	335	402	332	7,416	190,645
Mobile	Hank Aaron Stadium	1997	325	400	310	6,000	92,898
Montgomery	Riverwalk Stadium	2004	314	380	332	7,000	228,376
Pensacola	Blue Wahoos Stadium	2012	325	400	335	6,000	298,108
Tennessee	Smokies Stadium	2000	330	400	330	6,000	313,796

BILOXI SHUCKERS

Address: 105 Caillavet Street, Biloxi, MS 39530
Telephone: (228) 233-3465.
E-Mail Address: info@biloxishuckers.com. **Website:** www.biloxishuckers.com.
Affiliation (first year): Milwaukee Brewers (1999). **Years in League:** 1985-2015.

OWNERSHIP/MANAGEMENT
Operated By: Biloxi Baseball LLC.
President: Ken Young. **General Manager:** Hunter Reed. **Assistant General Manager:** Trevor Matifes. **Director, Media/Broadcaster:** TBA. **Creative Services & Production Manager:** Amy Johnson. **Business Development Manager:** Chris Birch. **Box Office Manager:** Allan Lusk. **Ticket Sales Executives:** Deven Matthews, Layton Markwood, Stephanie Chapman. **Community Relations & Promotions Manager:** Jenifer Truong. **Retail Manager:** Megan Ondrey. **Head Groundkeeper:** TBA. **Assistant Groundkeeper:** Quince Landry. **Human Resources & Accounting Manager:** Lisa Turner. **Administrative Assistant:** Jourdan Natale.

FIELD STAFF
Manager: Mike Guerrero. **Coach:** Chuckie Caufield. **Hitting Coach:** Al LeBouef. **Pitching Coach:** Dave Chavarria. **Athletic Trainer:** Kevan Creighton. **Strength/Conditioning Coach:** Nate Dine.

GAME INFORMATION
PA Announcer: Kyle Curley. **Official Scorer:** Scotty Berkowitz.
Stadium Name: MGM Park. **Location:** I-10 to I-110 South toward beach, take Ocean Springs exit onto US 90 (Beach Blvd), travel east one block, turn left on Caillavet Street, stadium is on left. **Ticket Price Range:** $7-$24. **Visiting Club Hotel:** Double Tree by Hilton Biloxi on Beach Blvd.

BIRMINGHAM BARONS

Office Address: 1401 1st Ave South, Birmingham, AL, 35233. **Mailing Address:** PO Box 877, Birmingham, AL, 35201.
Telephone: (205) 988-3200. **Fax:** (205) 988-9698.
E-Mail Address: barons@barons.com. **Website:** www.barons.com.
Affiliation (first year): Chicago White Sox (1986). **Years in League:** 1964-65, 1967-75, 1981-

OWNERSHIP/MANAGEMENT

Principal Owners: Don Logan, Jeff Logan, Stan Logan.
General Manager: Jonathan Nelson. **Vice President of Finance:** Randy Prince. **Director, Broadcasting:** Curt Bloom. **Director, Customer Service:** George Chavous. **Media Relations Assistants:** Unavailable. **Vice President of Marketing:** Erin O'Donnell. **Director of Retail Sales:** Nicole Siggers. **Vice President of Sales:** John Cook. **Director, Stadium Operations:** Timmy Hinds. **Director, Tickets & Community Relations:** Claire Griffith. **Director of Group Sales:** Jessica O'Rear. **Premium Sales Manager:** Brett Oates. **Director of Events:** Jennifer McGee. **Group Sales Managers:** Cory Ausderau, Tyler Gore, & Casey Sturgill. **Faith Based Outreach Coordinator:** Lindsey Shirley. **Head Groundskeeper:** Zach Van Voorhees. **Corporate Sales Manager:** Don Leo. **Manager of HR & Payroll:** Ty Reed. **GM of Food & Beverage:** David Madison. **Concessions Manager:** Andy Jackson. **Executive Chef:** Nick Tittle. **Catering Manager:** Matt Mullinax. **Premium Services Manager:** Sarah Spires.

FIELD STAFF

Manager: Julio Vinas. **Hitting Coach:** Cole Armstrong. **Pitching Coach:** Richard Dotson. **Head Athletic Trainer:** Corey Barton. **Strength and Conditioning Coach:** Tim Rodmaker.

GAME INFORMATION

Radio Announcer: Curt Bloom. **No of Games Broadcast:** 140. **Flagship Station:** News Radio 960 WERC-AM.
PA Announcers: Derek Scudder, Andy Parish. **Official Scorers:** AA Moore, David Tompkins.
Stadium Name: Regions Field. **Location:** I-65 (exit 259B) in Birmingham. **Standard Game Times:** 7:05 pm, Sat. 6:30, Sun 3:00. **Ticket Price Range:** $7-14.
Visiting Club Hotel: Sheraton Birmingham Hotel, 2101 Richard Arrington Junior Boulevard North, Birmingham, AL 35203. **Telephone:** (205) 324-5000.

CHATTANOOGA LOOKOUTS

Office Address: 201 Power Alley, Chattanooga, TN 37402.
Mailing Address: PO Box 11002, Chattanooga, TN 37401.
Telephone: (423) 267-2208. **Fax:** (423) 267-4258.
E-Mail Address: lookouts@lookouts.com. **Website:** www.lookouts.com.
Affiliation (first year): Minnesota Twins (2015). **Years in League:** 1964-65, 1976-

OWNERSHIP/MANAGEMENT

Operated By: Chattanooga Lookouts, LLC
Principal Owner: Hardball Capital, Managing Partner Jason Freier.
President: Rich Mozingo. **Public/Media Relations Manager:** Dan Kopf. **Head Groundskeeper:** Charlie Krips. **Marketing & Promotions Manager:** Alex Tainsh. **Director of Broadcasting:** Larry Ward. **Director, Food/Beverage:** Steve Sullivan. **Operations/Concessions Manager:** Anthony Polito. **Ticket Partnership Director:** Andrew Zito. **Ticket Partnership Manager:** Jennifer Crum. **Corporate Partnership Manager:** Coralee Bryan. **Ticket Operations Manager:** Bret Cranston. **Ticket Office Manager:** Aaron Glachman.

FIELD STAFF

Manager: Tommy Watkins. **Hitting Coach:** Javier Valentin. **Pitching Coach:** Ivan Arteaga. **Coach:** Richard Salazar. **Strength & Conditioning Coach:** Phil Hartt

GAME INFORMATION

Radio Announcers: Larry Ward. **No. of Games Broadcast:** 140. **Flagship Station:** 96.1.
PA Announcer: Ron Hall. **Official Scorers:** Andy Paul, David Jenkins.
Stadium Name: AT&T Field. **Location:** From I-24, take US 27 North to exit 1C (4th Street), first left onto Chestnut Street, left onto Third Street. **Ticket Price Range:** $5-10.
Visiting Club Hotel: Holiday Inn, 2232 Center Street, Chattanooga, TN 37421. **Telephone:** (423) 485-1185.

JACKSON GENERALS

Address: 4 Fun Place, Jackson, TN 38305.
Telephone: (731) 988-5299. **Fax:** (731) 988-5246.
E-Mail Address: sarge@jacksongeneralsbaseball.com.
Website: www.jacksongeneralsbaseball.com
Affiliation (first year): Arizona Diamondbacks (2017). **Years in League:** 1998-

OWNERSHIP/MANAGEMENT

Operated by: Jackson Baseball Club LP.

Chairman: David Freeman. **Owner:** Reese Smith III. **President:** Jason Compton. **Vice President, Finance:** Charles Ferrell. **General Manager:** Nick Hall. **Assistant General Manager:** Amanda Seimer. **Turf Manager:** Eric Taylor. **Manager, Media Relations/Broadcasting:** Tyler Springs. **Manager, Tickets & Merchandise:** Tory Goodman. **Manager, Stadium Operations & Security:** Lewis Crider. **Manager, Catering/Concessions:** Jeremy Wyatt. **Manager of Promotions/Production:** Robbie Perry. **Sales Exec:** Richard Coats. **Sales Exec:** Milt Canovan. **Sales Exec:** Marcus Sabata. **Sales Exec:** Mark Cunningham.

FIELD STAFF

Manager: Shelley Duncan. **Hitting Coach:** Vince Harrison. **Pitching Coach:** Doug Drabek. **Coach:** Javier Colina. Strength/ **Conditioning Coach:** Mike Locasto. **Trainer:** Joe Rosauer.

GAME INFORMATION

Radio Announcer: Tyler Springs. **No. of Games Broadcast:** 70 (Home). **PA Announcer:** Mike Coburn. **Official Scorer:** Mike Henson.

Stadium Name: The Ballpark at Jackson. **Location:** From I-40, take exit 85 South on FE Wright Drive, left onto Ridgecrest Road.

Standard Game Times: 6:05, Sun. 2:05 or 6:05.

Ticket Price Range: $8-12. **Visiting Club Hotel:** Doubletree by Hilton Jackson, 1770 Hwy 45 Bypass, Jackson, TN 38305. **Telephone:** (731) 664-6900.

JACKSONVILLE JUMBO SHRIMP

Office Address: 301 A. Philip Randolph Blvd, Jacksonville, FL 32202.

Telephone: (904) 358-2846. **Fax:** (904) 358-2845.

E-Mail Address: info@jaxshrimp.com. **Website:** www.jaxshrimp.com.

Affiliation (first year): Miami Marlins (2009). **Years In League:** 1970-

OWNERSHIP/MANAGEMENT

Operated by: Jacksonville Baseball LLC

Owner & Chief Executive Officer: Ken Babby. **Executive Assistant to Ken Babby:** Jill Popov.

President, Fast Forward Sports Group: Jim Pfander. **Chief Financial Officer:** Shawn Carlson. **General Manager:** Harold Craw. **Assistant General Manager:** Noel Blaha. **Vice President, Sales and Marketing:** Linda McNabb. **Director, Stadium Operations:** Weill Casey. **Director, Field Operations:** Christian Galen. **Director, Broadcasting:** Roger Hoover. **Director, Food & Beverage:** Ernest Hopkins. **Director, Ticket Operations:** Corey Marnik. **Director, Corporate Partnerships:** Gary Nevolis. **Director, Community Relations:** Andrea Williams. **Creative Services Manager:** Brian DeLettre. **Merchandise Manager:** Brennan Earley. **Box Office Manager:** Peter Ercey. **Food/Beverage Manager:** Chris Harper. **Media/Public Relations Manager:** Marco LaNave. **Accounting Manager:** Teresa Lively-Hall. **Partner Services Manager:** Ashley McCallen. **Senior Food & Beverage Manager:** Juanita Millhouse. **Promotions & Special Events Manager:** David Ratz. **Corporate Partnership Account Executive:** Joseph Roig Jr. **Military Liaison & Account Executive:** Theresa Viets. **Account Executives:** James Abbatinozzi, Justin Barnes, Alex Bell, Justin Lemminn, Tom Snyder. **Front Office Coordinator:** Lorie Tipton. **Accounting Assistant:** Jacob Yurdakul.

FIELD STAFF

Manager: Randy Ready. **Pitching Coach:** Storm Davis. **Hitting Coach:** Kevin Witt. **Coach:** Jose Ceballos. **Athletic Trainer:** Cesar Roman. **Strength/Conditioning Coach:** Julio Diaz. **Video Assistant:** Daniel Axelrod.

GAME INFORMATION

Radio Announcer: Roger Hoover. **No. of Games Broadcast:** 140. **Flagship Station:** 102.3 FM.

PA Announcer: John Leard. **Official Scorer:** Jason Eliopulos.

Stadium Name: Bragan Field at The Baseball Grounds of Jacksonville.

Location: I-95 South to Martin Luther King Parkway exit, follow Gator Bowl Blvd around Everbank Field; I-95 North to Exit 347 (Emerson Street), go right to Hart Bridge Expressway, take Sports Complex exit, left at light to stop sign, take left and follow around Everbank Field; From Mathews Bridge, take A Philip Randolph exit, right on A Philip Randolph, straight to stadium.

Standard Game Times: 7:05 pm, Sat. 6:35 pm, Sun. 3:05 pm. **Ticket Price Range:** $5-$18.

Visiting Club Hotel: Hyatt Regency Jacksonville Riverfront, 225 Coastline Drive, Jacksonville, FL 32202. **Telephone:** (904) 360-8665.

MISSISSIPPI BRAVES

Office Address: Trustmark Park, 1 Braves Way, Pearl, MS 39208.

Mailing Address: PO Box 97389, Pearl, MS 39288.

Telephone: (601) 932-8788. **Fax:** (601) 936-3567.

E-Mail Address: mississippibraves@braves.com. **Web site:** www.mississippibraves.com.

Affiliation (first year): Atlanta Braves (2005). **Years in League:** 2005-

OWNERSHIP/MANAGEMENT

Operated By: Atlanta National League Baseball Club Inc.

General Manager: Steve DeSalvo. **Assistant GM:** Dave Burke. **Director, Operations:** Jan Williams. **Merchandise Manager:** Sarah Banta. **Director, Communications, Media & Broadcasting:** Chris Harris. **Ticket Manager:** Jeff Flinn. **Concessions & Stadium Operations Manager:** Zach Evans. **Promotions Manager:** Dan Oleskowicz. **Director, Community Relations & Office Manager:** Christy Shaw. **Director, Field/Facility Operations:** Matt Taylor. **Suites, Catering & Special Events Manager:** Nancy Minev. **Graphic Design Manager:** Patrick Westrick. **Assistant Stadium Operations Manager:** Tony Duong.

FIELD STAFF

Manager: Chris Maloney. **Coach:** Carlos Mendez. **Pitching Coach:** Dennis Lewallyn. **Trainer:** TJ Saunders.

GAME INFORMATION

Radio Announcer: Chris Harris. **No. of Games Broadcast:** 140. **Flagship Station:** WYAB 103.9 FM. **PA Announcer:** Derrel Palmer. **Official Scorer:** Mark Beason.

Stadium Name: Trustmark Park. **Location:** I-20 to exit 48/Pearl (Pearson Road). **Ticket Price Range:** $6-$25.

Visiting Club Hotel: Hilton Garden Inn Jackson Flowood, 118 Laurel Park Cove, Flowood, MS 39232. **Telephone:** (601) 487-0800.

MOBILE BAYBEARS

Address: Hank Aaron Stadium, 755 Bolling Brothers Blvd., Mobile, AL 36606.
Telephone: (251) 479-2327. **Fax:** (251) 476-1147.
E-Mail Address: Info@mobilebaybears.com. **Web site:** www.MobileBayBears.com.
Affiliation (first year): Los Angeles Angels (2017). **Years in League:** 1966, 1970, 1997-current

OWNERSHIP/MANAGEMENT

Operated by: HWS Baseball Group. **Principal Owner:** Mike Savit.

Executive Vice President: Mike Gorrasi.

General Manager: Chris Morgan. **Assistant General Manager:** Ari Rosenbaum. **Director of Stadium Operations:** Stephen Warren. **Director of Food & Beverage:** Tom Pritzl. **Account Executive/Ticket Operations:** Jr Wittner. **Account Executive:** Brice Ballentine. **Account Executive:** Trish Miller. **Groundskeeper:** TurfPlus.

FIELD STAFF

Manager: Lou Marson. **Hitting Coach:** Lee Tinsley. **Pitching Coach:** Pat Rice. **Athletic Trainer:** Unavailable. **Strength Coach:** Unavailable.

GAME INFORMATION

Radio Announcer: Steve Goldberg **No. of Games Broadcast:** 140. **Website:** www.BayBearsRadio.com. MiLB.tv **PA Announcer:** Unavailable. **Official Scorer:** Unavailable.

Stadium Name: Hank Aaron Stadium. **Location:** I-65 to exit 1 (Government Blvd East), right at Satchel Paige Drive, right at Bolling Bros Blvd. **Standard Game Times:** 6:35pm (Weekday), 7:05 (Fri-Sat) 7:05 (Sun), 2:05 (April-May), Sunday: 5:05 pm (June-Sept). **Ticket Price Range:** $6-16. **Visiting Club Hotel:** Riverview Plaza, 64 S Water St, Mobile, AL 36602. **Telephone:** (251) 438-4000.

MONTGOMERY BISCUITS

Address: 200 Coosa St., Montgomery, AL 36104.
Telephone: (334) 323-2255. **Fax:** (334) 323-2225.
E-Mail address: info@biscuitsbaseball.com. **Web site:** www.biscuitsbaseball.com.
Affiliation (first year): Tampa Bay Rays (2004). **Years in League:** 1965-1980, 2004-

OWNERSHIP/MANAGEMENT

Operated By: Biscuits Baseball LLC. **Managing Owner:** Lou DiBella

President: Todd "Parney" Parnell. **Chief Operating Officer:** Brendon Porter. **General Manager:** Scott Trible. **Director of Marketing/Partnerships:** Michael Murphy. **Executive Consultant:** Greg Rauch. **Corporate Account Manager/Military Specialist:** Jay Jones. **Corporate Account Executive:** Matt Mulvanny. **Group Sales Manager:** Matt Baranofsky. **Group Sales Representative:** Katie Parker. **Box Office Manager, Season Ticket Coordinator:** Justin Ross. **Sales and Sponsorship Coordinator:** Alyssa Hudler. **Multimedia Specialist:** Jared McCarthy. **Marketing/Promotions Assistant:** Nathan Gunnels. **Broadcaster, Media Relations:** Chris Adams-Wall. **Director, Food & Beverage:** Risa Juliano. **Special Events/Catering Manager:** Sabrina Tew. **Executive Chef:** Mark Johnson. **Catering Supervisor:** Connie Edmondson. **Director, Stadium Operations:** Steve Blackwell. **Stadium Operations Assistant:** Thomas Constant. **Head Groundskeeper:** Alex English. **Business Manager:** Tracy Mims. **Sales Intern:** Kellsie Winkler. **Marketing Intern:** Tanya Hopson. **Retail Intern:** Ashley Williams. **Box Office Intern:** Spencer Valdespino. **Administrative Assistant:** Jeannie Burke.

FIELD STAFF

Manager: Brady Williams. **Pitching Coach:** RC Lichtenstein. **Coach:** Gary Redus. **Coach:** Jamie Nelson.

GAME INFORMATION

Radio Announcer: Chris Adams-Wall. **No of Games Broadcast:** 140. **Flagship Station:** WMSP 740-AM. **PA Announcer:** Rick Hendrick. **Official Scorer:** Brian Wilson. **Stadium Name:** Montgomery Riverwalk Stadium. **Location:** I-65 to exit 172, east on Herron Street, left on Coosa Street. **Ticket Price Range:** $9-13. **Visiting Club Hotel:** Candlewood Suites, 9151 Boyd-Cooper Pkwy, Montgomery, AL 36117. **Telephone:** (334) 277-0677.

PENSACOLA BLUE WAHOOS

Address: 351 West Cedar St., Pensacola, FL 32502.
Telephone: (850) 934-8444. **Fax:** (850) 791-6256.
E-Mail Address: info@bluewahoos.com. **Website:** www.bluewahoos.com.
Affiliation (first year): Cincinnati Reds (2012). **Years in League:** 2012-

OWNERSHIP/MANAGEMENT

Operated by: Northwest Florida Professional Baseball LLC. **Principal Owners:** Quint Studer, Rishy Studer. **Minority Owner:** Bubba Watson.
President: Jonathan Griffith. **Vice President of Operations:** Donna Kirby. **Receptionist:** Pam Handlin. **Operations Coordinator:** Mike Crenshaw. **Director, Sports Turf Management:** Dustin Hannah. **Director, Human Relations:** Candice Miller. **Media Relations Manager:** Ricki Stewart. **Broadcaster:** Tommy Thrall. **Creative Services Manager:** Adam Waldron. **Creative Services Assistant:** Derek Diamond. **Director, Merchandise:** Anna Striano. **Box Office Manager:** Joey DiChiara. **Sales Executives:** Jamie Briggs, Nick Castillo, Tyler Berridge. **Director, Food/Beverage:** Matt Risse. **CFO:** Amber McClure. **Assistant CFO:** Sally Jewell.

FIELD STAFF

Manager: Jody Bell. **Hitting Coach:** Gookie Dawkins. **Pitching Coach:** Danny Darwin. **Bench Coach:** Dick Schofield. **Athletic Trainer:** Tyler Moos. **Strength & Conditioning Coach:** Nate Tamargo.

GAME INFORMATION

Radio Announcer: Tommy Thrall. **No. of Games Broadcast:** 140. **Flagship Station:** The Ticket 97.1 FM. **PA Announcer:** Josh Gay. **Official Scorer:** Craig Cooper. **Stadium Name:** Blue Wahoos Stadium. **Standard Game Times:** 6:35 pm, Sat. 6:05, Sun. 5:05 pm. **Ticket Price Range:** $7-$19. **Visiting Club Hotels:** Hilton Garden Inn, Hampton Inn, Homewood Suites.

TENNESSEE SMOKIES

Address: 3540 Line Drive, Kodak, TN 37764.
Telephone: (865) 286-2300. **Fax:** (865) 523-9913.
E-Mail Address: info@smokiesbaseball.com. **Website:** www.smokiesbaseball.com.
Affiliation (first year): Chicago Cubs (2007-). **Years in League:** 1964-67, 1972-

OWNERSHIP/MANAGEMENT

Owners: Randy and Jenny Boyd.
CEO: Doug Kirchhofer. **President/COO:** Chris Allen. **Vice President:** Jeremy Boler. **General Manager, Baseball Operations:** Brian Cox. **General Manager, Business Operations:** Tim Volk. **Assistant General Manager, Stadium Operations:** Bryan Webster. **Director, Corporate Sales:** Chris Franklin. **Group Sales Manager:** Jason Moody. **Director, Field Maintenance:** Anthony DeFeo. **General Manager, Smokies Hospitality:** Scott Tallon. **Warehouse Manager:** John Felegy. **Director, Box Office/Merchandise:** Michael McMullen. **Stadium Operations Manager:** Josh Howe. **Merchandise Manager:** Matt Strutner. **Community Relations/Promotions Manager:** Allie Crain. **Creative Services/ Production Manager:** Drew Gibby. **Marketing/Media Relations Manager:** Connor Pearce. **Sponsorship Services Manager:** Baylor Love. **Sponsorship Services Coordinator:** Victoria Shillingsford. **Business Manager:** Suzanne French. **Account Executives:** Brad Dehler, Andrew O'Gara, Alex Ladd, Shelby Carter. **Senior Corporate Sales Executive:** Thomas Kappel.

FIELD STAFF

Manager: Mark Johnson. **Hitting Coach:** Jesus Feliciano. **Pitching Coach:** Terry Clark. **Coach:** Ben Carhart. **Strength Coach:** Jason Morriss. **Athletic Trainer:** Toby Williams.

GAME INFORMATION

Radio Announcer: Mick Gillispie. **No. of Games Broadcast:** 140. **Flagship Station:** WNML 99.1-FM/990-AM. **PA Announcer:** Unavailable. **Official Scorer:** Wade Mitchell. **Stadium Name:** Smokies Stadium. **Location:** I-40 to exit 407, Highway 66 North. **Standard Game Times:** 7:00 pm, Sat. 7:00 pm, Sun. 2/5:30. **Ticket Price Range:** $9-$14. **Visiting Club Hotel:** Hampton Inn & Suites Sevierville, 105 Stadium Drive, Kodak, TN 37764. **Telephone:** (865) 465-0590.

TEXAS LEAGUE

Mailing Address: 505 Main St., Suite 250, Fort Worth, TX 76102
Telephone: (682) 316-4100. **Fax:** (682) 316-4100.
E-Mail Address: office@texasleague.com **Website:** www.texasleague.com.
Years League Active: 1888-1890, 1892, 1895-1899, 1902-1942, 1946-.
President/Treasurer: Tim Purpura. **Vice President:** Justin Cole
Corporate Secretary: Monty Hoppel, **Assistant to the President:** Tyler King
Directors: Jon Dandes (Northwest Arkansas), Ken Schrom (Corpus Christi), Matt Gifford
(Springfield), Dale Hubbard (Tulsa), Chuck Greenberg (Frisco), Miles Prentice (Midland), Russ
Meeks (Arkansas), Burl Yarbrough (San Antonio).
Division Structure: North—Arkansas, Northwest Arkansas, Springfield, Tulsa. South—
Corpus Christi, Frisco, Midland, San Antonio.
Regular Season: 140 games (split-schedule). **2018 Opening Date:** April 5. **Closing Date:**
Sept 3.
All-Star Game: June 27 at Midland
Playoff Format: First-half division winners play second-half division winners in best-of-five
series. Winners meet in best-of-five series for league championship.

Tim Purpura

Roster Limit: 25. **Player Eligibility Rule:** No restrictions.
Brand of Baseball: Rawlings.
Umpires: Sean Allen (Fresno, CA), Grant Conrad (Carl Junction, MO), Jonathan Felczak (Bonney Lake, WA), Reid Gibbs
(Glendale, AZ), Jeff Gorman (Hayward, CA), Kyle McCrady Longview, WA), Malachi Moore (Compton, CA), Cody Oakes
(Oelwein, IA), Tyler Olson (Overland Park, KS), Justin Robinson (St. Louis, MO) Kyle Wallace (San Antonio, TX), Brian Walsh
(San Pedro, CA).

STADIUM INFORMATION

Club	Stadium	Opened	Dimensions			Capacity	2017 Att.
			LF	CF	RF		
Arkansas	Dickey-Stephens Park	2007	332	413	330	5,842	328,347
Corpus Christi	Whataburger Field	2005	325	400	315	5,362	331,242
Frisco	Dr Pepper Ballpark	2003	335	409	335	10,216	470,003
Midland	Security Bank Ballpark	2002	330	410	322	4,669	282,146
NW Arkansas	Arvest Ballpark	2008	325	400	325	6,500	304,026
San Antonio	Nelson Wolff Municipal Stadium	1994	310	402	340	6,200	305,351
Springfield	John Q. Hammons Field	2003	315	400	330	6,750	331,259
Tulsa	ONEOK Field	2010	330	400	307	7,833	374,976

ARKANSAS TRAVELERS

Office Address: Dickey-Stephens Park, 400 West Broadway, North Little Rock, AR 72114.
Mailing Address: PO Box 3177, Little Rock, AR 72203.
Telephone: (501) 664-1555. **Fax:** (501) 664-1834.
E-Mail address: travs@travs.com. **Website:** www.travs.com.
Affiliation (first year): Seattle Mariners (2017). **Years in League:** 1966-

OWNERSHIP/MANAGEMENT
Ownership: Arkansas Travelers Baseball Club, Inc.
President: Russ Meeks.
General Manager: Paul Allen. **Director, Assistant GM, Tickets:** Drew Williams. **Assistant GM, Merchandise:**
Rusty Meeks. **Broadcaster:** Steven Davis. **Controller:** Brad Eagle. **Director, Finance:** Patti Clark. **Director, In-Game
Entertainment:** Tommy Adam. **Park Superintendent:** Greg Johnston. **Assistant Park Superintendent:** Reggie
Temple. **Director, Stadium Operations:** Jay Borden. **Director of Guest Services:** Jared Schein. **Director, Marketing/
Media Relations:** Lance Restum. **Corporate Event Planners:** John Sjobeck, Sophie Ozier. **Director of Group Sales:** Eric
Schrader.

FIELD STAFF
Manager: Daren Brown. **Hitting Coach:** Roy Howell. **Pitching Coach:** Ethan Katz. **Assistant Hitting Coach/Mental
Skills:** Jimmy Van Ostrand.

GAME INFORMATION
Radio Announcer: Steven Davis. **No. of Games Broadcast:** 140. **Flagship Station:** KARN 920 AM.
PA Announcer: Russ McKinney. **Official Scorer:** Tim Cooper. **Stadium Name:** Dickey-Stephens Park. **Location:** I-30
to Broadway exit, proceed west to ballpark, located at Broadway Avenue and the Broadway Bridge. **Standard Game
Time:** 7:10 pm. **Ticket Price Range:** $3-13. **Visiting Club Hotel:** Crowne Plaza, 201 S. Shackleford Rd, Little Rock, AR
72211. **Telephone:** (501) 223-3000.

CORPUS CHRISTI HOOKS

Address: 734 East Port Ave, Corpus Christi, TX 78401.
Telephone: (361) 561-4665. **Fax:** (361) 561-4666.
E-Mail Address: info@cchooks.com. **Website:** www.cchooks.com.
Affiliation (first year): Houston Astros (2005). **Years in League:** 1958-59, 2005-

OWNERSHIP/MANAGEMENT

Owned/Operated By: Houston Astros.
President: Ken Schrom. **General Manager:** Wes Weigle.
Vice President of Sales/Marketing: Andy Steavens. **Senior Director, Finance:** Kim Harris. **Senior Director, Stadium Operations:** Jeremy Sturgeon. **Director, Media Relations/Broadcasting:** Michael Coffin. **Director, Marketing:** JD Davis. **Director, Business Development:** Maggie Freeborn. **Director, Premium/Membership Sales:** Zach Kaddatz. **Director, Ticketing:** Danielle O'Toole. **Field Superintendent:** Andrew Batts. **Account Executive:** Amanda Boman. **Ticket Operations Coordinator:** Ray Cervenka. **Accounting Manager:** Jessica Fearn. **Customer Service Manager:** Brett Howsley. **Special Events/Operations Coordinator:** Jorden Klaevemann. **Communications Coordinator:** Sam Levitt. **Community Outreach Coordinator:** Courtney Merritt. **Social Media Coordinator:** Gil Perez. **Account Executive:** Sean Phelan. **Video Production Coordinator:** Neil Rosan. **Senior Service Desk Technician:** Jonathan Santana. **Stadium Operations:** Michael Shedd. **Business Development Manager:** Diana Sleep. **Retail Manager:** Rudy Soliz. **Baseball Operations Manager:** Brad Starr. **Sr. Manager Premium Sales/Services:** Kelsey Thompson.

FIELD STAFF

Manager: Omar Lopez. **Hitting Coach:** Troy Snitker. **Pitching Coach:** Bill Murphy. **Development Coach:** Mycal Jones.

GAME INFORMATION

Radio Announcers: Michael Coffin, Sam Levitt, Gene Kasprzyk. **No. of Games Broadcast:** 140. **Flagship Station:** KKTX-AM 1360.
PA Announcer: TBA. **Stadium Name:** Whataburger Field. **Location:** I-37 to end of interstate, left at Chaparral, left at Hirsh Ave. **Ticket Price Range:** $6-20.
Visiting Club Hotel: Holiday Inn Corpus Christi Downtown Marina, 707 North Shoreline Blvd, Corpus Christi, Texas, 78401. **Telephone:** (361) 882-1700.

FRISCO ROUGHRIDERS

Address: 7300 RoughRiders Trail, Frisco, TX 75034.
Telephone: (972) 334-1900. **Fax:** (972) 731-5355.
E-Mail Address: info@ridersbaseball.com. **Website:** www.ridersbaseball.com.
Affiliation (first year): Texas Rangers (2003). **Years in League:** 2003-

OWNERSHIP/MANAGEMENT

Operated by: Frisco RoughRiders LP.
Chairman/CEO/General Partner: Chuck Greenberg. **Executive VP & General Manager:** Jason Dambach. **Chief Operating Officer:** Scott Burchett. **Chief Sales Officer:** John Alper. **Vice President, Marketing & Communications:** Matt Ratliff. **Vice President, Ticket Sales & Services:** Ross Lanford. **Vice President, Partner Services & Special Events:** Kathryne Buckley. **Vice President, Community Development/Executive Director of RoughRiders Foundation:** Breon Dennis. **Vice President, Accounting & Finance:** Dustin Alban. **Sr. Director, Game Entertainment:** Regina Pierce. **Sr. Director, Ticket Sales & Services:** David Dwyer. **Sr. Director, Sports Turf and Grounds Manager:** David Bicknell. **Director, Communications:** Art Garcia. **Director, Ticket Operations:** Brett Adams. **Director, Partner Activation:** David Kosydar. **Director, Human Resources:** Kenya Allen. **Director, Corporate Partnerships:** Mike Farrell. **Director, Maintenance:** Alfonso Bailon. **Executive Assistant and Office Manager:** Kelly Carr. **Operations Coordinator:** Ryan Wojdula. **Digital Marketing Manager:** Jennifer Johnson. **Managers, Game Entertainment:** Garret Young, Jordan Gracey. **Graphic Design Coordinator:** Trey Jackson. **Partner Services Coordinators:** Jenny Katlein, Alexis Summers. **Ticket Operations Coordinator:** Rebecca Spangler. **Premium Corporate Sales Managers:** Kasey Carlock, Joshua Bray, Tyler Ellis. **Premium Group Sales Manager:** Monica Man. **Sr. Corporate Sales Executive:** Tom Baker. **Sr. Group Sales Executive:** Johnny Coenen. **Corporate Sales Executives:** Andrew Dance, Crystal Vasquez, Ryan Williams, Jamaal Wilkins. **Group Sales Executives:** Tommy Burrell, Mikaya Carlisle, Nate Doederlein, Alex Sanborn, Enrique Saldana, Bailey Criado, Trevor Rolofson, Cameron Pipes.
Ticket Sales Coordinators: Joshua D'Penha D'Souza, Matthew Petrov, Sydney Ryan, Kyle Teegardin. **Human Resources/Accounting Assistant:** Laura Dama. **Customer Service Agents:** Claudia Kipp, Jean Scherer, Vicki Sohn.

FIELD STAFF

Manager: Joe Mikulik. **Hitting Coach:** Jason Hart. **Pitching Coach:** Greg Hibbard. **Trainer:** Jacob Newburn. **Strength/Conditioning:** Wade Lamont.

GAME INFORMATION

Broadcasters: Ryan Rouillard, Melanie Newman. **No. of Games Broadcast:** 140. **Flagship Station:** www. RidersBaseball.com. **PA Announcer:** Sean Heath. **Official Scorer:** Larry Bump.

Stadium Name: Dr Pepper Ballpark. **Location:** Intersection of Dallas North Tollway & State Highway 121. **Standard Game Times:** 7:05 pm, Sun. 4:05 (April-May). **Visiting Club Hotel:** Comfort Suites at Frisco Square, 9700 Dallas Parkway, Frisco, TX 75033. **Visiting Club Hotel Phone:** (972) 668-9700. **Visiting Club Hotel Fax:** (972) 668-9701.

MIDLAND ROCKHOUNDS

Address: Security Bank Ballpark, 5514 Champions Drive, Midland, TX 79706.
Telephone: (432) 520-2255. **Fax:** (432) 520-8326.
Website: www.midlandrockhounds.org.
Affiliation (first year): Oakland Athletics (1999). **Years in League:** 1972-

OWNERSHIP/MANAGEMENT

Operated By: Midland Sports, Inc. **Principal Owners:** Miles Prentice, Bob Richmond.
President: Miles Prentice. **Executive Vice President:** Bob Richmond. **General Manager:** Monty Hoppel.
Assistant GM: Jeff VonHolle. **Assistant GM, Marketing/Tickets:** Jamie Richardson. **Assistant GM, Operations:** Ray Fieldhouse. **Director, Broadcasting/Publications:** Bob Hards. **Director, Business Operations:** Eloisa Galvan. **Director, Sales:** Matthew Barnett. **Director, Ticketing/Office Manager:** Sabrina Banks. **Director, Client Services/Sports Complex Marketing:** Shelly Haenggi. **Director, Community Relations:** Courtnie Golden. **Director, Media Relations:** Frank Longobardo. **Director, Marketing:** Matt Bari. **Director, Facilities:** Joe Peters. **Director, Operations:** Cannon Schrank. **Head Groundskeeper:** Eric Peckham. **Game Entertainment/Video Board Coordinator:** Russ Pinkerton. **Sales Executive:** Mike Castillo. **Assistant Concessions Manager:** Al Melville. **Assistant Office/Ticket Manager:** Jordan Loya. **Home Clubhouse Manager:** Vernon Koslow. **Visiting Clubhouse Manager:** Seth Miller.

FIELD STAFF

Manager: Scott Steinmann. **Hitting Coach:** Tommy Everidge. **Pitching Coach:** Steve Connelly. **Trainer:** Justin Whitehouse. **Strength/Conditioning:** Omar Aguilar.

GAME INFORMATION

Radio Announcer: Bob Hards. **No. of Games Broadcast:** 140. **Flagship Station:** KCRS 550 AM.
PA Announcer: Wes Coles. **Official Scorer:** Steve Marcom.
Stadium Name: Security Bank Ballpark. **Location:** From I-20, exit Loop 250 North to Highway 191 intersection. **Standard Game Times:** Sunday: 2:00 pm, Monday-Wednesday: 6:30 pm, Thursday-Saturday: 7:00 pm. **Ticket Price Range:** $8-16.
Visiting Club Hotel: Springhill Suites by Marriott, 5716 Deauville Blvd, Midland, TX 79706. **Telephone:** (432) 695-6870.

NORTHWEST ARKANSAS
NATURALS

Address: 3000 Gene George Blvd, Springdale, AR 72762.
Telephone: (479) 927-4900. **Fax:** (479) 756-8088.
E-Mail Address: tickets@nwanaturals.com. **Website:** www.nwanaturals.com.
Affiliation (first year): Kansas City Royals (1995). **Years in League:** 2008-Present

OWNERSHIP/MANAGEMENT

Principal Owner: Rich Products Corp.
Chairman: Robert Rich Jr. **President, Rich Entertainment:** Melinda Rich. **President, Rich Baseball:** Jon Dandes.
General Manager: Justin Cole. **Sales Manager:** Mark Zaiger. **Business Manager:** Morgan Helmer. **Marketing/PR Manager:** Dustin Dethlefs. **Ballpark Operations Director:** Jeff Windle. **Ballpark Operations Assistant:** Corey Lewis.
Head Groundskeeper: Brock White. **Business Department Assistant:** Samantha Stawarz. **Ticket Office Coordinator:** Sam Ahern. **Broadcaster/Baseball Operations Coordinator:** Benjamin Kelly. **Event Coordinator:** Kristen Furlong.
Promotions Assistant: Roxanne Grundmeier. **Production Coordinator:** Adam Annaratone. **Ticket Sales Coordinator:** Jon Tucker. **Sr. Account Executive:** Brad Ziegler. **Account Executives:** Matt Fanning, Trey Garner. **Clubhouse Manager:** Danny Helmer.

FIELD STAFF

Manager: Mike Rojas. **Hitting Coach:** Leon Roberts. **Pitching Coach:** Steve Luebber. **Athletic Trainer:** Masa Koyanagi. **Strength & Conditioning Coach:** Jarret Abell.

GAME INFORMATION

Radio Announcer: Benjamin Kelly. **No. of Games Broadcast:** 140. **Flagship:** KQSM 92.1-FM. **PA Announcer:** Bill Rogers, John George, Jon Williams. **Official Scorers:** Kyle Stiles, Walter Woody & Paul Boyd. **Stadium Name:** Arvest Ballpark. **Location:** I-49 to US 412 West (Sunset Ave), Left on 56th St. **Ticket Price Range:** $8-13. **Standard Game Times:** 7:05 pm (Monday-Friday), 6:05 pm (Saturday), 2:05 pm (Sunday). **Visiting Club Hotel:** Holiday Inn Springdale, 1500 S 48th St, Springdale, AR 72762. **Telephone:** (479) 751-8300.

SAN ANTONIO MISSIONS

Address: 5757 Highway 90 West, San Antonio, TX 78227.
Telephone: (210) 675-7275. **Fax:** (210) 670-0001.
E-Mail Address: sainfo@samissions.com. **Website:** www.samissions.com.
Affiliation (first year): San Diego Padres (2007). **Years in League:** 1888, 1892, 1895-99, 1907-42, 1946-64, 1968-

OWNERSHIP/MANAGEMENT

Operated by: Elmore Sports Group. **Principal Owner:** David Elmore.
President: Burl Yarbrough. **General Manager:** Dave Gasaway. **Assistant GMs:** Mickey Holt, Jeff Long, Bill Gerlt.
GM, Diamond Concessions: Mike Lindal. **Controller:** Eric Olivarez. **Director, Broadcasting:** Mike Saeger. **Office Manager:** Delia Rodriguez. **Director, Operations:** John Hernandez. **Director, Public Relations:** Rich Weimert. **Field Superintendent:** Nic Kovacs. **Director, Ticketing:** Michael Ford.

FIELD STAFF

Manager: Phillip Wellman. **Hitting Coach:** Raul Padron. **Pitching Coach:** Jimmy Jones. **Trainer:** Isak Yoon. **Strength Coach:** Drew Heithoff

GAME INFORMATION

Radio Announcer: Mike Saeger. **No. of Games Broadcast:** 140. **Flagship Station:** 860-AM.
PA Announcer: Roland Ruiz. **Official Scorer:** David Humphrey.
Stadium Name: Nelson Wolff Stadium. **Location:** From I-10, I-35 or I-37, take US Hwy 90 West to Callaghan Road exit. **Standard Game Times:** 7:05 pm, Sun 2:05/6:05.
Visiting Club Hotel: Holiday Inn Northwest/Sea World. **Telephone:** (210) 520-2508.

SPRINGFIELD CARDINALS

Address: 955 East Trafficway, Springfield, MO 65802.
Telephone: (417) 863-0395. **Fax:** (417) 832-3004.
E-Mail Address: springfield@cardinals.com. **Website:** springfieldcardinals.com.
Affiliation (first year): St. Louis Cardinals (2005). **Years in League:** 2005-

OWNERSHIP/MANAGEMENT

Operated By: St. Louis Cardinals.
Vice President/General Manager: Dan Reiter. **VP, Baseball/Business Operations:** Scott Smulczenski. **Director, Ticket Operations:** Angela Deke. **Director, Stadium Operations:** Aaron Lowrey. **Director, Market Development:** Brad Beattie. **Manager, Production:** Kent Shelton. **Manager, Public Relations/Broadcaster:** Andrew Buchbinder. **Manager, Premium Sales/Marketing:** Zack Pemberton. **Manager, Fan Interaction:** Faith Lorhan. **Manager, Ticket Sales:** Eric Tomb. **Box Office Supervisor/Office Assistant:** Liz Blase. **Head Groundskeeper:** Brock Phipps. **Assistant Head Groundskeeper:** Derek Edwards.

FIELD STAFF

Manager: Johnny Rodriguez. **Hitting Coach:** Jobel Jimenez. **Pitching Coach:** Darwin Marrero. **Trainer:** TBA.

GAME INFORMATION

Radio Announcer: Andrew Buchbinder. **No. of Games Broadcast:** 140. **Flagship Station:** JOCK 98.7 FM.
PA Announcer: Unavailable. **Official Scorers:** Mark Stillwell, Tim Tourville.
Stadium Name: Hammons Field. **Location:** Highway 65 to Chestnut Expressway exit, west to National, south on National, west on Trafficway. **Standard Game Time:** 7:10 pm. **Ticket Price Range:** $6-28. **Visiting Club Hotel:** University Plaza Hotel, 333 John Q Hammons Parkway, Springfield, MO 65806. **Telephone:** (417) 864-7333.

TULSA DRILLERS

Address: 201 N. Elgin Ave, Tulsa, OK 74120.
Telephone: (918) 744-5998. **Fax:** (918) 747-3267.
E-Mail Address: mail@tulsadrillers.com. **Website:** www.tulsadrillers.com.
Affiliation (first year): Los Angeles Dodgers (2015). **Years in League:** 1933-42, 1946-65, 1977-present

OWNERSHIP/MANAGEMENT

Operated By: Tulsa Baseball Inc.
Co-Chairmen: Dale Hubbard, Jeff Hubbard.
President/GM: Mike Melega. **Executive VP/Assistant GM:** Jason George. **Bookkeeper:** Cheryll Couey. **Executive Assistant:** Kara Biden. **VP, Stadium Operations:** Mark Hilliard. **VP, Media/Public Relations:** Brian Carroll. **Director, Merchandise:** Tom Jones. **VP, Ticket Sales & Analytics:** Eric Newendorp. **Director, Marketing:** Justin Gorski. **Director, Video Production:** Alan Ramseyer. **Head Groundskeeper:** Gary Shepherd. **Assistant Bookkeeper:** Jenna Savill. **Manager, Ticket Sales:** Joanna Hubbard. **Manager, Group Sales:** John Rhodes. **Asst. Group Sales Manager:** Taylor Leavacy. **Account Executive:** Phil Sidoti. **Account Executive:** Cameron Gordon. **Mascot Coordinator:** Taylor Foote.

Manager, Facilities: Stevelan Hamilton. **Manager, Stadium Operations:** Marshall Schellhardt. **Manager, Graphic Design/Social Media:** Evan Brown. **Manager, Digital Media/Special Events:** Courtney Gemmett

   Ticket Sales Assistant: Nathan Cunningham. **Ticket Sales Assistant:** Colin Price. **Ticket Sales Assistant:** Joe Alexandrou. **Ticket Sales Assistant:** Katie Revlett. **Ticket Sales Assistant:** Nick Hill. **Social Media/Marketing Assistant:** Kyle Spinner. **Media/Public Relations Assistant:** Mark Verace. **Merchandise Assistant:** Jake Davis. **Promotions Assistant:** Alex Kossakoski. **Video Production Assistant:** Zhancheng Wu. **Director, Food Services:** Cody Malone. **Director, Concessions:** Wayne Campbell. **Concessions Manager:** Sara Bush. **Executive Chef:** Aloha Manahan. **Clubhouse Manager:** Rob Pierce.

FIELD STAFF

   Manager: Scott Hennessey. **Hitting Coach:** Terrmel Sledge. **Pitching Coach:** Dave Borkowski. **Coach:** Leo Garcia. **Trainer:** Kalie Swain. **Strength Coach:** Shaun Alexander. **Technology/Development Coach:** Peter Summerville.

GAME INFORMATION

   Radio Announcer: Dennis Higgins. **No. of Games Broadcast:** 140. **Flagship Station:** KTBZ 1430-AM.
   PA Announcer: Kirk McAnany. **Official Scorers:** Bruce Howard, Duane DaPron, Larry Lewis, Barry Lewis.
   Stadium Name: ONEOK Field. **Location:** I-244 to Cincinnati/Detroit Exit (6A), north on Detroit Ave, right onto John Hope Franklin Blvd, right on Elgin Ave. **Standard Game Times:** 7:05 pm, Sun. 1:05 (April-June), 7:05 (July-Aug). Mon. 11:05 am (May-June).
   Visiting Club Hotel: Marriott Tulsa Hotel Southern Hills, 1902 E 71st Street, Tulsa, OK 74136. **Telephone:** (918) 493-7000.

CALIFORNIA LEAGUE

Address: 3600 South Harbor Blvd, Suite 122, Oxnard, CA 93035.
Telephone: (805) 985-8585. **Fax:** (805) 985-8580.
Website: www.californialeague.com. **E-Mail:** info@californialeague.com.
Years League Active: 1941-1942, 1946-
President: Charlie Blaney. **Vice President:** Tom Volpe.
Directors: Bobby Brett (Rancho Cucamonga), Jake Kerr (Lancaster), Dave Elmore (Inland Empire), Gary Jacobs (Lake Elsinore), Mike Savit (Modesto), Tom Seidler (Visalia), Tom Volpe (Stockton), Dan Orum (San Jose).
Director, Operations/Marketing: Matt Blaney. **Historian:** Chris Lampe.
Legal Counsel: Jonathan Light. **CPA:** Mike Owen.
Division Structure: North—Modesto, San Jose, Stockton, Visalia. **South**—Inland Empire, Lake Elsinore, Lancaster, Rancho Cucamonga.
Regular Season: 140 games (split schedule).
2018 Opening Date: April 6. **Closing Date:** Sept 3.
Playoff Format: Four teams make the playoffs. First-half winners in each division play second-half winners (or wild card if the same team wins both halves) in best-of-five semifinals. Winners meet in best-of-five series for league championship.
All-Star Game: June 19 at Lancaster.
Roster Limit: 25 active (35 under control). **Player Eligibility:** No more than two players and one player/coach on active list may have more than six years experience.
Brand of Baseball: Rawlings. **Umpires:** TBD.

Charlie Blaney

STADIUM INFORMATION

			Dimensions				
Club	Stadium	Opened	LF	CF	RF	Capacity	2017 Att.
Inland Empire	San Manuel Stadium	1996	330	410	330	5,000	202,336
Lake Elsinore	The Diamond	1994	330	400	310	7,866	199,661
Lancaster	The Hangar	1996	350	410	350	4,500	169,237
Modesto	John Thurman Field	1952	312	400	319	4,000	147,562
Rancho Cucamo.	LoanMart Field	1993	335	400	335	6,615	171,622
San Jose	Municipal Stadium	1942	320	390	320	5,208	163,373
Stockton	Banner Island Ballpark	2005	300	399	326	5,200	184,164
Visalia	Recreation Ballpark	1946	320	405	320	2,468	126,419

INLAND EMPIRE 66ERS

Address: 280 South E St., San Bernardino, CA 92401.
Telephone: (909) 888-9922. **Fax:** (909) 888-5251. **Website:** www.66ers.com.
Affiliation (first year): Los Angeles Angels (2011). **Years in League:** 1941, 1987-

OWNERSHIP/MANAGEMENT
Operated by: Inland Empire 66ers Baseball Club of San Bernardino. **Principal Owners:** David Elmore, Donna Tuttle.
President: David Elmore. **Chairman:** Donna Tuttle. **General Manager:** Joe Hudson. **Director, Sales /Assistant GM:** Alex Groh. **Director, Broadcasting:** Steve Wendt. **Director, Corporate Sales/Marketing:** Steve Pelle. **Director, Promotions:** Adam Franey. **Director, Ticket Operations:** Sean Peterson. **Manager, Creative Services:** Dusty Ferguson. **Manager, Community Groups:** Stephanie O'Quinn. **Group Account Executive:** Jarrett Stark. **Coordinator, Promotions:** Aris Theofanopolous. **Coordinator, Group Sales:** Anna Forslin. **Coordinator, Ticket Operations:** Adam Zubiate. **Administrative Assistant:** Marlena Garcia. **Manager, Facility:** Richard Morales. **Head Groundskeeper:** Dominick Guerrero. **CFO:** John Fonseca. **Director, Food & Beverage (Diamond Creations):** Chris Henstra. **Operations Manager, Food & Beverage (Diamond Creations):** Mike Liotta.

FIELD STAFF
Manager: Ryan Barba. **Hitting Coach:** Brian Betancourth. **Pitching Coach:** Chris Seddon. **First Base Coach:** Steven Hernandez. **Athletic Trainer:** Yusuke Takahashi. **Strength & Conditioning Coach:** Adam Smith.

GAME INFORMATION
Radio Announcer: Steve Wendt. **Flagship Station:** 66ers Radio on TuneIn. **PA Announcer:** Renaldo Gonzales.
Official Scorer: Bill Maury-Holmes. **Stadium Name:** San Manuel Stadium. **Location:** From south, I-215 to 2nd Street exit, east on 2nd, right on G Street; from north, I-215 to 3rd Street exit, left on Rialto, right on G Street. **Standard Game Times:** Mon.-Fri. 7:05 pm; Sat. 6:05 pm; Sun. 2:05 pm (1st Half) 5:35 pm (2nd Half). **Ticket Price Range:** $8-$16. **Visiting Club Hotel:** Holiday Inn Express & Suites Loma Linda. **Telephone:** (909) 796-1000.

LAKE ELSINORE STORM

Address: 500 Diamond Drive, Lake Elsinore, CA 92530
Telephone: (951) 245-4487. **Fax:** (951) 245-0305.
E-Mail Address: info@stormbaseball.com. **Website:** www.stormbaseball.com.
Affiliation (first year): San Diego Padres (2001). **Years in League:** 1994-

OWNERSHIP/MANAGEMENT

Owners: Gary Jacobs, Len Simon.
General Manager/Director of Sales: Raj Narayanan. **Assistant GM (Operations/ Concessions):** Tim Arseneau. **Assistant GM (Marketing/Digital Media)/Senior Designer:** Mark Beskid. **Director of Finance & Business Administration:** Christine Kavic. **Director of Broadcasting:** Sean McCall. **VP of Business Development:** Paul Stiritz. **Director of Merchandising:** Donna Grunow. **Director of Ticketing:** Eric Colunga. **Assistant Director of Ticketing:** Lucas Wedgewood. **Assistant Director of Finance:** Andres Pagan. **Director of Communications/Sales Executive:** Eric Theiss. **Sales Executive:** Kasey Rawitzer. **Media Manager:** Matt Rodriguez. **Corporate Partnerships Sales Executive/Clubhouse Manager:** Terrance Tucker. **Assistant Director of Stadium Operations:** Daniel Limon. **Head Groundskeeper:** Joe Jimenez. **Assistant Groundskeeper:** Steven Frazier. **Director of Concessions/Food & Beverage:** Chris Kidder. **Director of Diamond Club Events:** Margie McCloskey.

FIELD STAFF

Manager: Edwin Rodriguez. **Hitting Coach:** Doug Banks. **Pitching Coach:** Pete Zamora. **Fielding Coach:** Freddy Flores.

GAME INFORMATION

Radio Announcer: Sean McCall. **No. of Games Broadcast:** 140. **Flagship Station:** Radio 94.5. **PA Announcer:** Unavailable. **Official Scorer:** Lloyd Nixon. **Stadium Name:** The Diamond. **Location:** From I-15, exit at Diamond Drive, west one mile to stadium. **Standard Game Times:** Mon.-Thurs. 6 p.m. Fri-Sat. 7 p.m. Sunday (first half): 1 p.m. (second half) 5 p.m. **Ticket Price Range:** $13-16. **Visiting Club Hotel:** Lake Elsinore Hotel and Casino, 20930 Malaga St, Lake Elsinore, CA 92530. **Telephone:** (951) 674-3101.

LANCASTER JETHAWKS

Address: 45116 Valley Central Way, Lancaster, CA 93536.
Telephone: (661) 726-5400. **Fax:** (661) 726-5406.
Email Address: info@jethawks.com. **Website:** www.jethawks.com.
Affiliation (first year): Colorado Rockies (2017). **Years in League:** 1996-

OWNERSHIP/MANAGEMENT

Operated By: JetHawks Baseball, LP. **Principal Owner/Managing General Partner:** Jake Kerr. **Partner:** Jeff Mooney. **President:** Andy Dunn. **Executive Vice President:** Tom Backemeyer. **General Manager:** William Thornhill. **Assistant General Manager:** Dylan Baker. **Director, Facility/Baseball Operations:** John Laferney. **Director, Broadcasting & Media Relations:** Jason Schwartz. **Director, Ticket Sales:** Jason Camp. **Box Office/Merchandise Manager:** Taylor Dunn. **Community Relations/Marketing Manager:** Julianna Clyne. **Manager, Sales & Special Events:** Veronica Hernandez

FIELD STAFF

Developmental Supervisor: Frank Gonzales. **Manager:** Fred Ocasio. **Hitting Coach:** Unavailable. **Pitching Coach:** Dave Burba. **Athletic Trainer:** Josh Guterman.

GAME INFORMATION

Radio Announcer: Jason Schwartz. **No. of Games Broadcast:** 140. **Flagship Station:** 1380AM & www.jethawks.com. **PA Announcer:** Paul Dybdahl. **Official Scorer:** David Guenther. **Stadium Name:** The Hangar. **Location:** Highway 14 in Lancaster to Avenue I exit, west one block to stadium. **Standard Game Times:** 6:35 pm, Sun. 2:05pm (April-June), 5:05pm (July-Sept). **Ticket Price Range:** $10-17. **Visiting Club Hotel:** Comfort Inn, 1825 W Avenue J-12, Lancaster CA 93534. **Telephone:** (661) 723-2001.

MODESTO NUTS

Office Address: 601 Neece Dr, Modesto, CA 95351.
Mailing Address: PO Box 883, Modesto, CA 95353.
Telephone: (209) 572-4487. **Fax:** (209) 572-4490.
E-Mail Address: fun@modestonuts.com. **Website:** www.modestonuts.com.
Affiliation (first year): Seattle Mariners (2017). **Years in League:** 1946-64, 1966-

OWNERSHIP/MANAGEMENT

Operated by: HWS Group IV. **Principal Owner:** Mike Savit.
Executive Vice President/General Manager: Michael Gorrasi. **Vice President, HWS Beverage:** Ed Mack. **General**

Manager: Zach Brockman. **Director, In-Game Entertainment:** Anthony Vallesteros. **Director, Marketing & Public Relations:** Natalie Winters. **Head Groundskeeper:** Chris Ambler. **Community Outreach Manager:** Sarah Lopes. **Director, Ticket Sales:** Chase Foster. **Account Executive:** Steven Webster. **Creative Services:** Charlie Magana. **Director, Broadcasting:** Keaton Gillogly. **Office Manager:** Kate Mendoza.

FIELD STAFF
Manager: Mitch Canham. **Hitting Coach:** Joe Thurston. **Pitching Coach:** Pete Woodworth.

GAME INFORMATION
Radio Announcer: Keaton Gillogly. **PA Announcer:** Unavailable. **Official Scorer:** Unavailable. **Stadium Name:** John Thurman Field. **Location:** Highway 99 in southwest Modesto to Tuolumne Boulevard exit, west on Tuolumne for one block to Neece Drive, left for 1/4 mile to stadium. **Standard Game Times:** 7:05 pm, Sun. 2:05pm/6:05 pm. **Ticket Price Range:** $8 -14. **Visiting Club Hotel:** Unavailable.

RANCHO CUCAMONGA
QUAKES

Office Address: 8408 Rochester Ave., Rancho Cucamonga, CA 91730.
Mailing Address: P.O. Box 4139, Rancho Cucamonga, CA 91729.
Telephone: (909) 481-5000. **Fax:** (909) 481-5005. **E-Mail Address:** info@rcquakes.com.
Website: www.rcquakes.com. **Affiliation (first year):** Los Angeles Dodgers (2011). **Years in League:** 1993-

OWNERSHIP/MANAGEMENT
Operated By: Bobby Brett. **Principal Owner:** Bobby Brett.
President: Brent Miles. **Vice President/General Manager:** Grant Riddle. **Vice President/Tickets:** Monica Ortega. **Assistant General Manager, Group Sales:** Linda Rathfon. **Assistant General Manager, Sponsorships:** Chris Pope. **Sponsorship Account Executive:** David Fields. **Sponsorship Account Executive:** Amy Gracia. **Sponsorship Account Executive:** Joey Huerta. **Director, Promotions:** Bobbi Salcido. **Director, Group Sales:** Kyle Burleson. **Director, Season Tickets/Operations:** Eric Jensen. **Group Sales Coordinator:** Trevor Morehead. **Group Sales Manager:** Mark Klopping, Kyle Nakama. **Director, Accounting:** Amara McCellan. **Director, Public Relations/Voice of the Quakes:** Mike Lindskog. **Office Manager:** Shelley Scebbi. **Director, Food/Beverage:** Austin Punzel.

FIELD STAFF
Manager: Drew Saylor. **Hitting Coach:** Justin Viele. **Pitching Coach:** Connor McGuiness. **Assistant Coach:** Petie Montero.

GAME INFORMATION
Radio Announcer: Mike Lindskog. **No. of Games Broadcast:** 140. **Flagship Station:** Fox Sports AM 1350 PA **Announcer:** Chris Albaugh. **Official Scorer:** Steve Wishek/Curt Christiansen. **Stadium Name:** LoanMart Field. **Location:** I-10 to I-15 North, exit at Foothill Boulevard, left on Foothill, left on Rochester to Stadium. **Standard Game Times:** 7:05 pm; Sun. 2:05 pm. **Visiting Club Hotel:** Best Western Heritage Inn, 8179 Spruce Ave, Rancho Cucamonga, CA 91730. **Telephone:** (909) 466-1111.

SAN JOSE GIANTS

Office Address: 588 E Alma Ave, San Jose, CA 95112.
Mailing Address: PO Box 21727, San Jose, CA 95151.
Telephone: (408) 297-1435. **Fax:** (408) 297-1453.
E-Mail Address: info@sjgiants.com. **Website:** www.sjgiants.com.
Affiliation (first year): San Francisco Giants (1988). **Years in League:** 1942, 1947-58, 1962-76, 1979-

OWNERSHIP/MANAGEMENT
Operated by: Progress Sports Management. **Principal Owners:** San Francisco Giants, Heidi Stamas, Richard Beahrs.
President/CEO: Daniel Orum. **Chief Operating Officer/General Manager:** Mark Wilson. **Senior VP, Communications/Chief Marketing Officer:** Juliana Paoli. **Senior VP, Ballpark Operations:** Lance Motch. **Director, Player Personnel:** Linda Pereira. **Director, Broadcasting:** Joe Ritzo. **Director, Group Sales:** Jeff Di Giorgio. **Director, Marketing/Media:** Jeff Black. **Director, Food and Beverage/HR:** Tara Tallman. **Manager, Accounting/ Payroll:** John Schember. **Manager, Food and Beverage:** Ramiro Mijares. **Senior Account Executive:** Justin Frederickson. **Account Executive:** Jimmy Quintanilla. **Coordinator, Ticket Operations:** Ryan Anthony. **Coordinator, Marketing/Community:** DJ Bettinger. **Coordinator, Retail/Merchandise:** Sierra Hanley. **Supervisor, Social Media/Community Relations:** Nicole Hernandez. **Head Groundskeeper:** Nathan Hobbs.

FIELD STAFF
Manager: Lipso Nava. **Hitting Coach:** Wilfredo Romero. **Pitching Coach:** Matt Yourkin. **Fundamentals Coach:** Gary Davenport. **Athletic Trainer:** Ryo Watanabe. **Strength & Conditioning Coach:** Mark Spadavecchia. **Bullpen Coach:** C.J. Picerni.

GAME INFORMATION

Radio Announcers: Joe Ritzo, Justin Allegri. **No. of Games Broadcast:** 140. **Flagship:** sjgiants.com. **Television Announcers:** Joe Ritzo, Joe Castellano. **No. of Games Broadcast:** 25 home games on Comcast Hometown Network (CHN), 70 home games on MiLB.TV. **PA Announcer:** Russ Call. **Official Scorer:** Mike Hohler. **Stadium Name:** Municipal Stadium. **Location:** South on I-280: Take 10th/11th Street Exit, turn right on 10th Street, turn left on Alma Ave. North on I-280: Take the 10th/11th Street Exit, Turn left on 10th Street, turn left on Alma Ave. **Standard Game Times:** 7 p.m., 6:30 p.m, Sat. 5 p.m., Sun 1 p.m. (5 p.m. after June 30). **Ticket Price Range:** $8-24.

STOCKTON PORTS

Address: 404 W Fremont St, Stockton, CA 95203. **Telephone:** (209) 644-1900.
Fax: (209) 644-1931. **E-Mail Address:** info@stocktonports.com.
Website: www.stocktonports.com.
Affiliation (first year): Oakland Athletics (2005). **Years in League:** 1941, 1946-72, 1978-

OWNERSHIP/MANAGEMENT

Operated By: 7th Inning Stretch LLC.
President: Pat Filippone. **General Manager:** Bryan Meadows. **Assistant General Manager:** Taylor McCarthy. **Senior Director, Ticket Sales and Service:** Mike Kim. **Director of Business Development:** Justice Hoyt. **Corporate Sales Manager:** Peter Fiorentino. **Community Relations Manager:** Allie Bakalar. **Stadium Operations Manager:** Seth Unger. **Ticket Operations Manager:** Markus Hagglund. **Group Sales Manager:** Riley Robar. **Ticket Sales Account Executive:** Vincent Zielen. **Corporate Sponsorship & Ticket Sales Executive:** Greg Bell. **Finance Manager:** Vang Hang. **Front Office Manager:** Christa Leri. **Spectra General Manager:** Mike Bristow.

FIELD STAFF

Manager: Rick Magnante. **Hitting Coach:** Brian McArn. **Pitching Coach:** Bryan Corey. **Athletic Trainer:** Shane Zdebiak. **Strength & Conditioning Coach:** Matt Mosiman. **Clubhouse Manager:** Vic Zapien.

GAME INFORMATION

Radio Announcer: Zack Bayrouty. **No of Games Broadcast:** 140. **Flagship Station:** KWSX 1280 AM. **TV:** Comcast Hometown Network, Channel 104, regional telecast. **PA Announcer:** Mike Conway. **Official Scorer:** Paul Muyskens. **Stadium Name:** Banner Island Ballpark. **Location:** From I-5/99, take Crosstown Freeway (Highway 4) exit El Dorado Street, north on El Dorado to Fremont Street, left on Fremont. **Standard Game Times:** 7:05 pm. **Ticket Price Range:** $7-$20. **Visiting Club Hotel:** Quality Inn Lathrop, 16855 Harlan Rd, Lathrop, CA 95330. **Telephone:** 209-598-1524.

VISALIA RAWHIDE

Address: 300 N Giddings St, Visalia, CA 93291.
Telephone: (559) 732-4433. **Fax:** (559) 739-7732.
E-Mail Address: info@rawhidebaseball.com. **Website:** www.rawhidebaseball.com.
Affiliation (first year): Arizona Diamondbacks (2007). **Years in League:** 1946-62, 1968-75, 1977-

OWNERSHIP/MANAGEMENT
President: Tom Seidler. **General Manager:** Jennifer Reynolds. **Assistant General Manager:** Jill Webb. **Baseball Operations Manager:** Julian Rifkind. **Director, Ticketing:** Heather Dominguez. **Director, Broadcasting & Media Relations:** Vinnie Longo. **Head Groundskeeper:** Mike Larson. **Manager, Ballpark Operations:** Jerry Verastegui. **Community Relations Manager:** Micolette Pena. **Ballpark Operations Coordinator:** Orlando Mendoza.

FIELD STAFF
Manager: Joe Mather. **Hitting Coach:** Franklin Stubbs. **Pitching Coach:** Jeff Bajenaru. **Bench Coach:** Travis Denker. **Trainer:** Chris Schepel.

GAME INFORMATION
Radio Announcers: Vinnie Longo. **No. of Games Broadcast:** 70. **Flagship Station:** Unavailable.
PA Announcer: Brian Anthony. **Official Scorer:** Harry Kargenian. **Stadium Name:** Rawhide Ballpark. **Location:** From Highway 99, take 198 East to Mooney Boulevard exit, left at second signal on Giddings; four blocks to ballpark. **Standard Game Times:** 7 pm, Sun. 1pm (first half), 6 pm (second half). **Ticket Price Range:** $7-30.
Visiting Club Hotel: Charter Inn & Suites, 1016 E Prosperity Ave, Tulare, CA 93274. **Telephone:** (559) 685-9500.

CAROLINA LEAGUE

Address: 3206 Buena Vista Road, Winston-Salem, NC 27106
Telephone: (336) 691-9030. **Fax:** (336) 464-2737.
 E-Mail Address: office@carolinaleague.com. **Website:** www.carolinaleague.com.
Years League Active: 1945-

President/Treasurer: Geoff Lassiter.
 Vice President: Billy Prim (Winston-Salem). **Executive VP:** Tim Zue (Salem). **Corporate Secretary:** Ken Young (Frederick). **Directors:** DG Elmore (Lynchburg), Chuck Greenberg (Myrle Beach), Dave Ziedelis (Frederick), Tyler Barnes (Carolina), Dave Heller (Wilmington), Billy Prum (Winston-Salem), Art Silber (Potomac), David Lane (Buies Creek), Joe Januszeswki (Down East).
Division Structure: North—Frederick, Lynchburg, Potomac, Salem, Wilmington.
 South—Buies Creek, Carolina, Down East, Myrtle Beach, Winston-Salem.
 Regular Season: 140 games (split schedule).
 2018 Opening Date: April 5. **Closing Date:** Sept 3.
 All-Star Game: South Division vs. North Division at Carolina, June 19.
 Playoff Format: First-half division winners play second-half division winners in best-of-three series. If a team wins both halves it plays division opponent with next-best second- half record. Division series winners meet in best-of-five series for Mills Cup. **Roster Limit:** 25 active. **Player Eligibility Rule:** No age limit. No more than two players and one player/coach on active list may have six or more years of prior minor league service. **Brand of Baseball:** Rawlings. **Umpires:** Isaias Barba (Hawthorne, CA), Matthew Brown (Conway, SC), Jason C. Johnson (Kingsport, TN), Thomas Hanahan, (Mentor, OH), Dave Martinez(Bayonne, NJ), Anthony Perez (Murrells Inlet, SC), Benjamin Phillips (Redondo Beach, CA), Austin D. Jones (Charleston, SC), Ryan Wilhelms (Rowlett, TX), Andrew J. Stukel (Duluth, MN).

Geoff Lassiter

STADIUM INFORMATION

| | | | Dimensions | | | | |
Club	Stadium	Opened	LF	CF	RF	Capacity	2017 Att.
Buies Creek	Jim Perry Stadium	2012	337	395	328	2,000	30,518
Carolina	Five County Stadium	1991	330	400	309	6,500	190,420
Down East	Grainger Stadium	1949	335	390	335	4,100	145,780
Frederick	Harry Grove Stadium	1990	325	400	325	5,400	303,930
Lynchburg	City Stadium	1939	325	390	325	4,000	137,566
Myrtle Beach	TicketReturn.com Field	1999	308	400	328	5,200	233,126
Potomac	Pfitzner Stadium	1984	315	400	315	6,000	236,010
Salem	Salem Memorial Stadium	1995	325	401	325	6,415	215,244
Wilmington	Frawley Stadium	1993	325	400	325	6,532	230,677
Winston-Salem	BB&T Ballpark	2010	315	399	323	5,500	304,607

BUIES CREEK ASTROS

Office Address: 76 Upchurch Ln, Lillington, NC, 27546.
 Mailing Address: PO Box 235, Buies Creek, NC 27506. **Telephone:** (910) 893-1459 .
 E-Mail Address: buiescreek@astros.com. **Website:** www.buiescreekastros.com
 Affiliation (first year): Houston Astros (2018). **Years In League:** 2018-

OWNERSHIP/MANAGEMENT
 Principal Owner: Houston Astros.
 General Manager: David Lane.

FIELD STAFF
 Manager: Morgan Ensberg. **Hitting Coach:** Ben Rosenthal. **Pitching Coach:** Drew Fench. **Development Coach:** Nate Shaver. **Athletic Trainer:** Unavailable. **Strengh & Conditioning Coach:** Unavailable.

GAME INFORMATION
 Radio: Unavailable. **Flagship Station:** Unavailable. **PA Announcer:** Unavailable. **Official Scorer:** Unavailable. **Stadium Name:** Jim Perry Stadium. **Location:** Campbell University. **Standard Game Time:** Mon.-Fri. 7:00pm. Sat. 6:00pm. Sun. 2:00 pm. **Ticket Price Range:** $7. **Visiting Club Hotel:** Fairfield Inn & Suites Dunn I-95. 513 Spring Branch Rd, Dunn, NC 28334. **Telephone:** (910) 891-4064.

CAROLINA MUDCATS

Office Address: 1501 NC Hwy 39, Zebulon, NC 27597.
Mailing Address: PO Drawer 1218, Zebulon, NC 27597. **Telephone:** (919) 269-2287.
Fax: (919) 269-4910. **E-Mail Address:** muddy@carolinamudcats.com.
Website: www.carolinamudcats.com.
Affiliation: Milwaukee Brewers (2018-). **Years in League:** 2012-

OWNERSHIP/MANAGEMENT
Ownership: Milwaukee Brewers Baseball Club, L.P. **Operated by:** Milwaukee Brewers Baseball Club, L.P.
Vice President/General Manager: Joe Kremer. **General Manager, Operations:** Eric Gardner. **Assistant GM, Sales:** David Lawrence. **Business Manager:** Joshua Perry. **Manager, Ticket Package Sales:** Taylor Gustafson. **Coordinator, Box Office:** Ryan Rainey. **Director, Group Sales:** Mike Link. **Associate, Group Sales:** Aaron Freeman, Andrew Houston, Jack Noble. **Director, Promotions and Fan Experience:** Patrick Ennis. **Coordinator, Community Relations:** Cassie Tomasello. **Coordinator, Special Events:** Nick Farmer. **Manager, Multimedia:** Evan Moesta. **Coordinator, Social Media/Marketing/Graphics:** Aaron Bayles. **Manager, Merchandise:** Amy Peterson. **Manager, Stadium Operations:** Cameron Olson. **Coordinator, Stadium Operations:** Michael Lincoln. **Director, Food and Beverage:** Dwayne Lucas. **Coordinator, Food and Beverage:** Josh Clark. **Director, Broadcasting and Media Relations:** Greg Young.

FIELD STAFF
Manager: Joe Ayrault. **Pitching Coach:** Dave Chavarria. **Hitting Coach:** Sandy Guerrero. **Coach:** Edwin Maysonet. **Athletic Trainer:** Jeff Bodenhamer. **Strength & Conditioning Coach:** Jonah Mergen.

GAME INFORMATION
Radio Announcer: Greg Young. **No. of Games Broadcast:** 140. **Flagship Station:** The Big Dawg 98.5 FM, WDWG. **PA Announcer:** Hayes Permar. **Official Scorer:** Bill Woodward. **Stadium Name:** Five County Stadium. **Location:** From Raleigh, US 64 East to 264 East, exit at Highway 39 in Zebulon. **Standard Game Times:** 7:00, Sat. 5:00, Sun. 2:00. **Ticket Price Range:** $10-12. **Visiting Club Hotel:** Holiday Inn Raleigh.

DOWN EAST WOOD DUCKS

Address: 400 East Grainger Avenue, Kinston, NC 28502
Telephone: (252) 686-5165
E-Mail Address: whowell@woodducksbaseball.com. **Website:** www.woodducksbaseball.com
Affiliation (first year): Texas Rangers (2018). Years in League 2018-

OWNERSHIP/MANAGEMENT
Operated By: Texas Rangers, LLC.
President: Neil Leibman. **General Manager:** Wade Howell. **Director of Operations:** Janell Bullock. **Head Groundskeeper:** Stephen Watson. **Public Relations Manager:** Alexa Kay. **Director of Ticket Sales:** Jon Clemmons.

FIELD STAFF
Manager: Spike Owen. **Hitting Coach:** Kenny Hook. **Pitching Coach:** Steve Mintz. **Coach:** Carlos Maldonado. **Trainer:** Alex Rodriguez. **Strength & Conditioning Coach:** Al Sandoval.

GAME INFORMATION
Radio Announcer: Dominic Cotroneo. **PA Announcer:** Bryan Hanks. **Stadium Name:** Grainger Stadium. **Standard Game Times:** 7:00 (weekdays), 6:00 (Saturdays), 2:00 (Sundays). **Ticket Price Range:** $5-12. **Visiting Club Hotel:** Mother Earth Motor Lodge, 501 N Herritage St., Kinston, NC 28501.

FREDERICK KEYS

Address: 21 Stadium Dr., Frederick, MD 21703.
Telephone: (301) 662-0013. **Fax:** (301) 662-0018.
E-Mail Address: info@frederickkeys.com. **Website:** www.frederickkeys.com.
Affiliation (first year): Baltimore Orioles (1989). **Years in League:** 1989-

OWNERSHIP/MANAGEMENT
Ownership: Maryland Baseball Holding LLC.
President: Ken Young. **General Manager:** Dave Ziedelis. **Director, Assistant General Manager Sales:** Matt Miller. **Director of Sponsorship:** Andrew Klein. **Director Broadcasting/ Public Relations:** Geoff Arnold. **Promotions and Creative Services Manager:** DeForest Garcia. **Director of Stadium Operations:** Kari Collins. **Sponsorship Sales Account Managers:** Casey O'Brien, Kelly Wallace. **Group Sales Account Managers:** Ellery Price, Ben Underwood, Marcus Jenkins. **Box Office Assistants:** Brady McIntosh, George Cluster. **Broadcasting/PR/Marketing Assistant:** Kyle Huson. **Marketing Assistant:** Kevin Hernandez. **Head Groundskeeper:** Mike Dunn. **Clubhouse Manager:** Jared Weiss. **Finance Manager:** Tami Hetrick. **General Manager, Ovations:** Alan Cranfill.

FIELD STAFF

Manager: Ryan Minor. **Hitting Coach:** Kyle Moore. **Pitching Coach:** Blaine Beatty. **Athletic Trainer:** Marty Brinker.

GAME INFORMATION

Radio Announcers: Geoff Arnold, Kyle Huson. **PA Announcer:** Andy Redmond. **Official Scorers:** Jason Lee, Luke Stillson, Dave Musil, Geoff Goyne, Bob Roberson, Dennis Hetrick. **Stadium Name:** Harry Grove Stadium. **Location:** From I-70, take exit 54 (Market Street), left at light; From I-270, take exit 32 (I-70Baltimore/Hagerstown toward Baltimore (I-70), to exit 54 at Market Street. **Ticket Price Range:** $9-15. **Visiting Club Hotel:** Comfort Inn Frederick, 7300 Executive Way, Frederick, MD 21704. **Telephone:** (301) 668-7272.

LYNCHBURG HILLCATS

Address: Lynchburg City Stadium, 3180 Fort Ave, Lynchburg, VA 24501. **Telephone:** (434) 528-1144. **Fax:** (434) 846-0768.
E-Mail Address: info@lynchburg-hillcats.com. **Website:** www.Lynchburg-hillcats.com.
Affiliation (first year): Cleveland Indians (2015). **Years in League:** 1966-

OWNERSHIP/MANAGEMENT

Operated By: Elmore Sports Group.
President: Chris Jones. **General Manager:** Ronnie Roberts. **Assistant General Manager:** Matt Klein. **General Manager of Concessions:** Jordan Speicher. **Director of Sales:** Max Rettig. **Head Groundskeeper:** Mike Georgiadis. **Director of Broadcasting and Communications:** Max Gun. **Director of Promotions:** Kestrel Kerl. **Director of Ticketing:** Lincoln Evans. **Operations/Clubhouse Manager:** Ryan Henson. **Team Reporter/On-Field Host:** Kestrel Kerl. **Account Executive:** Max Rettig. **Accountant:** Crystal Williamson.

FIELD STAFF

Manager: Rouglas Odor. **Hitting Coach:** Justin Toole. **Pitching Coach:** Tony Arnold. **Bench Coach:** Grant Fink. **Strength & Conditioning Coach:** Eric Ortego. **Athletic Trainer:** Bobby Ruiz.

GAME INFORMATION

Radio Announcer: Max Gun. **No. of Games Broadcast:** 140. **PA Announcer:** Chuck Young. **Official Scorers:** Malcolm Haley, Chuck Young. **Stadium Name:** Calvin Falwell Field at Lynchburg City Stadium. **Location:** US 29 Business South to Lynchburg City Stadium (exit 6); US 29 Business North to Lynchburg City Stadium (exit 4). **Ticket Price Range:** $6-9. **Visiting Club Hotel:** La Quinta Inn & Suites, 3320 Candlers Mountain Rd., Lynchburg, VA 24502. **Telephone:** (434) 847-8655.

MYRTLE BEACH PELICANS

Mailing Address: 1251 21st Avenue N. Myrtle Beach, SC 29577.
Telephone: (843) 918-6000. **Fax:** (843) 918-6001.
E-Mail Address: info@myrtlebeachpelicans.com.
Website: www.myrtlebeachpelicans.com.
Affiliation (first year): Chicago Cubs (2015). **Years in League:** 1999-

OWNERSHIP/MANAGEMENT

President/General Manager: Andy Milovich. **Merchandise Manager:** Dan Bailey. **AGM/Operations:** Mike Snow. **Senior Director of Finance:** Anne Frost. **Ticket Sales Manager:** Justin Bennett. **AGM/Community Development:** Jen Brunson. **Sr. Director of Marketing:** Kristin Call. **Corporate Marketing Manager:** Ryan Cannella. **Sports & Tourism Sales Manager:** Todd Chapman. **Administratice Assistant:** Beth Freitas. **President/Managing Partner:** Chuck Greenberg. **Community Partnership Manager:** Gandy Henry. **Corporate Sales Representative:** Robert Buchanan. **General Manager:** Ryan Moore. **Box Office Manager:** Shannon Samanka. **Sr. Director of Business Development:** Guy Schuman. **Sports Turf Manager:** Tradd Jones. **Media Relations/Broadcaster:** Scott Kornberg. **Director of Food and Beverage:** Brad Leininger. **Business Intelligence Analyst:** Ankit Agrawal.

FIELD STAFF

Manager: Buddy Bailey. **Pitching Coach:** Anderson Tavarez. **Hitting Coach:** Ty Wright. **Athletic Trainer:** Logan Severson.

GAME INFORMATION

PA Announcer: Jerrod Schmidt-Dubose. **Official Scorer:** B.J. Scott. **Stadium Name:** Ticketreturn.com Field at Pelicans Ballpark. **Location:** US Highway 17 Bypass to 21st Ave. North, half mile to stadium. **Standard Game Times:** 7:05 p.m. **Ticket Pirce Range:** $9-$15. **Visiting Club Hotel:** Courtyard Marriott Barefoot Landing, 1000 Commons Blvd., Myrtle Beach, S.C., 29572. **Telephone:** (843) 916-0600.

POTOMAC NATIONALS

Office Address: 7 County Complex Ct, Woodbridge, VA 22192.
Mailing Address: PO Box 2148, Woodbridge, VA 22195.
Telephone: (703) 590-2311. **Fax:** (703) 590-5716.
E-Mail Address: info@potomacnationals.com.
Website:www.potomacnationals.com.
Affiliation (first year): Washington Nationals (2005). **Years in League:** 1978-

OWNERSHIP/MANAGEMENT

Operated By: Potomac Baseball LLC. **Principal Owner:** Art Silber.
President: Lani Silber Weiss. **General Manager, Sales:** Bryan Holland. **General Manager, Operations:** Aaron Johnson. **Ticket Director:** Alec Manriquez. **Director, Media Relations & Broadcasting:** Mike Weisman. **Assistant General Manager/Director, Stadium Operations & Merchandising:** Arthur Bouvier. **Ticket Operations Manager:** Matt LeBlanc. **Corporate Partnership Fulfillment, Community Relations/Promotions Manager:** Brice Walker. **Group Sales Executive:** Meagan Rankin. **Director, Graphic Design:** Alexis Deegan. **Director, Finance:** Shawna Hooke.

FIELD STAFF

Manager: Tripp Keister. **Hitting Coach:** Luis Ordaz. **Pitching Coach:** Sam Narron. **Athletic Trainer:** Don Neidig. **Strength & Conditioning Coach:** Gabe Torres.

GAME INFORMATION

Radio Announcer: Mike Weisman. **No. of Games Broadcast:** 140. **Flagship:** www.potomacnationals.com. **PA Announcer:** Jeremy Whitham. **Official Scorer:** Jason Eichelberger, Ben Trittipoe. **Stadium Name:** G. Richard Pfitzner Stadium. **Location:** From I-95, take exit, 158B and continue on Prince William Parkway for five miles, right into County Complex Court. **Standard Game Times:** 7:05 pm, Sat. 6:35, Sun. 1:05. **Ticket Price Range:** $10-16. **Visiting Club Hotel:** Country Inn and Suites, Prince William Parkway, Woodbridge, VA 22192. **Telephone:** (703) 492-6868.

SALEM RED SOX

Office Address: 1004 Texas St., Salem, VA 24153.
Mailing Address: PO Box 842, Salem, VA 24153. **Telephone:** (540) 389-3333.
Fax: (540) 389-9710. **E-Mail Address:** info@salemsox.com.
Website: www.salemsox.com. **Affiliation (first year):** Boston Red Sox (2009).
Years in League: 1968-

OWNERSHIP/MANAGEMENT

Operated By: Carolina Baseball LLC/Fenway Sports Group.
Managing Director: Tim Zue. **President/General Manager:** Ryan Shelton. **VP/Assistant GM:** Allen Lawrence. **VP of Operations:** Tim Anderson. **VP of Ticket Sales/ Service:** Andrew Yarnall. **Director, Corporate Sponsorships:** Steven Elovich. **Marketing/Promotions Manager:** Maddy Tettelbach. **Facilities Manager/Head Groundskeeper:** Budgie Clark. **Group Sales Director:** Andrew Yarnall. **Ticket Operations/Retention Manager:** Dave Malerk. **Food/Beverage Manager:** Patrick Pelletier. **Premium Sales Account Executive:** Grant Harmon. **Retention & Group Sales Account Executive:** Bobby Howland. **Sr. Premium Sales Account Executive:** Alex Michel. **Accounting Manager:** Celeste Hotze. **Accounting Assistant:** Chandler Mackenhimer. **Clubhouse Manager:** Tom Wagner.

FIELD STAFF

Manager: Joe Oliver. **Hitting Coach:** Nelson Paulino. **Pitching Coach:** Lance Carter. **Trainer:** Nick Kuchwara.

GAME INFORMATION

Radio Announcer: Ben Gellman-Chomsky. **No. of Games Broadcast:** 140. **Flagship Station:** ESPN Radio 1240 AM. **PA Announcer:** Emile Brown. **Official Scorer:** Billy Wells. **Stadium Name:** Haley Toyota Field at Salem Memorial Ballpark. **Location:** I-81 to exit 141 (Route 419), follow signs to Salem Civic Center Complex. **Standard Game Times:** 7:05 pm, Sat./Sun. 6:05/4:05. **Ticket Price Range:** $7-14. **Visiting Club Hotel:** Comfort Suites Ridgewood Farms, 2898 Keagy Rd., Salem, VA 24153. **Telephone:** (540) 375-4800.

WILMINGTON BLUE ROCKS

Address: 801 Shipyard Drive, Wilmington, DE 19801.
Telephone: (302) 888-2015. **Fax:** (302) 888-2032.
E-Mail Address: info@bluerocks.com. **Website:** www.bluerocks.com.
Affiliation (first year): Kansas City Royals (2007). **Years in League:** 1993-

OWNERSHIP/MANAGEMENT

Operated by: Wilmington Blue Rocks LP. **Honorary President:** Matt Minker. **Owners:** Main Street Baseball, Clark Minker. **General Manager:** Andrew Layman. **Assistant GM:** Andrew Layman. Director, Broadcasting/Media **Relations:** Matt Janus. **Director, Merchandise:** Jim Beck. **Director, Community Affairs:** Kevin Linton.

Director of Web and Creative Services: Mike Diodati. **Director, Tickets:** Stefani Rash. **Marketing Manager:** Jason Estes. **Ticket Sales Manager:** Shea Macagnone. **Group Sales Manager:** Joe McCarthy. **Group Sales Executives:** Ryan Blaire, Alex Rella. **Box Office Manager:** Brent Kepner. **Group Sales Executives:** Joe McCarthy, Mike Cipolini, Mike Dailey. **Director, Field Operations:** Steve Gold. **Office Manager:** Marie Graney.

FIELD STAFF

Manager: Darryl Kennedy. **Hitting Coach:** Abraham Nunez. **Pitching Coach:** Doug Henry. **Athletic Trainer:** James Stone.

GAME INFORMATION

Radio Announcers: Matt Janus and Cory Nidoh. **No. of Games Broadcast:** 140. **Flagship Station:** 89.7 WGLS-FM. **PA Announcer:** Kevin Linton. **Official Scorer:** Dick Shute. **Stadium Name:** Judy Johnson Field at Daniel Frawley Stadium. **Location:** I-95 North to Maryland Ave (exit 6), right on Maryland Ave, and through traffic light onto Martin Luther King Blvd, right at traffic light on Justison St, follow to Shipyard Dr; I-95 South to Maryland Ave (exit 6), left at fourth light on Martin Luther King Blvd, right at fourth light on Justison St, follow to Shipyard Dr. **Standard Game Times:** 6:35 pm, (Mon-Thur) 7:05 (Fri/Sat), Sun. 1:35 p.m. **Ticket Price Range:** $6-$14. **Visiting Club Hotel:** Clarion Belle, 1612 N DuPont Hwy, New Castle, DE 19720. **Telephone:** (302) 299-1408.

WINSTON-SALEM DASH

Office Address: 926 Brookstown Ave, Winston-Salem, NC 27101.
Stadium Address: 951 Ballpark Way, Winston-Salem, NC 27101.
Telephone: (336) 714-2287. **Fax:** (336) 714-2288. **E-Mail Address:** info@wsdash.com. **Website:** www.wsdash.com.
Affiliation (first year): Chicago White Sox (1997). **Years in League:** 1945-

OWNERSHIP/MANAGEMENT

Operated by: W-S Dash. **Principal Owner:** Billy Prim.
President: CJ Johnson. **VP, Chief Financial Officer:** Kurt Gehsmann. **VP, Baseball Operations:** Ryan Manuel. **VP, Corporate Partnerships:** Corey Bugno. **Senior Director of Business Operations:** Russell Parmele. **Director, Entertainment/Community Relations:** Jessica Aveyard. **Director of Ticket Sales:** Paul Stephens. **Broadcast and Media Relations Manager:** Joe Weil. **Head Groundskeeper:** Paul Johnson. **Accounting Manager:** Amanda Elbert. **Creative Services Assistant:** Ryan Nicholson. **Corporate Partnerships Representatives:** Tanya Stevens and Ayla Acosta. **Group Sales Representative:** Brittany Daley. **Business Development Representative:** Shelby Cuthbertson. **Community Relations Manager:** Brittany Stewart. **Ticket Sales & Service Representatives:** Benjamin Kendrew and Hailey Lewan. **Box Office Manager:** Owen Wilson.

FIELD STAFF

Manager: Omar Vizquel. **Hitting Coach:** Charlie Poe. **Pitching Coach:** Matt Zaleski. **Coach:** Guillermo Quiroz. **Trainer:** Josh Fallin. **Strength Coach:** George Timke.

GAME INFORMATION

Radio Announcer: Joe Weil. **No. of Games Broadcast:** 140. **Flagship Station:** 600 AM-WSJS (Thursdays) or wsdash. com (all games). **PA Announcer:** Jeffrey Griffin. **Official Scorer:** Bill Grainger. **Stadium Name:** BB&T Ballpark. **Location:** I-40 Business to Peters Creek Parkway exit (exit 5A). **Standard Game Times:** M-F 7 p.m., Sat. 6 p.m., Sun. 2 p.m. **Visiting Club Hotel:** Unavailable.

FLORIDA STATE LEAGUE

Office Address: 3000 Gulf To Bay, Suite 219 Clearwater, FL 33759.
Mailing Address: 3000 Gulf To Bay, Suite 219 Clearwater, FL 33759.
Telephone: (727) 724-6146. **E-Mail Address:** office@floridastateleague.com.
Website: www.floridastateleague.com.

Years League Active: 1919-1927, 1936-1941, 1946- .

Chairman/President/Treasurer: Ken Carson.

Ken Carson

Executive Vice President: John Timberlake. **VPs: North**—Ron Myers. **South**—Mike Bauer.

Corporate Secretary: Steve Smith.

Directors: Mike Bauer (Jupiter/Palm Beach), Shelby Nelson (Dunedin), Jordan Kobritz (Charlotte), Jeff Podobnik (Bradenton), Jason Hochberg (Fort Myers), Reese Smith, III (Daytona), Ron Myers (Lakeland), Erik Anderson (Osceola), Vance Smith (Tampa), Traer Van Allen (St. Lucie), John Timberlake (Clearwater). **League Executive Assistant:** Laura LeCras.

Division Structure: North— Clearwater, Daytona, Dunedin, Lakeland, Osceola, Tampa. **South—**Bradenton, Charlotte, Fort Myers, Jupiter, Palm Beach, St. Lucie.

Regular Season: 140 games (split schedule). **2018 Opening Date:** April 5. **Closing Date:** September 2. **All-Star Game:** June 16 at Tampa.

Playoff Format: First-half division winners meet second-half winners in best of three series. Winners meet in best of five series for league championship. **Roster Limit:** 25. **Player Eligibility Rule:** No age limit. No more than two players and one player-coach on active list may have six or more years of prior minor league service.

Brand of Baseball: Rawlings.

Umpires: Jhonatan Biarreta Castillo, Samuel Burch, Donald Carlyon, Michael Carroll, Lorenz Evans, Emil Jimenez Pernalete, Tyler Jones, Reid Joyner, Jose Matamoros, Brandon Mooney, Robert Nunez, Gregory Roemer.

STADIUM INFORMATION

			Dimensions				
Club	**Stadium**	**Opened**	**LF**	**CF**	**RF**	**Capacity**	**2017 Att.**
Bradenton	McKechnie Field	1923	335	400	335	8,654	79,331
Charlotte	Charlotte Sports Park	2009	343	413	343	5,028	120,685
Clearwater	Spectrum Field	2004	330	400	330	8,500	200,201
Daytona	Jackie Robinson Ballpark	1930	317	400	325	4,200	136,224
Dunedin	Florida Auto Exchange Stadium	1977	335	400	327	5,509	38,956
Florida	Space Coast Stadium	1994	340	404	340	8,100	57,342
Fort Myers	Hammond Stadium	1991	330	405	330	7,900	121,438
Jupiter	Roger Dean Stadium	1998	330	400	325	6,871	69,064
Lakeland	Publix Field at Joker Marchant Stadium	1966	340	420	340	7,961	52,191
Palm Beach	Roger Dean Stadium	1998	330	400	325	6,871	58,832
St. Lucie	First Data Field	1988	338	410	338	7,000	132,359
Tampa	Steinbrenner Field	1996	318	408	314	10,270	93,823

BRADENTON MARAUDERS

Address: 1701 27th Street East, Bradenton, FL 34208.
Telephone: (941) 747-3031. **Fax:** (941) 747-9442.
E-Mail Address: MaraudersInfo@pirates.com. **Website:** www.BradentonMarauders.com.
Affiliation (first year): Pittsburgh Pirates (2010). **Years in League:** 1919-20, 1923-24, 1926, 2010-.

OWNERSHIP/MANAGEMENT

Operated By: Pittsburgh Associates.

Senior Director, Florida Operations: Jeff Podobnik. **Director, Operations:** A.J. Grant. **General Manager, Director of Sales:** Rachelle Madrigal. **Coordinator, Florida Operations:** Ray Morris. **Coordinator, Concessions:** Erika Rolando. **Assistant General Manager, Sales:** Craig Warzcecha. **Coordinator, Sponsorship/Tickets:** Sean Banks. **Coordinator, Sales:** Nolan Bialek. **Coordinator, Marketing/ Community Relations:** Katie Fritz. **Coordinator, Stadium Operations:** Nick Long. **Manager, Communications & In-Game Entertainment:** Nate March. **Head Groundskeeper:** Victor Madrigal.

FIELD STAFF

Manager: Gera Alvarez. **Hitting Coach:** Butch Wynegar. **Pitching Coach:** Matt Ford. **Athletic Trainer:** TBA.

GAME INFORMATION

PA Announcer: Jeff Phillips. **Official Scorer:** Dave Taylor. **Stadium Name:** LECOM Park. **Location:** I-75 to exit 220 (220B from I-75N) to SR 64 West/Manatee Ave, Left onto 9th St West, LECOM PARK on the left. **Standard Game Times:** 6:30 pm, Sun. 1:00 pm (1st half), 5 pm (second half). **Ticket Price Range:** $6-12. **Visiting Club Hotel:** Holiday Inn Express East Bradenton-Lakewood Ranch, 5464 Lena Road, Bradenton, FL 34211. **Telephone:** (941) 755-0055.

CHARLOTTE STONE CRABS

Address: 2300 El Jobean Road, Building A, Port Charlotte, FL 33948.
Telephone: (941) 206-4487. **Fax:** (941) 206-3599.
E-Mail Address: info@stonecrabsbaseball.com. **Website:** www.stonecrabsbaseball.com.
Affiliation (first year): Tampa Bay Rays (2009). **Years in League:** 2009-

OWNERSHIP/MANAGEMENT
Operated By: CBI-Rays.
General Manager: Jared Forma. **Assistant GM:** Jeff Cook. **Director, Finance:** Lori Engleman. **Director, Corporate Sponsorship:** Zach Jones. **Director, Group Sales:** Hallie Rubins. **Director, Food & Beverage:** Lynn Cleary. **Assistant Director, Food & Beverage:** Brittany Jones. **Stadium Operations Manager:** Andrew Crawford. **Broadcasting & Media Relations Manager:** John Vittas. **Fan Engagement Manager:** Ashley Stephenson. **Video Board Manager:** Chance Fernandez.

FIELD STAFF
Manager: Jim Morrison. **Pitching Coach:** Steve "Doc" Watson. **Coach:** Joe Szekely. **Coach:** German Melendez.

GAME INFORMATION
PA Announcer: Josh Grant. **Official Scorer:** Steve Posilovich. **Scoreboard Stats:** R.J. Fraser. **Gameday Stringer:** Jack Melton. **Stadium Name:** Charlotte Sports Park. **Location:** I-75 to Exit 179, turn left onto Toledo Blade Blvd then right on El Jobean Rd. **Ticket Price Range:** $7-12. **Visiting Club Hotel:** Sleep Inn, 806 Kings Hwy., Port Charlotte, FL 33980.
Phone: 941-613-6300.

CLEARWATER THRESHERS

Address: 601 N Old Coachman Road, Clearwater, FL 33765.
Telephone: (727) 712-4300. **Fax:** (727) 712-4498.
Website: www.threshersbaseball.com.
Affiliation (first year): Philadelphia Phillies (1985). **Years in League:** 1985-

OWNERSHIP/MANAGEMENT
Operated by: Philadelphia Phillies.
Director, Florida Operations/General Manager: John Timberlake. **Business Manager:** Dianne Gonzalez. **Assistant GM/Director, Sales:** Dan McDonough. **Assistant GM, Ticketing:** Jason Adams. **Office Administration:** DeDe Angelillis. **Manager, Group Sales:** Dan Madden. **Senior Sales Associate:** Bobby Mitchell. **Manager, Ballpark Operations:** Jay Warren. **Facilities and Operations Coordinator:** Sean McCarthy. **Corporate Sales Associate:** Cory Sipe. **Manager, Special Events and Suites Level:** Doug Kemp. **Manager, Community Engagement and Media:** Robert Stretch. **Clubhouse Manager:** Mark Meschede. **Manager, Food and Beverage:** Justin Gunsaulus. **Suites Coordinator:** Wendy Armstrong Smith. **Ticket Office Managers:** Pat Prevelige, Kyle Webb. **Group Sales Assistant:** Victoria Phipps. **Food and Beverage Operations Manager:** Kevin Smith. **Audio/Video:** Dominic Repper. **Manager, Merchandise:** Robin Warner.

FIELD STAFF
Manager: Shawn Williams. **Hitting Coach:** John Mizerock. **Pitching Coach:** Aaron Fultz. **Coach:** Ruben Gotay.

GAME INFORMATION
PA Announcer: Don Guckian. **Official Scorer:** Larry Wiederecht. **Stadium Name:** Spectrum Field. **Location:** US 19 North and Drew Street in Clearwater. **Standard Game Times:** Mon.-Thu. 7 pm, Fri.-Sat. 6:15, Sun. 1 p.m., most Wednesdays are day games. **Ticket Price Range:** $6-10. **Visiting Club Hotel:** La Quinta Inn, 21338 US Highway 19 N, Clearwater, FL 33765. **Telephone:** (727) 799-1565.

DAYTONA TORTUGAS

Address: 110 E Orange Ave, Daytona Beach, FL 32114. **Telephone:** (386) 257-3172.
Fax: (386) 523-9490. **E-Mail Address:** info@daytonatortugas.com.
Website: www.daytonatortugas.com. **Affiliation (first year):** Cincinnati Reds (201!
Years in League: 1920-24,1928, 1936-41, 1946-73, 1977-87, 1993-

OWNERSHIP/MANAGEMENT
Operated By: Tortugas Baseball Club LLC. **Principal Owner/President:** Reese Smith III.
President: Ryan Keur. **VP, Business Development:** Jim Jaworski. **Director, Broadcasting/Media/Communications:** Luke Mauro. **Director, Ticket Operations:** Paul Krenzer. **Manager, Food/Beverage:** Scot Masters. **Director, Community Relations:** Kristen Alford. **Director, Sales:** Austin Scher. **Stadium Ops/Merchandise Manager:** Kevin Trembley. **Marketing Coordinator:** Harolin Alvarez. **Director, Marketing/Entertainment:** James Wood. **Director, Corporate Partnerships:** Donna DiFiore. **Group Sales Manager:** Halle Fuerst. **Business Developer Manager:** Anderson Rathbun. **Controller:** David Manning.

FIELD STAFF
Manager: Ricky Gutierrez. **Hitting Coach:** Alex Pelaez. **Pitching Coach:** Tom Brown. **Bench Coach:** Desi Relaford. **Athletic Trainer:** Andrew Cleves.

GAME INFORMATION
Radio Announcer: Luke Mauro. **No. of Games Broadcast:** 140. **Flagship Station:** AM-1230 WSBB. **PA Announcer:** Tim Lecras. **Official Scorer:** Don Roberts. **Stadium Name:** Jackie Robinson Ballpark. **Location:** I-95 to International Speedway Blvd Exit, east to Beach Street, south to Magnolia Ave east to ballpark; A1A North/South to Orange Ave west to ballpark. **Standard Game Time:** 7:05 p.m. **Ticket Price Range:** $6-12.50. **Visiting Club Hotel:** Holiday Inn Resort Daytona Beach Oceanfront, 1615 S. Atlantic Ave Daytona Beach, FL 32118. **Telephone:** (386) 255-0921.

DUNEDIN BLUE JAYS

Address: 373 Douglas Ave Dunedin, FL 34698.
Telephone: (727) 733-9302. **Fax:** (727) 734-7661.
E-Mail Address: dunedin@bluejays.com. **Website:** dunedinbluejays.com.
Affiliation (first year): Toronto Blue Jays (1987). **Years in League:** 1978-79, 1987-

OWNERSHIP/MANAGEMENT
Director Florida Operations: Shelby Nelson. **General Manager:** Mike Liberatore. **Accounting Manager:** Gayle Gentry. **Manager, Retail Sales and Community Relations:** Kathi Beckman. **Manager, Ticket Operations:** Jackie Purcell. **Manager, Corporate and Group Sales:** Kelsey McIntosh. **Administrative Assistant/Receptionist:** Michelle Smith. **Supervisor, Stadium Operations:** Zac Phelps. **Head Superintendent:** Patrick Skunda.

FIELD STAFF
Manager: Casey Candaele. **Hitting Coach:** Donnie Murphy. **Pitching Coach:** Mark Riggins. **Coach:** Michel Abreu. **Strength & Conditioning Coach:** Kyle Edlhuber. **Athletic Trainer:** Dan Leja.

GAME INFORMATION
PA Announcer: Bill Christie. **Official Scorer:** Steven Boychuk. **Stadium Name:** Dunedin Stadium. **Location:** From I-275, north on Highway 19, left on Sunset Point Rd for 4.5 miles, right on Douglas Ave; stadium is on right. **Standard Game Times:** 6:30 pm, Sun. 1:00 pm. **Ticket Price Range:** $7. **Visiting Club Hotel:** La Quinta, 21338 US Highway 19 North, Clearwater, FL. **Telephone:** (727) 799-1565.

FLORIDA FIRE FROGS

Address: 631 Heritage Park Way Kissimmee, FL 34741
Telephone: (321) 697-3156 . **E-Mail Address:** info@floridafirefrogs.com.
Website: www.floridafirefrogs.com.
Affiliation (first year): Atlanta Braves (2017). **Years in League:** 2017-

OWNERSHIP/MANAGEMENT
Operated By: Manatees Baseball Club LLC.
Chairman: Tom Winters. **CEO:** Charlie Baumann. **President/GM:** Erik Anderson. **Assistant General Manager:** Adam Whitlow. **Community and Brand Awareness Manager:** Ryan Fitzgerald. **Director of Food and Beverage:** Helen Scholar. **Accounting Manager:** Matt Fasano. **Box Office Manager:** Garrett Washington. **Senior Director of Business Development/Group Sales:** Beth DeSimone. **Group Sales Manager:** Ian Ueltschi. **Corporate Sales Manager:** Matt Olinik. **Corporate/Group Sales Manager, Hispanic Market:** Enrique Guerra. **Clubhouse Manager:** Mike Pedrazas. **Head Groundskeeper:** Wayne Thompson.

FIELD STAFF
Manager: Luis Salazar. **Pitching Coach:** Mike Maroth. **Hitting Coach:** Rene Tosoni

GAME INFORMATION
PA Announcer: Unavailable. **Official Scorer:** Unavailable. **Stadium Name:** Osceola County Stadium. **Location:** Take either I-4 or the Florida Turnpike to US 192. Follow US 192 (Irlo Bronson Memorial Highway) to Bill Beck Boulevard. Turn onto Bill Beck Boulevard, then take a left onto Heritage Park Way. To get to US 192 from I-4, take Exit 64. From the Turnpike, take either Exit 242 (northbound) or Exit 244 (southbound).

FORT MYERS MIRACLE

Address: 14400 Six Mile Cypress Pkwy, Fort Myers, FL 33912.
Telephone: (239) 768-4210. **Fax:** (239) 768-4211.
E-Mail Address: miracle@miraclebaseball.com.
Website: www.miraclebaseball.com. **Affiliation (first year):** Minnesota Twins (1993).

Years in League: 1926, 1978-87, 1991-

OWNERSHIP/MANAGEMENT

Operated By: SJS Beacon Baseball. **Owner:** Jason Hochberg.

President/General Manager: Chris Peter. **Senior Director, Business Operations:** Suzanne Reaves. **Sales Manager:** Andy Wood. **Promotions Manager & Corporate Sales:** Whitley Patterson. **Sales Advisor:** Delroy Gay. **Group & Season Seat Executive:** Michael Burnette. **Account Executive & Box Office Assistant:** Ben Brown. **Marketing & Communications Specialist:** Niki Miranda-Dubay. **Broadcast & Media Relations Manager:** Marshall Kelner. **Food & Beverage Director:** Kevin Bush. **Assistant Food & Beverage Director:** Loren Merrigan. **Director of Operations:** Judd Loveland. **Merchandise Manager:** Lynn Izzo. **Front Office Manager:** Sylvia Meyer.

FIELD STAFF

Manager: Ramon Borrego. **Hitting Coach:** Steve Singleton. **Pitching Coach:** Henry Bonilla. **Trainer:** Steve Taylor. **Strength & Conditioning Coach:** Jacob Dean.

GAME INFORMATION

Radio Announcer: Marshall Kelner. **No. of Games Broadcast:** 140. **Internet Broadcast:** www.miraclebaseball.com. **PA Announcer:** Allen Woodard. **Official Scorer:** Scott Pedersen. **Stadium Name:** William H. Hammond Stadium at the CenturyLink Sports Complex. **Location:** Exit 131 off I-75, west on Daniels Parkway, left on Six Mile Cypress Parkway. **Standard Game Times:** Mon-Fri 7:00 pm, Sat. 6:00; Sun. 4:00. **Ticket Price Range:** $7.50-$13. **Visiting Club Hotel:** Four Points by Sheraton, 13600 Treeline Ave S, Fort Myers, FL 33913.

JUPITER HAMMERHEADS

Address: 4751 Main Street, Jupiter, FL 33458.
Telephone: (561) 775-1818. **Fax:** (561) 691-6886.
E-Mail Address: f.desk@rogerdeanstadium.com. **Website:** www.jupiterhammerheads.com.
Affiliation (first year): Miami Marlins (2002). **Years in League:** 1998-

OWNERSHIP/MANAGEMENT

Owned By: Miami Marlins, Jupiter Stadium, LTD.

General Manager, Jupiter Stadium, LTD: Mike Bauer. **General Manager:** Jamie Toole. **Executive Assistant:** Lynn Besaw. **Media Relations Assistant:** Tim Venus. **Director of Accounting:** Pam Satory. **Director of Corporate Partnrships:** Jamie Toole. **Director of Ticketing:** Andrew Seymour. **Marketing & Promotions Manager:** Sarah Campbell. **Building Manager:** Walter Herrera. **Event Services Manager:** Dan Knapinski. **Director, Grounds & Facilities:** Jordan Treadway. **Assistant Director, Grounds & Facilities:** Mitchell Moenster. **Merchandise Manager:** Taryn Taylor. **Ticket Office Manager:** Leighton Foster.

FIELD STAFF

Manager: Kevin Randel. **Pitching Coach:** Bruce Walton. **Hitting Coach:** Danny Santin. **Strength & Conditioning Coach:** Gregory Bourn. **Athletic Trainer:** Ben Cates.

GAME INFORMATION

PA Announcers: John Frost, Jay Zeager, Lou Palmer, Michael Brown. **Official Scorer:** Brennan McDonald. **Stadium Name:** Roger Dean Chevrolet Stadium. **Location:** I-95 to exit 83, east on Donald Ross Road for 1/4 mile. **Standard Game Times:** 6:30 pm, Sat. 5:30pm, Sun. 1:00/5:00 p.m. **Ticket Price Range:** $7- $10. **Visiting Club Hotel:** Fairfield Inn by Marriott, 6748 Indiantown Road, Jupiter, FL 33458. **Telephone:** (561) 748-5252.

LAKELAND FLYING TIGERS

Address: 2301 Lakeland Hills Blvd., Lakeland, FL 33805.
Telephone: (863) 686-8075. **Fax:** (863) 687-4127.
Website: www.lakelandflyingtigers.com.
Affiliation (first year): Detroit Tigers (1967). **Years in League:** 1919-26, 1953-55, 1960, 1962-64, 1967-.

OWNERSHIP/MANAGEMENT

Owned By: Detroit Tigers, Inc.

Principal and CEO of Illitch Holdings, Inc. and Detroit Tigers: Christoper Illitch. **Director, Florida Operations:** Ron Myers. **General Manager:** Zach Burek. **Manager, Administration/Operations Manager:** Shannon Follett. **Ticket Manager:** Ryan Eason. **Assistant General Manager:** Dan Lauer. **Administration/ Operations Assistant:** Alison Streicher. **Receptionist:** Maria Walls.

FIELD STAFF

Manager: Mike Rabelo. **Hitting Coach:** Tim Garland. **Pitching Coach:** Mark Johnson. **Coach:** Francisco Contreras. **Trainer:** Chris Vick. **Strength & Conditioning Coach:** Allan Williamson. **Video Coordinator:** Austin Reed. **Clubhouse Manager:** Bo Bianco.

GAME INFORMATION

PA Announcer: Unavailable. **Official Scorer:** Ed Luteran. **Stadium Name:** Publix Field at Joker Marchant Stadium. **Location:** Exit 33 on I-4 to 33 South (Lakeland Hills Blvd.), 1.5 miles on left. **Standard Game Times:** Mon.-Fri. 6:30, Sat. 6:00, Sun. 1:00. **Ticket Price Range:** $5-10. **Visiting Club Hotel:** Imperial Swan Hotel & Suites, 4141 South Florida Ave. Lakeland, FL 33813. **Telephone:** (863) 647-3000.

PALM BEACH CARDINALS

Address: 4751 Main Street, Jupiter, FL 33458.
Telephone: (561) 775-1818. **Fax:** (561) 691-6886.
E-Mail Address: frontdesk@rogerdeanchevroletstadium.com.
Website: www.palmbeachcardinals.com.
Affiliation (first year): St. Louis Cardinals (2003). **Years in League:** 2003-

OWNERSHIP/MANAGEMENT

Owned By: St. Louis Cardinals. **Operated By:** Jupiter Stadium LTD.
General Manager, Jupiter Stadium, LTD: Mike Bauer. **Executive Assistant:** Lynn Besaw. **Assistant GM, Jupiter Stadium:** Andrew Seymour. **Assistant GM, Jupiter Stadium:** Jamie Toole. **GM Palm Beach Cardinals:** Andrew Seymour. **Press Box/Media Relations:** Andrew Miller Director, **Accounting:** Pam Sartory. **Director, Corporate Partnerships:** Jamie Toole. **Manager, Marketing/ Promotions:** Sarah Campbell. **Coordinator, Event Services:** Dan Knapinski. **Director, Grounds:** Jordan Treadway. **Assistant Directors, Grounds:** Drew Wolcott. **Stadium Building Manager:** Walter Herrera. **Merchandise Manager:** Taryn Taylor. **Ticket Office Manager:** Leighton Foster. **Office Manager:** Dianne Detling.

FIELD STAFF

Manager: Dann Bilardello. **Hitting Coach:** Brandon Allen. **Pitching Coach:** Will Ohman. **Athletic Trainer:** Chris Whitman

GAME INFORMATION

PA Announcers: John Frost, Lou Palmer, Jay Zeager, Michael Brown. **Official Scorer:** Lou Villano. **Stadium Name:** Roger Dean Chevrolet Stadium. **Location:** I-95 to exit 83, east on Donald Ross Road for 1/4 mile. **Standard Game Times:** 6:30 pm, Sat. 5:30pm, Sun. 1:00/5:00 p.m. **Ticket Price Range:** $7- $10. **Visiting Club Hotel:** Fairfield Inn by Marriott, 6748 Indiantown Road, Jupiter, FL 33458. **Telephone:** (561) 748-5252.

ST. LUCIE METS

Address: 525 NW Peacock Blvd., Port St Lucie, FL 34986.
Telephone: (772) 871-2100. **Fax:** (772) 878-9802.
Website: www.stluciemets.com.
Affiliation (first year): New York Mets (1988). **Years in League:** 1988-

OWNERSHIP/MANAGEMENT

Operated by: Sterling Mets LP.
Chairman/CEO: Fred Wilpon. **President:** Saul Katz. **COO:** Jeff Wilpon. **Executive Director, Minor League Facilities:** Paul Taglieri. **General Manager:** Traer Van Allen. **Assistant General Manager:** Clint Cure. **Executive Assistant:** Mary O'Brien. **Coordinator, Group Sales:** Josh Sexton. **Staff Accountant:** Shannon Murray. **Accounting Clerk:** Christina Rivera. **Director, Sales/Corporate Partnerships:** Lauren DeAcetis. **Director, Ticketing/Merchandise:** Kyle Gleockler. **Manager, Food/Beverage Operations:** John Gallagher. **Manager, Media/Broadcast Relations:** Adam MacDonald. **Director, Group Sales/Community Relations:** Kasey Blair. **Maintenance:** Jerry Lanigan.

FIELD STAFF

Manager: Chad Kreuter. **Hitting Coach:** Joel Fuentes. **Pitching Coach:** Marc Valdes. **Trainer:** Matt Hunter. **Strength & Conditioning Coach:** Alex Tavarez. **Mental Skills Coach:** Sabrina Gomez.

GAME INFORMATION

PA Announcer: Evan Nine. **Official Scorer:** Bill Whitehead. **Stadium Name:** First Data Field. **Location:** Exit 121 (St Lucie West Blvd) off I-95, east 1/2 mile, left on NW Peacock Blvd. **Standard Game Times:** 6:30 pm, Sun 1pm. **Ticket Price Range:** $6 - $9. **Visiting Club Hotel:** Holiday Inn Express, 1601 NW Courtyard Circle, Port St Lucie, FL 34986. **Telephone:** (772) 879-6565.

TAMPA TARPONS

Address: One Steinbrenner Drive, Tampa, FL 33614.
Telephone: (813) 875-7753. **Fax:** (813) 673-3186
E-Mail Address: vsmith@yankees.com. **Website:** tarponsbaseball.com
Affiliation (first year): New York Yankees (1994).
Years in League: 1919-27, 1957-1988, 1994-

OWNERSHIP/MANAGEMENT

Operated by: Florida Bombers Baseball LLC. **VP Business Operations:** Vance Smith. **General Manager:** Matt Gess
Assistant GM: Jeremy Ventura. **Premium Ticket Services:** Jennifer Magliocchetti. **Ticket Operations & Promotions:**
Allison Stortz. **Digital Media Coordinator:** Maddie Erhardt. **Membership Services:** Kate Harvey.
Head Groundskeeper: Ritchie Anderson.

FIELD STAFF

Manager: Patrick Osborn. **Hitting Coach:** Eric Duncan. **Pitching Coach:** Jose Rosado. **Catching Coach:** Michel
Hernandez. **Defensive Coach:** Jose Javier. **Athletic Trainer:** Michael Becker. **Strength& Conditioning Coach:** Jacob
Dunning. **Video Coordinator:** Shea Wingate.

GAME INFORMATION

Radio: tarponsbaseball.com. **PA Announcer:** Unavailable. **Official Scorer:** Unavailable.
Stadium Name: George M Steinbrenner Field. **Location:** I-275 to Dale Mabry Hwy, North on Dale Mabry Hwy
(Facility is at corner of West Martin Luther King Blvd/Dale Mabry Hwy). **Standard Game Times:** Mon - Sat. 6:30pm,
Sun 1pm. **Ticket Price Range:** $5-8. **Visiting Club Hotel:** Unavailable.

MIDWEST LEAGUE

Address: 210 South Michigan St., 5th Floor-Plaza Building, South Bend, IN 46601. **Telephone:** (574) 234-3000. **Fax:** (574) 234-4220.
E-Mail Address: mwl@midwestleague.com, dickn@sni-law.com.
Website: www.midwestleague.com. **Years League Active:** 1947-

President/Legal Counsel/Secretary: Richard A. Nussbaum, II.

Vice President: Dave Walker.

Directors: Andrew Berlin (South Bend). Stuart Katzoff (Bowling Green). Chuck Brockett (Burlington). Lew Chamberlin (West Michigan). Dennis Conerton (Beloit). Paul Davis (Clinton). Tom Dickson (Lansing). Jason Freier (Fort Wayne). David Heller (Quad Cities). Doug Nelson (Cedar Rapids). Greg Rosenbaum (Dayton). Peter Carfagna (Lake County). Paul Barbeau (Great Lakes). Rocky Vonachen (Peoria). Bob Froehlich (Kane County). Rob Zerjav (Wisconsin).

League Administrator: Holly Voss.

Division Structure: East—Bowling Green, Dayton, Fort Wayne, Lake County, Lansing, South Bend, Great Lakes, West Michigan. **West**—Beloit, Burlington, Cedar Rapids, Clinton, Kane County, Peoria, Quad Cities, Wisconsin.

Regular Season: 140 games (split schedule). **Opening Date:** April 5. **Closing Date:** Sept 3.

All-Star Game: June 19 at Midland, Michigan.

Playoff Format: Eight teams qualify. First-half and second-half division winners and wild-card teams meet in best of three quarterfinal series. Winners meet in best of three series for division championships. Division champions meet in best-of-five series for league championship. **Roster Limit:** 25 active. **Player Eligibility Rule:** No age limit. No more than two players and one player-coach on active list may have more than five years experience.

Brand of Baseball: Rawlings ROM-MID.

Umpires: Unavailable.

Richard Nussbaum

STADIUM INFORMATION

Club	Stadium	Opened	Dimensions LF	CF	RF	Capacity	2017 Att.
Beloit	Pohlman Field	1982	325	380	325	3,500	67,975
Bowling Green	Bowling Green Ballpark	2009	318	400	326	4,559	174,722
Burlington	Community Field	1947	338	403	318	3,200	75,429
Cedar Rapids	Veterans Memorial Stadium	2002	315	400	325	5,300	166,413
Clinton	Ashford University Field	1937	335	401	325	5,000	124,161
Dayton	Fifth Third Field	2000	338	402	338	6,830	584,574
Fort Wayne	Parkview Field	2009	336	400	318	8,100	413,701
Great Lakes	Dow Diamond	2007	332	400	325	5,200	210,054
Kane County	Northwestern Medicine Field	1991	335	400	335	10,973	400,931
Lake County	Classic Park	2003	320	400	320	6,157	213,738
Lansing	Cooley Law School Stadium	1996	305	412	305	11,000	311,190
Peoria	Dozer Park	2002	310	400	310	7,000	230,277
Quad Cities	Modern Woodmen Park	1931	343	400	318	7,140	234,923
South Bend	Four Winds Fields	1987	336	405	336	5,000	350,803
West Michigan	Fifth Third Ballpark	1994	317	402	327	9,281	386,416
Wisconsin	Neuroscience Group Field	1995	325	400	325	5,170	243,767

BELOIT SNAPPERS

Office Address: 2301 Skyline Drive, Beloit, WI 53511.
Mailing Address: P.O. Box 855, Beloit, WI 53512.
Telephone: (608) 362-2272. **Fax:** (608) 362-0418.
E-Mail Address: snappy@snappersbaseball.com. **Website:** www.snappersbaseball.com.
Affiliation (first year): Oakland Athletics (2013). **Years in League:** 1982-

OWNERSHIP/MANAGEMENT

Operated by: Beloit Professional Baseball Association, Inc.

President: Dennis Conerton. **General Manager:** Seth Flolid. **Media Relations/Marketing:** Unavailable.
Director,Tickets/Community Relations/Merchandise: Jessica Swartz. **Head Groundskeeper:** Jayme Wilcox.

FIELD STAFF

Manager: Webster Garrison. **Hitting Coach:** Juan Dilone. **Pitching Coach:** Don Schulze. **Trainer:** Brian Thorson.

GAME INFORMATION

Radio Announcer: Josh Keener. **No. of Games Broadcast:** Home-40. **Flagship Station:** WADR 103.5 FM. **PA Announcer:** TBD. **Official Scorer:** Unavailable. **Stadium Name:** Pohlman Field. **Location:** I-90 to exit 185-A, right at Cranston Road for 1 1/2 miles; I-43 to Wisconsin 81 to Cranston Road, right at Cranston for 1 1/2 miles. **Standard Game**

Times: 7 pm, 6:30 pm (April-May), Sat. 4 pm (April-May), Sun 2 pm. **Ticket Price Range:** $6.50-$10. **Visiting Club Hotel:** Rodeway Inn, 2956 Milwaukee Rd, Beloit, WI 53511. **Telephone:** (608) 364-4000.

BOWLING GREEN HOT RODS

Address: Bowling Green Ballpark, 300 8th Avenue, Bowling Green, KY 42101.
Telephone: (270) 901-2121. **Fax:** (270) 901-2165.
E-Mail Address: fun@bghotrods.com. **Website:** www.bghotrods.com.
Affiliation (first year): Tampa Bay Rays (2009). **Years in League:** 2010-

OWNERSHIP/MANAGEMENT
Operated By: Manhattan Capital Sports Acquisition.
President/Managing Partner: Stuart Katzoff. **Partner:** Jerry Katzoff. **General Manager/COO:** Eric C. Leach.
Assistant General Manager: Matt Ingram. **Director, Creative Services:** Maggie Fields. **Director, Sales:** Kyle Wolz.
Director, Stadium Operations: Wallace Brown. **Assistant Director, Stadium Operations:** Brock Wilson. **Head Groundskeeper:** Coty Wells. **Manager, Promotions and Community Relations:** Laura Feese. **Senior Account Executive:** Daniel Kline. **Account Executive/Retail Store Manager:** Nate Card. **Manager, Box Office:** Jon Barhorst. **Manager, Broadcast/Media Relations:** Paul Taylor.

FIELD STAFF
Manager: Reinaldo Ruiz. **Pitching Coach:** Brian Reith. **Coach:** Manny Castillo. **Coach:** Jeremy Owens. **Athletic Trainer:** Brian Newman. **Conditioning Coach:** James McCallie.

GAME INFORMATION
Radio Announcer: Paul Taylor. **No. of Games Broadcast:** 140. **Flagship Station:** WBGN 94.1 FM. **PA Announcer:** Unavailable. **Official Scorer:** Unavailable. **Stadium Name:** Bowling Green Ballpark. **Location:** From I-65, take Exit 26 (KY-234/Cemetery Road) into Bowling Green for 3 miles, left onto College Street for .2 miles, right onto 8th Avenue. **Standard Game Times:** 6:35 pm, Sun. 4:05 pm. **Ticket Price Range:** $8-24. **Visiting Club Hotel:** Clarion Inn. **Telephone:** (270) 282-7130.

BURLINGTON BEES

Office Address: 2712 Mount Pleasant St., Burlington, IA 52601.
Mailing Address: PO Box 824, Burlington, IA 52601. **Telephone:** (319) 754-5705.
Fax: (319) 754-5882. **E-Mail Address:** staff@gobees.com.
Website: www.gobees.com. **Affiliation (first year):** Los Angeles Angels (2013).
Years in League: 1962-

OWNERSHIP/MANAGEMENT
Operated By: Burlington Baseball Association Inc.
President: Dave Walker. **General Manager:** Chuck Brockett. **Assistant GM/Director, Group Outings, Tickets, Merchandising:** Kim Parker. **Director, Broadcasting and Media/ Community Relations:** Wes Holtkamp.
Groundskeeper: Lance Weber. **Clubhouse Manager:** Tyler Doherty.

FIELD STAFF
Manager: Jack Howell. **Hitting Coach:** Matt Spring. **Pitching Coach:** Jonathan Van Eaton.

GAME INFORMATION
Radio Announcer: Michael Broskowski. **No. of Games Broadcast:** 140. **Flagship Station:** KBUR 1490-AM. **PA Announcer:** Unavailable. **Official Scorer:** Ted Gutman. **Stadium Name:** Community Field. **Location:** From US 34, take US 61 North to Mt. Pleasant Street, east 1/8 mile. **Standard Game Times:** 6:30 pm, Sun 2. April-May Sat. 5:00 pm. **Ticket Price Range:** $5-10. **Visiting Club Hotel:** Pzazz Best Western FunCity, 3001 Winegard Dr., Burlington, IA 52601. **Telephone:** (319) 753-2223.

CEDAR RAPIDS KERNELS

Office Address: 950 Rockford Road SW, Cedar Rapids, IA 52404.
Mailing Address: PO Box 2001, Cedar Rapids, IA 52406.
Telephone: (319) 363-3887. **Fax:** (319) 363-5631.
E-Mail Address: kernels@kernels.com. **Website:** www.kernels.com.
Affiliation (first year): Minnesota Twins (2013). **Years in League:** 1962-

OWNERSHIP/MANAGEMENT
President: Greg Seyfer. **Chief Executive Officer:** Doug Nelson. **General Manager:** Scott Wilson. **Manager, IT/ Communications:** Andrew Pantini. **Sports Turf Manager:** Jesse Roeder. **Director, Ticket/Group Sales:** Andrea Brommelkamp. **Director, Finance:** Tracy Barr. **Director, Broadcasting:** Morgan Hawk. **Director, Community Relations:** Ryne George. **Director, Corporate Sales/Marketing:** Jessica Fergesen. **Coordinator, History:** Marcia Moran. **Manager,**

Ticket Office: Peter Keleher. **Manager, Stadium Operations:** Joe Krumm. **Clubhouse Manager:** Zack Shickel.

FIELD STAFF

Manager: Toby Gardenhire. **Hitting Coach:** Brian Dinkelman. **Pitching Coach:** Cibney Bello, Justin Willard. **Athletic Trainer:** Davey LaCroix. **Strength & Conditioning Coach:** Phill Hartt.

GAME INFORMATION

Radio Announcer: Morgan Hawk, Chris Kleinhans-Schulz. **No. of Games Broadcast:** 140. **Flagship Station:** KMRY 1450-AM/93.1-FM. **PA Announcer:** Unavailable. **Official Scorers:** Steve Meyer, Shane Severson. **Stadium Name:** Perfect Game Field at Veterans Memorial Stadium. **Location:** From I-380 North, take the Wilson Ave exit, turn left on Wilson Ave, after the railroad tracks, turn right on Rockford Road, proceed .8 miles, stadium is on left; From I-380 South, exit at First Avenue, proceed to Eighth Avenue (first stop sign) and turn left, stadium entrance is on right. **Standard Game Times:** 6:35 pm, Sun. 2:05. **Ticket Price Range:** $8-12 in advance, $9-13 day of game. **Visiting Club Hotel:** Holiday Inn Express, 3320 Southgate Ct. SW, Cedar Rapids, IA 52404. **Telephone:** (319) 399-5025.

CLINTON LUMBERKINGS

Office Address: Ashford University Field, 537 Ball Park Drive, Clinton, IA 52732. **Mailing Address:** PO Box 1295, Clinton, IA 52733. **Telephone:** (563) 242-0727. **Fax:** (563) 242-1433. **E-Mail Address:** lumberkings@lumberkings.com. **Website:** www.lumberkings.com.

OWNERSHIP/MANAGEMENT

Operated By: Clinton Baseball Club Inc.
President: Paul Davis. **General Manager:** Ted Tornow. **Director, Broadcasting/Media Relations:** Erik Oas. **Director, Operations:** Tyler Oehmen. **Manager, Stadium Sportsturf:** Reid Olson. **Accountant:** Ryan Marcum. **Assistant Director, Operations:** Morty Kriner. **Director, Facility Compliance:** Tom Whaley. **Office Procurement Manager:** Les Moore. **Clubhouse Manager:** David Foura. **Community Service Representative:** Tammy Johnson. **Assistant Groundskeeper:** Matt Dunbar. **Special Events Coordinator:** Tom Krogman.

FIELD STAFF

Manager: Denny Hocking. **Hitting Coach:** Jose Umbria. **Pitching Coach:** Doug Mathis. **Bench Coach:** Unavailable.

GAME INFORMATION

Radio Announcer: Erik Oas. **No. of Games Broadcast:** 140. **Flagship Station:** WCCI 100.3 FM. **PA Announcer:** Brad Seward. **Official Scorer:** Alex Miller. **Stadium Name:** Ashford University Field. **Location:** Highway 67 North to Sixth Ave. North, right on Sixth, cross railroad tracks, stadium on right. **Standard Game Times:** 6:30 pm, Sun. 2:00. **Ticket Price Range:** $5-8. **Visiting Club Hotel:** AmericInn & Suites, 1301 17th Street, Fulton, Ill. 61252. **Telephone:** (815) 589-3333.

DAYTON DRAGONS

Office Address: Fifth Third Field, 220 N. Patterson Blvd., Dayton, OH 45402. **Mailing Address:** PO Box 2107, Dayton, OH 45401. **Telephone:** (937) 228-2287. **Fax:** (937) 228-2284. **E-Mail Address:** dragons@daytondragons.com. **Website:** www.daytondragons.com. **Affiliation (first year):** Cincinnati Reds (2000). **Years in League:** 2000-

OWNERSHIP/MANAGEMENT

Operated By: Palisades Arcadia Baseball LLC.
President & General Manager: Robert Murphy. **Executive Vice President:** Eric Deutsch. **Office Manager/Executive Assistant to the President:** Leslie Stuck. **VP, Accounting/ Finance:** Mark Schlein. **VP, Corporate Partnerships:** Jeff Webb, Brad Eaton. **VP, Sponsor Services:** Brandy Guinaugh. **Director, Media Relations & Broadcasting:** Tom Nichols. **Senior Director, Operations:** John Wallace. **Director, Facility Operations:** Jason Fleenor. **Senior Director, Entertainment:** Kaitlin Rohrer. **Director, Entertainment:** Katrina Hamilton. **Director, Creative Services:** James Westerheide. **Box Office Manager:** Stefanie Mitchell. **Director, Season Ticket Sales:** Trafton Eutsler. **Senior Group Sales Manager:** Carl Hertzberg. **Senior Corporate Marketing Managers:** Andrew Hayes, Sam Schneider. **Corporate Marketing Managers:** Sam Bowers, Matt Dombrowski, Andy Sheets, Ryan Tuttle, T.J. Wingo. **Corporate Partnerships Managers:** Christine Burns, Greg Brittany Snyder, Wesley Livesay, Lindsay Powell, Brandon Rexin. **Inside Sales Manager:** Mandy Roselli. **Inside Sales Representatives:** Zachary Millard. **Graphic Desinger:** Ali Beach. **Multimedia Desinger:** Connor Boyle. **Sports Turf Manager:** Britt Barry. **Operations Manager:** Tyler Dunton. **Operations Assistant:** Chandler Dawson. **Media Relations Assistant:** Josh Hess. **Clubhouse Manager:** Austin Coleman. **Staff Accountant:** Dorthy Day. **Administrative Secretary:** Barbara Van Schaik.

FIELD STAFF

Manager: Luis Bolivar. **Hitting Coach:** Daryle Ward. **Pitching Coach:** Seth Etherton. **Coach:** Kevin Mahar. **Trainer:** Andrew Cleves. **Strength & Conditioning Coach:** Trey Strickland.

GAME INFORMATION

Radio Announcers: Tom Nichols and Josh Hess. **No. of Games Broadcast:** 140. **Flagship Station:** WONE 980 AM. **Television Announcer:** Tom Nichols and Jack Pohl. **No. of Games Broadcast:** Home-25. **Flagship Station:** WBDT

Channel 26. **PA Announcer:** Ben Oburn. **Official Scorers:** Matt Lindsay, Mike Lucas, Matt Zircher. **Stadium Name:** Fifth Third Field. **Location:** I-75 South to downtown Dayton, left at First Street; I-75 North, right at First Street exit. **Ticket Price Range:** $9-$17. **Visiting Club Hotel:** Courtyard by Marriott, 100 Prestige Place, Miamisburg, OH 45342. **Phone:** 937-433-3131. **Fax:** 937-433-0285.

FORT WAYNE TINCAPS

Address: 1301 Ewing St., Fort Wayne, IN 46802. **Telephone:** (260) 482-6400.
Fax: (260) 471-4678. **E-Mail Address:** info@tincaps.com.
Website: www.tincaps.com. **Affiliation (first year):** San Diego Padres (1999). **Years in League:** 1993-

OWNERSHIP/MANAGEMENT

Operated By: Hardball Capital. **Owner:** Jason Freier.
President: Mike Nutter. **Vice President, Corporate Partnerships:** David Lorenz. **VP, Finance:** Brian Schackow. **VP, Marketing & Promotions:** Michael Limmer. **Creative Director:** Tony DesPlaines. **Director of Video Production:** Melissa Darby. **Assistant Video Production Manager:** Tim Bajema. **Broadcasting/Media Relations Manager:** John Nolan. **Community Engagement Manager:** Morgan Olson. **Group Sales Director:** Jared Parcell. **Group Sales Assistant Director:** Brent Harring. **Senior Ticket Account Manager:** Austin Allen. **Ticket Account Manager:** Dalton McGill. **Ticket Account Manager:** Jenn Sylvester. **Ticket Account Manager:** Tyler Lantz. **Ticketing Director:** Pat Ventura. **Reading Program Director/Assistant Director of Ticketing:** Paige Watson. **Corporate Partnerships Manager:** Tyler Baker. **Special Events Coordinator:** Holly Raney. **Banquet Event Manager:** Alexis Strabala. **Food/ Beverage Director:** Bill Lehn. **Executive Chef/Culinary Director:** Scott Kammerer. **VIP Services Manager:** Dominick Catanzarite. **Food/Beverage Operations Manager:** Nathan Seaman. **Commissary Manager:** Eric Sauer. **Head Groundskeeper:** Keith Winter. **Assistant Groundskeeper:** Ryan Lehrman. **Facilities Director:** Tim Burkhart. **Accounting Manager/Facilities Manager:** Erik Lose. **Groundskeeping/Ballpark Operations Assistant:** Jake Sperry. **Ballpark Cleaning Crew Supervisor:** Jeff Johnson. **Merchandise Manager:** Jen Klinker. **Human Resources/Office Manager:** Cathy Tinney.

FIELD STAFF

Manager: Anthony Contreras. **Hitting Coach:** Jonathan Matthews. **Pitching Coach:** Burt Hooton. **Fielding Coach:** Jhonny Carvajal. **Athletic Trainer:** Allyse Kramer. **Strength/Conditioning Coach:** Sam Hoffman.

GAME INFORMATION

Radio Announcers: John Nolan, Cory Stace, Mike Maahs. **No. of Radio GamesBroadcast:** 140. **Flagship Station:** WKJG 1380-AM/100.9-FM. **TV Announcers:** John Nolan, Dave Doster, Javi DeJesus, Bobby Pierce, Brett Rump, Tracy Coffman. **No. of TV Games Broadcast:** Home–70. **Flagship Station:** Comcast Network 81. **PA Announcer:** Jared Parcell. **Official Scorers:** Rich Tavierne, Bill Scott, Dave Coulter. **Stadium Name:** Parkview Field. **Location:** 1301 Ewing St., Fort Wayne, IN, 46802. **Ticket Price Range:** $5-$12.50. **Visiting Club Hotel:** Quality Inn, 1734 West Washington Center Rd., Fort Wayne, IN, 46818 (260-489-5554).

GREAT LAKES LOONS

Address: 825 East Main St., Midland, MI 48640.
Telephone: (989) 837-2255. **Fax:** (989) 837-8780.
E-Mail Address: info@loons.com. **Website:** www.loons.com.
Affiliation (first year): Los Angeles Dodgers (2007). **Years in League:** 2007-

OWNERSHIP/MANAGEMENT

Operated By: Michigan Baseball Operations.
Stadium Ownership: Michigan Baseball Foundation. **Founder:** William Stavropoulos. **Director, ESPN 100.9-FM Sales:** Jay Arons. **Manager, Concessions:** Andrew Booms. **Director, Gameday Experience & Community Outreach:** James Cahilellis. **Vice President, CFO:** Jana Chotivkova. **Vice President, Human Resources:** Ann Craig. **Assistant GM, Marketing & Communication:** Matt DeVries. **Director, Production:** Trent Elliott. **Manager, Group Venue Sales:** Tony Garant. **General Manager, Dow Diamond Events:** Dave Gomola. **Manager, ESPN 100.9-FM Business:** Robin Gover. **Adminstrative Support Assistant:** Melissa Kehoe. **Director, Partnership Activation:** Tyler Kring. **Manager, Ticket Operations:** John Metevia. **Vice President, Business Development:** Chris Mundhenk. **Executive Chief:** Andrea Noonan. **Director, ESPN 100.9-FM Production & Operations:** Jerry O'Donnell. **Coordinator, Group Ticket Sales:** Sam PeLong. **Assistant GM, Ticket Sales:** Thom Pepe. **Head Groundskeeper:** Kelly Rensel. **Manager, Creative Services:** Alex Seder. **Coordinator, Accounting:** Holly Snow. **Director, Accounting:** Jamie Start. **Director, Food & Beverage:** Gary Straight. **Assistant GM, Facility Operations:** Dan Straley. **Manager, Catering:** Ryan Teeple. **Manager, ESPN 100.9-FM Programming & Play-by-Play Broadcaster:** Brad Tunney. **Executive Assistant & MBF Grants:** Carol VanWert. **Corporate Account Executive:** Joe Volk. **Play-by-Play Broadcaster:** Chris Vosters. **Vice President, Baseball Operations & Gameday Experience:** Tiffany Wardynski.

FIELD STAFF

Manager: John Shoemaker. **Hitting Coach:** Jair Fernandez. **Pitching Coach:** Bobby Cuellar. **Bench Coach:** Seth Conner.

GAME INFORMATION

Play-by-Play Broadcaster: Chris Vosters & Brad Tunney. **No. of Games Broadcast:** 140. **Flagship Station:** WLUN, ESPN 100.9-FM (ESPN1009.com). **PA Announcer:** Jerry O'Donnell. **Official Scorers:** Matt Jones, Steve Robb. **Stadium Name:** Dow Diamond. **Location:** I-75 to US-10 W, Take the M-20/US-10 Business exit on the left toward downtown Midland, Merge onto US-10 W/MI-20 W (also known as Indian Street), Turn left onto State Street, the entrance to the stadium is at the intersection of Ellsworth and State Streets. **Standard Game Times:** 6:05 pm (April), 7:05 (May-Sept), Sun. 2:05. **Ticket Price Range:** $6-9. **Visiting Club Hotel:** Holiday Inn, 810 Cinema Drive, Midland, MI 48642. **Telephone:** (989) 794-8500.

KANE COUNTY COUGARS

Address: 34W002 Cherry Lane, Geneva, IL 60134. **Telephone:** (630) 232-8811. **Fax:** (630) 232-8815. **Website:** www.kccougars.com. **Affiliation (third year):** Arizona Diamondbacks (2015). **Years in League:** 1991-

OWNERSHIP/MANAGEMENT

Operated By: Cougars Baseball Partnership/American Sports Enterprises, Inc. **Chairman/Chief Executive Officer/ President:** Dr. Bob Froehlich. **Owners:** Dr. Bob Froehlich, Cheryl Froehlich. **Board of Directors:** Dr. Bob Froehlich, Cheryl Froehlich, Stephanie Froehlich, Chris Neidhart, Marianne Neidhart. **Vice President/General Manager:** Curtis Haug. **Senior Director, Finance/Administration:** Douglas Czurylo. **Finance/Accounting Manager:** Lance Buhmann. **Accounting:** Sally Sullivan. **Senior Director, Ticketing:** R. Michael Patterson. **Senior Ticket Sales Representative:** Alex Miller. **Sales Representatives:** Grace Mack, Sam Ostrowski, Dave Grochowski, Kelton Zimmerman. **Director, Ticket Services/Community Relations:** Amy Mason. **Senior Ticket Operations Representative:** Paul Quillia. **Ticket Operations Representative:** Jeff Weaver. **Director, Security:** Dan Klinkhamer. **Promotions Director/Office Manager:** Amy Bromann. **Communications Coordinator:** Jacquie Boatman. **Design/Graphics:** Emmet Broderick. **Media Placement Coordinator:** Bill Baker. **Video Director:** Mike Forrest. **Director, Food/Beverage:** Aaron Hammer. **Business Manager:** Robin Hull. **Executive Chef:** Ron Kludac. **Senior Director, Stadium Operations:** Mike Klafehn. **Director, Maintenance:** Jeff Snyder. **Head Groundskeeper:** Sean Ehlert.

FIELD STAFF

Manager: Blake Lalli. **Hitting Coach:** Rick Short. **Pitching Coach:** Rich Sauveur. **Coach:** Jorge Cortes. **Athletic Trainer:** Kelly Boyce. **Strength & Conditioning Coach:** Scott Shipman. **Clubhouse Manager:** Scott Anderson.

GAME INFORMATION

Radio Announcer: Joe Brand. **No. of Games Broadcast:** 140. **Flagship Station:** WBIG 1280-AM. **Official Scorer:** Joe Brand. **Stadium Name:** Northwestern Medicine Field. **Location:** From east or west, I-88 Ronald Reagan Memorial Tollway) to Farnsworth Ave. North exit, north five miles to Cherry Lane, left into stadium; from northwest, I-90 (Jane Addams Memorial Tollway) to Randall Rd. South exit, south to Fabayan Parkway, east to Kirk Rd., north to Cherry Lane, left into stadium complex. **Standard Game Times:** 6:30 pm, Sun. 1 pm. **Ticket Price Range:** $9-15. **Visiting Club Hotel:** Pheasant Run Resort, 4051 E Main St, St. Charles, IL 60174. **Telephone:** (630) 584-6300.

LAKE COUNTY CAPTAINS

Address: Classic Park, 35300 Vine St., Eastlake, OH 44095-3142. **Telephone:** (440) 975-8085. **Fax:** (440) 975-8958. **E-Mail Address:** nstein@captainsbaseball.com. **Website:** www.captainsbaseball.com. **Affiliation (first year):** Cleveland Indians (2003). **Years in League:** 2010-

OWNERSHIP/MANAGEMENT

Operated By: Cascia LLC. **Owners:** Peter and Rita Carfagna, Ray and Katie Murphy. **Chairman/Secretary/Treasurer:** Peter Carfagna. **Vice Chairman:** Rita Carfagna. **Vice President:** Ray Murphy. **General Manager:** Neil Stein. **Assistant GM:** Jen Yorko. **Sr. Director, Marketing & Promotions:** Drew LaFollette. **Director, Captains Concessions:** John Klein. **Director, Ticket Operations & Special Events:** Justin Cartor. **Manager, Stadium Operations:** Matt Boes. **Manager, Finance:** Nicole Ruggerio. **Manager, Media Relations & Sales:** Tim O'Brien. **Manager, Merchandise & Sales:** Christy Buchar. **Manager, Social Media & Corporate Sales:** Brent Pozza. **Ticket Sales Account Executive:** Kate Roth. **Coordinator, Marketing & Special Projects:** Devin Levan-Galang.

FIELD STAFF

Manager: Luke Carlin. **Hitting Coach:** Pete Lauritson. **Bench Coach:** Kyle Hudson. **Pitching Coach:** Joe Torres.

GAME INFORMATION

Radio Announcer: Andrew Luftglass. **No. of Games Broadcast:** 140. **Flagship Station:** allsportscleveland.net. **PA Announcer:** Jasen Sokol. **Official Scorers:** Mike Mohner, Chuck Murr. **Stadium Name:** Classic Park. **Location:** From Ohio State Route 2 East, exit at Ohio 91, go left and the stadium is 1/4 mile north on your right; From Ohio State Route 90 East, exit at Ohio 91, go right and the stadium in approximately five miles north on your right. **Standard Game Times:** 6:30 pm (April-May), 7 (May-Sept), Sun. 1:30. **Visiting Club Hotel:** Red Roof Inn 4166 State Route 306, Willoughby, Ohio 44094. **Telephone:** (440)-946-9872.

LANSING LUGNUTS

Address: 505 E. Michigan Ave., Lansing, MI 48912.
Telephone: (517) 485-4500. **Fax:** (517) 485-4518.
E-Mail Address: info@lansinglugnuts.com. **Website:** www.lansinglugnuts.com.
Affiliation (first year): Toronto Blue Jays (2005). **Years in League:** 1996-

OWNERSHIP/MANAGEMENT

Operated By: Take Me Out to the Ballgame LLC. **Principal Owners:** Tom Dickson, Sherrie Myers.
President: Nick Grueser. **General Manager:** Tyler Parsons. **Assistant GM:** Nick Brzezinski. **Executive Assistant:** Angela Sees. **Finance Manager:** Brianna Pfeil. **Corporate Sales Manager:** Alex Withorn. **Group Sales Manager:** Eric Pionk. **Season Ticket Specialist:** Greg Kruger. **Assistant Retail Director:** Matt Hicks. **Stadium Operations Manager:** Dennis Busse. **Assistant Stadium Operations Manager & Team Relations Manager:** Bill Getschman. **Senior VP of Operations Food & Beverage:** Jason Wilson. **Assistant Food/Beverage Director:** John Thompson. **Concessions Manager & Non-Profit Coordinator:** Paul Ciucci. **Events & Meetings Manager:** Malinda Barr. **Special Events Coordinator:** Monica Edwards. **Production Manager:** Ryan LeFevre. **Manager of Fan Engagement:** Mikaela Higgins. **Corporate Partnerships Manager:** Ashley Loudan. **Head Grounds Manager:** Zach Severns.

FIELD STAFF

Manager: Cesar Martin. **Hitting Coach:** Matt Young. **Pitching Coach:** Antonio Caceres. **Position Player Coach:** Dave Pano. **Athletic Trainer:** Caleb Daniel. **Strength & Conditioning Coach:** Aaron Spano.

GAME INFORMATION

Radio Announcer: Jesse Goldberg-Strassler. **No. of Games Broadcast:** 140. **Flagship Station:** WQTX 92.1-FM. **PA Announcer:** Unavailable. **Official Scorer:** Timothy Zeko. **Stadium Name:** Cooley Law School Stadium. **Location:** I-96 East/West to US 496, exit at Larch Street, north of Larch, stadium on left. **Ticket Price Range:** $8-$36. **Visiting Club Hotel:** Radisson Hotel.

PEORIA CHIEFS

Address: 730 SW Jefferson, Peoria, IL 61605.
Telephone: (309) 680-4000. **Fax:** (309) 680-4080.
E-Mail Address: feedback@chiefsnet.com. **Website:** www.peoriachiefs.com.
Affiliation (first year): St. Louis Cardinals (2013). **Years in League:** 1983-

OWNERSHIP/MANAGEMENT

Operated By: Peoria Chiefs Community Baseball Club LLC.
President: Rocky Vonachen. **General Manager:** Jason Mott. **Manager, Box Office:** Ryan Sivori. **Director, Media/Baseball Operations:** Nathan Baliva. **Marketing Manager:** Allison Rhoades. **Manager, Entertainment/Community Relations:** Patrick Walker. **Ticket Sales Manager:** Kate Voss. **Account Executives:** Kyle Belback; Kevin Kurowski, John Phelps. **Head Groundskeeper:** Mike Reno. **Director, Food/Beverage:** Nathan Weindruch. **Executive Chef:** Justin Uy.

FIELD STAFF

Manager: Chris Swauger. **Hitting Coach:** Russ Chambliss. **Pitching Coach:** Cale Johnson. **Coach:** Unavailable. **Trainer:** Dan Martin. **Strength & Conditioning Coach:** Frank Spinelli.

GAME INFORMATION

Radio Announcer: Nathan Baliva. **No. of Games Broadcast:** 140. **Flagship Station:** www.peoriachiefs.com, Tune-In Radio. **PA Announcer:** Unavailable. **Official Scorers:** Bryan Moore, Brad Kupiec, Nathan Baliva. **Stadium Name:** Dozer Park. **Location:** From South/East, I-74 to exit 93 (Jefferson St), continue one mile, stadium is one block on left; From North/West, I-74 to Glen Oak Exit, turn right on Glendale, which turns into Kumpf Blvd, turn right on Jefferson, stadium on left. **Standard Game Times:** 7 pm, 6:30 (April-May, after Aug. 26), Sat. 6:30, Sun. 2 p.m. **Ticket Price Range:** $7-14. **Visiting Club Hotel:** Quality Inn & Suites, 4112 Brandywine Dr, Peoria, IL, 61614. **Telephone:** (309) 685-2556.

QUAD CITIES RIVER BANDITS

Address: 209 S. Gaines St., Davenport, IA 52802.
Telephone: (563) 324-3000. **Fax:** (563) 324-3109.
E-Mail Address: bandit@riverbandits.com. **Website:** www.riverbandits.com.
Affiliation (first year): Houston Astros (2013). **Years in League:** 1960-

OWNERSHIP/MANAGEMENT

Operated by: Main Street Iowa LLC, David Heller, Roby Smith.
General Manager: Andrew Chesser. **VP, Sales:** Shawn Brown. **VP, Ticketing:** Mike Candela. **Assistant GM:** Jacqueline Holm. **Assistant GM, Special Events:** Amy Richey. **Director, Amusements:** Bill Duncan. **Manager, Baseball Finance:** Dawn Temple. **Account Manager, MSA:** Brenda Gibson. **Coordinator, HR and Finance:** Amy DeBoever.

Director, Community Relations: Crystal Bowen. **Manager, Promotions:** Aron Brecht. **Director, Media Relations:** Jason Kempf. **Manager, Stadium Operations:** Seth Reeve. **Manager, Creative Services and Production:** Jason Harrel. **Director, Merchandise:** Darren Pitra. **Manager, First Impressions:** Rae Mittan. **Manager, Special Events:** Allie Hudson. **Manager, Box Office:** Tyler Henderson. **Head Groundskeeper:** Andrew Marking. **Director, Food/Beverage:** Pete Cummins. **Account Executive, Group Sales:** Amanda Adee. **Account Executive, Group Sales:** Aaron Wilson. **Account Executive, Group Sales:** John Barrett.

FIELD STAFF

Manager: Mickey Storey. **Hitting Coach:** Graham Johnson. **Pitching Coach:** Dillon Lawson.

GAME INFORMATION

Radio Announcer: Jason Kempf. **No. of Games Broadcast:** 140. **Flagship Station:** 1170-AM KBOB. **PA Announcer:** TBA. **Official Scorer:** Unavailable. **Stadium Name:** Modern Woodmen Park. **Location:** From I-74, take Grant Street exit left, west onto River Drive, left on South Gaines Street; from I-80, take Brady Street exit south, right on River Drive, left on S. Gaines Street. **Standard Game Times:** 6:35 pm; Sun. 1:15 (April and Sept), Sun. 5:15 pm (May-August). **Ticket Price Range:** $5-13. **Visiting Club Hotel:** Radisson Quad City Plaza Hotel,111 E. 2nd St, Davenport, IA 52801. **Telephone:** (563) 322-2200.

SOUTH BEND CUBS

Office Address: 501 W. South St., South Bend, IN 46601.
Mailing Address: PO Box 4218, South Bend, IN 46634.
Telephone: (574) 235-9988. **Fax:** (574) 235-9950.
E-Mail Address: cubs@southbendcubs.com. **Website:** www.southbendcubs.com
Affiliation (first year): Chicago Cubs (2015). **Years in League:** 1988-

OWNERSHIP/MANAGEMENT

Owner: Andrew Berlin.
President: Joe Hart. **Vice President/General Manager, Business Development:** Nick Brown. **Assistant GM, Tickets:** Andy Beuster. **Director, Ticket Operations and Customer Service:** Devon Hastings. **Senior Account Executive:** Mitch McKamey. **Account Executives:** Kevin Drislane, Logan Lee, Brey Tyson. **Director, Finance/Human Resources:** Cheryl Carlson. **Director, Food/Beverage:** Nick Barkley. **Catering/Business Manager:** Jessica DuVall. **Executive Chief:** Josh Farmer. **Director, Media/Promotions:** Chris Hagstrom-Jones. **Promotions Assistant & Office Manager:** Kayla Smith. **Merchandise Manager:** Mary-Lou Pallo. **Assistant GM, Operations:** Peter Argueta. **Head Groundskeeper:** T.J. Wohlever. **Groundskeeper:** Jeremy Harper.

FIELD STAFF

Manager: Jimmy Gonzalez. **Hitting Coach:** Ricardo Medina. **Pitching Coach:** Brian Lawrence. **Bench Coach:** Unavailable. **Athletic Trainer:** James Edwards. **Strength & Conditiong Coach:** Unavailable.

GAME INFORMATION

Radio Announcer: Darin Pritchett. **Flagship Station:** 96.1 FM WSBT. **PA Announcer:** Gregg Sims, Jon Thompson. **Official Scorer:** Peter Yarbro. **Stadium Name:** Four Winds Field. **Location:** I-80/90 toll road to exit 77, take US 31/33 south to South Bend to downtown (Main Street), to Western Ave., right on Western, left on Taylor. **Standard Game Times:** 7:05 pm, Fri. 7:35, Sun. 2:05. **Ticket Price Range:** Advance $11-13, Day of Game $12-14. **Visiting Club Hotel:** DoubleTree by Hilton Hotel South Bend. **Telephone:** (574) 234-2000.

WEST MICHIGAN WHITECAPS

Office Address: 4500 West River Dr., Comstock Park, MI 49321. **Mailing Address:** PO Box 428, Comstock Park, MI 49321. **Telephone:** (616) 784-4131. **Fax:** (616) 784-4911. **E-Mail Address:** playball@whitecapsbaseball.com. **Website:** www.whitecapsbaseball.com. **Affiliation (first year):** Detroit Tigers (1997). **Years in League:** 1994-

OWNERSHIP/MANAGEMENT

Operated By: Whitecaps Professional Baseball Corp. **Principal Owners:** Denny Baxter, Lew Chamberlin. **President:** Scott Lane. **Vice President:** Jim Jarecki. **Vice President, Sales:** Steve McCarthy. **Facility Events Manager:** Mike Klint. **Operations Manager:** Mike Craven. **Director, Food/Beverage:** Matt Timon. **Community Relations Coordinator:** Jessica Muzevuca. **Director, Marketing/Media:** Mickey Graham. **Promotions Manager:** Matt Hoffman. **Multimedia Manager:** Elaine Cunningham. **Box Office Manager: Shaun Pynnonen Groundskeeper:** Mitch Hooten. **Facility Maintenance Manager:** Jason Ross. **Director, Ticket Sales:** Chad Sayen.

FIELD STAFF

Manager: Lance Parrish. **Coach:** Mariano Duncan. **Coach:** John Vander Wal. **Pitching Coach:** Jorge Cordova. **Trainer:** Jason Schwartzman.

GAME INFORMATION

Radio Announcers: Dan Hasty. **No. of Games Broadcast:** 140. **Flagship Station:** WBBL 107.3-FM. **PA Announcers:** Mike Newell, Bob Wells. **Official Scorers:** Mike Dean, Don Thomas. **Stadium Name:** Fifth Third Ballpark. **Location:** US 131 North from Grand Rapids to exit 91 (West River Drive). **Ticket Price Range:** $6-16. **Visiting Club Hotel:** Crowne Plaza 5700 28th Street SE Grand Rapids, MI 49546. **Telephone:** (616) 957-1770.

WISCONSIN TIMBER RATTLERS

Office Address: 2400 N. Casaloma Dr., Appleton, WI 54913. **Mailing Address:** PO Box 7464, Appleton, WI 54912. **Telephone:** (920) 733-4152. **Fax:** (920) 733-8032. **E-Mail Address:** info@timberrattlers.com. **Website:** www.timberrattlers.com. **Affiliation (first year):** Milwaukee Brewers (2009). **Years in League:** 1962-

OWNERSHIP/MANAGEMENT

Operated By: Appleton Baseball Club, Inc. **Chairman:** Jim Britt. **President/General Manager:** Rob Zerjav. **Vice President/Assistant GM:** Aaron Hahn. **Director, Food/Beverage:** Ryan Grossman. **Director, Stadium Operations/ Security:** Ron Kaiser. **Director, Community Relations:** Dayna Baitinger. **Director, Corporate Partnerships:** Ryan Cunniff. **Director of Grounds:** Jake Hannes. **Director, Group Sales:** Brittany Ezze. **Director, Merchandise:** Jay Grusznski. **Director, Media Relations:** Chris Mehring. **Group Sales:** Megan Chatterton, Kyle Fargen. **Corporate Marketing Manager:** Seth Merrill. **Box Office Manager:** Lance Kays. **Controller:** Cathy Spanbauer. **Banquet Sales/Events Manager:** Terry Lagarde. **Assistant Manager, Banquets/Events:** Kim Chonos. **Executive Chef:** Charles Behrmann. **Executive Sous Chef:** Derek Spranger. **Assistant, Food/Beverage Director:** Chris Prentice. **Stadium Operations Manager:** Aaron Johnson. **Creative Director:** Ann Lindeman. **Marketing Coordinator:** Hilary Bauer. **Entertainment Coordinator:** Jacob Jirschele. **Graphic Designer:** Nick Guenther. **Accounting/Human Resources Manager:** Sara Szablewski. **Production Manager:** Jerred Drake. **Clubhouse Manager:** Nate Sinnott. **Office Manager:** Mary Robinson.

FIELD STAFF

Manager: Matt Erickson. **Hitting Coach:** Hainley Statia. **Pitching Coach:** Steve Cline. **Athletic Trainer:** Jeff Paxson.

GAME INFORMATION

Radio Announcer: Chris Mehring. **No. of Games Broadcast:** 140. **Flagship Station:** WNAM 1280-AM. **Television Announcer:** Chris Mehring (Radio Simulcast). **Television Affiliates:** Spectrum Sports, WACY-TV. **No. of Games Broadcast:** TBA. **PA Announcer:** Joey D. **Official Scorer:** Jay Grusznski. **Stadium Name:** Neuroscience Group Field at Fox Cities Stadium. **Location:** Highway 41 to Highway 15 (00) exit, west to Casaloma Drive, left to stadium. **Standard Game Times:** 7:05 pm, 6:35 (April-May), Sat. 6:35, Sun. 1:05. **Ticket Price Range:** $7-36. **Visiting Club Hotel:** Country Inn & Suites; 355 N Fox River Dr, Appleton, WI 54913. **Telephone:** (920) 830-3240.

SOUTH ATLANTIC LEAGUE

Address: 2451 McMullen Booth Road, Suite 245, Clearwater, FL, 33759.
Telephone: (727) 538-4270. **Fax:** (727) 499-6853.
E-Mail Address: office@saloffice.com. **Website:** www.southatlanticleague.com.
Years League Active: 1904-1964, 1979-
President/Secretary/Treasurer: Eric Krupa.
First Vice President: Chip Moore (Rome). **Second VP:** Craig Brown (Greenville).
Directors: Cooper Brantley (Greensboro). Craig Brown (Greenville). Brian DeWine
(Asheville). Jason Freier (Columbia). Marvin Goldklang (Charleston). Neil Leibman (Hickory).
Art Matin (Lakewood). Chip Moore (Rome). Bruce Quinn (Hagerstown). Reese Smith
(Kannapolis). Andy Shea (Lexington). Jeff Eiseman (Augusta). Tom Volpe (Delmarva). Tim
Wilcox (West Virginia).
Division Structure: North—Delmarva, Greensboro, Hagerstown, Hickory, Kannapolis,
Lakewood, West Virginia. **South**—Asheville, Augusta, Charleston, Columbia, Greenville,
Lexington, Rome.
Regular Season: 140 games (split schedule).
2018 Opening Date: April 5. **Closing Date:** September 3.
All-Star Game: June 19 at Greensboro.
Playoff Format: First-half and second-half division winners meet in best-of-three series.
Winners meet in best of five series for league championship.
Roster Limit: 25 active. **Player Eligibility Rule:** No age limit. No more than two players and one player-coach on
active list may have more than five years of experience.
Brand of Baseball: Rawlings.
Umpires: Matthew Baldwin (Annapolis, MD). Reed Basner (Lawrenceville, GA). Mark Bass (Madisonville, LA). Jonathan
Benken (Lilburn, GA). Brandon Blome (Adairsville, GA). John Budka Jr. (Oradell, NJ). Dexter Kelly (Jonesboro, GA).
Jude Koury (Youngstown, OH), Forrest Ladd (Lafayette, LA). Scott Molloy (Cranston, RI). Zachary Neff (Greenville, SC).
Mark Stewart Jr. (Lake Worth, FL) Kelvis Velez Caminero (Ensenada, PR) Dillon Wilson (Clopton, AL).

Eric Krupa

STADIUM INFORMATION

Club	Stadium	Opened	Dimensions			Capacity	2017 Att.
			LF	CF	RF		
Asheville	McCormick Field	1992	326	373	297	4,000	184,019
Augusta	Lake Olmstead Stadium	1995	330	400	330	4,322	178,269
Charleston	Joseph P. Riley, Jr. Ballpark	1997	306	386	336	5,800	305,622
Columbia	Spirit Communications Park	2016	319	400	330	7,501	315,034
Delmarva	Arthur W. Perdue Stadium	1996	309	402	309	5,200	207,131
Greensboro	First National Bank Field	2005	322	400	320	7,599	350,743
Greenville	Fluor Field at the West End	2006	310	400	302	5,000	328,222
Hagerstown	Municipal Stadium	1931	335	400	330	4,600	84,181
Hickory	L.P. Frans Stadium	1993	330	401	330	5,062	136,225
Kannapolis	Intimidators Stadium	1995	330	400	310	4,700	69,112
Lakewood	FirstEnergy Park	2001	325	400	325	6,588	338,554
Lexington	Whitaker Bank Ballpark	2001	320	401	318	6,033	281,210
Rome	State Mutual Stadium	2003	335	400	330	5,100	161,444
West Virginia	Appalachian Power Park	2005	330	400	320	4,300	133,679

ASHEVILLE TOURISTS

Address: McCormick Field, 30 Buchanan Place, Asheville, NC 28801.
Telephone: (828) 258-0428. **E-Mail Address:** info@theashevilletourists.com.
Website: www.theashevilletourists.com. **Affiliation (first year):** Colorado Rockies
(1994). **Years in League:** 1976-

OWNERSHIP/MANAGEMENT
Operated By: DeWine Seeds Silver Dollar Baseball, LLC.
President: Brian DeWine. **General Manager:** Larry Hawkins. **Senior Sales Executive:** Chris Smith. **Business
Manager:** Ryan Straney. **Creative Marketing Manager:** Sam Fischer. **Director of Broadcasting/Media Relations:**
Doug Maurer. **Director of Ticket Operations:** Hannah Martin. **Group Sales Associates:** Michael Grimes, Matthew
Wisniewski, Robert Mantey, Samantha Cook. **Outside Sales Associate:** Bob Jones. **Stadium Operations Director:** Eliot
Williams. **Director of Food & Beverage:** Tyler Holt. **Head Groundskeeper:** Matt Dierdorff. **Merchandise Manager:** Kali
DeWine. **Publications:** Bill Ballew.

FIELD STAFF
Manager: Robinson Cancel. **Hitting Coach:** Norberto "Paco" Martín. **Pitching Coach:** Ryan Kibler. **Development
Supervisor:** Marv Foley. **Athletic Trainer:** Unavailable.

GAME INFORMATION

Radio Announcer: Doug Maurer. **No. of Games Broadcast:** 140. **Flagship Station:** WRES 100.7-FM. **PA Announcer:** Tim Lolley. **Official Scorer:** Jim Baker. **Stadium Name:** McCormick Field. **Location:** I-240 to Charlotte Street South exit, south one mile on Charlotte, left on McCormick Place. **Ticket Price Range:** $6-13. **Visiting Club Hotel:** Brookstone Lodge. **Telephone:** (828) 398-5888.

AUGUSTA GREENJACKETS

Office Address: 187 Railroad Ave. North Augusta, SC 29841.
Mailing Address: PO Box 3746 Hill Station, Augusta, GA 30914.
Telephone: (706) 736-7889. **Fax:** (706) 736-1122.
E-Mail Address: info@greenjacketsbaseball.com. **Web site:** www.greenjacketsbaseball.com.
Affiliation (first year): San Francisco Giants (2005). **Years in League:** 1988-

OWNERSHIP/MANAGEMENT

Ownership Group: AGON Sports & Entertainment. **Owner:** Chris Schoen.
President: Jeff Eiseman. **Vice President:** Tom Denlinger. **General Manager:** Brandon Greene. **Mgr., Ticket Sales:** Matt Szczupakowski. **Accounting:** Debbie Brown. **Stadium Operations Director:** Billy Nowak. **Marketing/Promotions/Community Relations:** Shannon Mitchell. **Mgr, Corporate Partnerships:** Greg Dietz. **Ticket Sales Account Executive:** Troy Pakusch. **Mgr., Group Sales:** Yari Natal. **Group Sales Account Executive:** James Mullins. **Ticket Operations Specialists and Supervisor:** Tyler Wilcox. **Retail Sales Manager:** Chelsea Galbraith. **Food & Beverage Director:** Tyler Glynn. **Food & Beverage Supervisor:** David Hutto. **Groundskeeper:** Trey Altman.

FIELD STAFF

Manager: Jolbert Cabrera. **Hitting Coach:** Thomas Neal. **Pitching Coach:** Clay Rapada. **Coach:** Ydwin Villegas.

GAME INFORMATION

PA Announcer: Unavailable. **Stadium Name:** SRP Park. **Location:** I-20 to Washington Road exit, east to Broad Street exit, left on Milledge Road. **Standard Game Times:** 7:05 pm, Sat. 6:05pm; Sun. 2:**05 through May, 5:**05 pm on Memorial Day. **Ticket Price Range:** $9-$28. **Visiting Club Hotel:** Comfort Suites, 2911 Riverwest Dr, Augusta, GA. **Telephone:** (706) 434-2540.

CHARLESTON RIVERDOGS

Office Address: 360 Fishburne St, Charleston, SC 29403.
Mailing Address: PO Box 20849, Charleston, SC 29403.
Telephone: (843) 723-7241. **Fax:** (843) 723-2641.
E-Mail Address: admin@riverdogs.com. **Website:** www.riverdogs.com.
Affiliation (first year): New York Yankees (2005). **Years in League:** 1973-78, 1980-

OWNERSHIP/MANAGEMENT

Operated by: The Goldklang Group/South Carolina Baseball Club LP.
Chairman: Marv Goldklang. **President:** Jeff Goldklang. **Club President/General Manager:** Dave Echols. **President Emeritus:** Mike Veeck. **Director, Fun:** Bill Murray. **Co-Owners:** Peter Freund, Gene Budig, Al Phillips. **VP, Business and Marketing Development:** Scott Bush. **VP, Corporate Sales:** Andy Lange. **VP, Special Events:** Melissa Azevedo. **Assistant GM:** Ben Abzug. **Director, Promotions:** Nate Kurant. **Director, Broadcasting/Media Relations:** Matt Dean. **Director, Food/Beverage:** Josh Shea. **Director, Merchandise:** Mike DeAntonio. **Director, Community Relations:** Walter Nolan-Cohn. **Director, Ticket Sales:** Garret Randle. **Director, Operations:** Philip Guiry. **Director, Video Production:** Jeremy Schrank. **Business Manager:** Dale Stickney. **Box Office Manager:** Morgan Powell. **Marketing & Creative Services Coordinator:** Bradley Moore. **Special Events Manager:** Megan Blackman. **Riley Park Club Events Manager:** Bailey Linderman. **Food/Beverage Manager:** Kristina Wilkins. **Sales Representative:** Daniel Armas, Mike Ryan, Serg Saradjian, Jake Terrell, Will Senn. **Office Manager:** Cynthia Linhart. **Head Groundskeeper:** Mike Williams. **Clubhouse Manager:** Harris Seletsky.

FIELD STAFF

Manager: Julio Mosquera. **Hitting Coach:** Scott Seabol. **Pitching Coach:** Justin Pope. **Defensive Coach:** Dan Fiorito. **Athletic Trainer:** Michael Sole. **Strength & Conditioning Coach:** Danny Russo.

GAME INFORMATION

Radio Announcer: Matt Dean. **No. of Games Broadcast:** 140. **Flagship Station:** WTMA 1250-AM. **PA Announcer:** Ken Carrington. **Official Scorer:** Mike Hoffman. **Stadium Name:** Joseph Riley Jr. **Location:** 360 Fishburne St, Charleston, SC 29403, From US 17, take Lockwood Dr. North, right on Fishburne St. **Standard Game Times:** 7:05pm, Sat. 6:05pm, Sun. 5:05. **Ticket Price Range:** $8-20. **Visiting Club Hotel:** Sleep Inn Airport.

COLUMBIA FIREFLIES

Office Address: 1640 Freed Street, Columbia, SC 29201.
Mailing Address: 1640 Freed Street, Columbia, SC 29201.
Telephone: (803) 726-4487. **Fax:** (803) 726-3126.
E-Mail Address: info@columbiafireflies.com. **Website:** www.columbiafireflies.com.
Affiliation (first year): New York Mets (2016). **Years in League:** 2016-

OWNERSHIP/MANAGEMENT

Operated By: Columbia Fireflies Baseball, LLC.
President: John Katz. **Executive Vice President:** Brad Shank. **Senior Vice President/Food & Beverage:** Scott Burton. **Vice President, Marketing & Public Relations:** Abby Naas. **Director of Corporate Partnerships:** Blake Buchanan. **Director, Accounting & Baseball Operations:** Jonathan Mercier. **Office Manager:** Sabriya Brooks. **Director, Ticketing:** Joe Shepard. **Director, Group Sales:** Kaylee Swanson. **Assistant Director, Ticketing/Reading Program Manager:** Kyle Williamson. **Ticket Account Manager:** Stephanie Keane, Jeff Berger, Dalton Tresvant, Scott Rhodes, Elena Hooven. **Graphics Manager:** Marcus Walker. **New Media Engagement & Promotions Manager:** Kyle Martin. **Video Production Manager:** Jared Law. **Community Engagement Manager:** Elliott Anderson. **Marketing/Client Services Manager:** Ashlie DeCarlo. **Business Analytics Manager:** Corey Marchesini. **Director of Broadcasting/Media Relations:** Kevin Fitzgerald. **Merchandise Manager:** Alex Watson. **Executive Chef:** Bobby Hunter. **Catering Manager:** Terry Stevenson. **Luxury Suite & Club Level Manager:** Maranda Holliday. **Director of Facilities:** Anthony Altamura. **Head Groundskeeper:** Danny Losito. **Assistant Groundskeeper:** Dalton Workman.

FIELD STAFF

Manager: Pedro Lopez. **Pitching Coach:** Jonathan Hurst. **Hitting Coach:** Ender Chavez. **Trainer:** Hiroto Kawamura. **Strength & Conditioning Coach:** Tanner Miracle.

GAME INFORMATION

Radio Announcer: Kevin Fitzgerald. **No. of Games Broadcast:** 140. **Flagship Station:** Unavailable.
PA Announcer: Bryan Vacchio. **Official Scorer:** Unavailable. **Stadium Name:** Spirit Communications Park.
Location: 1640 Freed Street, Columbia, SC 29201. **Standard Game Times:** 7:05pm, Sun. 2:05 pm.
Ticket Price Range: $5-$10. **Visiting Club Hotel:** Hyatt Place Columbia/Harbison, 1130 Kinley Road, Irmo, SC 29063.

DELMARVA SHOREBIRDS

Office Address: 6400 Hobbs Rd, Salisbury, MD 21804.
Mailing Address: PO Box 1557, Salisbury, MD 21802.
Telephone: (410) 219-3112. **Fax:** (410) 219-9164. **E-Mail Address:** info@theshorebirds.com.
Website: www.theshorebirds.com. **Affiliation (first year):** Baltimore Orioles (1997). **Years in League:** 1996-

OWNERSHIP/MANAGEMENT

Operated By: 7th Inning Stretch, LP. **Owner:** Tom Volpe.
President: Pat Filippone. **General Manager:** Chris Bitters. **Assistant GM:** Jimmy Sweet. **Director, Promotions & Marketing:** Eric Sichau. **Director, Business Development:** Andrew Bryda. **Director, Tickets:** Brandon Harms. **Box Office Manager:** Benjamin Posner. **Group Sales Manager:** Josh Knupp. **Ticket Sales Account Executive:** Skip Krantz. **Community Relations Manager:** Kathy Damato. **Director, Stadium Operations:** Will Schaap. **Head Groundskeeper:** Tim Young. **Director, Broadcasting:** Will DeBoer. **Communication Services Coordinator:** Bobby Coon. **Accounting Manager:** Gail Potts. **Merchandise & Office Manager:** Audrey Vane.

FIELD STAFF

Manager: Buck Britton. **Pitching Coach:** Unavailable. **Hitting Coach:** Unavailable.

GAME INFORMATION

Radio Announcer: Will DeBoer. **No. of Games Broadcast:** 140. **Flagship Station:** Fox Sports 960 WTGM. **PA Announcer:** Tyler Horton. **Stadium Name:** Arthur W. Perdue Stadium. **Location:** From US 50 East, right on Hobbs Rd; From US 50 West, left on Hobbs Road. **Standard Game Time:** 7:05 pm. **Ticket Price Range:** $8-13. **Visiting Club Hotel:** Sleep Inn, 406 Punkin Court, Salisbury, MD 21804. **Telephone:** (410) 572-5516.

GREENSBORO GRASSHOPPERS

Address: 408 Bellemeade St, Greensboro, NC 27401.
Telephone: (336) 268-2255. **Fax:** (336) 273-7350.
E-Mail Address: info@gsohoppers.com. **Website:** www.gsohoppers.com.
Affiliation (first year): Miami Marlins (2003). **Years in League:** 1979-

OWNERSHIP/MANAGEMENT

Operated By: Greensboro Baseball LLC. **Principal Owners:** Cooper Brantley, Wes Elingburg, Len White.
President/General Manager: Donald Moore. **Vice President, Baseball Operations:** Katie Dannemiller. **Assistant**

General Manager: Tim Vangel. **Chief Financial Officer:** Brad Falkiewicz. **Director of Sales:** Todd Olson. **Director, Ticket/Box Office Operations:** Andy Webb. **Director, Production/Partnership Services:** Josh Feldman. **Director, Creative Services:** Amanda Williams. **Cooridnator, Promotions/Community Relations:** Mary DeFriest. **Manager, Video Production:** Jak Kerley. **Office Administrator:** Brooke Kingston. **Sales Associates:** Erich Dietz, Stephen Johnson. **Director, Stadium Operations:** Chris Naiberk. **Head Groundskeeper:** Jordan Billingsley. **Assistant Groundskeeper:** Anthony Alejo.

FIELD STAFF
Manager: Todd Pratt. **Pitching Coach:** Mark DiFelice. **Coach:** Frankie Moore. **Coach:** Angel Espada. **Trainer:** Mike Bibbo.

GAME INFORMATION
Radio Announcer: Andy Durham. **No. of Games Broadcast:** 140. **Flagship Station:** WPET 950-AM. **PA Announcer:** TBD. **Official Scorer:** Wesley Gullet/Chris Fenisey. **Stadium Name:** First National Bank Field. **Location:** From I-85, take Highway 220 South (exit 36) to Coliseum Blvd, continue on Edgeworth Street, ballpark at corner of Edgeworth and Bellemeade Streets. **Standard Game Times:** 7 pm, Sun. 4 pm. **Ticket Price Range:** $7-11. **Visiting Club Hotel:** Days Inn 6102 Landmark Center Boulevard, Greensboro, NC 27407. **Telephone:** (336) 553-2763.

GREENVILLE DRIVE

Address: 935 South Main St, Suite 202, Greenville, SC 29601
Telephone: (864) 240-4500.
E-Mail Address: info@greenvilledrive.com. **Website:** www.greenvilledrive.com.
Affiliation (first year): Boston Red Sox (2005). **Years in League:** 2005-

OWNERSHIP/MANAGEMENT
Operated By: Greenville Drive, LLC. **Owner/President:** Craig Brown.
General Manager: Eric Jarinko. **VP, Marketing:** Jeff Brown. **VP, Operations/Grounds:** Greg Burgess. **VP, Finance:** Jordan Smith. **Director, Sponsorships & Community Engagement:** Katie Batista. **Director, Sales:** Thomas Berryhill. **Director, Food & Beverage:** Mike Agostino. **Director, Merchandise:** Corey Brothers. **Director, Operations:** Russell Bennett. **Media Relations Manager:** Cameron White. **Sponsor Services & Activations Manager:** Matthew Tezza. **Sponsorship & Community Events Manager:** Melissa Welch. **Special Events Coordinator:** Grace Mann. **Accountant Executive:** Houghton Flanagan, Micah Gold, Ned Kennedy, Jeb Maloney. **Inside Sales Representative:** Craig Houghton. **Assistant Director, Food and Beverage:** Rebekah Miller. **Box Office Manager:** Katie Cox. **Clubhouse Manager:** Bob Wagner. **Assistant Groundskeeper:** Richard Douglas. **Accounting Manager:** Adam Baird. **Office Manager:** Amanda Medlin.

FIELD STAFF
Manager: Iggy Suarez. **Hitting Coach:** Wilton Veras. **Pitching Coach:** Bob Kipper. **Head Athletic Trainer:** Phil Millan.

GAME INFORMATION
Radio Announcer: Ed Jenson. **No. of Games Broadcast:** Home-70, Away-21. **Flagship Station:** www.greenville drive.com. **PA Announcer:** Chuck Hussion. **Official Scorer:** Jordan Caskey. **Stadium Name:** Fluor Field at the West End. **Location:** From south, I-85N to exit 42 toward downtown Greenville, turn left onto Augusta Road, stadium is two miles on the left; From north, I-85S to I-385 toward Greenville, turn left onto Church Street, turn right onto University Ridge. **Standard Game Times:** 7:05 PM, Sun 4:05 PM. **Ticket Price Range:** $7-10. **Visiting Club Hotel:** Wingate by Wyndham, 246 Congaree Road, Greenville, SC 29607. **Telephone:** (864) 288-1200.

HAGERSTOWN SUNS

HAGERSTOWN SUNS

Address: 274 E Memorial Blvd, Hagerstown, MD 21740.
Telephone: (301) 791-6266. **Fax:** (301) 791-6066.
E-Mail Address: info@hagerstownsuns.com. **Website:** www.hagerstownsuns.com.
Affiliation (first year): Washington Nationals (2007). **Years in League:** 1993-

OWNERSHIP/MANAGEMENT
Principal Owner/Operated by: Hagerstown Baseball LLC.
President: Bruce Quinn. **General Manager:** Travis Painter. **Assistant GM/Head Groudnskeeper:** Brian Saddler. **Director, Media Relations:** Shawn Murnin. **F&B Operations:** Center Plate. **Manager, Promotions/Game Day Production:** Tom Burtman. **Manager, Box Office/Ticket Operations:** Unavailable. **Director of Sale:** Ross Combs. **Assistant Head Groundskeeper:** Mark Rabideau.

FIELD STAFF
Manager: Patrick Anderson. **Hitting Coach:** Amaury Garcia. **Pitching Coach:** Tim Redding. **Trainer:** Darren Yoos.

GAME INFORMATION
Radio Announcer: Kevin Gehl. **No. of Games Broadcast:** Home-70. **Flagship Station:** Unavailable. **PA Announcer:** Johnny Castle. **Official Scorer:** Will Kauffman. **Stadium Name:** Municipal Stadium. **Location:** Exit 32B (US 40 West) on I-70 West, left at Eastern Boulevard; Exit 6A (US 40 East) on I-81, right at Eastern Boulevard. **Standard Game Times:** 7:05 pm, Sun. 2:05 pm. **Ticket Price Range:** $10-13.

HICKORY CRAWDADS

Office Address: 2500 Clement Blvd. NW, Hickory, NC 28601. **Mailing Address:**
PO Box 1268, Hickory, NC 28603. **Telephone:** (828) 322-3000. **Fax:** (828) 322-6137.
E-Mail Address: crawdad@hickorycrawdads.com.
Website: www.hickorycrawdads.com. **Affiliation (first year):** Texas Rangers (2009).
Years in League: 1952, 1960, 1993-

OWNERSHIP/MANAGEMENT
Operated by: Hickory Baseball Inc. **Principal Owners:** Texas Rangers.
President: Neil Leibman. **General Manager:** Mark Seaman. **Assistant GM:** Charlie Downs. **Business Manager:**
Donna White. **Executive Director of Sales and Merchandise:** Douglas Locascio. **Director of Promotions and
Community Relations:** Chris Dillon. **Creative Services Specialist:** Ashley Salinas. **Director of Group Sales:** Robby
Willis. **Head Groundskeeper:** Andrew Tallent. **Director, Food/Beverage:** Kevin McAlee. **Group Sales Executives:**
Mitchell Lister, John Ryan.

FIELD STAFF
Manager: Matt Hagen. **Hitting Coach:** Chase Lambin. **Pitching Coach:** Jose Jaimes. **Coach:** Turtle Thomas. **Athletic
Trainer:** Luke Teeters. **Strength/Conditioning:** Adam Noel.

GAME INFORMATION
PA Announcers: Ralph Mangum, Jason Savage. **Official Scorers:** Mark Parker, Paul Fogelman. **Stadium Name:** LP
Frans Stadium. **Location:** I-40 to exit 123 (Lenoir North), 321 North to Clement Blvd, left for 1/2 mile. **Standard Game
Times: 1st half**—6pm Mon–Wed & Sat., Thur & Fri 7pm, Sun 3pm; **2nd half**—7pm, Sun 5pm. **Visiting Club Hotel:**
Crowne Plaza, 1385 Lenior-Rhyne Boulevard SE, Hickory, NC 28602. **Telephone:** (828) 323-1000.

KANNAPOLIS INTIMIDATORS

Office Address: 2888 Moose Road, Kannapolis, NC 28083. **Mailing Address:** PO Box
64, Kannapolis, NC 28082. **Telephone:** (704) 932-3267. **Fax:** (704) 938-7040.
E-Mail Address: info@intimidatorsbaseball.com.
Website: www.intimidatorsbaseball.com.
Affiliation (first year): Chicago White Sox (2001). **Years in League:** 1995-

OWNERSHIP/MANAGEMENT
Operated by: Intimidators Baseball Club, LLC.
President/General Manager: Brian Radle. **Vice President of Operations:** Randy Long. **Vice President of Corporate
Partnerships & Sales:** Ben Knapple. **Director of Finance:** Kyle Raskin. **Group Sales Executive:** Jenna Brunnhoelzl.
Account Executive: Spencer Severs. **Community Marketing Manager:** Blair Jewell. **Promotions & New Media
Manager:** Mary Ann Maestre. **Box Office Manager:** Mike Wolf. **Stadium Operations & Account Executive:** Andrew
Gibson. **Head Groundskeeper:** Billy Ball. **Assistant Groundskeeper:** Brian Mroz.

FIELD STAFF
Manager: Justin Jirschele. **Hitting Coach:** Jamie Dismuke. **Pitching Coach:** Matt Zaleski. **Athletic Trainer:** Joe Geck.
Strength & Conditioning Coach: Goldy Simmons.

GAME INFORMATION
Radio Announcer: Trevor Wilt. **No. of Games Broadcast:** 70. **Flagship Station:** www.intimidatorsbaseball.com. **PA
Announcer:** Bill Jones. **Official Scorer:** Brent Stastny. **Stadium Name:** Intimidators Stadium. **Location:** Exit 63 on I-85,
west on Lane Street to Stadium Drive. **Standard Game Times:** Weekdays until Daylight Savings, 6:30 p.m., Weekends &
Weekdays After Daylight Savings, 7:05 p.m., Sun. 5:05pm. **Ticket Price Range:** $6-$10. **Visiting Club Hotel:** Uptown
Suites, 7850 Commons Park Cir NW, Concord, NC 28027.

LAKEWOOD BLUECLAWS

Address: 2 Stadium Way, Lakewood, NJ 08701.
Telephone: (732) 901-7000. **Fax:** (732) 901-3967.
E-Mail Address: info@blueclaws.com. **Website:** www.blueclaws.com
Affiliation (first year): Philadelphia Phillies (2001). **Years in League:** 2001-

OWNERSHIP/MANAGEMENT
Managing Partner/Shore Town Baseball: Art Matin. **President/General Manager:** Joe Ricciutti. **VP, Ticket Sales
& Service:** Jim McNamara. **VP, Community Relations:** Jim DeAngelis. **VP, Events & Operations:** Kevin Fenstermacher.
Director of Communications: Greg Giombarrese. **Director of Sponsorship:** Rob Vota. **Director of Food & Beverage:**
Kevin O'Byrne. **Director of Merchandise:** Ben Cecil. **Director of Season Ticket Sales:** Rob McGillick. **Director of
Group Sales:** Mike Kasel. **Director of Production:** Kirsten Boye. **Director of Marketing & Promotions:** Jamie Stone.
Director of Partnership Services: Zack Nicol. **Senior Sales Executive:** Craig Ebinger. **Group Sales Manager:** Ryan

Shaughnessy, Kevin Litus, Jacob Tannen, Courtney Boyle, Tyler Odle. **Ticket Sales Manager:** Joel Podos, Ellen Hartigan. **Sponsorship Sales Manager:** Anthony Arena. **Partnership Services Manager:** Dylan Citron. **Hospitality Manager:** Jared Takacs. **Ticket Operations Manager:** Garrett Herr. **Ticket Service Coordinator:** Cameron Mitchell. **Data & CRM Coordinator:** Joe Pepio. **Events & Operations Manager:** Steven Woloshin, Kevin McNellis. **Accounting Manager:** Annette Clark. **Front Office Manager:** JoAnne Bell.

FIELD STAFF

Manager: Marty Malloy. **Hitting Coach:** Tyler Henson. **Pitching Coach:** Brad Bergesen. **Coach:** Milver Reyes. **Athletic Trainer:** Kris Terrian. **Strength & Conditioning Coach:** Henry Aleck.

GAME INFORMATION

Radio Announcers: Greg Giombarrese. **No. of Games Broadcast:** 140. **Flagship Station:** WOBM 1160-AM. **PA Announcers:** Kevin Clark. **Official Scorers:** Joe Bellina. **Stadium Name:** FirstEnergy Park. **Location:** Route 70 to New Hampshire Avenue, North on New Hampshire for 2.5 miles to ballpark. **Standard Game Times:** 7:05 pm, 6:35 pm (April-May); Sun. 1:**05, 5:**05 (July-Aug). **Ticket Price Range:** $7-13. **Visiting Team Hotel:** Clarion Hotel Toms River, 815 Route 37 West, Toms River, NJ 08755. **Telephone:** (732) 341-3400.

LEXINGTON LEGENDS

Address: 207 Legends Lane, Lexington, KY 40505.
Telephone: (859) 252-4487. **Fax:** (859) 252-0747.
E-Mail Address: webmaster@lexingtonlegends.com.
Website: www.lexingtonlegends.com.
Affiliation (first year): Kansas City Royals (2013). **Years in League:** 2001-

OWNERSHIP/MANAGEMENT

Operated By: STANDS LLC. **Principal:** Susan Martinelli.
President/CEO: Andy Shea. **Executive Vice President:** Gary Durbin. **Vice President, Business Development:** Sarah Bosso. **Director, Stadium Operations/Manager, Human Resources:** Shannon Kidd. **Accounting and Business Operations Manager:** Leslie Taylor. **Special Projects Manager:** Anne Mapson. **Director, Corporate Sales:** Jesse Scaglion. **Senior Corporate Sales Executive/ Promotions Manager:** April Smith. **Ticket Operations Manager:** Mark Costagliola. **Creative Marketing Director:** Ty Cobb. **Director, Broadcasting/Media Relations:** Emma Tiedemann. **Director of Group Sales:** Mike Allison. **Senior Account Executive:** Ron Borkowski. **Director, Video Operations/IT:** Nick Juhasz. **Head Groundskeeper:** Johnny Youngblood. **Facility Specialist:** Steve Moore.

FIELD STAFF

Manager: Scott Thorman. **Hitting Coach:** Jesus Azuaje. **Pitching Coach:** Mitch Stetter. **Bench Coach:** Glenn Hubbard. **Athletic Trainer:** Saburo Hagihara.

GAME INFORMATION

Radio Announcer: Emma Tiedemann. **No. of Games Broadcast:** 140. **Flagship Station:** WLXG 1300-AM. **PA Announcer:** Ty Cobb. **Official Scorer:** Hugh Davis. **Stadium Name:** Whitaker Bank Ballpark. **Location:** From I-64/75, take exit 113, right onto North Broadway toward downtown Lexington for 1.2 miles, past New Circle Road (Highway 4), right into stadium, located adjacent to Northland Shopping Center. **Standard Game Times:** Monday, Tuesday, Thursday, **Friday, 7:**05 pm; **most Wednesdays, 12:**35 p.m.; **Saturdays, 6:**35 p.m.; **Sundays, 2:**05 p.m. **Ticket Price Range:** $5-$25. **Visiting Club Hotel:** Clarion Hotel Conference Center South, 5532 Athens-Boonesboro Rd, Lexington, KY 40509. **Phone:** (859) 263-5241.

ROME BRAVES

Office Address: State Mutual Stadium, 755 Braves Blvd, Rome, GA 30161.
Mailing Address: PO Box 1915, Rome, GA 30162-1915. **Telephone:** (706) 378-5100.
Fax: (706) 368-6525. **E-Mail Address:** rome.braves@braves.com.
Website: www.romebraves.com. **Affiliation (first year):** Atlanta Braves (2003).
Years in League: 2003

OWNERSHIP MANAGEMENT

Operated By: Atlanta National League Baseball Club Inc.
VP and General Manager: Jim Bishop. **Assistant GM:** Jim Jones. **Director, Stadium Operations:** Brad Smith. **Director, Ticket Manager:** Jeff Fletcher. **Community Relations and Special Events:** Lori George. **Director, Business Operations:** Miranda Black. **Digital Manager:** Libby Chambers. **Account Representative:** Katie Aspin. **Director, Head Groundskeeper:** Bryant Powers. **Retail Manager:** Starla Roden. **Warehouse Operations Manager:** Morgan McPherson. **Food and Beverage Director:** Jonathan Jackson. **Culinary Director:** Owen Reppert.

FIELD STAFF

Manager: Rocket Wheeler. **Coach:** Bobby Moore. **Pitching Coach:** Dan Meyer. **Trainer:** Vic Scarpone.

GAME INFORMATION

Radio Announcer: Kevin Karel. **No. of Games Broadcast:** 140. **Flagship Station:** 99.5 FM The Jock, RomeBraves. com (home games). **PA Announcer:** Tony McIntosh. **Official Scorers:** Jim O'Hara, Lyndon Huckaby. **Stadium Name:**

State Mutual Stadium. **Location:** I-75 North to exit 190 (Rome/Canton), left off exit and follow Highway 411/Highway 20 to Rome, right at intersection on Highway 411 and Highway 1 (Veterans Memorial Highway), stadium is at intersection of Veterans Memorial Highway and Riverside Parkway. **Ticket Price Range:** $5-12. **Visiting Club Hotel:**Days Inn, 840 Turner McCall Blvd, Rome, GA 30161. **Telephone:** (706) 295-0400.

WEST VIRGINIA POWER

Address: 601 Morris St, Suite 201, Charleston, WV 25301.
Telephone: (304) 344-2287. **Fax:** (304) 344-0083.
E-Mail Address: info@wvpower.com. **Website:** www.wvpower.com.
Affiliation (first year): Pittsburgh Pirates (2009). **Years in League:** 1987-

OWNERSHIP MANAGEMENT

Operated By: West Virginia Baseball, LLC. **Managing Partner:** Tim Wilcox.
Executive Vice President: Ken Fogel. **General Manager:** Tim Mueller. **Assistant GM:** Jeremy Taylor. **Social Media and Merchandise Manager:** Hannah Frenchick. **Accountant:** Darren Holstein. **Director of Ticket Sales:** George Levandoski. **Broadcast and Media Relations Manager:** David Kahn. **Head Groundskeeper:** Paul Kuhna. **Box Office Manager:** Zach Kurdin. **Assistant, Food/Beverage:** Nathan Richard. **Director, Food/Beverage:** Aaron Simmons. **Community Relations Manager:** Haley Townsend.

FIELD STAFF

Manager: Wyatt Toregas. **Hitting Coach:** Chris Petersen. **Pitching Coach:** Joel Hanrahan.

GAME INFORMATION

Radio Announcer: David Kahn. **No. of Games Broadcast:** 140. **Flagship Stations:** The Jock- WJYP- 1300 AM & WMON- 1340 AM. **PA Announcer:** Unavailable. **Official Scorer:** Unavailable. **Stadium Name:** Appalachian Power Park. **Location:** I-77 South to Capitol Street exit, left on Lee Street, left on Brooks Street. **Standard Game Times:** 7:05 pm, Sat 6:05, Sun 2:05. **Ticket Price Range:** $6-11. **Visiting Club Hotel:** Holiday Inn Civic Center, 100 Civic Center Drive, Charleston, WV 25301. **Telephone:** (304) 345-0600.

NEW YORK-PENN LEAGUE

Address: 204 37th Ave. North, #366, St. Petersburg, Florida 33704.
Telephone: (727) 289-7111. **Fax:** (727) 683-9691.
Website: www.newyork-pennleague.com.

Years League Active: 1939-
President: Ben Hayes.
President Emeritus: Robert Julian. **Treasurer:** Jon Dandes (West Virginia). **Corporate Secretary:** Doug Estes (Williamsport). **League Administrator:** Laurie Hayes. **League Historian:** Charlie Wride. **Directors:** Matt Slatus (Aberdeen), Jeff Dygert (Auburn), Naomi Silver (Batavia), Steve Cohen (Brooklyn), E. Miles Prentice (Connecticut), Marvin Goldklang (Hudson Valley), Dave Heller (Lowell), Michael Savit (Mahoning Valley), Chuck Greenberg (State College), Glenn Reicin (Staten Island), Bill Gladstone (Tri-City), Kyle Bostwick (Vermont), Jon Dandes (West Virginia), Peter Freund (Williamsport).
Division Structure: McNamara—Aberdeen, Brooklyn, Hudson Valley, Staten Island. **Pinckney—**Auburn, Batavia, Mahoning Valley, State College, West Virginia, Williamsport. **Stedler—**Lowell, Connecticut, Tri-City, Vermont. **Regular Season:** 76 games.
2018 Opening Date: June 15. **Closing Date:** Sept 3. **All-Star Game:** Aug. 14, State College.
Playoff Format: Division winners and wild-card team meet in best of three series. Winners meet in best of three series for league championship. **Roster Limit:** 35 active and eligible to play in any given game.
Player Eligibility Rule: No more than four players 23 or older; no more than three players on active list may have four or more years of prior service. **Brand of Baseball:** Rawlings. **Umpires:** Unavailable.

Ben Hayes

STADIUM INFORMATION

Club	Stadium	Opened	Dimensions LF	CF	RF	Capacity	2017 Att.
Aberdeen	Ripken Stadium	2002	310	400	310	6,000	130,823
Auburn	Falcon Park	1995	330	400	330	2,800	46,132
Batavia	Dwyer Stadium	1996	325	400	325	2,600	27,389
Brooklyn	KeySpan Park	2001	315	412	325	7,500	186,853
Connecticut	Dodd Stadium	1995	309	401	309	6,270	73,439
Hudson Valley	Dutchess Stadium	1994	325	400	325	4,494	147,936
Lowell	Edward LeLacheur Park	1998	337	400	301	4,842	126,565
Mahoning Valley	Eastwood Field	1999	335	405	335	6,000	107,894
State College	Medlar Field at Lubrano Park	2006	325	399	320	5,412	123,401
Staten Island	Richmond County Bank Ballpark	2001	325	400	325	6,500	71,401
Tri-City	Joseph L. Bruno Stadium	2002	325	400	325	5,000	142,922
Vermont	Centennial Field	1922	323	405	330	4,000	82,674
West Virginia	WVU Baseball Park	2015	325	400	325	3,500	75,064
Williamsport	Bowman Field	1923	345	405	350	4,200	61,082

ABERDEEN IRONBIRDS

Address: 873 Long Drive, Aberdeen, MD 21001
Telephone: (410) 297-9292. **Fax:** (210) 297-6653
E-Mail address: Info@ironbirdsbaseball.com. **Website:** ironbirdsbaseball.com
Affiliation (first year): Baltimore Orioles (2002). **Years in league:** 2002-

OWNERSHIP/MANAGEMENT

Operated By: Ripken Professional Baseball LLC. **Principal Owner:** Cal Ripken Jr. **Co-Owner/Executive Vice President:** Bill Ripken.

General Manager: Matt Slatus. **Director, Ticketing:** Justin Johnson. **Director, Creative Services:** Kevin Jimenez. **Director, Game & Team Operations:** Jack Graham. **Sr. Director, Business Development:** Vince Bulik. **Director, Human Resources:** Lavorette Preston. **Director, Retail Merchandise:** Don Eney. **Grounds Superintendent:** Todd Bradley. **Manager, Facilities:** Larry Gluch. **Facilities Assistant:** David Dawson. **Manager, Ticket Operations & Analytics:** Joe Burgess. **Manager, Accounting:** Elly Ripken. **Coordinator, Business Development:** Ashley Nalley. **Coordinator, Marketing & Promotions:** David Kendrick. **Coordinator, Corporate Partnerships:** Sarah Mrochinski. **Group Events Specialists:** Justin Gentilcore, Tyler Weingandt. **Fan Experience Specialists:** Andrew Geckle, Nina Heinlein, Lauren Carrig. **Accounting Assistant:** Austyn Ripken. **Office Coordinator:** Amelia Adams.

FIELD STAFF

Unavailable

GAME INFORMATION

Radio Announcer: Daniel Kurish. **No. of Games Broadcast:** 76. **Flagship Station:** WAMD 970 AM. **PA Announcer:** Unavailable. **Official Scorer:** Joe Stetka. **Stadium Name:** Leidos Field at Ripken Stadium. **Location:** I-95 to exit 85 (route 22), west on 22, right onto long drive. **Ticket Price range:** $5-$39. **Visiting Club Hotel:** Comfort Inn-Aberdeen,

Marriott Courtyard-Aberdeen, Residence Inn-Aberdeen.

AUBURN DOUBLEDAYS

Address: 130 N Division St, Auburn, NY 13021. **Telephone:** (315) 255-2489
E-Mail Address: info@auburndoubledays.com. **Website:** www.auburndoubledays.com.
Affiliation (first year): Washington Nationals (2011). **Years in League:** 1958-80, 1982-

OWNERSHIP/MANAGEMENT
Owned by: City of Auburn. **Operated by:** Auburn Community Baseball LLC.
President: Jeff Dygert. **General Manager:** Adam Winslow. **Assistant General Managers:** Andy Collier, Shane Truman.

FIELD STAFF
Manager: Jerad Head. **Hitting Coach:** Mark Harris. **Pitching Coach:** Franklin Bravo.

GAME INFORMATION
Radio Announcer: Drew Carter. **No. of Games Broadcast:** 76. **Flagship Station:** WAUB. **PA Announcer:** Mike DeForrest. **Official Scorer:** Robert Coogan. **Stadium Name:** Falcon Park. **Location:** I-90 to exit 40, right on Route 34 South for 8 miles to York Street, right on York, left on North Division Street. **Standard Game Times:** 6:30 pm (Mon- Sat), 2:00 pm (Sun). **Ticket Price Range:** $6-11. **Visiting Club Hotel:** Unavailable.

BATAVIA MUCKDOGS

Address: Dwyer Stadium, 299 Bank St, Batavia, NY 14020.
Telephone: Unavailable. **Fax:** Unavailable.
E-Mail Address: Unavailable. **Website:** www.muckdogs.com.
Affiliation (first year): Miami Marlins (2013). **Years in League:** 1939-53, 1957-59, 1961-

OWNERSHIP/MANAGEMENT
Operated By: Muckdogs Baseball, INC. **General Manager:** Dave Chase.

FIELD STAFF
Manager: Mike Jacobs. **Hitting Coach:** Jesus Merchan. **Pitching Coach:** Jason Erickson. **Defensive Coach:** Ronnie Richardson. **Athletic Trainer:** Jordan Wheat. **Strength & Conditioning Coach:** Spencer Clevenger. **Video Assistant:** Trey McNickle.

GAME INFORMATION
Radio Announcer: Unavailable. **No. of Games Broadcast:** Home-37 Away-5. **Flagship Station:** WBTA 1490-AM/100.1 FM. **PA Announcer:** Unavailable. **Official Scorer:** Paul Spiotta. **Stadium Name:** Dwyer Stadium. **Location:** I-90 to exit 48, left on Route 98 South, left on Richmond Avenue, left on Bank Street. **Standard Game Times:** 7:05 pm, Sun. 1:05/5:05. **Ticket Price Range:** $6.00-8.00. **Visiting Club Hotel:** Unavailable.

BROOKLYN CYCLONES

Address: 1904 Surf Ave, Brooklyn, NY 11224. **Telephone:** (718) 372-5596.
Fax: (718) 449-6368. **E-Mail Address:** info@brooklyncyclones.com.
Website: www.brooklyncyclones.com. **Affiliation (first year):** New York Mets (2001
Years in League: 2001-

OWNERSHIP/MANAGEMENT
Chairman, CEO: Fred Wilpon. **President:** Saul Katz. **COO:** Jeff Wilpon. **Vice President:** Steve Cohen. **General Manager:** Kevin Mahoney. **Assistant GM:** Gary Perone. **Director, Communications:** Billy Harner. **Director, Ticketing:** Greg Conway. **Operations Manager:** Vladimir Lipsman. **Marketing Manager:** Alyssa Morel. **Community Relations:** Christina Moore. **Community Outreach/Promotions:** King Henry. **Account Executives:** Tommy Cardona, Nicole Kneessy, Craig Coughlin, Rafael Guerreo, Joe Sensi, Ricky Viola. **Staff Accountant:** Tatiana Isdith. **Administrative Assistant, Community Relations:** Sharon Lundy.

FIELD STAFF
Manager: Edgardo Alfonzo. **Coach:** Marlon Anderson. **Pitching Coach:** Royce Ring. **Coach:** David Davallilo.

GAME INFORMATION
Radio Announcer: Keith Raad. **No. of Games Broadcast:** 76. **Flagship Station:** WKRB 90.3-FM. **PA Announcer:** Mark Frotto. **Official Scorer:** Unavailable. **Stadium Name:** MCU Park. **Location:** Belt Parkway to Cropsey Ave South, continue on Cropsey until it becomes West 17th St, continue to Surf Ave, stadium on south side of Surf Ave; By subway, west/south to Stillwell Ave./Coney Island station. **Ticket Price Range:** $10-17. **Visiting Club Hotel:** Unavailable.

CONNECTICUT TIGERS

Address: 14 Stott Avenue, Norwich, CT 06360.
Telephone: (860) 887-7962. **Fax:** (860) 886-5996.
E-Mail Address: info@cttigers.com. **Website:** www.cttigers.com.
Affiliation (first year): Detroit Tigers (1999). **Years in League:** 2010-

OWNERSHIP/MANAGEMENT

Operated By: Oneonta Athletic Corp.
President: Miles Prentice. **Senior Vice President:** CJ Knudsen. **General Manager:** Dave Schermerhorn. **Director, Concessions/Merchandise:** Heather Bartlett. **Director, Ticket Operations:** Josh Postler. **Community Relations & Promotions Manager:** Ed McMahon. **Head Groundskeeper:** Ryan Lefler.

FIELD STAFF

Manager: Gerald Laird. **Hitting Coach:** Rafael Martinez. **Pitching Coach:** Ace Adams. **Trainer:** Shane McFarland. **Strength & Conditioning Coach:** Edwin Ortiz.

GAME INFORMATION

PA Announcer: Ed Weyant. **Official Scorer:** Chris Cote. **Stadium Name:** Dodd Stadium. **Location:** Exit 14 (old exit 82) off I-395. **Standard Game Times:** 7:05 pm, Sun. 4:05. **Ticket Price Range:** $10-20. **Visiting Club Hotel:** Holiday Inn Norwich.

HUDSON VALLEY RENEGADES

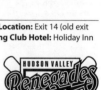

Office Address: Dutchess Stadium, 1500 Route 9D, Wappingers Falls, NY 12590.
Mailing Address: PO Box 661, Fishkill, NY 12524.
Telephone: (845) 838-0094. **Fax:** (845) 838-0014.
E-Mail Address: info@hvrenegades.com. **Website:** www.hvrenegades.com.
Affiliation (first year): Tampa Bay Rays (1996). **Years in League:** 1994-

OWNERSHIP/MANAGEMENT

Operated by: Keystone Professional Baseball Club Inc. **Principal Owner:** Marv Goldklang.
President: Steve Gliner. **Executive Vice President/General Manager:** Eben Yager. **Vice President:** Rick Zolzer. **Assistant GM:** Kristen Huss. **Assistant GM:** Sean Kammerer. **Director, Baseball Operations:** Joe Ausanio. **Director, Business Operations:** Vicky DeFreese. **Director of Ticket Sales:** Bryan Viggiano. **Director, Food & Beverage/ Merchandise:** Teri Bettencourt. **Manager, New Business Development:** Dave Neff. **Marketing Manager:** Rachel Wallbrown. **Manager, Stadium Operations:** Chris Lynch. **Head Groundskeeper:** Tim Merante. **Ticket Sales Executives:** Nick Leitner, Michael Schaeffer, Jeremiah DeLine.

FIELD STAFF

Manager: Craig Albernaz. **Hitting Coach:** Alejandro Freire. **Pitching Coach:** Jose Gonzalez. **Assistant Coach:** Rafael Valenzuela. **Athletic Trainer:** Tsutomu Kamiya. **Strength & Conditioning Coach:** Dan Rousseau.

GAME INFORMATION

Radio Announcer: Josh Carey. **No. of Games Broadcast:** Home-38. **Flagship Stations:** WKIP 1450-AM. **PA Announcer:** Rick Zolzer. **Official Scorers:** Unavailable. **Stadium Name:** Dutchess Stadium. **Location:** I-84 to exit 11 (Route 9D North), north one mile to stadium. **Standard Game Times:** 7:05 pm, Sun. 5:05. **Visiting Club Hotel:** Magnuson Hotel, 20 Schuyler Blvd and Route 9, Fishkill, NY 12524. **Telephone:** (845) 896-4995. **Umpire Hotel:** Springhill Suites, 500 Westage Business Center Dr, Fishkill, NY 12524. (845) 896-8100.

LOWELL SPINNERS

Address: 450 Aiken St, Lowell, MA 01854.
Telephone: (978) 459-2255. **Fax:** (978) 459-1674.
E-Mail Address: info@lowellspinners.com. **Website:** www.lowellspinners.com.
Affiliation (first year): Boston Red Sox (1996). **Years in League:** 1996-

OWNERSHIP/MANAGEMENT

Operated by: Main Street Baseball. **Owner:** Dave Heller.
President/General Manager: Shawn Smith **Vice President:** Brian Lindsay. **VP, Finance:** Priscilla Harbour. **Box Office Manager:** TJ Konstant. **Creative Services Representative:** Connor Sullivan. **Grounds Manager:** Jon Sheehan. **Director of Grounds Managemnet:** Jack Schmidgall. **Director of Merchandise & Community Relations:** Jamie Arthur. **Group Sales Manager:** Julia McNeil. **Ticket Sales Executive:** Dave O'Brien. **Coordinator of Marketing Partnerships:** Frank Pimentel. **Coordinator of Operations:** Tracy Taylor

FIELD STAFF

Manager: Corey Wimberly. **Hitting Coach:** Nate Spears. **Pitching Coach:** Nick Green. **Athletic Trainer:** Joel Harris.

GAME INFORMATION
Radio Announcer: John Leahy. **No. of Games Broadcast:** 76. **Flagship Station:** WCAP 980-AM. **PA Announcer:** Unavailable. **Official Scorer:** David Rourke. **Stadium Name:** Edward A LeLacheur Park. **Location:** From Route 495 and 3, take exit 35C (Lowell Connector), follow connector to exit 5B (Thorndike Street) onto Dutton Street, left onto Father Morrissette Boulevard, right on Aiken Street. **Standard Game Times:** 7:05 pm. **Ticket Price Range:** $7-10 (advance); $9-12 (day of game). **Visiting Club Hotel:** Radisson of Chelmsford, 10 Independence Dr, Chelmsford, MA 01879. **Telephone:** (978) 356-0800.

MAHONING VALLEY
SCRAPPERS

Address: 111 Eastwood Mall Blvd, Niles, OH 44446.
Telephone: (330) 505-0000. **Fax:** (303) 505-9696.
E-Mail Address: info@mvscrappers.com. **Website:** www.mvscrappers.com.
Affiliation (first year): Cleveland Indians (1999). **Years in League:** 1999-

OWNERSHIP/MANAGEMENT
Operated By: HWS Baseball Group.
Managing General Partner: Michael Savit. **Vice President, HWS Baseball/ General Manager:** Jordan Taylor. **Assistant GM, Marketing:** Heather Sahli. **Assistant GM, Sales:** Matt Thompson. **Director of Tickets & Game Operations:** Kate Walsh. **Director of Ticket Sales:** Tyler Adams. **Manager, Box Office:** Clayton Sibilla. **Assistant GM, Operations:** Brad Hooser. **Head Groundskeeper:** Ryan Olszewski. **Manager, Accounting & Human Resources:** Roxanne Herrington. **Manager, Production:** Drew Masirovits

FIELD STAFF
Manager: Jim Pankovits. **Hitting Coach:** Unavailable. **Pitching Coach:** Jason Blanton. **Bench Coach:** Omir Santos. **Athletic Trainer:** Gabriel Garcia. **Strength & Conditioning Coach:** Moises Cuevas.

GAME INFORMATION
Radio Announcer: Tim Pozsgai. **No. of Games Broadcast:** 76. **Flagship Station:** SportsRadio 1240 AM. **PA Announcer:** Unavailable. **Official Scorer:** Craig Antush. **Stadium Name:** Eastwood Field. **Location:** I-80 to 11 North to 82 West to 46 South; stadium located behind Eastwood Mall. **Ticket Price Range:** $8-12. **Visiting Club Hotel:** Days Inn & Suites, 1615 Liberty St, Girard, OH 44429. **Telephone:** (330) 759-9820.

STATE COLLEGE SPIKES

Address: 112 Medlar Field at Lubrano Park, University Park, PA 16802.
Telephone: (814) 272-1711. **Fax:** (814) 272-1718.
Website: www.statecollegespikes.com.
Affiliation (first year): St. Louis Cardinals (2013). **Years in League:** 2006-.

OWNERSHIP/MANAGEMENT
Operated By: Spikes Baseball LP.
Chairman/Managing Partner: Chuck Greenberg. **President:** Jason Dambach. **General Manager:** Scott Walker. **Assistant GM, Operations:** Dan Petrazzolo. **Director of Ticket Sales:** Mike Frissore. **Senior Ticket Account Executive:** Seth English. **Ticket Account Executive:** Brittany Ferrizzi. **Ticket Account Executive:** Taylor Young. **Accounting Manager:** Karen Mahon. **Senior Director, Box Office/Business Ops:** Steve Christ. **Director, Promotions/In-Game Entertainment:** Ben Love. **Manager of Communications:** Joe Putnam. **Senior Sports Turf Manager:** Matt Neri. **Off the Rack Outfitters Team Store Manager:** Julie Henry.

FIELD STAFF
Manager: Joe Kruzel. **Hitting Coach:** Roger LaFrancois. **Pitching Coach:** Adrian Martin. **Athletic Trainer:** Unavailable. **Strength & Conditioning Coach:** Don Trapp.

GAME INFORMATION
PA Announcer: Jeff Brown. **Official Scorers:** Dave Baker, John Dixon. **Stadium Name:** Medlar Field at Lubrano Park. **Location:** From west, US 322 to Mount Nittany Expressway, I-80 to exit 158 (old exit 23/Milesburg), follow Route 150 South to Route 26 South; From east, I-80 to exit 161 (old exit 24/Bellefonte) to Route 26 South or US 220/I-99 South. **Standard Game Times:** 7:05 pm, Sun. 6:05. **Ticket Price Range:** $8-18. **Visiting Club Hotel:** Ramada Conference & Golf Hotel, 1450 Atherton St, State College, PA 16801. **Telephone:** (814) 238-3001.

STATEN ISLAND YANKEES

Stadium Address: 75 Richmond Terrace, Staten Island, NY 10301
Telephone: (718) 720-9265. Fax: (718) 273-5763. Website: www.siyank.com.
Affiliation (first year): New York Yankees (1999). Years in League: 1999-Present

OWNERSHIP/MANAGEMENT

Principal Owners: Nostalgic Partners.
President/Operating Partner: Will Smith. General Manager: Jane Rogers. Vice President of Business
Development: Adam Lorber. CFO: Jason Nazzaro. Vice President of Operations: T.J. Jahn. Group Sales Manager:
David Percarpio. Group Sales Executives: Jesse Lopresti, David Budash, Alex Alberque, James Maloney. Director
of Communications & Entertainment: Ian Fontenot. Production & Marketing Manager: Matt Kruth. Head
Groundskeeper: Ray Levan. Stadium Operations Manager: Anthony Silvia

FIELD STAFF

Manager: Unavailable. Hitting Coach: Unavailable. Pitching Coach: Unavailable. Defensive Coach: Unavailable.

GAME INFORMATION

Radio Announcer: Unavailable. No. of Games Broadcast: 38 (home games). Flagship Station: WSIA 88.9 FM. PA
Announcer: Jeff Fromm. Official Scorer: Unavailable. Stadium Name: Richmond County Bank Ballpark at St George.
Location: 75 Richmond Terrace, Staten Island, NY 10301 (located next to Staten Island Ferry and Staten Island Railway-
St. George) Standard Game Times: Mon-Sat 7 p.m., Sundays 4 p.m. Visiting Club Hotel: Unavailable.

TRI-CITY VALLEYCATS

Office Address: Joseph L Bruno Stadium, 80 Vandenburg Ave, Troy, NY 12180.
Mailing Address: PO Box 694, Troy, NY 12181. Telephone: (518) 629-2287.
Fax: (518) 629-2299. E-Mail Address: info@tcvalleycats.com.
Website: www.tcvalleycats.com. Affiliation (first year): Houston Astros (2002).
Years in League: 1999-

OWNERSHIP/MANAGEMENT

Operated By: Tri-City ValleyCats Inc. Principal Owners: Martin Barr, John Burton, William Gladstone, Rick Murphy,
Alfred Roberts, Stephen Siegel.
President: William Gladstone. Executive Vice President/Chief Operating Officer: Rick Murphy. General
Manager: Matt Callahan. Assistant GM: Michelle Skinner. Media Relations Manager: Chris Chenes. Ticket Office
and Operations Manager: Jessica Guido. Food & Beverage Coordinator: Missy Henry. Account Executive: Adam
Migirditch. Administrative Assistant: Elyse Zima.

FIELD STAFF

Manager: Jason Bell. Hitting Coach: Jeremy Barnes. Pitching Coach: Erick Abreu. Athletic Trainer: Daniel Cerquera.
Strength & Conditioning Coach: Mike Myers.

GAME INFORMATION

Radio Announcer: Unavailable. No. of Games Broadcast: 38. Flagship Station: MiLB.com. PA Announcer:
Anthony Pettograsso. Official Scorer: Dave Vatz. Stadium Name: Joseph Bruno Stadium. Location: From north, I-87
to exit 7 (Route 7), go east 1 1/2 miles to I-787 South, to Route 378 East, go over bridge to Route 4, right to Route 4
South, one mile to Hudson Valley Community College campus on left; From south, I-87 to exit 23 (I-787), I-787 north six
miles to exit for Route 378 east, over bridge to Route 4, right to Route 4 South, one mile to campus on left; From east,
Massachusetts Turnpike to exit B-1 (I-90), nine miles to Exit 8 (Defreestville), left off ramp to Route 4 North, five miles
to campus on right; From west, I-90 to exit 24 (I-90 East), I-90 East for six miles to I-787 North (Troy), 2.2 miles to exit for
Route 378 East, over bridge to Route 4, right to Route 4 south for one mile to campus on left. Standard Game Times:
7pm, Sun. 5 pm. Ticket Price Range: $5.25-$12. Visiting Club Hotel: The Desmond Hotel & Conference Center, 660
Albany-Shaker Road, Albany, NY 12211. Telephone: (518) 869-8100.

VERMONT LAKE MONSTERS

Address: 1 King Street Ferry Dock, Burlington, VT 05401.
Telephone: (802) 655-4200. Fax: (802) 655-5660.
E-Mail Address: info@vermontlakemonsters.com.
Website: www.vermontlakemosters.com.
Affiliation (first year): Oakland Athletics (2011). Years in League: 1994-

OWNERSHIP/MANAGEMENT

Operated by: Vermont Expos Inc. Principal Owner/President: Ray Pecor Jr.
Vice President: Kyle Bostwick. General Manager: Joe Doud. Assistant General Manager: Adam Matth. Executive
Director, Sales & Marketing: Nate Cloutier. Director, Marketing & Promotions: Maria Valentyn. Director, Team
Operations & Community Outreach, Box Office Manager: Derek McCabe. Staff Accountant: Heather Regnuad.

Director, Media Relations: Paul Stanfield. **Clubhouse Operations:** Max Pudvar, Cam Zagursky. **Head Groundskeeper:** Wylie Coseo.

FIELD STAFF

Manager: Aaron Nieckula. **Hitting Coach:** Lloyd Turner. **Pitching Coach:** Carlos Chavez.

GAME INFORMATION

Radio Announcers: George Commo. **No. of Games Broadcast:** Home-38 (Internet Only). **PA Announcer:** Jamey McGowan. **Official Scorer:** Bruce Bosley. **Stadium Name:** Centennial Field. **Location:** I-89 to exit 14W, right on East Avenue for one mile, right at Colchester Avenue. **Standard Game Times:** 7:05 pm, Sat. 6:05, Sun. 5:05. **Ticket Price Range:** $5-8. **Visiting Club Hotel:** Doubletree By Hilton (formerly Sheraton). **Telephone:** (802) 865-6600.

WEST VIRGINIA BLACK BEARS

Office Address: 2040 Jedd Gyorko Drive, Granville, WV 26534
Mailing Address: PO Box 4680 Morgantown, WV 26504.
Telephone: (304) 293-7910. **Website:** www.westvirginiablackbears.com
Affiliation (first year): Pittsburgh Pirates (2015). **Years in League:** 2015-

OWNERSHIP/MANAGEMENT

Operated By: Rich Baseball Operations.
President: Robert Rich Jr. **Chief Operating Officer:** Jonathan Dandes. **General Manager:** Matthew Drayer.
Assistant GM: Jackie Riggleman. **Sponsorship and Promotions Manager:** Unavailable. **Stadium Manager:** Craig McIntosh. **Grounds Keeper:** Justin Gibson.

FIELD STAFF

Manager: Brian Esposito. **Hitting Coach:** Jonathan Prieto. **Pitching Coach:** Tom Filer.

GAME INFORMATION

PA Announcer: Bill Nevlin. **Official Scorer:** Unavailable. **Stadium Name:** Monongalia County Ballpark. **Standard Game Times:** 7:05 pm, Sun. 4:05. **Visiting Club Hotel:** Unavailable.

WILLIAMSPORT CROSSCUTTERS

Office Address: BB&T Ballpark at Historic Bowman Field, 1700 W Fourth St, Williamsport, PA 17701. **Mailing Address:** PO Box 3173, Williamsport, PA 17701.
Telephone: (570) 326-3389. **Fax:** (570) 326-3494.
E-Mail Address: mail@crosscutters.com. **Website:** www.crosscutters.com.
Affiliation (first year): Philadelphia Phillies (2007). **Years in League:** 1968-72, 1994-

OWNERSHIP/MANAGEMENT

Operated By: Cutting Edge Baseball, LLC. **Principal Owner:** Peter Freund.
Vice President/General Manager: Doug Estes. **Vice-President, Marketing/Public Relations:** Gabe Sinicropi. **Director, Food/Beverage:** Bill Gehron. **Director, Ticket Operations/Community Relations:** Sarah Budd. **Director, Client Services:** Nate Schneider.

FIELD STAFF

Manager: Pat Borders. **Pitching Coach:** Hector Berrios. **Coach:** Christian Marrero. **Coach:** Greg Brodzinski.

GAME INFORMATION

Radio Announcers: Todd Bartley, Ian Catherine. **No. of Games Broadcast:** 76. **Flagship Station:** WLYC 1050-AM & 104.1 FM (FoxSports Williamsport). **Stadium Name:** BB&T Ballpark at Historic Bowman Field. **Location:** 1700 W. Fourth St., Williamsport, PA. **From the North:** Follow Route 15 South. Take the Fourth Street exit. Turn left onto Fourth Street. Ballpark will be on your left. **From the South:** Follow Route 15 North. Cross the Susquehanna River via the Market Street Bridge and follow into Downtown Williamsport. At the second traffic light, turn left onto Fourth Street. Follow approx. 3 miles. Ballpark will be on your right. Ballpark will be your right. **Ticket Price Range:** $7-$15. **Visiting Club Hotel:** Best Western, 1840 E Third St, Williamsport, PA 17701. **Telephone:** (570) 326-1981.

NORTHWEST LEAGUE

Mike Ellis

Address: 140 N Higgins Ave., No. 211, Missoula, MT, 59802.
Telephone: (406) 541-9301. **Fax:** (406) 543-9463.
E-Mail Address: mellisnwl@aol.com. **Website:** www.northwestleague.com
Years League Active: 1954-
President/Treasurer: Mike Ellis. **Vice President:** Derrek Ebert (Tri-City).
Corporate Secretary: Jerry Walker (Salem-Keizer).
Directors: Dave Elmore (Eugene), Bobby Brett (Spokane), Tom Volpe (Everett), Jake Kerr (Vancouver), Mike McMurray (Hillsboro), Brent Miles (Tri-City), Jerry Walker (Salem-Keizer), Jeff Eiseman (Boise). **Administrative Assistant:** Judy Ellis.
Division Structure: South—Boise, Hillsboro, Eugene, Salem-Keizer. **North**—Everett, Spokane, Tri-City, Vancouver.
Regular Season: 76 games (split schedule).
2018 Opening Date: June 15. **Closing Date:** Sept. 3.
All-Star Game: Aug. 7 at Grand Junction (Northwest League vs. Pioneer Baseball League).
Playoff Format: First-half division winners meet second-half division winners in best of three series. Winners meet in best of five series for league championship.
Roster Limit: 35 active, 35 under control. **Player Eligibility Rule:** No more than three players on active list may have four or more years of prior service.
Brand of Baseball: Rawlings. **Umpires:** Unavailable.

STADIUM INFORMATION

Club	Stadium	Opened	Dimensions LF	CF	RF	Capacity	2017 Att.
Boise	Memorial Stadium	1989	335	400	335	3,426	121,455
Eugene	PK Park	2010	335	400	325	4,000	125,297
Everett	Everett Memorial Stadium	1984	324	380	330	3,682	110,161
Hillsboro	Hillsboro Ballpark	2013	325	400	325	4,500	128,416
Salem-Keizer	Volcanoes Stadium	1997	325	400	325	4,100	81,011
Spokane	Avista Stadium	1958	335	398	335	7,162	196,653
Tri-City	Dust Devils Stadium	1995	335	400	335	3,700	86,461
Vancouver	Nat Bailey Stadium	1951	335	395	335	6,500	239,527

BOISE HAWKS

Address: 5600 N. Glenwood St. Boise, ID 83714.
Telephone: (208) 322-5000. **Fax:** (208) 322-6846.
Website: www.boisehawks.com. **Affiliation:** Colorado Rockies (2015).
Years in League: 1975-76, 1978, 1987-

OWNERSHIP/MANAGEMENT

Operated by: Boise Professional Baseball LLC. **President:** Jeff Eiseman. **Vice President, Operations:** Missy Martin **General Manager:** Bob Flannery. **Assistant General Manager:** Mike Van Hise. **Director, Stadium Ops/Food & Beverage:** Jake Lusk. **Manager, Accounting/Office:** Judy Peterson. **Corporate Sales Manager:** Brooke Bedgood **Assistant Manager, Ticket Sales:** Jon Jensen. **Account Executive:** Matt Osbon, Colton Hampson, Mikayla Leroue **Sales/Operations Specialist:** Jacob Cluff. **Stadium Operations Manager:** Carl Koster. **Media Relations/Marketing Manager:** Carly McCullough. **Marketing Coordinator:** Rachel Moir. **Graphics/Video Production Coordinator:** Collyn Lackey. **Media Relations/Play-by-Play Broadcaster:** Rylan Kobre. **Head Groundskeeper:** Mike Savage

FIELD STAFF

Development Supervisor: John Pierson. **Manager:** Scott Little. **Hitting Coach:** Cesar Galvez. **Pitching Coach:** Bob Apodaca. **Athetic Trainer:** Mickey Clarizio.

GAME INFORMATION

Radio Announcer: Rylan Kobre. **No. of Games Broadcast:** 76. **Flagship Station:** None. **PA Announcer:** Jeremy Peterson. **Official Scorer:** Curtis Haines. **Stadium Name:** Memorial Stadium. **Location:** I-84 to Cole Rd., north to Western Idaho Fairgrounds at 5600 North Glenwood St. **Standard Game Time:** 7:15 PM. **Ticket Price Range:** $8-35 **Visiting Club Hotel:** Wyndham Garden Hotel, 3300 South Vista Ave. Boise, ID

EUGENE EMERALDS

Office Address: 2760 Martin Luther King Jr. Blvd, Eugene, OR 97401.
Mailing Address: PO Box 10911, Eugene, OR 97440.
Telephone: (541) 342-5367. **Fax:** (541) 342-6089.
E-Mail Address: info@emeraldsbaseball.com. **Website:** www.emeraldsbaseball.com.
Affiliation (first year): Chicago Cubs (2015). **Years in League:** 1955-68, 1974-

OWNERSHIP/MANAGEMENT

Operated By: Elmore Sports Group Ltd. **Principal Owner:** David Elmore.
General Manager: Allan Benavides. **Assistant GM:** Matt Dompe. **Director, Food/Beverage:** Turner Elmore.
Director, Tickets: Peter Billups. **Event Manager:** Chris Bowers. **Group Sales:** Patrick Zajac. **Graphic Designer:**
Danny Cowley. **Director, Community Affairs:** Anne Culhane. **Ticket Sales:** David Roth, Cam LaFerle, Kindra Bates.
Sponsorship Sales: Brian Vucovich. **Home Radio:** Matt Dompe. **Away Radio:** Patrick Zajac.

FIELD STAFF

Manager: Steve Lerud. **Hitting Coach:** Osmin Melendez. **Pitching Coach:** Armando Gabino. **Assistant Coach:** Jacob
Rogers. **Athletic Trainer:** Sean Folan.

GAME INFORMATION

Radio Announcer: Matt Dompe. **No. of Games Broadcast:** 76. **Flagship Station:** 95.3-FM The Score. **PA
Announcer:** Ted Welker. **Official Scorer:** George McPherson. **Stadium Name:** PK Park. **Standard Game Time:** 7:05 p.m.,
Sun. 1:05pm. **Ticket Price Range:** $7-$13. **Visiting Club Hotel:** Candlewood Suites Eugene Springfield.

EVERETT AQUASOX

Mailing Address: 3802 Broadway, Everett, WA 98201.
Telephone: (425) 258-3673. **Fax:** (425) 258-3675.
E-Mail Address: info@aquasox.com. **Website:** www.aquasox.com.
Affiliation (first year): Seattle Mariners (1995). **Years in League:** 1984-

OWNERSHIP/MANAGEMENT

Operated by: 7th Inning Stretch, LLC.
Directors: Tom Volpe, Pat Filippone. **General Manager:** Danny Tetzlaff. **Assistant GM:** Rick Maddox. **Director,
Corporate Partnerships/Broadcasting:** Pat Dillon. **Director, Tickets:** Gary Olson. **Corporate Partnership and Team
Operations Manager:** Alex Clausius. **Director of Community Relations & Merchandise:** Ashlea LaPlant. **Marketing &
Creative Manager:** Jason Grohoske. **Account Executives:** Bryan Martin, Marco Rodriguez, Sasha Siks.

FIELD STAFF

Manager: Jose Moreno. **Hitting Coach:** Eric Farris. **Pitching Coaches:** Danielin Acevedo, Moises Hernandez.

GAME INFORMATION

Radio Announcer: Pat Dillon. **No. of Games Broadcast:** 76. **Flagship Station:** KRKO 1380-AM. **PA Announcer:** Tom
Lafferty. **Official Scorer:** Pat Castro. **Stadium Name:** Everett Memorial Stadium. **Location:** I-5, exit 192. **Standard Game
Times:** 7:05 pm, Sun. 4:05. **Ticket Price Range:** $8-18. **Visiting Club Hotel:** Best Western Cascadia Inn, 2800 Pacific Ave,
Everett, WA 98201. **Telephone:** (425) 258-4141.

HILLSBORO HOPS

Address: 4460 NE Century Blvd., Hillsboro, OR, 97124. **Telephone:** (503) 640-0887.
E-Mail Address: info@hillsborohops.com. **Website:** www.hillsborohops.com.
Affiliation (first year): Arizona Diamondbacks (2001). **Years in League:** 2013-

OWNERSHIP/MANAGEMENT

Operated by: Short Season LLC. **Managing Partners:** Mike McMurray, Josh Weinman, Myron Levin.
Chairman and CEO: Mike McMurray. **President and General Manager:** K.L. Wombacher. **Chief Financial Officer:**
Laura McMurray. **Director, Ballpark Operations:** Ryan Kees. **Vice President, Tickets:** Jason Gavigan. **Senior Director,
Merchandise:** Lauren Wombacher. **Director, Communications:** Preston Toulon. **Director, Broadcasting:** Rich Burk.

FIELD STAFF

Manager: Shawn Roof. **Hitting Coach:** Micah Franklin. **Pitching Coach:** Mike Parrott. **Coach:** Carlos Mesa.
Coach: Ben Petrick.

GAME INFORMATION

PA Announcer: Brian Rogers. **Official Scorer:** Blair Cash. **Stadium Name:** Ron Tonkin Field. **Location:** 4460 NE
Century Blvd., Hillsboro, OR. 97124. **Standard Game Times:** 7:05 pm, Sat. 5:03, Sun. 4:05. **Ticket Price Range:** $7-$18.
Visiting Club Hotel: Extended Stay America—Portland/Hillsboro, Hillsboro, OR. **Telephone:** (503) 221-0140.

SALEM-KEIZER VOLCANOES

Office Address: 6700 Field of Dreams Way, Keizer, OR 97303.
Mailing Address: PO Box 20936, Keizer, OR 97307.
Telephone: (503) 390-2225. **Fax:** (503) 390-2227.
E-Mail Address: Volcanoes@volcanoesbaseball.com.
Website: www.volcanoesbaseball.com.
Affiliation (first year): San Francisco Giants (1997). **Years in League:** 1997-.

OWNERSHIP/MANAGEMENT

Operated By: Sports Enterprises Inc. **Principal Owners:** Jerry Walker, Lisa Walker. **President/General Manager:** Jerry Walker. **Vice President:** Lisa Walker. **President, Operations:** Rick Nelson. **Senior Account Executive/Game Day Operations:** Jerry Howard. **Director, Business Development:** Justin Lacche.

FIELD STAFF

Manager: Hector Borg. **Pitching Coach:** Dwight Bernard. **Hitting Coach:** Jake Fox. **Fundamentals Coach:** Mark Hallberg. **Strength and Conditioning Coach:** Joe Palazzolo. **Athletic Trainer:** Charlene Wichman.

GAME INFORMATION

Radio Announcer: Wes Tucker. **No. of Games Broadcast:** 76. **Flagship Station:** KBZY Radio 1490AM. **PA Announcer:** Unavailable. **Official Scorer:** Scott Sepich. **Stadium Name:** Volcanoes Stadium. **Location:** I-5 to exit 260 (Chemawa Road), west one block to Stadium Way NE, north six blocks to stadium. **Standard Game Times:** 6:35 pm, Sun. 5:05. **Ticket Price Range:** $7-30. **Visiting Club Hotel:** Comfort Suites, 630 Hawthorne Ave SE, Salem, OR 97301. **Telephone:** (503) 585-9705.

SPOKANE INDIANS

Office Address: Avista Stadium, 602 N Havana, Spokane, WA 99202. **Mailing Address:** PO Box 4758, Spokane, WA 99220.
Telephone: (509) 535-2922. **Fax:** (509) 534-5368.
E-Mail Address: mail@spokaneindians.com. **Website:** www.spokaneindians.com.
Affiliation (first year): Texas Rangers (2003). **Years in League:** 1972, 1983-Present -

OWNERSHIP/MANAGEMENT

Operated By: Longball Inc. **Principal Owner:** Bobby Brett. **Co-Owner/Senior Advisor:** Andrew Billig. **Vice President/General Manager:** Chris Duff. **Senior Vice President:** Otto Klein. **VP, Development:** Josh Roys. **Director, Business Operations:** Lesley DeHart. **Assistant GM, Sponsorships:** Kyle Day. **Assistant GM, Tickets:** Nick Gaebe. **Corporate Partnerships Manager:** Darby Moore. **Business Operations Coordinator:** MacKenzie White. **Director of Public Relations:** John Collett. **Communications Consultant:** Bud Bareither. **Assistant Director, Tickets:** Sean Bozigian. **Account Executives:** Jake Forsman, Jake Browne, Tim O'Leary. **Directory of Group Sales:** Olivia Handwerk. **Group Sales Coordinator:** Gina Giesseman. **Personal Account Manager:** Forest Salgado. **CFO:** Greg Sloan. **Controller:** Tim Gittel. **Director of Facilities & Grounds:** Tony Lee. **Assistant Director, Stadium Operations:** Larry Blumer.

FIELD STAFF

Manager: Kenny Holmberg. **Hitting Coach:** Jared Goedert. **Pitching Coach:** Jono Armold. **Strength/Conditioning Coach:** Ed Yong. **Trainer:** Bronson Santillan.

GAME INFORMATION

Radio Announcer: Mike Boyle. **No. of Games Broadcast:** 76. **Flagship Station:** 1510 KGA. **PA Announcer:** Scott Lewis. **Official Scorer:** Todd Gilkey. **Stadium Name:** Avista Stadium. **Location:** From west, I-90 to exit 283B (Thor/Freya), east on Third Avenue, left onto Havana; From east, I-90 to Broadway exit, right onto Broadway, left onto Havana. **Standard Game Time:** 6:30 pm, Sun. 3:30 pm. **Ticket Price Range:** $5-13. **Visiting Club Hotel:** Mirabeau Park Hotel & Convention Center, 1100 N. Sullivan Rd, Spokane, WA 99037. **Telephone:** (509) 924-9000.

TRI-CITY DUST DEVILS

Address: 6200 Burden Blvd, Pasco, WA 99301.
Telephone: (509) 544-8789. **Fax:** (509) 547-9570.
E-Mail Address: info@dustdevilsbaseball.com. **Website:** www.dustdevilsbaseball.com.
Affiliation (first year): San Diego Padres (2015). **Years in League:** 1955-1974, 1983-1986, 2001-

OWNERSHIP/MANAGEMENT

Operated by: Northwest Baseball Ventures. **Principal Owners:** George Brett, Yoshi Okamoto, Brent Miles.
President: Brent Miles. **Vice President/General Manager:** Derrel Ebert. **Assistant General Manager, Business Operations:** Trevor Shively. **Assistant General Manager, Sponsorships:** Ann Shaffer. **Promotions Manager:** Samantha Beck. **Sponsorships Account Executive:** Trenton Dupré. **Dircetor of Ticket Sales:** Riley Shintaffer. **Group Sales Coordinator:** Ben McEnderfer. **Ticket Sales Coordinator:** Marcus Manderbach. **Ticket Operations Coordinator:** Taylor Fraise. **Head Groundskeeper:** Michael Angel.

FIELD STAFF

Manager: Aaron Levin. **Hitting Coach:** Oscar Salazar. **Pitching Coach:** Giancarlo Alvarado.

GAME INFORMATION

Radio Announcer: Chris King. **No. of Games Broadcast:** 76. **Flagship Station:** 870-AM KFLD. **PA Announcer:** Patrick Harvey. **Official Scorers:** Tony Wise, Scott Tylinski. **Stadium Name:** Gesa Stadium. **Location:** I-182 to exit 9 (Road 68), north to Burden Blvd, right to stadium. **Standard Game Time:** 7:15 pm. **Ticket Price Range:** $7-11. **Visiting Club Hotel:** Hampton Inn & Suites Pasco/Tri-Cities, 6826 Burden Blvd., Pasco, WA 99301. **Telephone:** (509) 792-1660

VANCOUVER CANADIANS

Address: Scotiabank Field at Nat Bailey Stadium, 4601 Ontario St, Vancouver, British Columbia V5V 3H4. **Telephone:** (604) 872-5232. **Fax:** (604) 872-1714.
E-Mail Address: staff@canadiansbaseball.com. **Website:** www.canadiansbaseball.com.
Affiliation (first year): Toronto Blue Jays (2011). **Years in League:** 2000-

OWNERSHIP/MANAGEMENT

Operated by: Vancouver Canadians Professional Baseball LLP. **Managing General Partner:** Jake Kerr. **Partner:** Jeff Mooney.
President: Andy Dunn. **General Manager:** JC Fraser. **Assistant General Manager:** Allan Bailey. **Financial Controller:** Brenda Chmiliar. **VP, Sales/Marketing:** Graham Wall. **Director, Communications:** Rob Fai. **Director, Sales/Game Day Operations:** Michael Richardson. **Manager, Sales & Marketing:** Lindsay Scharf. **Manager, Group Sales & Social Media:** Stephani Ellis. **Manager, Community Relations:** Oscar Duran. **Manager, Ticket Operations:** Reilly Simmonds. **Coordinator, Sales:** Mackenzie Hunter. **Coordinator, Sales:** Lori Stankiewicz. **Head Groundskeeper:** Ross Baron. **Manager, Ballpark Operations/Home Clubhouse Attendant:** John Stewart. **Manager, Concessions:** Iain Graham (Aramark).

FIELD STAFF

Manager: Dallas McPherson. **Hitting Coach:** Aaron Mathews. **Pitching Coach:** Jim Czajkowski.

GAME INFORMATION

Radio Announcer: Rob Fai. **No. of Games Broadcast:** 76. **Flagship Station:** TSN 1040-AM/1410 AM. **PA Announcer:** Don Andrews/John Ashbridge. **Official Scorer:** Mike Hanafin. **Stadium Name:** Scotiabank Field at Nat Bailey Stadium. **Location:** From downtown, take Cambie Street Bridge, left on East 29th Ave., left on Ontario St to stadium; From south, take Highway 99 to Oak Street, right on 41st Ave, left on Cambie St. right on East 29th Ave., left on Ontario St to stadium. **Standard Game Times:** 7:05 pm, Sun. 1:05. **Ticket Price Range:** $16-27. **Visiting Club Hotel:** Accent Inns, 10551 Edwards Dr, Richmond, BC V6X 3L8. **Telephone:** (604) 273-3311.

APPALACHIAN LEAGUE

APPALACHIAN LEAGUE
of professional baseball clubs

Mailing Address: 759 182nd Ave. E., Redington Shores, FL 33708.
Telephone: 704-252-2656. **E-Mail Address:** office@appyleague.net.
Website: www.appyleague.com. **Years League Active:** 1921-25, 1937-55, 1957-
President/Treasurer: Lee Landers. **Corporate Secretary:** David Cross (Danville).
Directors: Charlie Wilson (Bluefield), Larry Broadway (Bristol), J.J. Picollo
(Burlington), Dom Chiti (Danville), Jeremy Zoll (Elizabethton), Jeff Graupe (Greeneville), Gary
LaRocque (Johnson City), Ian Levin (Kingsport), Mitch Lukevics (Princeton), Eric Schmitt
(Pulaski). **Executive Committee:** Mike Mains (Elizabethton), Brian Paupeck (Pulaski),
Dan Moushon(Burlington), Gary La Rocque (St. Louis), Charlie Wilson (Toronto), Larry
Broadway(Pittsburgh). **Board of Trustees Representative:** Mitch Lukevics (Tampa Bay).
   League Administrator: Bobbi Landers.
   Division Structure: East—Bluefield, Burlington, Danville, Princeton, Pulaski. **West**—Bristol,
Elizabethton, Greeneville, Johnson City, Kingsport.
   Regular Season: 68 games. **2018 Opening Date:** June 22. **Closing Date:** August 29.
   All-Star Game: None.
   Playoff Format: First-and second-place teams in each division play each other in best-of-
three series. Winners meet in best-of-three series for league championship. **Roster Limit:** 35
active, 35 under control. **Player Eligibility Rule:** No more than three play ers on the active
roster may have three or more years of prior minor league service.
   Brand of Baseball: Rawlings. **Umpires:** Uavailable.

Lee Landers

STADIUM INFORMATION

Club	Stadium	Opened	LF	Dimensions CF	RF	Capacity	2017 Att.
Bluefield	Bowen Field	1939	335	400	335	2,250	21,595
Bristol	DeVault Memorial Stadium	1969	325	400	310	2,000	20,813
Burlington	Burlington Athletic Stadium	1960	335	410	335	3,000	34,483
Danville	Dan Daniel Memorial Park	1993	330	400	330	2,588	32,634
Elizabethton	Joe O'Brien Field	1974	335	414	326	1,500	18,746
Greeneville	Pioneer Park	2004	331	400	331	2,400	35,305
Johnson City	TVA Credit Union Ballpark	1956	320	410	320	2,500	29,742
Kingsport	Hunter Wright Stadium	1995	330	410	330	2,500	29,742
Princeton	Hunnicutt Field	1988	330	396	330	1,950	17,690
Pulaski	Calfee Park	1935	335	405	310	2,500	77,880

BLUEFIELD BLUE JAYS

Office Address: Stadium Drive, Bluefield, WV 24701. **Mailing Address:** PO Box 356,
Bluefield, WV 24701. **Telephone:** (304) 324-1326. **Fax:** (304) 324-1318.
E-Mail Address: babybirds1@comcast.net. **Website:** www.bluefieldjays.com.
Affiliation (first year): Toronto Blue Jays (2011). **Years in League:** 1946-55, 1957-

OWNERSHIP/MANAGEMENT
   Director: Charlie Wilson (Toronto Blue Jays). **President:** George McGonagle. **Vice President:** David Kersey. **Counsel:**
Brian Cochran.

FIELD STAFF
   Manager: Dennis Holmberg. **Hitting Coach:** Carlos Villalobos. **Pitching Coach:** Adam Bernero. **Position Player
Coach:** Chris Schaeffer.

GAME INFORMATION
   PA Announcer: Unavailable. **Official Scorer:** Unavailable. **Stadium Name:** Bowen Field. **Location:** I-77 to Bluefield
exit 1, Route 290 to Route 460 West, fourth light right onto Leatherwood Lane, left at first light, past Hometown Shell
station and turn right, stadium quarter-mile on left. **Ticket Price Range:** $6. **Visiting Club Hotel:** Quality Inn Bluefield,
3350 Big Laurel Highway/460 West, Bluefield, WV 24701. **Telephone:** (304) 325-6170.

BRISTOL PIRATES

Ballpark Location: 1501 Euclid Ave, Bristol, VA 24201. **Mailing Address:** PO Box 1434, Bristol, VA 24203. **Telephone:** (276) 206-9946. **Fax:** (423)-968-2636.
E-Mail Address: gm@bristolbaseball.com. **Website:** www.bristolpiratesbaseball.com.
Twitter: @BriBucs. **Facebook:** www.facebook.com/bristolpiratesbaseball.
Affiliation (first year): Pittsburgh Pirates (2014). **Years in League:** 1921-25, 1940-55, 1969-

OWNERSHIP/MANAGEMENT
Owned by: Pittsburgh Pirates.
Director: Larry Broadway (Pittsburgh Pirates). **Operated by:** Bristol Baseball Inc. **President/General Manager:** Mahlon Luttrell. **Vice Presidents:** Craig Adams, Mark Young & Travis DeBusk. **Treasurer:** Jean Luttrell. **Secretary:** Connie Kinkead.

FIELD STAFF
Manager: Miguel Perez. **Hitting Coach:** Austin McClune. **Pitching Coach:** Joey Seaver. **Trainer:** Tyler Brooks. **Strength & Conditioning Coach:** Unavailable.

GAME INFORMATION
Radio: milb.com. **PA Announcer:** Unavailable. **Official Scorer:** Connie Kinkead. **Stadium Name:** DeVault Memorial Stadium. **Location:** I-81 to exit 3 onto Commonwealth Ave, right on Euclid Ave for half-mile. **Standard Game Time:** 7 pm, 6 pm Sunday. **Ticket Price Range:** $4-$8. **Visiting Club Hotel:** Holiday Inn, 3005 Linden Drive Bristol, VA 24202. **Telephone:** (276) 466-4100.

BURLINGTON ROYALS

Office Address: 1450 Graham St, Burlington, NC 27217. **Mailing Address:** PO Box 1143, Burlington, NC 27216.
Telephone: (336) 222-0223. **Fax:** (336) 226-2498.
E-Mail Address: info@burlingtonroyals.com. **Website:** www.burlingtonroyals.com
Affiliation (first year): Kansas City Royals (2007). **Years in League:** 1986-

OWNERSHIP/MANAGEMENT
Operated by: Burlington Baseball Club Inc.
Director: Ronnie Richardson (Kansas City). **President:** Miles Wolff. **Vice President:** Dan Moushon. **General Manager:** Mikie Morrison. **Assistant GM:** Tyler Cockerille. **Sales & Marketing Coordinator:** Lauren Wagaman. **Manager, Corporate Partnerships & Group Sales:** Katie Soraghan.

FIELD STAFF
Manager: Brooks Conrad. **Hitting Coach:** Nelson Liriano. **Pitching Coach:** Carlos Martinez.

GAME INFORMATION
Radio Announcer: Justin Gallanty. **No. of Games Broadcast:** Home-34, Away-34. **Flagship:** www.burlingtonroyals.com. **PA Announcer:** Unavailable. **Official Scorer:** Unavailable. **Stadium Name:** Burlington Athletic Stadium. **Location:** I-40/85 to exit 145, north on Route 100 (Maple Avenue) for 1.5 miles, right on Mebane Street for 1.5 miles, right on Beaumont, left on Graham. **Standard Game Time:** 7 p.m. **Ticket Price Range:** $5-9. **Visiting Club Hotel:** Ramada Burlington Hotel.

DANVILLE BRAVES

Office Address: Dan Daniel Memorial Park, 302 River Park Dr, Danville, VA 24540.
Mailing Address: PO Box 378, Danville, VA 24543.
Telephone: (434) 797-3792. **Fax:** (434) 797-3799.
E-Mail Address: danvillebraves@braves.com. **Website:** www.dbraves.com.
Affiliation (first year): Atlanta Braves (1993). **Years in League:** 1993-

OWNERSHIP/MANAGEMENT
Operated by: Atlanta National League Baseball Club LLC.
Director: Jonathan Schuerholz (Atlanta Braves). **General Manager:** David Cross. **Assistant GM:** Brandon Bennett. **Community Relations & Sales Manager:** Betsy Haugh. **Head Groundskeeper:** Ryan Brown.

FIELD STAFF
Manager: Barrett Kleinknecht. **Coach:** Barbaro Garbey. **Pitching Coach:** Kanekoa Texeira. **Athletic Trainer:** Drew Garner. **Strength/Conditioning Coach:** Unavailable.

GAME INFORMATION
Radio Announcer: Nick Pierce. **No. of Games Broadcast:** Home-34. **Flagship Station:** www.dbraves.com. **PA Announcer:** Jay Stephens. **Official Scorer:** Mark Bowman. **Stadium Name:** American Legion Field Post 325 Field at

Dan Daniel Memorial Park. **Location:** US 29 Bypass to River Park Drive/Dan Daniel Memorial Park exit; follow signs to park. **Standard Game Times:** 7 pm, Sun. 4. pm. **Ticket Price Range:** $5-9. **Visiting Club Hotel:** Comfort Inn & Suites, 100 Tower Drive, Danville, VA 24540.

ELIZABETHTON TWINS

Office Address: 300 West Mill St., Elizabethton, TN 37643. **Stadium Address:** 208 N. Holly Lane, Elizabethton, TN 37643. **Mailing Address:** 300 West Mill St., Elizabethton, TN 37643. **Telephone:** (423) 547-6441. **Fax:** (423) 547-6442. **Affiliation (first year):** Minnesota Twins (1974. **Years in League:** 1937-42, 1945-51, 1974-

OWNERSHIP/MANAGEMENT
Operator: City of Elizabethton.
Director: Jeremy Zoll. **President:** Harold Mains. **General Manager:** Mike Mains. **Clubhouse Operations/Head Groundskeeper:** David McQueen.

FIELD STAFF
Manager: Ray Smith. **Coach:** Jeff Reed. **Pitching Coach:** Luis Ramirez. **Athletic Trainer:** Ben Myers. **Strength & Conditioning Coach:** Travis Koon.

GAME INFORMATION
Radio Announcer: Mike Gallagher. **No. of Games Broadcast:** 34–Home, 6–Away. **Flagship Station:** WBEJ 1240-AM. **PA Announcer:** Tom Banks. **Official Scorer:** Gene Renfro. **Stadium Name:** Joe O'Brien Field. **Location:** I-81 to Highway I-26, exit at Highway 321/67, left on Holly Lane. **Standard Game Times:** 7 pm. **Ticket Price Range:** $3-6. **Visiting Club Hotel:** Holiday Inn, 101 W Springbrook Dr, Johnson City, TN 37601. **Telephone:** (423) 282-4611.

GREENEVILLE REDS

Office Address: 135 Shiloh Road, Greeneville, TN 37743.
Mailing Address: 135 Shiloh Road, Greeneville, TN 37743.
Telephone: Unavailable. **Fax:** (423) Unavailable.
E-Mail Address: Unavailable. **Website:** www.greenevillereds.com.

OWNERSHIP/MANAGEMENT
Owned by: Cincinnati Reds, LLC.
Director: Jeff Graupe (Cincinnati Reds). **General Manager:** Paul Kleinhans-Schulz.

FIELD STAFF
Manager: Gookie Dawkins. **Hitting Coach:** Darryl Brinkley. **Pitching Coach:** Chad Cordero. **Bench Coach:** Reggie Williams. **Athletic Trainer:** Ryan Ross. **Strength & Conditioning Coach:** Blaine Taylor.

GAME INFORMATION
Radio Announcer: Steve Wilhoit. **Flagship Station:** greenevillereds.com. **PA Announcer:** Unavailable. **Official Scorer:** Johnny Painter. **Stadium Name:** Pioneer Park. **Location:** On the campus of Tusculum College, 135 Shiloh Rd Greeneville, TN 37743. **Standard Game Time:** Mon-Fri: 7 p.m., Sat: 6 p.m., Sun: 2 p.m. **Ticket Price Range:** $5-11. **Visiting Club Hotel:** Quality Inn, 3160 E Andrew Johnson Hwy, Greeneville, TN 37745. **Telephone:** (423) 638-7511.

JOHNSON CITY CARDINALS

Office Address: 510 Bert St., Johnson City, TN 37601. **Mailing Address:** PO Box 179, Johnson City, TN 37605. **Telephone:** (423) 461-4866. **Fax:** (423) 461-4864. **E-Mail Address:** contact@jccardinals.com. **Website:** www.jccardinals.com. **Affiliation (first year):** St. Louis Cardinals (1975). **Years in League:** 1911-13, 1921-24, 1937-55, 1957-61, 1964-

OWNERSHIP/MANAGEMENT
Owned by: St. Louis Cardinals. **Operated by:** Boyd Sports, LLC.
President: Chris Allen. **Director:** Gary Larocque. **General Manager:** Zac Clark.

FIELD STAFF
Manager: Roberto Espinoza. **Hitting Coach:** Cody Gabella. **Pitching Coach:** Rick Harig.

GAME INFORMATION
PA Announcer: Unavailable. **Official Scorer:** Unavailable. **Stadium Name:** TVA Credit Union Ballpark. **Location:** I-26 to exit 23, left on East Main, through light onto Legion Street. **Standard Game Time:** 7 pm. **Ticket Price Range:** $6-$9. **Visiting Club Hotel:** Holiday Inn, 101 W Springbrook Dr, Johnson City, TN 37601. **Telephone:** (423) 282-4611.

KINGSPORT METS

Address: 800 Granby Rd, Kingsport, TN 37660. **Telephone:** (423) 224-2626.
Fax: (423) 224-2625. **E-Mail Address:** info@kmets.com. **Website:** www.kmets.com
Affiliation (first year): New York Mets (1980). **Years in League:** 1921-25, 1938-52,
1957, 1960-63, 1969-82, 1984-

OWNERSHIP/MANAGEMENT

Owner/Operated By: New York Mets. **Director:** Ian Levin. **General Manager:** Brian Paupeck. **Staff:** Josh Lawson.
Clubhouse Manager: Carlos Martell.

FIELD STAFF

Manager: Sean Ratliff. **Hitting Coach:** Delwyn Young. **Pitching Coach:** Josue Matos. **Athletic Trainer:** Vanessa
Weisbach. **Strength & Conditioning Coach:** John Perry.

GAME INFORMATION

PA Announcer: Reese Williams. **Official Scorer:** Zeke Newton. **Stadium Name:** Hunter Wright Stadium. **Location:**
I-26, Exit 1 (Stone Drive), left on West Stone Drive (US 11W), right on Granby Road. **Standard Game Times:** Mon-Sat.
6:30pm, Sun. 4pm, Doubleheader: Mon-Sat., 5pm, Sun., 4pm. **Ticket Price Range:** $5-$8. **Visiting Club Hotel:** Quality
Inn, 3004 Bays Mountain Plaza, Kingsport, TN 37664. **Telephone:** (423) 230-0534.

PRINCETON RAYS

Office Address: 345 Old Bluefield Rd, Princeton, WV 24739.
Mailing Address: PO Box 5646, Princeton, WV 24740. **Telephone:** (304) 487-2000.
Fax: (304) 487-8762. **E-Mail Address:** princetonrays@frontier.com. **Website:** www.princetonrays.net.
Affiliation (first year): Tampa Bay Rays (1997). **Years in League:** 1988-

OWNERSHIP/MANAGEMENT

Operated By: Princeton Baseball Association Inc. **Director:** Mitch Lukevics. **President:** Dewey Russell. **General
Manager:** Danny Shingleton. **Director, Stadium Operations:** Dewey Russell, Adam Sarver. **Clubhouse Manager:**
Anthony Dunagan. **Administrative Assistant:** Courtney Longworth. **Chaplain:** Craig Stout.

FIELD STAFF

Manager: Danny Sheaffer. **Coach:** Wuarnner Rincones. **Coach:** Blake Butera. **Pitching Coach:** Jim Paduch. **Athletic
Trainer:** Ruben Santiago.

GAME INFORMATION

Radio Announcer: Kyle Cooper. **No. of Games Broadcast:** 34–Away. **Flagship Station:** WAEY-103.3FM. **PA
Announcer:** Eric Lester. **Official Scorer:** Unavailable. **Stadium Name:** Hunnicutt Field. **Location:** Exit 9 off I-77, US
460 West to downtown exit, left on Stafford Drive; stadium located behind Mercer County Technical Education Center.
Standard Game Times: 7 PM, Sun. 5 pm. **Ticket Price Range:** $5-8. **Visiting Club Hotel:** Days Inn, I-77 and Ambrose
Lane, Princeton, WV 24740. **Telephone:** (304) 425-8100.

PULASKI YANKEES

PULASKI

Office Address: 529 Pierce Avenue, Pulaski, VA 24301.
Mailing Address: PO Box 852, Pulaski, VA 24301. **Telephone:** (540) 980-1070.
Email Address: info@pulaskiyankees.net. **Affiliation (first season):** New York Yankees (2015).
Years in League: 1942-1951, 1952-55, 1957-58, 1969-77, 1982-92, 1997-2002, 2003-2006, 2008-2014, 2015-

OWNERSHIP/MANAGEMENT

Operated By: Calfee Park Baseball Inc. **Park Owners:** David Hagan, Larry Shelor. **General Manager:** Christina Edney.

FIELD STAFF

Manager: Nick Ortiz. **Hitting Coach:** Francisco Leandro. **Pitching Coach:** Gerardo Casadiego. **Defensive Coach:**
Teuris Olivares. **Athletic Trainer:** Manny Ozoa. **Strength & Conditioning Coach:** Larry Adegoke.

GAME INFORMATION

PA Announcer: Unavailable. **Official Scorer:** Unavailable. **Stadium Name:** Historic Calfee Park. **Location:** Interstate
81 to Exit 89-B (Route 11), north to Pulaski, right on Pierce Avenue. **Ticket Price Range:** $5-11. **Visiting Club Hotel:**
Quality Inn, Dublin, VA.

PIONEER LEAGUE

Office Address: 180 S Howard Street, Spokane, WA 99201.
Mailing Address: PO Box 2564, Spokane, WA 99220.
Telephone: (509) 456-7615. **Fax:** (509) 456-0136.
E-Mail Address: fanmail@pioneerleague.com. **Website:** www.pioneerleague.com.
Years League Active: 1939-42, 1946-

President: Jim McCurdy.
Directors: Dave Baggott (Ogden), Matt Ellis (Missoula), DG Elmore (Helena), Kevin Greene (Idaho Falls), Michael Baker (Grand Junction), Jeff Katofsky (Orem), Vinny Purpura (Great Falls), Dave Heller (Billings). **League Administrator:** Teryl MacDonald. **Executive Director:** Mary Ann McCurdy.
Division Structure: North—Billings, Great Falls, Helena, Missoula. **South**—Grand Junction, Idaho Falls, Ogden, Orem.
Regular Season: 76 games (split schedule).
2018 Opening Date: June 15. **Closing Date:** Sept. 6.
All-Star Game: Aug. 7 at Grand Junction (Pioneer League vs. Northwest League).
Playoff Format: First-half division winners meet second-half division winners in best of three series. Winners meet in best-of-three series for league championship. **Roster Limit:** 35 active, 35 dressed for each game. **Player Eligibility Rule:** No player on active list may have three or more years of prior minor league service.
Brand of Baseball: Rawlings.
Umpires: Unavailable.

Jim McCurdy

STADIUM INFORMATION

Club	Stadium	Opened	Dimensions LF	CF	RF	Capacity	2017 Att.
Billings	Dehler Park	2008	329	410	350	3,071	110,311
Grand Junction	Sam Suplizio Field	1949	302	400	333	7,014	79,547
Great Falls	Centene Stadium at Legion Park	1956	335	414	335	3,800	47,260
Helena	Kindrick Field	1939	335	400	325	1,700	33,843
Idaho Falls	Melaleuca Field	1976	340	400	350	3,400	90,816
Missoula	Ogren Park at Allegiance Field	2004	309	398	287	3,500	71,936
Ogden	Lindquist Field	1997	335	396	334	5,000	128,348
Orem	Home of the Owlz	2005	305	408	312	4,500	55,981

BILLINGS MUSTANGS

Office Address: Dehler Park, 2611 9th Avenue North, Billings, MT 59101.
Mailing Address: PO Box 1553, Billings, MT 59103-1553.
Telephone: (406) 252-1241. **Fax:** (406) 252-2968.
E-Mail Address: mustangs@billingsmustangs.com. **Website:** billingsmustangs.com.
Affiliation (first year): Cincinnati Reds (1974). **Years in League:** 1948-63, 1969-

OWNERSHIP/MANAGEMENT
Operated By: Mustangs Baseball LLC.
President/CEO: Dave Heller. **General Manager:** Gary Roller. **Director, Corporate Sales/Partnerships:** Chris Marshall. **Director, Stadium Operations:** Matt Schoonover. **Director, Broadcasting/Media Relations:** Dustin Daniel. **Director, Food and Beverage Services:** Curt Prchal. **Director, Field Operations:** Jeff Limburg.

FIELD STAFF
Manager: Ray Martinez. **Hitting Coach:** Bryan LaHair. **Pitching Coach:** Derrin Ebert. **Strength Coach:** Justin Bucko. **Athletic Trainer:** Josh Hobson. **Athletic Trainer:** Brandon Blascak.

GAME INFORMATION
Radio Broadcaster: Dustin Daniel. **No. of Games Broadcast:** 76. **Flagship Station:** ESPN 910-AM KBLG. **PA Announcer:** Sara Spangle. **Official Scorer:** George Kimmet. **Stadium Name:** Dehler Park. **Location:** I-90 to Exit 450, north on 27th Street North to 9th Avenue North. **Standard Game Times:** Mon-Fri 7:05 pm, Sat. 6:05 pm, Sun. 1:05 pm. **Ticket Price Range:** $5-$11.

GRAND JUNCTION ROCKIES

Address: 1315 North Ave., Grand Junction, CO, 81501
Telephone: (970) 255-7625. **Fax:** (970) 241-2374
Email: mritter@gjrockies.com. **Website:** www.gjrockies.com
Affiliation (first year): Colorado Rockies (2001). **Years in League:** 2001–

OWNERSHIP/MANAGEMENT
   Principal Owners/Operated by: GJR, LLC
   President: Joe Kubly. **Assistant GM:** Mick Ritter. **Concessions Manager:** Matt Allen. **Marketing Manager:** Jarah Wright. **Community Ambassador:** Tim Ray.

FIELD STAFF
   Manager: Unavailable. **Hitting Coach:** Jake Opitz. **Pitching Coach:** Doug Jones.

GAME INFORMATION
   Radio Announcer: Adam Spolane. **Number of Games Broadcast:** 76. **Flagship Station:** KNZZ, 1100-AM. **Television Announcer:** Adam Spolane. **Number of Games Televised:** Unavailable. **Flagship:** KGJT—My Network, Dish Network. **Produced by:** Colorado Mesa University. **PA Announcer:** Tim Ray. **Official Scorers:** Chris Hanks, Dan Kenyon, Tyler Ehlers. **Stadium Name:** Suplizio Field. **Location:** 1315 North Ave. Grand Junction, CO 81501. **Standard Game Times:** 6:40 pm. **Ticket Price Range:** $7-$11.

GREAT FALLS VOYAGERS

Address: 1015 25th St N, Great Falls, MT 59401.
Telephone: (406) 452-5311. **Fax:** (406) 454-0811.
E-Mail Address: voyagers@gfvoyagers.com. **Website:** www.gfvoyagers.com.
Affiliation (first year): Chicago White Sox (2003). **Years in League:** 1948-1963, 1969-

OWNERSHIP/MANAGEMENT
   Operated By: Great Falls Baseball.
   President: Vinny Purpura. **General Manager:** Scott Reasoner. **Assistant General Manager:** Scott Lettre.

FIELD STAFF
   Manager: Tim Esmay. **Hitting Coach:** Eric Richardson. **Pitching Coach:** John Ely.

GAME INFORMATION
   Radio Announcer: Shawn Tiemann. **No. of Games Broadcast:** 76. **Flagship Station:** KXGF-1400 AM. **PA Announcer:** Chris Evans. **Official Scorer:** Mike Lewis. **Stadium Name:** Centene Stadium. **Location:** From I-15 to exit 281 (10th Ave S), left on 26th, left on Eighth Ave North, right on 25th, ballpark on right, past railroad tracks. **Ticket Price Range:** $5-10. **Visiting Club Hotel:** Days Inn, 101 14th Ave NW, Great Falls, MT 59404. **Telephone:** (406) 727-6565.

HELENA BREWERS

Office Address: 1300 N. Ewing, Helena, MT 59601.
Mailing Address: PO Box 6756, Helena, MT 59604.
Telephone: (406) 495-0500. **Fax:** (406) 495-0900.
E-Mail Address: info@helenabrewers.net. **Website:** www.helenabrewers.net.
Affiliation (first year): Milwaukee Brewers (2003). **Years in League:** 1978-2000, 2003-

OWNERSHIP/MANAGEMENT
   Operated by: Helena Baseball Club LLC. **Principal Owner:** David Elmore.
   General Manager: Paul Fetz. **Director, Operations & Ticketing:** James Van Dyke. **Director, Group Sales/ Marketing:** Matt Ramstead. **Radio Announcer/Director, Broadcasting/Media Relations:** Garrett Greene.

FIELD STAFF
   Manager: Nestor Corredor. **Hitting Coach:** Liu Rodriguez. **Pitching Coach:** Rolando Valles.

GAME INFORMATION
   Radio Announcer: Dustin Daniel. **No. of Games Broadcast:** 76. **Flagship Station:** Unavailable. **PA Announcer:** Kevin Smith. **Official Scorers:** Unavailable. **Stadium Name:** Kindrick Field. **Location:** Cedar Street exit off I-15, west to Last Chance Gulch, left at Memorial Park. **Standard Game Time:** 7:05 pm, Sun. 1:05. **Ticket Price Range:** $6-10. **Visiting Club Hotel:** Red Lion Colonial. **Telephone:** (406) 443-2100.

IDAHO FALLS CHUKARS

Office Address: 900 Jim Garchow Way, Idaho Falls, ID 83402.
Mailing Address: PO 2183, Idaho, ID 83403.
Telephone: (208) 522-8363. **Fax:** (208) 522-9858.
E-Mail Address: chukars@ifchukars.com. **Website:** www.ifchukars.com.
Affiliation (first year): Kansas City Royals (2004). **Years in League:** 1940-42, 1946-

OWNERSHIP/MANAGEMENT

Operated By: The Elmore Sports Group. **Principal Owner:** David Elmore.
President/General Manager: Kevin Greene. **Vice President:** Paul Henderson. **Assistant GM:** Josh Michalsen.
Director, Operations: Aaron Madero. **Clubhouse Manager:** Jared Trorscher. **Head Groundskeeper:** Unavailable.

FIELD STAFF

Manager: Omar Ramirez. **Hitting Coach:** Damon Hollins. **Pitching Coach:** Jeff Suppan.

GAME INFORMATION

Radio Announcer: John Balginy. **No. of Games Broadcast:** 76. **Flagship Station:** ESPN 980-AM & 94.5 and 105.1FM.
PA Announcer: Javier Hernandez. **Official Scorer:** John Balginy. **Stadium Name:** Melaleuca Field. **Location:** I-15 to
West Broadway exit, left onto Memorial Drive, right on Mound Avenue, 1/4 mile to stadium. **Standard Game Times:**
7:15 pm, Sun. 4:00. **Ticket Price Range:** $6-12. **Visiting Club Hotel:** Fairbridge Inn & Suites, 850 Lindsay Blvd, Idaho
Falls, ID 83402. **Telephone:** (208) 522-6260.

MISSOULA OSPREY

Address: 140 N Higgins, Suite 201, Missoula, MT 59802.
Telephone: (406) 543-3300. **Fax:** (406) 543-9463.
E-Mail Address: info@missoulaosprey.com. **Website:** www.missoulaosprey.com.
Affiliation (first year): Arizona Diamondbacks (1999). **Years in League:** 1956-60, 1999-

OWNERSHIP/MANAGEMENT

Operated By: Mountain Baseball LLC.
President: Mike Ellis. **Executive Vice President:** Judy Ellis. **Executive Vice President:** Matt Ellis. **Retail Manager:**
Kim Klages Johns. **Office Manager/Bookkeeper, Director of Ticketing:** Nola Hunter. **Sales Executive:** Taylor Rush.

FIELD STAFF

Manager: Mike Benjamin. **Hitting Coach:** Jose Amado. **Pitching Coach:** Shane Loux. **Strength/Conditioning:**
Derek Clovis. **Trainer:** Damon Reel. **Bullpen Coach:** Eddie Oropesa.

GAME INFORMATION

Radio Announcer: Unavailable. **No. of Games Broadcast:** 76. **Flagship Station:** ESPN 102.9 FM. **PA Announcer:**
Unavailable. **Official Scorer:** Unavailable. **Stadium Name:** Ogren Park Allegiance Field. **Location:** Take Orange Street
to Cregg Lane, west on Cregg Lane, stadium west of McCormick Park past railroad trestle. **Standard Game Times:** 7:05
pm, Sun. 5:05. **Ticket Price Range:** $6-13. **Visiting Club Hotel:** Comfort Inn-University, 1021 E. Broadway, Missoula, MT
59802. **Telephone:** (406) 549-7600.

OGDEN RAPTORS

Address: 2330 Lincoln Ave, Ogden, UT 84401. **Telephone:** (801) 393-2400.
Fax: (801) 393-2473. **E-Mail Address:** homerun@ogden-raptors.com.
Website: www.ogden-raptors.com. **Affiliation (first year):** Los Angeles Dodgers
(2003). **Years in League:** 1939-42, 1946-55, 1966-74, 1994-

OWNERSHIP/MANAGEMENT
Operated By: Ogden Professional Baseball, Inc. **Principal Owners:** Dave Baggott,
John Lindquist.
President/General Manager: Dave Baggott. **Director, Media Relations/Broadcaster:** Andrew Haynes. **Director,
Food Services:** Stacy Oliver. **Director, Security:** Scott McGregor. **Director, Social Media:** Kevin Johnson. **Director,
Ticket Operations:** Trevor Wilson. **Director, Information Technology:** Chris Greene. **Public Relations:** Pete Diamond.
Groundskeeper: Kenny Kopinski. **Assistant Groundskeeper:** Bob Richardson.

FIELD STAFF
Manager: Jeremy Rodriguez. **Hitting Coach:** Dustin Kelly. **Pitching Coach:** Dean Stiles. **Clubhouse Manager:** Dave
"MacGyver" Ackerman

GAME INFORMATION
Radio Announcer: Andrew Haynes. **No. of Games Broadcast:** 76. **Flagship Station:** ogden-raptors.com. **PA
Announcer:** Pete Diamond. **Official Scorer:** Dennis Kunimura. **Stadium Name:** Lindquist Field. **Location:** I-15 North to
21th Street exit, east to Lincoln Avenue, south three blocks to park. **Standard Game Times:** 7 pm, Sun. 4. **Ticket Price
Range:** $4-10. **Visiting Club Hotel:** Unavailable.

OREM OWLZ

Address: 970 W. University Parkway, Orem, UT 84058. **Telephone:** (801) 377-2255.
E-Mail Address: matt@oremowlz.com. **Website:** www.oremowlz.com.
Affiliation: Los Angeles Angels (2001). **Years in League:** 2001-

OWNERSHIP/MANAGEMENT
Operated By: Bery Bery Gud To Me LLC. **Principal Owner:** Jeff Katofsky.
General Manager: Rick Berry. **Assistant GM:** Julie Hatch. **Director, Sales & Marketing:** Matt Potts. **Director, Public
Relations:** Sydney Cluff.

FIELD STAFF
Manager: Dave Stapleton. **Hitting Coach:** D. Ortega/M. Del Campo. **Pitching Coach:** M. Wuertz/C. Seddon.

GAME INFORMATION
Radio Announcer: Michael Broskowski. **No. of Games Broadcast:** 76. **Flagship Station:** Unavailable. **PA
Announcer:** Unavailable. **Official Scorer:** Adrianne. **Stadium Name:** Home of the Owlz. **Location:** Exit 269 (University
Parkway) off I-15 at Utah Valley University campus. **Ticket Price Range:** $6-12. **Visiting Club Hotel:** Unavailable.

ARIZONA LEAGUE

Office Address: 620 W Franklin St., Boise, ID 83702. **Mailing Address:** PO Box 1645, Boise, ID 83701.
Telephone: (208) 429-1511. **Fax:** (208) 429-1525. **E-Mail Address:** bobrichmond@qwestoffice.net
Years League Active: 1988- **President/Treasurer:** Bob Richmond. **Vice President:** Mike Bell (Diamondbacks).
Corporate Secretary: Ted Polakowski (Athletics). **Administrative Assistant:** Rob Richmond.
Divisional Alignment: East—Angels, Athletics, Cubs, Diamondbacks, Giants, Giants 2.
Central—Brewers, Dodgers, Indians, Indians 2, Reds, White Sox. **West**—Mariners, Padres1, Padres2, Rangers, Royals.
Regular Season: 56 games (split schedule). **2018 Opening Date:** June 18. **Closing Date:** Aug. 25.
Playoff Format: Six teams qualify. The three division champions from each half qualify for the single-elimination playoffs. If the same team wins a division in both halves, the team with the second-best overall record from the other division teams would qualify as the second team from that division. The two clubs with the best overall records receive first-round byes. Quarterfinal winners advance to a one-game playoff against one of the clubs that received a bye. Semifinal winners meet in a one-game final for the league championship. **All-Star Game:** None.
Roster Limit: 35 active. **Player Eligibility Rule:** No player may have three or more years of prior minor league service.

Clubs	Playing Site	Manager	Coach(es)	Pitching Coach
Angels	Angels Complex, Tempe	Jack Santora	A. Gomez/R. Sebra	J. Cuevas/J. Oseguera
Athletics	Papago Park, Phoenix	Eddie Menchaca	Ruben Escalera	Gabriel Ozuna
Brewers	Maryvale Baseball Complex, Phoenix	Rafael Neda	B. Del Chiaro/T. Diggs	Nat Ballenberg
Cubs	Fitch Park, Mesa	Carmelo Martinez	Unavailable	Unavailable
D-backs	Salt River Fields at Talking Stick	Darrin Garner	Jonny Gomes	Manny Garcia
Dodgers	Camelback Ranch, Glendale	Mark Kertenian	Jarek Cunningham	Luis Meza
Giants	Giants complex, Scottsdale	Carlos Valderrama	Travis Ishikawa	M. Rodriguez/Lee Smith
Giants	Giants complex, Scottsdale	Billy Horton	Doug Clark	Mike Couchee
Indians	Goodyear Ballpark	Larry Day	J. Esposito/K. Correa	Joel Mangrum
Indians	Goodyear Ballpark	Jerry Owens	J. Betances/M. Weiner	Owen Dew
Mariners	Peoria Sports Complex	Zac Livingston	TBD	Yoel Monzon
Padres	Peoria Sports Complex	Vinny Lopez	Pat O'Sullivan	Leo Rosales
Padres	Peoria Sports Complex	Unavailable	Raul Gonzalez	Unavailable
Rangers	Surprise Recreation Campus	Matt Siegel	S. Manriquez/J. Moore/	H. Lugo/C. Egelston
Reds	Goodyear Ballpark	Jose Nieves	Todd Takayoshi	Elmer Dessens
Royals	Surprise Recreation Campus	Tony Pena Jr.	A. David/R. Castro	Mark Davis
White Sox	Camelback Ranch	Ryan Newman	Gary Ward	Felipe Lira

GULF COAST LEAGUE

Operated By: Minor League Baseball. **Office Address:** 9550 16th Street North, St Petersburg, FL 33716.
Telephone: 727-456-1734. **Fax:** 727-456-1745. **Website:** www.milb.com. **Email Address:** gcl@milb.com.
Vice President, Baseball & Business Operations: Tim Brunswick. **Assistant Director, Baseball & Business Operations:** Andy Shultz. **2018 Opening Date:** June 18. **Closing Date:** August 25. **Regular Season:** 56 Games (East, South)/54 Games (Northeast, Northwest). **Divisional Alignment: East**—Astros, Cardinals, Marlins, Mets, Nationals.
Northeast—Braves, Phillies East, Tigers East, Yankees East. **Northwest**—Blue Jays, Phillies West, Pirates, Tigers West, Yankees West. **South**—Orioles, Rays, Red Sox, Twins. **Playoff Format:** The division winner with the best record plays the division winner with the lowest record and the other two division winners meet in a one game semifinal. The winners meet in a best-of-three series for the Gulf Coast League championship. **All-Star Game:** None. **Roster Limit:** 35 active and in uniform and eligible to play. At least 10 must be pitchers as of July 1. **Player Eligibility Rule:** No player may have three or more years of prior minor league service. **Brand of Baseball:** Rawlings.

Clubs	Playing Site	Manager	Hitting Coach	Pitching Coach
Astros	Ballpark of the Palm Beaches	Wladimir Sutil	C. Cedeno/R. Rojas	Jose Rada
Blue Jays	Bobby Mattick Training Center	Luis Hurtado	P Elliott/G. Carroll	Rafael Lazo
Braves	ESPN Wide World of Sports	Nestor Perez Jr.	Rick Albert	Elvin Nina
Cardinals	Cardinals Complex	Steve Turco	Jose Leon	Giovanni Carrara
Marlins	Roger Dean Stadium Complex	John Pachot	Rigoberto Silverio	Manny Olivera
Mets	Mets Complex	Jose Carreno	Rafael Fernandez	Ariel Prieto
Nationals	The Ballpark of the Palm Beaches	Mario Lisson	J. Mejia/L. Jeronimo	Larry Pardo
Orioles	Ed Smith Stadium Complex	Unavailable	Unavailable	Unavailable
Phillies East	Carpenter Complex	Roly deArmas	Rafael DeLima	Hector Mercado
Phillies West	Carpenter Complex	Nelson Prada	Chris Heintz	Matt Hockenberry
Pirates	Pirate City	Dave Turgeon	Kory DeHaan	Drew Benes
Rays	Charlotte Sports Park	Tomas Francisco	R.Guerrero/S. Smedley	M. DeMerritt/ A.Bastardo
Red Sox	Jet Blue Park, Fort Myers	Tom Kotchman	Junior Zamora	Dick Such
Tigers East	Tigertown, Lakeland	Luis Lopez	Rafael Gil	Carlos Bohorquez
Tigers West	Tigertown, Lakeland	Gary Cathcart	Bill Springman	Mike Alvarez
Twins	Lee County Sports Complex	Dan Ramsay	M. Borgschulte/L. Rodriguez	V. Vasquez/F. Jagoda
Yankees East	Himes Complex, Tampa	Unavailable	Unavailable	Unavailable
Yankees West	Himes Complex, Tampa	Unavailable	Unavailable	Unavailable

TEAM SCHEDULES

TRIPLE-A

INTERNATIONAL LEAGUE

BUFFALO BISONS

APRIL
6-8 . . . . at Rochester
9-11 . . . . at Pawtucket
12-15 . . . . . . Indianapolis
16-18 . . . . Louisville
20-22 . . . . at Norfolk
23-25 . . . . at Durham
27-29 . . . . Pawtucket
30 . . . . . . at Scranton/WB

MAY
1-2 . . . . . . at Scranton/WB
3-6 . . . . Syracuse
7-9 . . . . Rochester
10-13 . . . . at Lehigh Valley
14-16 . . . . . . at Pawtucket
18-20 . . . . . . Scranton/WB
21-24 . . . . Syracuse
25-28 . . . . . . at Rochester
29-31 . . . . Columbus

JUNE
1-3 . . . . Charlotte
5-7 . . . . at Toledo
8-10 . . . . at Columbus
11-13 . . . . at Lehigh Valley
14-17 . . . . Rochester
19-21 . . . . . . at Pawtucket
22-24 . . . . . . Lehigh Valley
25-28 . . . . Pawtucket
29-30 . . . . at Syracuse

JULY
1 . . . . at Syracuse
2-3 . . . . Scranton/WB
4-5 . . . . . . at Scranton/WB
6-8 . . . . Syracuse
12-15 . . . . at Lehigh Valley
16-18 . . . . Norfolk
19-22 . . . . Durham
24-26 . . . . at Louisville
27-29 . . . . . at Indianapolis
30-31 . . . . . . Lehigh Valley

AUGUST
1-2 . . . . Lehigh Valley
3-5 . . . . . . at Scranton/WB
7-9 . . . . Gwinnett
10-12 . . . . Toledo
13-15 . . . . at Charlotte
16-19 . . . . at Gwinnett
21-23 . . . . . . Scranton/WB
24-27 . . . . Pawtucket
28-30 . . . . . . at Rochester
31 . . . . at Syracuse

SEPTEMBER
1-3 . . . . at Syracuse

CHARLOTTE KNIGHTS

APRIL
5-8 . . . . at Durham
9-11 . . . . at Norfolk
12-15 . . . . . . Scranton/WB
16-18 . . . . Rochester
20-22 . . . . . at Indianapolis
23-25 . . . . at Louisville
27-29 . . . . Norfolk
30 . . . . Gwinnett

MAY
1-2 . . . . Gwinnett
3-6 . . . . at Columbus
7-10 . . . . at Gwinnett
11-13 . . . . Durham
15-17 . . . . at Toledo
18-20 . . . . at Columbus
21-24 . . . . Norfolk
25-28 . . . . Indianapolis
29-31 . . . . at Lehigh Valley

JUNE
1-3 . . . . at Buffalo
5-7 . . . . Syracuse
8-10 . . . . Lehigh Valley
12-13 . . . . at Durham
14-17 . . . . at Norfolk
19-21 . . . . Columbus
22-24 . . . . Toledo
25-27 . . . . at Durham
28-30 . . . . Gwinnett

JULY
1 . . . . Gwinnett
2-3 . . . . at Norfolk
4-5 . . . . Durham
6-8 . . . . at Gwinnett
12-15 . . . . at Durham
16-19 . . . . Pawtucket
20-22 . . . . Indianapolis
24-26 . . . . at Scranton/WB
27-29 . . . . at Pawtucket
30-31 . . . . Norfolk

AUGUST
1-2 . . . . Norfolk
3-5 . . . . Durham
7-9 . . . . at Syracuse
10-12 . . . . at Rochester
13-15 . . . . Buffalo
16-19 . . . . Louisville
21-23 . . . . at Norfolk
24-27 . . . . Gwinnett
28-30 . . . . Durham
31 . . . . at Gwinnett

SEPTEMBER
1-3 . . . . at Gwinnett

COLUMBUS CLIPPERS

APRIL
6-8 . . . . at Indianapolis
9-11 . . . . at Louisville
12-15 . . . . Durham
16-18 . . . . Pawtucket
20-22 . . . . at Rochester
23-25 . . . . at Scranton/WB
27-29 . . . . Indianapolis
30 . . . . at Louisville

MAY
1-2 . . . . at Louisville
3-6 . . . . Charlotte
7-10 . . . . at Toledo
11-13 . . . . . at Indianapolis
15-17 . . . . Gwinnett
18-20 . . . . Charlotte
21-24 . . . . Toledo
25-28 . . . . at Gwinnett
29-31 . . . . at Buffalo

JUNE
1-3 . . . . at Syracuse
5-7 . . . . Norfolk
8-10 . . . . Buffalo
11-14 . . . . at Louisville
15-17 . . . . Indianapolis
19-21 . . . . at Charlotte
22-24 . . . . at Gwinnett
25-27 . . . . Louisville
28-30 . . . . Indianapolis

JULY
1 . . . . Indianapolis
2-3 . . . . at Toledo
4-5 . . . . Toledo
6-8 . . . . at Indianapolis
12-15 . . . . at Louisville
16-18 . . . . . . Lehigh Valley
19-22 . . . . . . Scranton/WB
24-26 . . . . at Pawtucket
27-29 . . . . at Lehigh Valley
30-31 . . . . Indianapolis

AUGUST
1 . . . . Indianapolis
2-5 . . . . Louisville
7-9 . . . . at Durham
10-12 . . . . at Norfolk
13-15 . . . . Rochester
16-19 . . . . Syracuse
21-23 . . . . . at Indianapolis
24-27 . . . . at Toledo
28-30 . . . . Louisville
31 . . . . Toledo

SEPTEMBER
1-3 . . . . Toledo

DURHAM BULLS

APRIL
5-8 . . . . Charlotte
9-11 . . . . Gwinnett
12-15 . . . . . . at Columbus
16-18 . . . . at Toledo
20-22 . . . . . . Lehigh Valley
23-25 . . . . Buffalo
27-29 . . . . at Gwinnett
30 . . . . at Norfolk

MAY
1-2 . . . . at Norfolk
3-6 . . . . Toledo
7-10 . . . . Norfolk
11-13 . . . . at Charlotte
15-17 . . . . Louisville
18-20 . . . . Indianapolis
21-24 . . . . at Gwinnett
25-28 . . . . at Louisville
29-31 . . . . Rochester

JUNE
1-3 . . . . Pawtucket
5-7 . . . . . . at Scranton/WB
8-10 . . . . at Rochester
12-13 . . . . Charlotte
14-17 . . . . Gwinnett
19-21 . . . . at Louisville
22-24 . . . . . at Indianapolis
25-27 . . . . Charlotte
28-30 . . . . at Norfolk

JULY
1 . . . . at Norfolk
2-3 . . . . Gwinnett
4-5 . . . . at Charlotte
6-8 . . . . Norfolk
12-15 . . . . Charlotte
16-18 . . . . at Syracuse
19-22 . . . . at Buffalo
24-26 . . . . Toledo
27-29 . . . . Syracuse
30-31 . . . . at Gwinnett

AUGUST
1-2 . . . . at Gwinnett
3-5 . . . . at Charlotte
7-9 . . . . Columbus
10-12 . . . . Scranton/WB
13-15 . . . . at Lehigh Valley
16-19 . . . . at Pawtucket
21-23 . . . . Gwinnett
24-27 . . . . at Norfolk
28-30 . . . . at Charlotte
31 . . . . Norfolk

SEPTEMBER
1-3 . . . . Norfolk

GWINNETT STRIPERS

APRIL
6-8 . . . . at Norfolk
9-11 . . . . at Durham
12-15 . . . . Rochester
16-18 . . . . . . Scranton/WB
20-22 . . . . at Pawtucket
23-25 . . . . at Rochester
27-29 . . . . Durham
30 . . . . at Charlotte

MAY
1-2 . . . . at Charlotte
3-6 . . . . at Indianapolis
7-10 . . . . Charlotte
11-13 . . . . Norfolk
15-17 . . . . at Columbus
18-20 . . . . at Toledo
21-24 . . . . Durham
25-28 . . . . Columbus
29-31 . . . . . at Indianapolis

JUNE
1-3 . . . . at Louisville
5-7 . . . . Lehigh Valley
8-10 . . . . Syracuse
11-13 . . . . at Norfolk
14-17 . . . . at Durham
19-21 . . . . Toledo
22-24 . . . . Columbus
25-27 . . . . at Norfolk
28-30 . . . . at Charlotte

JULY	**AUGUST**
1 . . . . at Charlotte	1-2 . . . . Durham
2-3 . . . . .at Durham	3-5 . . . . .Norfolk
4-5 . . . . .Norfolk	7-9 . . . . at Buffalo
6-8 . . . . Charlotte	10-12 . . . . . . at Syracuse
12-15 . . . . at Norfolk	13-15 . . . . Louisville
16-19 . . . . . .Indianapolis	16-19 . . . . Buffalo
20-22 . . . . Pawtucket	21-23 . . . . . . .at Durham
24-26 . . . . at Lehigh Valley	24-27 . . . . . .at Charlotte
27-29 . . . . at Scranton/WB	28-30 . . . . .Norfolk
30-31 . . . . Durham	31 . . . . Charlotte
	SEPTEMBER
	1-3 . . . . Charlotte

INDIANAPOLIS INDIANS

APRIL	28-30 . . . . . . at Columbus
6-8 . . . . .Columbus	**JULY**
9-11 . . . . Toledo	1 . . . . at Columbus
12-15 . . . . at Buffalo	2-3 . . . . at Louisville
16-18 . . . . . . at Syracuse	4-5 . . . . Louisville
20-22 . . . . Charlotte	6-8 . . . . Columbus
23-25 . . . . Syracuse	12-15 . . . . Toledo
27-29 . . . . at Columbus	16-19 . . . . . at Gwinnett
30 . . . . .at Toledo	20-22 . . . . . at Charlotte
MAY	24-26 . . . . Rochester
1-2 . . . . .at Toledo	27-29 . . . . Buffalo
3-6 . . . . Gwinnett	30-31 . . . . at Columbus
7-10 . . . . . . .at Louisville	**AUGUST**
11-13 . . . . .Columbus	1 . . . . at Columbus
15-17 . . . . at Norfolk	2-5 . . . . .at Toledo
18-20 . . . . . . .at Durham	7-9 . . . . . Lehigh Valley
21-24 . . . . . . Louisville	10-12 . . . . .Pawtucket
25-28 . . . . at Charlotte	13-15 . . . . at Scranton/WB
29-31 . . . . Gwinnett	16-19 . . . at Lehigh Valley
JUNE	21-23 . . . . Columbus
1-3 . . . . . . Scranton/WB	24-25 . . . . . at Louisville
5-7 . . . . . . at Rochester	26-27 . . . . Louisville
8-10 . . . . at Pawtucket	28-30 . . . . Toledo
11-14 . . . . Toledo	31 . . . . Louisville
15-17 . . . . at Columbus	**SEPTEMBER**
19-21 . . . . . . .Norfolk	1 . . . . Louisville
22-24 . . . . Durham	2-3 . . . . . . at Louisville
25-27 . . . . . . .at Toledo	

LEHIGH VALLEY IRONPIGS

APRIL	25-28 . . . . . Scranton/WB
6-8 . . . . at Pawtucket	29-30 . . . . . at Rochester
9-11 . . . . at Scranton/WB	**JULY**
12-15 . . . . Louisville	1 . . . . at Rochester
16-18 . . . . .Norfolk	2-3 . . . . Syracuse
20-22 . . . . . . .at Durham	4-5 . . . . . . at Syracuse
23-25 . . . . . at Norfolk	6-8 . . . . Rochester
27-29 . . . . . Scranton/WB	12-15 . . . . Buffalo
30 . . . . Syracuse	16-18 . . . . . at Columbus
MAY	19-22 . . . . . .at Toledo
1-2 . . . . Syracuse	24-26 . . . . Gwinnett
3-6 . . . . at Rochester	27-29 . . . . . . Columbus
7-9 . . . . .Pawtucket	30-31 . . . . at Buffalo
10-13 . . . . Buffalo	**AUGUST**
15-17 . . . . at Scranton/WB	1-2 . . . . at Buffalo
18-20 . . . . . at Syracuse	3-5 . . . . Syracuse
21-24 . . . . Rochester	7-9 . . . . . . at Indianapolis
25-28 . . . . . at Pawtucket	10-12 . . . . . .at Louisville
29-31 . . . . Charlotte	13-15 . . . . Durham
JUNE	16-19 . . . . . .Indianapolis
1-3 . . . . Toledo	21-23 . . . . . at Syracuse
5-7 . . . . . . .at Gwinnett	24-27 . . . . Scranton/WB
8-10 . . . . . .at Charlotte	28-30 . . . . . at Pawtucket
11-13 . . . . Buffalo	31 . . . . at Rochester
14-17 . . . . . .Pawtucket	**SEPTEMBER**
19-21 . . . at Scranton/WB	1-3 . . . . . . at Rochester
22-24 . . . . . at Buffalo	

LOUISVILLE BATS

APRIL	28-30 . . . . .at Toledo
6-8 . . . . Toledo	**JULY**
9-11 . . . . .Columbus	1 . . . . .at Toledo
12-15 . . . at Lehigh Valley	2-3 . . . . .Indianapolis
16-18 . . . . at Buffalo	4-5 . . . . . at Indianapolis
20-22 . . . . Syracuse	6-8 . . . . Toledo
23-25 . . . . Charlotte	12-15 . . . . .Columbus
27-29 . . . . . . .at Toledo	16-18 . . . . . at Rochester
30 . . . . .Columbus	19-22 . . . . . at Syracuse
MAY	24-26 . . . . Buffalo
1-2 . . . . .Columbus	27-29 . . . . Rochester
3-6 . . . . at Norfolk	30-31 . . . . . . .at Toledo
7-10 . . . . .Indianapolis	**AUGUST**
11-13 . . . . Toledo	1 . . . . .at Toledo
15-17 . . . . . .at Durham	2-5 . . . . at Columbus
18-20 . . . . . . at Norfolk	7-9 . . . . .Pawtucket
21-24 . . . . at Indianapolis	10-12 . . . . . Lehigh Valley
25-28 . . . . Durham	13-15 . . . . . .at Gwinnett
29-31 . . . . . . Scranton/WB	16-19 . . . . . .at Charlotte
JUNE	21-23 . . . . Toledo
1-3 . . . . Gwinnett	24-25 . . . . . . .Indianapolis
5-7 . . . . . . at Pawtucket	26-27 . . . . at Indianapolis
8-10 . . . . at Scranton/WB	28-30 . . . . at Columbus
11-14 . . . . .Columbus	31 . . . . . . at Indianapolis
15-17 . . . . . . .at Toledo	**SEPTEMBER**
19-21 . . . . Durham	1 . . . . at Indianapolis
22-24 . . . . . . .Norfolk	2-3 . . . . . . .Indianapolis
25-27 . . . . . at Columbus	

NORFOLK TIDES

APRIL	25-27 . . . . Gwinnett
6-8 . . . . Gwinnett	28-30 . . . . Durham
9-11 . . . . Charlotte	**JULY**
12-15 . . . . . at Syracuse	1 . . . . Durham
16-18 . . . at Lehigh Valley	2-3 . . . . Charlotte
20-22 . . . . Buffalo	4-5 . . . . .at Gwinnett
23-25 . . . . . Lehigh Valley	6-8 . . . . .at Durham
27-29 . . . . . .at Charlotte	12-15 . . . . Gwinnett
30 . . . . Durham	16-18 . . . . . . at Buffalo
MAY	19-22 . . . . at Rochester
1-2 . . . . Durham	24-26 . . . . Syracuse
3-6 . . . . Louisville	27-29 . . . . Toledo
7-10 . . . . . . .at Durham	30-31 . . . . . at Charlotte
11-13 . . . . . . at Gwinnett	**AUGUST**
15-17 . . . . . .Indianapolis	1-2 . . . . .at Charlotte
18-20 . . . . . . Louisville	3-5 . . . . at Gwinnett
21-24 . . . . at Charlotte	7-9 . . . . . Scranton/WB
25-28 . . . . . .at Toledo	10-12 . . . . Columbus
29-31 . . . . . .Pawtucket	13-15 . . . . . at Pawtucket
JUNE	16-19 . . . at Scranton/WB
1-3 . . . . Rochester	21-23 . . . . Charlotte
5-7 . . . . . . at Columbus	24-27 . . . . Durham
8-10 . . . . .at Toledo	28-30 . . . . at Gwinnett
11-13 . . . . Gwinnett	31 . . . . .at Durham
14-17 . . . . . . Charlotte	**SEPTEMBER**
19-21 . . . at Indianapolis	1-3 . . . . .at Durham
22-24 . . . . . at Louisville	

PAWTUCKET RED SOX

APRIL	**MAY**
6-8 . . . . Lehigh Valley	1-2 . . . . Rochester
9-11 . . . . Buffalo	3-4 . . . . . at Scranton/WB
12-15 . . . . . . .at Toledo	5-6 . . . . . . Scranton/WB
16-18 . . . . at Columbus	7-9 . . . . at Lehigh Valley
20-22 . . . . Gwinnett	10-13 . . . . at Syracuse
23-25 . . . . Toledo	14-16 . . . . Buffalo
27-29 . . . . . . at Buffalo	18-20 . . . . at Rochester
30 . . . . Rochester	21-24 . . . . . Scranton/WB
	25-28 . . . . . Lehigh Valley

29-31 . . . . at Norfolk

JUNE
1-3 . . . . .at Durham
5-7 . . . . Louisville
8-10 . . . . . . .Indianapolis
11-13 . . . . at Syracuse
14-17 . . . . at Lehigh Valley
19-21 . . . . Buffalo
22-24 . . . . Syracuse
25-28 . . . . . . at Buffalo
29-30 . . . . at Scranton/WB

JULY
1 . . . . . . at Scranton/WB
2-3 . . . . Rochester
4-5 . . . . . . at Rochester
6-8 . . . . . . Scranton/WB
12-15 . . . . Syracuse
16-19 . . . . . . at Charlotte

ROCHESTER RED WINGS

APRIL
6-8 . . . . Buffalo
9-11 . . . . Syracuse
12-15 . . . . at Gwinnett
16-18 . . . . . at Charlotte
20-22 . . . . . . Columbus
23-25 . . . . . Gwinnett
27-29 . . . . . at Syracuse
30 . . . . . . at Pawtucket

MAY
1-2 . . . . . . at Pawtucket
3-6 . . . . . . Lehigh Valley
7-9 . . . . at Buffalo
10-13 . . . at Scranton/WB
15-17 . . . . Syracuse
18-20 . . . . . . Pawtucket
21-24 . . . at Lehigh Valley
25-28 . . . . Buffalo
29-31 . . . . .at Durham

JUNE
1-3 . . . . at Norfolk
5-7 . . . . . .Indianapolis
8-10 . . . . Durham
11-13 . . . at Scranton/WB
14-17 . . . . . . at Buffalo
19-21 . . . . . . Syracuse
22-24 . . . . . Scranton/WB

SCRANTON/WILKES-BARRE RAILRIDERS

APRIL
6-8 . . . . Syracuse
9-11 . . . . . . Lehigh Valley
12-15 . . . . . at Charlotte
16-18 . . . . . at Gwinnett
20-22 . . . . Toledo
23-25 . . . . . . Columbus
27-29 . . at Lehigh Valley
30 . . . . Buffalo

MAY
1-2 . . . . Buffalo
3-4 . . . . . . Pawtucket
5-6 . . . . . at Pawtucket
7-9 . . . . . at Syracuse
10-13 . . . . . Rochester
15-17 . . . . Lehigh Valley
18-20 . . . . . . at Buffalo
21-24 . . . at Pawtucket
25-28 . . . . Syracuse
29-31 . . . . . .at Louisville

JUNE
1-3 . . . . . at Indianapolis

20-22 . . . . . .at Gwinnett
24-26 . . . . Columbus
27-29 . . . . . . Charlotte
30-31 . . . . . . at Syracuse

AUGUST
1-2 . . . . . . at Syracuse
3-5 . . . . Rochester
7-9 . . . . . . .at Louisville
10-12 . . . at Indianapolis
13-15 . . . . .Norfolk
16-19 . . . . Durham
21-23 . . . . . at Rochester
24-27 . . . . . at Buffalo
28-30 . . . . . Lehigh Valley
31 . . . . . at Scranton/WB

SEPTEMBER
1 . . . . . . at Scranton/WB
2-3 . . . . . . Scranton/WB

25-28 . . . . . . at Syracuse
29-30 . . . . . Lehigh Valley

JULY
1 . . . . Lehigh Valley
2-3 . . . . . at Pawtucket
4-5 . . . . .Pawtucket
6-8 . . . . . at Lehigh Valley
12-15 . . . at Scranton/WB
16-18 . . . . Louisville
19-22 . . . . . . .Norfolk
24-26 . . . at Indianapolis
27-29 . . . . .at Louisville
30-31 . . . . . Scranton/WB

AUGUST
1-2 . . . . Scranton/WB
3-5 . . . . . at Pawtucket
7-9 . . . . Toledo
10-12 . . . . Charlotte
13-15 . . . . . at Columbus
16-19 . . . . . .at Toledo
21-23 . . . . . . .Pawtucket
24-27 . . . . at Syracuse
28-30 . . . . Buffalo
31 . . . . Lehigh Valley

SEPTEMBER
1-3 . . . . . . Lehigh Valley

5-7 . . . . Durham
8-10 . . . . Louisville
11-13 . . . . Rochester
14-17 . . . . . at Syracuse
19-21 . . . . . Lehigh Valley
22-24 . . . . . at Rochester
25-28 . . . at Lehigh Valley
29-30 . . . . . . .Pawtucket

JULY
1 . . . . .Pawtucket
2-3 . . . . at Buffalo
4-5 . . . . Buffalo
6-8 . . . . . at Pawtucket
12-15 . . . . Rochester
16-18 . . . . . .at Toledo
19-22 . . . . . at Columbus
24-26 . . . . . . Charlotte
27-29 . . . . . Gwinnett
30-31 . . . . . at Rochester

AUGUST
1-2 . . . . . . at Rochester
3-5 . . . . Buffalo

7-9 . . . . at Norfolk
10-12 . . . . .at Durham
13-15 . . . . . .Indianapolis
16-19 . . . . . .Norfolk
21-23 . . . . . at Buffalo
24-27 . . . at Lehigh Valley

SYRACUSE CHIEFS

APRIL
6-8 . . . . . at Scranton/WB
9-11 . . . . . . at Rochester
12-15 . . . . . . .Norfolk
16-18 . . . . . .Indianapolis
20-22 . . . . .at Louisville
23-25 . . . at Indianapolis
27-29 . . . . . . Rochester
30 . . . . . at Lehigh Valley

MAY
1-2 . . . . at Lehigh Valley
3-6 . . . . at Buffalo
7-9 . . . . . . Scranton/WB
10-13 . . . . . . .Pawtucket
15-17 . . . . . at Rochester
18-20 . . . . . Lehigh Valley
21-24 . . . . . at Buffalo
25-28 . . . at Scranton/WB
29-31 . . . . Toledo

JUNE
1-3 . . . . Columbus
5-7 . . . . . .at Charlotte
8-10 . . . . . .at Gwinnett
11-13 . . . . .Pawtucket
14-17 . . . . . Scranton/WB
19-21 . . . . at Rochester
22-24 . . . . . at Pawtucket

TOLEDO MUD HENS

APRIL
6-8 . . . . .at Louisville
9-11 . . . . at Indianapolis
12-15 . . . . . . .Pawtucket
16-18 . . . . Durham
20-22 . . . at Scranton/WB
23-25 . . . . at Pawtucket
27-29 . . . . . Louisville
30 . . . . .Indianapolis

MAY
1-2 . . . . .Indianapolis
3-6 . . . . .at Durham
7-10 . . . . Columbus
11-13 . . . . . .at Louisville
15-17 . . . . . . Charlotte
18-20 . . . . . . Gwinnett
21-24 . . . . at Columbus
25-28 . . . . . .Norfolk
29-31 . . . . . at Syracuse

JUNE
1-3 . . . . at Lehigh Valley
5-7 . . . . Buffalo
8-10 . . . . Norfolk
11-14 . . . at Indianapolis
15-17 . . . . . Louisville
19-21 . . . .at Gwinnett
22-24 . . . . . .at Charlotte

28-30 . . . . Syracuse
31 . . . . .Pawtucket

SEPTEMBER
1 . . . . .Pawtucket
2-3 . . . . at Pawtucket

25-28 . . . . . . Rochester
29-30 . . . . Buffalo

JULY
1 . . . . Buffalo
2-3 . . . . at Lehigh Valley
4-5 . . . . . . Lehigh Valley
6-8 . . . . at Buffalo
12-15 . . . . at Pawtucket
16-18 . . . . Durham
19-22 . . . . . . Louisville
24-26 . . . . at Norfolk
27-29 . . . . . . .at Durham
30-31 . . . . . . .Pawtucket

AUGUST
1-2 . . . . .Pawtucket
3-5 . . . . . at Lehigh Valley
7-9 . . . . Charlotte
10-12 . . . . . . Gwinnett
13-15 . . . . . . .at Toledo
16-19 . . . . . at Columbus
21-23 . . . . . Lehigh Valley
24-27 . . . . . . Rochester
28-30 . . . . at Scranton/WB
31 . . . . Buffalo

SEPTEMBER
1-3 . . . . Buffalo

25-27 . . . . . .Indianapolis
28-30 . . . . Louisville

JULY
1 . . . . Louisville
2-3 . . . . Columbus
4-5 . . . . . at Columbus
6-8 . . . . . . .at Louisville
12-15 . . . . .at Indianapolis
16-18 . . . . Scranton/WB
19-22 . . . . Lehigh Valley
24-26 . . . . . .at Durham
27-29 . . . . at Norfolk
30-31 . . . . Louisville

AUGUST
1 . . . . Louisville
2-5 . . . . . . .Indianapolis
7-9 . . . . at Rochester
10-12 . . . . . at Buffalo
13-15 . . . . Syracuse
16-19 . . . . . . Rochester
21-23 . . . . .at Louisville
24-27 . . . . . Columbus
28-30 . . . . at Indianapolis
31 . . . . at Columbus

SEPTEMBER
1-3 . . . . at Columbus

PACIFIC COAST LEAGUE

ALBUQUERQUE ISOTOPES

APRIL
5-9 . . . . at Salt Lake
10-12 . . . . Las Vegas
13-16 . . . . Salt Lake
17-20 . . . . at Tacoma
21-23 . . . . . at Salt Lake
25-29 . . . . . Las Vegas
30 . . . . at Tacoma

MAY
1-3 . . . . at Tacoma
4-7 . . . . El Paso
8-11 . . . . at Reno
12-15 . . . . .at Las Vegas
17-20 . . . . Reno
21-24 . . . . Salt Lake
25-29 . . . at Sacramento
30-31 . . . . Fresno

JUNE
1-3 . . . . Fresno
5-7 . . . . .at Iowa
8-11 . . . . . at Omaha
13-15 . . . . . Memphis
16-19 . . . . . .Nashville

21-23 . . . . .at Fresno
25-28 . . . . . . .Sacramento
29-30 . . . . at El Paso

JULY
1-3 . . . . at El Paso
4-8 . . . . .Tacoma
12-15 . . . .at Las Vegas
16-19 . . . . El Paso
20-22 . . . . Fresno
24-26 . . . at Oklahoma City
27-30 . .at Colorado Springs

AUGUST
1-3 . . . . .Round Rock
4-7 . . . . New Orleans
9-12 . . . . . . .at Fresno
13-15 . . . . .Tacoma
16-19 . . . . . . .Sacramento
21-23 . . . . . at El Paso
24-27 . . . . Reno
28-30 . . . . at Sacramento
31 . . . . .at Reno

SEPTEMBER
1-3 . . . . .at Reno

COLORADO SPRINGS SKY SOX

APRIL
5-9 . . . . at Omaha
10-12 . . . New Orleans
13-16 . . . . . .Round Rock
17-20 . . .at New Orleans
21-23 . . at Round Rock
25-29 . . . . . . .Omaha
30 . . . . .Nashville

MAY
1-3 . . . . .Nashville
4-7 . . . . at Oklahoma City
8-11 . . . . . at Nashville
12-15 . . . Oklahoma City
17-20 . . . . Memphis
21-24 . . . . at Nashville
25-29 . . . . .at Memphis
30-31 . . . . Iowa

JUNE
1-3 . . . . Iowa
5-7 . . . . at Fresno
8-11 . . . . . at Sacramento
13-15 . . . . . . Las Vegas
16-19 . . . . Salt Lake

21-24 . . . . .at Iowa
25-28 . . . . . . Memphis
29-30 . . . at Round Rock

JULY
1-3 . . . . . . at Round Rock
4-8 . . . . New Orleans
12-15 . . . .at New Orleans
16-19 . . . . .Round Rock
20-22 . . . . at Memphis
24-26 . . . . . . El Paso
27-30 . . . . . Albuquerque

AUGUST
1-3 . . . . .at Reno
4-7 . . . . at Tacoma
9-12 . . . . . . .Nashville
14-16 . . . . . . at Iowa
17-19 . . . . . .Omaha
21-23 . . . . Iowa
24-27 . . at Oklahoma City
28-30 . . . . . at Omaha
31 . . . . . . Oklahoma City

SEPTEMBER
1-3 . . . . . Oklahoma City

EL PASO CHIHUAHUAS

APRIL
5-9 . . . . .at Las Vegas
10-12 . . . . Salt Lake
13-16 . . . . . Las Vegas
17-20 . . . . .at Reno
21-23 . . . . .at Las Vegas
25-29 . . . . Salt Lake
30 . . . . Reno

MAY
1-3 . . . . Reno
4-7 . . . . . at Albuquerque
8-11 . . . . .Tacoma
12-15 . . . . .at Reno
17-20 . . . . Fresno
21-24 . . . . at Tacoma

25-29 . . . . . . .at Fresno
30-31 . . . . . .Sacramento

JUNE
1-3 . . . . .Sacramento
5-7 . . . . at Omaha
8-11 . . . . at Iowa
13-15 . . . . . . .Nashville
16-19 . . . . . Memphis
21-24 . . . . at Sacramento
25-28 . . . . . . Fresno
29-30 . . . . . Albuquerque

JULY
1-3 . . . . Albuquerque
4-8 . . . . at Salt Lake
12-15 . . . . Reno

16-19 . . . . at Albuquerque
20-22 . . . . . . .Sacramento
24-26 . .at Colorado Springs
27-30 . . . at Oklahoma City

AUGUST
1-3 . . . . New Orleans
4-7 . . . . .Round Rock
9-12 . . . . . . at Sacramento

FRESNO GRIZZLIES

APRIL
5-9 . . . . .at Reno
10-12 . . . . .Tacoma
13-16 . . . . Reno
17-20 . . . .at Las Vegas
21-23 . . . . .at Reno
25-29 . . . . .Tacoma
30 . . . . at Salt Lake

MAY
1-3 . . . . . at Salt Lake
4-7 . . . . .Sacramento
8-11 . . . . .at Las Vegas
12-15 . . . . . . .Salt Lake
17-20 . . . . at El Paso
21-24 . . . . Reno
25-29 . . . . . El Paso
30-31 . . . at Albuquerque

JUNE
1-3 . . . . . at Albuquerque
5-7 . . . . Colorado Springs
8-11 . . . .Oklahoma City
13-15 . . . .at New Orleans
16-19 . . . . at Round Rock

21-23 . . . . . Albuquerque
25-28 . . . . . at El Paso
29-30 . . . . at Sacramento

JULY
1-3 . . . . . at Sacramento
4-7 . . . . Las Vegas
12-15 . . . . . at Tacoma
16-19 . . . . . .Sacramento
20-22 . . . . at Albuquerque
24-26 . . . . Iowa
27-30 . . . . . . .Omaha

AUGUST
1-3 . . . . at Nashville
4-7 . . . . .at Memphis
9-12 . . . . . . Albuquerque
13-15 . . . . . Las Vegas
16-19 . . . . . at Tacoma
21-23 . . . . at Sacramento
24-27 . . . . . . .Salt Lake
28-30 . . . . El Paso
31 . . . . at Salt Lake

SEPTEMBER
1-3 . . . . at Salt Lake

IOWA CUBS

APRIL
5-9 . . . . . .Oklahoma City
10-12 . . . . . at Nashville
13-16 . . . . .at Memphis
17-20 . . . . .Nashville
21-23 . . . . . . Memphis
25-29 . . at Oklahoma City
30 . . . . .Omaha

MAY
1-3 . . . . .Omaha
4-7 . . . . . . at Round Rock
8-11 . . . . . . at Omaha
12-15 . . . . . .Round Rock
17-20 . . . . .Omaha
21-24 . . . . at Round Rock
25-29 . . . New Orleans
30-31 . .at Colorado Springs

JUNE
1-3 . . . .at Colorado Springs
5-7 . . . . Albuquerque
8-11 . . . . El Paso
13-15 . . . . .at Reno
16-19 . . . . at Tacoma

21-24 . . . Colorado Springs
25-28 . . . .at New Orleans
29-30 . . . . Memphis

JULY
1-3 . . . . Memphis
4-8 . . . . . . at Nashville
12-15 . . . . . . .Nashville
16-19 . . . . . .at Memphis
20-22 . . . . . New Orleans
24-26 . . . . . .at Fresno
27-30 . . . . . at Sacramento

AUGUST
1-3 . . . . Salt Lake 4-7
Las Vegas
9-12 . . . . .at New Orleans
14-16 . . . Colorado Springs
17-19 . . at Oklahoma City
21-23 . .at Colorado Springs
24-27 . . . . at Omaha
28-30 . . . Oklahoma City
31 . . . . .Round Rock

SEPTEMBER
1-3 . . . . .Round Rock

LAS VEGAS 51S

APRIL
5-9 . . . . El Paso
10-12 . . . at Albuquerque
13-16 . . . . at El Paso
17-20 . . . . Fresno
21-23 . . . . . . El Paso
25-29 . . at Albuquerque
30 . . . . . . .Sacramento

MAY
1-3 . . . . .Sacramento
4-7 . . . . . . at Salt Lake
8-11 . . . . Fresno
12-15 . . . . . Albuquerque
17-20 . . . . . . at Tacoma
21-24 . . . at Sacramento
25-29 . . . . .Tacoma

30-31 . . . . .at Reno

JUNE
1-3 . . . . .at Reno
5-7 . . . . . . New Orleans
8-11 . . . . . . .Round Rock
13-15 . .at Colorado Springs
16-19 . . . at Oklahoma City
21-24 . . . . Reno
25-28 . . . . . at Tacoma
29-30 . . . . . . .Salt Lake

JULY
1-3 . . . . .Salt Lake
4-7 . . . . .at Fresno
12-15 . . . . . Albuquerque
16-19 . . . . at Salt Lake

MEMPHIS REDBIRDS

APRIL
5-9 . . . . . . at Round Rock
10-12 . . . . .Omaha
13-16 . . . . Iowa
17-20 . . . . at Omaha
21-23 . . . . . . .at Iowa
25-29 . . . .Round Rock
30 . . . . . . Oklahoma City

MAY
1-3 . . . . . . Oklahoma City
4-7 . . . . at Nashville
8-11 . . . . at Oklahoma City
12-15 . . . . . . .Nashville
17-20 . .at Colorado Springs
21-24 . . . .Oklahoma City
25-29 . . . Colorado Springs
30-31 . . . .at New Orleans

JUNE
1-3 . . . . . .at New Orleans
5-7 . . . . .Tacoma
8-11 . . . . Reno
13-15 . . . . at Albuquerque
16-19 . . . . . at El Paso

NASHVILLE SOUNDS

APRIL
5-9 . . . . . .at New Orleans
10-12 . . . . Iowa
13-16 . . . . .Omaha
17-20 . . . . .at Iowa
21-23 . . . . . . at Omaha
25-29 . . . . . New Orleans
30 . . . .at Colorado Springs

MAY
1-3 . . .at Colorado Springs
4-7 . . . . Memphis
8-11 . . . . Colorado Springs
12-15 . . . . . .at Memphis
17-20 . . . at Oklahoma City
21-24 . . . Colorado Springs
25-29 . . . .Oklahoma City
30-31 . . . at Round Rock

JUNE
1-3 . . . . . . at Round Rock
5-7 . . . . Reno
8-11 . . . . .Tacoma
13-15 . . . . . . at El Paso
16-19 . . . . at Albuquerque

20-22 . . . . .at Reno
24-26 . . . . .Nashville
27-30 . . . . Memphis

AUGUST
1-3 . . . . at Omaha
4-7 . . . . .at Iowa
9-12 . . . . Reno
13-15 . . . . .at Fresno
16-19 . . . . . . at El Paso
21-23 . . . . .Salt Lake
24-27 . . . . at Sacramento
28-30 . . . . .Tacoma
31 . . . . .Sacramento

SEPTEMBER
1-3 . . . . .Sacramento

21-24 . . . . . New Orleans
25-28 . .at Colorado Springs
29-30 . . . . .at Iowa

JULY
1-3 . . . . .at Iowa
4-8 . . . . .Omaha
12-15 . . . . . . at Omaha
16-19 . . . . Iowa
20-22 . . . Colorado Springs
24-26 . . . . . . at Salt Lake
27-30 . . . . . .at Las Vegas

AUGUST
1-3 . . . . .Sacramento
4-7 . . . . Fresno
9-12 . . . at Oklahoma City
13-16 . . . . . New Orleans
17-19 . . . . . .Round Rock
21-23 . . . .at New Orleans
24-27 . . . . .Nashville
28-30 . . . . at Round Rock
31 . . . . at Nashville

SEPTEMBER
1-3 . . . . at Nashville

21-24 . . . . . .Round Rock
25-28 . . . at Oklahoma City
29-30 . . . . at Omaha

JULY
1-3 . . . . at Omaha
4-8 . . . . Iowa
12-15 . . . . .at Iowa
16-19 . . . . .Omaha
20-22 . . . . .Oklahoma City
24-26 . . . . . .at Las Vegas
27-30 . . . . . . at Salt Lake

AUGUST
1-3 . . . . Fresno
4-7 . . . . .Sacramento
9-12 . . .at Colorado Springs
13-16 . . . . . .Round Rock
17-19 . . . . . New Orleans
21-23 . . . . at Round Rock
24-27 . . . . at Memphis
28-30 . . . .at New Orleans
31 . . . . Memphis

SEPTEMBER
1-3 . . . . Memphis

NEW ORLEANS BABY CAKES

APRIL
5-9 . . . . .Nashville
10-12 . .at Colorado Springs
13-16 . . at Oklahoma City
17-20 . . . Colorado Springs
21-23 . . . .Oklahoma City
25-29 . . . . . at Nashville
30 . . . . .Round Rock

MAY
1-3 . . . . . . .Round Rock
4-7 . . . . at Omaha
8-11 . . . at Round Rock
12-15 . . . . .Omaha
17-20 . . . . .Round Rock
21-24 . . . . . . at Omaha
25-29 . . . . . . .at Iowa
30-31 . . . . . Memphis

JUNE
1-3 . . . . Memphis
5-7 . . . .at Las Vegas
8-11 . . . at Salt Lake
13-15 . . . . . . Fresno
16-19 . . . . . .Sacramento

21-24 . . . . . . at Memphis
25-28 . . . . Iowa
29-30 . . . . .Oklahoma City

JULY
1-3 . . . . . .Oklahoma City
4-8 . . . .at Colorado Springs
12-15 . . . Colorado Springs
16-19 . . at Oklahoma City
20-22 . . . . .at Iowa
24-26 . . . . Reno
27-30 . . . . .Tacoma

AUGUST
1-3 . . . . at El Paso
4-7 . . . . at Albuquerque
9-12 . . . . Iowa
13-16 . . . . . .at Memphis
17-19 . . . . at Nashville
21-23 . . . . . . Memphis
24-27 . . . . at Round Rock
28-30 . . . . . . .Nashville
31 . . . . .Omaha

SEPTEMBER
1-3 . . . . .Omaha

OKLAHOMA CITY DODGERS

APRIL
5-9 . . . . .at Iowa
10-12 . . . . . .Round Rock
13-16 . . . . . New Orleans
17-20 . . . . at Round Rock
21-23 . . .at New Orleans
25-29 . . . . Iowa
30 . . . . at Memphis

MAY
1-3 . . . . at Memphis
4-7 . . . . Colorado Springs
8-11 . . . . Memphis
12-15 . .at Colorado Springs
17-20 . . . . .Nashville
21-24 . . . . . at Memphis
25-29 . . . . at Nashville
30-31 . . . . .Omaha

JUNE
1-3 . . . . .Omaha
5-7 . . . . . . at Sacramento
8-11 . . . . . . .at Fresno
13-15 . . . . . .Salt Lake
16-19 . . . . . . Las Vegas

21-24 . . . . at Omaha
25-28 . . . . .Nashville
29-30 . . .at New Orleans

JULY
1-3 . . . . .at New Orleans
4-8 . . . . .Round Rock
12-15 . . . at Round Rock
16-19 . . . . . New Orleans
20-22 . . . . . . at Nashville
24-26 . . . . . Albuquerque
27-30 . . . . El Paso

AUGUST
1-3 . . . . at Tacoma
4-7 . . . . .at Reno
9-12 . . . . Memphis
13-16 . . . . . at Omaha
17-19 . . . . Iowa
21-23 . . . . .Omaha
24-27 . . . Colorado Springs
28-30 . . . . .at Iowa
31 . . . .at Colorado Springs

SEPTEMBER
1-3 . . . .at Colorado Springs

OMAHA STORM CHASERS

APRIL
5-9 . . . . . Colorado Springs
10-12 . . . . . . .at Memphis
13-16 . . . . . at Nashville
17-20 . . . . Memphis
21-23 . . . . .Nashville
25-29 . .at Colorado Springs
30 . . . . .at Iowa

MAY
1-3 . . . . .at Iowa
4-7 . . . . New Orleans
8-11 . . . . Iowa
12-15 . . . . .at New Orleans
17-20 . . . . .at Iowa
21-24 . . . . . New Orleans
25-29 . . . . . .Round Rock
30-31 . . . at Oklahoma City

JUNE
1-3 . . . . at Oklahoma City
5-7 . . . . El Paso
8-11 . . . . . . Albuquerque
13-15 . . . . . at Tacoma
16-19 . . . . .at Reno
21-24 . . . .Oklahoma City
25-28 . . . at Round Rock
29-30 . . . . .Nashville

JULY
1-3 . . . . .Nashville
4-8 . . . . .at Memphis
12-15 . . . . Memphis
16-19 . . . . at Nashville
20-22 . . . . . .Round Rock
24-26 . . . . . at Sacramento
27-30 . . . . .at Fresno

AUGUST
1-3 . . . . Las Vegas
4-7 . . . . .Salt Lake
9-12 . . . . . at Round Rock
13-16 . . . . .Oklahoma City
17-19 . .at Colorado Springs

RENO ACES

APRIL
5-9 . . . . Fresno
10-12 . . . at Sacramento
13-16 . . . . .at Fresno
17-20 . . . . El Paso
21-23 . . . . Fresno
25-29 . . . . at Sacramento
30 . . . . at El Paso

MAY
1-3 . . . . at El Paso
4-7 . . . . .Tacoma
8-11 . . . . . Albuquerque
12-15 . . . . El Paso
17-20 . . at Albuquerque
21-24 . . . . . . .at Fresno
25-29 . . . . at Salt Lake
30-31 . . . . . Las Vegas

JUNE
1-3 . . . . Las Vegas
5-7 . . . . at Nashville
8-11 . . . . . .at Memphis
13-15 . . . . Iowa
16-19 . . . . Omaha

ROUND ROCK EXPRESS

APRIL
5-9 . . . . Memphis
10-12 . . . at Oklahoma City
13-16 . .at Colorado Springs
17-20 . .Oklahoma City
21-23 . . . Colorado Springs
25-29 . . . . . .at Memphis
30 . . . . . .at New Orleans

MAY
1-3 . . . . .at New Orleans
4-7 . . . . Iowa
8-11 . . . . . . New Orleans
12-15 . . . . .at Iowa
17-20 . . .at New Orleans
21-24 . . . . Iowa
25-29 . . . . at Omaha
30-31 . . . . . . .Nashville

JUNE
1-3 . . . . .Nashville
5-7 . . . . at Salt Lake
8-11 . . .at Las Vegas
13-15 . . .Sacramento
16-19 . . . . Fresno

SACRAMENTO RIVER CATS

APRIL
5-9 . . . . at Tacoma
10-12 . . . . Reno
13-16 . . . . .Tacoma
17-20 . . . at Salt Lake
21-23 . . . . . . at Tacoma
25-29 . . . . Reno
30 . . . . . . .at Las Vegas

21-23 . . . at Oklahoma City
24-27 . . . . Iowa
28-30 . . . Colorado Springs
31 . . . . . .at New Orleans

SEPTEMBER
1-3 . . . . . .at New Orleans

21-24 . . . . .at Las Vegas
25-28 . . . . .Salt Lake
29-30 . . . . . . at Tacoma

JULY
1-3 . . . . at Tacoma
4-8 . . . . .Sacramento
12-15 . . . . . . at El Paso
16-19 . . . . .Tacoma
20-22 . . . . Las Vegas
24-26 . . . .at New Orleans
27-30 . . . . at Round Rock

AUGUST
1-3 . . . . . . Colorado Springs
4-7 . . . . . .Oklahoma City
9-12 . . . . .at Las Vegas
13-15 . . . . . .Sacramento
16-19 . . . . .Salt Lake
21-23 . . . . . . at Tacoma
24-27 . . . at Albuquerque
28-30 . . . . at Salt Lake
31 . . . . Albuquerque

SEPTEMBER
1-3 . . . . Albuquerque

21-24 . . . . . . at Nashville
25-28 . . . . Omaha
29-30 . . . Colorado Springs

JULY
1-3 . . . . . . Colorado Springs
4-8 . . . . . at Oklahoma City
12-15 . . . .Oklahoma City
16-19 . .at Colorado Springs
20-22 . . . . at Omaha
24-26 . . . . .Tacoma
27-30 . . . . Reno

AUGUST
1-3 . . . . . at Albuquerque
4-7 . . . . at El Paso
9-12 . . . . Omaha
13-16 . . . . . . at Nashville
17-19 . . . . .at Memphis
21-23 . . . . .Nashville
24-27 . . . . . New Orleans
28-30 . . . . . . Memphis
31 . . . . .at Iowa

SEPTEMBER
1-3 . . . . .at Iowa

MAY
1-3 . . . . . . .at Las Vegas
4-7 . . . . .at Fresno
8-11 . . . . .Salt Lake
12-15 . . . . .Tacoma
17-20 . . . . . . at Salt Lake
21-24 . . . . . . Las Vegas
25-29 . . . . . Albuquerque
30-31 . . . . at El Paso

JUNE
1-3 . . . . at El Paso
5-7 . . . . . .Oklahoma City
8-11 . . . . Colorado Springs
13-15 . . . . at Round Rock
16-19 . . . .at New Orleans
21-24 . . . . El Paso
25-28 . . . at Albuquerque
29-30 . . . . Fresno

JULY
1-3 . . . . Fresno
4-8 . . . . at Reno
12-15 . . . . . . .Salt Lake
16-19 . . . . . . .at Fresno
20-22 . . . . . at El Paso

SALT LAKE BEES

APRIL
5-9 . . . . Albuquerque
10-12 . . . . . at El Paso
13-16 . . . . at Albuquerque
17-20 . . . . . . .Sacramento
21-23 . . . . Albuquerque
25-29 . . . . . at El Paso
30 . . . . Fresno

MAY
1-3 . . . . Fresno
4-7 . . . . Las Vegas
8-11 . . . . . at Sacramento
12-15 . . . . . . .at Fresno
17-20 . . . . . . .Sacramento
21-24 . . . at Albuquerque
25-29 . . . . Reno
30-31 . . . . . at Tacoma

JUNE
1-3 . . . . at Tacoma
5-7 . . . . .Round Rock
8-11 . . . . . . New Orleans
13-15 . . . at Oklahoma City
16-19 . .at Colorado Springs

TACOMA RAINIERS

APRIL
5-9 . . . . .Sacramento
10-12 . . . . .at Fresno
13-16 . . . at Sacramento
17-20 . . . . . . Albuquerque
21-23 . . . . .Sacramento
25-29 . . . . . . .at Fresno
30 . . . . Albuquerque

MAY
1-3 . . . . Albuquerque
4-7 . . . . .at Reno
8-11 . . . . . . at El Paso
12-15 . . . . at Sacramento
17-20 . . . . . Las Vegas
21-24 . . . . . . El Paso
25-29 . . . . .at Las Vegas
30-31 . . . . .Salt Lake

JUNE
1-3 . . . . .Salt Lake
5-7 . . . . . .at Memphis
8-11 . . . at Nashville
13-15 . . . . Omaha
16-19 . . . . Iowa

24-26 . . . . Omaha
27-30 . . . . Iowa

AUGUST
1-3 . . . . .at Memphis
4-7 . . . . at Nashville
9-12 . . . . El Paso
13-15 . . . . .at Reno
16-19 . . . . at Albuquerque
21-23 . . . . Fresno
24-27 . . . . . . Las Vegas
28-30 . . . Albuquerque
31 . . . . .at Las Vegas

SEPTEMBER
1-3 . . . . . . .at Las Vegas

21-24 . . . . .Tacoma
25-28 . . . . .at Reno
29-30 . . . . at Las Vegas

JULY
1-3 . . . . . . .at Las Vegas
4-8 . . . . El Paso
12-15 . . . at Sacramento
16-19 . . . . Las Vegas
20-22 . . . . . at Tacoma
24-26 . . . . . . Memphis
27-30 . . . . . . .Nashville

AUGUST
1-3 . . . . .at Iowa
4-7 . . . . at Omaha
9-12 . . . . .Tacoma
13-15 . . . . . . El Paso
16-19 . . . . .at Reno
21-23 . . . . .at Las Vegas
24-27 . . . . . . .at Fresno
28-30 . . . . Reno
31 . . . . Fresno

SEPTEMBER
1-3 . . . . Fresno

21-24 . . . . . . at Salt Lake
25-28 . . . . Las Vegas
29-30 . . . . Reno

JULY
1-3 . . . . Reno
4-8 . . . . . at Albuquerque
12-15 . . . . Fresno
16-19 . . . . .at Reno
20-22 . . . . .Salt Lake
24-26 . . . . at Round Rock
27-30 . . . .at New Orleans

AUGUST
1-3 . . . . . .Oklahoma City
4-7 . . . . . Colorado Springs
9-12 . . . . . at Salt Lake
13-15 . . . at Albuquerque
16-19 . . . . Fresno
21-23 . . . . Reno
24-27 . . . . El Paso
28-30 . . . .at Las Vegas
31 . . . . at El Paso

SEPTEMBER
1-3 . . . . at El Paso

MAY
1-3 . . . . . . .at Las Vegas
4-7 . . . . .at Fresno
8-11 . . . . .Salt Lake
12-15 . . . . .Tacoma
17-20 . . . . . . at Salt Lake
21-24 . . . . . . Las Vegas
25-29 . . . . . Albuquerque
30-31 . . . . at El Paso

DOUBLE-A

EASTERN LEAGUE

AKRON RUBBERDUCKS

APRIL
5-8 . . . . .at Altoona
9-11 . . . . . .at Binghamton
13-15 . . . . Trenton
16-19 . . . . Altoona
20-22 . . . . . . at Bowie
23-25 . . . . . . .at Reading
27-29 . . . . .Bowie
30 . . . . . . Binghamton

MAY
1-2 . . . . . . Binghamton
3-6 . . . . at Bowie
7-9 . . . . . at Richmond
10-13 . . . . Erie
14-16 . . . . . . at Trenton
17-20 . . . . . at Hartford
22-24 . . . . . . Trenton
25-28 . . . . . .Richmond
29-31 . . . . .at Altoona

JUNE
1-3 . . . . Erie
5-7 . . . at New Hampshire
8-10 . . . . . . at Portland
12-14 . . . New Hampshire
15-17 . . . .at Reading
19-21 . . . . . . Hartford

ALTOONA CURVE

APRIL
5-8 . . . . .Akron
9-11 . . . . . . .Harrisburg
13-15 . . . . . . at Erie
16-19 . . . . . at Akron
20-22 . . . . .Richmond
23-25 . . . . Erie
27-29 . . . at Harrisburg
30 . . . . at Richmond

MAY
1-2 . . . . . . at Richmond
3-6 . . . . Erie
7-9 . . . . .Bowie
10-13 . . . . . at Reading
14-16 . . . . . . Richmond
17-20 . . . . . . Portland
22-24 . . . . . . at Bowie
25-28 . . . at Harrisburg
29-31 . . . . .Akron

JUNE
1-3 . . . . at Hartford
5-7 . . . . Reading
8-10 . . . . Hartford
12-14 . . . .at Binghamton
15-17 . . . New Hampshire
19-21 . . . . . at Richmond

BINGHAMTON RUMBLE PONIES

APRIL
5-8 . . . . Portland
9-11 . . . . .Akron
13-15 . . . . . at Portland
16-19 . . at New Hampshire
20-22 . . . . Erie

22-24 . . . . . .Harrisburg
25-28 . . . . at Bowie
29-30 . . . . . . Altoona

JULY
1-3 . . . . Altoona
4-8 . . . . . at Richmond
12-15 . . . . Binghamton
16-18 . . . at Harrisburg
19-22 . . . . .Richmond
23-25 . . . . . . Altoona
26-29 . . . . . . at Erie
31 . . . . .Bowie

AUGUST
1-2 . . . . .Bowie
3-5 . . . . . . .at Altoona
7-9 . . . . Reading
10-12 . . . . . . Portland
14-16 . . . at Binghamton
17-19 . . . . at Harrisburg
20-21 . . . . . . at Erie
22-23 . . . . Erie
24-26 . . . .Harrisburg
27-30 . . . . . . .Bowie
31 . . . . at Erie

SEPTEMBER
1-3 . . . . at Erie

22-24 . . . . . . at Erie
25-28 . . . .Harrisburg
29-30 . . . . at Akron

JULY
1-3 . . . . at Akron
4-8 . . . . Trenton
12-15 . . . . . . at Erie
16-18 . . . . . . .Bowie
19-22 . . . . . .at Reading
23-25 . . . . . at Akron
26-29 . . . . Binghamton
31 . . . . . . at Harrisburg

AUGUST
1-2 . . . . . . at Harrisburg
3-5 . . . . .Akron
7-9 . . . . .at Trenton
10-12 . . . . Erie
14-16 . . at New Hampshire
17-19 . . . . . at Portland
20-21 . . . . .at Binghamton
22-23 . . . . . .Harrisburg
24-26 . . . . . .Richmond
27-30 . . . . . . Trenton
31 . . . . at Bowie

SEPTEMBER
1-3 . . . . at Bowie

7-9 . . . . at Hartford
10-13 . . . . . at Portland
14-16 . . . . Erie
17-20 . . at New Hampshire
22-24 . . . . . . .Richmond
25-28 . . . . .Bowie
29-31 . . . . at Erie

JUNE
1-3 . . . . . New Hampshire
5-7 . . . at Harrisburg
8-10 . . . . . .at Trenton
12-14 . . . . . . Altoona
15-17 . . . . at Hartford
19-21 . . . . .at Trenton
22-24 . . . . . . Hartford
25-28 . . . . . . Trenton
29-30 . . . . at Portland

JULY
1-3 . . . . at Portland
4-8 . . . . Erie

BOWIE BAYSOX

APRIL
5-8 . . . . .Harrisburg
9-11 . . . . Erie
13-15 . . . at Harrisburg
16-19 . . . at Richmond
20-22 . . . . .Akron
23-25 . . . . . .Richmond
27-29 . . . . . at Akron
30 . . . . at Erie

MAY
1-2 . . . . at Erie
3-6 . . . . .Akron
7-9 . . . . . .at Altoona
10-13 . . . . . . Hartford
14-16 . . . . . .Harrisburg
17-20 . . . . . .at Trenton
22-24 . . . . . . Altoona
25-28 . . . at Binghamton
29-31 . . . . at Richmond

JUNE
1-3 . . . . Trenton
5-7 . . . . . . at Portland
8-10 . . . at New Hampshire
12-14 . . . . Trenton
15-17 . . . . Portland
19-21 . . . . at Harrisburg

ERIE SEAWOLVES

APRIL
5-8 . . . . .at Reading
9-11 . . . . at Bowie
13-15 . . . . Altoona
16-19 . . . . Trenton
20-22 . . .at Binghamton
23-25 . . .at Altoona
27-29 . . . . Binghamton
30 . . . . .Bowie

MAY
1-2 . . . . .Bowie
3-6 . . . . .at Altoona
7-9 . . . . .Harrisburg
10-13 . . . . . at Akron
14-16 . . . .at Binghamton
18-21 . . . . . Reading
22-24 . . . . . at Harrisburg

12-15 . . . . at Akron
16-18 . . . . Portland
19-22 . . . . Trenton
23-25 . . . . . at Bowie
26-29 . . . . . . at Altoona
31 . . . . Hartford

AUGUST
1-2 . . . . Hartford
3-5 . . . . .Harrisburg
7-9 . . . . . . at Richmond
10-12 . . . .at Reading
14-16 . . . . .Akron
17-19 . . . . . . Reading
20-21 . . . . . . Altoona
22-23 . . . . . at Hartford
24-26 . . at New Hampshire
27-30 . . . . at Hartford
31 . . . . Portland

SEPTEMBER
1-3 . . . . Portland

22-24 . . . . . at Richmond
25-28 . . . . .Akron
29-30 . . . . . . at Erie

JULY
1-3 . . . . at Erie
4-8 . . . . .Harrisburg
12-15 . . . . .at Reading
16-18 . . . . .at Altoona
19-22 . . . . Erie
23-25 . . . . . Binghamton
26-29 . . . at Harrisburg
31 . . . . at Akron

AUGUST
1-2 . . . . at Akron
3-5 . . . . Reading
7-9 . . . . . New Hampshire
10-12 . . . . . at Hartford
14-16 . . . . . . Richmond
17-19 . . . . . . at Erie
20-21 . . . . . at Richmond
22-23 . . . . . . .Richmond
24-26 . . . . Erie
27-30 . . . . . at Akron
31 . . . . Altoona

SEPTEMBER
1-3 . . . . Altoona

25-28 . . . . Trenton
29-31 . . . . . Binghamton

JUNE
1-3 . . . . at Akron
5-7 . . . . Hartford
8-10 . . . . Reading
12-14 . . . . at Hartford
15-17 . . . . .at Trenton
18-20 . . . New Hampshire
22-24 . . . . . . Altoona
25-28 . . . . .at Reading
29-30 . . . . .Bowie

JULY
1-3 . . . . .Bowie
4-8 . . . . . .at Binghamton
12-15 . . . . . . Altoona
16-18 . . . at Richmond

19-22 . . . . at Bowie	13-15 . . . . .Harrisburg
23-25 . . . . Richmond	17-19 . . . . .Bowie
26-29 . . . . .Akron	20-21 . . . . .Akron
31 . . . . at Portland	22-23 . . . . at Akron

AUGUST

1-2. . . . . Bowie	24-26 . . . . at Bowie
3-5. . at New Hampshire	27-30 . . . . at Harrisburg
7-9. . . . . Portland	31 . . . . .Akron
10-12 . . . . . .at Altoona	

SEPTEMBER

1-3. . . . . .Akron

HARRISBURG SENATORS

APRIL

5-8. . . . . at Bowie	22-24 . . . . at Akron
9-11 . . . . .at Altoona	25-28 . . . . . . .at Altoona
13-15 . . . . .Bowie	29-30 . . . . Richmond
16-19 . . . . Reading	**JULY**
20-22 . . . . . at Hartford	1-3. . . . . Richmond
23-25 . . . . . at Trenton	4-8. . . . . at Bowie
27-29 . . . . Altoona	12-15 . . . . Hartford
30 . . . . Hartford	16-18 . . . . .Akron

MAY

1-2. . . . . Hartford	19-22 . at New Hampshire
3-6. . . . . . . at Trenton	23-25 . . . . . at Portland
7-9. . . . . at Erie	26-29 . . . . .Bowie
10-13 . . . New Hampshire	31 . . . . Altoona
14-16 . . . . . at Bowie	**AUGUST**
17-20 . . . . at Richmond	1-2. . . . . Altoona
22-24 . . . . Erie	3-5. . . . .at Binghamton
25-28 . . . . Altoona	7-9. . . . . Hartford
29-31 . . . . . at Hartford	10-12 . . . . Trenton

JUNE

1-3. . . . . Portland	13-15 . . . . at Erie
5-7. . . . . . . Binghamton	17-19 . . . . .Akron
8-10. . . . . . at Richmond	20-21 . . . . Reading
12-14 . . . . . .at Reading	22-23 . . . . . .at Altoona
15-17 . . . . . Richmond	24-26 . . . . . . at Akron
19-21 . . . . .Bowie	27-30 . . . . Erie
	31 . . . . at Richmond

SEPTEMBER

1-3. . . . . . . at Richmond

HARTFORD YARD GOATS

APRIL

5-8. . . . . New Hampshire	22-24 . . . .at Binghamton
9-11 . . . . Richmond	25-28 . . . . . . Richmond
13-15 . . at New Hampshire	29-30 . . . . . . .at Reading
16-19 . . . . . at Portland	**JULY**
20-22 . . . . . . .Harrisburg	1-3. . . . . at Reading
23-25 . . . . Portland	4-8. . . . . Portland
27-29 . . . . . at Richmond	12-15 . . . at Harrisburg
30 . . . . . . at Harrisburg	16-18 . . . . Reading

MAY

1-2. . . . . . . at Binghamton	19-22 . . . . . at Portland
3-6. . . . . Portland	23-25 . . . . . . at Trenton
7-9. . . . . . . Binghamton	26-29 . . . New Hampshire
10-13 . . . . . . at Bowie	31 . . . . . .at Binghamton
14-16 . . . New Hampshire	**AUGUST**
17-20 . . . . .Akron	1-2. . . . . . .at Binghamton
22-24 . . . . . . at Portland	3-5. . . . . Trenton
25-28 . at New Hampshire	7-9. . . . . at Harrisburg
29-31 . . . . . .Harrisburg	10-12 . . . . .Bowie

JUNE

1-3. . . . . Altoona	14-16 . . . . . .at Reading
5-7. . . . . at Erie	17-19 . . . . at Richmond
8-10. . . . . . .at Altoona	20-21 . . . . . . at Trenton
12-14 . . . . Erie	22-23 . . . . . Binghamton
15-17 . . . . . Binghamton	24-26 . . . . Trenton
19-21 . . . . .at Akron	27-30 . . . . . Binghamton
	31 . . at New Hampshire

SEPTEMBER

1-3. . . . at New Hampshire

NEW HAMPSHIRE FISHER CATS

APRIL

5-8. . . . . . at Hartford	22-24 . . . . Reading
9-11 . . . . . . at Trenton	25-28 . . . . Portland
13-15 . . . . . . Hartford	29-30 . . . . . . at Trenton
16-19 . . . . . Binghamton	**JULY**
20-22 . . . . . .at Reading	1-3. . . . . at Trenton
23-25 . . . .at Binghamton	4-8. . . . . Reading
27-29 . . . . . . Trenton	12-15 . . . . . at Portland
30 . . . . Reading	16-18 . . . . Trenton

MAY

1-2. . . . . Reading	19-22 . . . . . . .Harrisburg
3-6. . . . . .at Binghamton	23-25 . . . . . . .at Reading
7-9. . . . . Portland	26-29 . . . . . at Hartford
10-13 . . . at Harrisburg	31 . . . . Richmond
14-16 . . . . . at Hartford	**AUGUST**
17-20 . . . . . Binghamton	1-2. . . . . Richmond
22-24 . . . . . .at Reading	3-5. . . . . Erie
25-28 . . . . Hartford	7-9. . . . . at Bowie
29-31 . . . . Portland	10-12 . . . . at Richmond

JUNE

1-3. . . . . .at Binghamton	14-16 . . . . Altoona
5-7. . . . . .Akron	17-19 . . . . . at Trenton
8-10. . . . . .Bowie	20-21 . . . . . at Portland
12-14 . . . . . at Akron	22-23 . . . . Portland
15-17 . . . . . .at Altoona	24-26 . . . . . Binghamton
18-20 . . . . . . at Erie	27-30 . . . . . at Portland
	31 . . . . Hartford

SEPTEMBER

1-3. . . . . Hartford

PORTLAND SEA DOGS

APRIL

5-8. . . . . .at Binghamton	22-24 . . . . Trenton
9-11 . . . . . .at Reading	25-28 . . at New Hampshire
13-15 . . . . . Binghamton	29-30 . . . . . Binghamton
16-19 . . . . . . Hartford	**JULY**
20-22 . . . . . at Trenton	1-3. . . . . Binghamton
23-25 . . . . . at Hartford	4-8. . . . . at Hartford
27-29 . . . . Reading	12-15 . . . New Hampshire
30 . . . . Trenton	16-18 . . . .at Binghamton

MAY

1-2. . . . . Trenton	19-22 . . . . Hartford
3-6. . . . . . . at Hartford	23-25 . . . . . . .Harrisburg
7-9. . . at New Hampshire	26-29 . . . . . . at Trenton
10-13 . . . . . Binghamton	31 . . . . Erie
14-16 . . . . . .at Reading	**AUGUST**
17-20 . . . .at Altoona	1-2. . . . . Erie
22-24 . . . . Hartford	3-5. . . . . Richmond
25-28 . . . . Reading	7-9. . . . . at Erie
29-31 . at New Hampshire	10-12 . . . . . . at Akron

JUNE

1-3. . . . . . . at Harrisburg	14-16 . . . . Trenton
5-7. . . . . .Bowie	17-19 . . . . Altoona
8-10. . . . . .Akron	20-21 . . . New Hampshire
12-14 . . . . at Richmond	22-23 . . at New Hampshire
15-17 . . . . . at Bowie	24-26 . . . . . .at Reading
19-21 . . . . Reading	27-30 . . . New Hampshire
	31 . . . . . . .at Binghamton

SEPTEMBER

1-3. . . . . .at Binghamton

READING FIGHTIN PHILS

APRIL

5-8. . . . . Erie	7-9. . . . . at Trenton
9-11 . . . . Portland	10-13 . . . . Altoona
13-15 . . . . at Richmond	14-16 . . . . Portland
16-19 . . . at Harrisburg	18-21 . . . . at Erie
20-22 . . . New Hampshire	22-24 . . . New Hampshire
23-25 . . . . .Akron	25-28 . . . . . at Portland
27-29 . . . . at Portland	29-31 . . . . . . at Trenton
30 . . . . at New Hampshire	**JUNE**
MAY	1-4. . . . . Richmond
1-2. . . . at New Hampshire	5-7. . . . . .at Altoona
4-6. . . . . Richmond	8-10. . . . . at Erie
	12-14 . . . . . . .Harrisburg

15-17 . . . . .Akron	
19-21 . . . . . . at Portland	
22-24 . . at New Hampshire	
25-28 . . . . Erie	
29-30 . . . . Hartford	

JULY

1-3. . . . . Hartford
4-8. . . . at New Hampshire
12-15 . . . . .Bowie
16-18 . . . . . . at Hartford
19-22 . . . . Altoona
23-25 . . . New Hampshire
26-29 . . . . . at Richmond
31 . . . . Trenton

AUGUST

1-2. . . . . Trenton
3-5. . . . . at Bowie
7-9. . . . . at Akron
10-12 . . . . . Binghamton
14-16 . . . . Hartford
17-19 . . .at Binghamton
20-21 . . . at Harrisburg
22-23 . . . . Trenton
24-26 . . . . Portland
27-30 . . . . at Richmond
31 . . . . at Trenton

SEPTEMBER

1-3. . . . . at Trenton

RICHMOND FLYING SQUIRRELS

APRIL

5-8. . . . . at Trenton
9-11. . . . . . . at Hartford
13-15 . . . . Reading
16-19 . . . . .Bowie
20-22 . . . . . .at Altoona
23-25 . . . . . . at Bowie
27-29 . . . . . . Hartford
30 . . . . Altoona

MAY

1-2. . . . . Altoona
4-6. . . . . .at Reading
7-9. . . . . .Akron
10-13 . . . . Trenton
14-16 . . . . .at Altoona
17-20 . . . . .Harrisburg
22-24 . . . .at Binghamton
25-28 . . . . . at Akron
29-31 . . . . . . .Bowie

JUNE

1-4. . . . . .at Reading
5-7. . . . . at Trenton
8-10 . . . . . . .Harrisburg
12-14 . . . . Portland
15-17 . . . at Harrisburg
19-21 . . . . Altoona

22-24 . . . . .Bowie
25-28 . . . . . . at Hartford
29-30 . . . . . at Harrisburg

JULY

1-3. . . . . . at Harrisburg
4-8. . . . . .Akron
12-15 . . . . at Trenton
16-18 . . . . Erie
19-22 . . . . at Akron
23-25 . . . . at Erie
26-29 . . . . Reading
31 . . . . at New Hampshire

AUGUST

1-2. . . . at New Hampshire
3-5. . . . . at Portland
7-9. . . . . Binghamton
10-12 . . . . New Hampshire
14-16 . . . . at Bowie
17-19 . . . . . . Hartford
20-21 . . . . .Bowie
22-23 . . . . at Bowie
24-26 . . . . .at Altoona
27-30 . . . . Reading
31 . . . . .Harrisburg

SEPTEMBER

1-3. . . . . .Harrisburg

TRENTON THUNDER

APRIL

5-8. . . . . .Richmond
9-11. . . . New Hampshire
13-15 . . . . at Akron
16-19 . . . . at Erie
20-22 . . . . Portland
23-25 . . . . . .Harrisburg
27-29 . . at New Hampshire
30 . . . . at Portland

MAY

1-2. . . . . at Portland
3-6. . . . . .Harrisburg
7-9. . . . . Reading
10-13 . . . . . at Richmond
14-16 . . . . . . .Akron
17-20 . . . . .Bowie
22-24 . . . . at Akron
25-28 . . . . . at Erie
29-31 . . . . . Reading

JUNE

1-3. . . . . at Bowie
5-7. . . . . .Richmond
8-10 . . . . . . Binghamton
12-14 . . . . at Bowie
15-17 . . . . Erie
19-21 . . . . . . Binghamton

22-24 . . . . . . at Portland
25-28 . . .at Binghamton
29-30 . . . . New Hampshire

JULY

1-3. . . . . New Hampshire
4-8. . . . . .at Altoona
12-15 . . . . . . .Richmond
16-18 . . at New Hampshire
19-22 . . . .at Binghamton
23-25 . . . . Hartford
26-29 . . . . Portland
31 . . . . .at Reading

AUGUST

1-2. . . . . .at Reading
3-5. . . . . . at Hartford
7-9. . . . . Altoona
10-12 . . . .at Harrisburg
14-16 . . . . at Portland
17-19 . . . New Hampshire
20-21 . . . . Hartford
22-23 . . . .at Reading
24-26 . . . . at Hartford
27-30 . . . . .at Altoona
31 . . . . Reading

SEPTEMBER

1-3. . . . . Reading

SOUTHERN LEAGUE

BILOXI SHUCKERS

APRIL

5-9. . . . . at Montgomery
11-15 . . . . . .Mississippi
16-20 . . . . . at Mobile
21-25 . . . . Montgomery
26-30 . . . .at Birmingham

MAY

2-6. . . . . Jacksonville
7-11. . . . at Montgomery
12-16 . . . . Pensacola
17-21 . . . . Chattanooga
23-27 . . . . at Mobile
29-31 . . . . . .Mississippi

JUNE

1-2. . . . . .Mississippi
3-7. . . . . . at Pensacola
8-12. . . . at Jacksonville
13-17 . . . . . .Mississippi
21-26 . . . at Chattanooga
28-30 . . . . . Mobile

JULY

1-3. . . . . Mobile
4-7. . . . . . at Mississippi
8-11. . . . . Jackson
12-16 . . . at Jacksonville
18-22 . . . . . .Tennessee
23-27 . . . . .at Jackson
28-31 . . . . at Pensacola

AUGUST

1 . . . . at Pensacola
2-6. . . . . . . Jacksonville
8-12. . . . at Tennessee
14-18 . . . . Mobile
19-23 . . . . . Pensacola
24-28 . . . . at Mississippi
30-31 . . . . Birmingham

SEPTEMBER

1-3. . . . . Birmingham

BIRMINGHAM BARONS

APRIL

5-9. . . . . at Chattanooga
11-15 . . . . . Montgomery
16-20 . . . . .at Jackson
21-25 . . . . at Pensacola
26-30 . . . . . Biloxi

MAY

2-6. . . . . . at Tennessee
7-11. . . . . Pensacola
12-16 . . . . . at Mobile
17-21 . . . . Montgomery
23-27 . . . .at Jackson
29-31 . . . . Chattanooga

JUNE

1-2. . . . . . Chattanooga
3-7. . . . . . .Jacksonville
8-12. . . . . . at Tennessee
13-17 . . . Chattanooga
21-26 . . . at Montgomery
28-30 . . . . Jackson

JULY

1-3. . . . . Jackson
4-7. . . . . at Chattanooga
8-11. . . . . . . .Mississippi
12-16 . . . . at Tennessee
18-22 . . . . Jackson
23-27 . . . . . .Tennessee
28-31 . . . . at Mississippi

AUGUST

1 . . . . .at Mississippi
2-6. . . . . Mobile
8-12. . . . at Montgomery
14-18 . . . . . .Tennessee
19-23 . . . . at Jacksonville
24-28 . . . . Jackson
30-31 . . . . at Biloxi

SEPTEMBER

1-3. . . . . at Biloxi

CHATTANOOGA LOOKOUTS

APRIL

5-9. . . . . . Birmingham
11-15 . . . . . at Pensacola
16-20 . . . . .Jacksonville
21-25 . . . .at Jackson
26-30 . . . . Tennessee

MAY

2-6. . . . . . . at Mobile
7-11. . . . . Jackson
12-16 . . . . .Tennessee
17-21 . . . . at Biloxi
23-27 . . . . Montgomery
29-31 . . .at Birmingham

JUNE

1-2. . . . . .at Birmingham
3-7. . . . . Mobile
8-12. . . . at Montgomery
13-17 . . .at Birmingham
21-26 . . . . Biloxi
28-30 . . . . . at Tennessee

JULY

1-3. . . . . . at Tennessee
4-7. . . . . . . Birmingham
8-11. . . . . at Jacksonville
12-16 . . . . Montgomery
18-22 . . . . at Mobile
23-27 . . . . . Pensacola
28-31 . . . . at Tennessee

AUGUST

1 . . . . at Tennessee
2-6. . . . . . .Mississippi
8-12. . . . . . Jackson
14-18 . . . . at Mississippi
19-23 . . . . at Montgomery
24-28 . . . . Jacksonville
30-31 . . . . . at Jackson

SEPTEMBER

1-3. . . . . .at Jackson

JACKSON GENERALS

APRIL
5-9 . . . . Jacksonville
11-15 . . . . . at Tennessee
16-20 . . . . . Birmingham
21-25 . . . . . Chattanooga
26-30 . . . . at Mississippi

MAY
2-6 . . . . . . Montgomery
7-11 . . . . at Chattanooga
12-16 . . . . Mississippi
17-21 . . . . at Pensacola
23-27 . . . . . Birmingham
29-31 . . . . at Montgomery

JUNE
1-2 . . . . at Montgomery
3-7 . . . . Tennessee
8-12 . . . . . at Mobile
13-17 . . . . at Jacksonville
21-26 . . . . Pensacola
28-30 . . . . at Birmingham

JULY
1-3 . . . . . at Birmingham
4-7 . . . . Tennessee
8-11 . . . . at Biloxi
12-16 . . . . Mobile
18-22 . . . at Birmingham
23-27 . . . . Biloxi
28-31 . . . at Montgomery

AUGUST
1 . . . . at Montgomery
2-6 . . . . Tennessee
8-12 . . . . at Chattanooga
14-18 . . . . . Montgomery
19-23 . . . . at Tennessee
24-28 . . . at Birmingham
30-31 . . . . Chattanooga

SEPTEMBER
1-3 . . . . Chattanooga

JACKSONVILLE JUMBO SHRIMP

APRIL
5-9 . . . . at Jackson
11-15 . . . . . . Mobile
16-20 . . . . at Chattanooga
21-25 . . . . at Tennessee
26-30 . . . . . Pensacola

MAY
2-6 . . . . at Biloxi
7-11 . . . . Tennessee
12-16 . . at Montgomery
17-21 . . . . . . Mobile
23-27 . . . . at Mississippi
29-31 . . . . . Pensacola

JUNE
1-2 . . . . . . Pensacola
3-7 . . . . . at Birmingham
8-12 . . . . Biloxi
13-17 . . . . . . Jackson
21-26 . . . . at Mississippi
28-30 . . . . . Montgomery

JULY
1-3 . . . . . . Montgomery
4-7 . . . . . . at Mobile
8-11 . . . . . Chattanooga
12-16 . . . . Biloxi
18-22 . . . at Pensacola
23-27 . . . . Montgomery
28-31 . . . . at Mobile

AUGUST
1 . . . . at Mobile
2-6 . . . . at Biloxi
8-12 . . . . . .Mississippi
14-18 . . . at Pensacola
19-23 . . . . Birmingham
24-28 . . . at Chattanooga
30-31 . . . . . .Mississippi

SEPTEMBER
1-3 . . . . .Mississippi

MISSISSIPPI BRAVES

APRIL
5-9 . . . . Tennessee
11-15 . . . . at Biloxi
16-20 . . . . . Pensacola
21-25 . . . . . . at Mobile
26-30 . . . . Jackson

MAY
2-6 . . . . at Pensacola
7-11 . . . . Mobile
12-16 . . . . . at Jackson
17-21 . . . at Tennessee
23-27 . . . . . Jacksonville
29-31 . . . . . at Biloxi

JUNE
1-2 . . . . . . at Biloxi
3-7 . . . . . Montgomery
8-12 . . . . . Pensacola
13-17 . . . . . at Biloxi
21-26 . . . . . Jacksonville
28-30 . . . . at Pensacola

JULY
1-3 . . . . . at Pensacola
4-7 . . . . Biloxi
8-11 . . . . at Birmingham
12-16 . . . . . . Pensacola
18-22 . . at Montgomery
23-27 . . . . Mobile
28-31 . . . . Birmingham

AUGUST
1 . . . . Birmingham
2-6 . . . . at Chattanooga
8-12 . . . . at Jacksonville
14-18 . . . . Chattanooga
19-23 . . . . at Mobile
24-28 . . . . Biloxi
30-31 . . . at Jacksonville

SEPTEMBER
1-3 . . . . . at Jacksonville

MOBILE BAYBEARS

APRIL
5-9 . . . . Pensacola
11-15 . . at Jacksonville
16-20 . . . . Biloxi
21-25 . . . . .Mississippi
26-30 . . . at Montgomery

MAY
2-6 . . . . . . Chattanooga
7-11 . . . . at Mississippi
12-16 . . . . Birmingham
17-21 . . at Jacksonville
23-27 . . . . Biloxi
29-31 . . . at Tennessee

JUNE
1-2 . . . . . at Tennessee
3-7 . . . . at Chattanooga
8-12 . . . . . . Jackson
13-17 . . . at Pensacola
21-26 . . . . .Tennessee

JULY
28-30 . . . . at Biloxi

JULY
1-3 . . . . at Biloxi
4-7 . . . . Jacksonville
8-11 . . . at Pensacola
12-16 . . . . .at Jackson
18-22 . . . . Chattanooga
23-27 . . at Mississippi
28-31 . . . . Jacksonville

AUGUST
1 . . . . Jacksonville
2-6 . . . . at Birmingham
8-12 . . . . . . Pensacola
14-18 . . . . at Biloxi
19-23 . . . .Mississippi
24-28 . . at Pensacola
30-31 . . . Montgomery

SEPTEMBER
1-3 . . . . . . Montgomery

MONTGOMERY BISCUITS

APRIL
5-9 . . . . Biloxi
11-15 . . . at Birmingham
16-20 . . . . . Tennessee
21-25 . . . . at Biloxi
26-30 . . . . . . Mobile

MAY
2-6 . . . . . . at Jackson
7-11 . . . . Biloxi
12-16 . . . . Jacksonville
17-21 . . at Birmingham
23-27 . . at Chattanooga
29-31 . . . . . Jackson

JUNE
1-2 . . . . . . Jackson
3-7 . . . . . at Mississippi
8-12 . . . . Chattanooga
13-17 . . . at Tennessee
21-26 . . . . Birmingham
28-30 . . at Jacksonville

JULY
1-3 . . . . at Jacksonville
4-7 . . . . . . Pensacola
8-11 . . . . . at Tennessee
12-16 . . . at Chattanooga
18-22 . . . .Mississippi
23-27 . . at Jacksonville
28-31 . . . . . . Jackson

AUGUST
1 . . . . Jackson
2-6 . . . . at Pensacola
8-12 . . . . . Birmingham
14-18 . . . at Jackson
19-23 . . . . Chattanooga
24-28 . . . . .Tennessee
30-31 . . . at Mobile

SEPTEMBER
1-3 . . . . at Mobile

PENSACOLA BLUE WAHOOS

APRIL
5-9 . . . . at Mobile
11-15 . . . . Chattanooga
16-20 . . . . at Mississippi
21-25 . . . Birmingham
26-30 . . at Jacksonville

MAY
2-6 . . . . .Mississippi
7-11 . . . . at Birmingham
12-16 . . . . . at Biloxi
17-21 . . . . . Jackson
23-27 . . . . .Tennessee
29-31 . . at Jacksonville

JUNE
1-2 . . . . at Jacksonville
3-7 . . . . Biloxi
8-12 . . . . at Mississippi
13-17 . . . . . . Mobile
21-26 . . . . .at Jackson
28-30 . . . . . .Mississippi

JULY
1-3 . . . . . . .Mississippi
4-7 . . . . at Montgomery
8-11 . . . . Mobile
12-16 . . . . at Mississippi
18-22 . . . . .Jacksonville
23-27 . . . at Chattanooga
28-31 . . . . Biloxi

AUGUST
1 . . . . Biloxi
2-6 . . . . . . Montgomery
8-12 . . . . . . at Mobile
14-18 . . . .Jacksonville
19-23 . . . . . . at Biloxi
24-28 . . . . . . Mobile
30-31 . . . at Tennessee

SEPTEMBER
1-3 . . . . . at Tennessee

TENNESSEE SMOKIES

APRIL
5-9 . . . . at Mississippi
11-15 . . . . Jackson
16-20 . . . . at Montgomery
21-25 . . . . . . Jacksonville
26-30 . . . at Chattanooga

MAY
2-6 . . . . Birmingham
7-11 . . . . . at Jacksonville
12-16 . . . at Chattanooga
17-21 . . . . . . .Mississippi
23-27 . . . . at Pensacola
29-31 . . . . Mobile

JUNE
1-2 . . . . Mobile
3-7 . . . . .at Jackson
8-12 . . . . . Birmingham
13-17 . . . . . Montgomery
21-26 . . . . . at Mobile
28-30 . . . . . Chattanooga

JULY
1-3 . . . . . Chattanooga
4-7 . . . . .at Jackson
8-11 . . . . . . Montgomery
12-16 . . . . . Birmingham
18-22 . . . . . . at Biloxi
23-27 . . . . at Birmingham
28-31 . . . . . Chattanooga

AUGUST
1 . . . . Chattanooga
2-6 . . . . . . .at Jackson
8-12 . . . . Biloxi
14-18 . . . at Birmingham
19-23 . . . . Jackson
24-28 . . . at Montgomery
30-31 . . . . . Pensacola

SEPTEMBER
1-3 . . . . Pensacola
Texas League

ARKANSAS TRAVELERS

APRIL
5-7 . . . . San Antonio
8-10 . . . . . Corpus Christi
12-14 . . . . .at San Antonio
15-17 . . .at Corpus Christi
19-22 . . . . . . Springfield
23-26 . . . . Tulsa
27-30 . . . . .at Springfield

MAY
1-4 . . . . .at Tulsa
5-8 . . . . . . NW Arkansas
10-13 . . . . . . Springfield
14-17 . . . at NW Arkansas
18-21 . . . . .at Tulsa
22-24 . . . . . . Midland
25-27 . . . . .Frisco
29-31 . . . . at Midland

JUNE
1-3 . . . . at Frisco
5-8 . . . . Tulsa
9-12 . . . . . . NW Arkansas
13-16 . . . . .at Springfield
17-20 . . . . at NW Arkansas
21-24 . . . . .at Springfield
28-30 . . . . . Corpus Christi

JULY
1-3 . . . . . . San Antonio
4-6 . . . .at Corpus Christi
7-9 . . . . . .at San Antonio
11-14 . . . . . Springfield
15-18 . . . . .at Tulsa
19-22 . . . . . Springfield
23-25 . . at NW Arkansas
26-29 . . . . Tulsa
30-31 . . . . . NW Arkansas

AUGUST
1 . . . . NW Arkansas
2-5 . . . . .at Tulsa
7-9 . . . . Frisco
10-12 . . . . . Midland
14-16 . . . . at Frisco
17-19 . . . . . . at Midland
21-24 . . . . Tulsa
25-27 . . . . NW Arkansas
28-31 . . . . .at Springfield

SEPTEMBER
1-3 . . . . . at NW Arkansas

CORPUS CHRISTI HOOKS

APRIL
5-7 . . . . at NW Arkansas
8-10 . . . . at Arkansas
12-14 . . . . . NW Arkansas
15-17 . . . . .Arkansas
19-22 . . . . . . at Frisco
23-26 . . . . . . Midland
27-30 . . . . .Frisco

MAY
1-4 . . . . at Midland
5-8 . . . . . .at San Antonio
10-13 . . . . Midland
14-17 . . . . . San Antonio
18-21 . . . . . . at Frisco
22-24 . . . . . Springfield
25-27 . . . . Tulsa
29-31 . . . . .at Springfield

JUNE
1-3 . . . . .at Tulsa
5-8 . . . . .Frisco
9-12 . . . . . . San Antonio
13-16 . . . . . . at Midland
17-20 . . . . at San Antonio
21-24 . . . . .Frisco
28-30 . . . . . at Arkansas

JULY
1-3 . . . . . at NW Arkansas
4-6 . . . . .Arkansas
7-9 . . . . . . NW Arkansas
11-14 . . . . . at Midland
15-18 . . . . .Frisco
19-22 . . . . at Midland
23-25 . . . at San Antonio
26-29 . . . . Midland
30-31 . . . . . San Antonio

AUGUST
1 . . . . San Antonio
2-5 . . . . at Frisco
7-9 . . . . Tulsa
10-12 . . . . . Springfield

FRISCO ROUGHRIDERS

APRIL
5-7 . . . . Tulsa
8-10 . . . . Springfield
12-14 . . . . .at Tulsa
15-17 . . .at Springfield
19-22 . . . Corpus Christi
23-26 . . .at San Antonio
27-30 . . . .at Corpus Christi

MAY
1-4 . . . . San Antonio
5-8 . . . . Midland
10-13 . . . at San Antonio
14-17 . . . . . at Midland
18-21 . . . Corpus Christi
22-24 . . at NW Arkansas
25-27 . . . . at Arkansas
29-31 . . . NW Arkansas

JUNE
1-3 . . . . .Arkansas
5-8 . . . . .at Corpus Christi
9-12 . . . . Midland
13-16 . . . . . San Antonio
17-20 . . . . at Midland
21-24 . . . .at Corpus Christi

14-16 . . . . .at Tulsa
17-19 . . .at Springfield
21-24 . . . . . Midland
25-27 . . . . . San Antonio

28-31 . . . . at Frisco

SEPTEMBER
1-3 . . . . . .at San Antonio

28-30 . . . . . . Springfield

JULY
1-3 . . . . Tulsa
4-6 . . . . .at Springfield
7-9 . . . . .at Tulsa
11-14 . . . . . San Antonio
15-18 . . .at Corpus Christi
19-22 . . . . . San Antonio
23-25 . . . . Midland
26-29 . . . .at San Antonio
30-31 . . . . at Midland

AUGUST
1 . . . . at Midland
2-5 . . . . . . Corpus Christi
7-9 . . . . at Arkansas
10-12 . . . at NW Arkansas
14-16 . . . . .Arkansas
17-19 . . . . . NW Arkansas
21-24 . . . .at San Antonio
25-27 . . . . Midland
28-31 . . . . Corpus Christi

SEPTEMBER
1-3 . . . . at Midland

MIDLAND ROCKHOUNDS

APRIL
5-7 . . . . Springfield
8-10 . . . . Tulsa
12-14 . . .at Springfield
15-17 . . . . .at Tulsa
19-22 . . . . San Antonio
23-26 . . .at Corpus Christi
27-30 . . . .at San Antonio

MAY
1-4 . . . . . . Corpus Christi
5-8 . . . . at Frisco
10-13 . . . .at Corpus Christi
14-17 . . . . .Frisco
18-21 . . . . San Antonio
22-24 . . . . . . at Arkansas
25-27 . . . at NW Arkansas
29-31 . . . . .Arkansas

JUNE
1-3 . . . . NW Arkansas
5-8 . . . . . .at San Antonio
9-12 . . . . at Frisco
13-16 . . . . Corpus Christi
17-20 . . . . .Frisco
21-24 . . . .at San Antonio

28-30 . . . . Tulsa

JULY
1-3 . . . . Springfield
4-6 . . . . .at Tulsa
7-9 . . . . . .at Springfield
11-14 . . . . Corpus Christi
15-18 . . .at San Antonio
19-22 . . . Corpus Christi
23-25 . . . . at Frisco
26-29 . . .at Corpus Christi
30-31 . . . . .Frisco

AUGUST
1 . . . . .Frisco
2-5 . . . . San Antonio
7-9 . . . . at NW Arkansas
10-12 . . . . . at Arkansas
14-16 . . . NW Arkansas
17-19 . . . . .Arkansas
21-24 . . . .at Corpus Christi
25-27 . . . . at Frisco
28-31 . . . . . San Antonio

SEPTEMBER
1-3 . . . . .Frisco

NORTHWEST ARKANSAS NATURALS

APRIL
5-7 . . . . . Corpus Christi
8-10 . . . . . San Antonio
12-14 . . . .at Corpus Christi
15-17 . . . . .at San Antonio
19-20 . . . . Tulsa
21-22 . . . . .at Tulsa
23-26 . . . . .at Springfield
27 . . . . .at Tulsa
28-29 . . . . Tulsa
30 . . . . .at Tulsa

MAY
1-4 . . . . Springfield
5-8 . . . . . . at Arkansas
10-13 . . . . Tulsa
14-17 . . . . .Arkansas
18-21 . . . .at Springfield
22-24 . . . . .Frisco
25-27 . . . . . . Midland
29-31 . . . . at Frisco

JUNE
1-3 . . . . at Midland

5-8 . . . . Springfield	26-29 . . . . . at Springfield	**MAY**	4-6 . . . . Frisco
9-12 . . . . . . at Arkansas	30-31 . . . . . . at Arkansas	1-4 . . . . . at NW Arkansas	7-9 . . . . Midland
13-16 . . . . at Tulsa		5-8 . . . . Tulsa	11-14 . . . . . at Arkansas
17-20 . . . . Arkansas	**AUGUST**	10-13 . . . . . at Arkansas	15-18 . . . . . NW Arkansas
21-24 . . . . at Tulsa	1 . . . . at Arkansas	14-17 . . . . . . at Tulsa	19-22 . . . . . at Arkansas
28-30 . . . . San Antonio	2-5 . . . . Springfield	18-21 . . . . NW Arkansas	23-25 . . . . at Tulsa
	7-9 . . . . Midland	22-24 . . . at Corpus Christi	26-29 . . . . . NW Arkansas
JULY	10-12 . . . . Frisco	25-27 . . . . at San Antonio	30-31 . . . . Tulsa
1-3 . . . . . Corpus Christi	14-16 . . . . . . at Midland	29-31 . . . . Corpus Christi	
4-6 . . . . . at San Antonio	17-19 . . . . . . at Frisco		**AUGUST**
7-9 . . . at Corpus Christi	21-24 . . . . . . Springfield	**JUNE**	1 . . . . Tulsa
11-14 . . . . Tulsa	25-27 . . . . . at Arkansas	1-3 . . . . . . San Antonio	2-5 . . . . . at NW Arkansas
15-18 . . . . at Springfield	28-31 . . . . at Tulsa	5-8 . . . . . at NW Arkansas	7-9 . . . . . at San Antonio
19-22 . . . . Tulsa		9-12 . . . . Tulsa	10-12 . . . at Corpus Christi
23-25 . . . . Arkansas	**SEPTEMBER**	13-16 . . . . . . Arkansas	14-16 . . . . San Antonio
	1-3 . . . . Arkansas	17-20 . . . . at Tulsa	17-19 . . . . Corpus Christi
		21-24 . . . . . . Arkansas	21-24 . . . at NW Arkansas
SAN ANTONIO MISSIONS		28-30 . . . . at Frisco	25-27 . . . . at Tulsa
			28-31 . . . . Arkansas
APRIL	28-30 . . . at NW Arkansas	**JULY**	
5-7 . . . . at Arkansas	**JULY**	1-3 . . . . at Midland	**SEPTEMBER**
8-10 . . . . at NW Arkansas	1-3 . . . . at Arkansas		1-3 . . . . Tulsa
12-14 . . . . Arkansas	4-6 . . . . . NW Arkansas	**TULSA DRILLERS**	
15-17 . . . . NW Arkansas	7-9 . . . . . . Arkansas		
19-22 . . . . . at Midland	11-14 . . . . . . at Frisco	**APRIL**	17-20 . . . . . Springfield
23-26 . . . . Frisco	15-18 . . . . . . Midland	5-7 . . . . at Frisco	21-24 . . . . NW Arkansas
27-30 . . . . . . Midland	19-22 . . . . . at Frisco	8-10 . . . . . at Midland	28-30 . . . . at Midland
	23-25 . . . . Corpus Christi	12-14 . . . . Frisco	
MAY	26-29 . . . . Frisco	15-17 . . . . . Midland	**JULY**
1-4 . . . . at Frisco	30-31 . . at Corpus Christi	19-20 . . at NW Arkansas	1-3 . . . . at Frisco
5-8 . . . . Corpus Christi		21-22 . . . NW Arkansas	4-6 . . . . Midland
10-13 . . . . Frisco	**AUGUST**	23-26 . . . . at Arkansas	7-9 . . . . Frisco
14-17 . . at Corpus Christi	1 . . . . . at Corpus Christi	27 . . . . . NW Arkansas	11-14 . . at NW Arkansas
18-21 . . . . . at Midland	2-5 . . . . . at Midland	28-29 . . at NW Arkansas	15-18 . . . . . Arkansas
22-24 . . . . Tulsa	7-9 . . . . . . Springfield	30 . . . . . NW Arkansas	19-22 . . at NW Arkansas
25-27 . . . . . Springfield	10-12 . . . . Tulsa		23-25 . . . . . Springfield
29-31 . . . . . . at Tulsa	14-16 . . . at Springfield	**MAY**	26-29 . . . . at Arkansas
	17-19 . . . . . . at Tulsa	1-4 . . . . Arkansas	30-31 . . at Springfield
JUNE	21-24 . . . . . . Frisco	5-8 . . . . . at Springfield	
1-3 . . . . . at Springfield	25-27 . at Corpus Christi	10-13 . . at NW Arkansas	**AUGUST**
5-8 . . . . . . Midland	28-31 . . . . at Midland	14-17 . . . . . Springfield	1 . . . . . . at Springfield
9-12 . . at Corpus Christi		18-21 . . . . Arkansas	2-5 . . . . . . Arkansas
13-16 . . . . . at Frisco	**SEPTEMBER**	22-24 . . at San Antonio	7-9 . . . . at Corpus Christi
17-20 . . . . Corpus Christi	1-3 . . . . . Corpus Christi	25-27 . . at Corpus Christi	10-12 . . . at San Antonio
21-24 . . . . . . Midland		29-31 . . . . San Antonio	14-16 . . . Corpus Christi
			17-19 . . . . San Antonio
SPRINGFIELD CARDINALS		**JUNE**	21-24 . . . . at Arkansas
		1-3 . . . . . Corpus Christi	25-27 . . . . . Springfield
APRIL	15-17 . . . . Frisco	5-8 . . . . . at Arkansas	28-31 . . . NW Arkansas
5-7 . . . . . at Midland	19-22 . . . . . at Arkansas	9-12 . . . . at Springfield	
8-10 . . . . at Frisco	23-26 . . . . NW Arkansas	13-16 . . . NW Arkansas	**SEPTEMBER**
12-14 . . . . . . Midland	27-30 . . . . Arkansas		1-3 . . . . . . at Springfield

HIGH CLASS A

CALIFORNIA LEAGUE

INLAND EMPIRE 66ERS

		JUNE	24-26 . . . . Visalia
		1-3 . . . . . at Lake Elsinore	27-29 . . . . at San Jose
		5-7 . . . . . . Lake Elsinore	31 . . . . Lancaster
		8-10 . at Rancho Cucamonga	
		11-14 . . . . Lancaster	**AUGUST**
APRIL	**MAY**	15-17 . Rancho Cucamonga	1-2 . . . . Lancaster
5-8 . . . . San Jose	1-3 . . . . . . Lake Elsinore	21-24 . . . . . at Lancaster	3-5 . . . . Modesto
9-11 . . . . Modesto	4-6 . . . . at Stockton	25-28 . . . . . . Visalia	7-9 . . . . . . at Lancaster
12-15 at Rancho Cucamonga	8-10 . . . . at Lancaster	29-30 at Rancho Cucamonga	10-12 . . . . Lake Elsinore
16-18 . . . at Lake Elsinore	11-14 . . . . . . Stockton		13-15 . . . . . San Jose
19-22 . . . . . . Lancaster	15-17 . . at Lake Elsinore	**JULY**	17-19 . . . . at Modesto
24-26 . . . . at Modesto	18-20 . . . . . Lancaster	1-3 . at Rancho Cucamonga	21-23 . . at Lake Elsinore
27-29 . . . . . . at Visalia	22-24 . . . . . at Visalia	4-8 . . . . Stockton	24-27 . Rancho Cucamonga
30 . . . . . . Lake Elsinore	25-27 . Rancho Cucamonga	9-12 . . at Lake Elsinore	28-30 . . . Lake Elsinore
	28-31 . . . . . at Lancaster	13-16 . Rancho Cucamonga	31 . at Rancho Cucamonga
		18-20 . . . . . at Visalia	
		21-23 . . . . . at Stockton	**SEPTEMBER**
			1-3 . at Rancho Cucamonga

LAKE ELSINORE STORM

APRIL
5-8 . . . . at Stockton
9-11 . . . . at Visalia
12-15 . . . . Lancaster
16-18 . . . . . Inland Empire
19-22 at Rancho Cucamonga
23-25 . . . . at San Jose
27-29 . . . . . . Stockton
30 . . . . . at Inland Empire

MAY
1-3 . . . . . at Inland Empire
4-6 . . . . Modesto
8-10 . . Rancho Cucamonga
11-14 . . . . . at Modesto
15-17 . . . . Inland Empire
18-20 at Rancho Cucamonga
22-24 . . . . . . Lancaster
25-27 . . . . . . San Jose
28-31 at Inland Empire

JUNE
1-3 . . . . . . Inland Empire
5-7 . . . . at Inland Empire
8-10 . . . . at Lancaster
11-14 . Rancho Cucamonga
15-17 . . . . . . Lancaster
21-24 . . . . at Visalia

25-28 . Rancho Cucamonga
29-30 . . . . . . at Modesto

JULY
1-3 . . . . at Modesto
4-8 . . . . Visalia
9-12 . . . . Inland Empire
13-16 . . . . . at Lancaster
18-20 . . . . . . Modesto
21-23 . . . . . San Jose
24-26 . . . . at Lancaster
27-29 . . . . . . Stockton
31 . at Rancho Cucamonga

AUGUST
1-2 . at Rancho Cucamonga
3-5 . . . . . . at San Jose
7-9 . . . . Visalia
10-12 . . . at Inland Empire
14-16 at Rancho Cucamonga
17-19 . Rancho Cucamonga
21-23 . . . . Inland Empire
24-27 . . . . at Lancaster
28-30 . . . at Inland Empire
31 . . . . Lancaster

SEPTEMBER
1-3 . . . . Lancaster

LANCASTER JETHAWKS

APRIL
5-8 . . . . Modesto
9-11 . . . . San Jose
12-15 . . . . at Lake Elsinore
16-18 . Rancho Cucamonga
19-22 . . . at Inland Empire
24-26 . . . . . at Visalia
27-29 . Rancho Cucamonga
30 . . . . at Stockton

MAY
1-3 . . . . . at Stockton
4-6 . . . . San Jose
8-10 . . . . . Inland Empire
11-14 . . . . at San Jose
15-17 . . . . Visalia
18-20 . . . at Inland Empire
22-24 . . at Lake Elsinore
25-27 . . . . . . Stockton
28-31 . . . . Inland Empire

JUNE
1-3 . at Rancho Cucamonga
5-7 . . Rancho Cucamonga
8-10 . . . . Lake Elsinore
11-14 . . . at Inland Empire
15-17 . . . at Lake Elsinore
21-24 . . . . Inland Empire

25-28 . . . . . . at Modesto
29-30 . . . . . . at Stockton

JULY
1-3 . . . . at Stockton
4-8 . . . . Modesto
9-12 . at Rancho Cucamonga
13-16 . . . . . Lake Elsinore
18-20 . . . . at Stockton
21-23 . . . . . . at Visalia
24-26 . . . . Lake Elsinore
27-29 . . . . . . Visalia
31 . . . . . at Inland Empire

AUGUST
1-2 . . . . . at Inland Empire
3-5 . . Rancho Cucamonga
7-9 . . . . . Inland Empire
10-12 at Rancho Cucamonga
14-16 . . . . . . Stockton
17-19 . . . . . at San Jose
21-23 at Rancho Cucamonga
24-27 . . . . Lake Elsinore
28-30 . Rancho Cucamonga
31 . . . . . at Lake Elsinore

SEPTEMBER
1-3 . . . . at Lake Elsinore

MODESTO NUTS

APRIL
5-8 . . . . at Lancaster
9-11 . . . . at Inland Empire
12-15 . . . . Visalia
16-18 . . . . Stockton
19-22 . . . at San Jose
24-26 . . . . Inland Empire
27-29 . . . . . . San Jose
30 . at Rancho Cucamonga

MAY
1-3 . at Rancho Cucamonga
4-6 . . . . . at Lake Elsinore

8-10 . . . . San Jose
11-14 . . . . Lake Elsinore
15-17 . . . . at San Jose
18-20 . . . . . at Visalia
22-24 . . . . . San Jose
25-27 . . . . . San Jose
28-31 . . . . at Stockton

JUNE
1-3 . . . . . . at San Jose
5-7 . . . . Visalia
8-10 . . . . San Jose
11-14 . . . . . at Visalia

APRIL
15-17 . . . . Stockton
21-24 . . . . . . at Stockton
25-28 . . . . . . Lancaster
29-30 . . . . . Lake Elsinore

JULY
1-3 . . . . . . Lake Elsinore
4-8 . . . . . . at Lancaster
9-12 . . . . . . at Visalia
13-16 . . . . Stockton
18-20 . . at Lake Elsinore
21-23 at Rancho Cucamonga
24-26 . . . . . . Stockton
27-29 . Rancho Cucamonga
31 . . . . at Stockton

AUGUST
1-2 . . . . at Stockton
3-5 . . . . at Inland Empire
7-9 . . . . Stockton
10-12 . . . . at Visalia
14-16 . . . . . . Visalia
17-19 . . . Inland Empire
21-23 . . . . at Stockton
24-27 . . . . . San Jose
28-30 . . . . . . Visalia
31 . . . . . at San Jose

SEPTEMBER
1-3 . . . . at San Jose

RANCHO CUCAMONGA QUAKES

APRIL
5-8 . . . . at Visalia
9-11 . . . . . . at Stockton
12-15 . . . . Inland Empire
16-18 . . . at Lancaster
19-22 . . . . . Lake Elsinore
24-26 . . . . . . Stockton
27-29 . . . . Lancaster
30 . . . . Modesto

MAY
1-3 . . . . Modesto
4-6 . . . . . . at Visalia
8-10 . . . . at Lake Elsinore
11-14 . . . . Visalia
15-17 . . . at Stockton
18-20 . . . . . Lake Elsinore
22-24 . . . . . . Stockton
25-27 . at Inland Empire
28-31 . . . . . Lake Elsinore

JUNE
1-3 . . . . Lancaster
5-7 . . . . . . at Lancaster
8-10 . . . . Inland Empire
11-14 . . at Lake Elsinore
15-17 . at Inland Empire
21-24 . . . . . . San Jose

25-28 . . . . at Lake Elsinore
29-30 . . . . . Inland Empire

JULY
1-3 . . . . . . Inland Empire
4-8 . . . . . . at San Jose
9-12 . . . . . . Lancaster
13-16 . . . at Inland Empire
18-20 . . . . . San Jose
21-23 . . . . . . Modesto
24-26 . . . . at San Jose
27-29 . . . . at Modesto
31 . . . . . . Lake Elsinore

AUGUST
1-2 . . . . . Lake Elsinore
3-5 . . . . . at Lancaster
6-8 . . . . . at San Jose
10-12 . . . . Lancaster
14-16 . . . . Lake Elsinore
17-19 . . at Lake Elsinore
21-23 . . . . . Lancaster
24-27 . . . at Inland Empire
28-30 . . . at Inland Empire
31 . . . . . Inland Empire

SEPTEMBER
1-3 . . . . . Inland Empire

SAN JOSE GIANTS

APRIL
5-8 . . . . at Inland Empire
9-11 . . . . . . at Lancaster
12-15 . . . . . . Stockton
16-18 . . . . . at Visalia
19-22 . . . . . . Modesto
23-25 . . . . Lake Elsinore
27-29 . . . . at Modesto
30 . . . . Visalia

MAY
1-3 . . . . Visalia
4-6 . . . . . . at Lancaster
8-10 . . . . . at Modesto
11-14 . . . . . Lancaster
15-17 . . . . . . Modesto
18-20 . . . . . at Stockton
22-24 . . . . at Modesto
25-27 . at Lake Elsinore
28-31 . . . . . . Visalia

JUNE
1-3 . . . . Modesto
5-7 . . . . Stockton
8-10 . . . . at Modesto
11-14 . . . . at Stockton
15-17 . . . . . . Visalia
21-24 at Rancho Cucamonga

25-28 . . . . . Stockton
29-30 . . . . at Visalia

JULY
1-3 . . . . at Visalia
4-8 . . Rancho Cucamonga
9-12 . . . . at Stockton
13-16 . . . . . . Visalia
18-20 at Rancho Cucamonga
21-23 . . at Lake Elsinore
24-26 . Rancho Cucamonga
27-29 . . . Inland Empire
31 . . . . at Visalia

AUGUST
1-2 . . . . . . at Visalia
3-5 . . . . Lake Elsinore
6-8 . . . Rancho Cucamonga
10-12 . . . . at Stockton
13-15 . . . at Inland Empire
17-19 . . . . Lancaster
21-23 . . . . . at Visalia
24-27 . . . at Modesto
28-30 . . . . Stockton
31 . . . . Modesto

SEPTEMBER
1-3 . . . . Modesto

STOCKTON PORTS

APRIL
5-8 . . . . Lake Elsinore
9-11 . . Rancho Cucamonga
12-15 . . . . . . at San Jose
16-18 . . . . . . at Modesto
19-22 . . . . Visalia
24-26 at Rancho Cucamonga
27-29 . . . . at Lake Elsinore
30 . . . . Lancaster

MAY
1-3 . . . . Lancaster
4-6 . . . . . . Inland Empire
8-10 . . . . at Visalia
11-14 . . . at Inland Empire
15-17 . Rancho Cucamonga
18-20 . . . . San Jose
22-24 at Rancho Cucamonga
25-27 . . . . . . at Lancaster
28-31 . . . . Modesto

JUNE
1-3 . . . . at Visalia
5-7 . . . . . . at San Jose
8-10 . . . . Visalia
11-14 . . . . San Jose
15-17 . . . . . at Modesto
21-24 . . . . Modesto

VISALIA RAWHIDE

APRIL
5-8 . . . Rancho Cucamonga
9-11 . . . . . . Lake Elsinore
12-15 . . . . . . at Modesto
16-18 . . . . . . at San Jose
19-22 . . . . . at Stockton
24-26 . . . . . . Lancaster
27-29 . . . . Inland Empire
30 . . . . at San Jose

MAY
1-3 . . . . at San Jose
4-6 . . . Rancho Cucamonga
8-10 . . . . Stockton
11-14 at Rancho Cucamonga
15-17 . . . . . . at Lancaster
18-20 . . . . Modesto
22-24 . . . . Inland Empire
25-27 . . . . . at Modesto
28-31 . . . . . at San Jose

JUNE
1-3 . . . . Stockton
5-7 . . . . . . at Modesto
8-10 . . . . . . at Stockton
11-14 . . . . Modesto
15-17 . . . . . at San Jose
21-24 . . . . . Lake Elsinore

CAROLINA LEAGUE

BUIES CREEK ASTROS

APRIL
5-8 . . . . at Salem
9-11 . . . . . . at Lynchburg
12-15 . . . . Salem
16-18 . . . . . Myrtle Beach
19-22 . . . . at Carolina
24-26 . . . . . Down East
27-29 . . . . Frederick

MAY
1-3 . . . . . . at Down East
4-6 . . . . . at Winston-Salem
7-9 . . . . Carolina
10-13 . . at Myrtle Beach
15-17 . . . Winston-Salem
18-20 . . . . Carolina
21-24 at Winston-Salem
25-28 . . . . . . Lynchburg
29-31 . . . . at Down East

APRIL (Stockton continued)
25-28 . . . . . . at San Jose
29-30 . . . . Lancaster

JULY
1-3 . . . . Lancaster
4-8 . . . . at Inland Empire
9-12 . . . . San Jose
13-16 . . . . . at Modesto
18-20 . . . . . . Lancaster
21-23 . . . . Inland Empire
24-26 . . . . . at Modesto
27-29 . . . at Lake Elsinore
31 . . . . Modesto

AUGUST
1-2 . . . . Modesto
3-5 . . . . at Visalia
7-9 . . . . at Modesto
10-12 . . . . San Jose
14-16 . . . . . at Lancaster
17-19 . . . . Visalia
21-23 . . . . Modesto
24-27 . . . . . . at Visalia
28-30 . . . . at San Jose
31 . . . . Visalia

SEPTEMBER
1-3 . . . . Visalia

JULY (Visalia continued)
1-3 . . . . at San Jose
4-8 . . . at Lake Elsinore
9-12 . . . . Modesto
13-16 . . . . . at San Jose
18-20 . . . . Inland Empire
21-23 . . . . Lancaster
24-26 . . . at Inland Empire
27-29 . . . . . at Lancaster
31 . . . . San Jose

AUGUST
1-2 . . . . San Jose
3-5 . . . . Stockton
7-9 . . . . at Lake Elsinore
10-12 . . . . Modesto
14-16 . . . . . at Modesto
17-19 . . . . . at Stockton
21-23 . . . . San Jose
24-27 . . . . Stockton
28-30 . . . . . at Modesto
31 . . . . at Stockton

SEPTEMBER
1-3 . . . . at Stockton

MAY (Buies Creek continued)
1-3 . . . . . . at Down East
4-6 . . . . at Winston-Salem
7-9 . . . . Carolina
10-13 . . at Myrtle Beach
15-17 . . . Winston-Salem
18-20 . . . . Carolina
21-24 at Winston-Salem
25-28 . . . . . . Lynchburg
29-31 . . . . at Down East

CAROLINA MUDCATS

APRIL
5-8 . . . . . Winston-Salem
9-11 . . . . Frederick
12-15 . . at Winston-Salem
16-18 . . . at Wilmington
19-22 . . . . Buies Creek
24-26 . . . . . Myrtle Beach
27-29 . . at Down East

MAY
1-3 . . . . . at Myrtle Beach
4-6 . . . . Down East
7-9 . . . . at Buies Creek
10-13 . . . . Wilmington
15-17 . . . at Down East
18-20 . . . at Buies Creek
21-24 . . . . . . Down East
25-28 . . . Myrtle Beach
29-31 . . . . at Lynchburg

JUNE
1-3 . . . . at Winston-Salem
5-7 . . . . Down East
8-10 . . . . Winston-Salem
11-13 . . . at Buies Creek
14-17 . . at Myrtle Beach
21-22 . . . . at Buies Creek
23-24 . . . . Buies Creek
26-29 . . . . at Salem
30 . . . . . at Buies Creek

DOWN EAST WOOD DUCKS

APRIL
5-8 . . . . at Lynchburg
9-11 . . . . . . at Potomac
12-15 . . . Myrtle Beach
16-18 . . . . Winston-Salem
19-22 . . at Myrtle Beach
24-26 . . . at Buies Creek
27-29 . . . . Carolina

MAY
1-3 . . . . . . Buies Creek
4-6 . . . . at Carolina
7-9 . . . . . Myrtle Beach
10-13 . . at Winston-Salem
15-17 . . . . Carolina
18-20 . . . . Winston-Salem
21-24 . . . . at Carolina
25-28 . . . . . Frederick
29-31 . . . . . Buies Creek

JUNE
1-3 . . . . at Myrtle Beach
5-7 . . . . at Carolina

JUNE (Stockton continued)
24-26 . . . . . . at Potomac
27-29 . . . . at Wilmington
31 . . . . . . at Wilmington

AUGUST
1-2 . . . . Wilmington
3-5 . . . . Lynchburg
7-9 . . . . . at Down East
10-12 . . . . at Frederick
14-16 . . . Winston-Salem
17-19 . . at Myrtle Beach
21-22 . . . . Carolina
23 . . . . at Carolina
24-26 . . . Winston-Salem
27-30 . . at Myrtle Beach
31 . . . . at Carolina

SEPTEMBER
1 . . . . at Carolina
2-3 . . . . Carolina

JULY (Carolina Mudcats)
1 . . . . at Buies Creek
2-3 . . . . Buies Creek
4-8 . . . . Frederick
9-12 . . . at Myrtle Beach
13-16 . . . . . . Lynchburg
18-20 . . . Winston-Salem
21-23 . . . . at Lynchburg
24-26 . . . Myrtle Beach
27-29 . . . . . at Potomac
31 . . . . at Winston-Salem

AUGUST
1-2 . . . . at Winston-Salem
3-5 . . . . Salem
6-8 . . . . Lynchburg
10-13 . . . . . . at Salem
14-16 . . . at Down East
17-19 . . . . Potomac
21-22 . . . at Buies Creek
23 . . . . Buies Creek
24-26 . . . . at Frederick
27-30 . . . . Down East
31 . . . . . . Buies Creek

SEPTEMBER
1 . . . . Buies Creek
2-3 . . . . . at Buies Creek

JUNE (Down East continued)
8-10 . . . . . . Buies Creek
11-13 . . . . . Wilmington
14-17 . . . . at Frederick
21-24 . . at Winston-Salem
25-29 . . . . Potomac
30 . . . . Salem

JULY
1-3 . . . . Salem
4-8 . . . . at Winston-Salem
9-12 . . . at Buies Creek
13-16 . . . Myrtle Beach
18-20 . . . . at Frederick
21-23 . . . at Buies Creek
24-26 . . . . Lynchburg
27-29 . . . . . Frederick
31 . . . . at Myrtle Beach

AUGUST
1-2 . . . at Myrtle Beach
3-5 . . . . . Winston-Salem
7-9 . . . . Buies Creek
10-12 . . . . at Lynchburg

14-16 . . . . Carolina
17-19 . . . . at Salem
20-22 . . . at Wilmington
24-26 . . . . Myrtle Beach

27-30 . . . . . . .at Carolina
31 . . . . . . Winston-Salem
SEPTEMBER
1-3 . . . . . Winston-Salem

FREDERICK KEYS

APRIL
5-8 . . . . . at Myrtle Beach
9-11 . . . . .at Carolina
12-15 . . . . . . .Potomac
16-18 . . . . . at Lynchburg
19-22 . . . . . . Wilmington
24-26 . . . . at Salem
27-29 . . . . at Buies Creek

MAY
1-3 . . . . .Salem
4-6 . . . . at Wilmington
7-9 . . . . .Lynchburg
10-13 . . . . . . .Potomac
15-17 . . . at Lynchburg
18-20 . . . Myrtle Beach
21-24 . . . . .Salem
25-28 . . . at Down East
29-31 . . . at Wilmington

JUNE
1-3 . . . . .Lynchburg
5-7 . . . . at Potomac
8-10 . . . at Wilmington
11-13 . . . . . . .Lynchburg
14-17 . . . . . . .Down East
21-24 . . . . . . at Salem

25-29 . . . .Winston-Salem
30 . . . . .Lynchburg

JULY
1-3 . . . . .Lynchburg
4-8 . . . . .at Carolina
9-12 . . . . Wilmington
13-16 . . . at Potomac
18-20 . . . .Down East
21-23 . . . . Wilmington
24-26 . . . at Winston-Salem
27-29 . . . . at Down East
31 . . . . .Potomac

AUGUST
1-2 . . . . .Potomac
3-5 . . . . . . at Wilmington
7-9 . . . . . . at Potomac
10-12 . . . Buies Creek
14-16 . . . . . . .Salem
17-19 . . . at Lynchburg
21-23 . . . . . at Salem
24-26 . . . . . Carolina
27-30 . . . at Potomac
31 . . . . . . Myrtle Beach

SEPTEMBER
1-3 . . . . Myrtle Beach

LYNCHBURG HILLCATS

APRIL
5-8 . . . . .Down East
9-11 . . . . . . Buies Creek
12-15 . . . . at Wilmington
16-18 . . . . Frederick
19-22 . . . . at Potomac
24-26 . . . .Winston-Salem
27-29 . . . . Potomac

MAY
1-3 . . . at Winston-Salem
4-6 . . . . Myrtle Beach
7-9 . . . . at Frederick
10-13 . . . . . at Salem
15-17 . . . . . Frederick
18-20 . . . . Potomac
21-24 . . . at Myrtle Beach
25-28 . . . at Buies Creek
29-31 . . . . Carolina

JUNE
1-3 . . . . at Frederick
5-7 . . . . . at Wilmington
8-10 . . . . . Potomac
11-13 . . . . . at Frederick
14-17 . . . . . .Salem
21-24 . . . . . Myrtle Beach

25-29 . . . . at Wilmington
30 . . . . at Frederick

JULY
1-3 . . . . at Frederick
4-8 . . . . Wilmington
9-12 . . . . . . .Potomac
13-16 . . . . . . .at Carolina
18-20 . . . . . Wilmington
21-23 . . . . . . Carolina
24-26 . . . at Down East
27-29 . . . at Myrtle Beach
31 . . . . .Salem

AUGUST
1-2 . . . . .Salem
3-5 . . . . at Buies Creek
6-8 . . . . .at Carolina
10-12 . . . .Down East
14-16 . . . at Wilmington
17-19 . . . . Frederick
21-23 . . . . .Potomac
24-26 . . . at Potomac
27-30 . . . . . Wilmington
31 . . . . at Salem

SEPTEMBER
1-3 . . . . at Salem

MYRTLE BEACH PELICANS

APRIL
5-8 . . . . .Frederick
9-11 . . . . .Winston-Salem
12-15 . . . at Down East
16-18 . . . . at Buies Creek
19-22 . . . .Down East
24-26 . . . . .at Carolina
27-29 . . . . . at Salem

MAY
1-3 . . . . Carolina
4-6 . . . . . . at Lynchburg
7-9 . . . . . at Down East
10-13 . . . . . Buies Creek
15-17 . . . at Wilmington
18-20 . . . . . at Frederick
21-24 . . . . .Lynchburg

25-28 . . . . .at Carolina
29-31 . . . . Winston-Salem

JUNE
1-3 . . . . .Down East
5-7 . . . . . . at Buies Creek
8-10 . . . . .Salem
11-13 . . . at Winston-Salem
14-17 . . . . Carolina
21-24 . . . . at Lynchburg
25-29 . . . . Buies Creek
30 . . . . Potomac

JULY
1-3 . . . . .Potomac
4-8 . . . . . . at Buies Creek
9-12 . . . . Carolina
13-16 . . . . . at Down East
18-20 . . . . .Potomac

POTOMAC NATIONALS

APRIL
5-8 . . . . Wilmington
9-11 . . . . .Down East
12-15 . . . . at Frederick
16-18 . . . . . . at Salem
19-22 . . . . . .Lynchburg
24-26 . . . at Wilmington
27-29 . . . . at Lynchburg

MAY
1-3 . . . . . . Wilmington
4-6 . . . . .Salem
7-9 . . . . . at Wilmington
10-13 . . . at Frederick
15-17 . . . . .Salem
18-20 . . . at Lynchburg
21-24 . . . . Wilmington
25-28 . . . .Winston-Salem
29-31 . . . . at Salem

JUNE
1-3 . . . . . at Buies Creek
5-7 . . . . .Frederick
8-10 . . . . . at Lynchburg
11-13 . . . . . at Salem
14-17 . . . Buies Creek
21-24 . . . . Wilmington

25-29 . . . . at Down East
30 . . . . . at Myrtle Beach

JULY
1-3 . . . at Myrtle Beach
4-8 . . . . .Salem
9-12 . . . at Lynchburg
13-16 . . . . . . Frederick
18-20 . . . at Myrtle Beach
21-23 . . . . at Salem
24-26 . . . . . Buies Creek
27-29 . . . . . Carolina
31 . . . . . . at Frederick

AUGUST
1-2 . . . . . . at Frederick
3-5 . . . . Myrtle Beach
7-9 . . . . .Frederick
10-12 . . at Winston-Salem
14-16 . . . Myrtle Beach
17-19 . . . . . .at Carolina
21-23 . . . . at Lynchburg
24-26 . . . . .Lynchburg
27-30 . . . . . . Frederick
31 . . . . . . at Wilmington

SEPTEMBER
1-3 . . . . . . at Wilmington

SALEM RED SOX

APRIL
5-8 . . . . . . Buies Creek
9-11 . . . . Wilmington
12-15 . . . at Buies Creek
16-18 . . . . . .Potomac
19-22 . . . at Winston-Salem
24-26 . . . . . .Frederick
27-29 . . . . . Myrtle Beach

MAY
1-3 . . . . at Frederick
4-6 . . . . at Potomac
7-9 . . . .Winston-Salem
10-13 . . . .Lynchburg
15-17 . . . at Potomac
18-20 . . . . . Wilmington
21-24 . . . at Frederick
25-28 . . . at Wilmington
29-31 . . . . Potomac

JUNE
1-3 . . . . Wilmington
5-7 . . . . at Winston-Salem
8-10 . . . at Myrtle Beach
11-13 . . . . . .Potomac
14-17 . . . at Lynchburg
21-24 . . . . . .Frederick

21-23 . . . . .Winston-Salem
24-26 . . . . . .at Carolina
27-29 . . . . . . .Lynchburg
31 . . . . .Down East

AUGUST
1-2 . . . . .Down East
3-5 . . . . . . at Potomac
6-8 . . . . at Winston-Salem
10-12 . . . . Wilmington
14-16 . . . at Potomac
17-19 . . . . . Buies Creek
21-23 . . . at Winston-Salem
24-26 . . . at Down East
27-30 . . . . . Buies Creek
31 . . . . at Frederick

SEPTEMBER
1-3 . . . . at Frederick

26-29 . . . . Carolina
30 . . . . at Down East

JULY
1-3 . . . . at Down East
4-8 . . . . at Potomac
9-12 . . . .Winston-Salem
13-16 . . . . at Wilmington
18-20 . . . at Buies Creek
21-23 . . . . .Potomac
24-26 . . . at Wilmington
27-29 . . . .Winston-Salem
31 . . . . .at Lynchburg

AUGUST
1-2 . . . . . at Lynchburg
3-5 . . . . .at Carolina
7-9 . . . . . . Wilmington
10-13 . . . . . Carolina
14-16 . . . . at Frederick
17-19 . . . .Down East
21-23 . . . . . .Frederick
24-26 . . . . at Wilmington
27-30 . . at Winston-Salem
31 . . . . .Lynchburg

SEPTEMBER
1-3 . . . . .Lynchburg

WILMINGTON BLUE ROCKS

APRIL
5-8 . . . . at Potomac
9-11 . . . . at Salem
12-15 . . . . . . .Lynchburg
16-18 . . . . Carolina
19-22 . . . . at Frederick
24-26 . . . . . . .Potomac
27-29 . . . .Winston-Salem

MAY
1-3 . . . . at Potomac
4-6 . . . . .Frederick
7-9 . . . . .Potomac
10-13 . . . . . . at Carolina
15-17 . . . . . Myrtle Beach
18-20 . . . . . . at Salem
21-24 . . . . . at Potomac
25-28 . . . . . . .Salem
29-31 . . . . . . .Frederick

JUNE
1-3 . . . . at Salem
5-7 . . . . .Lynchburg
8-10 . . . . .Frederick
11-13 . . . . at Down East
14-17 . . at Winston-Salem
21-24 . . . . . . at Potomac

25-29 . . . . . . .Lynchburg
30 . . . . . .Winston-Salem

JULY
1-3 . . . . . . .Winston-Salem
4-8 . . . . at Lynchburg
9-12 . . . . . . at Frederick
13-16 . . . . .Salem
18-20 . . . . . at Lynchburg
21-23 . . . . . at Frederick
24-26 . . . . .Salem
27-29 . . . . . Buies Creek
31 . . . . at Buies Creek

AUGUST
1-2 . . . . . . at Buies Creek
3-5 . . . . .Frederick
7-9 . . . . at Salem
10-12 . . at Myrtle Beach
14-16 . . . . . .Lynchburg
17-19 . . at Winston-Salem
20-22 . . . . . . .Down East
24-26 . . . . .Salem
27-30 . . . at Lynchburg
31 . . . . .Potomac

SEPTEMBER
1-3 . . . . .Potomac

WINSTON-SALEM DASH

APRIL
5-8 . . . . .at Carolina
9-11 . . . . at Myrtle Beach
12-15 . . . . Carolina
16-18 . . . . at Down East
19-22 . . . . .Salem
24-26 . . . at Lynchburg
27-29 . . . at Wilmington

MAY
1-3 . . . . .Lynchburg
4-6 . . . . . Buies Creek
7-9 . . . . . . at Salem
10-13 . . . . . . .Down East
15-17 . . . . at Buies Creek
18-20 . . . . at Down East
21-24 . . . . . Buies Creek
25-28 . . . . . . at Potomac
29-31 . . at Myrtle Beach

JUNE
1-3 . . . . Carolina
5-7 . . . . .Salem
8-10 . . . . . at Carolina
11-13 . . . . . Myrtle Beach
14-17 . . . . . .Wilmington
21-24 . . . . . . .Down East

25-29 . . . . . . at Frederick
30 . . . . . at Wilmington

JULY
1-3 . . . . . . at Wilmington
4-8 . . . . .Down East
9-12 . . . . . . at Salem
13-16 . . . . . . Buies Creek
18-20 . . . . . .at Carolina
21-23 . . . at Myrtle Beach
24-26 . . . . . . .Frederick
27-29 . . . . . at Salem
31 . . . . Carolina

AUGUST
1-2 . . . . Carolina
3-5 . . . . . at Down East
6-8 . . . . . Myrtle Beach
10-12 . . . . . . .Potomac
14-16 . . at Buies Creek
17-19 . . . . . .Wilmington
21-23 . . . . . Myrtle Beach
24-26 . . . at Buies Creek
27-30 . . . . .Salem
31 . . . . at Down East

SEPTEMBER
1-3 . . . . at Down East

FLORIDA STATE LEAGUE

BRADENTON MARAUDERS

APRIL
5-6 . . . . . . at St. Lucie
7-8 . . . . St. Lucie
9-12 . . . . . . at Lakeland
13-15 . . . at Clearwater
17-19 . . . . . Palm Beach
20-22 . . . . . . .Fort Myers
23-25 . . . . Tampa
26-29 . . . . . . at Jupiter

MAY
1-3 . . . . Dunedin

4-6 . . . . at Charlotte
7-9 . . . . at Dunedin
10-12 . . . . . Palm Beach
14-17 . . . . . . Daytona
18-20 . . . at Palm Beach
21-23 . . . at Fort Myers
24-27 . . . . Jupiter
29-31 . . . . . at Daytona

JUNE
1-3 . . . . Charlotte
4-7 . . . . Florida
8-10 . . . . .at Tampa

11-14 . . . . at Florida
18-20 . . . . . Clearwater
21-24 . . . . . .Fort Myers
26-28 . . . at Palm Beach
29-30 . . . . . at Dunedin

JULY
1 . . . . at Dunedin
2-3 . . . . . . Palm Beach
4-5 . . . . . at St. Lucie
6-8 . . . . . . .Fort Myers
9-12 . . . . . . .Lakeland
13-15 . . . . at Daytona
16-18 . . . . . . Jupiter
19-21 . . . . . Daytona
23-25 . . . . . .at Tampa

JULY
1 . . . . Tampa
2-3 . . . . .Fort Myers
4-5 . . . . at Florida
6-8 . . . . at Clearwater
9-12 . . . . St. Lucie
13-15 . . . . . at Jupiter
16-18 . . . . . . Tampa
19-21 . . . . Jupiter
23-25 . . . . . at Florida
26-29 . . . . at St. Lucie
31 . . . . Florida

AUGUST
1-2 . . . . Florida
3-5 . . . . . . at Dunedin
6-8 . . . . .Bradenton
9-12 . . . . Dunedin
13-16 . . . at Fort Myers
17-19 . . . Palm Beach
21-23 . . . . . at Bradenton
24-26 . . . .at Clearwater
27-30 . . . . . . Daytona
31 . . . . Florida

SEPTEMBER
1-2 . . . . Florida

CHARLOTTE STONE CRABS

APRIL
5-6 . . . . . . at Fort Myers
7-8 . . . . .Fort Myers
9-12 . . . . . at Daytona
13-15 . . . at Lakeland
17-19 . . . . Clearwater
20-22 . . . . . Palm Beach
23-25 . . . . at St. Lucie
26-29 . . . . . .at Tampa

MAY
1-3 . . . . St. Lucie
4-6 . . . . .Bradenton
7-9 . . . . . . at Fort Myers
10-12 . . . . . at Jupiter
14-17 . . . . . .Lakeland
18-20 . . . . . . Jupiter
21-23 . . . . . .at Tampa
24-27 . . . . . .Fort Myers
29-31 . . . at Palm Beach

JUNE
1-3 . . . . . . at Bradenton
4-7 . . . . Dunedin
8-10 . . . . . . Clearwater
11-14 . . . . at Dunedin
18-20 . . . . . . .Lakeland
21-24 . . . at Palm Beach
26-28 . . . . at Lakeland

29-30 . . . . Tampa

JULY
1 . . . . Tampa
2-3 . . . . .Fort Myers
4-5 . . . . at Florida
6-8 . . . .at Clearwater
9-12 . . . . St. Lucie
13-15 . . . . . at Jupiter
16-18 . . . . . . Tampa
19-21 . . . . Jupiter
23-25 . . . . . at Florida
26-29 . . . . at St. Lucie
31 . . . . Florida

AUGUST
1-2 . . . . Florida
3-5 . . . . . . at Dunedin
6-8 . . . . .Bradenton
9-12 . . . . Dunedin
13-16 . . . at Fort Myers
17-19 . . . Palm Beach
21-23 . . . . . at Bradenton
24-26 . . . .at Clearwater
27-30 . . . . . . Daytona
31 . . . . Florida

SEPTEMBER
1-2 . . . . Florida

CLEARWATER THRESHERS

APRIL
5-6 . . . . Dunedin
7-8 . . . . at Dunedin
9-12 . . . . Jupiter
13-15 . . . . .Bradenton
17-19 . . . . . at Charlotte
20-22 . . . . . .at Tampa
23-25 . . . . . .Fort Myers
26-29 . . . . . at Dunedin

MAY
1-2 . . . . .Lakeland
3 . . . . at Lakeland
4-6 . . . . Dunedin
7-9 . . . . . . at Lakeland
10-12 . . . . . . Daytona
14-17 . . . . . . Palm Beach
18-20 . . . . . at Florida
21-23 . . . . . at St. Lucie
24-27 . . . . at Palm Beach
29-31 . . . . . . .Fort Myers

JUNE
1-3 . . . . Florida
4-7 . . . . at Daytona
8-10 . . . . .at Charlotte
11-14 . . . . Tampa

18-20 . . . . . at Bradenton
21-24 . . . . . . Dunedin
26-28 . . . . at Daytona
29-30 . . . . . . St. Lucie

JULY
1 . . . . St. Lucie
2-3 . . . . .Lakeland
4-5 . . . . .at Tampa
6-8 . . . . Charlotte
9-12 . . . . . at Dunedin
13-15 . . . . . at Florida
16-18 . . . . . Daytona
19-21 . . . . Florida
23-25 . . . . at St. Lucie
26 . . . . .Lakeland
27-29 . . . at Lakeland
31 . . . . Tampa

AUGUST
1-2 . . . . Tampa
3-5 . . . . . . at Bradenton
6-8 . . . . .at Tampa
9-12 . . . . St. Lucie
13-16 . . . . . . .Bradenton
17-19 . . . at Fort Myers
21-23 . . . . Dunedin

24-26 . . . . Charlotte
27-30 . . . . at Jupiter
31 . . . . at Fort Myers

DAYTONA TORTUGAS

APRIL
5-6 . . . . Florida
7-8 . . . . at Florida
9-12 . . . . Charlotte
13-15 . . . . Jupiter
17-19 . . . . at Tampa
20-22 . . . . at Dunedin
23-25 . . . . Florida
26-29 . . . . at Fort Myers

MAY
1-3 . . . . at Jupiter
4-6 . . . . Lakeland
7-9 . . . . Tampa
10-12 . . . at Clearwater
14-17 . . . . . at Bradenton
18-20 . . . . Dunedin
21-23 . . . . . . at Jupiter
24-27 . . . . St. Lucie
29-31 . . . . Bradenton

JUNE
1-3 . . . . at Lakeland
4-7 . . . . Clearwater
8-10 . . . at Palm Beach
11-14 . . . . . at St. Lucie
18-20 . . . . . Palm Beach
21-24 . . . . Florida
26-28 . . . . . . Clearwater

DUNEDIN BLUE JAYS

APRIL
5-6 . . . . . . at Clearwater
7-8 . . . . Clearwater
9-12 . . . . . at Palm Beach
13-15 . . . . at St. Lucie
17-19 . . . . . . Fort Myers
20-22 . . . . . . Daytona
23-25 . . . . at Lakeland
26-29 . . . . . Clearwater

MAY
1-3 . . . . at Bradenton
4-6 . . . . . at Clearwater
7-9 . . . . Bradenton
10-12 . . . . . Fort Myers
14-17 . . . . . . at Tampa
18-20 . . . . at Daytona
21-23 . . . . . . Florida
24-27 . . . . Lakeland
29-31 . . . . . at Florida

JUNE
1-3 . . . . Tampa
4-7 . . . . . . at Charlotte
8-10 . . . at Fort Myers
11-14 . . . . . Charlotte
18-20 . . . . . St. Lucie
21-24 . . . at Clearwater
26-28 . . . . at Florida

FLORIDA FIRE FROGS

APRIL
5-6 . . . . . . at Daytona
7-8 . . . . Daytona
9-12 . . . at Fort Myers
13-15 . . . at Palm Beach
17-19 . . . . . . St. Lucie

29-30 . . . . . . at Florida
JULY
1 . . . . at Florida
2-3 . . . . St. Lucie
4-5 . . . . at Palm Beach
6-8 . . . . Jupiter
9-12 . . . . . at Florida
13-15 . . . . . Bradenton
16-18 . . . at Clearwater
19-21 . . . . at Bradenton
23-25 . . . Palm Beach
26-29 . . . . . Fort Myers
31 . . . at Palm Beach

AUGUST
1-2 . . . . at Palm Beach
3-5 . . . . at St. Lucie
6-8 . . . . . . Dunedin
9-12 . . . . . Jupiter
13-16 . . . at Lakeland
17-19 . . . at Tampa
21-23 . . . . Lakeland
24-26 . . . . . . Tampa
27-30 . . . at Charlotte
31 . . . . . at Dunedin

SEPTEMBER
1-2 . . . . at Dunedin

29-30 . . . . . Bradenton
JULY
1 . . . . Bradenton
2-3 . . . . Tampa
4-5 . . . . at Fort Myers
6-8 . . . . at St. Lucie
9-12 . . . . Clearwater
13-15 . . . . at Tampa
16-18 . . . . Florida
19-21 . . . . . Tampa
23-25 . . . at Lakeland
26-29 . . . at Jupiter
31 . . . . . Lakeland

AUGUST
1-2 . . . . Lakeland
3-5 . . . . Charlotte
6-8 . . . at Daytona
9-12 . . . at Charlotte
13-16 . . . . Jupiter
17-19 . . . . St. Lucie
21-23 . . . at Clearwater
24-26 . . . at Bradenton
27-30 . . . Palm Beach
31 . . . . . Daytona

SEPTEMBER
1-2 . . . . . Daytona

20-22 . . . . . Lakeland
23-25 . . . at Daytona
26-29 . . . at Lakeland
MAY
1-3 . . . . Palm Beach
4-6 . . . . . Tampa

7-9 . . . . at St. Lucie
10-12 . . . at Tampa
14-17 . . . . St. Lucie
18-20 . . . . Clearwater
21-23 . . . at Dunedin
24-27 . . . . Tampa
29-31 . . . Dunedin

JUNE
1-3 . . . . at Clearwater
4-7 . . . at Bradenton
8-10 . . . Jupiter
11-14 . . . Bradenton
18-20 . . . at Jupiter
21-24 . . . at Daytona
26-28 . . . Dunedin
29-30 . . . . Daytona

JULY
1 . . . . . Daytona
2-3 . . . at Jupiter
4-5 . . . Charlotte
6-8 . . . at Palm Beach

FORT MYERS MIRACLE

APRIL
5-6 . . . . . . Charlotte
7-8 . . . . at Charlotte
9-12 . . . . Florida
13-15 . . . . Tampa
17-19 . . . at Dunedin
20-22 . . . at Bradenton
23-25 . . . at Clearwater
26-29 . . . Daytona

MAY
1-3 . . . at Tampa
4-6 . . . . Jupiter
7-9 . . . . Charlotte
10-12 . . . at Dunedin
14-17 . . . at Jupiter
18-20 . . . St. Lucie
21-23 . . . Bradenton
24-27 . . . at Charlotte
29-31 . . . at Clearwater

JUNE
1-3 . . . at St. Lucie
4-7 . . . Palm Beach
8-10 . . . Dunedin
11-14 . . . at Palm Beach
18-20 . . . Tampa
21-24 . . . at Bradenton
26-28 . . . at Tampa

29-30 . . . Lakeland
JULY
1 . . . . Lakeland
2-3 . . . at Charlotte
4-5 . . . Dunedin
6-8 . . . at Bradenton
9-12 . . . Palm Beach
13-15 . . . at Lakeland
16-18 . . . St. Lucie
19-21 . . . Lakeland
23-25 . . . at Jupiter
26-29 . . . at Daytona
31 . . . . Jupiter

AUGUST
1-2 . . . Jupiter
3-5 . . . Florida
6-8 . . . at Lakeland
9-12 . . . at Florida
13-16 . . . Charlotte
17-19 . . . Clearwater
21-23 . . . at Palm Beach
24-26 . . . at St. Lucie
27-30 . . . Bradenton
31 . . . . Clearwater

SEPTEMBER
1-2 . . . Clearwater

JUPITER HAMMERHEADS

APRIL
5-6 . . . at Palm Beach
7-8 . . . Palm Beach
9-12 . . . at Clearwater
13-15 . . . at Daytona
17-19 . . . Lakeland
20-22 . . . St. Lucie
23-25 . . . at Palm Beach
26-29 . . . Bradenton

MAY
1-3 . . . Daytona
4-6 . . . at Fort Myers
7-9 . . . at Palm Beach
10-12 . . . Charlotte
14-17 . . . Fort Myers
18-20 . . . at Charlotte
21-23 . . . Daytona
24-27 . . . at Bradenton
29-31 . . . at St. Lucie

JUNE
1-3 . . . Palm Beach
4-7 . . . Lakeland
8-10 . . . at Florida
11-14 . . . at Lakeland
18-20 . . . Florida
21-24 . . . at Tampa
26-28 . . . at St. Lucie
29-30 . . . Palm Beach

JULY
1 . . . Palm Beach
2-3 . . . Florida
4-5 . . . at Lakeland
6-8 . . . at Daytona
9-12 . . . Tampa
13-15 . . . Charlotte
16-18 . . . at Bradenton
19-21 . . . at Charlotte
23-25 . . . Fort Myers

9-12 . . . Daytona
13-15 . . . Clearwater
16-18 . . . at Dunedin
19-21 . . . at Clearwater
23-25 . . . Charlotte
26-29 . . . Bradenton
31 . . . at Charlotte

AUGUST
1-2 . . . at Charlotte
3-5 . . . at Fort Myers
6-8 . . . Palm Beach
9-12 . . . Fort Myers
13-16 . . . at St. Lucie
17-19 . . . at Lakeland
21-23 . . . Jupiter
24-26 . . . Lakeland
27-30 . . . at Tampa
31 . . . at Charlotte

SEPTEMBER
1-2 . . . at Charlotte

26-29 . . . . Dunedin	17-19 . . . . . . .Bradenton
31 . . . . at Fort Myers	21-23 . . . . at Florida
AUGUST	24-26 . . . . . at Palm Beach
1-2. . . . . . at Fort Myers	27-30 . . . . . . Clearwater
3-5. . . . . Palm Beach	31 . . . . St. Lucie
6-8. . . . . St. Lucie	**SEPTEMBER**
9-12 . . . . at Daytona	1-2. . . . . St. Lucie
13-16 . . . . . . at Dunedin	

LAKELAND FLYING TIGERS

APRIL	29-30 . . . . . at Fort Myers
5-6. . . . . Tampa	**JULY**
7-8. . . . . .at Tampa	1 . . . . at Fort Myers
9-12 . . . . . . .Bradenton	2-3. . . . . . at Clearwater
13-15 . . . . Charlotte	4-5. . . . . Jupiter
17-19 . . . . at Jupiter	6-8. . . . . Tampa
20-22 . . . . . . at Florida	9-12 . . . . at Bradenton
23-25 . . . . . . .Dunedin	13-15 . . . . . . .Fort Myers
26-29 . . . . Florida	16-18 . . . . at Palm Beach
MAY	19-21 . . . . at Fort Myers
1-2. . . . . .at Clearwater	23-25 . . . . Dunedin
3 . . . . Clearwater	26 . . . . at Clearwater
4-6. . . . . . . at Daytona	27-29 . . . . . . Clearwater
7-9. . . . . Clearwater	31 . . . . at Dunedin
10-12 . . . . at St. Lucie	**AUGUST**
14-17 . . . . . .at Charlotte	1-2. . . . . at Dunedin
18-20 . . . . Tampa	3-5. . . . . .at Tampa
21-23 . . . . Palm Beach	6-8. . . . . . . .Fort Myers
24-27 . . . . . . at Dunedin	9-12 . . . . at Palm Beach
29-31 . . . . .at Tampa	13-16 . . . . Daytona
JUNE	17-19 . . . . at Florida
1-3. . . . . Daytona	21-23 . . . . at Daytona
4-7. . . . . at Jupiter	24-26 . . . . . . at Florida
8-10 . . . . St. Lucie	27-30 . . . . St. Lucie
11-14 . . . . Jupiter	31 . . . . Palm Beach
18-20 . . . . . .at Charlotte	**SEPTEMBER**
21-24 . . . . . at St. Lucie	1-2. . . . . . . Palm Beach
26-28 . . . . Charlotte	

PALM BEACH CARDINALS

APRIL	29-30 . . . . at Jupiter
5-6. . . . . Jupiter	**JULY**
7-8. . . . . at Jupiter	1 . . . . at Jupiter
9-12 . . . . .Dunedin	2-3. . . . . . at Bradenton
13-15 . . . . Florida	4-5. . . . . . . Daytona
17-19 . . . . . at Bradenton	6-8. . . . . Florida
20-22 . . . . . .at Charlotte	9-12 . . . . at Fort Myers
23-25 . . . . Jupiter	13-15 . . . . . at St. Lucie
26-29 . . . . . at St. Lucie	16-18 . . . . . . .Lakeland
MAY	19-21 . . . . St. Lucie
1-3. . . . . at Florida	23-25 . . . . . at Daytona
4-6. . . . . St. Lucie	26-29 . . . . . . .at Tampa
7-9. . . . . Jupiter	31 . . . . Daytona
10-12 . . . . . at Bradenton	**AUGUST**
14-17 . . . . .at Clearwater	1-2. . . . . Daytona
18-20 . . . . . .Bradenton	3-5. . . . . at Jupiter
21-23 . . . . . . at Lakeland	6-8. . . . . . . at Florida
24-27 . . . . . . Clearwater	9-12 . . . . .Lakeland
29-31 . . . . . . Charlotte	13-16 . . . . Tampa
JUNE	17-19 . . . . . .at Charlotte
1-3. . . . . at Jupiter	21-23 . . . . . .Fort Myers
4-7. . . . . . at Fort Myers	24-26 . . . . Jupiter
8-10 . . . . Daytona	27-30 . . . . . at Dunedin
11-14 . . . . . . .Fort Myers	31 . . . . at Lakeland
18-20 . . . . . . at Daytona	**SEPTEMBER**
21-24 . . . . . . Charlotte	1-2. . . . . . . at Lakeland
26-28 . . . . . . .Bradenton	

ST. LUCIE METS

APRIL	29-30 . . . . . at Clearwater
5-6. . . . . .Bradenton	**JULY**
7-8. . . . . . at Bradenton	1 . . . . at Clearwater
9-12 . . . . Tampa	2-3. . . . . at Daytona
13-15 . . . . Dunedin	4-5. . . . . . . .Bradenton
17-19 . . . . . . at Florida	6-8. . . . . Dunedin
20-22 . . . . . . at Jupiter	9-12 . . . . . .at Charlotte
23-25 . . . . . . Charlotte	13-15 . . . . Palm Beach
26-29 . . . . . Palm Beach	16-18 . . . . at Fort Myers
MAY	19-21 . . . . at Palm Beach
1-3. . . . . . . .at Charlotte	23-25 . . . . . . Clearwater
4-6. . . . at Palm Beach	26-29 . . . . . . Charlotte
7-9. . . . . Florida	31 . . . . at Bradenton
10-12 . . . . .Lakeland	**AUGUST**
14-17 . . . . . at Florida	1-2. . . . . . . at Bradenton
18-20 . . . . at Fort Myers	3-5. . . . . Daytona
21-23 . . . . . Clearwater	6-8. . . . . at Jupiter
24-27 . . . . . at Daytona	9-12 . . . . .at Clearwater
29-31 . . . . Jupiter	13-16 . . . . Florida
JUNE	17-19 . . . . . . at Dunedin
1-3. . . . . .Fort Myers	21-23 . . . . Tampa
4-7. . . . . .at Tampa	24-26 . . . . . .Fort Myers
8-10 . . . . . . at Lakeland	27-30 . . . . . at Lakeland
11-14 . . . . Daytona	31 . . . . at Jupiter
18-20 . . . . . at Dunedin	**SEPTEMBER**
21-24 . . . . .Lakeland	1-2. . . . . at Jupiter
26-28 . . . . Jupiter	

TAMPA TARPONS

APRIL	**JULY**
5-6. . . . . . . at Lakeland	1 . . . . .at Charlotte
7-8. . . . . . . .Lakeland	2-3. . . . . at Dunedin
9-12 . . . . . . at St. Lucie	4-5. . . . . Clearwater
13-15 . . . . at Fort Myers	6-8. . . . . . . at Lakeland
17-19 . . . . Daytona	9-12 . . . . at Jupiter
20-22 . . . . . . Clearwater	13-15 . . . . Dunedin
23-25 . . . . at Bradenton	16-18 . . . . .at Charlotte
26-29 . . . . . . Charlotte	19-21 . . . . . . at Dunedin
MAY	23-25 . . . . . . .Bradenton
1-3. . . . . .Fort Myers	26-29 . . . . . Palm Beach
4-6. . . . . at Florida	31 . . . . . . .at Clearwater
7-9. . . . . at Daytona	**AUGUST**
10-12 . . . . Florida	1-2. . . . . . .at Clearwater
14-17 . . . . Dunedin	3-5. . . . . .Lakeland
18-20 . . . . . at Lakeland	6-8. . . . . . . Clearwater
21-23 . . . . . . Charlotte	9-12 . . . . at Bradenton
24-27 . . . . . . at Florida	13-16 . . . . at Palm Beach
29-31 . . . . . . .Lakeland	17-19 . . . . Daytona
JUNE	21-23 . . . . . . at St. Lucie
1-3. . . . . at Dunedin	24-26 . . . . . . at Daytona
4-7. . . . . St. Lucie	27-30 . . . . Florida
8-10 . . . . . . .Bradenton	31 . . . . .Bradenton
11-14 . . . . .at Clearwater	**SEPTEMBER**
18-20 . . . . at Fort Myers	1-2. . . . . .Bradenton
21-24 . . . . Jupiter	
26-28 . . . . . .Fort Myers	
29-30 . . . . . at Charlotte	

LOW CLASS A

MIDWEST LEAGUE

BELOIT SNAPPERS

APRIL

5-6	. . . . Wisconsin
7-8	. . . . at Wisconsin
9-12	. . . . . at Burlington
13-15	. . . . at Kane County
17-19	. . . . Cedar Rapids
20-22	. . . . . . at Clinton
23-26	. . . . Peoria
27-29	. . . . Clinton

MAY

1-3	. . . . . . .at Fort Wayne
4-6	. . . .at Lake County
7-9	. . . . . . Great Lakes
10-12	. . . . Lansing
14-17	. . . . . at Wisconsin
18-20	. . . . . Quad Cities
21-24	. . . . Peoria
25-28	. . . . . at Burlington
29-31	. . . . . Kane County

JUNE

1-3	. . . . . at Quad Cities
5-7	. . . . at Cedar Rapids
8-11	. . . . .Burlington
12-14	. . . . at Peoria
15-17	. . . . Clinton
21-24	. . . . at Quad Cities

BOWLING GREEN HOT RODS

APRIL

5-6	. . . . Dayton
7-8	. . . . at Dayton
9-12	. . . . . at South Bend
13-15	. . . . . . Fort Wayne
17-19	. . at West Michigan
20-22	. . .at Lake County
23-26	. . . . . . South Bend
27-29	. . . . . Lake County

MAY

1-3	. . . . at Clinton
4-6	. . . . . . at Burlington
7-9	. . . . Peoria
10-12	. . . . . Cedar Rapids
14-17	. . . . at Great Lakes
18-20	. . . . at Lansing
21-24	. . . . . Great Lakes
25-28	. . . . Dayton
29-31	. . . . .at Fort Wayne

JUNE

1-3	. . . . . West Michigan
5-7	. . . . Lansing
8-11	. . . . at Dayton
12-14	. . . . . . Fort Wayne
15-17	. . . .at Lake County
21-24	. . . . . Lake County

BURLINGTON BEES

APRIL

5-6	. . . . Peoria
7-8	. . . . at Peoria
9-12	. . . . Beloit
13-15	. . . . . Quad Cities
17-19	. . . . . . at Clinton
20-22	. . . . . Quad Cities

10-12	. . . at West Michigan
14-17	. . . . Kane County
18-20	. . . . . at Wisconsin
21-24	. . . . . . at Clinton
25-28	. . . . Beloit
29-31	. . . . at Peoria

JUNE

1-3	. . . . Cedar Rapids
5-7	. . . . Clinton
8-11	. . . . at Beloit
12-14	. . . . . . Wisconsin
15-17	. . . at Quad Cities
21-24	. . . . . . at Peoria
25-27	. . . . . at Kane County
28-30	. . . . Cedar Rapids

JULY

1	. . . . Cedar Rapids
2-3	. . . . Peoria
4-5	. . . . at Peoria

CEDAR RAPIDS KERNELS

APRIL

5-6	. . . . . at Quad Cities
7-8	. . . . . at Quad Cities
9-12	. . . . . . at Peoria
13-15	. . . . Clinton
17-19	. . . . at Beloit
20-22	. . . . Kane County
23-26	. . . . . .Burlington
27-29	. . . . at Quad Cities

MAY

1-3	. . . . South Bend
4-6	. . . . . . West Michigan
7-9	. . . . at Dayton
10-12	. . . at Bowling Green
14-17	. . . . Quad Cities
18-20	. . . . at Clinton
21-24	. . . at Kane County
25-28	. . . . Clinton
29-31	. . . . . . Wisconsin

JUNE

1-3	. . . . . . at Burlington
5-7	. . . . Beloit
8-11	. . . . at Wisconsin
12-14	. . . at Kane County
15-17	. . . . Peoria
21-24	. . . . . . Wisconsin
25-27	. . . . Beloit

CLINTON LUMBERKINGS

APRIL

5-6	. . . . . at Kane County
7-8	. . . . Kane County
9-12	. . . . Wisconsin
13-15	. . . at Cedar Rapids
17-19	. . . . . .Burlington
20-22	. . . . Beloit
23-26	. . . . at Wisconsin
27-29	. . . . . at Beloit

MAY

1-3	. . . . . .Bowling Green
4-6	. . . . .Dayton
7-9	. . at West Michigan
10-12	. . at South Bend
14-17	. . . . . at Peoria
18-20	. . . . Cedar Rapids
21-24	. . . . . .Burlington
25-28	. . . . at Cedar Rapids

6-9	. . . . . at Quad Cities
11-13	. . . . Lansing
14-16	. . . . Great Lakes
18-20	. . .at Fort Wayne
21-23	. . .at Lake County
25-27	. . . . Quad Cities
28-31	. . . . .Beloit

AUGUST

1-3	. . . . at Wisconsin
4-6	. . . . . . Kane County
8-10	. . . . . at Wisconsin
11-14	. . at Kane County
15-17	. . . . . . Wisconsin
18-20	. . . . . . at Beloit
21-23	. . . . Clinton
24-27	. . . . . Quad Cities
29-31	. . . at Cedar Rapids

SEPTEMBER

1-3	. . . . Clinton

JULY

1	. . . . Cedar Rapids
2-3	. . . . Peoria
4-5	. . . . at Peoria

28-30	. . . . . at Burlington

JULY

1	. . . . at Burlington
2-3	. . . . . . at Wisconsin
4-5	. . . . Wisconsin
6-9	. . . . at Kane County
11-13	. . . . . Fort Wayne
14-16	. . . . Lake County
18-20	. . at Great Lakes
21-23	. . . . .at Lansing
25-27	. . . . Clinton
28-29	. . . . Quad Cities
30-31	. . . at Quad Cities

AUGUST

1-3	. . . . .at Peoria
4-6	. . . . Beloit
8-10	. . . . at Clinton
11-12	. . . at Quad Cities
13-14	. . . . Quad Cities
15-17	. . . . Peoria
18-20	. . . . at Wisconsin
21-23	. . . . . . at Beloit
24-27	. . . . Kane County
29-31	. . . . . .Burlington

SEPTEMBER

1-3	. . . . at Beloit

29-31	. . . . . . Quad Cities

JUNE

1-3	. . . . Peoria
5-7	. . . . . at Burlington
8-11	. . . . . Kane County
12-14	. . . at Quad Cities
15-17	. . . . . . at Beloit
21-24	. . . . Kane County
25-27	. . . . . .Burlington
28-30	. . . . . at Wisconsin

JULY

1	. . . . at Wisconsin
2-3	. . . . . at Kane County
4-5	. . . . . Kane County
6-9	. . . . at Beloit
11-13	. . . . . Great Lakes
14-16	. . . . Lansing

BELOIT (JULY continued)

25-27	. . . . at Cedar Rapids
28-30	. . . . Peoria

JULY

1	. . . . Peoria
2-3	. . . . . . Quad Cities
4-5	. . . . . at Quad Cities
6-9	. . . . Clinton
11-13	. . . at South Bend
14-16	. . at West Michigan
18-20	. . . . Bowling Green
21-23	. . . . Dayton
25-27	. . . at Kane County
28-31	. . . . . at Burlington

AUGUST

1-3	. . . . . . Kane County
4-6	. . . . at Cedar Rapids
8-10	. . . . . . Quad Cities
11-14	. . . . . . Wisconsin
15-17	. . . . . . at Clinton
18-20	. . . . . .Burlington
21-23	. . . . Cedar Rapids
24-27	. . . . . .at Peoria
29-31	. . . . at Wisconsin

SEPTEMBER

1-3	. . . . . Cedar Rapids

BOWLING GREEN (continued)

25-27	. . . . .at Fort Wayne
28-30	. . at West Michigan

JULY

1	. . . . at West Michigan
2-3	. . . . . at South Bend
4-5	. . . . South Bend
6-9	. . . . . .at Fort Wayne
11-13	. . . . . Kane County
14-16	. . . . . . Quad Cities
18-20	. . . . at Beloit
21-23	. . . . . at Wisconsin
25-27	. . . . . . Great Lakes
28-31	. . . . . . Fort Wayne

AUGUST

1-3	. . . .at Lake County
4-6	. . . . . . South Bend
8-10	. . . West Michigan
11-14	. . . . . . .at Lansing
15-17	. . . . at Great Lakes
18-20	. . . . . . at Dayton
21-23	. . . . Lansing
24-27	. . . . . Lake County
29-31	. . . . at South Bend

SEPTEMBER

1-3	. . . . .Dayton

BURLINGTON (continued)

23-26	. . . at Cedar Rapids
27-29	. . . at Kane County

MAY

1-3	. . . . .Dayton
4-6	. . . . . . Bowling Green
7-9	. . . at South Bend

18-20 . . . . . .at Lake County	11-14 . . . . at Peoria
21-23 . . . . . .at Fort Wayne	15-17 . . . . .Beloit
25-27 . . . at Cedar Rapids	18-20 . . . . . at Kane County
28-31 . . . . Peoria	21-23 . . . . . . at Burlington
AUGUST	24-27 . . . . Wisconsin
1-3 . . . . . . at Quad Cities	29-31 . . . . Quad Cities
4-6 . . . . Wisconsin	**SEPTEMBER**
8-10 . . . . . . Cedar Rapids	1-3 . . . . at Burlington

DAYTON DRAGONS

APRIL	25-27 . . . . . . Great Lakes
5-6. . . . . at Bowling Green	28-30 . . . . . at South Bend
7-8. . . . . . Bowling Green	**JULY**
9-12 . . . . . . Lake County	1 . . . . at South Bend
13-15 . . . . . at Great Lakes	2-3. . . . . .at Lake County
17-19 . . . . . . South Bend	4-5. . . . . . Lake County
20-22 . . . .at Fort Wayne	6-9. . . . . at Great Lakes
23-26 . . . . . . .at Lansing	11-13 . . . . . Quad Cities
27-29 . . . . . . Fort Wayne	14-16 . . . . . Kane County
MAY	18-20 . . . . . at Wisconsin
1-3. . . . . . . at Burlington	21-23 . . . . at Beloit
4-6. . . . . at Clinton	25-27 . . . . . . Fort Wayne
7-9. . . . . . . Cedar Rapids	28-31 . . . . Lansing
10-12 . . . . Peoria	**AUGUST**
14-17 . . . . . . .at Lansing	1-3. . . . . . .at Fort Wayne
18-20 . . . . . Great Lakes	4-6. . . . . at West Michigan
21-24 . . . . . Lake County	8-10 . . . . .at Lansing
25-28 . . . at Bowling Green	11-14 . . . . at Great Lakes
29-31 . . . . West Michigan	15-17 . . . . . Lake County
JUNE	18-20 . . . . . Bowling Green
1-3. . . . . Lansing	21-23 . . . . at West Michigan
5-7. . . . . .at Lake County	24-27 . . . . Lansing
8-11. . . . . . Bowling Green	29-31 . . . . West Michigan
12-14 . . . . at South Bend	**SEPTEMBER**
15-17 . . . at West Michigan	1-3. . . . . at Bowling Green
21-24 . . . . . . South Bend	

FORT WAYNE TINCAPS

APRIL	25-27 . . . . .Bowling Green
5-6. . . . . .at Lake County	28-30 . . . . .at Lake County
7-8. . . . . Lake County	**JULY**
9-12 . . . . Lansing	1 . . . . . . .at Lake County
13-15 . . . at Bowling Green	2-3. . . . . . at Great Lakes
17-19 . . . . . . Great Lakes	4-5. . . . . . . Great Lakes
20-22 . . . . . . .Dayton	6-9. . . . . . Bowling Green
23-26 . . . . at Great Lakes	11-13 . . . at Cedar Rapids
27-29 . . . . at Dayton	14-16 . . . . .at Peoria
MAY	18-20 . . . . . . .Burlington
1-3. . . . . .Beloit	21-23 . . . . Clinton
4-6. . . . . Wisconsin	25-27 . . . . at Dayton
7-9. . . . . at Quad Cities	28-31 . . . at Bowling Green
10-12 . . . at Kane County	**AUGUST**
14-17 . . . . West Michigan	1-3. . . . . .Dayton
18-20 . . . . . . South Bend	4-6. . . . . Lansing
21-24 . . . at West Michigan	8-10 . . . .at Lake County
25-28 . . . . .at Lansing	11-14 . . . . West Michigan
29-31 . . . . . Bowling Green	15-17 . . . . . South Bend
JUNE	18-20 . . . . . . .at Lansing
1-3. . . . . at Great Lakes	21-23 . . . . . at Great Lakes
5-7. . . . . at South Bend	24-27 . . . . at South Bend
8-11. . . . . . . Lansing	29-31 . . . . . Lake County
12-14 . . . at Bowling Green	**SEPTEMBER**
15-17 . . . . . . Great Lakes	1-3. . . . . at West Michigan
21-24 . . . . West Michigan	

GREAT LAKES LOONS

APRIL	13-15 . . . . .Dayton
5-6. . . . . Lansing	17-19 . . . .at Fort Wayne
7-8. . . . . .at Lansing	20-22 . . . . West Michigan
9-12 . . . at West Michigan	23-26 . . . . . . Fort Wayne

27-29 . . . . . at South Bend	2-3. . . . . Fort Wayne
MAY	4-5. . . . . . . .at Fort Wayne
1-3. . . . . Quad Cities	6-9. . . . . .Dayton
4-6. . . . . . . Kane County	11-13 . . . . . . at Clinton
7-9. . . . . at Beloit	14-16 . . . . at Burlington
10-12 . . . . at Wisconsin	18-20 . . . . Cedar Rapids
14-17 . . . .Bowling Green	21-23 . . . . Peoria
18-20 . . . . at Dayton	25-27 . . . at Bowling Green
21-24 . . . at Bowling Green	28-31 . . .at Lake County
25-28 . . . .at Lake County	**AUGUST**
29-31 . . . . . . South Bend	1-3. . . . . . West Michigan
JUNE	4-6. . . . . . . Lake County
1-3. . . . . Fort Wayne	8-10 . . . . . at South Bend
5-7. . . . at West Michigan	11-14 . . . . . . .Dayton
8-11. . . . . . Lake County	15-17 . . . . . Bowling Green
12-14 . . . . West Michigan	18-20 . . . . at South Bend
15-17 . . .at Fort Wayne	21-23 . . . . . . Fort Wayne
21-24 . . . . .at Lansing	24-27 . . . at West Michigan
25-27 . . . . . . at Dayton	29-31 . . . . . . .at Lansing
28-30 . . . . Lansing	**SEPTEMBER**
JULY	1-3. . . . . South Bend
1 . . . . Lansing	

KANE COUNTY COUGARS

APRIL	25-27 . . . . .at Peoria
5-6. . . . . Clinton	28-30 . . . . . . Quad Cities
7-8. . . . . . at Clinton	**JULY**
9-12 . . . at Quad Cities	1 . . . . Quad Cities
13-15 . . . . .Beloit	2-3. . . . . .Clinton
17-19 . . . . at Wisconsin	4-5. . . . . at Clinton
20-22 . . . at Cedar Rapids	6-9. . . . . . . Cedar Rapids
23-26 . . . . Quad Cities	11-13 . . . at Bowling Green
27-29 . . . . . .Burlington	14-16 . . . . . . at Dayton
MAY	18-20 . . . West Michigan
1-3. . . . . . . .at Lansing	21-23 . . . . . South Bend
4-6. . . . . . at Great Lakes	25-27 . . . . .Beloit
7-9. . . . . Lake County	28-31 . . . . . at Wisconsin
10-12 . . . . Fort Wayne	**AUGUST**
14-17 . . . . at Burlington	1-3. . . . . at Beloit
18-20 . . . . at Peoria	4-6. . . . . . . at Burlington
21-24 . . . Cedar Rapids	8-10 . . . . Peoria
25-28 . . . . . . Wisconsin	11-14 . . . . . . .Burlington
29-31 . . . . . at Beloit	15-17 . . . at Quad Cities
JUNE	18-20 . . . . Clinton
1-3. . . . . . . at Wisconsin	21-23 . . . . Peoria
5-7. . . . . Peoria	24-27 . . . at Cedar Rapids
8-11. . . . . . at Clinton	29-31 . . . . . .at Peoria
12-14 . . . . Cedar Rapids	**SEPTEMBER**
15-17 . . . . . Wisconsin	1-3. . . . . Wisconsin
21-24 . . . . at Clinton	

LAKE COUNTY CAPTAINS

APRIL	**JUNE**
5-6. . . . . Fort Wayne	1-3. . . . . . at South Bend
7-8. . . . . . .at Fort Wayne	5-7. . . . . Dayton
9-12 . . . . . at Dayton	8-11. . . . at Great Lakes
13-15 . . . . . . South Bend	12-14 . . . . Lansing
17-19 . . . . . at Lansing	15-17 . . . . Bowling Green
20-22 . . . Bowling Green	21-24 . . . at Bowling Green
23-26 . . . . West Michigan	25-27 . . . .at Lansing
27-29 . . . at Bowling Green	28-30 . . . . . Fort Wayne
MAY	**JULY**
1-3. . . . . Wisconsin	1 . . . . Fort Wayne
4-6. . . . . .Beloit	2-3. . . . . .Dayton
7-9. . . . . at Kane County	4-5. . . . . at Dayton
10-12 . . . at Quad Cities	6-9. . . . . West Michigan
14-17 . . . . . . South Bend	11-13 . . . . . . .at Peoria
18-20 . . . at West Michigan	14-16 . . . at Cedar Rapids
21-24 . . . . at Dayton	18-20 . . . . Clinton
25-28 . . . . . . Great Lakes	21-23 . . . . . .Burlington
29-31 . . . . . . .at Lansing	25-27 . . . at West Michigan
	28-31 . . . . . Great Lakes

AUGUST
1-3 . . . . . . .Bowling Green
4-6 . . . . . . at Great Lakes
8-10 . . . . Fort Wayne
11-14 . . . . at South Bend
15-17 . . . . at Dayton

18-20 . . . . . West Michigan
21-23 . . . . . . South Bend
24-27 . . . at Bowling Green
29-31 . . . .at Fort Wayne

SEPTEMBER
1-3 . . . . Lansing

LANSING LUGNUTS

APRIL
5-6 . . . . . . at Great Lakes
7-8 . . . . Great Lakes
9-12 . . . . .at Fort Wayne
13-15 . . . . West Michigan
17-19 . . . . Lake County
20-22 . . . at South Bend
23-26 . . . . Dayton
27-29 . . at West Michigan

MAY
1-3 . . . . . . Kane County
4-6 . . . . . . Quad Cities
7-9 . . . . at Wisconsin
10-12 . . . . . . at Beloit
14-17 . . . . .Dayton
18-20 . . . . Bowling Green
21-24 . . . at South Bend
25-28 . . . . . Fort Wayne
29-31 . . . . Lake County

JUNE
1-3 . . . . at Dayton
5-7 . . . . at Bowling Green
8-11 . . . .at Fort Wayne
12-14 . . . .at Lake County
15-17 . . . . South Bend
21-24 . . . . . Great Lakes

25-27 . . . . . Lake County
28-30 . . . . at Great Lakes

JULY
1 . . . . . . at Great Lakes
2-3 . . . at West Michigan
4-5 . . . . . West Michigan
6-9 . . . . . . South Bend
11-13 . . . at Burlington
14-16 . . . . . at Clinton
18-20 . . . . Peoria
21-23 . . . Cedar Rapids
25-27 . . . at South Bend
28-31 . . . . at Dayton

AUGUST
1-3 . . . . . . South Bend
4-6 . . . . . .at Fort Wayne
8-10 . . . . .Dayton
11-14 . . . .Bowling Green
15-17 . . . at West Michigan
18-20 . . . . . Fort Wayne
21-23 . . at Bowling Green
24-27 . . . . . at Dayton
29-31 . . . . Great Lakes

SEPTEMBER
1-3 . . . . . .at Lake County

PEORIA CHIEFS

APRIL
5-6 . . . . at Burlington
7-8 . . . . Burlington
9-12 . . . . . Cedar Rapids
13-15 . . . . Wisconsin
17-19 . . . . at Quad Cities
20-22 . . . . . . Wisconsin
23-26 . . . . at Beloit
27-29 . . . . . at Wisconsin

MAY
1-3 . . . . . West Michigan
4-6 . . . . South Bend
7-9 . . . at Bowling Green
10-12 . . . . . at Dayton
14-17 . . . . .Clinton
18-20 . . . . . Kane County
21-24 . . . . . at Beloit
25-28 . . . . at Quad Cities
29-31 . . . .Burlington

JUNE
1-3 . . . . at Clinton
5-7 . . . . . at Kane County
8-11 . . . . . . Quad Cities
12-14 . . . . .Beloit
15-17 . . . Cedar Rapids
21-24 . . . . . . .Burlington

25-27 . . . . . Kane County
28-30 . . . . at Beloit

JULY
1 . . . . at Beloit
2-3 . . . . . at Burlington
4-5 . . . . . .Burlington
6-9 . . . . . . at Wisconsin
11-13 . . . . . Lake County
14-16 . . . . . . Fort Wayne
18-20 . . . . . . .at Lansing
21-23 . . . at Great Lakes
25-27 . . . . Wisconsin
28-31 . . . . . . at Clinton

AUGUST
1-3 . . . . Cedar Rapids
4-6 . . . . Quad Cities
8-10 . . . at Kane County
11-14 . . . . .Clinton
15-17 . . . at Cedar Rapids
18-20 . . . . at Quad Cities
21-23 . . . at Kane County
24-27 . . . . .Beloit
29-31 . . . . Kane County

SEPTEMBER
1-3 . . . . . . at Quad Cities

QUAD CITIES RIVER BANDITS

APRIL
5-6 . . . . Cedar Rapids
7-8 . . . . . at Cedar Rapids
9-12 . . . . . . Kane County
13-15 . . . . . at Burlington
17-19 . . . . Peoria

20-22 . . . . . at Burlington
23-26 . . . at Kane County
27-29 . . . . Cedar Rapids

MAY
1-3 . . . . . at Great Lakes

APRIL
4-6 . . . . .at Lansing
7-9 . . . . Fort Wayne
10-12 . . . . . Lake County
14-17 . . . at Cedar Rapids
18-20 . . . . . . at Beloit
21-24 . . . . . . Wisconsin
25-28 . . . . Peoria
29-31 . . . . . . at Clinton

JUNE
1-3 . . . . Beloit
5-7 . . . . at Wisconsin
8-11 . . . . at Peoria
12-14 . . . . Clinton
15-17 . . . . .Burlington
21-24 . . . . Beloit
25-27 . . . . . . Wisconsin
28-30 . . . at Kane County

JULY
1 . . . . . . at Kane County
2-3 . . . . at Beloit
4-5 . . . . .Beloit

SOUTH BEND CUBS

APRIL
5-6 . . . . at West Michigan
7-8 . . . . . . West Michigan
9-12 . . . . Bowling Green
13-15 . . . .at Lake County
17-19 . . . . . at Dayton
20-22 . . . . Lansing
23-26 . . . at Bowling Green
27-29 . . . Great Lakes

MAY
1-3 . . . . . at Cedar Rapids
4-6 . . . . .at Peoria
7-9 . . . . .Burlington
10-12 . . . . .Clinton
14-17 . . . .at Lake County
18-20 . . . .at Fort Wayne
21-24 . . . . Lansing
25-28 . . . . West Michigan
29-31 . . . at Great Lakes

JUNE
1-3 . . . . . Lake County
5-7 . . . . . Fort Wayne
8-11 . . . at West Michigan
12-14 . . . . Dayton
15-17 . . . . at Lansing
21-24 . . . . at Dayton

25-27 . . . . West Michigan
28-30 . . . . Dayton

JULY
1 . . . . .Dayton
2-3 . . . . Bowling Green
4-5 . . . . at Bowling Green
6-9 . . . . . . at Lansing
11-13 . . . . .Beloit
14-16 . . . . . . Wisconsin
18-20 . . . . at Quad Cities
21-23 . . . at Kane County
25-27 . . . . Lansing
28-31 . . . at West Michigan

AUGUST
1-3 . . . . .at Lansing
4-6 . . . at Bowling Green
8-10 . . . . Great Lakes
11-14 . . . . Lake County
15-17 . . . .at Fort Wayne
18-20 . . . . . Great Lakes
21-23 . . . .at Lake County
24-27 . . . . . Fort Wayne
29-31 . . . .Bowling Green

SEPTEMBER
1-3 . . . . . . at Great Lakes

WEST MICHIGAN WHITECAPS

APRIL
5-6 . . . . South Bend
7-8 . . . . . . at South Bend
9-12 . . . . . . Great Lakes
13-15 . . . . .at Lansing
17-19 . . . . Bowling Green
20-22 . . . . at Great Lakes
23-26 . . .at Lake County
27-29 . . . . . Lansing

MAY
1-3 . . . . . . .at Peoria
4-6 . . . . . at Cedar Rapids
7-9 . . . . .Clinton
10-12 . . . . . .Burlington
14-17 . . . .at Fort Wayne
18-20 . . . . Lake County
21-24 . . . . . Fort Wayne
25-28 . . . at South Bend
29-31 . . . . . . at Dayton

JUNE
1-3 . . . . at Bowling Green
5-7 . . . . Great Lakes
8-11 . . . . South Bend
12-14 . . . at Great Lakes
15-17 . . . . .Dayton
21-24 . . . .at Fort Wayne
25-27 . . . at South Bend
28-30 . . . . Bowling Green

JULY
1 . . . . Bowling Green
2-3 . . . . Lansing
4-5 . . . . . . .at Lansing
6-9 . . . . . .at Lake County
11-13 . . . . . Wisconsin
14-16 . . . . .Beloit
18-20 . . . at Kane County
21-23 . . . at Quad Cities
25-27 . . . . Lake County
28-31 . . . . . . South Bend

AUGUST
1-3 . . . . Clinton
4-6 . . . . at Peoria
8-10 . . . . at Beloit
11-12 . . . . Cedar Rapids
13-14 . . at Cedar Rapids
15-17 . . . . Kane County
18-20 . . . . Peoria
21-23 . . . . at Wisconsin
24-27 . . . . at Burlington
29-31 . . . . . at Clinton

SEPTEMBER
1-3 . . . . Peoria

AUGUST
1-3 . . . . . at Great Lakes
4-6 . . . . Dayton
8-10 . . . at Bowling Green
11-14 . . . . . .at Fort Wayne
15-17 . . . . Lansing
18-20 . . . . .at Lake County
21-23 . . . . .Dayton
24-27 . . . . . . Great Lakes
29-31 . . . . at Dayton

SEPTEMBER
1-3 . . . . Fort Wayne

WISCONSIN TIMBER RATTLERS

APRIL
5-6 . . . . at Beloit
7-8 . . . . Beloit
9-12 . . . . at Clinton
13-15 . . . . at Peoria
17-19 . . . . . Kane County
20-22 . . . . . . at Peoria
23-26 . . . . Clinton
27-29 . . . . Peoria

MAY
1-3 . . . . . .at Lake County
4-6 . . . . . . .at Fort Wayne
7-9 . . . . Lansing
10-12 . . . . . . Great Lakes
14-17 . . . . Beloit
18-20 . . . . .Burlington
21-24 . . . . at Quad Cities
25-28 . . . . at Kane County
29-31 . . . . at Cedar Rapids

JUNE
1-3 . . . . . . Kane County
5-7 . . . . Quad Cities
8-11 . . . . . Cedar Rapids
12-14 . . . . . at Burlington
15-17 . . . . at Kane County
21-24 . . . . at Cedar Rapids

25-27 . . . . . at Quad Cities
28-30 . . . . .Clinton

JULY
1 . . . . .Clinton
2-3 . . . . Cedar Rapids
4-5 . . . . . at Cedar Rapids
6-9 . . . . Peoria
11-13 . . . at West Michigan
14-16 . . . . at South Bend
18-20 . . . . .Dayton
21-23 . . . . Bowling Green
25-27 . . . . at Peoria
28-31 . . . . . . Kane County

AUGUST
1-3 . . . . .Burlington
4-6 . . . . at Clinton
8-10 . . . . .Burlington
11-14 . . . . at Beloit
15-17 . . . . . at Burlington
18-20 . . . . . Cedar Rapids
21-23 . . . . . Quad Cities
24-27 . . . . . . at Clinton
29-31 . . . . .Beloit

SEPTEMBER
1-3 . . . . . at Kane County

SOUTH ATLANTIC LEAGUE

ASHEVILLE TOURISTS

APRIL
5-8 . . . . .at Delmarva
9-11 . . . . . .at Kannapolis
12-15 . . . . Columbia
16-18 . . . . Rome
19-22 . . . . at West Virginia
23-26 . . . . Lexington
27-29 . . . . . . .Greensboro

MAY
1-3 . . . . at Charleston
4-7 . . . . at Rome
9-11 . . . . Greensboro
12-15 . . . . . . Kannapolis
17-20 . . . . at Rome
21-24 . . . . Greenville
25-28 . . . . Lexington
29-31 . . . . at Rome

JUNE
1-3 . . . . . . at Greenville
5-7 . . . . Rome
8-10 . . . . Lexington
11-14 . . . .at Charleston
15-17 . . . . Augusta
21-23 . . . . . . Charleston
24-26 . . . . . . Charleston

27-29 . . . . . .at Columbia
30 . . . . at Lexington

JULY
1-3 . . . . . . at Lexington
4-6 . . . . .Rome
7-9 . . . . Greenville
11-13 . . . . at Lakewood
14-17 . . . . at Greensboro
19-22 . . . . . Greenville
23-26 . . . . . . Lexington
27-29 . . . . at West Virginia
30-31 . . . . at Greenville

AUGUST
1 . . . . at Greenville
2-5 . . . . Columbia
7-9 . . . . at Lexington
10-13 . . . . at Greensboro
15-17 . . . . .Hickory
18-21 . . . . Augusta
23-26 . . . .at Columbia
27-30 . . . . .at Kannapolis
31 . . . . .Rome

SEPTEMBER
1-3 . . . . .Rome

AUGUSTA GREENJACKETS

APRIL
5-8 . . . . .at Columbia
9-11 . . . . . at Greensboro
12-15 . . . . Lexington
16-18 . . . . . . Kannapolis
19-22 . . . . . . at Rome
23-26 . . . . . at Greenville
27-29 . . . . Columbia

MAY
1-3 . . . . . at West Virginia
4-7 . . . . . . .at Delmarva
9-11 . . . . .Rome
12-15 . . . . . . Greensboro
17-20 . . . . at Greenville
21-24 . . . . . Charleston
25-28 . . . . .Rome
29-31 . . . . at Greenville

JUNE
1-3 . . . . at Lexington
5-7 . . . . Greenville
8-10 . . . . . .at Columbia
11-14 . . . . West Virginia
15-17 . . . . . at Asheville
21-23 . . . . Rome
24-26 . . . . . at Hickory
27-29 . . . . . Greenville
30 . . . . Columbia

JULY
1-3 . . . . Columbia
4-6 . . . . at Charleston
7-9 . . . . at Rome
11-13 . . . . . . Lexington
14-17 . . . . .Rome
19-22 . . . .at Columbia
23-26 . . . . at Charleston
27-29 . . . . . . Columbia
30-31 . . . . . Kannapolis

AUGUST
1 . . . . Kannapolis
2-5 . . . . at West Virginia
7-9 . . . . .Hagerstown
10-13 . . . . . . Greenville
15-17 . . . .at Kannapolis
18-21 . . . . . at Asheville
23-26 . . . . . Kannapolis
27-30 . . . . . at Lexington
31 . . . . Columbia

SEPTEMBER
1-3 . . . . Columbia

CHARLESTON RIVERDOGS

APRIL
5-8 . . . . . at Lexington
9-11 . . . . at Rome
12-15 . . . . . Kannapolis
16-18 . . . . . West Virginia
19-22 . . . . at Greensboro
23-26 . . . . . . Columbia
27-29 . . . . at Greenville

MAY
1-3 . . . . .Asheville
4-7 . . . . Lexington
9-11 . . . . . . at Lakewood
12-15 . . . . at Hagerstown
17-20 . . . . Columbia
21-24 . . . . . at Augusta
25-28 . . . . . . at Hickory
29-31 . . . . Columbia

JUNE
1-3 . . . . Delmarva
5-7 . . . . .at Columbia
8-10 . . . . . at Greenville
11-14 . . . . .Asheville
15-17 . . . . . . Greenville
21-23 . . . . at Lexington
24-26 . . . . . at Asheville
27-29 . . . . .Rome
30 . . . . at Greenville

JULY
1-3 . . . . . . at Greenville
4-6 . . . . Augusta
7-9 . . . . . . .at Columbia
11-13 . . . . . Delmarva
14-17 . . . . .Hickory
19-22 . . . . . . at Rome
23-26 . . . . . . Augusta
27-29 . . . . . Greenville
30-31 . . . . . at Hickory

AUGUST
1 . . . . at Hickory
2-5 . . . . .at Delmarva
7-9 . . . . .Lakewood
10-13 . . . . .Hagerstown
15-17 . . . . at Delmarva
18-21 . . . . at West Virginia
23-26 . . . . . Greenville
27-30 . . . . at Columbia
31 . . . . West Virginia

SEPTEMBER
1-3 . . . . . . West Virginia

COLUMBIA FIREFLIES

APRIL
5-8 . . . . Augusta
9-11 . . . . . . .Hagerstown
12-15 . . . . at Asheville
16-18 . . . . at Greenville
19-22 . . . . . . .Hickory
23-26 . . . . .at Charleston
27-29 . . . . . at Augusta

MAY
1-3 . . . . Lexington
4-7 . . . . .Lakewood
9-11 . . . . . . at Hickory
12-15 . . . . . Delmarva
17-20 . . . . .at Charleston
21-24 . . . . West Virginia
25-28 . . . . . Greenville
29-31 . . . . .at Charleston

JUNE
1-3 . . . . at Rome
5-7 . . . . Charleston
8-10 . . . . Augusta
11-14 . . . . . at Lexington
15-17 . . . . at Hagerstown
21-23 . . . . . Lakewood
24-26 . . . . at Lexington
27-29 . . . . . Asheville
30 . . . . at Augusta

JULY
1-3 . . . . at Augusta
4-6 . . . . . . Greenville
7-9 . . . . Charleston
11-13 . . . at Hagerstown
14-17 . . . . at Lakewood
19-22 . . . . . Augusta
23-26 . . . . . at Rome
27-29 . . . . at Augusta
30-31 . . . . West Virginia

AUGUST
1 . . . . West Virginia
2-5 . . . . at Asheville
7-9 . . . . Greenville
10-13 . . . . . . Delmarva

15-17 . . . . at West Virginia
18-21 . . . . . at Hagerstown
23-26 . . . . .Asheville
27-30 . . . . . . Charleston

DELMARVA SHOREBIRDS

APRIL
5-8. . . . . . . .Asheville
9-11 . . . . .Hickory
12-15 . . . . . at Lakewood
16-18 . . . . at Hagerstown
19-22 . . . . . . Lakewood
23-26 . . . . Kannapolis
27-29 . . . . at Hickory

MAY
1-3 . . . . Greenville
4-7 . . . . Augusta
9-11 . . . . . . at Lexington
12-15 . . . .at Columbia
17-20 . . .Hagerstown
21-24 . . . . at Hickory
25-28 . . . . .Lakewood
29-31 . . . .at Kannapolis

JUNE
1-3 . . . . . . at Charleston
5-7 . . . . .Greensboro
8-10 . . . . .Hagerstown
11-14 . . . at Kannapolis
15-17 . . . . at West Virginia
21-23 . . . . Kannapolis
24-26 . . . . . .Hagerstown

27-29 . . . . at Greensboro
30 . . . . . at Lakewood

JULY
1-3 . . . . . . at Lakewood
4-6 . . . . . .Hagerstown
7-9 . . . . .Hickory
11-13 . . . . .at Charleston
14-17 . . . at West Virginia
19-22 . . . . .Greensboro
23-26 . . . . at Hagerstown
27-29 . . . .at Kannapolis
30-31 . . . . . .Lakewood

AUGUST
1 . . . . .Lakewood
2-5 . . . . . . Charleston
7-9 . . . . at Rome
10-13 . . . . .at Columbia
15-17 . . . . . Charleston
18-21 . . . . .Rome
23-26 . . . . at Greensboro
27-30 . . . . . . .Hickory
31 . . . . . at Lakewood

SEPTEMBER
1-3 . . . . at Lakewood

GREENSBORO GRASSHOPPERS

APRIL
5-8 . . . . .Hickory
9-11 . . . . Augusta
12-15 . . . . at Hagerstown
16-18 . . . . at Lakewood
19-22 . . . . Charleston
23-26 . . . . . at Hickory
27-29 . . . . . at Asheville

MAY
1-3 . . . . . . .Hagerstown
4-7 . . . . .Greenville
9-11 . . . . . . at Asheville
12-15 . . . . at Augusta
17-20 . . . . .Lakewood
21-24 . . . . Kannapolis
25-28 . . at Hagerstown
29-31 . . . . at Lakewood

JUNE
1-3 . . . . West Virginia
5-7 . . . . . . .at Delmarva
8-10 . . . . . . .Lakewood
11-14 . . . . . .Hickory
15-17 . . . .at Kannapolis
21-23 . . . . at Hagerstown
24-26 . . . . Kannapolis

27-29 . . . . Delmarva
30 . . . . at Hickory

JULY
1-3 . . . . .at Hickory
4-6 . . . . .Lakewood
7-9 . . . . . . at Lexington
11-13 . . . . . Kannapolis
14-17 . . . . .Asheville
19-22 . . . . .at Delmarva
23-26 . . . . at Lakewood
27-29 . . . . . . .Hickory
30-31 . . . . . at Rome

AUGUST
1 . . . . at Rome
2-5 . . . . . .at Kannapolis
7-9 . . . . . West Virginia
10-13 . . . . . . .Asheville
15-17 . . . . at Greenville
18-21 . . . .at Kannapolis
23-26 . . . . . Delmarva
27-30 . . . . .Lakewood
31 . . . . at Hickory

SEPTEMBER
1-3 . . . . . . at Hickory

GREENVILLE DRIVE

APRIL
5-8 . . . . . at West Virginia
9-11 . . . . . . at Lexington
12-15 . . . . .Rome
16-18 . . . . . Columbia
19-22 . . . . .at Kannapolis
23-26 . . . . . . Augusta
27-29 . . . . . . Charleston

MAY
1-3 . . . . .at Delmarva

4-7 . . . . . . at Greensboro
9-11 . . . . . Kannapolis
12-15 . . . . at Lexington
17-20 . . . . Augusta
21-24 . . . . . at Asheville
25-28 . . .at Columbia
29-31 . . . . . . Augusta

JUNE
1-3 . . . . .Asheville
5-7 . . . . at Augusta

8-10 . . . . Charleston
11-14 . . . . .Rome
15-17 . . . at Charleston
21-23 . . . . . . .Asheville
24-26 . . . . at Rome
27-29 . . . . at Augusta
30 . . . . Charleston

JULY
1-3 . . . . Charleston
4-6 . . . . . . .at Columbia
7-9 . . . . . at Asheville
11-13 . . . . .Rome
14-17 . . . . . Lexington
19-22 . . . at Asheville
23-26 . . . . .Hickory

HAGERSTOWN SUNS

APRIL
5-8. . . . . at Rome
9-11 . . . .at Columbia
12-15 . . . . . .Greensboro
16-18 . . . . . . Delmarva
19-22 . . . at Lexington
23-26 . . . . .Lakewood
27-29 . . . . . . Rome

MAY
1-3 . . . . . at Greensboro
4-7 . . . . . .at Kannapolis
9-11 . . . . . West Virginia
12-15 . . . . . Charleston
17-20 . . . .at Delmarva
21-24 . . . at Lakewood
25-28 . . . . .Greensboro
29-31 . . . . . . .Hickory

JUNE
1-3 . . . . .at Kannapolis
5-7 . . . . . . .Lakewood
8-10 . . . . .at Delmarva
11-14 . . . at Lakewood
15-17 . . . . Columbia
21-23 . . . . Greensboro
24-26 . . . .at Delmarva

HICKORY CRAWDADS

APRIL
5-8 . . . . . . at Greensboro
9-11 . . . . . .at Delmarva
12-15 . . . . West Virginia
16-18 . . . . . Lexington
19-22 . . . .at Columbia
23-26 . . . . . Greensboro
27-29 . . . . . Delmarva

MAY
1-3 . . . . . .at Kannapolis
4-7 . . . . at West Virginia
9-11 . . . . . Columbia
12-15 . . . . . . .Rome
17-20 . . .at Kannapolis
21-24 . . . . . Delmarva
25-28 . . . . . Charleston
29-31 . . . .at Hagerstown

JUNE
1-3 . . . . . at Lakewood
5-7 . . . . . . Kannapolis
8-10 . . . . West Virginia
11-14 . . . at Greensboro
15-17 . . . . . at Lakewood
21-23 . . . West Virginia
24-26 . . . . Augusta

27-29 . . . . at Charleston
30-31 . . . . . . .Asheville

AUGUST
1 . . . . .Asheville
2-5 . . . . .Rome
7-9 . . . . .at Columbia
10-13 . . . . at Augusta
15-17 . . . .Greensboro
18-21 . . . . . . .Hickory
23-26 . . . at Charleston
27-30 . . . . at Rome
31 . . . . Lexington

SEPTEMBER
1-3 . . . . Lexington

27-29 . . . . . at Lakewood
30 . . . . . West Virginia

JULY
1-3 . . . . . West Virginia
4-6 . . . . . .at Delmarva
7-9 . . . . . at West Virginia
11-13 . . . . . Columbia
14-17 . . . . .at Kannapolis
19-22 . . . . .Lakewood
23-26 . . . . Delmarva
27-29 . . . . at Lakewood
30-31 . . . . . Lexington

AUGUST
1 . . . . Lexington
2-5 . . . . .Hickory
7-9 . . . . . at Augusta
10-13 . . .at Charleston
15-17 . . . . . Lexington
18-21 . . . . . Columbia
23-26 . . . at Lexington
27-30 . . at West Virginia
31 . . . . Kannapolis

SEPTEMBER
1-3 . . . . Kannapolis

27-29 . . . . at West Virginia
30 . . . . Greensboro

JULY
1-3 . . . . Greensboro
4-6 . . . . . . .at Kannapolis
7-9 . . . . . . .at Delmarva
11-13 . . . . . West Virginia
14-17 . . . . .at Charleston
19-22 . . . . . Kannapolis
23-26 . . . . at Greenville
27-29 . . . at Greensboro
30-31 . . . . . Charleston

AUGUST
1 . . . . Charleston
2-5 . . . . . . at Hagerstown
7-9 . . . . . . Kannapolis
10-13 . . . . .Lakewood
15-17 . . . . at Asheville
18-21 . . . . at Greenville
23-26 . . . . .Lakewood
27-29 . . . at Greensboro
30-31 . . . . . Charleston

SEPTEMBER
1-3 . . . . Greensboro

KANNAPOLIS INTIMIDATORS

APRIL
5-8. . . . . . . .Lakewood
9-11. . . . . . . .Asheville
12-15 . . . . .at Charleston
16-18 . . . . . at Augusta
19-22 . . . . . . Greenville
23-26 . . . . . .at Delmarva
27-29 . . . . . at Lakewood

MAY
1-3. . . . . .Hickory
4-7. . . . . . . .Hagerstown
9-11. . . . . at Greenville
12-15 . . . . at Asheville
17-20 . . . . .Hickory
21-24 . . . . at Greensboro
25-28 . . . at West Virginia
29-31 . . . . Delmarva

JUNE
1-3. . . . . . . .Hagerstown
5-7. . . . . . . .at Hickory
8-10 . . . . at Rome
11-14 . . . . Delmarva
15-17 . . . . . . Greensboro
21-23 . . . . . .at Delmarva
24-26 . . . . at Greensboro

27-29 . . . . . . Lexington
30 . . . . at Rome

JULY
1-3. . . . . at Rome
4-6. . . . . .Hickory
7-9. . . . . . . .Lakewood
11-13 . . . . . at Greensboro
14-17 . . . . .Hagerstown
19-22 . . . . . at Hickory
23-26 . . . . West Virginia
27-29 . . . . . Delmarva
30-31 . . . . . at Augusta

AUGUST
1 . . . . at Augusta
2-5. . . . . . . Greensboro
7-9. . . . . . .at Hickory
10-13 . . . . . at Lexington
15-17 . . . . . . Augusta
18-21 . . . . . Greensboro
23-26 . . . . at Augusta
27-30 . . . . . .Asheville
31 . . . . . at Hagerstown

SEPTEMBER
1-3. . . . . . at Hagerstown

LAKEWOOD BLUECLAWS

APRIL
5-8. . . . .at Kannapolis
9-11. . . at West Virginia
12-15 . . . . . . Delmarva
16-18 . . . . . Greensboro
19-22 . . . . .at Delmarva
23-26 . . . . at Hagerstown
27-29 . . . . . . Kannapolis

MAY
1-3. . . . . at Rome
4-7. . . . . . . .at Columbia
9-11. . . . . . Charleston
12-15 . . . . West Virginia
17-20 . . . . at Greensboro
21-24 . . . . . .Hagerstown
25-28 . . . . .at Delmarva
29-31 . . . . . . Greensboro

JUNE
1-3. . . . . .Hickory
5-7. . . . . at Hagerstown
8-10 . . . . at Greensboro
11-14 . . . . . .Hagerstown
15-17 . . . . . . .Hickory
21-23 . . . . . .at Columbia
24-26 . . . at West Virginia

27-29 . . . . . .Hagerstown
30 . . . . Delmarva

JULY
1-3. . . . . Delmarva
4-6. . . . . at Greensboro
7-9. . . . . .at Kannapolis
11-13 . . . . . . .Asheville
14-17 . . . . Columbia
19-22 . . . . at Hagerstown
23-26 . . . . . . Greensboro
27-29 . . . . . .Hagerstown
30-31 . . . . at Delmarva

AUGUST
1 . . . . .at Delmarva
2-5. . . . . Lexington
7-9. . . . . at Charleston
10-13 . . . . . . at Hickory
15-17 . . . . .Rome
18-21 . . . . . Lexington
23-26 . . . . at Hickory
27-30 . . . . at Greensboro
31 . . . . Delmarva

SEPTEMBER
1-3. . . . . Delmarva

LEXINGTON LEGENDS

APRIL
5-8. . . . . Charleston
9-11. . . . . . . Greenville
12-15 . . . . . at Augusta
16-18 . . . . . . at Hickory
19-22 . . . . .Hagerstown
23-26 . . . . at Asheville
27-29 . . . . . West Virginia

MAY
1-3. . . . . . . .at Columbia
4-7. . . . . . . .at Charleston
9-11. . . . . . . Delmarva
12-15 . . . . . Greenville
17-20 . . . . at West Virginia
21-24 . . . . Rome

25-28 . . . . . . at Asheville
29-31 . . . . . West Virginia

JUNE
1-3. . . . . Augusta
5-7. . . . . at West Virginia
8-10 . . . . . . at Asheville
11-14 . . . . Columbia
15-17 . . . . . . at Rome
21-23 . . . . . . Charleston
24-26 . . . . . . Columbia
27-29 . . . . .at Kannapolis
30 . . . . .Asheville

JULY
1-3. . . . . .Asheville

APRIL
4-6. . . . . at West Virginia
7-9. . . . . Greensboro
11-13 . . . . . at Augusta
14-17 . . . . at Greenville
19-22 . . . . West Virginia
23-26 . . . . at Asheville
27-29 . . . . .Rome
30-31 . . . at Hagerstown

AUGUST
1 . . . . at Hagerstown

ROME BRAVES

APRIL
5-8. . . . . . . .Hagerstown
9-11. . . . . . . Charleston
12-15 . . . . at Greenville
16-18 . . . . at Asheville
19-22 . . . . . Augusta
23-26 . . . at West Virginia
27-29 . . . at Hagerstown

MAY
1-3. . . . . .Lakewood
4-7. . . . . .Asheville
9-11. . . . . . at Augusta
12-15 . . . . at Hickory
17-20 . . . . . . .Asheville
21-24 . . . . at Lexington
25-28 . . . . at Augusta
29-31 . . . . . . .Asheville

JUNE
1-3. . . . . . . Columbia
5-7. . . . . . at Asheville
8-10 . . . . . . Kannapolis
11-14 . . . . at Greenville
15-17 . . . . . Lexington
21-23 . . . . at Augusta
24-26 . . . . . Greenville

WEST VIRGINIA POWER

APRIL
5-8. . . . . . . Greenville
9-11. . . . . . . .Lakewood
12-15 . . . . . at Hickory
16-18 . . . .at Charleston
19-22 . . . . . . .Asheville
23-26 . . . . . . .Rome
27-29 . . . . . at Lexington

MAY
1-3. . . . . Augusta
4-7. . . . . .Hickory
9-11. . . . . at Hagerstown
12-15 . . . . at Lakewood
17-20 . . . . . . Lexington
21-24 . . . . .at Columbia
25-28 . . . . . . Kannapolis
29-31 . . . . at Lexington

JUNE
1-3. . . . . at Greensboro
5-7. . . . . . . Lexington
8-10 . . . . . . .at Hickory
11-14 . . . . . at Augusta
15-17 . . . . . . Delmarva
21-23 . . . . at Hickory
24-26 . . . . . .Lakewood

2-5. . . . . at Lakewood
7-9. . . . . .Asheville
10-13 . . . . . . Kannapolis
15-17 . . . at Hagerstown
18-21 . . . . at Lakewood
23-26 . . . . .Hagerstown
27-30 . . . . Augusta
31 . . . . . at Greenville

SEPTEMBER
1-3. . . . . at Greenville

27-29 . . . .at Charleston
30 . . . . Kannapolis

JULY
1-3. . . . . . . Kannapolis
4-6. . . . . . at Asheville
7-9. . . . . Augusta
11-13 . . . . at Greenville
14-17 . . . . at Augusta
19-22 . . . . . Charleston
23-26 . . . . . Columbia
27-29 . . . at Lexington
30-31 . . . . . Greensboro

AUGUST
1 . . . . Greensboro
2-5. . . . . . at Greenville
7-9. . . . . . . Delmarva
10-13 . . . . West Virginia
15-17 . . . . at Lakewood
18-21 . . . .at Delmarva
23-26 . . . West Virginia
27-30 . . . . . Greenville
31 . . . . at Asheville

SEPTEMBER
1-3. . . . . . . at Asheville

27-29 . . . . .Hickory
30 . . . . . at Hagerstown

JULY
1-3. . . . . .at Hagerstown
4-6. . . . . Lexington
7-9. . . . . . . .Hagerstown
11-13 . . . . . at Hickory
14-17 . . . . . Delmarva
19-22 . . . . at Lexington
23-26 . . . . .at Kannapolis
27-29 . . . . . . .Asheville
30-31 . . . .at Columbia

AUGUST
1 . . . . .at Columbia
2-5. . . . . Augusta
7-9. . . . . at Greensboro
10-13 . . . . at Rome
15-17 . . . . . . Columbia
18-21 . . . . . Charleston
23-26 . . . . . at Rome
27-30 . . . .Hagerstown
31 . . . . . at Charleston

SEPTEMBER
1-3. . . . . . . at Charleston

SHORT SEASON

NEW YORK-PENN LEAGUE

ABERDEEN IRONBIRDS

JUNE	
15-17	Hudson Valley
18-20	Tri-City
21-23	at Staten Island
24-26	Vermont
28-30	at Lowell

JULY	
1-3	Hudson Valley
4-6	at Brooklyn
7-9	at Tri-City
11-13	Brooklyn
14-16	Auburn
17-19	at Lowell
20-22	Connecticut
24-26	at West Virginia
27-29	Mahoning Valley
30-31	at Staten Island

AUGUST	
1	at Staten Island
2-4	at Brooklyn
5-7	Staten Island
8-10	Vermont
11-12	at Hudson Valley
15-16	Lowell
17-19	at Connecticut
20-22	at Vermont
23-25	Staten Island
26-28	at Tri-City
29-31	Connecticut

SEPTEMBER	
1-3	at Hudson Valley

AUBURN DOUBLEDAYS

JUNE	
15-17	Batavia
18-20	at Williamsport
21-23	at Mahoning Valley
24-26	West Virginia
28	at Batavia
29-30	Batavia

JULY	
1-3	at Williamsport
4-6	State College
7-9	at West Virginia
11-13	Lowell
14-16	at Aberdeen
17-19	Mahoning Valley
20-22	at State College
24-26	at Tri-City
27-29	Connecticut
30-31	West Virginia

AUGUST	
1	West Virginia
2-4	at State College
5-7	Williamsport
8	Batavia
9-10	at Batavia
11-12	State College
15-16	at Mahoning Valley
17-19	Batavia
20-22	Mahoning Valley
23-25	at State College
26-28	at West Virginia
29-31	Williamsport

SEPTEMBER	
1-3	at Batavia

BATAVIA MUCKDOGS

JUNE	
15-17	at Auburn
18-20	West Virginia
21-23	Williamsport
24-26	at State College
28	Auburn
29-30	at Auburn

JULY	
1-3	West Virginia
4-6	at Mahoning Valley
7-9	State College
11-13	at Connecticut
14-16	Lowell
17-19	at Williamsport
20-22	Mahoning Valley
24-26	Staten Island
27-29	at Vermont
30-31	at State College

AUGUST	
1	at State College
2-4	Mahoning Valley
5-7	at West Virginia
8	at Auburn
9-10	Auburn
11-12	at Williamsport
15-16	West Virginia
17-19	at Auburn
20-22	at West Virginia
23-25	Williamsport
26-28	State College
29-31	at Mahoning Valley

SEPTEMBER	
1-3	Auburn

BROOKLYN CYCLONES

JUNE	
15	at Staten Island
16	Staten Island
17	at Staten Island
18-20	Hudson Valley
21-23	at Connecticut
24-26	Lowell
28-30	at Vermont

JULY	
1	Staten Island
2	at Staten Island
3	Staten Island
4-6	Aberdeen
7	at Staten Island
8	Staten Island
9	at Staten Island
11-13	at Aberdeen
14-16	Williamsport
17-19	at Tri-City
20-22	Lowell
24-26	at Mahoning Valley
27-29	at West Virginia
30-31	Tri-City

AUGUST	
1	Tri-City
2-4	Aberdeen
5-7	at Hudson Valley
8-10	Connecticut
11-12	at Lowell
15-16	Vermont
17-19	at Hudson Valley
20-22	at Tri-City
23-25	Connecticut
26-28	at Vermont
29-31	Hudson Valley

SEPTEMBER	
1	Staten Island
2	at Staten Island
3	Staten Island

CONNECTICUT TIGERS

JUNE	
15-17	Lowell
18-20	at Vermont
21-23	Brooklyn
24-26	at Hudson Valley
28-30	Staten Island

JULY	
1-3	at Lowell
4-6	Lowell
7-9	at Vermont
11-13	Batavia
14-16	Vermont
17-19	at Hudson Valley
20-22	at Aberdeen
24-26	State College
27-29	at Auburn
30-31	Vermont

AUGUST	
1	Vermont
2-4	at Staten Island
5-7	Tri-City
8-10	at Brooklyn
11-12	Staten Island
15-16	at Tri-City
17-19	Aberdeen
20-22	Hudson Valley
23-25	at Brooklyn
26-28	Lowell
29-31	at Aberdeen

SEPTEMBER	
1-3	at Lowell

HUDSON VALLEY RENEGADES

JUNE	
15-17	at Aberdeen
18-20	at Brooklyn
21-23	Vermont
24-26	Connecticut
28-30	at Tri-City

JULY	
1-3	at Aberdeen
4	at Staten Island
5-6	Staten Island
7-9	at Lowell
11-13	West Virginia
14-16	at Mahoning Valley
17-19	Connecticut
20-22	Vermont
24-26	at Lowell
27-29	at Williamsport
30-31	Lowell

AUGUST	
1	Lowell
2-4	at Vermont
5-7	Brooklyn
8-10	at Tri-City
11-12	Aberdeen
15	at Staten Island
16	Staten Island
17-19	Brooklyn
20-22	at Connecticut
23-25	Tri-City
26-28	Staten Island
29-31	at Brooklyn

SEPTEMBER	
1-3	Aberdeen

LOWELL SPINNERS

JUNE	
15-17	at Connecticut
18-20	Staten Island
21-23	at Tri-City
24-26	at Brooklyn
28-30	Aberdeen

JULY	
1-3	Connecticut
4-6	at Connecticut
7-9	Hudson Valley
11-13	at Auburn
14-16	at Batavia
17-19	Aberdeen
20-22	at Brooklyn
24-26	Hudson Valley
27-29	State College
30-31	at Hudson Valley

AUGUST	
1	at Hudson Valley
2-4	at Tri-City
5-7	Vermont
8-10	at Staten Island

11-12 . . . . .Brooklyn
15-16 . . . . . at Aberdeen
17-19 . . . . .Tri-City
20-22 . . at Staten Island
23-25 . . . . .Vermont

26-28 . . . . . at Connecticut
29-31 . . . . .Tri-City
SEPTEMBER
1-3 . . . . .Connecticut

MAHONING VALLEY SCRAPPERS

JUNE
15-17 . . . . . West Virginia
18-20 . . . . at State College
21-23 . . . . .Auburn
24-26 . . . . . Williamsport
28-30 . . . at West Virginia

JULY
1-3 . . . . at State College
4-6 . . . . .Batavia
7-9 . . . . . . Williamsport
11-13 . . . . at Staten Island
14-16 . . . . Hudson Valley
17-19 . . . . . . at Auburn
20-22 . . . . . at Batavia
24-26 . . . . . . .Brooklyn
27-29 . . . . at Aberdeen

30-31 . . . . . Williamsport
AUGUST
1 . . . . Williamsport
2-4 . . . . at Batavia
5-7 . . . . . State College
8-10 . . . .at Williamsport
11-12 . . . at West Virginia
15-16 . . . . .Auburn
17-19 . . . . State College
20-22 . . . . . at Auburn
23-25 . . . . West Virginia
26-28 . . . .at Williamsport
29-31 . . . . .Batavia

SEPTEMBER
1-3 . . . . . at West Virginia

STATE COLLEGE SPIKES

JUNE
15 . . . . .at Williamsport
16 . . . . . . Williamsport
17 . . . . .at Williamsport
18-20 . . .Mahoning Valley
21-23 . . . at West Virginia
24-26 . . . . Batavia
28 . . . . . .at Williamsport
29 . . . . . . Williamsport
30 . . . . . .at Williamsport

JULY
1-3 . . . .Mahoning Valley
4-6 . . . . at Auburn
7-9 . . . . . . at Batavia
11-13 . . . . . .Vermont
14-16 . . . . . . Tri-City
17-19 . . at West Virginia
20-22 . . . . .Auburn

24-26 . . . . at Connecticut
27-29 . . . . .at Lowell
30-31 . . . . .Batavia

AUGUST
1 . . . . Batavia
2-4 . . . . .Auburn
5-7 . . . at Mahoning Valley
8-10 . . . . . West Virginia
11-12 . . . . . . at Auburn
15-16 . . . . . Williamsport
17-19 . . at Mahoning Valley
20 . . . . Williamsport
21-22 . . . .at Williamsport
23-25 . . . . .Auburn
26-28 . . . . . at Batavia
29-31 . . . . . West Virginia

SEPTEMBER
1-3 . . . . . .at Williamsport

STATEN ISLAND YANKEES

JUNE
15 . . . . .Brooklyn
16 . . . . at Brooklyn
17 . . . . .Brooklyn
18-20 . . . . . .at Lowell
21-23 . . . . . Aberdeen
24-26 . . . . Tri-City
28-30 . . . .at Connecticut

JULY
1 . . . . at Brooklyn
2 . . . . .Brooklyn
3 . . . . at Brooklyn
4 . . . . . . Hudson Valley
5-6 . . .at Hudson Valley
7 . . . . .Brooklyn
8 . . . . at Brooklyn
9 . . . . .Brooklyn
11-13 . . .Mahoning Valley
14-16 . . . . . West Virginia
17-19 . . . . at Vermont
20-22 . . . . Tri-City

24-26 . . . . at Batavia
27-29 . . . . at Tri-City
30-31 . . . . Aberdeen

AUGUST
1 . . . . Aberdeen
2-4 . . . . .Connecticut
5-7 . . . . . . at Aberdeen
8-10 . . . . Lowell
11-12 . . . . at Connecticut
15 . . . . . Hudson Valley
16 . . . . .at Hudson Valley
17-19 . . . . . . at Vermont
20-22 . . . . Lowell
23-25 . . . . at Aberdeen
26-28 . . .at Hudson Valley
29-31 . . . . Vermont

SEPTEMBER
1 . . . . at Brooklyn
2 . . . . .Brooklyn
3 . . . . at Brooklyn

TRI-CITY VALLEYCATS

JUNE
15-17 . . . . . . .Vermont
18-20 . . . . . at Aberdeen
21-23 . . . . Lowell
24-26 . . . at Staten Island
28-30 . . . . Hudson Valley

JULY
1-3 . . . . . . at Vermont
4-6 . . . . .Vermont
7-9 . . . . Aberdeen
11-13 . . .at Williamsport
14-16 . . at State College
17-19 . . . . . . .Brooklyn
20-22 . . at Staten Island
24-26 . . . . .Auburn
27-29 . . . . . Staten Island

30-31 . . . . . . at Brooklyn
AUGUST
1 . . . . at Brooklyn
2-4 . . . . Lowell
5-7 . . . . . at Connecticut
8-10 . . . . . Hudson Valley
11-12 . . . . . . at Vermont
15-16 . . . . . .Connecticut
17-19 . . . . . . .at Lowell
20-22 . . . . . . .Brooklyn
23-25 . . .at Hudson Valley
26-28 . . . . . . Aberdeen
29-31 . . . . . . .at Lowell

SEPTEMBER
1-3 . . . . at Vermont

VERMONT LAKE MONSTERS

JUNE
15-17 . . . . at Tri-City
18-20 . . . . . .Connecticut
21-23 . . . .at Hudson Valley
24-26 . . . . . at Aberdeen
28-30 . . . . . . .Brooklyn

JULY
1-3 . . . . Tri-City
4-6 . . . . at Tri-City
7-9 . . . . .Connecticut
11-13 . . at State College
14-16 . . . at Connecticut
17-19 . . . . . Staten Island
20-22 . . .at Hudson Valley
24-26 . . . . . Williamsport
27-29 . . . . Batavia

30-31 . . . . at Connecticut
AUGUST
1 . . . . .at Connecticut
2-4 . . . . . . Hudson Valley
5-7 . . . . .at Lowell
8-10 . . . . . . at Aberdeen
11-12 . . . . Tri-City
15-16 . . . . . at Brooklyn
17-19 . . . . . Staten Island
20-22 . . . . . Aberdeen
23-25 . . . . . . .at Lowell
26-28 . . . . . . .Brooklyn
29-31 . . . . at Staten Island

SEPTEMBER
1-3 . . . . Tri-City

WEST VIRGINIA BLACK BEARS

JUNE
15-17 . . at Mahoning Valley
18-20 . . . . at Batavia
21-23 . . . . . State College
24-26 . . . . at Auburn
28-30 . . . .Mahoning Valley

JULY
1-3 . . . . at Batavia
4-6 . . . . Williamsport
7-9 . . . . .Auburn
11-13 . . .at Hudson Valley
14-16 . . . at Staten Island
17-19 . . . . . State College
20-22 . . .at Williamsport
24-26 . . . . . . Aberdeen
27-29 . . . . .Brooklyn

30-31 . . . . at Auburn
AUGUST
1 . . . . at Auburn
2-4 . . . . . .at Williamsport
5-7 . . . . .Batavia
8-10 . . . . at State College
11-12 . . . .Mahoning Valley
15-16 . . . . . . at Batavia
17-19 . . . . . Williamsport
20-22 . . . . Batavia
23-25 . . at Mahoning Valley
26-28 . . . . .Auburn
29-31 . . . at State College

SEPTEMBER
1-3 . . . .Mahoning Valley

WILLIAMSPORT CROSSCUTTERS

JUNE
15 . . . . State College
16 . . . . at State College
17 . . . . State College
18-20 . . . . .Auburn
21-23 . . . . . at Batavia
24-26 . . at Mahoning Valley
28 . . . . State College
29 . . . . . . State College
30 . . . . State College

JULY
1-3 . . . . .Auburn
4-6 . . . . . at West Virginia

7-9 . . . . at Mahoning Valley
11-13 . . . . Tri-City
14-16 . . . . . . at Brooklyn
17-19 . . . . Batavia
20-22 . . . . . West Virginia
24-26 . . . . . at Vermont
27-29 . . . . . Hudson Valley
30-31 . . at Mahoning Valley

AUGUST
1 . . . . . at Mahoning Valley
2-4 . . . . West Virginia
5-7 . . . . at Auburn
8-10 . . . .Mahoning Valley

11-12 . . . . Batavia	23-25 . . . . at Batavia
15-16 . . . . at State College	26-28 . . .Mahoning Valley
17-19 . . . at West Virginia	29-31 . . . . . . at Auburn
20 . . . . . at State College	**SEPTEMBER**
21-22 . . . . . State College	1-3 . . . . State College

NORTHWEST LEAGUE

BOISE HAWKS

JUNE		24-26 . . . . . . at Hillsboro
15-19 . . . . . . at Spokane		27-31 . . . . Tri-City
20-22 . . . . . Salem-Keizer		**AUGUST**
23-25 . . . . at Eugene		1-5 . . . . at Everett
26-28 . . . . .Hillsboro		9-13 . . . . Spokane
29-30 . . . . at Tri-City		14-16 . . . . . Salem-Keizer
JULY		17-19 . . . . . . at Eugene
1-3 . . . . at Tri-City		20-22 . . . at Salem-Keizer
4-6 . . . . .Eugene		23-27 . . . . . at Vancouver
7-9 . . . . at Salem-Keizer		29-31 . . . . .Hillsboro
11-15 . . . . . . .Vancouver		**SEPTEMBER**
16-18 . . . . at Hillsboro		1-3 . . . . .Eugene
19-23 . . . . Everett		

EUGENE EMERALDS

JUNE		24-26 . . . . . Salem-Keizer
15-19 . . . . . .Vancouver		27-31 . . . . at Vancouver
20-22 . . . . . . at Hillsboro		**AUGUST**
23-25 . . . . Boise		1-5 . . . . .Spokane
26-28 . . . . at Salem-Keizer		9-13 . . . . at Everett
29-30 . . . . Everett		14-16 . . . . . . .Hillsboro
JULY		17-19 . . . . Boise
1-3 . . . . Everett		20-22 . . . at Hillsboro
4-6 . . . . at Boise		23-27 . . . . Tri-City
7-9 . . . . .Hillsboro		29-31 . . at Salem-Keizer
11-15 . . . . . . at Spokane		**SEPTEMBER**
16-18 . . . Salem-Keizer		1-3 . . . . at Boise
19-23 . . . . at Tri-City		

EVERETT AQUASOX

JUNE		24-26 . . . . . . .Vancouver
15-19 . . . . .Hillsboro		27-31 . . . . at Salem-Keizer
20-22 . . . . at Vancouver		**AUGUST**
23-25 . . . . Tri-City		1-5 . . . . Boise
26-28 . . . . . . at Spokane		9-13 . . . . .Eugene
29-30 . . . . . . at Eugene		14-16 . . . . . . at Spokane
JULY		17-19 . . . . . at Tri-City
1-3 . . . . at Eugene		20-22 . . . . Spokane
4-6 . . . . . . .Vancouver		23-27 . . . . . at Hillsboro
7-9 . . . . at Tri-City		29-31 . . . . at Vancouver
11-15 . . . . . Salem-Keizer		**SEPTEMBER**
16-18 . . . . . Spokane		1-3 . . . . Tri-City
19-23 . . . . at Boise		

HILLSBORO HOPS

JUNE		24-26 . . . . Boise
15-19 . . . . . . at Everett		27-31 . . . . . at Spokane
20-22 . . . . . . .Eugene		**AUGUST**
23-25 . . . . . Salem-Keizer		1-5 . . . . .Vancouver
26-28 . . . . at Boise		9-13 . . . . . . at Tri-City
29-30 . . . . Spokane		14-16 . . . . . at Eugene
JULY		17-19 . . . . at Salem-Keizer
1-3 . . . . Spokane		20-22 . . . . . . .Eugene
4-6 . . . . at Salem-Keizer		23-27 . . . . Everett
7-9 . . . . at Eugene		29-31 . . . . at Boise
11-15 . . . . Tri-City		**SEPTEMBER**
16-18 . . . . . Boise		1-3 . . . . Salem-Keizer
19-23 . . . . . at Vancouver		

SALEM-KEIZER VOLCANOES

JUNE		24-26 . . . . at Eugene
15-19 . . . . Tri-City		27-31 . . . . Everett
20-22 . . . . at Boise		**AUGUST**
23-25 . . . . . . at Hillsboro		1-5 . . . . at Tri-City
26-28 . . . . .Eugene		9-13 . . . . .Vancouver
29-30 . . . . at Vancouver		14-16 . . . . . . at Boise
JULY		17-19 . . . . . . .Hillsboro
1-3 . . . . . at Vancouver		20-22 . . . . Boise
4-6 . . . . .Hillsboro		23-27 . . . . at Spokane
7-9 . . . . Boise		29-31 . . . . .Eugene
11-15 . . . . at Everett		**SEPTEMBER**
16-18 . . . . at Eugene		1-3 . . . . at Hillsboro
19-23 . . . . Spokane		

SPOKANE INDIANS

JUNE		24-26 . . . . Tri-City
15-19 . . . . Boise		27-31 . . . . .Hillsboro
20-22 . . . . at Tri-City		**AUGUST**
23-25 . . . . .Vancouver		1-5 . . . . at Eugene
26-28 . . . . Everett		9-13 . . . . at Boise
29-30 . . . at Hillsboro		14-16 . . . . Everett
JULY		17-19 . . . . . at Vancouver
1-3 . . . . at Hillsboro		20-22 . . . . . . at Everett
4-6 . . . . Tri-City		23-27 . . . . Salem-Keizer
7-9 . . . . at Vancouver		29-31 . . . . . at Tri-City
11-15 . . . . .Eugene		**SEPTEMBER**
16-18 . . . . at Everett		1-3 . . . . .Vancouver
19-23 . . . . at Salem-Keizer		

TRI-CITY DUST DEVILS

JUNE		24-26 . . . . . . at Spokane
15-19 . . . at Salem-Keizer		27-31 . . . . . at Boise
20-22 . . . . Spokane		**AUGUST**
23-25 . . . . . at Everett		1-5 . . . . Salem-Keizer
26-28 . . . . at Vancouver		9-13 . . . . .Hillsboro
29-30 . . . . Boise		14-16 . . . . at Vancouver
JULY		17-19 . . . . Everett
1-3 . . . . Boise		20-22 . . . . . .Vancouver
4-6 . . . . . . at Spokane		23-27 . . . . . at Eugene
7-9 . . . . Everett		29-31 . . . . . Spokane
11-15 . . . . at Hillsboro		**SEPTEMBER**
16-18 . . . . . .Vancouver		1-3 . . . . at Everett
19-23 . . . . .Eugene		

VANCOUVER CANADIANS

JUNE		24-26 . . . . at Everett
15-19 . . . . . . at Eugene		27-31 . . . . .Eugene
20-22 . . . . Everett		**AUGUST**
23-25 . . . . . at Spokane		1-5 . . . . . . at Hillsboro
26-28 . . . . Tri-City		9-13 . . . . at Salem-Keizer
29-30 . . . . Salem-Keizer		14-16 . . . . Tri-City
JULY		17-19 . . . . Spokane
1-3 . . . . . Salem-Keizer		20-22 . . . . at Tri-City
4-6 . . . . . . at Everett		23-27 . . . . . Boise
7-9 . . . . Spokane		29-31 . . . . Everett
11-15 . . . . . . at Boise		**SEPTEMBER**
16-18 . . . at Tri-City		1-3 . . . . at Spokane
19-23 . . . . . . .Hillsboro		

ROOKIE

APPALACHIAN LEAGUE

BLUEFIELD BLUE JAYS

JUNE
19-21 . . . . . . Johnson City
22-24 . . . . . at Burlington
25-26 . . . . Princeton
28-30 . . .at Greeneville

JULY
1-3 . . . . .Burlington
4-5 . . . . at Pulaski
6 . . . . Pulaski
7-9 . . . . Kingsport
10-12 . . . . . .at Princeton
13 . . . . Princeton
14-16 . . . . Danville
18-20 . . . . at Johnson City
21-23 . . . . Pulaski
24-26 . . . . Bristol

27-29 . . . . . .at Princeton
31 . . . . at Bristol

AUGUST
1-2 . . . . .at Bristol
3-5 . . . . Danville
6-8 . . . . Greeneville
9-11 . . . . .at Elizabethton
12-14 . . . . . at Kingsport
16-18 . . . . . Elizabethton
19 . . . . Princeton
20 . . . . .at Princeton
21-23 . . . . . .at Danville
24 . . . . at Pulaski
25-26 . . . . Pulaski
27-29 . . . . . at Burlington

BRISTOL PIRATES

JUNE
19-21 . . . .at Greeneville
22-24 . . . . Elizabethton
25-26 . . . . Pulaski
28-30 . . . . . .at Princeton

JULY
1-3 . . . . .at Danville
4-6 . . . . . . Johnson City
7-9 . . . . Princeton
10-13 . . . . . . at Pulaski
14-16 . . .at Greeneville
18-20 . . . . . .Burlington
21-23 . . . . . . Kingsport
24-26 . . . . . . at Bluefield

27-29 . . . .at Elizabethton
31 . . . . .Bluefield

AUGUST
1-2 . . . . .Bluefield
3-5 . . . . at Kingsport
6-8 . . . . Johnson City
9-11 . . . . . . Greeneville
12-14 . . . at Johnson City
16-18 . . . . at Burlington
19-20 . . . . Pulaski
21-23 . . . . at Kingsport
24-26 . . . . . Elizabethton
27-29 . . . . Danville

BURLINGTON ROYALS

JUNE
19-21 . . . .at Elizabethton
22-24 . . . . Bluefield
25-26 . . . . Danville
28-30 . . . . . . at Pulaski

JULY
1-3 . . . . at Bluefield
4-6 . . . . Princeton
7-9 . . . . Greeneville
10-13 . . . . .at Danville
14-16 . . . . Johnson City
18-20 . . . . . . at Bristol
21-23 . . .at Greeneville
24-26 . . . . . Elizabethton

27-29 . . . . . . Kingsport
31 . . . . at Pulaski

AUGUST
1-2 . . . . at Pulaski
3-5 . . . . Princeton
6-8 . . . . .at Danville
9-11 . . . . Bluefield
12-14 . . . . .at Princeton
16-18 . . . . . . Bristol
19-20 . . . . . . Danville
21-23 . . . at Johnson City
24-26 . . . . at Kingsport
27-29 . . . . . . .Bluefield

DANVILLE BRAVES

JUNE
19-21 . . . . Pulaski
22-24 . . . . . .at Princeton
25-26 . . . at Burlington
28-30 . . . . . Elizabethton

JULY
1-3 . . . . Bristol
4-6 . . . . . .at Greeneville
7-9 . . . .at Elizabethton
10-13 . . . . .Burlington
14-16 . . . . . at Bluefield

18-20 . . . . Pulaski
21-23 . . . . . Johnson City
24-26 . . . . at Kingsport
27-29 . . . at Johnson City
31 . . . . Princeton

AUGUST
1-2 . . . . Princeton
3-5 . . . . at Bluefield
6-8 . . . . .Burlington
9-11 . . . . Kingsport
12-14 . . . . . . at Pulaski

16-18 . . . . . . Greeneville
19-20 . . . . . at Burlington
21-23 . . . . .Bluefield

ELIZABETHTON TWINS

JUNE
19-21 . . . . . . .Burlington
22-24 . . . . . . at Bristol
25-26 . . . . . Johnson City
28-30 . . . . . .at Danville

JULY
1-3 . . . . . . .at Princeton
4-6 . . . . Kingsport
7-9 . . . . Danville
10-13 . . . at Johnson City
14-16 . . . . at Kingsport
18-20 . . . . . . Greeneville
21-23 . . . . . . Princeton
24-26 . . . . . at Burlington

27-29 . . . . Bristol
31 . . . . . at Johnson City

AUGUST
1-2 . . . . . at Johnson City
3-5 . . . . at Pulaski
6-8 . . . . Kingsport
9-11 . . . . . . .Bluefield
12-14 . . . . .at Greeneville
16-18 . . . . . at Bluefield
19-20 . . . . . Johnson City
21-23 . . . . . Greeneville
24-26 . . . . . . at Bristol
27-29 . . . . Pulaski

GREENEVILLE ASTROS

JUNE
19-21 . . . . Bristol
22-24 . . . . at Pulaski
25-26 . . . . . Kingsport
28-30 . . . . . .Bluefield

JULY
1 . . . . Johnson City
2-3 . . . at Johnson City
4-6 . . . . Danville
7-9 . . . . . at Burlington
10-13 . . . . at Kingsport
14-16 . . . . Bristol
18-20 . . .at Elizabethton
21-23 . . . . . .Burlington
24-26 . . . . . .at Princeton

27-29 . . . . Pulaski
31 . . . . at Kingsport

AUGUST
1-2 . . . . at Kingsport
3-5 . . . . Johnson City
6-8 . . . . . . at Bluefield
9-11 . . . . . . .at Bristol
12-14 . . . . . Elizabethton
16-18 . . . . .at Danville
19-20 . . . . . Kingsport
21-23 . . .at Elizabethton
24 . . . . . . Johnson City
25 . . . . . at Johnson City
26 . . . . Johnson City
27-29 . . . . Princeton

JOHNSON CITY CARDINALS

JUNE
19-21 . . . . . at Bluefield
22-24 . . . . . . Kingsport
25-26 . . . .at Elizabethton
28-30 . . . . . at Kingsport

JULY
1 . . . . . . .at Greeneville
2-3 . . . . Greeneville
4-6 . . . . at Bristol
7-9 . . . . Pulaski
10-13 . . . . . Elizabethton
14-16 . . . . at Burlington
18-20 . . . . . . Bluefield
21-23 . . . . . . .at Danville
24-26 . . . . . . at Pulaski

27-29 . . . . Danville
31 . . . . Elizabethton

AUGUST
1-2 . . . . Elizabethton
3-5 . . . . . . .at Greeneville
6-8 . . . . at Bristol
9-11 . . . . Princeton
12-14 . . . . Bristol
16-18 . . . . .at Princeton
19-20 . . . .at Elizabethton
21-23 . . . . . .Burlington
24 . . . . . .at Greeneville
25 . . . . Greeneville
26 . . . . . .at Greeneville
27-29 . . . . Kingsport

KINGSPORT METS

JUNE
19-21 . . . . Princeton
22-24 . . . at Johnson City
25-26 . . . . .at Greeneville
28-30 . . . . . Johnson City

JULY
1-3 . . . . Pulaski
4-6 . . . . . .at Elizabethton
7-9 . . . . at Bluefield

10-13 . . . . . . Greeneville
14-16 . . . . . Elizabethton
18-20 . . . .at Princeton
21-23 . . . . . . at Bristol
24-26 . . . . Danville
27-29 . . . at Burlington
31 . . . . Greeneville

AUGUST
1-2 . . . . Greeneville

3-5 . . . . Bristol
6-8 . . . . .at Elizabethton
9-11 . . . . . . .at Danville
12-14 . . . . Bluefield
16-18 . . . . at Pulaski

PRINCETON RAYS

JUNE	
19-21	at Kingsport
22-24	Danville
25-26	at Bluefield
28-30	Bristol

JULY	
1-3	Elizabethton
4-6	at Burlington
7-9	at Bristol
10-12	Bluefield
13	at Bluefield
14-16	at Pulaski
18-20	Kingsport
21-23 . . . . .at Elizabethton
24-26	Greeneville

PULASKI YANKEES

JUNE	
19-21 . . . . . . .at Danville
22-24	Greeneville
25-26	at Bristol
28-30	Burlington

JULY	
1-3	at Kingsport
4-5	Bluefield
6	at Bluefield
7-9	at Johnson City
10-13	Bristol
14-16	Princeton
18-20 . . . . . . .at Danville
21-23	at Bluefield
24-26	Johnson City

PIONEER LEAGUE

BILLINGS MUSTANGS

JUNE	
15-18	Missoula
19-21	at Great Falls
22-24	at Helena
25-27	Great Falls
28-29	Helena
30	at Missoula

JULY	
1-3	at Missoula
4-6	Helena
7-8	at Helena
10-13	Grand Junction
14-16	Orem
18-20 . . .at Grand Junction
21-24	at Orem

GRAND JUNCTION ROCKIES

JUNE	
15-18	Orem
19-22 . . . . .Idaho Falls
23-25	at Ogden
26-29 . . . . at Idaho Falls
30	at Orem

JULY	
1-3	at Orem

19-20 . . . . .at Greeneville
21-23 . . . . Bristol
24-26 . . . . .Burlington
27-29 . . . . at Johnson City

27-29 . . . . .Bluefield
31 . . . . .at Danville

AUGUST	
1-2 . . . . .at Danville
3-5 . . . . at Burlington
6-8 . . . . Pulaski
9-11 . . . . . at Johnson City
12-14 . . . . . . .Burlington
16-18 . . . . . . Johnson City
19 . . . . at Bluefield
20 . . . . Bluefield
21-23 . . . . at Pulaski
24-26 . . . . Danville
27-29 . . . . . .at Greeneville

27-29 . . . . .at Greeneville
31 . . . . .Burlington

AUGUST	
1-2 . . . . .Burlington
3-5 . . . . Elizabethton
6-8 . . . . .at Princeton
9-11 . . . . . at Burlington
12-14 . . . . Danville
16-18 . . . . Kingsport
19-20 . . . . at Bristol
21-23 . . . . Princeton
24 . . . . .Bluefield
25-26 . . . . . . at Bluefield
27-29 . . . . .at Elizabethton

26-29 . . . . Missoula
30-31 . . . . . . .Great Falls

AUGUST	
1-2 . . . . at Great Falls
3-5 . . . . at Helena
9-12 . . . . Ogden
13-15 . . . . . . .Idaho Falls
17-19 . . . . at Ogden
20-23 . . . . . at Idaho Falls
24-26 . . . . Helena
28-31 . . . . . . at Missoula

SEPTEMBER	
1-3 . . . . at Great Falls
4-6 . . . . .Great Falls

4-8 . . . . Ogden
10-13 . . . . at Billings
14-16 . . . . . at Great Falls
18-20 . . . . Billings
21-24 . . . . .Great Falls
25-27 . . . . at Ogden
28-29 . . . . .Orem
30-31 . . . . Ogden

AUGUST	
1 . . . . Ogden
2-5 . . . . . at Idaho Falls
9-12 . . . . Helena
13-15 . . . . Missoula
17-19 . . . . . . at Helena
20-23 . . . . . . at Missoula

GREAT FALLS VOYAGERS

JUNE	
15 . . . . Helena
16-17 . . . . . . at Helena
18 . . . . Helena
19-21 . . . . Billings
22-24 . . . . . at Missoula
25-27 . . . . . at Billings
28-29 . . . . . . Missoula
30 . . . . Helena

JULY	
1 . . . . Helena
2-3 . . . . at Helena
4-6 . . . . Missoula
7-8 . . . . . . at Missoula
10-13 . . . . .Orem
14-16 . . . . Grand Junction

HELENA BREWERS

JUNE	
15 . . . . . at Great Falls
16-17 . . . .Great Falls
18 . . . . . at Great Falls
19-21 . . . . . at Missoula
22-24 . . . . Billings
25-27 . . . . . . Missoula
28-29 . . . . . at Billings
30 . . . . . at Great Falls

JULY	
1 . . . . . at Great Falls
2-3 . . . . .Great Falls
4-6 . . . . . . at Billings
7-8 . . . . Billings
10-13 . . . . . at Idaho Falls
14-16 . . . . at Ogden

IDAHO FALLS CHUKARS

JUNE	
15-18 . . . . Ogden
19-22 . .at Grand Junction
23-25 . . . . . . at Orem
26-29 . . . . Grand Junction
30 . . . . at Ogden

JULY	
1-3 . . . . at Ogden
4-6 . . . . .Orem
7-8 . . . . at Orem
10-13 . . . . Helena
14-16 . . . . Missoula
18-20 . . . . . . at Helena
21-24 . . . . at Missoula
25-27 . . . . .Orem

MISSOULA OSPREY

JUNE	
15-18 . . . . . . at Billings
19-21 . . . . Helena
22-24 . . . . . . .Great Falls

25-28 . . . . . . .Idaho Falls
29-30 . . . . . . at Orem
31 . . . . at Ogden

SEPTEMBER	
1 . . . . at Ogden
3-4 . . . . .Orem
5-6 . . . . at Orem

18-20 . . . . at Orem
21-24 . . .at Grand Junction
26-29 . . . . Helena
30-31 . . . . at Billings

AUGUST	
1-2 . . . . Billings
3-5 . . . . at Missoula
9-12 . . . . .Idaho Falls
13-15 . . . . Ogden
17-19 . . . . . at Idaho Falls
20-23 . . . . at Ogden
25-27 . . . . .Missoula
28-31 . . . . at Helena

SEPTEMBER	
1-3 . . . . Billings
4-6 . . . . at Billings

18-20 . . . . . . .Idaho Falls
21-24 . . . . Ogden
26-29 . . . . . at Great Falls
30-31 . . . . .Missoula

AUGUST	
1-2 . . . . at Missoula
3-5 . . . . Billings
9-12 . . . .at Grand Junction
13-15 . . . . at Orem
17-19 . . . . Grand Junction
20-23 . . . . Orem
24-26 . . . . . at Billings
28-31 . . . . . .Great Falls

SEPTEMBER	
1-3 . . . . .Missoula
4-6 . . . . at Missoula

28-29 . . . . at Ogden
30-31 . . . . at Orem

AUGUST	
1 . . . . at Orem
2-5 . . . . . Grand Junction
9-12 . . . . . at Great Falls
13-15 . . . . . . at Billings
17-19 . . . . . .Great Falls
20-23 . . . . Billings
25-28 . . .at Grand Junction
29-30 . . . . . . at Ogden
31 . . . . Orem

SEPTEMBER	
1 . . . . Orem
3-6 . . . . Ogden

25-27 . . . . . . at Helena
28-29 . . . . . at Great Falls
30 . . . . Billings

JULY
1-3	. . . . Billings
4-6	. . . . at Great Falls
7-8	. . . . Great Falls
10-13	. . . . at Ogden
14-16	. . . . . at Idaho Falls
18-20	. . . . Ogden
21-24	. . . . . . .Idaho Falls
26-29	. . . . at Billings
30-31	. . . . at Helena

AUGUST
1-2	. . . . Helena
3-5	. . . . Great Falls
9-12	. . . . at Orem
13-15	. . at Grand Junction
17-19	. . . . Orem
20-23	. . . . Grand Junction
25-27	. . . . at Great Falls
28-31	. . . . Billings

SEPTEMBER
1-3	. . . . at Helena
4-6	. . . . Helena

OGDEN RAPTORS

JUNE
15-18	. . . . . at Idaho Falls
19-20	. . . . Orem
21-22	. . . . at Orem
23-25	. . . . Grand Junction
26-27	. . . . Orem
28-29	. . . . . . at Orem
30	. . . . . . .Idaho Falls

JULY
1-3	. . . . .Idaho Falls
4-8	. . at Grand Junction
10-13	. . . . Missoula
14-16	. . . . Helena
18-20	. . . . . . at Missoula
21-24	. . . . at Helena
25-27	. . . . Grand Junction

28-29	. . . . . . .Idaho Falls
30-31	. . at Grand Junction

AUGUST
1	. . . . . at Grand Junction
2-5	. . . . Orem
9-12	. . . . at Billings
13-15	. . . at Great Falls
17-19	. . . . Billings
20-23	. . . . Great Falls
24-28	. . . . at Orem
29-30	. . . . . .Idaho Falls
31	. . . . . . Grand Junction

SEPTEMBER
1	. . . . Grand Junction
3-6	. . . . . . at Idaho Falls

OREM OWLZ

JUNE
15-18	. . at Grand Junction
19-20	. . . . at Ogden
21-22	. . . . Ogden
23-25	. . . . . . .Idaho Falls
26-27	. . . . at Ogden
28-29	. . . . Ogden
30	. . . . . . Grand Junction

JULY
1-3	. . . . . Grand Junction
4-6	. . . . . at Idaho Falls
7-8	. . . . .Idaho Falls
10-13	. . . . . at Great Falls
14-16	. . . . at Billings
18-20	. . . . . . Great Falls
21-24	. . . . Billings
25-27	. . . . . at Idaho Falls

28-29	. . .at Grand Junction
30-31	. . . . . . .Idaho Falls

AUGUST
1	. . . . .Idaho Falls
2-5	. . . . at Ogden
9-12	. . . . Missoula
13-15	. . . . Helena
17-19	. . . . . at Missoula
20-23	. . . . at Helena
24-28	. . . . Ogden
29-30	. . . . Grand Junction
31	. . . . at Idaho Falls

SEPTEMBER
1	. . . . at Idaho Falls
3-4	. . . . .at Grand Junction
5-6	. . . . . Grand Junction

ARIZONA LEAGUE

AZL ANGELS

JUNE
20	. . . . Cubs 1
22	. . . . Giants Orange
26	. . . . Athletics
27	. . . . D-backs
30	. . . . .Indians 2

JULY
3	. . . . Mariners
5	. . . . .Giants Black
7	. . . . Padres1
10	. . . . Royals
12	. . . . Rangers
16	. . . . D-backs
18	. . . . Padres2
21	. . . . Dodgers
23	. . . . .Indians 1

26	. . . . Cubs 1
28	. . . . . . Giants Orange

AUGUST
1	. . . . Athletics
3	. . . . White Sox
6	. . . . Brewers
8	. . . . Cubs 2
10	. . . . Reds
11	. . . . .Giants Black
16	. . . . Giants Orange
18	. . . . Athletics
21	. . . . D-backs
23	. . . . Cubs 2
26	. . . . Cubs 1
27	. . . . .Indians 2

AZL ATHLETICS

JUNE
18	. . . . Angels
20	. . . . .Indians 2
23	. . . . Cubs 1
25	. . . . . . Giants Orange
29	. . . . . . .Giants Black

JULY
18	. . . . Angels
20	. . . . .Indians 2
23	. . . . Cubs 1
25	. . . . . . Giants Orange
29	. . . . . . .Giants Black

AUGUST
4	. . . . Royals
6	. . . . Padres2
9	. . . . Mariners
11	. . . . Padres1
14	. . . . D-backs
16	. . . . . . .Giants Black
20	. . . . Angels
21	. . . . . Giants Orange
25	. . . . Cubs 1
26	. . . . D-backs

AZL BREWERS

JUNE
18	. . . . .Indians 1
20	. . . . Reds
24	. . . . Padres2
26	. . . . Padres1
28	. . . . White Sox

JULY
1	. . . . .Indians 2
3	. . . . Cubs 2
5	. . . . Giants Orange
9	. . . . Mariners
11	. . . . Athletics
14	. . . . D-backs
15	. . . . .Giants Black
19	. . . . Dodgers
22	. . . . Cubs 1

24	. . . . .Indians 1
26	. . . . Reds
30	. . . . White Sox
31	. . . . Angels

AUGUST
4	. . . . Cubs 2
5	. . . . Royals
10	. . . . Rangers
11	. . . . .Indians 2
14	. . . . Reds
16	. . . . Padres2
19	. . . . Cubs 2
20	. . . . .Indians 2
23	. . . . Reds
25	. . . . Padres1

AZL CUBS 1

JUNE
18	. . . . D-backs
21	. . . . Angels
22	. . . . . .Giants Black
25	. . . . .Indians 1
28	. . . . Athletics
30	. . . . White Sox

JULY
1	. . . . Giants Orange
5	. . . . Padres1
7	. . . . .Indians 2
12	. . . . Cubs 2
13	. . . . Reds
15	. . . . Padres2
18	. . . . Royals
21	. . . . Rangers

24	. . . . D-backs
27	. . . . Brewers
28	. . . . . .Giants Black

AUGUST
2	. . . . Dodgers
3	. . . . Athletics
6	. . . . . . Giants Orange
7	. . . . Angels
10	. . . . Athletics
13	. . . . Mariners
17	. . . . Rangers
18	. . . . D-backs
21	. . . . . . .Giants Black
23	. . . . .Indians 2
27	. . . . .Indians 1

AZL CUBS 2

JUNE
18	. . . . Reds
22	. . . . White Sox
23	. . . . .Indians 1
27	. . . . .Indians 2
29	. . . . Brewers

JULY
1	. . . . Padres2
4	. . . . D-backs
7	. . . . Rangers
9	. . . . Athletics
11	. . . . .Indians 1
13	. . . . White Sox
16	. . . . Cubs 1
20	. . . . . . Giants Orange
23	. . . . Royals

24	. . . . Reds
29	. . . . .Indians 1
30	. . . . Mariners

AUGUST
2	. . . . .Indians 2
3	. . . . Brewers
6	. . . . . . .Giants Black
9	. . . . Dodgers
12	. . . . Angels
14	. . . . Padres1
17	. . . . .Indians 2
18	. . . . .Indians 1
21	. . . . Brewers
24	. . . . White Sox
26	. . . . .Indians 2

AZL D-BACKS

JUNE
19 . . . . . . Giants Orange
22 . . . . Royals
23 . . . . Angels
26 . . . . . . .Giants Black
29 . . . . . Giants Orange

JULY
2 . . . . Cubs 1
3 . . . . Rangers
7 . . . . Dodgers
8 . . . . .Indians 1
11 . . . . Angels
13 . . . . Brewers
18 . . . . . . White Sox
20 . . . . Padres2
23 . . . . . . .Indians 2

25 . . . . Athletics
28 . . . . Cubs 2
29 . . . . Angels

AUGUST
1 . . . . . . .Giants Black
3 . . . . Reds
6 . . . . Padres1
8 . . . . Mariners
11 . . . . . Giants Orange
13 . . . . Angels
16 . . . . Cubs 1
19 . . . . Athletics
23 . . . . Athletics
24 . . . . . .Giants Black
27 . . . . . Giants Orange

AZL DODGERS

JUNE
18 . . . . Rangers
20 . . . . Mariners
24 . . . . Royals
25 . . . . Padres1
27 . . . . . Giants Orange
30 . . . . Reds

JULY
3 . . . . . . White Sox
4 . . . . Padres2
8 . . . . Angels
10 . . . . Brewers
13 . . . . Mariners
14 . . . . Royals
18 . . . . Cubs 2
20 . . . . Padres1

24 . . . . Rangers
26 . . . . . . .Indians 2
30 . . . . Royals
31 . . . . Padres1

AUGUST
3 . . . . .Indians 1
4 . . . . White Sox
7 . . . . D-backs
10 . . . . . .Giants Black
12 . . . . Cubs 1
13 . . . . Athletics
17 . . . . Padres2
19 . . . . Mariners
22 . . . . Angels
23 . . . . Rangers

AZL GIANTS BLACK

JUNE
19 . . . . Athletics
21 . . . . . . .Indians 1
24 . . . . D-backs
27 . . . . Cubs 1
30 . . . . Athletics

JULY
1 . . . . Angels
6 . . . . Mariners
7 . . . . Padres2
9 . . . . Dodgers
11 . . . . Cubs 1
14 . . . . Cubs 2
16 . . . . Padres1
21 . . . . . . .Indians 2
22 . . . . . Giants Orange

25 . . . . . Giants Orange
27 . . . . Angels
30 . . . . D-backs
31 . . . . Reds

AUGUST
4 . . . . Rangers
7 . . . . Royals
9 . . . . Brewers
12 . . . . Royals
15 . . . . Athletics
17 . . . . Angels
20 . . . . . . White Sox
22 . . . . D-backs
25 . . . . Angels
27 . . . . Cubs 2

AZL GIANTS ORANGE

JUNE
20 . . . . . . .Giants Black
21 . . . . D-backs
24 . . . . Athletics
26 . . . . Cubs 1
30 . . . . Rangers

JULY
2 . . . . Angels
4 . . . . Brewers
6 . . . . Cubs 2
9 . . . . Padres2
11 . . . . . . .Indians 2
15 . . . . Mariners

16 . . . . .Indians 1
21 . . . . Royals
23 . . . . Cubs 1
26 . . . . . .Giants Black
27 . . . . D-backs
30 . . . . Athletics

AUGUST
1 . . . . Cubs 1
5 . . . . Dodgers
7 . . . . Padres1
9 . . . . Reds
12 . . . . . . White Sox
15 . . . . Angels

AZL INDIANS 1

17 . . . . D-backs
19 . . . . . .Giants Black
22 . . . . Cubs 1

JUNE
20 . . . . White Sox
22 . . . . . .Indians 2
26 . . . . Cubs 2
28 . . . . Angels
30 . . . . Brewers

JULY
1 . . . . Reds
6 . . . . Cubs 1
7 . . . . . Giants Orange
10 . . . . . .Giants Black
12 . . . . Royals
15 . . . . Rangers
19 . . . . D-backs
21 . . . . Reds
22 . . . . Padres1

24 . . . . Athletics
26 . . . . . .Giants Black

26 . . . . . . White Sox
27 . . . . Athletics

AUGUST
1 . . . . Cubs 2
2 . . . . Padres2
5 . . . . Mariners
8 . . . . Dodgers
10 . . . . . . White Sox
13 . . . . . .Indians 2
15 . . . . Brewers
16 . . . . Reds
21 . . . . Padres2
23 . . . . . . White Sox
25 . . . . Reds
26 . . . . Brewers

AZL INDIANS 2

JUNE
18 . . . . White Sox
21 . . . . Brewers
23 . . . . Reds
25 . . . . Angels
28 . . . . Cubs 2

JULY
2 . . . . .Indians 1
3 . . . . Athletics
6 . . . . D-backs
8 . . . . Cubs 1
10 . . . . . Giants Orange
12 . . . . Dodgers
18 . . . . . .Giants Black
19 . . . . Rangers
22 . . . . Cubs 2

24 . . . . White Sox
27 . . . . Padres1
29 . . . . Reds
31 . . . . Royals

AUGUST
3 . . . . Mariners
5 . . . . Athletics
8 . . . . Brewers
10 . . . . Padres2
12 . . . . . .Indians 1
16 . . . . Cubs 2
18 . . . . . . White Sox
21 . . . . Reds
22 . . . . . .Indians 1
25 . . . . . Giants Orange

AZL MARINERS

JUNE
19 . . . . Royals
21 . . . . Padres2
23 . . . . Rangers
25 . . . . Brewers
28 . . . . Dodgers
30 . . . . Padres1

JULY
4 . . . . . .Giants Black
5 . . . . Reds
10 . . . . . . White Sox
11 . . . . Padres2
14 . . . . Athletics
16 . . . . . .Indians 2
19 . . . . Angels
22 . . . . D-backs

25 . . . . Royals
27 . . . . Padres2
29 . . . . Rangers
31 . . . . Cubs 1

AUGUST
4 . . . . . Giants Orange
6 . . . . .Indians 1
10 . . . . Padres1
11 . . . . Cubs 2
14 . . . . Dodgers
15 . . . . Rangers
18 . . . . Royals
21 . . . . Padres1
24 . . . . Dodgers
26 . . . . Padres1

AZL PADRES1

JUNE
20 . . . . Padres2
21 . . . . Athletics
24 . . . . Cubs 2
27 . . . . Rangers

JULY
1 . . . . Mariners
2 . . . . Dodgers
4 . . . . Royals

6 . . . . Brewers
10 . . . . Rangers
12 . . . . . .Giants Black
15 . . . . . .Indians 2
18 . . . . . .Indians 1
21 . . . . . . White Sox
23 . . . . Dodgers
26 . . . . Mariners
28 . . . . Rangers

AUGUST		
1 . . . . Brewers		
2 . . . . Giants Orange		
4 . . . . Reds		
5 . . . . Angels		
9 . . . . D-backs		
12 . . . . Padres2		

AZL PADRES2

JUNE		
19 . . . . Padres1	25 . . . . Padres1	
22 . . . . Dodgers	28 . . . . Dodgers	
25 . . . . Rangers	31 . . . . White Sox	
26 . . . . Mariners	AUGUST	
30 . . . . Royals	1 . . . . Mariners	
JULY	4 . . . . D-backs	
2 . . . . . . .Giants Black	7 . . . . Cubs 2	
5 . . . . Rangers	9 . . . . Royals	
6 . . . . Angels	11 . . . . Cubs 1	
10 . . . . Reds	14 . . . . . . .Giants Black	
12 . . . . . Giants Orange	15 . . . . .Indians 2	
14 . . . . Padres1	19 . . . . Rangers	
16 . . . . Brewers	20 . . . . .Indians 1	
21 . . . . Mariners	24 . . . . Royals	
22 . . . . Athletics	25 . . . . Dodgers	

AZL RANGERS

JUNE		
19 . . . . Dodgers	25 . . . . Dodgers	
22 . . . . Padres1	30 . . . . Padres1	
24 . . . . Mariners	31 . . . . .Indians 1	
28 . . . . Royals	AUGUST	
29 . . . . Padres2	2 . . . . .Giants Black	
JULY	5 . . . . Cubs 1	
2 . . . . Cubs 2	7 . . . . .Indians 2	
4 . . . . Reds	8 . . . . Athletics	
8 . . . . Brewers	12 . . . . D-backs	
9 . . . . D-backs	14 . . . . Royals	
13 . . . . Angels	18 . . . . Dodgers	
14 . . . . White Sox	20 . . . . Mariners	
18 . . . . . Giants Orange	22 . . . . Padres1	
20 . . . . Mariners	25 . . . . Royals	
23 . . . . Padres2	27 . . . . Padres2	

AZL REDS

JUNE		
19 . . . . Brewers	25 . . . . Brewers	
21 . . . . Cubs 2	27 . . . . Cubs 2	
24 . . . . White Sox	30 . . . . Padres2	
26 . . . . .Indians 2	AUGUST	
28 . . . . D-backs	1 . . . . .Indians 2	
29 . . . . Mariners	5 . . . . .Giants Black	
JULY	6 . . . . .Indians 2	
3 . . . . .Indians 1	8 . . . . Cubs 1	
6 . . . . Athletics	11 . . . . .Indians 1	
8 . . . . Royals	13 . . . . Rangers	
11 . . . . Padres1	15 . . . . White Sox	
14 . . . . . Giants Orange	18 . . . . Brewers	
15 . . . . Dodgers	20 . . . . Cubs 1	
19 . . . . Cubs 2	24 . . . . Brewers	
22 . . . . Angels	26 . . . . Padres2	

AZL ROYALS

JUNE		
18 . . . . Mariners	27 . . . . Padres2	
20 . . . . Rangers	29 . . . . Padres1	
23 . . . . Dodgers	JULY	
25 . . . . . . .Giants Black	3 . . . . Cubs 1	
	5 . . . . .Indians 1	

15 . . . . Cubs 1	7 . . . . White Sox
16 . . . . Mariners	9 . . . . Reds
19 . . . . Royals	13 . . . . .Indians 2
20 . . . . Dodgers	15 . . . . Angels
24 . . . . Rangers	19 . . . . Athletics
27 . . . . Royals	20 . . . . Brewers
	24 . . . . Mariners
	26 . . . . Padres2
	28 . . . . .Indians 1
	29 . . . . Dodgers

AZL WHITE SOX

JUNE		
19 . . . . Cubs 2	25 . . . . Cubs 2	
23 . . . . Brewers	28 . . . . .Indians 2	
25 . . . . Reds	29 . . . . Brewers	
27 . . . . .Indians 1	AUGUST	
29 . . . . Dodgers	2 . . . . Angels	
JULY	5 . . . . Padres2	
2 . . . . Royals	7 . . . . .Indians 1	
5 . . . . .Indians 2	9 . . . . Rangers	
8 . . . . Mariners	13 . . . . Brewers	
9 . . . . Padres1	14 . . . . . Giants Orange	
12 . . . . D-backs	17 . . . . .Indians 1	
15 . . . . Athletics	19 . . . . Reds	
19 . . . . Cubs 1	22 . . . . Cubs 2	
20 . . . . Reds	25 . . . . Mariners	
23 . . . . . . .Giants Black	27 . . . . Dodgers	

GULF COAST LEAGUE

GCL ASTROS

JUNE		
19 . . . . .Cardinals	23 . . . . Mets	
23 . . . . Mets	26 . . . . Marlins	
26 . . . . Marlins	27 . . . . Nationals	
27 . . . . Nationals	29 . . . . .Cardinals	
29 . . . . .Cardinals	AUGUST	
JULY	2 . . . . Mets	
3 . . . . Mets	5 . . . . Marlins	
6 . . . . Marlins	6 . . . . Nationals	
7 . . . . Nationals	8 . . . . .Cardinals	
9 . . . . .Cardinals	12 . . . . Mets	
13 . . . . Mets	15 . . . . Marlins	
16 . . . . Marlins	16 . . . . Nationals	
17 . . . . Nationals	18 . . . . .Cardinals	
19 . . . . .Cardinals	22 . . . . Mets	
	25 . . . . Marlins	

GCL BLUE JAYS

JUNE		
20 . . . . Phillies West	25 . . . . . . .Yankees West	
21 . . . . Phillies East	27 . . . . Tigers West	
25 . . . . Braves	28 . . . . Phillies West	
JULY	AUGUST	
2 . . . . Tigers West	1 . . . . Phillies East	
3 . . . . .Tigers East	4 . . . . Pirates	
5 . . . . Yankees East	7 . . . . Phillies West	
6 . . . . . . .Yankees West	8 . . . . Braves	
9 . . . . Phillies West	9 . . . . .Tigers East	
10 . . . . Braves	11 . . . . Yankees East	
13 . . . . Phillies East	13 . . . . . . .Yankees West	
17 . . . . Pirates	15 . . . . Tigers West	
21 . . . . . . .Tigers East	20 . . . . Phillies East	
24 . . . . Yankees East	23 . . . . Pirates	
	25 . . . . Phillies West	

GCL BRAVES

JUNE		
20	. . . . Tigers West
22	. . . . Yankees West
26	. . . . Phillies East
27	. . . . Phillies West
30	. . . . .Blue Jays

JULY	
2	. . . . Pirates
4	. . . . Yankees East
7	. . . . .Tigers East
9	. . . . Tigers West
11	. . . . . . .Yankees West
14	. . . . Phillies East
16	. . . . Phillies West
19	. . . . .Blue Jays

23	. . . . Yankees East
26	. . . . .Tigers East
27	. . . . Pirates
30	. . . . . .Yankees West

AUGUST	
2	. . . . Phillies East
3	. . . . Phillies West
7	. . . . Tigers West
10	. . . . Yankees East
14	. . . . .Tigers East
15	. . . . Pirates
17	. . . . .Blue Jays
21	. . . . Phillies East
22	. . . . Phillies West
25	. . . . Tigers West

GCL CARDINALS

JUNE	
20	. . . . Marlins
24	. . . . .Astros
26	. . . . Nationals
27	. . . . Mets
30	. . . . Marlins

JULY	
4	. . . . .Astros
6	. . . . Nationals
7	. . . . Mets
10	. . . . Marlins
14	. . . . Astros
16	. . . . Nationals
17	. . . . Mets
20	. . . . Marlins

24	. . . . .Astros
26	. . . . Nationals
27	. . . . Mets
30	. . . . .Marlins

AUGUST	
3	. . . . .Astros
5	. . . . Nationals
6	. . . . Mets
9	. . . . Marlins
13	. . . . Astros
15	. . . . Nationals
16	. . . . Mets
19	. . . . Marlins
23	. . . . .Astros
25	. . . . Nationals

GCL MARLINS

JUNE	
19	. . . . Mets
21	. . . . Astros
23	. . . . Nationals
25	. . . . .Cardinals
29	. . . . Mets

JULY	
1	. . . . .Astros
3	. . . . Nationals
5	. . . . .Cardinals
9	. . . . Mets
11	. . . . Astros
13	. . . . Nationals
15	. . . . .Cardinals
19	. . . . Mets
21	. . . . Astros

23	. . . . Nationals
25	. . . . .Cardinals
29	. . . . Mets
31	. . . . .Astros

AUGUST	
2	. . . . Nationals
4	. . . . .Cardinals
8	. . . . Mets
10	. . . . .Astros
12	. . . . Nationals
14	. . . . .Cardinals
18	. . . . Mets
20	. . . . .Astros
22	. . . . Nationals
24	. . . . .Cardinals

GCL METS

JUNE	
18	. . . . .Astros
20	. . . . Nationals
22	. . . . .Cardinals
24	. . . . Marlins
28	. . . . Astros
30	. . . . Nationals

JULY	
2	. . . . .Cardinals
4	. . . . Marlins
8	. . . . Astros
10	. . . . Nationals
12	. . . . .Cardinals
14	. . . . Marlins
18	. . . . Astros
20	. . . . Nationals

22	. . . . .Cardinals
24	. . . . .Marlins
28	. . . . .Astros
30	. . . . Nationals

AUGUST	
1	. . . . .Cardinals
3	. . . . .Marlins
7	. . . . .Astros
9	. . . . Nationals
11	. . . . .Cardinals
13	. . . . Marlins
17	. . . . Astros
19	. . . . Nationals
21	. . . . .Cardinals
23	. . . . Marlins

GCL NATIONALS

JUNE	
18	. . . . .Marlins
21	. . . . .Cardinals
22	. . . . .Astros
25	. . . . Mets
28	. . . . .Marlins

JULY	
1	. . . . .Cardinals
2	. . . . .Astros
5	. . . . Mets
8	. . . . .Marlins
11	. . . . .Cardinals
12	. . . . .Astros
15	. . . . Mets
18	. . . . .Marlins
21	. . . . .Cardinals

22	. . . . .Astros
25	. . . . Mets
28	. . . . .Marlins
31	. . . . .Cardinals

AUGUST	
1	. . . . .Astros
4	. . . . Mets
7	. . . . .Marlins
10	. . . . .Cardinals
11	. . . . .Astros
14	. . . . Mets
17	. . . . .Marlins
20	. . . . .Cardinals
21	. . . . .Astros
24	. . . . Mets

GCL ORIOLES

JUNE	
19	. . . . Twins
23	. . . . .Rays
26	. . . . Red Sox
28	. . . . Red Sox
29	. . . . .Rays

JULY	
2	. . . . Twins
4	. . . . Twins
7	. . . . .Rays
9	. . . . Red Sox
11	. . . . Red Sox
13	. . . . .Rays
17	. . . . Twins
19	. . . . Twins
21	. . . . .Rays

24	. . . . Red Sox
26	. . . . Red Sox
27	. . . . .Rays
30	. . . . Twins

AUGUST	
1	. . . . Twins
4	. . . . .Rays
6	. . . . Red Sox
8	. . . . Red Sox
10	. . . . .Rays
14	. . . . Twins
16	. . . . Twins
18	. . . . .Rays
21	. . . . Red Sox
24	. . . . .Rays

GCL PHILLIES EAST

JUNE	
18	. . . . . . .Yankees West
20	. . . . Yankees East
22	. . . . Pirates
23	. . . . Tigers West
27	. . . . .Tigers East
30	. . . . Phillies West

JULY	
4	. . . . .Blue Jays
5	. . . . Braves
9	. . . . Yankees East
11	. . . . Pirates
12	. . . . Tigers West
16	. . . . .Tigers East
17	. . . . . . .Yankees West

19	. . . . Phillies West
23	. . . . .Blue Jays
24	. . . . Braves
30	. . . . Pirates
31	. . . . Tigers West

AUGUST	
3	. . . . .Tigers East
4	. . . . . . .Yankees West
7	. . . . Yankees East
10	. . . . .Blue Jays
11	. . . . Braves
17	. . . . Phillies West
22	. . . . .Tigers East
23	. . . . . . .Yankees West
25	. . . . Yankees East

GCL PHILLIES WEST

JUNE	
19	. . . . Yankees East
21	. . . . Pirates
25	. . . . Phillies East
26	. . . . .Tigers East
28	. . . . Tigers West
29	. . . . .Blue Jays
30	. . . . Phillies East

JULY	
3	. . . . .Yankees West
6	. . . . Braves
10	. . . . Phillies East
13	. . . . Pirates
14	. . . . .Tigers East
18	. . . . Yankees East

20	. . . . Tigers West
21	. . . . . . .Yankees West
25	. . . . Braves

AUGUST	
1	. . . . Pirates
2	. . . . .Tigers East
6	. . . . Yankees East
8	. . . . Phillies East
9	. . . . . . .Yankees West
13	. . . . Braves
16	. . . . .Blue Jays
18	. . . . Tigers West
20	. . . . Pirates
21	. . . . .Tigers East
24	. . . . Yankees East

GCL PIRATES

JUNE
18 . . . . .Blue Jays
19 . . . . Braves
23 . . . . Yankees East
26 . . . . . .Yankees West
28 . . . . Phillies East
29 . . . . .Tigers East

JULY
4 . . . . Phillies West
6 . . . . Tigers West
7 . . . . .Blue Jays
12 . . . . Yankees East
14 . . . . . .Yankees West
18 . . . . Braves
20 . . . . Phillies East
23 . . . . Phillies West
25 . . . . Tigers West
26 . . . . .Blue Jays
28 . . . . .Tigers East
31 . . . . Yankees East

AUGUST
2 . . . . .Yankees West
6 . . . . Braves
10 . . . . Phillies West
13 . . . . Tigers West
14 . . . . .Blue Jays
16 . . . . .Tigers East
18 . . . . Phillies East
21 . . . . . .Yankees West
24 . . . . Braves

GCL RAYS

JUNE
18 . . . . Red Sox
20 . . . . Red Sox
22 . . . . Orioles
25 . . . . Twins
27 . . . . Twins
30 . . . . Orioles

JULY
3 . . . . Red Sox
5 . . . . Red Sox
6 . . . . Orioles
10 . . . . Twins
14 . . . . Orioles
16 . . . . Red Sox
18 . . . . Red Sox
20 . . . . Orioles
23 . . . . Twins
25 . . . . Twins
28 . . . . Orioles
31 . . . . Red Sox

AUGUST
3 . . . . Orioles
7 . . . . Twins
9 . . . . Twins
11 . . . . Orioles
13 . . . . Red Sox
15 . . . . Red Sox
17 . . . . Orioles
20 . . . . Twins
22 . . . . Twins
25 . . . . Orioles

GCL RED SOX

JUNE
19 . . . . .Rays
23 . . . . Twins
25 . . . . Orioles
27 . . . . Orioles
29 . . . . Twins

JULY
2 . . . . .Rays
4 . . . . .Rays
7 . . . . Twins
10 . . . . Orioles
13 . . . . Twins
17 . . . . .Rays
19 . . . . .Rays
21 . . . . Twins
23 . . . . Orioles
25 . . . . Orioles
27 . . . . Twins
30 . . . . .Rays

AUGUST
1 . . . . .Rays
4 . . . . Twins
7 . . . . Orioles
9 . . . . Orioles
10 . . . . Twins
14 . . . . .Rays
16 . . . . .Rays
18 . . . . Twins
20 . . . . Orioles
22 . . . . Orioles
24 . . . . Twins

GCL TIGERS EAST

JUNE
18 . . . . Braves
20 . . . . Pirates
23 . . . . .Blue Jays
25 . . . . Tigers West
28 . . . . . . Yankees East
30 . . . . Tigers West

JULY
2 . . . . . . .Yankees West
5 . . . . Phillies West
6 . . . . Phillies West
9 . . . . Pirates
10 . . . . Tigers West
12 . . . . .Blue Jays
17 . . . . Braves
20 . . . . . . Yankees East
24 . . . . . . Phillies West
25 . . . . Phillies East
27 . . . . . . .Yankees West
31 . . . . .Blue Jays

AUGUST
4 . . . . Braves
7 . . . . Pirates
8 . . . . Tigers West
11 . . . . Phillies West
13 . . . . Phillies East
15 . . . . . . .Yankees West
18 . . . . . . Yankees East
23 . . . . Braves
25 . . . . Pirates

GCL TIGERS WEST

JUNE
19 . . . . .Blue Jays
21 . . . . . .Yankees West
22 . . . . Phillies West
27 . . . . Pirates
29 . . . . Braves
30 . . . . .Tigers East

JULY
3 . . . . Phillies East
7 . . . . Yankees East
11 . . . . Phillies West
13 . . . . . .Yankees West
16 . . . . Pirates
18 . . . . .Blue Jays
19 . . . . .Tigers East
21 . . . . Phillies East
26 . . . . Yankees East
28 . . . . Braves
30 . . . . Phillies West

AUGUST
1 . . . . . . .Yankees West
3 . . . . Pirates
6 . . . . .Blue Jays
9 . . . . Phillies East
14 . . . . Yankees East
16 . . . . Braves
17 . . . . .Tigers East
20 . . . . . .Yankees West
22 . . . . Pirates
24 . . . . .Blue Jays

GCL TWINS

JUNE
18 . . . . Orioles
20 . . . . Orioles
22 . . . . Red Sox
26 . . . . .Rays
28 . . . . .Rays
30 . . . . Red Sox

JULY
3 . . . . Orioles
5 . . . . Orioles
6 . . . . Red Sox
9 . . . . .Rays
11 . . . . .Rays
14 . . . . Red Sox
16 . . . . Orioles
18 . . . . Orioles
20 . . . . Red Sox
24 . . . . .Rays
26 . . . . .Rays
28 . . . . Red Sox
31 . . . . Orioles

AUGUST
3 . . . . Red Sox
6 . . . . .Rays
8 . . . . .Rays
11 . . . . Red Sox
13 . . . . Orioles
15 . . . . Orioles
17 . . . . Red Sox
21 . . . . .Rays
25 . . . . Red Sox

GCL YANKEES EAST

JUNE
18 . . . . . Tigers West
21 . . . . Braves
22 . . . . . . .Tigers East
26 . . . . . . .Blue Jays
29 . . . . . Phillies East
30 . . . . . .Yankees West

JULY
2 . . . . . . Phillies West
3 . . . . Pirates
11 . . . . .Tigers East
13 . . . . Braves
14 . . . . . .Blue Jays
17 . . . . . Tigers West
19 . . . . . .Yankees West
21 . . . . Pirates
27 . . . . Phillies West
28 . . . . Phillies East
30 . . . . .Tigers East

AUGUST
1 . . . . Braves
2 . . . . .Blue Jays
4 . . . . Tigers West
9 . . . . Pirates
15 . . . . . . Phillies West
16 . . . . . . Phillies East
17 . . . . . .Yankees West
20 . . . . Braves
21 . . . . .Blue Jays
23 . . . . Tigers West

GCL YANKEES WEST

JUNE
19 . . . . . . .Tigers East
23 . . . . Phillies West
25 . . . . Yankees East
27 . . . . .Blue Jays
28 . . . . Braves
30 . . . . Yankees East

JULY
4 . . . . Tigers West
5 . . . . Pirates
7 . . . . Phillies East
10 . . . . . . Yankees East
12 . . . . . . Phillies West
16 . . . . . . .Blue Jays
18 . . . . . . .Tigers East
20 . . . . Braves
23 . . . . Tigers West
24 . . . . Pirates
26 . . . . . . Phillies East
31 . . . . Phillies West

AUGUST
3 . . . . .Blue Jays
6 . . . . .Tigers East
8 . . . . Yankees East
10 . . . . Tigers West
11 . . . . Pirates
14 . . . . . . Phillies East
18 . . . . Braves
22 . . . . .Blue Jays
24 . . . . .Tigers East

INDEPENDENT

AMERICAN ASSOCIATION

CHICAGO
MAY
25-27 . . . . . . Kansas City
JUNE
1-3 . . . . Winnipeg
4-6 . . . . Sioux Falls
15-17 . . . . St. Paul
19-21 . . . . Texas
25-26 . . .Gary Southshore
29-30 . . .Fargo-Moorhead
JULY
1 . . . . .FM
2-3 . . . . .Gary Southshore
6-8 . . . . .Cleburne
9-11 . . . . Sioux City
20-22 . . . . . . .Sioux Falls
23-25 . . . .Fargo-Moorhead
30-31 . . . . Wichita
AUGUST
1-2 . . . . .Wichita
10-12 . . . . Winnipeg
20-22 . . . .Gary Southshore
23-25 . . . . .St. Paul
SEPTEMBER
1-3 . . . . Lincoln

CLEBURNE
MAY
18-20 . . . . . Winnipeg
21-23 . . .Fargo-Moorhead
JUNE
1-3 . . . . .St. Paul
4-6 . . . . Sioux City
11-14 . . . . . . .Wichita
15-17 . . . . Lincoln
26-28 . . . . . Sioux Falls
29-30 . . . . . . Kansas City
JULY
1 . . . . Kansas City
2, 4 . . . . Texas
13-15 . . . . Chicago
16-18 . . . . . . Kansas City
27-30 . . . .Gary Southshore
31 . . . . Sioux City
AUGUST
1 . . . . Sioux City
10-13 . . . . Wichita
20-21 . . . . Texas
23-25 . . . . Lincoln
SEPTEMBER
1, 3 . . . . Texas

FARGO-MOORHEAD
MAY
25-27 . . . . .Lincoln
28-30 . . . . .Sioux Falls
JUNE
7-10 . . . .Gary Southshore
15-17 . . . . Kansas City
22-24 . . . . .Wichita
26-28 . . . . Texas
JULY
3-4 . . . . St. Paul
5-8 . . . . Winnipeg
17-19 . . .Gary Southshore
20-22 . . . . Winnipeg
30-31 . . . . St. Paul
AUGUST
1-2 . . . . St. Paul
3-5 . . . . .Cleburne
6-8 . . . . Chicago
20-22 . . . . Sioux City
26-28 . . . . Chicago
SEPTEMBER
1-3 . . . . Sioux Falls

GARY SOUTHSHORE
MAY
18-20 . . . . St. Paul
28-31 . . . . Chicago
JUNE
1-3 . . . . .Fargo-Moorhead
4-6 . . . . Winnipeg
15-17 . . . . . Sioux City
19-21 . . . . . . .Cleburne
27-28 . . . . Chicago
JULY
4 . . . . Chicago
9-11 . . . . Texas
20-22 . . . . St. Paul
23-25 . . . . . . .Sioux Falls
AUGUST
3-5 . . . . .Wichita
6-8 . . . . Lincoln
13-15 . . . . Winnipeg
17-19 . . . . . . .Sioux Falls
23-25 . . . .Fargo-Moorhead
SEPTEMBER
1-3 . . . . Kansas City

LINCOLN
MAY
17-20 . . . . . Sioux City
22-24 . . . . .Wichita
JUNE
4-6 . . . . .Fargo-Moorhead
8-10 . . . . . . .Cleburne
18-20 . . . . St. Paul
22-24 . . . . Chicago
29-30 . . .Gary Southshore
JULY
1 . . . . . .Gary Southshore
9-11 . . . . Kansas City
16-18 . . . . .Wichita
20-22 . . . . . . Sioux City
31 . . . . Winnipeg
AUGUST
1-2 . . . . Winnipeg
3-5 . . . . Sioux Falls
9-12 . . . . Texas
21-22 . . . . . . Kansas City
26-28 . . . . Texas
29-31 . . . . .Cleburne

KANSAS CITY
MAY
22-24 . . .Gary Southshore
JUNE
1-3 . . . . .Wichita
11-14 . . . . . Sioux City
22-24 . . . . . . .Cleburne
26-28 . . . . .Lincoln
JULY
2-4 . . . . .Sioux Falls
12-15 . . . . .St. Paul
20-22 . . . . Texas
24-26 . . . . .Lincoln
27-29 . . . . Chicago
AUGUST
6-8 . . . . Texas
14-16 . . .Fargo-Moorhead
17-19 . . . . .Cleburne
23-25 . . . . . . Winnipeg
26-28 . . . . . . Sioux City
29-31 . . . . .Wichita

ST. PAUL
MAY
21-23 . . . . Chicago
25-27 . . .Gary Southshore
JUNE
8-10 . . . . Sioux Falls
11-13 . . .Fargo-Moorhead
21-24 . . . . . . Winnipeg
25-27 . . . . . Sioux City
JULY
2 . . .Fargo-Moorhead
6-8 . . . . .Lincoln
9-11 . . . . .Cleburne
25-26 . . . . .Wichita
27-29 . . . . Texas
AUGUST
3-5 . . . . Kansas City
9-12 . . . .Gary Southshore
13-16 . . . . . . .Sioux Falls
17-18 . . .Fargo-Moorhead
29-31 . . . . Chicago
SEPTEMBER
1-3 . . . . Winnipeg

TEXAS
MAY
18-20 . . .Fargo-Moorhead
21-23 . . . . Winnipeg
28-31 . . . . .St. Paul
JUNE
1-3 . . . . Sioux City
5-7 . . . . Kansas City
11-14 . . . . .Lincoln
15-17 . . . . .Wichita
29-30 . . . . . .Sioux Falls
JULY
1 . . . . Sioux Falls
3 . . . . .Cleburne
5-7 . . . . Kansas City
16-18 . . . . Chicago
31 . . . .Gary Southshore
AUGUST
1 . . . . . .Gary Southshore
2-5 . . . . Sioux City
14-16 . . . . . . .Cleburne
17-19 . . . . .Lincoln
22 . . . . .Cleburne
23-25 . . . . .Wichita
SEPTEMBER
2 . . . . .Cleburne

SIOUX CITY
MAY
25-27 . . . . . . .Cleburne
28-31 . . . . . . Kansas City
JUNE
8-10 . . . . Texas
19-21 . . .Fargo-Moorhead
22-24 . . .Gary Southshore
JULY
2-4 . . . . Winnipeg
6-8 . . . . .Wichita
13-15 . . . . .Lincoln
17-19 . . . . .St. Paul
23-26 . . . . .Cleburne
27-29 . . . . .Lincoln
AUGUST
6-8 . . . . .Wichita
9-12 . . . . Kansas City
15-16 . . . . Chicago
23-25 . . . . Sioux Falls
29-31 . . . . Texas

SIOUX FALLS
MAY
18-20 . . . . Chicago
22-24 . . . . Sioux City
JUNE
1-3 . . . . Lincoln
11-14 . . . . Chicago
15-17 . . . . . . Winnipeg
22-24 . . . . Texas
JULY
6-8 . . . . . . .Gary Southshore
13-16 . . . .Fargo-Moorhead
17-19 . . . . Winnipeg
27-29 . . . . .Wichita
31 . . . . Kansas City

AUGUST

1-2 . . . . Kansas City	20-22 . . . . St. Paul
6-8 . . . . St. Paul	27-28 . . . . .Cleburne
9-12 . . . . .Fargo-Moorhead	29-31 . . . .Gary Southshore

WICHITA

MAY

18-20 . . . . . . Kansas City	3-5 . . . . .Lincoln
25-27 . . . . Texas	9-11 . . . .Fargo-Moorhead
28-31 . . . . .Cleburne	12-15 . . . . Texas

JUNE

4-6 . . . . St. Paul	19-22 . . . . .Cleburne
8-10 . . . . Kansas City	**AUGUST**
19-21 . . . . Sioux Falls	14-16 . . . . .Lincoln
29-30 . . . . Sioux City	17-19 . . . . Chicago
JULY	20-22 . . . . Winnipeg
1 . . . . Sioux City	27-28 . . . .Gary Southshore
	SEPTEMBER
	1-3 . . . . Sioux City

WINNIPEG

MAY

25-27 . . . . . . .Sioux Falls	9-12 . . . . .Sioux Falls
28-31 . . . . .Lincoln	13-15 . . .Gary Southshore
JUNE	24-26 . . . . Texas
8-10 . . . . Chicago	27-29 . . . .Fargo-Moorhead
11-13 . . .Gary Southshore	**AUGUST**
18-20 . . . . . Kansas City	3-5 . . . . Chicago
25-27 . . . . .Wichita	6-8 . . . . .Cleburne
28-30 . . . . St. Paul	17-19 . . . . Sioux City
JULY	27-28 . . . . St. Paul
1 . . . . St. Paul	29-31 . . . .Fargo-Moorhead

ATLANTIC LEAGUE

LONG ISLAND DUCKS

MAY

		JULY	
4-6 . . . Southern Maryland		1 . . . . Road Warriors	
11-13 . . . . . . Sugar Land		6-8 . . . . Sugar Land	
15-17 . . . . Road Warriors		17-19 . . . . . . New Britain	
22-24 . . . . Road Warriors		20-22 . . . . Somerset	
25-27 . . . . Somerset		30-31 . . . . Somerset	
JUNE		**AUGUST**	
1-3 . . . . New Britain		1 . . . . Somerset	
4-6 . . . . Lancaster		2-5 . . . . . . Road Warriors	
12-14 . . Southern Maryland		9-12 . . . . .York	
15-17 . . . . Lancaster		13-15 . . Southern Maryland	
18-20 . . . . . . Sugar Land		24-26 . . . . Road Warriors	
25-28 . . . . .York		28-30 . . . . Lancaster	
29-30 . . . . Road Warriors		**SEPTEMBER**	
		4-6 . . . . New Britain	
		7-9 . . . . Road Warrior	

LANCASTER

MAY

4-6 . . . . .York		6-8 . . . . New Britain	
8-10 . . . . Sugar Land		16-19 . . . . .York	
18-20 . . . . Road Warriors		23-26 . . . . . . Long Island	
22-24 . . . . .York		27-29 . . . . . . New Britain	
29-31 . . . . Somerset		**AUGUST**	
JUNE		3-5 . . . . Sugar Land	
1-3 . . . Southern Maryland		7-9 . . . . . . Road Warriors	
8-10 . . . . . . Road Warriors		13-15 . . . . Road Warriors	
12-14 . . . . . . New Britain		17-19 . . . . . . Sugar Land	
18-20 . . . . Somerset		24-26 . . . . Somerset	
21-24 . . . . . . Long Island		**SEPTEMBER**	
JULY		5-6 . . . . Somerset	
3-5 . . . . . . Road Warriors		7-9 . . . Southern Maryland	
		14-16 . . . . Road Warriors	

NEW BRITAIN

MAY

4-6 . . . . . . Road Warriors		3-5 . . . . Long Island	
8-10 . . . . Long Island		13-15 . . Southern Maryland	
15-17 . . . . Lancaster		20-22 . . . . Road Warriors	
18-20 . . . . .York		24-26 . . . . . . Sugar Land	
25-27 . . . . . . Sugar Land		30-31 . . . . Road Warriors	
29-31 . . . . Road Warriors		**AUGUST**	
JUNE		1 . . . . Road Warriors	
4-6 . . . . .York		10-12 . . . . Lancaster	
7-10 . . . . Somerset		17-19 . . . . . . Long Island	
19-21 . . Southern Maryland		20-23 . . . . Road Warriors	
22-24 . . . . Road Warriors		28-30 . . . . .York	
29-30 . . Southern Maryland		31 . . . . Somerset	
JULY		**SEPTEMBER**	
1 . . . . Southern Maryland		1-2 . . . . Somerset	
		7-9 . . . . Sugar Land	
		11-12 . . . . Lancaster	

SOUTHERN MARYLAND

APRIL

27-29 . . . . . . Long Island		17-19 . . . . Somerset	
1-3 . . . . Lancaster		20-22 . . . . Lancaster	
8-9 . . . . .York		27-29 . . . . . . Long Island	
11-13 . . . . Road Warriors		31 . . . . Lancaster	
21-24 . . . . . New Britain		**AUGUST**	
25-27 . . . . Lancaster		1-2 . . . . Lancaster	
JUNE		7-9 . . . . Sugar Land	
4-6 . . . . . . Road Warriors		10-12 . . . . Road Warriors	
8-10 . . . . . . Sugar Land		17-19 . . . . Road Warriors	
15-17 . . . . .York		21-23 . . . . . . Long Island	
26-28 . . . . Road Warriors		31 . . . . . . Road Warriors	
JULY		**SEPTEMBER**	
2-5 . . . . Somerset		1-2 . . . . . . Road Warriors	
6-8 . . . . .York		4-6 . . . . Sugar Land	
		13-16 . . . . . . New Britain	

SOMERSET

APRIL

		JULY	
27-29 . . . . Road Warriors		6-8 . . . . . Road Warriors	
MAY		13-15 . . . . Lancaster	
1-3 . . . . Long Island		23-26 . . Southern Maryland	
8-10 . . . . . Road Warriors		27-29 . . . . Road Warriors	
11-12 . . . . Lancaster		**AUGUST**	
18-20 . . . . . . Long Island		2-5 . . . . New Britain	
22-24 . . . . . . Sugar Land		6-8 . . . . Long Island	
JUNE		17-19 . . . . .York	
1-3 . . . . . . Road Warriors		21-23 . . . . . . Sugar Land	
5-6 . . . . Sugar Land		28-30 . . . . Road Warriors	
12-14 . . . . .York		**SEPTEMBER**	
15-17 . . . . . New Britain		7-9 . . . . .York	
22-24 . . Southern Maryland		11-12 . . Southern Maryland	
26-28 . . . . . . New Britain			

SUGAR LAND

APRIL

		JULY	
27-30 . . . . . . New Britain		1 . . . . Lancaster	
MAY		13-19 . . . . Road Warriors	
1-2 . . . . New Britain		27-31 . . . . .York	
4-6 . . . . Somerset		**AUGUST**	
14-20 . . Southern Maryland		1-2 . . . . .York	
29-31 . . . . . . Long Island		10-16 . . . . Somerset	
JUNE		24-26 . . . . . . New Britain	
1-3 . . . . .York		28-30 . . Southern Maryland	
11-17 . . . . Road Warriors		31 . . . . Lancaster	
25-30 . . . . Lancaster		**SEPTEMBER**	
		1-2 . . . . Lancaster	
		11-16 . . . . . . Long Island	

YORK

APRIL	
26-29 . . . . Lancaster	
1-2. . . . . . Road Warriors	
11-13 . . . . . . New Britain	
15-16 . . . . Somerset	
25-27 . . . . . Road Warriors	
28-31 . Southern Maryland	

JUNE	
7-10 . . . . Long Island	
18-21 . . . . . Road Warriors	
22-24 . . . . . . Sugar Land	
29-30 . . . . Somerset	

JULY	
1 . . . . Somerset	

3-5 . . . . Sugar Land
13-15 . . . . . . Long Island
20-22 . . . . . . Sugar Land
24-26 . . . Road Warriors
3-5. . . Southern Maryland
6-8. . . . . . . New Britain
14-16 . . . . . . New Britain
20-23 . . . . Lancaster
24-26 . Southern Maryland
31 . . . . Long Island

SEPTEMBER	
1-2. . . . . Long Island	
4-6. . . . . . Road Warriors	
11-12 . . . . Road Warriors	
14-16 . . . . Somerset	

CAN-AM LEAGUE

OTTAWA

MAY	
18-21 . . . . . . New Jersey	
28-31 . . . . Rockland	

JUNE	
1-3. . . . . . Trois-Rivieres	
12-14 . . . . Quebec	
15-17 . . . . International#2	
19-21 . . . . Trois-Rivieres	
26-28 . Dominican Republic	
29-30 . . . . Sussex	

JULY	
1 . . . . Sussex	

9-11 . . . . . . Trois-Rivieres
12-15 . . . . Rockland
23-25 . . . . Quebec
31 . . . . Rockland

AUGUST	
1-2. . . . . Rockland	
3-5. . . . . . . New Jersey	
9-12 . . . . Sussex	
20-23 . . . . Quebec	
31 . . . . New Jersey	

SEPTEMBER	
1-3. . . . . . . New Jersey	

QUEBEC

MAY	
17-20 . . . . . Trois-Rivieres	
22-24 . . . . . New Jersey	
17-May . . . . TR	

JUNE	
1-3. . . . . Sussex	
5-7. . . . . Ottawa	
8-10 . . . . . International#2	
15-17 . . . . Sussex	
19-21 . . . . International#1	
29-30 . . . . . . New Jersey	

JULY	
1 . . . . New Jersey	

9-11 . . . . Sussex
16-18 . . . . Ottawa
19 . . . . . . Trois-Rivieres
21-22 . . . . . Trois-Rivieres
31 . . . . New Jersey

AUGUST	
1-2. . . . . . . New Jersey	
3-5. . . . . Sussex	
9-12 . . . . Rockland	
24-26 . . . . Trois-Rivieres	
28-30 . . . . Ottawa	
31 . . . . Rockland	

SEPTEMBER	
1-3. . . . . Rockland	

TROIS-RIVIERES

MAY	
25-27 . . . . Rockland	
28-31 . . . . Sussex	

JUNE	
8-10 . . . . Ottawa	
11-14 . . . . International#2	
15-17 . . . . . New Jersey	
22-24 . . . . International#1	
26-28 . . . . Quebec	

JULY	
3-5. . . . . Ottawa	

6-8. . . . . Rockland
12-15 . . . . Quebec
20 . . . . Quebec
23-25 . . . . . . New Jersey
26-29 . . . . Quebec

AUGUST	
6-8. . . . . Sussex	
13-15 . . . . Ottawa	
16-19 . . . . Sussex	
28-30 . . . . Rockland	

SUSSEX

MAY	
17 . . . . Rockland	
22-24 . . . . . Trois-Rivieres	
25-27 . . . . Quebec	

JUNE	
5-7. . . . . New Jersey	

8-10 . . . . International#1
19-21 . . . . International#2
22-25 . . . . Quebec
26-28 . . . . Rockland

JULY	
2-4. . . . . . . New Jersey	

6-8. . . . . Ottawa
12-15 . . . . . New Jersey
17-18 . . . . Rockland
26-29 . . . . Ottawa
31 . . . . . . Trois-Rivieres

AUGUST	
1-2. . . . . . Trois-Rivieres	

ROCKLAND

MAY	
18-20 . . . . Sussex	
22-24 . . . . Ottawa	
JUNE	
1-4. . . . . . New Jersey	
5-7. . . . . Trois-Rivieres	
12-14 . . . . Sussex	
15-17 . . . . International#1	
22-24 . . . . International#2	
29-30 . . . . Trois-Rivieres	

JULY	
1 . . . . Trois-Rivieres	

NEW JERSEY

MAY	
25-27 . . . . Ottawa	
28-31 . . . . Quebec	

JUNE	
8-10 . . . . Rockland	
11-14 . . . . International#1	
19-21 . . . . Rockland	
22-24 . . . . Ottawa	
26-28 . . . . International#2	

13-15 . . . . Quebec
21-23 . . . . Rockland
24-26 . . . . Ottawa
31 . . . . . . Trois-Rivieres

SEPTEMBER	
1-3. . . . . . Trois-Rivieres	

2-4. . . . . Quebec
9-11 . . . . . New Jersey
16 . . . . Sussex
19-22 . . . . Ottawa
23-25 . . . . Sussex

AUGUST	
3-5. . . . . . Trois-Rivieres	
6-8. . . . . Ottawa	
13-15 . . . . . New Jersey	
16-19 . . . . Quebec	
24-26 . . . . . New Jersey	

JULY	
5-7. . . . . Quebec	
16-18 . . . . Trois-Rivieres	
19-22 . . . . Sussex	
26-29 . . . . Rockland	

AUGUST	
6-8. . . . . Quebec	
9-12 . . . . . Trois-Rivieres	
16-19 . . . . Ottawa	
21-23 . . . . Trois-Rivieres	
27-30 . . . . Sussex	

FRONTIER LEAGUE

EVANSVILLE

MAY	
11-13 . . . . . .Washington	
18-20 . . . . .Normal	
30-31 . . . . Florence	

JUNE	
5-7. . . . . Gateway	
15-17 . . . . Traverse City	
22-24 . . . Southern Illinois	
26-28 . . . . Gateway	
29-30 . . . . . . River City	

JULY	
1 . . . . River City	
17-19 . . . . .Lake Erie	
20-22 . . . . . . Windy City	
31 . . . . Joliet	

AUGUST	
1-2. . . . . Joliet	
3-5. . . . . . . Schaumburg	
10-12 . . . . Florence	
14-16 . . . . .Normal	
21-23 . . . . Southern Illinois	
24-26 . . . . River City	

FLORENCE

MAY	
10-12 . . . . Joliet	
18-20 . . . . Gateway	

JUNE	
1-3. . . . . River City	
5-7. . . . . Southern Illinois	
13-14 . . . . . Windy City	
15-17 . . . . Schaumburg	
19-21 . . . . . Evansville	

JULY	
3-5. . . . . . . .Washington	
13-15 . . . . Southern Illinois	
17-19 . . . . Traverse City	
24-26 . . . . .Normal	

AUGUST	
3-5. . . . . .Lake Erie	
7-9. . . . . River City	
17-19 . . . . Evansville	
24-26 . . . . .Gateway	
29-30 . . . . .Normal	

GATEWAY

MAY	
11-13 . . . . . Schaumburg	
22-24 . . . . . . .Lake Erie	
29-31 . . . . . . River City	

JUNE	
1-3. . . . . .Normal	
8-10 . . . . Florence	
12-14 . . . . . .Washington	
22-24 . . . . .Normal	

JULY

2-4	Windy City
13-15	River City
20-22	Traverse City
24-26	Evansville

AUGUST

3-5	Joliet

JOLIET

MAY

15-17	Evansville
18-20	Windy City
25-27	Southern Illinois
29-31	Washington

JUNE

5-7	Lake Erie
15-17	Gateway
19-21	Windy City
22-24	Traverse City
29-30	Lake Erie

JULY

1	Lake Erie
3-5	Normal
17-19	River City
20-22	Florence
27-29	Schaumburg

AUGUST

7-9	Washington
17-19	Traverse City
31	Schaumburg

SEPTEMBER

1-2	Schaumburg

LAKE ERIE

MAY

15-17	Normal
18-20	Washington
29-31	Traverse City

JUNE

8-10	Schaumburg
15-17	River City
19-21	Schaumburg

JULY

3-5	Evansville
6-8	Florence
20-22	Southern Illinois
27-29	Windy City
31	Gateway

AUGUST

1-2	Gateway
10-12	Traverse City
14-16	Joliet
21-23	Joliet
28-30	Windy City
31	Washington

SEPTEMBER

1-2	Washington
11-13	Traverse City
22-24	Joliet
25-27	Windy City

NORMAL

JUNE

8-10	Southern Illinois
12-14	Lake Erie
19-21	Southern Illinois
26-28	River City
29-30	Florence

JULY

1	Florence
6-8	Schaumburg
13-15	Evansville
17-19	Washington
27-29	Gateway

AUGUST

7-9	Gateway
10-12	River City
21-23	Florence
31	Evansville

SEPTEMBER

1-2	Evansville

RIVER CITY

MAY

15-17	Traverse City
22-24	Schaumburg
25-27	Lake Erie

JUNE

5-7	Normal
8-10	Evansville
19-21	Gateway
22-24	Florence
25	Gateway

JULY

6-8	Joliet
20-22	Washington
27-29	Evansville
31	Windy City

AUGUST

1-2	Windy City
14-16	Southern Illinois
17-19	Normal
22-23	Gateway
28-30	Southern Illinois
31	Florence

SEPTEMBER

1-2	Florence

SCHAUMBURG

MAY

15-17	Southern Illinois
18-20	Traverse City
25-27	Gateway

JUNE

1-3	Lake Erie
5-7	Windy City
12-14	Evansville
22-24	Washington

10-12	Southern Illinois
15-16	Florence
28-30	Evansville
31	Southern Illinois

SEPTEMBER

1-2	Southern Illinois

26-28	Joliet

JULY

3-5	River City
20-22	Normal

JULY

31	Florence

SOUTHERN ILLINOIS

MAY

11-13	Lake Erie
18-20	River City
29-31	Normal

JUNE

1-3	Evansville
12-14	Joliet
15-17	Washington
26-28	Florence
29-30	Gateway

JULY

1	Gateway
6-8	Windy City
17-19	Schaumburg
24-26	River City
27-29	Florence

AUGUST

1-2	Traverse City
7,9	Evansville
17-19	Gateway
24-26	Normal

TRAVERSE CITY

MAY

23-24	Florence
25-27	Evansville

JUNE

1-3	Joliet
8-10	Windy City
13-14	River City
28	Lake Erie

JULY

3-5	Southern Illinois
6-8	Gateway
13-15	Schaumburg
25-27	Lake Erie
27-29	Washington

AUGUST

3-5	Normal
15-16	Washington
29-30	Joliet
31	Windy City

SEPTEMBER

1-2	Windy City

WASHINGTON

MAY

15-17	Gateway
23-24	Southern Illinois
25-27	Florence

JUNE

5-7	Traverse City
8-10	Joliet
19-21	Traverse City
26-28	Windy City
29-30	Schaumburg

JULY

1	Schaumburg
6-8	Evansville
13-15	Lake Erie
24-26	Joliet
31	Normal

AUGUST

1-2	Normal
3-5	River City
10-12	Windy City
21-23	Schaumburg
24-26	Lake Erie

WINDY CITY

MAY

10-12	River City
15-17	Florence
22-24	Evansville
30-31	Schaumburg

JUNE

1-3	Washington
15-17	Normal
20	Joliet
22-24	Lake Erie
29-30	Traverse City

JULY

1	Traverse City
13-15	Joliet
17-19	Gateway
23-26	Schaumburg

AUGUST

3-5	Southern Illinois
7-9	Lake Erie
17-19	Washington
21-23	Traverse City
24-25	Joliet

AUGUST

10-12	Joliet
14-16	Windy City
17-19	Lake Erie
24-26	Traverse City
28-30	Washington

SEPTEMBER

1-2	Florence

SPRING TRAINING SCHEDULES

AMERICAN LEAGUE

BALTIMORE ORIOLES

FEBRUARY
23	Tampa Bay
24	at Philadelphia
24	Minnesota
25	at Boston
26	Detroit
27	at Tampa Bay
28	St. Louis

MARCH
1	at Tampa Bay
2	Pittsburgh
3	at Philadelphia
4	Boston
6	at Minnesota
7	at Tampa Bay
8	Toronto
9	at Toronto
10	Pittsburgh
11	at Boston
11	Philadelphia
12	at Pittsburgh
13	at Minnesota
14	New York (AL)
15	at St. Louis
16	at New York (NL)
17	Toronto
18	New York (NL)
19	at Detroit
20	Tampa Bay
21	at New York (NL)
22	Boston
23	Tampa Bay
24	Minnesota
25	at Philadelphia

BOSTON RED SOX

FEBRUARY
23	Minnesota
24	Tampa Bay
25	Baltimore
26	at Pittsburgh
27	St. Louis
27	at Minnesota
28	Pittsburgh

MARCH
1	at Houston
2	at St. Louis
3	New York (AL)
4	at Baltimore
6	at Tampa Bay
7	at Philadelphia
7	Minnesota
8	Tampa Bay
9	at Miami
10	at Minnesota
11	Baltimore
12	at Toronto
14	at Minnesota
15	Toronto
16	Minnesota
17	Tampa Bay
18	at Pittsburgh
19	Philadelphia
20	Pittsburgh
21	at Tampa Bay
22	at Baltimore
23	at New York (AL)
24	Houston
25	at Minnesota
26-27	Chicago (NL)

CHICAGO WHITE SOX

FEBRUARY
23	at Los Angeles (NL)
24	at Seattle
25	Cincinnati
26	Oakland
27	at Chicago (NL)
28	Texas

MARCH
1	at Cincinnati
2	Los Angeles (NL)
3	at Kansas City
4	San Diego
5	at Oakland
6	Milwaukee
7	Cincinnati
8	at Texas
8	Kansas City
9	at San Diego
10	at Chicago (NL)
11	Arizona
12	at Seattle
14	at Milwaukee
15	at Los Angeles (AL)
16	Chicago (NL)
17	Los Angeles (NL)
18	at Oakland
19	at Arizona
20	Texas
21	San Diego
22	at Arizona
23	Seattle
24	at Los Angeles (NL)
25	Milwaukee

CLEVELAND INDIANS

FEBRUARY
23	Cincinnati
24	at Arizona
25	at Cincinnati
26	at Milwaukee
27	Oakland
28	Seattle
28	at Los Angeles (AL)

MARCH
1	at Los Angeles (NL)
2	Texas
3	San Francisco
4	at Milwaukee
5	at Los Angeles (NL)
6	at Cincinnati
7	Chicago (NL)
8	Los Angeles (NL)
9	at Colorado
10	at San Diego
11	at Kansas City
11	Milwaukee
12	Texas
14	Los Angeles (AL)
15	Cincinnati
16	at Oakland
17-18	at Chicago (NL)
18	at Seattle
19	at San Francisco
21	Kansas City
22	San Diego
23	Arizona
24	at Texas
25	Cincinnati
26-27	at Arizona

DETROIT TIGERS

FEBRUARY
23	at New York (AL)
24	Toronto
25	Pittsburgh
25	at Toronto
26	at Baltimore
27	at Philadelphia
28	at New York (AL)

MARCH
1	Atlanta
2	Miami
3	Tampa Bay
4	at Washington
5	at New York (NL)
6	New York (AL)
7	Toronto
8	at Pittsburgh
9	New York (NL)
10	at Toronto
11	Atlanta
12	Washington
13	at New York (AL)
15	at Atlanta
16	Philadelphia
17	New York (AL)
18	at Tampa Bay
19	Baltimore
20	New York (AL)
21	at Atlanta
22	at Philadelphia
23	at Atlanta
24	Philadelphia
25	Atlanta
26	Tampa Bay
27	at Tampa Bay

HOUSTON ASTROS

FEBRUARY
23	Washington
24	Atlanta
25	at St. Louis
26	at Miami
26	New York (NL)
27	at New York (NL)
28	Minnesota

MARCH
1	Boston
2	New York (NL)
3	Washington
4	at St. Louis
5	Miami
6	at Washington
6	at New York (NL)
7	Miami
8	at Atlanta
9	St. Louis
10	Washington
11,13	at New York (NL)
14	St. Louis
15	at Washington
16	at New York (AL)
17	at Miami
18	Atlanta
19	New York (NL)
21	at Washington
22	Miami
23	at Minnesota
23	at Washington
24	at Boston
25	at Miami
26-27	Milwaukee

KANSAS CITY ROYALS

FEBRUARY

24	Los Angeles (NL)
25	at Oakland
26	at San Francisco
27	Seattle
28	Cincinnati

MARCH

1	at Seattle
2	at San Diego
3	Chicago (AL)
4	at Cincinnati
6	San Diego
7	Milwaukee
8	at Chicago (AL)
9	Arizona
9	at Los Angeles (NL)
10	at Arizona
11	Cleveland
12	San Diego
12	Texas
13	Oakland
14	Chicago (NL)
15	at Los Angeles (NL)
16	at San Diego
17	Texas
17	at Texas
18	at Chicago (NL)
20	San Francisco
21	at Cleveland
22	at Milwaukee
23	at San Francisco
23	Los Angeles (NL)
24	at Arizona
25	Chicago (NL)

NEW YORK YANKEES

FEBRUARY

23	Detroit
24	at Pittsburgh
25	at Philadelphia
26	Philadelphia
27	at Toronto
28	Detroit

MARCH

1	at Philadelphia
2	Atlanta
3	at Boston
4	Tampa Bay
6	at Detroit
7	at New York (NL)
8	Philadelphia
9	at Atlanta
10	New York (NL)
11	at Miami
12	Minnesota
13	Detroit
14	at Baltimore
15	Pittsburgh
16	Houston
17	at Detroit
18	Miami
19	Tampa Bay
20	at Detroit
21	Baltimore
22	at Minnesota
23	Boston
24	at Atlanta
24	Toronto
25	at Tampa Bay
26	at Atlanta

LOS ANGELES ANGELS OF ANAHEIM

FEBRUARY

23	at Oakland
24	Milwaukee
25	San Diego
26	at San Diego
27	at Colorado
28	Cleveland

MARCH

1	at San Francisco
2	Chicago (NL)
3	at Seattle
4	Colorado
5	at Cincinnati
6	at Arizona
7	Los Angeles (NL)
8	at Oakland
9	at Chicago (NL)
10	at San Francisco
10	San Francisco
11	Texas
12	Cincinnati
14	at Cleveland
15	at Colorado
15	Chicago (AL)
16	Colorado
17	at Seattle
18	at Texas
19	Seattle
20	Arizona
22	at Los Angeles (NL)
23	Oakland
24	Arizona
25	Los Angeles (NL)
26-27	at Los Angeles (NL)

OAKLAND ATHLETICS

FEBRUARY

23	Los Angeles (AL)
24	San Diego
25	Kansas City
26	at Chicago (AL)
27	at Cleveland
28	at Chicago (NL)

MARCH

1	Texas
3	San Diego
4	at San Diego
5	Chicago (AL)
6	Texas
7	at Seattle
8	Los Angeles (AL)
9	at Milwaukee
10	at Texas
11	Chicago (NL)
12	San Francisco
13	at Kansas City
15	Seattle
16	Cleveland
17	Seattle
17	at San Francisco
18	Chicago (AL)
19	at Los Angeles (NL)
20	Los Angeles (NL)
21	at Milwaukee
22	Colorado
23	at Los Angeles (AL)
24	Milwaukee
25	San Francisco
26-27	at San Francisco

MINNESOTA TWINS

FEBRUARY

23	at Boston
24	at Baltimore
25	Tampa Bay
26	St. Louis
27	Boston
28	at Houston
28	Tampa Bay

MARCH

1	at St. Louis
2	Toronto
3	at Toronto
4	Pittsburgh
5	at Philadelphia
6	Baltimore
7	at Boston
9	at Tampa Bay
10	Boston
11	at Tampa Bay
12	at New York (AL)
13	Baltimore
14	Boston
15	at Tampa Bay
16	Tampa Bay
16	at Boston
17	at Pittsburgh
18	Philadelphia
19	at Pittsburgh
21	Pittsburgh
22	New York (AL)
23	Houston
24	at Baltimore
25	Boston
27	at Washington

SEATTLE MARINERS

FEBRUARY

23	at San Diego
24	Chicago (AL)
25	Los Angeles (NL)
26	at Chicago (NL)
27	at Kansas City
27	San Diego
28	at Cleveland

MARCH

1	Kansas City
2	at Milwaukee
3	Los Angeles (NL)
4	at Texas
6	Colorado
7	Oakland
8	San Francisco
9	at San Francisco
10	at Cincinnati
11	Cincinnati
12	Chicago (AL)
13	at Colorado
14	San Francisco
15	at Oakland
16	at Texas
17	at Oakland
17	Los Angeles (AL)
18	Cleveland
19	at Los Angeles (AL)
21	Milwaukee
22	Texas
23	at Chicago (AL)
24	Chicago (NL)
25	at San Diego
27	at Colorado

TAMPA BAY RAYS

FEBRUARY
23 . . . . .Pittsburgh
23 . . . . .at Baltimore
24 . . . . at Boston
25 . . . . . . at Minnesota
26 . . . . Toronto
27 . . . . Baltimore
28 . . . . . at Minnesota

MARCH
1 . . . . Baltimore
2 . . . . Philadelphia
3 . . . . at Detroit
4 . . . . . at New York (AL)
6 . . . . Boston
7 . . . . Baltimore
8 . . . . at Boston
9 . . . . .Minnesota

10 . . . . . .at Philadelphia
11 . . . . . . .Minnesota
13 . . . . . .at Philadelphia
14 . . . . . . at Pittsburgh
15 . . . . . . .Minnesota
16 . . . . . . at Minnesota
17 . . . . . . at Boston
18 . . . . Detroit
19 . . . . .at New York (AL)
20 . . . . . .at Baltimore
21 . . . . Boston
22 . . . . . . at Toronto
23 . . . . . .at Baltimore
23 . . . . Toronto
24 . . . . . at Pittsburgh
25 . . . . . New York (AL)
26 . . . . . . at Detroit
27 . . . . Detroit

TEXAS RANGERS

FEBRUARY
24 . . . . . .at Chicago (NL)
25 . . . . .Colorado
26 . . . .Los Angeles (NL)
27 . . . at Los Angeles (NL)
28 . . . . . .at Chicago (AL)

MARCH
1 . . . . San Diego
1 . . . . at Oakland
2 . . . . at Cleveland
3 . . . . . at San Francisco
4 . . . . Seattle
5 . . . . . . .San Francisco
6 . . . . . . at Oakland
7 . . . . . . .at Colorado
8 . . . . Chicago (AL)
9 . . . . at Cincinnati

10 . . . . Oakland
11 . . . at Los Angeles (AL)
12 . . . . . at Cleveland
12 . . . . at Kansas City
13 . . . . at Milwaukee
15 . . . . . Milwaukee
16 . . . . Seattle
17 . . . . . at Kansas City
17 . . . . . Kansas City
18 . . . . .Los Angeles (AL)
19 . . . . . . .Colorado
20 . . . . . .at Chicago (AL)
21 . . . . . Chicago (NL)
22 . . . . Cincinnati
22 . . . . . . at Seattle
23 . . . . . . at San Diego
24 . . . . . . Cleveland
26-27 . . . . . . Cincinnati

TORONTO BLUE JAYS

FEBRUARY
23 . . . . Philadelphia
24 . . . . at Detroit
25 . . . . Detroit
26 . . . . . . at Tampa Bay
27 . . . . . New York (AL)
28 . . . . Philadelphia

MARCH
1 . . . . . . at Pittsburgh
2 . . . . . . at Minnesota
3 . . . . .Minnesota
4 . . . .at Philadelphia
6 . . . . .Atlanta
7 . . . . . . at Detroit
7 . . . . .Pittsburgh
8 . . . .at Baltimore
9 . . . . Baltimore

10 . . . . Detroit
11 . . . . .Pittsburgh
12 . . . . Boston
13 . . . . at Atlanta
15 . . . . at Boston
16 . . . . .at Philadelphia
17 . . . . . .at Baltimore
18 . . . . .Pittsburgh
19 . . . . . . at Atlanta
20 . . . . .at Philadelphia
21 . . . . . . Philadelphia
22 . . . . . . Tampa Bay
22 . . . . . at Pittsburgh
23 . . . . .at Tampa Bay
24 . . . . .at New York (AL)
25 . . . . .Pittsburgh
26-27 . . . . . . St. Louis

NATIONAL LEAGUE

ARIZONA D-BACKS

FEBRUARY
23 . . . . at Colorado
24 . . . . Cleveland
25 . . . . Milwaukee
26 . . . . . at Cincinnati
26 . . . . .Colorado
27 . . . . at San Francisco
28 . . . . . .Colorado

MARCH
1 . . . . Milwaukee
2 . . . . . . at Colorado
3 . . . . at Los Angeles (NL)
4 . . . . . Chicago (NL)
5 . . . . . . at San Diego
6 . . . . . .Los Angeles (AL)
8 . . . . . .at Milwaukee
9 . . . . . at Kansas City

10 . . . . Kansas City
11 . . . . . .at Chicago (AL)
12 . . . . .Colorado
14 . . . . Cincinnati
15 . . . . . .at Chicago (NL)
16 . . . .Los Angeles (NL)
17 . . . . San Diego
18 . . . . . at Cincinnati
19 . . . . . . Chicago (AL)
20 . . . at Los Angeles (AL)
21 . . . . . . .San Francisco
22 . . . . . . Chicago (AL)
23 . . . . . at Cleveland
24 . . . at Los Angeles (AL)
24 . . . . . . Kansas City
25 . . . . at Colorado
26-27 . . . . . . Cleveland

ATLANTA BRAVES

FEBRUARY
23 . . . . .at New York (NL)
24 . . . . at Houston
25 . . . . at Washington
26 . . . . . . .Washington
27 . . . . . . .Pittsburgh
28 . . . . . New York (NL)

MARCH
1 . . . . at Detroit
1 . . . . .Washington
2 . . . at New York (AL)
3 . . . . St. Louis
4 . . . . Miami
5 . . . . . . .Pittsburgh
6 . . . . . .at Toronto
8 . . . . Houston
9 . . . . . . New York (NL)

10 . . . . at Pittsburgh
11 . . . . at Detroit
12 . . . . Philadelphia
13 . . . . Toronto
14 . . . . Philadelphia
15 . . . . Detroit
16 . . . . . at Pittsburgh
17 . . . .at Philadelphia
17 . . . . St. Louis
18 . . . . . . at Houston
19 . . . . Toronto
21 . . . . Detroit
22 . . . . . at St. Louis
23 . . . . Detroit
24 . . . . New York (AL)
25 . . . . at Detroit
26 . . . . . New York (AL)

CHICAGO CUBS

FEBRUARY
23 . . . . . .at Milwaukee
24 . . . . Texas
25 . . . . at San Francisco
26 . . . . Seattle
27 . . . . . . Chicago (AL)
28 . . . . Oakland

MARCH
1 . . . . .Colorado
2 . . . . at Los Angeles (AL)
3 . . . . Cincinnati
4 . . . . at Arizona
5 . . . . . . at Colorado
6 . . . .Los Angeles (NL)
7 . . . . . . at Cleveland
8 . . . . San Diego
9 . . . . . .Los Angeles (AL)

10 . . . . Chicago (AL)
10 . . . . at Los Angeles (NL)
11 . . . . at Oakland
13 . . . . . . at San Diego
13 . . . . . .San Francisco
14 . . . . at Kansas City
15 . . . . .Arizona
16 . . . . . .at Chicago (AL)
17-18 . . . . Cleveland
18 . . . . Kansas City
19 . . . . . at Cincinnati
21 . . . . at Texas
22 . . . at San Francisco
23 . . . . Milwaukee
24 . . . . at Seattle
24 . . . . .Colorado
25 . . . . . at Kansas City
26-27 . . . . . . at Boston

CINCINNATI REDS

FEBRUARY
23 . . . . at Cleveland
24 . . . . .Colorado
25 . . . . . .at Chicago (AL)
25 . . . . Cleveland
26 . . . . .Arizona
27 . . . . . . at Milwaukee
28 . . . . . . at Kansas City

MARCH
1 . . . . Chicago (AL)
2 . . . at San Francisco
3 . . . . .at Chicago (NL)
4 . . . . . . Kansas City
5 . . . . . .Los Angeles (AL)
6 . . . . Cleveland
7 . . . . . .at Chicago (AL)

8 . . . . at Colorado
9 . . . . Texas
10 . . . . Seattle
11 . . . . at Seattle
12 . . . . at Los Angeles (AL)
14 . . . . at Arizona
15 . . . . at Cleveland
16 . . . . Milwaukee
17 . . . . . . .San Francisco
18 . . . . .Arizona
19 . . . . . . Chicago (NL)
20 . . . . . . at San Diego
22 . . . . at Texas
23 . . . . at Colorado
24 . . . . San Diego
25 . . . . at Cleveland
26-27 . . . . at Texas

COLORADO ROCKIES

FEBRUARY
23 . . . . .Arizona
24 . . . . at Cincinnati
25 . . . . at Texas
26 . . . . at Arizona
27 . . . . .Los Angeles (AL)
28 . . . . at Arizona

MARCH
1 . . . . . . .at Chicago (NL)
2 . . . . .Arizona
3 . . . . Milwaukee
4 . . . . at Los Angeles (AL)
5 . . . . . Chicago (NL)
6 . . . . at Seattle
7 . . . . Texas
8 . . . . Cincinnati

9 . . . . Cleveland
10 . . . . .at Milwaukee
11 . . . . . .Los Angeles (NL)
12 . . . . at Arizona
13 . . . . Seattle
14 . . . . at Los Angeles (NL)
15 . . . . .Los Angeles (AL)
16 . . . . at Los Angeles (AL)
17 . . . . at Milwaukee
18 . . . . .San Francisco
19 . . . . at Texas
20 . . . . Milwaukee
22 . . . . at Oakland
23 . . . . Cincinnati
24 . . . . . .at Chicago (NL)
25 . . . . .Arizona
27 . . . . Seattle

LOS ANGELES DODGERS

FEBRUARY
23 . . . . Chicago (AL)
24 . . . . . . at Kansas City
24 . . . . . .San Francisco
25 . . . . at Seattle
26 . . . . at Texas
27 . . . . Texas
28 . . . . . . at San Diego

MARCH
1 . . . . Cleveland
2 . . . . .at Chicago (AL)
3 . . . . .Arizona
4 . . . at San Francisco
5 . . . . Cleveland
6 . . . . . .at Chicago (NL)
7 . . . . at Los Angeles (AL)
8 . . . . at Cleveland

9 . . . . Kansas City
10 . . . . Chicago (NL)
11 . . . . at Colorado
12 . . . . Milwaukee
14 . . . . .Colorado
15 . . . . Kansas City
16 . . . . at Arizona
17 . . . . . .at Chicago (AL)
18 . . . . at Milwaukee
18 . . . . San Diego
19 . . . . Oakland
20 . . . . at Oakland
22 . . . . . .Los Angeles (AL)
23 . . . . . . at Kansas City
24 . . . . Chicago (AL)
25 . . . . at Los Angeles (AL)
26-27 . . . .Los Angeles (AL)

MIAMI MARLINS

FEBRUARY
23 . . . . St. Louis
24 . . . . .Washington
25 . . . . .at New York (NL)
26 . . . . Houston
27 . . . at Washington
28 . . . . .Washington

MARCH
1 . . . . . .at New York (NL)
2 . . . . at Detroit
3 . . . . . New York (NL)
4 . . . . at Atlanta
5 . . . . at Houston
6 . . . . St. Louis
7 . . . . at Houston
8 . . . . . . at St. Louis

9 . . . . Boston
10 . . . . at St. Louis
11 . . . . . . New York (AL)
13 . . . . St. Louis
14 . . . . New York (NL)
15 . . . . .at New York (NL)
16 . . . . at St. Louis
17 . . . . .Houston
18 . . . . .at New York (AL)
19 . . . . .Washington
20 . . . . . at Washington
21 . . . . St. Louis
22 . . . . at Houston
23 . . . . .Washington
24 . . . . . at Washington
25 . . . . .at New York (NL)
25 . . . . Houston

MILWAUKEE BREWERS

FEBRUARY
23 . . . . Chicago (NL)
23 . . . . . . at San Francisco
24 . . . . at Los Angeles (AL)
25 . . . . at Arizona
26 . . . . Cleveland
27 . . . . Cincinnati
28 . . . . . . .San Francisco

MARCH
1 . . . . at Arizona
2 . . . . Seattle
3 . . . . at Colorado
4 . . . . Cleveland
6 . . . . . .at Chicago (AL)
7 . . . . . . at Kansas City
8 . . . . .Arizona
9 . . . . Oakland

10 . . . . .Colorado
11 . . . . at Cleveland
12 . . . at Los Angeles (NL)
13 . . . . Texas
14 . . . . Chicago (AL)
15 . . . . at Texas
16 . . . . . . at Cincinnati
17 . . . . .Colorado
18 . . . .Los Angeles (NL)
20 . . . . at Colorado
21 . . . . Oakland
21 . . . . at Seattle
22 . . . . . . Kansas City
23 . . . .at Chicago (NL)
24 . . . . . . at Oakland
25 . . . .at Chicago (AL)
26-27 . . . . . at Houston

NEW YORK METS

FEBRUARY
23 . . . . .Atlanta
24 . . . . St. Louis
25 . . . . Miami
26 . . . . at Houston
27 . . . . Houston
28 . . . . at Atlanta

MARCH
1 . . . . Miami
2 . . . . .Washington
2 . . . . at Houston
3 . . . . at Miami
4 . . . . .Washington
5 . . . . Detroit
6 . . . . Houston
7 . . . . . . New York (AL)

8 . . . . at Washington
9 . . . . at Detroit
10 . . . . .at New York (AL)
11,13 . . . . Houston
13 . . . . at Washington
14 . . . . .at Miami
15 . . . . Miami
16 . . . . Baltimore
17 . . . . . . at Washington
18 . . . . . . .at Baltimore
19 . . . . at Houston
20 . . . . . . at St. Louis
22 . . . . .Washington
23 . . . . St. Louis
24 . . . . . . at St. Louis
25 . . . . Miami

PHILADELPHIA PHILLIES

FEBRUARY
23	at Toronto
24	Baltimore
25	New York (AL)
26	at New York (AL)
27	Detroit
28	at Toronto

MARCH
1	New York (AL)
2	at Tampa Bay
3	Baltimore
3	at Pittsburgh
4	Toronto
5	Minnesota
7	Boston
8	at New York (AL)
9	Pittsburgh
10	Tampa Bay
11	at Baltimore
12	at Atlanta
13	Tampa Bay
14	at Atlanta
16	at Detroit
16	Toronto
17	Atlanta
18	at Minnesota
19	at Boston
20	Toronto
21	at Toronto
22	Detroit
23	at Pittsburgh
24	at Detroit
25	Baltimore
26	at Pittsburgh
27	Pittsburgh

PITTSBURGH PIRATES

FEBRUARY
23	at Tampa Bay
24	New York (AL)
25	at Detroit
26	Boston
27	at Atlanta
28	at Boston

MARCH
1	Toronto
2	at Baltimore
3	Philadelphia
4	at Minnesota
5	at Atlanta
7	at Toronto
8	Detroit
9	at Philadelphia
10	Atlanta
10	at Baltimore
11	at Toronto
12	Baltimore
14	Tampa Bay
15	at New York (AL)
16	Atlanta
17	Minnesota
18	Boston
18	at Toronto
19	Minnesota
20	at Boston
21	at Minnesota
22	Toronto
23	Philadelphia
24	Tampa Bay
25	at Toronto
26	Philadelphia
27	at Philadelphia

SAN DIEGO PADRES

FEBRUARY
23	Seattle
24	at Oakland
25	at Los Angeles (AL)
26	Los Angeles (AL)
27	at Seattle
28	Los Angeles (NL)

MARCH
1	at Texas
2	Kansas City
3	at Oakland
4	at Chicago (AL)
4	Oakland
5	Arizona
6	at Kansas City
7	at San Francisco
8	at Chicago (NL)
9	Chicago (AL)
10	Cleveland
11	at San Francisco
12	at Kansas City
13	Chicago (NL)
15	San Francisco
16	Kansas City
17	at Arizona
18	at Los Angeles (NL)
20	Cincinnati
21	at Chicago (AL)
22	at Cleveland
23	Texas
24	at Cincinnati
25	Seattle
26	at El Paso

SAN FRANCISCO GIANTS

FEBRUARY
23	Milwaukee
24	at Los Angeles (NL)
25	Chicago (NL)
26	Kansas City
27	Arizona
28	at Milwaukee

MARCH
1	Los Angeles (AL)
2	Cincinnati
3	at Cleveland
3	Texas
4	Los Angeles (NL)
5	at Texas
7	San Diego
8	at Seattle
9	Seattle
10	Los Angeles (AL)
10	at Los Angeles (AL)
11	San Diego
12	at Oakland
13	at Chicago (NL)
14	at Seattle
15	at San Diego
17	at Cincinnati
17	Oakland
18	at Colorado
19	Cleveland
20	at Kansas City
21	at Arizona
22	Chicago (NL)
23	Kansas City
25	at Oakland
26-27	Oakland

ST. LOUIS CARDINALS

FEBRUARY
23	at Miami
24	at New York (NL)
25	Houston
26	at Minnesota
27	at Boston
28	at Baltimore

MARCH
1	Minnesota
2	Boston
3	at Atlanta
4	Houston
5	Washington
6	at Miami
7	Washington
8	Miami
9	at Houston
10	Miami
11	at Washington
13	at Miami
14	at Houston
15	Baltimore
16	Miami
16	at Washington
17	at Atlanta
18	Washington
20	New York (NL)
21	at Miami
22	Atlanta
23	at New York (NL)
24	New York (NL)
25	at Washington
26-27	at Toronto

WASHINGTON NATIONALS

FEBRUARY
23	at Houston
24	at Miami
25	Atlanta
26	at Atlanta
27	Miami
28	at Miami

MARCH
1	at Atlanta
2	at New York (NL)
3	at Houston
4	Detroit
4	at New York (NL)
5	at St. Louis
6	Houston
7	at St. Louis
8	New York (NL)
10	at Houston
11	St. Louis
12	at Detroit
13	New York (NL)
15	Houston
16	St. Louis
17	New York (NL)
18	at St. Louis
19	at Miami
20	Miami
21	Houston
22	at New York (NL)
23	Houston
23	at Miami
24	Miami
25	St. Louis
27	Minnesota

INDEPENDENT LEAGUES

AMERICAN ASSOCIATION

Office Address: 1415 Hwy 54 West, Suite 210, Durham, NC 27707.
Telephone: (919) 401-8150. **Fax:** (919) 401-8152. **Website:** www.americanassociationbaseball.com.
Year Founded: 2006.
Commissioner: Miles Wolff.
Director, Umpires: Kevin Winn.
Division Structure—North Division: Fargo-Moorhead RedHawks, St. Paul Saints, Sioux Falls Canaries, Winnipeg Goldeyes.
South Division: Gary SouthShore RailCats, Kansas City T-Bones, Lincoln Saltdogs, Sioux City Explorers.
South Division: Cleburne Railroaders, Laredo Lemurs, Texas AirHogs, Wichita Wingnuts.
Regular Season: 100 games.
2018 Opening Date: May 17. **Closing Date:** Sept. 3.
Playoff Format: Top two finishers in each division play in best-of-five series. Winners play for best-of-five American Association championship.
Roster Limit: 22.
Eligibility Rule: Minimum of four first-year players; maximum of five veterans (at least six or more years of professional service).
Brand of Baseball: Rawlings.
Statistician: Pointstreak.com, 602-1595 16th Avenue, Richmond Hill, ON Canada L4B 3N9.

STADIUM INFORMATION

Club	Stadium	Opened	Dimensions LF	CF	RF	Capacity	2017 Att.
Chicago	Impact Field			6,300		New	
Cleburne	The Depot at Cleburne Station	2017	335	400	320	3,200	103,264
Fargo-Moorhead	Newman Outdoor Field	1996	318	408	314	4,513	176,086
Gary SouthShore	U.S. Steel Yard	2002	320	400	335	6,139	181,612
Kansas City	CommunityAmerica Ballpark	2003	300	396	328	6,537	211,599
Lincoln	Haymarket Park	2001	335	395	325	4,500	172,712
St. Paul	CHS Field	2015	330	396	320	7,140	406,501
Sioux City	Mercy Field at Lewis and Clark Park	1993	330	400	330	3,630	58,407
Sioux Falls	Sioux Falls Stadium	1964	312	410	312	4,656	113,506
Texas	AirHogs Stadium	2008	330	400	330	5,445	65,672
Wichita	Lawrence-Dumont Stadium	1934	344	401	312	6,055	157,995
Winnipeg	Shaw Park	1999	325	400	325	7,481	219,556

CHICAGO DOGS

Office Address: 5505 Pearl Street, 4th Floor, Rosemont, IL, 60018
Telephone: (847) 260-2544.
E-mail: info@thechicagodogs.com. **Website:** www.thechicagodogs.com.
Owners: Shawn Hunter, Steven Gluckstern. **Field Manager:** Butch Hobson.

GAME INFORMATION
Stadium Name: Impact Field. **Capacity:** 6,300.
Standard Game Times: 7:05, Sunday 1:05.

CLEBURNE RAILROADERS

Office Address: 1906 Brazzle Boulevard, Cleburne, TX 76033.
Telephone: (817) 945-8705.
Email address: info@railroaderbaseball.com. **Website:** www.railroaderbaseball.com.
General Manager: Bill Adams. **Assistant General Manager:** John Stark. **Ticket Office:** Patty Hicks. **Manager, Front Office:** Sara Williams. **Manager, Media Relations:** Michael Dixon. **Field Manager:** Gabe Suarez. **Pitching Coach:** Ed Pruitt. **Hitting Coach:** Ron Fenwick.

GAME INFORMATION
Broadcasters: Michael Dixon & Brad Allred. **No. of Games Broadcast:** 100. **Webcast Address:** www.railroaderbaseball.com.
Stadium Name: The Depot at Cleburne Station. **Capacity:** 3,020. **Directions:** From Chisholm Trail Parkway (Toll road) continue south across US HWY 67, turn left onto Hedrick Road. From US HWY 67 South, exit Nolan River Road, turn left onto Nolan River Road, turn left onto Hedrick Road. From US HWY 67 North, exit Nolan River Road, turn right onto Nolan River Road. Turn left onto Hedrick Road.
Standard Game Times: 7:06, Sunday 6:05.

FARGO-MOORHEAD REDHAWKS

Office Address: 1515 15th Ave N, Fargo, ND 58102.
Telephone: (701) 235-6161. **Fax:** (701) 297-9247.
Email Address: redhawks@fmredhawks.com. **Website:** www.fmredhawks.com.
Operated by: Fargo Baseball LLC.
Chairman of the Board: Bruce Thom. **President & CEO:** Brad Thom.
Director, Accounting: Matt Moen. **Assistant General Manager:** Karl Hoium. **Head Groundskeeper:** Tim Jallen.
Director, Ticket Operations: Isaac Olson. **Director, Communications:** Chad Ekren. **Coordinator, Group Sales:** Cole Milberger. **Director, Stadium Operations:** Michael Stark. **Manager:** Michael Schlact. **Coaches:** Chris Coste, Robbie Lopez. **Trainer:** Matt McManus. **Clubhouse Manager:** Chris "Bambino" Krick. **Player Personnel Consultant:** Jeff Bittiger.

GAME INFORMATION

Radio Announcers: Jack Michaels, Brad Anderson. **No. of Games Broadcast:** 100. **Flagship Station:** 740-AM The FAN.
Stadium Name: Newman Outdoor Field. **Location:** I-29 North to exit 67, east on 19th Ave North, right on Albrecht Boulevard. **Standard Game Times:** 7:02 pm, Sat 6, Sun 1.

GARY SOUTHSHORE RAILCATS

Office Address: One Stadium Plaza, Gary, IN 46402.
Telephone: (219) 882-2255. **Fax:** (219) 882-2259.
Email Address: info@railcatsbaseball.com. **Website:** www.railcatsbaseball.com.
Operated by: Salvi Sports Enterprises.
Owner/CEO: Pat Salvi. **Owner:** Lindy Salvi.
President, Salvi Sports Enterprises: Will Salvi. **General Manager:** Brian Lyter. **Assistant GM/Director, Tickets:** David Kay. **Director, Marketing/Promotions:** David Kerr. **Manager, Box Office/Account Executive:** Kevin Edgington. **Marketing Consultant:** Renee Connelly. **Head Groundskeeper/Operations:** Noah Simmons.
Manager: Greg Tagert. **Pitching Coach:** Alain Quijano. **Coaches:** Bobby Spain, J.T. Scara, Mike Habas.

GAME INFORMATION

Broadcaster: Jared Shlensky. **No. of Games Broadcast:** 100. **Flagship Station:** WEFM 95.9-FM.
Stadium Name: US Steel Yard. **Location:** Take I-65 North to end of highway at U.S. 12/20 [Dunes Highway]. Turn left on U.S. 12/20 heading west for 1.5 miles (three stoplights). Stadium is on left side. **Standard Game Times:** 7:10 p.m., Sat 6:10, Sun 2:10.

KANSAS CITY T-BONES

Office Address: 1800 Village West Parkway, Kansas City, KS 66111.
Telephone: (913) 328-5618. **Fax:** (913) 328-5674.
Email Address: tickets@tbonesbaseball.com.
Website: www.tbonesbaseball.com.
Operated By: T-Bones Baseball Club, LLC; Ehlert Development.
Owner: John Ehlert. **President:** Adam Ehlert.
VP/General Manager: Chris Browne. **VP, Corporate Sponsorships/Sales:** Scott Steckly. **Director, Group Sales:** Stephen Hardwick. **Director, Marketing/Promotions:** Morgan Kolenda. **Director, Ticket Sales/Merchandise:** Kacy Muller. **Account Executive/Group Sales:** Scott Hull. **Group Sales Associate:** Nick Restivo. **Sponsorship Sales Executive:** Bryan Porting. **Coordinator, Stadium Operations:** Kyle Disney. **Head Groundskeeper:** Nathan Miller. **Bookkeeper:** Karen Slaughter.
Manager: Joe Calfapietra. **Coaches:** Frank White, Bill Sobbe. **Clubhouse Manager:** John West.

GAME INFORMATION

Radio Announcer: Dan Vaughan. **No. of Games Broadcast:** 100. **Flagship Station:** KMBZ 1660-AM.
Stadium Name: CommunityAmerica Ballpark. **Location:** State Avenue West off I-435 and State Avenue. **Standard Game Times:** 7:05 p.m., 1:05 p.m. (Sun).

LINCOLN SALTDOGS

Office Address: 403 Line Drive Circle, Suite A, Lincoln, NE 68508.
Telephone: (402) 474-2255. **Fax:** (402) 474-2254.
Email Address: info@saltdogs.com. **Website:** www.saltdogs.com.
Chairman: Jim Abel. **President/GM:** Charlie Meyer.
Director, Marketing: Bret Beer. **Director, Broadcasting/Communications:** Drew Bontadelli. **Director, Stadium Operations:** Dave Aschwege. **Director, Sales:** Steve Zoucha. Director, **Merchandise & Promotions:** Shelby Meier. **Director, Video Production:** Cade McFadden. **Assistant Director, Stadium Operations:** Dan Busch. **Manager, Ticket Sales:** Colter Clarke, Taylor Wyatt. **Turf Manager:** Jeremy Johnson. **Assistant Turf Manager:** Jen Roeber. **Office Manager:** Kaydra Brodine.
Manager: Bobby Brown. **Coaches:** Tom Carcione, Jim Haller. **Trainers:** Corey Courtney, Ryan Pederson, Matt Honerman.

GAME INFORMATION

Radio Announcer: TBA. **No. of Games Broadcast:** 100. **Flagship Station:** KLMS 1480AM & ESPN101.5FM. **Webcast Address:** www.americanassociationbaseball.com.
Stadium Name: Haymarket Park. **Location:** I-80 to Cornhusker Highway West, left on First Street, right on Sun Valley Boulevard, left on Line Drive.
Standard Game Times: 6:35 p.m., Sunday 5:05.

ST. PAUL SAINTS

Office Address: 360 Broadway Street, St. Paul, MN 55101.
Telephone: (651) 644-3517. **Fax:** (651) 644-1627.
Email Address: funisgood@saintsbaseball.com.
Website: www.saintsbaseball.com.
Principal Owners: Marv Goldklang, Bill Murray, Mike Veeck. **Chairman:** Marv Goldklang. **President:** Jeff Goldklang.
Executive VP/General Manager: Derek Sharrer. **Executive VP:** Tom Whaley. **Senior VP/Assistant GM:** Chris Schwab. Business Manager; Krista Schnelle. **Vice President/Director, Broadcast/Media Relations:** Sean Aronson. **Director, Promotions/Marketing:** Sierra Bailey. **Director, Corporate Sales:** Tyson Jeffers. **Senior Account Executive:** Mark Jeffrey. **Corporate Sales Manager:** Zane Heinselman. **Ticket Office Manager:** Darion Fletcher. **Director, Operations:** Curtis Nachtsheim. **Manager, Marketing Services:** Kelly Hagenson. **Director, Digital Media and Video Production:** Jordan Lynn. **Office Manager:** Gina Kray. **Events Manager:** Anna Gutknecht. **Director, Food/Beverage:** Justin Grandstaff. **Head Groundskeeper:** Nick Baker. **Director, Community Partnerships/Fan Services:** Eddie Coblentz.
Manager: George Tsamis. **Coaches:** Kerry Ligtenberg, Ole Sheldon. **Trainer:** Jason Ellenbecker. **Clubhouse Manager:** Danny Wilson.

GAME INFORMATION

Radio Announcer: Sean Aronson. **No. of Games Broadcast:** 100. **Flagship Station:** Club 1220 AM. **Webcast Address:** www.saintsbaseball.com.
Stadium Name: CHS Field. **Location:** From the west take I-94 to the 7th St. Exit and head south to 5th & Broadway. From the east take I-94 to the Mounds Blvd/US-61N exit. Turn left on Kellogg and a right on Broadway until you reach 5th St.
Standard Game Times: 7:05 pm, Sun 5:05.

SIOUX CITY EXPLORERS

Office Address: 3400 Line Drive, Sioux City, IA 51106.
Telephone: (712) 277-9467. **Fax:** (712) 277-9406.
Email Address: promotions@xsbaseball.com. **Website:** www.xsbaseball.com.
President: Matt Adamski.
VP/General Manager: Shane M Tritz. **Director, Marketing:** Tyler Hinker. **Director, Ticketing:** Connor Ryan. **Groundskeeper/Director, Stadium Operations:** Brent Recker. **Manager, Promotions/Community Relations:** Julie Targy.
Field Manager: Steve Montgomery. **Coaches:** Bobby Post, Matt Passerelle.

GAME INFORMATION

Radio Announcer: TBA. **No. of Games Broadcast:** 100. **Flagship Station:** KSCJ 1360-AM. **Webcast Address:** www.xsbaseball.com.
Stadium Name: Mercy Field at Lewis and Clark Park. **Location:** I-29 to Singing Hills Blvd, North, right on Line Drive.
Standard Game Times: 7:05 p.m., **Sun 6:**05.

SIOUX FALLS CANARIES

Office Address: 1001 N West Ave, Sioux Falls, SD 57104.
Telephone: (605) 336-6060. **Fax:** (605) 333-0139.
Email Address: info@sfcanaries.com. **Website:** www.sfcanaries.com.
Operated by: Canaries Baseball, LLC.
CEO/Managing Partner: Tom Garrity.
General Manager: Duell Higbe. **Director, Sales:** Brian Olthoff.
Manager: Mike Meyer. **Coach:** Ben Moore, Eddie Gerald, Landon Danelson.

GAME INFORMATION

Radio Announcer: JJ Hartigan. **No. of Games Broadcast:** 100. **Flagship Station:** KWSN 1230-AM. **Webcast Address:** www.kwsn.com.

Stadium Name: Sioux Falls Stadium. **Location:** I-29 to Russell Street, east one mile, south on West Avenue.
Standard Game Times: 7:05 p.m., Sat 6:05, Sun 1:05.

TEXAS AIRHOGS

Office Address: 1600 Lone Star Parkway, Grand Prairie, TX 75050.
Telephone: (972) 504-9383. **Fax:** (972) 504-2288.
Website: www.airhogsbaseball.com. **Email:** info@airhogsbaseball.com.
VP/General Manager: J.T. Onyett. **Directors, Business Development:** George Howington, Nate Gutierrez. **Coordinator, Digital Marketing:** Molly Onyett.
Manager: Billy Martin Jr. **Coach:** Troy Conkle. **Trainer:** Ainsley Capra. **Clubhouse Manager:** John Witt.

GAME INFORMATION

Broadcaster: Joey Zanaboni. **No of Games Broadcast:** 100. **Webcast:** www.airhogsbaseball.com.

Stadium Name: AirHogs Stadium. **Location:** From I-30, take Beltline Road exit going north, take Lone Star Park entrance towards the stadium.

Standard Game Times - 7:05 p.m., Sun (May-June) 2:05, (July-September) 6:05.

WICHITA WINGNUTS

Office Address: 300 South Sycamore, Wichita, KS 67213.
Telephone: (316) 264-6887. **Fax:** (316) 264-2129.
Website: www.wichitawingnuts.com.
Owners: Steve Ruud, Gary Austerman, Nate Robertson.
General Manager: Brian Turner. **Assistant General Manager/Director, Finance:** Aaron McMullin. **Director, Stadium Operations:** Kyle Baldwin. **Manager, Marketing & Community Relations:** Megan Looper. **Corporate Sales Executive:** Tim Slack. **Manager, Group & Season Tickets:** Tyler Harrison. **Manager, Game Day Staff & Merchandise:** Ashley Binder. **Director, Food & Beverage:** Greg Read.
Manager: Brent Clevlen. **Coaches:** Anthony Capra, Jim Foltz.

GAME INFORMATION

Broadcaster: Denning Gerig. **No. of Games Broadcast:** 100. **Flagship Station:** KGSO 1410-AM.
Webcast Address: www.wichitawingnuts.com.
Stadium Name: Lawrence-Dumont Stadium. **Location:** 135 North to Kellogg (54) West, Take Seneca Street exit North to Maple, Go East on Maple to Sycamore, Stadium is located on corner of Maple and Sycamore.
Standard Game Times: 7:05 p.m., Sun 1:05.

WINNIPEG GOLDEYES

Office Address: One Portage Ave E, Winnipeg, Manitoba R3B 3N3.
Telephone: (204) 982-2273. **Fax:** (204) 982-2274.
Email Address: goldeyes@goldeyes.com. **Website:** www.goldeyes.com.
Operated by: Winnipeg Goldeyes Baseball Club, Inc.
Principal Owner/President: Sam Katz.
General Manager: Andrew Collier. **Vice President & COO:** Regan Katz. **CFO:** Jason McRae-King. **Director, Sales/Marketing:** Dan Chase. **Manager, Box Office:** Kevin Arnst. **Coordinator, Food/Beverage:** Melissa Schlichting.
Account Executive: Steve Schuster. **Suite Manager/Sales & Marketing:** Angela Sanche. **Manager, Promotions:** Tara Maslowsky. **Manager, Retail:** Kendra Gibson. **Controller:** Judy Jones. **Facility Manager:** Don Ferguson. **Executive Assistant:** Sherri Rheubottom. **Administrative Assistant:** Bonnie Benson.
Manager/Director, Player Procurement: Rick Forney. **Coach:** Tom Vaeth. **Trainer:** Derek McClennan.

Clubhouse Manager: Jamie Samson.

GAME INFORMATION

Radio Announcer: Steve Schuster. **No. of Games Broadcast:** 100. **Flagship Station:** CJNU 93.7 FM.

Stadium Name: Shaw Park. **Location:** North on Pembina Highway to Broadway, East on Broadway to Main Street, North on Main Street to Water Avenue, East on Water Avenue to Westbrook Street, North on Westbrook Street to Lombard Avenue, East on Lombard Avenue to Mill Street, South on Mill Street to ballpark.

Standard Game Times: 7:00 p.m., Sat 6:00, Sun 1:00.

ATLANTIC LEAGUE

Mailing Address: PO Box 5190, Lancaster, Pa., 17606.
Telephone: (720) 389-6992 or (978) 790-5421
Email Address: info@atlanticleague.com. **Website:** www.atlanticleague.com.
Year Founded: 1998.
Founder/Chairman: Frank Boulton.
Senior Vice Presidents/Executive Committee: Frank Boulton, Bill Shipley, Bob Zlotnik.
President: Rick White. **League Administrator:** Emily Merrill.
Division Structure:
Freedom Division—Lancaster, Southern Maryland, Sugar Land, York. **Liberty Division**—Long Island, New Britain, Road Warriors, Somerset. **Regular Season:** 126 games (split-schedule).
2018 Opening Date: April 26. **Closing Date:** Sept 16. **All-Star Game:** July 11, at Long Island.
Playoff Format: First-half division winners meet second-half winners in best-of-five series; Winners meet in best-of-five final for league championship.
Roster Limit: 25. Teams may keep 27 players from start of season until May 31. **Eligibility Rule:** No restrictions; MLB and MiLB suspensions honored.
Brand of Baseball: Rawlings. **Statistical Service:** Pointstreak.

STADIUM INFORMATION

Club	Stadium	Opened	Dimensions LF	CF	RF	Capacity	2017 Att.
Lancaster	Clipper Magazine Stadium	2005	372	400	300	6,000	255,251
Long Island	Bethpage Ballpark	2000	325	400	325	6,002	341,830
New Britain	New Britain Stadium	1996	330	400	330	6,146	194,744
Somerset	TD Bank Ballpark	1999	317	402	315	6,100	342,231
So. Maryland	Regency Furniture Stadium	2008	305	400	320	6,000	210,007
Sugar Land	Constellation Field	2012	348	405	325	7,500	317,721
York	PeoplesBank Park	2007	300	400	325	5,000	212,624

LANCASTER BARNSTORMERS

Mailing Address: 650 North Prince Street Lancaster, PA 17603
Telephone: (717) 509-4487. **Fax:** (717) 509-4486
Email Address: info@lancasterbarnstormres.com.
Website: www.lancasterbarnstormers.com.
General Manager: Michael Reynolds. **VP, Marketing:** Kristen Simon. **Accounting Manager:** Leanne Beaghan. **Senior Business Development Representative:** John Erisman. **Senior Business Development Representative:** Dawn Rissmiller. **Senior Business Development Representative:** Melissa Tucker. Director, **Skyboxes & Ticket Services:** Maureen Wheeler. **Director, Media Relations/Broadcasting:** Dave Collins. **Director, Stadium Operations:** Andrew Wurst. **Director, Ticket Sales & Service:** Michael Kalchick. **Human Resource Generalist:** Tania Atkinson. **On Field Host/Business Development Specialist:** Alex Einhorn. **Business Development Specialist:** Adam Smith. **Promotions & Sponsorship Fulfillment Coordinator:** Alexandra Bunn. **Business Development Specialist:** Andrew Spanos. **Stadium Operations Coordinator:** Chris Hauck. **Box Office Coordinator/Client Services Representative:** Doug Condran. **Business Development Specialist:** Holly Shelton. **Business Development Specialist:** Kyle Witman. **Mascot & Seasonal Staff Coordinator:** Lori Krchnar. **Business Development Specialist:** Michael Wiese. **Cleaning Services Supervisor:** Miggy Rosado. **Business Development Specialist & Game Presentation Coordinator:** Rachel Deyle. **Creative Services Coordinator:** Ryan Cortazzo. **Business Development Specialist:** Samantha Biastre.

Manager: Ross Peeples. **Hitting Coach:** Josh Bell. **OAL Team Doctor:** Joel A. Horning. **MD Head Trainer:** Jarred Binner, MS, LAT, ATC, PES, CES; **Medical Consultant:** Patrick J. Moreno, MD.

   Radio Announcer: Dave Collins. **No. of Games Broadcast:** 140 on www.lancasterbarnstormers.com. **PA Announcer: John Witwer Official Scorer:** Joel Schreiner, Bill Hoffman.

LONG ISLAND DUCKS

   Mailing Address: 3 Court House Dr, Central Islip, NY 11722.
   Telephone: (631) 940-3825. **Fax:** (631) 940-3800.
   Email Address: info@liducks.com. **Website:** www.liducks.com.
   Operated by: Long Island Ducks Professional Baseball, LLC.
   Founder/CEO: Frank Boulton. **Owner/Chairman:** Seth Waugh. **Owner/Senior Vice President, Baseball Operations:** Bud Harrelson.
   President/General Manager: Michael Pfaff. **Assistant GM/Senior VP, Sales:** Doug Cohen. **Senior Director, Administration:** Gerry Anderson. **VP, Sales/Operations:** John Wolff. **Director, Season Sales:** Brad Kallman. **Manager, Box Office:** Ben Harper. **Director, Media Relations/Broadcasting:** Michael Polak. **Director, Marketing/Promotions:** Jordan Schiff. **Staff Accountant:** Annmarie DeMasi. **Head Groundskeeper:** Brett Franklin. **Manager, Group Sales:** Anthony Rubino. **Senior Account Executive:** Sean Smith. **Manager, Merchandise/Client Services:** Will Sorrentino. **Manager, Stadium Operations:** Ryan Mariotti. **Coordinator, Administration:** Michelle Jensen. **Account Executive:** Daniel Bornschein.
   Manager: Kevin Baez. **Coaches:** Bud Harrelson. **Coordinator, Medical Services:** Tony Amin. **Head Trainer:** Dotty Pitchford.

GAME INFORMATION
   Radio Announcers: Michael Polak, Chris King, David Weiss. **No. of Games Broadcast:** 126 on www.liducks.com. **PA Announcer:** Bob Ottone. **Official Scorer:** Michael Polak.

NEW BRITAIN BEES

   Office Address: 230 John Karbonic Way, New Britain, CT 06051
   Telephone: (860) 826-2337.
   Email Address: info@nbbees.com. **Website:** www.nbbees.com.
   Operated by: Hard Hittin' Professional Baseball, LLC.
   Principal Owner: Anthony Iacovone. **Partner:** Frank Boulton. **Partner:** Michael Pfaff.
   General Manager: Brad Smith. **Assistant General Manager:** Paul Herrmann. **Director, Corporate Sales/General League Counsel:** Jamie Goldman. **Business Manager:** Allison Farrell. **Manager, Group Sales:** J.P. Mccooe. **Account Executive:** Andrea Tolisano. **Account Executive:** Jon Galgano.
   Manager: Wally Backman.

GAME INFORMATION
   Stadium Name: New Britain Stadium. **Location:** 230 John Karbonic Way, New Britain, CT 06051.
   Directions: From Route 9, take the ramp left towards New Britain, Merge onto CT-571 via exit 24 on left toward CT-71/CT-371/ Kensington. Take the CT-71 ramp toward Kensington, and then make slight left onto John Karbonic Way.
   Standard Game Times: 6:35. Sunday: 1:35.

ROAD WARRIORS

   Mailing Address: PO Box 5190, Lancaster, Pa., 17606
   Telephone: (720) 389-6992 or (978) 790-5421

   Operated by: Travel team operated by the Atlantic League.

SOMERSET PATRIOTS

   Office Address: One Patriots Park, Bridgewater, NJ 08807.
   Telephone: (908) 252-0700. **Fax:** (908) 252-0776.
   Website: www.somersetpatriots.com.
   Operated by: Somerset Baseball Partners, LLC.
   Principal Owners: Steve Kalafer, Josh Kalafer, Jonathan Kalafer.
   Chairman: Steve Kalafer.
   President/General Manager: Patrick McVerry. **Senior Vice President, Marketing:** Dave Marek. **VP, Public Relations:** Marc Russinoff.
   VP, Operations: Bryan Iwicki. **VP, Ticket Operations:** Matt Kopas. **Senior Director, Merchandise:** Rob Crossman.

Director, Operations: Tom McCartney.

Director, Group Sales: Deanna Liotard. **Director, Marketing:** Hal Hansen. **Media Relations Manager:** Marc Schwartz.

Ticket Office Manager: Nick Cherrillo. **Corporate Sales Manager:** Ken Smith.

Group Sales Managers: Zach Keller, Chris Dillon, Ian Gatehouse. **Executive Assistant to GM:** Michele DaCosta. **Senior VP/Treasurer:** Ron Schulz. **Accountant:** Stephanie DePass. **Receptionist:** Lorraine Ott.

GM, HomePlate Catering/Hospitality: Mike McDermott. **Operations Manager, HomePlate Catering/Hospitality:** Jimmy Search. **Head Groundskeeper:** Dan Purner.

Manager: Brett Jodie. **Hitting/Third Base Coach:** Glen Barker. **Pitching Coach/ Director, Baseball Operations:** Jon Hunton.

Trainer: Phil Lee. **Manager Emeritus:** Sparky Lyle.

GAME INFORMATION

Radio Announcer: Marc Schwartz. **No. of Games Broadcast:** Home-72, Away-54.

Flagship Station: WCTC 1450-AM. **Live Video Streams:** Home-20 (SPN.tv).

PA Announcer: Paul Spychala. **Official Scorer:** John Nolan.

Ballpark Name: TD Bank Ballpark. **GPS Location:** 860 East Main Street Bridgewater, NJ. **Standard Game Times:** 7:05. Sun: 1:05./5:05.

Visiting Club Hotel: Clarion Hotel.

SOUTHERN MARYLAND
BLUE CRABS

Office Address: 11765 St. Linus Drive
Telephone: 301-638-9788
Principal Owners: Crabs On Deck LLC.
General Manager: Courtney Knichel. **Marketing Manager:** Kristine Perry.
Director, Sales: Wade Johnson. **Creative Services Coordinator:** Hayley Bingham. **Director of Business Operations:** Theresa Coffey. **Account Executive:** Devin Monahan. **Director, Facility Operations:** Jason Sproesser.
Facility Operations Coordinator: Nick Woolford. **Corporate Sales Manager:** Tim Lillis.
Manager: James Frisbie. **Hitting Coach:** Kash Beauchamp

GAME INFORMATION

Radio Announcer: Brandon Bulanda. **No of Games broadcast:** Unavailable. **Radio Station:** Unavailable. **Stadium Name:** Blue Crabs Stadium.

Standard Game Times: 6:35. Sunday: 2:05.

SUGAR LAND SKEETERS

Office Address: 1 Stadium Drive, Sugar Land, Texas, 77498.
Telephone: (281) 240-4487.
Owners: Marcie & Bob Zlotnik. **Special Advisor:** Deacon Jones.
President: Jay Miller. **Assistant General Manager, Community:** Kyle Dawson.
Assistant General Manager: Tyler Stamm. **Executive Administrator:** Kailee Kubicek. **Director, Finances:** Greg Hodges. **Director, Ticket Sales:** Jennifer Schwarz. **Box Office Manager:** Wesley Barnes. **Operations Director:** Donnie Moore. **Operations Manager:** Clayton Lemke. **Head Groundskeeper:** Brad Detmore. **Assistant Groundskeeper:** Robert Croteau. **Senior Director, Broadcasting/Sales:** Ira Liebman. **Special Events Director:** Matt Thompson.
Special Events Manager: Eddy Juarez. **Senior Director Sales:** Scott Podsim.
Senior Sales Managers: Sunny Okpon. **Sales Managers:** Robbie Weinhardt, Ashley Richter, Dolores Townley. **Customer Service Manager:** Adam Mettler. **Group Services Manager:** Chris Parsons. **Marketing/Digital Media Coordinator:** Megan Murnane. **Community Relations Manager:** Sallie Weir. **Video Production Coordinator:** Troy Young. **Graphics Coordinator:** Shay Villarreal. **Mascot Coordinator:** Megan Brown. **Director of Merchandise:** Candace Nix. **Skeeters Stop Attendant:** Kaitlin Klinchock. **Legends General Manager:** Greg Hernandez. **Legends Events Manager:** Jay Lero. **Legends Accountant:** Andrea Jennings. **Legends Operations Manager:** Ginavieve Strickland. **Legends Staffing Coordinator:** Tiffany Freeman. **Executive Chef:** Eric Robison.
Manager: Pete Incaviglia. **Pitching Coach:** Raffy Montalvo. **Team Doctor:** Dr. Bhojani. **Team Trainer:** Max Mahaffey.

GAME INFORMATION

Radio Announcer: Ira Liebman. **No. of Games Broadcast:** 138. **Flagship Radio Station:** 1560 AM. **Standard Game Times:** 7:05. Sat: 6:05. Sun: 2:05./6:05.

Directions to Ballpark: Southbound HWY 59-Take the exit toward Corporate Dr/US-90/Stafford/Sugar Land. Turn right onto HWY 6. Travel northbound to Imperial Blvd. Turn right onto Imperial Blvd from HWY 6.

Visiting Club Hotel: Sugar Land Marriott Town Square. **Telephone:** (281) 275-8400.

YORK REVOLUTION

Office Address: 5 Brooks Robinson Way, York, PA 17401.
Telephone: (717) 801-4487. **Fax:** (717) 801-4499.
Email Address: info@yorkrevolution.com. **Website:** www.yorkrevolution.
com.
   Operated by: York Professional Baseball Club, LLC. **Principal Owners:** York Professional Baseball Club, LLC.
   President: Eric Menzer. **General Manager/Vice President, Operations:** John Gibson. **VP, Business Development:** Nate Tile. **Finance Coordinator:** Jen Martin. **Director, Ticketing:** Cindy Brown. **Box Office Manager:** Bob Gibson. **Director, Marketing/Communications:** Doug Eppler. **Creative Director:** Cody Bannon. **Director, Group Sales/ Hospitality:** Reed Gunderson. **Senior Account Executives:** Mary Beth Ching, Brandon Tesluk. **Account Executives:** Brett Pietrzak, Matt Hawn, Karly Spangle, Taylor Cubbler. **Season Ticket Account Executives:** Jordan Haidle, Zac Getz. **Coordinator, Hospitality & Group Sales:** Emily Udit. **Coordinator, Client Services:** Alison Beddia. **Director, Special Events:** Adam Nugent. **Stadium Operations Manager:** David Dicce. **Legends Hospitality GM, Concessions/ Merchandise/Catering:** Brett Herman. **Legends Hospitality Catering Manager:** Lou Rivera. **Legends Hospitality Chef:** Tiffany Livering. **Legends Hospitality Concessions Manager:** Amanda Shusko.
   Manager: Mark Mason. **Pitching Coach:** Paul Fletcher. **Bench/Third-Base Coach:** Enohel Polanco.

GAME INFORMATION
   Radio Announcer: Darrell Henry. **No. of Games Broadcast:** 128. **Flagship Station:** WOYK 1350 AM. **Official Scorer:** Brian Wisler.
   Stadium Name: PeoplesBank Park. **Location:** Take Route 30 West to North George Street. **Directions:** Turn left onto North George Street; follow that straight for four lights, PeoplesBank Park is on left. **Standard Game Times:** 6:30. **Sun:** 1. **Visiting Club Hotel:** Wyndham Garden York, 2000 Loucks Road, York, PA 17408. **Telephone:** (717) 846-9500.

CAN-AM LEAGUE

Office Address: 1415 Hwy 54 West, Suite 210, Durham, NC 27707.
Telephone: (919) 401-8150. **Fax:** (919) 401-8152. **Website:** www.canamleague.com.
Year Founded: 2005.
Commissioner: Miles Wolff. **Director, Umpires:** Kevin Winn.
Regular Season: 100 games. **2018 Opening Date:** May 17. **Closing Date:** Sept. 3. **Playoff Format:** Top four teams meet in best-of-five semifinals; winners meet in best-of-five finals. **Roster Limit:** 22. **Eligibility Rule:** Minimum of five and maximum of eight first-year players; minimum of five players must be an LS-4 or higher; a maximum of four may be veterans. **Brand of Baseball:** Rawlings. **Statistician:** Pointstreak.com.

STADIUM INFORMATION

Club	Stadium	Opened	Dimensions LF	CF	RF	Capacity	2017 Att.
New Jersey	Yogi Berra Stadium	1998	308	398	308	3,784	91,892
Ottawa	RCGT Park	1993	325	404	325	10,332	92,654
Quebec	Stade Canac de Québec	1938	315	385	315	4,500	141,923
Rockland	Provident Bank Park	2011	323	403	313	4,750	145,005
Sussex County	Skylands Stadium	1994	330	392	330	4,200	80,442
Trois-Rivieres	Stade Stereo+	1938	342	372	342	4,500	79,228

NEW JERSEY JACKALS

Office Address: 8 Yogi Berra Drive, Little Falls, NJ 07424. **Telephone:** (973) 746-7434.
Email Address: contact@jackals.com. **Website:** www.jackals.com.
Owner/President: Al Dorso. **President, Baseball Operations:** Gregory Lockard.
Sr. Vice President, Operations: Al Dorso Jr. **Vice President, Marketing:** Mike Dorso.
General Manager: Joe Redmon. **Coordinators, Group Sales:** A.J. Gammaro, Kristopher Jones. **Director, Creative Services:** Dennis Mark. **Public Relations:** Steven Solomon. **Manager, Facilities:** Mark Murphy.
Manager: Brooks Carey.

GAME INFORMATION

Webcast Announcer: Alex Cammarata. **No. of Games Broadcast:** 100. **Webcast Address:** www.jackals.com.
Stadium Name: Yogi Berra Stadium.
Location: On the campus of Montclair State University; Route 80 or Garden State Parkway to Route 46, take Valley Road exit to Montclair State University.
Standard Game Times: 7:05 p.m., Sat: 6:05., Sun: 2:05.

OTTAWA CHAMPIONS

Office Address: 300 Coventry Road, Ottawa, ON K1K 4P5. **Telephone:** (613) 745-2255. **Fax:** (613) 745-3289. **Email Address:** info@ottawachampions.com. **Website:** www.ottawachampions.com.
Owner: Miles Wolff. **President:** David Gourlay.
Assistant General Manager: Davyd Balloch. **Director, Business Operations and Ticketing:** Ian Hooper. **Director of Communications:** Michael Nellis. **Graphic Design:** Sofia Polimenakos. **Chief Financial Officer:** Scott Gibeault. **Director of Game Ops/Promotions:** Spencer Rodd. **Baseball Operations:** Chuck Dufton.
Manager: Hal Lanier. **Coaches:** Sebastien Boucher, Jared Lemieux.

GAME INFORMATION

Broadcaster—English: Mike Nellis. **Broadcaster—French:** Dominic Murray. **Webcast—English/French. Webcast Address:** www.ottawachampions.com.
Stadium Name: Raymond Chabot Grant Thornton Park. **Location:** From Hwy #417 (Queensway), take Vanier Parkway (Exit #117). Turn right on to Coventry Road. Raymond Chabot Grant Thornton Park is at your immediate right.
Standard Game Times: Mon-Sat: 7:05 p.m., Sun: 1:35.

QUEBEC CAPITALES

Office Address: 100 Rue du Cardinal Maurice-Roy, Quebec City, QC G1K 8Z1.
Telephone: (418) 521-2255. **Fax:** (418) 521-2266. **Email Address:** info@capitalesde quebec.com. **Website:** www.capitalesdequebec.com.
Owners: Jean Tremblay, Pierre Tremblay and Marie-Pierre Simard. **President:** Michel Laplante. **General Manager:** Bobby Baril. **Accountant:** Julie Lefrançois. **Director, Communications:** Maxime Aubry.
Box Office Supervisor/Merchandise Director: Jean-Philippe Otis. **Coordinator, Marketing:** Annie-Pier Couture.

Coordinator, Promotions and Community Relations: Janel Laplante. Coordinator, Baseball Operations: Charles Demers.

Manager: Patrick Scalabrini. Coaches: Karl Gélinas, Jean-Philippe Roy. Trainer: Jean-François Brochu.

GAME INFORMATION

Broadcaster: François Paquet. Stadium Name: Stade Canac de Québec. Location: Highway 40 to Highway 173 (Centre-Ville) exit 2 to Parc Victoria. Standard Game Times: 7:05 p.m., Sat: 6:05., Sun: 1:05.

ROCKLAND BOULDERS

Office Address: 1 Palisades Credit Union Park Drive, Pomona, NY 10970. Telephone: (845) 364-0009. Fax: (845) 364-0001. E-Mail Address: info@rockland-boulders.com. Website: www.rocklandboulders.com.

President: Ken Lehner. Executive Vice President/General Manager: Shawn Reilly. VP, Business Development: Seth Cantor. Director of Finance: Michele Almash. Manager, Box Office: Megan Ciampo. Manager, Retail Store: Deidra Verona. Manager, Ticket Sales: Karen McCombs. Assistant Manager, Ticket Sales: Courtney Vardi. Account Executive: Staush Zamoyta. Consultant, Public Relations and Media: Steve Balsan. Manager, Concessions: George McElroy. Director, Security: Jeff Rinaldi. Audio/Visual Specialist: Jim Houston.

Manager: Jamie Keefe. Coach: Richard Salazar. Trainer: Lori Rahaim.

GAME INFORMATION

Broadcaster: Seth Cantor. No. of Games Broadcast: 70. Flagship Station: WRCR 1700-AM. TV – Verizon FIOS1, Optimum (select games). Webcast Address: www.rocklandboulders.com. Stadium Name: Palisades Credit Union Park. Location: Take Palisades Parkway Exit 12 towards Route 45, make left at stop sign on Conklin Road, make left on Route 45, turn right on Pomona Road, take 1st right on Fireman's Memorial Drive. Standard Game Times: Monday-Saturday: 6:30. Sunday (May 20-July 1) 1:35, (July 22-August 26) 5:00.

SUSSEX COUNTY MINERS

Office Address: 94 Championship Place, Suite 11, Augusta, NJ 07822. Telephone: (973) 383-7644. Fax : (973) 383-7522. Email Address : contact@scminers.com. Website: www.scminers.com

Owner, President: Al Dorso, Sr. Vice President, Operations: Al Dorso, Jr. Vice President, Marketing: Mike Dorso. General Manager: Justin Ferrarella. Director, Creative Services: Dennis Mark. Manager, Corporate Partnerships: Joann Ciancitto. Account Executive, Corporate Sales: Scott Goriscak. Coordinators, Group Sales: Marina Agacinski, Adrienne Lina. Graphic Designers: Will Romano, Georgina Fakhoury.

Manager: Bobby Jones. Coach: Simon Walters.

GAME INFORMATION

Broadcaster: Bret Leuthner. No. of Games Broadcast: 100. Webcast Address: www.scminers.com. Stadium Name: Skylands Stadium. Location: In New Jersey, I-80 to exit 34B (Route 15 North) to Route 565 North; From Pennsylvania, I-84 to Route 6 (Matamoras) to Route 206 North to Route 565 North. Standard Game Times: Monday-Friday: 7:05., Saturday: 6:05., Sunday: 2:05 (May, June, Sept.), 4:05 (July-August).

TROIS-RIVIÈRES AIGLES

Office Address: 1760 Avenue Gilles-Villeneuve, Trois-Rivières, QC G9A 5K8. Telephone: (819) 379-0404. Email Address: info@lesaiglestr.com. Website:www.lesaiglestr.com

President: Marc-André Bergeron. General Manager: René Martin. Director, Communications/Marketing: Simon Laliberté. Director, Sales/Operations: Guillaume Boyer. Coordinator, Group Sales: Virginie Lamothe. Coordinator, Box Office: Frédérik Bélanger. Accounting: Geneviève Lavigueur.

Manager: T.J. Stanton. Coaches: Matthew Rusch, Chris Torres.

GAME INFORMATION

Broadcaster: Simon Laliberté. No. of Games Broadcast: 65.

Webcast Address: www.cfou.ca/direct.php

Stadium Name: Stade Stereo+. Location: Take Hwy 40 West, exit Boul. des Forges/Centre-ville, keep right, turn right at light, turn right at stop sign.

Standard Game Times: Mon-Sat: 7:05., Sun: 1:05.

FRONTIER LEAGUE

Office Address: 2041 Goose Lake Rd Suite 2A, Sauget, IL 62206.
Telephone: (618) 215-4134. **Fax:** (618) 332-2115.
Email Address: office@frontierleague.com. **Website:** www.frontierleague.com.
Year Founded: 1993.
Commissioner: Bill Lee.
Deputy Commissioner: Steve Tahsler.
President: Rich Sauget (Gateway). **Vice President, Operations:** Pat Salvi (Schaumburg). **Vice President, Marketing:** Tom Kramig.
Board of Directors: John Stanley (Evansville), Clint Brown (Florence), Nick Semaca (Joliet), Steve Malliet (Normal/River City), Mike Pinto (Southern Illinois), Leslye Wuerfel (Traverse City), Steve Zavacky (Washington), Al Oremus (Windy City).
Division Structure: East—Joliet, Lake Erie, Schaumburg, Traverse City, Washington, Windy City. **West**—Evansville, Florence, Gateway, Normal, River City, Southern Illinois.
Regular Season: 96 games. **2018 Opening Date:** May 10. **Closing Date:** Sept 2.
All-Star Game: Wednesday, July 11 at River City.
Playoff Format: Two division winners and next two best records; two best-of-five rounds.
Roster Limit: 24. **Eligibility Rule:** Minimum of twelve Rookie 1/Rookie 2 players. No player may be 27 prior to Jan. 1 of current season.
Brand of Baseball: Rawlings.
Statistician: Pointstreak, 602-1595 16th Avenue, Richmond Hill, ONT L4B 3N9.

STADIUM INFORMATION

Club	Stadium	Opened	Dimensions LF	CF	RF	Capacity	2017 Att.
Evansville	Bosse Field	1915	315	415	315	5,110	100,337
Florence	UC Health Stadium	2004	325	395	325	4,200	87,545
Gateway	GCS Ballpark	2002	318	395	325	5,500	148,176
Joliet	Slammers Stadium	2002	330	400	327	6,229	100,160
Lake Erie	Sprenger Stadium	2009	325	400	325	5,000	94,035
Normal	The Corn Crib	2010	356	400	344	7,000	75,804
River City	CarShield Field	1999	320	382	299	4,989	94,958
Schaumburg	Schaumburg Stadium	1999	355	400	353	8,107	160,644
So. Illinois	Rent One Park	2007	325	400	330	4,500	151,521
Traverse City	Wuerfel Park	2006	320	400	320	4,600	119,544
Washington	Wild Things Park	2002	325	400	325	3,200	77,233
Windy City	Standard Bank Stadium	1999	335	390	335	2,598	78,585

EVANSVILLE OTTERS

Mailing Address: 23 Don Mattingly Way, Evansville, IN 47711.
Telephone: (812) 435-8686.
Operated by: Evansville Baseball, LLC.
Owner: Bussing family. **President:** John Stanley. **Vice President, Sales:** Joel Padfield.
Assistant General Manager: Josh Hack Wilson. **Director of Operations:** Jeff Roos.
Director of Marketing/Community Relations: Elspeth Urbina. **Media Relations Manager:** Zane Clodfelter. **Director of Communications:** Preston Leinenbach. **Assistant Director of Operations/Finance Manager:** John Rumble. **Gift Shop Manager:** Rhonda Trail. **Account Executive:** Keith Millikan. **Controller:** Casie Williams. **Sports Turf Manager:** Lance Adler.
Manager: Andy McCauley.

GAME INFORMATION

No. of Games Broadcast: Home-48, Away-48. **Flagship Station:** WUEV 91.5-FM. **PA Announcer:** Zane Clodfelter.
Stadium Name: Bosse Field. **Location:** US 41 to Lloyd Expressway West (IN-62), Main St Exit, Right on Main St, ahead 1 mile to Bosse Field. **Standard Game Times:** 6:35 p.m., Sun: 5:05., Doubleheaders: 5:35 p.m.
Visiting Club Hotel: Comfort Inn & Suites, 3901 Hwy 41 N, Evansville, IN 47711..

FLORENCE FREEDOM

Office Address: 7950 Freedom Way, Florence, KY, 41042.
Telephone: (859) 594-4487. **Fax:** (859) 594-3194.
Email Address: info@florencefreedom.com.
Operated by: Canterbury Baseball, LLC.

VP/General Manager: Josh Anderson. Assistant GM, Operations: Kim Brown. Director, Ticket Sales: Zach Ziler. Groups Sales Manager: Amanda Sipple, Business Manager: Shelli Bitter. Director, Amateur Baseball: Matt Blankenship. Box Office Manager: Max Johnson. Director, Marketing & Promotions: Knicko Hartung. Manager: Dennis Pelfrey. Pitching Coach: Brian White. Hitting Coach: Zac Mitchell.

GAME INFORMATION
Official Scorer: Joe Gall.
Stadium: UC Health Stadium. Location: I71/75 South to exit 180, left onto US 42, right on Freedom Way; I-71/75 North to exit 180. Standard Game Times: 6:35 p.m., Fri: 7:05, Sat-Sun: 6:05.
Visiting Club Hotel: Microtel Inn & Suites, Florence, KY

GATEWAY GRIZZLIES

Telephone: (618) 337-3000. Fax: (618) 332-3625.
Email Address: info@gatewaygrizzlies.com. Website: www.gatewaygrizzlies.com
Operated by: Gateway Baseball, LLC. Managing Officer: Richard Sauget.
General Manager: Steven Gomric. Assistant General Manager: Alex Wilson. Director of Stadium Operations and Events: Kurt Ringkamp. Director of Corporate Partnerships: James Caldwell. Radio & Media Broadcaster: Nate Gatter. Director of Community Relations: Shannon Lacker. Director of Promotions: Gayle Lymer. Box Office Manager: Brett Helfrich. Assistant Director Stadium Operations: Jacob Vantrees
Manager: Phil Warren. Trainer: Geof Manzo.

GAME INFORMATION
Radio Announcer: Nate Gatter. No. of Games Broadcast: Home-50, Away-48.
PA Announcer: Tom Calhoun. Stadium Name: GCS Ballpark. Location: I-255 at exit 15 (Mousette Lane). Standard Game Times: 7:05 p.m., Sun: 6:05 p.m.

JOLIET SLAMMERS

Office Address: 1 Mayor Art Schultz Dr, Joliet, IL 60432
Telephone: (815) 722-2287
E-Mail Address: info@jolietslammers.com. Website: www.jolietslammers.com
Owner: Joliet Community Baseball & Entertainment, LLC.
General Manager: Heather Mills. Director of Food/Beverage: Tom Fremarek. Director, Community Relations: Ken Miller. Manager, Corporate Sales: Porscha Johnson. Account Executive: Lauren Rhodes. Account Executive: TJ Propp
Manager: Jeff Isom.

GAME INFORMATION
No. of Games Broadcast: 96. Flagship Station: www.jolietslammers.com. Official Scorer: Dave Laketa. Stadium Name: Joliet Route 66 Stadium. Location: 1 Mayor Art Schultz Drive, Joliet, IL 60432. Standard Game Times: 7:05 p.m.; Sat: 6:05 p.m. Sun: 1:05 p.m. Visiting Club Hotel: Harrah's Casino Joliet & Joliet Super 8.

LAKE ERIE CRUSHERS

Address: 2009 Baseball Boulevard. Avon, Ohio 44011.
Telephone: 440-934-3636. Website: www.lakeeriecrushers.com.
Operated by: Blue Dog Baseball, LLC
Managing Officer: Tom Kramig. VP Operations: Paul Siegwarth. Accountant: DJ Saylor. Box Office Manager: Collin DeJong. Director, Concessions/Catering: Greg Kobunski. Director, Marketing & Promotions: Catie Graf. Director of Ticketing: Jay Miller. Account Executive: Matt Moos, Mike Mays. Chris Meyer, Ryan Acus. Director, Broadcasting: Andy Barch.
Manager: Cam Roth

GAME INFORMATION
Stadium Name: Sprenger Health Care Stadium
Location: Intersection of I-90 and Colorado Ave in Avon, OH.
Standard Game Times: 7:05 p.m., Sun: 2:05.

NORMAL CORNBELTERS

Mailing Address: 1000 West Raab Road, Normal, IL 61761.
Telephone: 309-454-2255 (BALL). Fax: 309- 454-2287 (BATS).
Ownership: Normal Baseball Group.

President/General Manager: Steve Malliet. VP, Corporate Sales: Mike Petrini. VP, Ticket Sales: Ryan Eucker. Ticket Sales Director: Sean Mendyk. Business Manager: Deana Roberts. Box Office Manager: Sean Mendyk. Public Address Announcer: Greg Halblieb.

Field Manager: Billy Horn.

GAME INFORMATION

Stadium Name: The Corn Crib. Location: From I-55 North, go south on I-55 and take the 165 exit, turn left at light, turn right on Raab Road to ballpark on right; From I-55 South, go north on I-55 and take the 165 exit, merge onto Route 51 (Main Street), turn right on Raab Road to ballpark on right. Standard Game Times: 6:35 p.m., Sun: 3:05.

RIVER CITY RASCALS

Office Address: 900 TR Hughes Blvd, O'Fallon, MO 63366.
Telephone: (636) 240-2287. Fax: (636) 240-7313.
Email Address: info@rivercityrascals.com. Website: www.rivercityrascals.com.
Operated by: PS and J Professional Baseball Club LLC.
Owners: Tim Hoeksema, Jan Hoeksema, Fred Stratton, Anne Stratton, Pam Malliet, Steve Malliet, Michael Veeck, Greg Wendt.
President: Dan Dial. General Manager: Lisa Ferreira. VP of Ticket Sales: David Schmoll. Director of Stadium Operations: Tom Bauer. Director, Food/Beverage: Seth Schoem. Business Manager: Carrie Green. Promotions & Social Media Manager: Leigha Dempsey. Box Office Manager/Account Executive: Nicole Anderson. Account Executive: Ryan Alwell
Manager: Steve Brook.

GAME INFORMATION

No. of Games Broadcast: Home-48, Away-48. PA Announcer: Mike Kromer.
Stadium Name: CarShield Field. Location: I-70 to exit 219, north on TR Hughes Road, follow signs to ballpark.
Standard Game Times: 6:35 p.m., Sun: 4:05.
Visiting Club Hotel: America's Best Value Inn 1310 Bass Pro Drive St Charles, MO. Telephone: (636) 947-5900..

SCHAUMBURG BOOMERS

Office Address: 1999 Springinsguth Road, Schaumburg, IL 60193
Email Address: info@boomersbaseball.com. Website: www.boomersbaseball.com
Owned by: Pat and Lindy Salvi.
General Manager: Michael Larson. Business Manager: Todd Fulk. Director of Facilities: Mike Tlusty. Director Food/Beverage: Chris Wojtkiewicz. Broadcaster: Tim Calderwood. Box Office Manager: Anthony Giammanco. Director of Promotions: Riley Anderson. Director of Community Relations: Peter Long. Director of Stadium Operations: Collin Cunningham. Account Executive: Hanna Olson. Account Executive: Drew Winter. Head Chef: Devin Maney
Manager: Jamie Bennett

GAME INFORMATION

Broadcaster: Tim Calderwood. No. of Games Broadcast: Home-48, Away-48. Flagship Station: WRMN 1410 AM Elgin. Official Scorer: Ken Trendel.
Stadium: Schaumburg Boomers Stadium. Location: I-290 to Thorndale Ave Exit, head West on Elgin-O'Hare Expressway until Springinsguth Road Exit, second left at Springinsguth Road (shared parking lot with Schaumburg Metra Station).
Visiting Club Hotel: AmericInn Hotel & Suites, 1300 East Higgins Road, Schaumburg IL 60173.

SOUTHERN ILLINOIS MINERS

Office Address: Rent One Park, 1000 Miners Drive, Marion, IL 62959.
Telephone: (618) 998-8499. Fax: (618) 969-8550.
Email Address: info@southernillinoisminers.com. Website: www.southernillinoisminers.com.
Operated by: Southern Illinois Baseball Group. Owner: Jayne Simmons.
Chief Operating Officer: Mike Pinto. General Manager: John Wilson. Assistant General Manager/Director of Finance: Cathy Perry. Director, Stadium Operations: Will Niermann. Director, Ticket Operations: Kirby Spangler. Director, Video Production/Creative Services: Heath Hooker. Director, Promotions: Katie Basil. Director, Radio Broadcasting/Media Relations: Jason Guerette. Sponsorship/Group Coordinator: Skyler Hoth. Account Executives: Brent O'Bold, Casey Rose.
Field Manager: Mike Pinto. Hitting Coach: Steve Marino. Pitching Coach: TBA. Bullpen Coach: Roy Perez.
Instructor: Ralph Santana. Coach/Advance Scout: John Lakin. Strength/Conditioning Coordinator: Chris Stone.

GAME INFORMATION

No. of Games Broadcast: 96. Flagship Station: 97.7 WHET-FM.

Stadium Name: Rent One Park. Location: US 57 to Route 13 East, right at Halfway Road to Fairmont Drive.
Standard Game Times: 7:05 p.m., Sat: 6:05., Sun: 5:05.

Visiting Club Hotel: EconoLodge, 1806 Bittle Place, Marion, IL 62959 618-993-1644

TRAVERSE CITY BEACH BUMS

Office Address: 333 Stadium Dr, Traverse City, MI 49685.
Telephone: (231) 943-0100. Fax: (231) 943-0900.
Email Address: info@tcbeachbums.com. Website: www.tcbeachbums.com.
Operated by: Traverse City Beach Bums, LLC.
Managing Member/President/COO: John Wuerfel. Member/GM: Leslye Wuerfel.
Vice President/Director, Baseball Operations: Jason Wuerfel. Director, Ticketing: Michael Ward. Promotions Director: Courtne Stuck.
Field Manager: Dan Rohn.

GAME INFORMATION

No. of Games Broadcast: 96. PA Announcer: Gary Langley.

Stadium Name: Wuerfel Park. Location: Three miles south of the Grand Traverse Mall just off US-31 and M-37 in Chums Village. Stadium is visible from the highway. Standard Game Times: 7:05 p.m., Sun: 5:05.

WASHINGTON WILD THINGS

Office Address: One Washington Federal Way, Washington, PA 15301.
Telephone: (724) 250-9555. Fax: (724) 250-2333.
Email Address: info@washingtonwildthings.com. Website: www.washingtonwild things.com.
Owned by: Sports Facility, LLC. Operated by: Washington Frontier League Baseball, LLC.
President/Chief Executive Officer: Stuart Williams. Managing Partner: Francine W. Williams. General Manager: Steven Zavacky. Director, Marketing/Communications/Corporate Relations: Christine Blaine. Corporate Partnership Ticket Manager: Austin Snodgrass. Controller: JJ Heider. Assistant GM: Jordan Millorino. Creative Services: Sadie Rylander. Director of Baseball Operations: Tony Buccilli. Digital Media Manager: Kyle Dawson.
Manager: Gregg Langbehn.

GAME INFORMATION

Stadium Name: Wild Things Park. Location: I-70 to exit 15 (Chestnut. Street), right on Chestnut Street to Washington Crown Center Mall, right at mall entrance, right on to Mall Drive to stadium. Standard Game Times: 7:05 p.m., Sun: 5:35.

Visiting Club Hotel: Red Roof Inn.

WINDY CITY THUNDERBOLTS

Office Address: 14011 South Kenton Avenue, Crestwood, IL 60418 (Old Zip 60445)
Telephone: (708) 489-2255. Fax: (708) 489-2999.
Email Address: info@wcthunderbolts.com. Website: www.wcthunderbolts.com.
Owned by: Crestwood Professional Baseball, LLC.
General Manager: Mike Lucas. Assistant GM: Mike VerSchave. Senior Sales Executive: Bill Waliewski. Director, Community Relations: Johnny Sole. Director, Group Sales: Kenny Thorne.
Field Manager: Ron Biga. Hitting Coach: Erik Lis. Assistant Coach: Devin DeYoung.

GAME INFORMATION

Radio Announcer: Terry Bonadonna. No. of Games Broadcast: 96. Flagship Station: WXAV, 88.3 FM. Official Scorer: Chris Gbur

Stadium Name: Standard Bank Stadium. Location: I-294 to South Cicero Ave, exit (Route 50), south for 1 1/2 miles, left at Midlothian Turnpike, right on Kenton Ave; I-57 to 147th Street, west on 147th to Cicero, north on Cicero, right on Midlothian Turnpike, right on Kenton. Standard Game Times: 7:05 p.m., Sat: 6:05., Sun: 2:05./5:05.

Visiting Club Hotel: Georgioís Comfort Inn, 8800 W 159th St, Orland Park, IL 60462. Telephone: (708) 403-1100.

ADDITIONAL LEAGUES

PACIFIC ASSOCIATION OF PROFESSIONAL BASEBALL CLUBS

Mailing address: 1379 Canyon Road, Geyserville CA 95441.
Telephone: (707) 857-1780 or (925) 588-3047
Year Founded: 2013.
Teams: San Rafael Pacifics, Sonoma Stompers, Vallejo Admirals and Pittsburg Diamonds.
Roster Limit: 22. **Eligibility Rules:** None.
2016 Start Date: June 1
Playoff Format: First-half winner plays second half winner (if different teams win each half), play one-game playoff.
Playoff Start Date: Aug. 31.
Brand of Baseball: Rawlings.
Statistician: Pointstreak.

PECOS LEAGUE

Website: www.PecosLeague.com.
Address: PO Box 271489, Houston, Tx 77277. **Telephone:** 575-680-2212.
E-mail: info@pecosleague.com
Commissioner: Andrew Dunn.
Teams: Alpine Cowboys, Alpine, Texas; Garden City Wind, Garden City, Kan.; Santa Fe Fuego, Santa Fe, N.M.; Trinidad Triggers, Trinidad, Colo.; Roswell Invaders, Roswell, N.M.; Ruidoso Osos, Ruidoso, N.M.; Tucson Saguaros, Tucson, Ariz.; White Sands Pupfish, Alamogordo, N.M.; Pacific Bakersfield Train Robbers, Bakersfield, Calif.; California City Whiptails, California City, Calif; High Desert Yardbirds, Adelanto, Calif; Monterey Amberjacks, Monterey, Calif.
Year Founded: 2010.
Regular Season: 64 games. **Start Date:** May 17. **Playoff Format:** Best of 5 in first round, best of 3 in finals.
Roster Limit: 22 (no designated hitter).
Eligibility Rules: 25 and under.
Brand of Baseball: National League.

UNITED SHORE PROFESSIONAL BASEBALL LEAGUE

Location: Jimmy Johns Field. 7171 Auburn Rd, Utica MI.
Website: www.uspbl.com. **Telephone:** (248) 327-4829. **Email:** baseballoperations@uspbl.com
Ownership Group: General Sports & Entertainment.
CEO: Andrew D. Appelby. **COO:** Dana L. Schmitt. **VP of Corporate Sponsorship:** Matthew J. Schul. **VP of Marketing and Public Relations:** Scott MacDonald. **VP of Ticket Sales & Premium Seating:** Zack Phillips. **VP of Groups Sales & Events:** Theresa Doan. **Director of Client Services:** Jeremiah Hergott. **Director of Ballpark Operations:** Mark Albertson. **Promotions and Marketing Coordinator:** Haylee Podrasky

BASEBALL OPERATIONS STAFF

Director of Baseball Operations: Justin Orenduff. **Deputy Director of Baseball Operations:** Mike Zielinski.
Fielding Coordinator: Paul Niggebrugge. **Catching and Throwing Coordinator:** Ray Ortega.
Teams: Birmingham-Bloomfield Beavers, Eastside Diamond Hoppers, Utica Unicorns, Westside Woolly Mammoths. Managers
Birmingham-Bloomfield Beavers: Chris Newell; **Eastside Diamond Hoppers:** Paul Noce; **Utica Unicorns:** Jim Essian; **Westside Woolly Mammoths:** Shane McCatty.
Roster Limit: (20).
Eligibility Rules: (Age limits 18-26)
2018 Start Date: May 11th.
No of Games: 75. Each Team plays 50 games.
Playoff Format: Single-game elimination.

INTERNATIONAL

AMERICAS

MEXICO

MEXICAN LEAGUE

MEMBER, NATIONAL ASSOCIATION

NOTE: The Mexican League is a member of the National Association of Professional Baseball Leagues and has a Triple-A classification. However, its member clubs operate largely independent of the 30 major league teams, and for that reason the league is listed in the international section.

Address: Av Insurgentes Sur #797 3er. piso. Col. Napoles. C.P. 03810, Benito Juarez, Mexico, D.F. **Telephone:** 52-55-5557-1007. **Fax:** 52-55-5395-2454. **E-Mail Address:** oficina@lmb.com.mx. **Website:** www. lmb.com.mx.

Years League Active: 1955-.
President: Javier Salinas. **Director, Administration:** Oscar Neri Rojas Salazar.

Division Structure: North—Aguascalientes, Durango, Laguna, Mexico City, Monclova, Monterrey, Saltillo, Tijuana. **South**—Campeche, Laredo, Leon, Oaxaca, Puebla, Quintana Roo, Tabasco, Yucatan.

Regular Season: 114 games (split-schedule). **2018 Opening Date:** March 22. **Closing Date:** Oct. 8.

All-Star Game: June 29, Merida, Yucatan.

Playoff Format: Eight teams qualify, including the top three teams in each division. The fourth and fifth place teams in each division will hold a wild-card elimination game, as long as they are separated by no more than three games.

Roster Limit: 28. **Roster Limit, Imports:** 7.

AGUASCALIENTES RIELEROS

Office Address: López Mateos # 101 Torre "A" Int 214 y 215, Plaza Cristal, Colonia San Luis, CP 20250. **Telephone:** (52) 449-915-1596. **Fax:** (52) 614-459-0336. **E-Mail Address:** Not available. **Website:** www.rielerosags.com.

President: Mario Rodriguez. **General Manager:** Iram Campos Lara.

Manager: Homar Rojas.

CAMPECHE PIRATAS

Office Address: Calle Filiberto Qui Farfan No. 2, Col. Camino Real, CP 24020, Campeche, Campeche. **Telephone:** (52) 981-827-4759. **Fax:** (52) 981-827-4767. **E-Mail Address:** piratas@prodigy.net.mx. **Website:** www. piratasdecampeche.mx.

President: Gabriel Escalante Castillo. **General Manager:** Gabriel Lozano Berron.

Manager: Daniel Fernandez.

DURANGO GENERALES

Office Address: De Los Deportes, Unidad Deportiva, 98065_00 Zacatecas, ZAC. **Telephone:** (52) 496-105-3940. **E-Mail Address:** contacto@generalesbeisbol.com. mx. **Website:** http://generalesbeisbol.com.mx/

President: Virgilio Ruiz Isassi.

Manager: Matias Carrillo.

LAGUNA VAQUEROS

Office Address: Juan Gutenberg s/n, Col Centro, CP 27000, Torreon, Coahuila. **Telephone:** (52) 871-718-5515. **Fax:** (52) 871-717-4335. **E-Mail Address:** Not available. **Website:** www.clubvaqueroslaguna.com.

President: Ricardo Martin Bringas. **General Manager:** Roberto Cota Camacho.

Manager: Ramon Orantes.

LAREDO TECOLOTES

Office Address: Lib. de Nuevo Laredo 20, Tamaulipas. **Website:** http://www.facebook.com/ TecolotesNvoLdo.

President: Jose Antonio Mansur Beltran. **General Manager:** Grimaldo Martinez Gonzalez.

Manager: Eddy Castro.

MEXICO CITY DIABLOS ROJOS

Office Address: Av Cuauhtemoc #451-101, Col Narvarte, CP 03020, Mexico DF. **Telephone:** (56) 398-722-9722. **E-Mail Address:** contacto@diablos-rojos.com. **Website:** www.diablos.com.mx.

President: Alfredo Harp Helu. **General Manager:** Francisco Minjarez.

Manager: Victor Bojorquez.

MONCLOVA ACEREROS

Office Address: Cuauhtemoc #299, Col Ciudad Deportiva, CP 25750, Monclova, Coahuila. **Telephone:** (52) 866-636-2650. **Fax:** (52) 866-636-2688. **E-Mail Address:** acereros2014@live.com. **Website:** www. acereros.com.mx.

General Manager: Donaciano Garza Gutierrez.

Manager: Dan Firova.

MONTERREY SULTANES

Office Address: Av Manuel Barragan s/n, Estadio Monterrey, Apartado Postal 870, Monterrey, Nuevo Leon, CP 66460. **Telephone:** (52) 81-8351-2015. **Fax:** (52) 81-8351-8022. **E-Mail Address:** sultanes@sultanes.com. mx. **Website:** www.sultanes.com.mx.

President: José Maiz Garcia. **General Manager:** Roberto Magdaleno.

Manager: Roberto Kelly.

OAXACA GUERREROS

Office Address: M Bravo 417 Col Centro 68000, Oaxaca, Oaxaca. **Telephone:** (52) 951-515-5522. **Fax:** (52) 951-515-4966. **E-Mail Address:** oaxacaguerreros@gmail. com. **Website:** www.guerreros.mx.

President: Lorenzo Peón Escalante. **General Manager:** Guillermo Spindola Morales.

Manager: Jose Luis Sandoval.

PUEBLA PERICOS

Office Address: Calz Zaragoza S/N, Unidad Deportiva 5 de Mayo, Col Maravillas, CP 72220, Puebla, Puebla. **Telephone:** (52) 222-222-2116. **Fax:** (52) 222-222-2117. **E-Mail Address:** oficina@pericosdepuebla.com.mx. **Website:** www.pericosdepuebla.com.mx.

President: Juan Villareal. **General Manager:** Jose Raul Melendez Habib.

Manager: Lorenzo Bundy.

QUINTANA ROO TIGRES

Office Address: Av Mayapan Mz 4 Lt 1 Super Mz 21, CP 77500, Cancun, Quintana Roo. **Telephone:** (52) 998-887-3108. **Fax:** (52) 998-887-1313. **E-Mail Address:** tigres@tigrescapitalinos.com.mx. **Website:** www.tigresqr. mx.

President: Carlos Peralta Quintero. **General Manager:** Francisco Minjarez Garcia.

Manager: Tim Johnson.

SALTILLO SARAPEROS

Office Address: Blvd Nazario Ortiz Esquina con Blvd Jesus Sanchez, CP 25280, Saltillo, Coahuila. **Telephone:** (52) 844-416-9455. **Fax:** (52) 844-439-1330. **E-Mail Address:** aley@grupoley.com. **Website:** www.saraperos. com.mx.

President: Alvaro Ley Lopez. **General Manager:** Eduardo Valenzuela Guajardo.
Manager: Not Available.

TABASCO OLMECAS

Office Address: Avenida Velodromo de la Ciudad Deportiva S/N, Atasta, 86100 Villahermosa, Tabasco. **Telephone:** (52) 993-352-2787. **Fax:** (52) 993-352-2788. **E-Mail Address:** hola@olmecastasco.mx. **Website:** www.olmecastabasco.mx.
President: Raul Gonzalez Rodriguez. **General Manager:** Luis Guzman Ramos.
Manager: Enrique Reyes.

TIJUANA TOROS

Office Address: Blvd Agua Caliente #11720, Col Hipodromo 22020, Tijuana, BC. **Telephone:** (52) 664-635-5600. **E-Mail Address:** contacto@torosdetijuana.com. **Website:** www.torosdetijuana.com.
General Manager: Antonio Cano.
Manager: Pedro Mere.

YUCATAN LEONES

Office Address: Calle 50 #406-B, Entre 35 y 37, Col Jesus Carranza, CP 97109, Merida, Yucatán. **Telephone:** (52) 999-926-3022. **Fax:** (52) 999-926-3631. **E-Mail Addresses:** mserrano@leones.mx. **Website:** www.leones.mx.
President: Erick Ernesto Arellano Hernández. **General Manager:** Alejandro Orozco Garcia.
Manager: Roberto Vizcarra.

MEXICAN ACADEMY

Rookie Classification
Mailing Address: Ubicación: Av. El Fundador #100, Col. San Miguel, El Carmen N.L., C.P. 66550. **Telephone:** (81) 8158-7900. **Fax:** (52) 555-395-2454. **E-Mail Address:** pgarza@academia-lmb.com. **Website:** www.academia-lmb.com.
President: C.P. **Plinio Escalante Bolio. Director General:** Salvador Viera Higuera.
Regular Season: 50 games. **Opening Date:** Not available. **Closing Date:** Not available.

DOMINICAN REPUBLIC

DOMINICAN SUMMER LEAGUE

Member, National Association
Rookie Classification
Mailing Address: Calle Segunda No 64, Reparto Antilla, Santo Domingo, Dominican Republic. **Telephone/ Fax:** (809) 532-3619. **Website:** www.dominicansummer league.com. **E-Mail Address:** ligadeverano@codetel.net.do.
Years League Active: 1985-.
President: Orlando Diaz.
Member Clubs/Division Structure: Boca Chica North—Astros Orange, Brewers/Indians, Cubs, Dodgers, Indians, Pirates, Rangers 1, Rays 2. Boca Chica. **South—** Angels, Cardinals, Mets 1, Nationals, Phillies 1, Rockies Twins, Yankees. Boca Chica. **Northwest—**Astros Blue, Athletics, Braves, Dodgers 1, Marlins, Rays 1, Red Sox 1, Royals. Boca Chica. **Baseball City—**Blue Jays, Diamondbacks 1, Giants, Mariners 1, Orioles 1, Padres, Reds, White Sox. **San Pedro de Macoris—**Brewers, Cubs 2, Diamondbacks, Mets 2, Phillies 2, Rangers 2, Tigers.
Regular Season: 72 games. **Opening Date:** Unavailable. **Closing Date:** Unavailable.
Playoff Format: Six teams qualify for playoffs, including four division winners and two wild-card teams. Teams with two best records receive a bye to the semifinals; four other playoff teams play best-of-three series. Winners advance to best-of-three semifinals. Winners advance to best-of-five championship series.
Roster Limit: 35 active. **Player Eligibility Rule:** No player may have four or more years of prior minor league service. No draft-eligible player from the U.S. or Canada (not including players from Puerto Rico) may participate in the DSL. No age limits apply.

CHINA

CHINA BASEBALL LEAGUE

Mailing Address: 5, Tiyuguan Road, Beijing 100763, China. **Telephone:** (86) 010-8718-3534. **Fax:** (86) 010-6711-7596. **Website:** baseball.sport.org.cn.
Years League Active: 2002-.
Chairman: Hu Jian Guo.
Member Clubs: Division 1: Beijing Tigers, Guangdong Leopards, Jiangsu Pegasus, Shanghai Golden Eagles, Sichuan Dragons, Tianjin Lions. **Division 2:** Henan Elephants. Shandong Institute of Commerce and Technology Baseball Club. China Society Baseball Club. People's Liberation Army Baseball Club.
Email: chinabaseball2008@aliyun.com.
Regular Season: 15 games.
Playoff Format: Top two teams meet in a best-of-three championship.

JAPAN

Mailing Address: Mita Bellju Building, 11th Floor, 5-36-7 Shiba, Minato-ku, Tokyo 108-0014. **Telephone:** 03-6400-1189. **Fax:** 03-6400-1190.
Website: www.npb.or.jp, www.npb.or.jp/eng
Commissioner: Atsushi Saito.
Executive Secretary: Atsushi Ihara. **Executive Director, Baseball Operations:** Minoru Hata. **Executive Director, NPB Rules & Labor:** Nobuhisa "Nobby" Ito.
Executive Director, Central League Operations: Kazuhide Kinefuchi. **Executive Director, Pacific League Operations:** Kazuo Nakano.
Nippon Series: Best-of-seven series between Central and Pacific League champions, begins Oct 27.
All-Star Series: July 13 at Kyocera Dome; July 14 at Fujisaki Prefectural Baseball Stadium.
Roster Limit: 70 per organization (one major league club, one minor league club). Major league club is permitted to register 28 players at a time, though just 25 may be available for each game.
Roster Limit, Imports: Four in majors (no more than three position players or pitchers); unlimited in minors.

CENTRAL LEAGUE

Regular Season: 143 games.
2017 Opening Date: March 31. **Closing Date:** Oct. 1.
Playoff Format: Second-place team meets third-place team in best-of-three series. Winner meets first-place team in best-of-seven series to determine representative in Japan Series (first-place team has one-game advantage to begin series).

CHUNICHI DRAGONS

Mailing Address: Chunichi Bldg 6F, 4-1-1 Sakae, Naka-ku, Nagoya 460-0008. **Telephone:** 052-261-8811. **Chairman:** Bungo Shirai. **President:** Takao Sasaki. **Field Manager:** Shigekazu Mori.

HANSHIN TIGERS

Mailing Address: 2-33 Koshien-cho, Nishinomiya-shi, Hyogo-ken 663-8152. **Telephone:** 0798-46-1515. **Chairman:** Shinya Sakai. **President:** Keiichiro Yotsufuji. **Field Manager:** Tomoaki Kanemoto.

HIROSHIMA TOYO CARP

Mailing Address: 2-3-1 Minami Kaniya, Minami-ku, Hiroshima 732-8501. **Telephone:** 082-554-1000. **President:** Hajime Matsuda. **General Manager:** Kiyoaki Suzuki. **Field Manager:** Koichi Ogata.

TOKYO YAKULT SWALLOWS

Mailing Address: Seizan Bldg, 4F, 2-12-28 Kita Aoyama, Minato-ku, Tokyo 107-0061. **Telephone:** 03-3405-8960.
Chairman: Sumiya Hori. **President:** Tsuyoshi Klnugasa. **Senior Director:** Junji Ogawa. **Field Manager:** Mitsuru Manaka.

YOKOHAMA DENA BAYSTARS

Mailing Address: Kannai Arai Bldg, 7F, 1-8 Onoe-cho, Naka-ku, Yokohama 231-0015. **Telephone:** 045-681-0811.
Chairman: Makoto Haruta. **President:** Shingo Okamura. **General Manager:** Shigeru Takada. **Field Manager:** Alex Ramirez.

YOMIURI GIANTS

Mailing Address: Yomiuri Shimbun Bldg, 26F, 1-7-1 Otemachi, Chiyoda-ku, Tokyo 100-8151. **Telephone:** 03-3246-7733. **Fax:** 03-3246-2726.
Chairman: Kojiro Shiraishi. **President:** Hiroshi Kubo. **General Manager:** Tatsuyoshi Tsutsumi. **Field Manager:** Yoshinobu Takahashi.

PACIFIC LEAGUE

Regular Season: 143 games.
2017 Opening Date: March 31. **Closing Date:** Oct. 5.
Playoff Format: Second-place team meets third-place team in best-of-three series. Winner meets first-place team in best-of-seven series to determine league's representative in Japan Series (first-place team has one-game advantage to begin series).

CHIBA LOTTE MARINES

Mailing Address: 1 Mihama, Mihama-ku, Chiba-shi, Chiba-ken 261-8587. **Telephone:** 03-5682-6341.
Chairman: Takeo Shigemitsu. **President:** Shinya Yamamuro. **Field Manager:** Tsutomu Ito.

FUKUOKA SOFTBANK HAWKS

Mailing Address: Fukuoka Yahuoku Japan Dome, Hawks Town, 2-2-2 Jigyohama, Chuo-ku, Fukuoka 810-0065. **Telephone:** 092-847-1006. **Owner:** Masayoshi Son. **Chairman:** Sadaharu Oh. **President:** Yoshimitsu Goto. **Field Manager:** Kimiyasu Kudo.

HOKKAIDO NIPPON HAM FIGHTERS

Mailing Address: 1 Hitsujigaoka, Toyohira-ku, Sapporo 062-8655. **Telephone:** 011-857-3939.

Chairman: Juichi Suezawa. **President:** Kenso Takeda. **General Manager:** Hiroshi Yoshimura. **Field Manager:** Hideki Kuriyama.

ORIX BUFFALOES

Mailing Address: 3-Kita-2-30 Chiyozaki, Nishi-ku, Osaka 550-0023. **Telephone:** 06-6586-0221. **Fax:** 06-6586-0240.
Chairman: Yoshihiko Miyauchi. **President:** Hiroaki Nishina. **General Manager:** Hiroyuki Nagamura. **Field Manager:** Junichi Fukura.

SAITAMA SEIBU LIONS

Mailing Address: 2135 Kami-Yamaguchi, Tokorozawa-shi, Saitama-ken 359-1189. **Telephone:** 04-2924-1155. **Fax:** 04-2928-1919.
President: Hajime Igo. **Field Manager:** Hatsuhiko Tsuji.

TOHOKU RAKUTEN GOLDEN EAGLES

Mailing Address: 2-11-6 Miyagino, Miyagino-ku, Sendai-shi, Miyagi-ken 983-0045. **Telephone:** 022-298-5300. **Fax:** 022-298-5360.
Chairman: Hiroshi Mikitani. **President:** Yozo Tachibana. **Field Manager:** Masataka Nashida.

KOREA

KOREA BASEBALL ORGANIZATION

Mailing Address: 946-16 Dokokdong, Kangnam-gu, Seoul, Korea. **Telephone:** (02) 3460-4600. **Fax:** (02) 3460-4639.
Years League Active: 1982-.
Website: www.koreabaseball.com.
Commissioner: Koo Bon-Neung. **Secretary General:** Yang Hae-Young.
Member Clubs: Doosan Bears, Hanwha Eagles, Kia Tigers, KT Wiz, LG Twins, Lotte Giants, NC Dinos, Nexen Heroes, Samsung Lions, SK Wyverns.
Regular Season: 128 games. **2018 Opening Date:** April 1.
Playoffs: Third- and fourth-place teams meet in best-of-three series; winner advances to meet second-place team in best-of-five series; winner meets first-place team in best-of-seven Korean Series for league championship.
Roster Limit: 26 active through Sept 1, when rosters expand to 31. **Imports:** Two active.

TAIWAN

CHINESE PROFESSIONAL BASEBALL LEAGUE

Mailing Address: 2F, No 32, Pateh Road, Sec 3, Taipei, Taiwan 10559. **Telephone:** 886-2-2577-6992. **Fax:** 886-2-2577-2606. **Website:** www.cpbl.com.tw.
Years League Active: 1990-.
Commissioner: Jenn-Tai Hwang. **Deputy Secretary General:** Hueimin Wang. **E-Mail Address:** richard.wang@cpbl.com.tw.
Member Clubs: Chinatrust Brothers, Fubon Guardians, Lamigo Monkeys, Uni-President 7-Eleven Lions.
Regular Season: 120 games. Each team plays 60 games in the first and second halves of the season. **2018 Opening Date:** Not available. **Playoffs:** Half-season winners are eligible for the postseason. If a non-half-season winner team possesses a higher overall winning percentage than any other half-season winner, then this team gains a wild card and will play a best-of-five series against the half-season winner with the lower winner percentage. The winner of the playoff series advances to Taiwan Series (best-of-seven). If the same team clinches both first- and second-half seasons, then that team is awarded one win to start the Taiwan Series.

EUROPE

NETHERLANDS

DUTCH MAJOR LEAGUE

Mailing Address: Koninklijke Nederlandse Baseball en Softball Bond (Royal Dutch Baseball and Softball Association), Postbus 2650, 3430 GB Nieuwegein, Holland. **Telephone:** 31-30-751-3650. **Fax:** 31-30-751-3651. **Website:** www.knbsb.nl.

Member Clubs: Curacao Neptunus, De Glaskoning Twins, DSS, HCAW, Hoofddorp Pioniers, L&D Amsterdam, Pickles UVV.

Regular season: 42 games.

President: Bob Bergkamp.

ITALY

ITALIAN BASEBALL LEAGUE

Mailing Address: Federazione Italiana Baseball Softball, Viale Tiziano 74, 00196 Roma, Italy. **Telephone:** 39-06-32297201. **Fax:** 39-06-36858201. **Website:** www.fibs.it.

Member Clubs: Bologna, Nettuno, Novara, Parma, Padulo. Rimini, San Marino, Tomassin. **President:** Riccardo Fraccari.

Regular season: 34 games.

Playoffs: Top four teams advance to best-of-five semi-finals. Semifinal winners play best-of-five Italian Series.

WINTER BASEBALL

CARIBBEAN BASEBALL CONFEDERATION

Mailing Address: Frank Feliz Miranda No 1 Naco, Santo Domingo, Dominican Republic. **Telephone:** (809) 381-2643. **Fax:** (809) 565-4654.

Commissioner: Juan Francisco Puello. **Secretary:** Benny Agosto.

Member Countries: Cuba, Colombia, Dominican Republic, Mexico, Nicaragua, Puerto Rico, Venezuela (Colombia and Nicaragua do not play in the Caribbean Series).

2019 Caribbean Series: Barquisimeto, Venezuela, February.

DOMINICAN LEAGUE

Office Address: Ave. Tiradentes, Ensanche La Fé, Estadio Quisqueya, Santo Domingo, Dominican Republic. **Telephone:** (809) 567-6371. **Fax:** (809) 567-5720. **E-Mail Address:** ligadom@hotmail.com. **Website:** www.lidom.com.

Years League Active: 1951-.

President: Leonardo Matos Berrido. **Vice President:** Winston Llenas Davila.

Member Clubs: Aguilas Cibaenas, Estrellas de Oriente, Gigantes del Cibao, Leones del Escogido, Tigres del Licey, Toros del Este.

Regular Season: 50 games.

Playoff Format: Top four teams meet in 18-game round-robin. Top two teams advance to best-of-nine series for league championship. Winner advances to Caribbean Series.

Roster Limit: 30. **Imports:** 7.

MEXICAN PACIFIC LEAGUE

Mailing Address: Blvd Solidaridad No 335, Plaza las Palmas, Edificio A, Nivel 1, Local 4, Hermosillo, Sonora, Mexico CP 83246. **Telephone:** (52) 662-310-9714. **Fax:** (52) 662-310-9715. **E-Mail Address:** medios@lmp.mx. **Website:** www.lmp.mx.

Years League Active: 1958-.

President: Omar Canizales Soto. **General Manager:** Christian Veliz Valencia. **Administrative Manager:**
Remigio Valencia Navarro.

Member Clubs: Culiacan Tomateros, Hermosillo Naranjeros, Jalisco Charros, Los Mochis Caneros, Mazatlan Venados, Mexicali Aguilas, Navojoa Mayos, Obregon Yaquis.

Regular Season: 68 games.

Playoff Format: Six teams advance to best-of-seven quarterfinals. Three winners and losing team with best record advance to best-of-seven semifinals. Winners meet in best-of-seven series for league championship. Winner advances to Caribbean Series.

Roster Limit: 30. **Imports:** 5.

PUERTO RICAN LEAGUE

Office Address: Avenida Munoz Rivera 1056, Edificio First Federal, Suite 501, Rio Piedras, PR 00925. **Mailing Address:** PO Box 191852, San Juan, PR 00019. **Telephone:** (786) 244-1146. **Fax:** (787) 767-3028. **Website:** www.ligapr.com. **E-mail address:** info@ligapr.com

Years League Active: 1938-2007; 2008-

President: Hector Rivera. **Managing Director:** Jose Ariel Nazario Alvarez. **Press Director:** Ricardo Valero Viruet.

Member Clubs: Aguadilla Tiburones, Caguas Criollos, Carolina Gigantes, Mayaguez Indios, Santurce Cangrejeros.

Regular Season: 40 games.

Playoff Format: Top three teams meet in round robin series, with top two teams advancing to best-of-seven final. Winner advances to Caribbean Series.

Roster Limit: 30. **Imports:** 5.

VENEZUELAN LEAGUE

Mailing Address: Avenida Casanova, Centro Comercial "El Recreo," Torre Sur, Piso 3, Oficinas 6 y 7, Sabana Grande, Caracas, Venezuela. **Telephone:** (58) 212-761-6408. **Fax:** (58) 212-761-7661. **Website:** www.lvbp.com.

Years League Active: 1946-.

President: Juan Jose Avila. **Vice Presidents:** Esteban Palacios Lozada, Domingo Santander. **General Manager:** Domingo Alvarez.

Member Clubs: Anzoategui Caribes, Aragua Tigres, Caracas Leones, La Guaira Tiburones, Lara Cardenales, Magallanes Navegantes, Margarita Bravos, Zulia Aguilas.

Regular Season: 64 games.

Playoff Format: Top two teams in each division, plus a wild-card team, meet in 16-game round-robin series. Top two finishers meet in best-of-seven series for league championship. Winner advances to Caribbean Series.

Roster Limit: 26. **Imports:** 7.

COLOMBIAN LEAGUE

Office/Mailing Address: Hotel Eslait Cra 53 No. 72-27 2do piso, Baranquilla. **Telephone:** (57) 368-6561. **E-mail Address:** prensa@lcbp.com.co. **Website:** www.lcbp.com.co.

President: Edinson Renteria. **Director, Operations:** Harold Herrera. **Director, Communications:** Jose Barraza.

Member Clubs: Barranquilla Caimanes, Cartegena Tigres, Monteria Leones, Sincelejo Toros.

Regular season: 42 games.

Playoff Format: Top three teams play eight-game round robin. Top two teams meet in best-of-seven finals for league championship.

AUSTRALIA

AUSTRALIAN BASEBALL LEAGUE

Street Address: Suite 5/65-67 Thomas Drive Chevron Island QLD 4217. **Postal Address:** PO Box 218 Chevron Island QLD 4217. **Telephone:** (07) 5510 6800. **Fax:** (07) 5510 6855. **E-Mail Address:** abfadmin@baseball.org.au. **Website:** web.theabl.com.au.

CEO: Cam Vale. **General Manager:** Ben Foster.

Teams: Adelaide Bite, Brisbane Bandits, Canberra Cavalry, Melbourne Aces, Perth Heat, Sydney Blue Sox.

2018 Opening Date: Unavailable. Play usually opens in November with playoffs in February.

Playoff Format: The teams with the best four records qualify for the playoffs. Teams are seeded 1-4, with the top two seeds hosting all three games of the best-of-three semifinal series. Winners advance to a best-of-three championship series.

DOMESTIC LEAGUE

ARIZONA FALL LEAGUE

Mailing Address: 2415 E Camelback Road, Suite 850, Phoenix, AZ 85016. **Telephone:** (602) 281-7250. **Fax:** (602) 281-7313. **E-Mail Address:** afl@mlb.com. **Website:** mlb.mlb.com/mlb/events/afl/.

Years League Active: 1992-.

Operated by: Major League Baseball.

Executive Director: Steve Cobb. **Administrator:** Darlene Emert. **Communications:** Paul Jensen.

Teams: Glendale Desert Dogs, Mesa Solar Sox, Peoria Javelinas, Salt River Rafters, Scottsdale Scorpions, Surprise Saguaros.

Regular season: 32 games. **2018 Opening Date:** Unavailable. Play usually opens in mid-October. **Playoff Format:** Division champions meet in one-game championship.

Roster Limit: 30. Each major league organization is required to provide six players. All Triple-A and Double-A players are eligible provided they are on Double-A rosters no later than Aug. 1. Each organization is permitted to send one player below the Double-A level. One foreign player is allowed, as long as the player does not resides in a country that participates in winter ball, as part of the Caribbean Confederation or the Australian winter league. No players with more than one year active or two years total of credited major league service as of Aug. 31 are eligible, though a club can send one player picked in the previous Rule 5 Draft. Players on minor league disabled lists must be activated at least 45 days before the conclusion of their respective seasons to be eligible.

COLLEGES

COLLEGE ORGANIZATIONS

NATIONAL COLLEGIATE ATHLETIC ASSOCIATION

Mailing Address: 700 W. Washington Street, PO Box 6222, Indianapolis, IN 46206. **Telephone:** (317) 917-6222. **Fax:** (317) 917-6826 (championships), (317) 917-6710 (baseball).

E-mail Addresses: Division I Championship: rprettyman@ncaa.org (Ron Prettyman), rlburhr@ncaa.org (Randy Buhr), ctolliver@ncaa.org (Chad Tolliver), thalpin@ncaa.org (Ty Halpin), jhamilton@ncaa.org (JD Hamilton), kgiles@ncaa.org (Kim Giles). **Division II Championship:** ebreece@ncaa.org (Eric Breece). **Division III:** jpwilliams@ncaa.org (J.P. Williams).

Websites: www.ncaa.org, www.ncaa.com.

President: Dr. Mark Emmert. **Managing director, Division I Championships/Alliances:** Ron Prettyman. **Director, Division I Championships/Alliances:** Randy Buhr. **Associate Director, Championships/Alliances:** Chad Tolliver. **Division II Assistant Director, Championshps/Alliances:** Eric Breece. **Division III Assistant Director, Championships/Alliances:** J.P. Williams. **Media Contact, Division I Championships, Alliances/College World Series:** J.D. Hamilton. **Playing Rules Contact:** Ty Halpin. **Statistics Contacts:** Jeff Williams (Division I and RPI); Mark Bedics (Division II); Sean Straziscar (Division III).

Chairman, Division I Baseball Committee: Ray Tanner (Director of Athletics, South Carolina).

Division I Baseball Committee: Kevin Anderson (Director of Athletics, Maryland); Whit Babcock (Director of Athletics, Virginia Tech); David Blank (Director of Athletics, Elon); Mike Buddie (Director of Athletics, Furman); Christopher Del Conte (Director of Athletics, Texas); Joe Karlgaard (Director of Athletics, Rice); Steve Robertello (Co-Interim Director of Athletics, Fresno State); Benjamin Shove (Assistant Commissioner, Northeast Conference); Scott Sidwell (Director of Athletics, University of San Francisco); Ray Tanner (Director of Athletics, South Carolina).

Chairman, Division II Baseball Committee: Mark Clements (Associate Director of Athletics, Northwest Missouri State). **Chairman, Division III Baseball Committee:** Jim Peeples (Head Baseball Coach, Piedmont College).

2019 National Convention: Jan. 23-26 at Orlando, Fla.

2018 CHAMPIONSHIP TOURNAMENTS

NCAA DIVISION I
College World Series: Omaha, Neb., June 16-26/27
Super Regionals (8): Campus sites, June 8-11
Regionals (16): Campus sites, June 1-4

NCAA DIVISION II
World Series: USA Baseball National Training Complex, Cary, N.C. May 26-June 2
Regionals (8): Campus sites, May 17-21

NCAA DIVISION III
World Series: Fox Cities Stadium, Appleton, Wis., May 25-29
Regionals (8): Campus sites, May 17-21

NATIONAL JUNIOR COLLEGE ATHLETIC ASSOCIATION

Mailing Address: 1631 Mesa Ave., Suite B, Colorado Springs, CO 80906. **Telephone:** (719) 590-9788. **Fax:** (719) 590-7324. **E-Mail Address:** mkrug@njcaa.org. **Website:** www.njcaa.org.

Executive Director: Mary Ellen Leicht. **Director, Division I Baseball Tournament:** Jamie Hamilton. **Director, Division II Baseball Tournament:** Billy Mayberry. **Director, Division III Baseball Tournament:** Bill Ellis. **Director Media Relations:** Mark Krug.

2018 CHAMPIONSHIP TOURNAMENTS

DIVISION I
World Series: Grand Junction, CO, May 26-June 1/2

DIVISION II
World Series: Enid, OK, May 26-June 1/2

DIVISION III
World Series: Greeneville, TN, May 26-May 30/31

CALIFORNIA COMMUNITY COLLEGE ATHLETIC ASSOCIATION

Mailing Address: 2017 O St., Sacramento, CA 95811. **Telephone:** (916) 444-1600. **Fax:** (916) 444-2616. **E-Mail Addresses:** ccarter@cccaasports.org, jboggs@cccaasports.org. **Website:** www.cccaasports.org.

Executive Director: Carlyle Carter. **Director, Membership Services:** Jennifer Cardone. **Director, Championships:** George Mategakis. **Director, Membership Services:** Jennifer Cardone, jcardone@cccaasports.org. **Buisness Operations Specialist:** Rina Kasim, rkasim@cccaasports.org. **Administrative Assistant:** Rima Trotter, rtrotter@cccaasports.org.

2018 CHAMPIONSHIP TOURNAMENT

State Championship: Stockton, CA, May 9-12.

NORTHWEST ATHLETIC CONFERENCE

Mailing Address: Clark College TGB 121, 1933 Fort Vancouver Way, Vancouver, WA 98663. **Telephone:** (360) 992-2833. **Fax:** (360) 696-6210. **E-Mail Address:** nwaacc@clark.edu. **Website:** www.nwacsports.org.

Executive Director: Marco Azurdia. **Executive Assistant:** Carol Hardin. **Sports Information Director:** Tracy Swisher. **Director, Operations:** Garet Studer. **Compliance Manager:** Jim Jackson.

2018 CHAMPIONSHIP TOURNAMENT

NWAC Championship: Lower Columbia College, Longview, WA, May 24-28.

AMERICAN BASEBALL COACHES ASSOCIATION

Office Address: 4101 Piedmont Parkway, Suite C, Greensboro, NC 27410. **Telephone:** (336) 821-3140. **Fax:** (336) 886-0000. **E-Mail Address:** abca@abca.org. **Website:** www.abca.org.

Executive Director: Craig Keilitz. **Director, Exhibits/Branding:** Juahn Clark. **Communications/Business Coordinator:** Jon Litchfield. **Membership/Convention Coordinator:** Zach Haile.

Chairman: Mark Johnson. **President:** Rich Maloney (Ball State).

2019 National Convention: Jan. 3-6 in Dallas

NCAA DIVISION I CONFERENCES

AMERICA EAST CONFERENCE

Mailing Address: 451 D Street, Suite 702, Boston, MA 02127. **Telephone:** (617) 695-6369. **Fax:** (617) 695-6380.
E-Mail Address: hager@americaeast.com.
Website: www.americaeast.com.
Baseball Members (First Year): Albany (2002), Binghamton (2002), Hartford (1990), Maine (1990), Maryland-Baltimore County (2004), Massachusetts-Lowell (2014), Stony Brook (2002). **Director, Strategic Media/ Baseball Contact:** Jared Hager. **2018 Tournament:** Six teams, double-elimination, May 23-26 at Mahaney Diamond, Orono, Me.

AMERICAN ATHLETIC CONFERENCE

Mailing Address: 15 Park Row West, Providence, RI 02903. **Telephone:** (401) 453-0660. **Fax:** (401) 751-8540.
E-Mail Address: csullivan@theamerican.org.
Website: www.theamerican.org.
Baseball Members (First Year): Central Florida (2014), Cincinnati (2014), Connecticut (2014), East Carolina (2015), Houston (2014), Memphis (2014), South Florida (2014), Tulane (2015), Wichita State (2018). **Director, Communications:** Chuck Sullivan. **2018 Tournament:** Eight teams, double-elimination until the final, May 22-27 at Spectrum Field, Clearwater, Fla.

ATLANTIC COAST CONFERENCE

Mailing Address: 4512 Weybridge Ln., Greensboro, NC 27407. **Telephone:** (336) 851-6062. **Fax:** (336) 854-8797.
E-Mail Address: sphillips@theacc.org.
Website: www.theacc.com.
Baseball Members (First Year): Boston College (2006), Clemson (1954), Duke (1954), Florida State (1992), Georgia Tech (1980), Maryland (1954), Miami (2005), North Carolina (1954), North Carolina State (1954), Notre Dame (2014), Pittsburgh (2014), Virginia (1955), Virginia Tech (2005), Wake Forest (1954). **Associate Director, Communications:** Steve Phillips. **2018 Tournament:** 12 teams, group play followed by single-elimination semifinals and finals. May 22-27 at Durham Bulls Athletic Park, Durham.

ATLANTIC SUN CONFERENCE

Mailing Address: 3370 Vineville Ave., Suite 108-B, Macon, GA 31204. **Telephone:** (478) 474-3394. **Fax:** (478) 474-4272.
E-Mail Addresses: pmccoy@atlanticsun.org.
Website: www.atlanticsun.org.
Baseball Members (First Year): Florida Gulf Coast (2008), Jacksonville (1999), Kennesaw State (2006), Lipscomb (2004), New Jersey Tech (2016), North Florida (2006), South Carolina-Upstate (2008), Stetson (1986). **Director, Sports Information:** Patrick McCoy. **2018 Tournament:** Eight teams, double-elimination. May 23-26 at Harmon Stadium, Jacksonville.

ATLANTIC 10 CONFERENCE

Mailing Address: 11827 Canon Blvd., Suite 200, Newport News, VA 23606. **Telephone:** (757) 706-3059. **Fax:** (757) 706-3042.
E-Mail Address: ckilcoyne@atlantic10 .org.
Website: www.atlantic10.com.
Baseball Members (First Year): Davidson (2015), Dayton (1996), Fordham (1996), George Mason (2014), George Washington (1977), La Salle (1996), Massachu-

setts (1977), Rhode Island (1981), Richmond (2002), St. Bonaventure (1980), Saint Joseph's (1983), Saint Louis (2006), Virginia Commonwealth (2013). **Commissioner:** Bernadette V. McGlade. **Director, Communications:** Drew Dickerson. **Assistant Director, Communications/ Baseball Contact:** Chris Kilcoyne. **2018 Tournament:** Seven teams, double elimination. May 23-26 at Barcroft Park, Arlington, Va.

BIG EAST CONFERENCE

Mailing Address: BIG EAST Conference, 655 3rd Avenue, 7th Floor, New York, NY 10017. **Telephone:** (212) 969-3181. **Fax:** (212) 969-2900.
E-Mail Address: kquinn@bigeast.com.
Website: www.bigeast.com.
Baseball Members (First Year): Butler (2014), Creighton (2014), Georgetown (1985), St. John's (1985), Seton Hall (1985), Villanova (1985), Xavier (2014). **Assistant Commissioner, Olympic Sports/Marketing Communications:** Kristin Quinn. **2018 Tournament:** Four teams, modified double-elimination. May 24-27 at Prasco Park, Mason, Ohio.

BIG SOUTH CONFERENCE

Mailing Address: 7233 Pineville-Matthews Rd., Suite 100, Charlotte, NC 28226. **Telephone:** (704) 341-7990. **Fax:** (704) 341-7991.
E-Mail Address: brianv@bigsouth.org.
Website: www.bigsouthsports.com.
Baseball Members (First Year): Campbell (2012), Charleston Southern (1983), Gardner-Webb (2009), High Point (1999), Liberty (1991), Longwood (2013), UNC Asheville (1985), Presbyterian (2009), Radford (1983), Winthrop (1983). **Assistant Director, Public Relations/Baseball Contact:** Brian Verdi. **2018 Tournament:** Eight teams, double-elimination. May 22-26, at Lynchburg, Va.

BIG TEN CONFERENCE

Mailing Address: 5440 Park Place, Rosemont, IL 60018. **Telephone:** (847) 696-1010. **Fax:** (847) 696-1110.
E-Mail Addresses: kkane@bigten.org.
Website: www.bigten.org.
Baseball Members (First Year): Illinois (1896), Indiana (1906), Iowa (1906), Maryland (2015), Michigan (1896), Michigan State (1950), Minnesota (1906), Nebraska (2012), Northwestern (1898), Ohio State (1913), Penn State (1992), Purdue (1906), Rutgers (2015). **2018 Tournament:** Eight teams, double-elimination. May 23-27 at TD Ameritrade Park, Omaha.

BIG 12 CONFERENCE

Mailing Address: 400 E. John Carpenter Freeway, Irving, TX 75062. **Telephone:** (469) 524-1009.
E-Mail Address: lrasmussen@big12sports.com.
Website: www.big12sports.com.
Baseball Members (First Year): Baylor (1997), Kansas (1997), Kansas State (1997), Oklahoma (1997), Oklahoma State (1997), Texas Christian (2013), Texas (1997), Texas Tech (1997), West Virginia (2013). **Director, Communications:** Rob Carolla. **2018 Tournament:** Eight teams, double-elimination. May 23-27 at Chickasaw Bricktown Ballpark, Oklahoma City.

BIG WEST CONFERENCE

Mailing Address: 2 Corporate Park, Suite 206, Irvine, CA 92606. **Telephone:** (949) 261-2525. **Fax:** (949) 261-2528.

E-Mail Address: jstcyr@bigwest.org.
Website: www.bigwest.org.
Baseball Members (First Year): Cal Poly (1997), UC Davis (2008), UC Irvine (2002), UC Riverside (2002), UC Santa Barbara (1970), Cal State Fullerton (1975), Cal State Northridge (2001), Hawaii (2013), Long Beach State (1970). **Director, Communications:** Julie St. Cyr. **2018 Tournament:** None.

COLONIAL ATHLETIC ASSOCIATION

Mailing Address: 8625 Patterson Ave., Richmond, VA 23229. **Telephone:** (804) 754-1616. **Fax:** (804) 754-1973.
E-Mail Address: rwashburn@caasports.com.
Website: www.caasports.com.
Baseball Members (First Year): College of Charleston (2014), Delaware (2002), Elon (2015), Hofstra (2002), James Madison (1986), UNC Wilmington (1986), North-eastern (2006), Towson (2002), William & Mary (1986).
Associate Commissioner/Communications: Rob Washburn. **2018 Tournament:** Six teams, double-elimination. May 23-26 at Eagle Field at Veterans Memorial Park, Harrisonburg, Va.

CONFERENCE USA

Mailing Address: 5201 N. O'Connor Blvd., Suite 300, Irving, TX 75039. **Telephone:** (214) 774-1300. **Fax:** (214) 496-0055.
E-Mail Address: rdanderson@c-usa.org.
Website: www.conferenceusa.com.
Baseball Members (First Year): Alabama-Birmingham (1996), Charlotte (2014), Florida Atlantic (2014), Florida International (2014), Louisiana Tech (2014), Marshall (2006), Middle Tennessee State (2014), Old Dominion (2014), Rice (2006), Southern Mississippi (1996), Texas-San Antonio (2014), Western Kentucky (2015). **Assistant Commissioner, Baseball Operations:** Russell Anderson. **2018 Tournament:** Eight teams, double-elimination. May 23-27 at MGM Park, Biloxi, Miss.

HORIZON LEAGUE

Mailing Address: 201 S. Capitol Ave., Suite 500, Indianapolis, IN 46225. **Telephone:** (317) 237-5604. **Fax:** (317) 237-5620.
E-Mail Address: bpotter@horizonleague.org.
Website: www.horizonleague.org.
Baseball Members (First Year): Illinois-Chicago (1994), Northern Kentucky (2016), Oakland (2014), Wright State (1994), Wisconsin-Milwaukee (1994), Youngstown State (2002). **2018 Tournament:** Six teams, modified double-elimination. May 23-26, hosted by No. 1 seed.

IVY LEAGUE

Mailing Address: 228 Alexander Rd., Second Floor, Princeton, NJ 08544. **Telephone:** (609) 258-6426. **Fax:** (609) 258-1690.
E-Mail Address: trevor@ivyleaguesports.com.
Website: www ivyleaguesports.com.
Baseball Members (First Year): Rolfe—Brown (1948), Dartmouth (1930), Harvard (1948), Yale (1930). Gehrig—Columbia (1930), Cornell (1930), Pennsylvania (1930), Princeton (1930). **Assistant Executive Director, Communications/Championships:** Trevor Rutledge-Leverenz. **2018 Tournament:** Best-of-three series between division champions. Team with best Ivy League record hosts. May 19-20.

METRO ATLANTIC ATHLETIC CONFERENCE

Mailing Address: 712 Amboy Ave., Edison, NJ 08837. **Telephone:** (732) 738-5455.
E-Mail Address: sean.radu@maac.org.
Website: www.maacsports.com.
Baseball Members (First Year): Canisius (1990), Fairfield (1982), Iona (1982), Manhattan (1982), Marist (1998), Monmouth (2014), Niagara (1990), Quinnipiac (2014), Rider (1998), Saint Peter's (1982), Siena (1990). **Assistant Commissioner, New Media:** Lily Rodriguez. **Director, New Media (Baseball Contact):** Ruben Perez Jr. **2018 Tournament:** Six teams, double-elimination. May 22-27 at Richmond County Bank Ballpark, Staten Island, N.Y.

MID-AMERICAN CONFERENCE

Mailing Address: 24 Public Square, 15th Floor, Cleveland, OH 44113. **Telephone:** (216) 566-4622. **Fax:** (216) 858-9622.
E-Mail Address: jguy@mac-sports.com.
Website: www.mac-sports.com.
Baseball Members (First Year): Ball State (1973), Bowling Green State (1952), Central Michigan (1971), Eastern Michigan (1971), Kent State (1951), Miami (1947), Northern Illinois (1997), Ohio (1946), Toledo (1950), Western Michigan (1947). **Assistant Commissioner, Communications and Social Media:** Jeremy Guy. **2018 Tournament:** Eight teams, double-elimination. May 23-27 at Springer Stadium, Avon, Ohio.

MID-EASTERN ATHLETIC CONFERENCE

Mailing Address: 2730 Ellsmere Ave., Norfolk, VA 23513. **Telephone:** (757) 951-2055. **Fax:** (757) 951-2077.
E-Mail Address: brian.howard@themeac.com; porterp@themeac.com.
Website: www.meacsports.com.
Baseball Members (First Year): Bethune-Cookman (1979), Coppin State (1985), Delaware State (1970), Florida A&M (1979), Maryland Eastern Shore (1970), Norfolk State (1998), North Carolina A&T (1970), North Carolina Central (2012), Savannah State (2012). **Assistant Director, Media Relations/Baseball Contact:** Brian Howard. **2018 Tournament:** six-teams, double-elimination. May 16-19 at Jackie Robinson Stadium, Daytona Beach, Fla.

MISSOURI VALLEY CONFERENCE

Mailing Address: 1818 Chouteau Ave., St. Louis, MO 63103. **Telephone:** (314) 444-4300. **Fax:** (314) 444-4333.
E-Mail Address: kbriscoe@mvc.org.
Website: www.mvc-sports.com.
Baseball Members (First Year): Bradley (1955), Dallas Baptist (2014), Evansville (1994), Illinois State (1980), Indiana State (1976), Missouri State (1990), Southern Illinois (1974), Valparaiso (2018). **Assistant Commissioner, Communications:** Ashley Dickerson. **2018 Tournament:** Eight-teams, double-elimination. May 23-26 at Dallas.

MOUNTAIN WEST CONFERENCE

Mailing Address: 10807 New Allegiance Dr., Suite 250, Colorado Springs, CO 80921. **Telephone:** (719) 488-4052. **Fax:** (719) 487-7241.
E-Mail Address: jwillson@themw.com.
Website: www.themw.com.
Baseball Members (First Year): Air Force (2000), Fresno State (2013), Nevada (2013), Nevada-Las Vegas (2000), New Mexico (2000), San Diego State (2000), San Jose State (2014). **Associate Director, Communications:** Judy Willson. **2018 Tournament:** Four teams,

double-elimination. May 24-27 at Tony Gwynn Stadium, San Diego.

NORTHEAST CONFERENCE

Mailing Address: 200 Cottontail Lane, Vantage Court South, Somerset, NJ 08873. **Telephone:** (732) 469-0440. **Fax:** (732) 469-0744.

E-Mail Address: rventre@northeast conference.org. **Website:** www.northeastconference.org.

Baseball Members (First Year): Bryant (2010), Central Connecticut State (1999), Fairleigh Dickinson (1981), Long Island -Brooklyn (1981), Mount St. Mary's (1989), Sacred Heart (2000), Wagner (1981). **Director, Communications/ Social Media:** Ralph Ventre. **2018 Tournament:** Four teams, double-elimination. May 24-27 at Dodd Stadium, Norwich, Conn.

OHIO VALLEY CONFERENCE

Mailing Address: 215 Centerview Dr., Suite 115, Brentwood, TN 37027. **Telephone:** (615) 371-1698. **Fax:** (615) 891-1682.

E-Mail Address: kschwartz@ovc.org. **Website:** www.ovcsports.com.

Baseball Members (First Year): Austin Peay State (1962), Belmont (2013), Eastern Illinois (1996), Eastern Kentucky (1948), Jacksonville State (2003), Morehead State (1948), Murray State (1948), Southeast Missouri State (1991), Southern Illinois-Edwardsville (2012), Tennessee-Martin (1992), Tennessee Tech (1949). **Assistant Commissioner:** Kyle Schwartz. **2018 Tournament:** Eight teams. May 22-27 at Oxford, Ala.

PAC-12 CONFERENCE

Mailing Address: Pac-12 Conference 360 3rd Street, 3rd Floor San Francisco, CA 94107. **Telephone:** (415) 580-4200. **Fax:** (415)549-2828.

E-Mail Address: jolivero@pac-12.org. **Website:** www.pac-12.com.

Baseball Members (First Year): Arizona (1979), Arizona State (1979), California (1916), UCLA (1928), Oregon (2009) Oregon State (1916), Southern California (1923), Stanford (1918), Utah (2012), Washington (1916), Washington State (1919). **Public Relations Contact:** Jon Olivero. **2018 Tournament:** None.

PATRIOT LEAGUE

Mailing Address: 3773 Corporate Pkwy., Suite 190, Center Valley, PA 18034. **Telephone:** (610) 289-1950. **Fax:** (610) 289-1951.

E-Mail Address: mdougherty@patriotleague.com. **Website:** www.patriotleague.org.

Baseball Members (First Year): Army (1993), Bucknell (1991), Holy Cross (1991), Lafayette (1991), Lehigh (1991), Navy (1993). **Assistant Executive Director, Communications:** Matt Dougherty. **2018 Tournament:** Four teams, best-of-three semifinals May 12-13 and best-of-three finals May 18-20 at higher seeds.

SOUTHEASTERN CONFERENCE

Mailing Address: 2201 Richard Arrington Blvd. N., Birmingham, AL 35203. **Telephone:** (205) 458-3000. **Fax:** (205) 458-3030.

E-Mail Address: scartell@sec.org. **Website:** www.secsports.com.

Baseball Members (First Year): East Division— Florida (1933), Georgia (1933), Kentucky (1933), Missouri (2013), South Carolina (1992), Tennessee (1933), Vander-

bilt (1933). **West Division—**Alabama (1933), Arkansas (1992), Auburn (1933), Louisiana State (1933), Mississippi (1933), Mississippi State (1933), Texas A&M (2013). **Director, Communications:** Chuck Dunlap. **2018 Tournament:** 12 teams, modified single/double-elimination. May 22-27 at Hoover, Ala.

SOUTHERN CONFERENCE

Mailing Address: 702 N. Pine St., Spartanburg, SC 29303. **Telephone:** (864) 591-5100. **Fax:** (864) 591-3448. **E-Mail Address:** pperry@socon.org. **Website:** www.soconsports.com.

Baseball Members (First Year): The Citadel (1937), East Tennessee State (1979-2005, 2015), Furman (1937), Mercer (2015), UNC Greensboro (1998), Samford (2009), VMI (1925-2003, 2015), Western Carolina (1977), Wofford (1998). **Media Relations:** Phil Perry. **2018 Tournament:** Nine teams, single-game play-in for bottom two seeds, followed by double-elimination bracket play. May 22-27 at Fluor Field, Greenville, S.C.

SOUTHLAND CONFERENCE

Mailing Address: 2600 Network Blvd, Suite 150, Frisco, Texas 75034. **Telephone:** (972) 422-9500. **Fax:** (972) 422-9225.

E-Mail Address: mcebold@southland.org **Website:** southland.org.

Baseball Members (First Year): Abilene Christian (2014), Central Arkansas (2007), Houston Baptist (2014), Incarnate Word (2014), Lamar (1999), McNeese State (1973), New Orleans (2014), Nicholls State (1992), Northwestern State (1988), Sam Houston State (1988), Southeastern Louisiana (1998), Stephen F. Austin State (2006), Texas A&M-Corpus Christi (2007). **Baseball Contact/ Assistant Director:** Melissa Cebold. **2018 Tournament:** Two four-team brackets, double-elimination. May 23-26 at Constellation Field, Sugar Land, Texas.

SOUTHWESTERN ATHLETIC CONFERENCE

Mailing Address: 2101 6th Ave. North, Suite 700, Birmingham, AL 35203. **Telephone:** (205) 251-7573. **Fax:** (205) 297-9820.

E-Mail Address: j.jones@swac.org. **Website:** www.swac.org.

Baseball Members (First Year): East Division—Alabama A&M (2000), Alabama State (1982), Alcorn State (1962), Jackson State (1958), Mississippi Valley State (1968). **West Division—**Arkansas-Pine Bluff (1999), Grambling State (1958), Prairie View A&M (1920), Southern (1934), Texas Southern (1954). **Director, Communications:** Bridgette Robles. **2018 Tournament:** Eight teams, double-elimination. May 16-20 at Wesley Barrow Stadium, New Orleans, La.

SUMMIT LEAGUE

Mailing Address: 340 W. Butterfield Rd., Suite 3D, Elmhurst, IL 60126. **Telephone:** (630) 516-0661. **Fax:** (630) 516-0673.

E-Mail Address: mette@thesummitleague.org. **Website:** www.thesummitleague.org.

Baseball Members (First Year): IPFW (2008), Nebraska-Omaha (2013), North Dakota State (2008), Oral Roberts (1998), South Dakota State (2008), Western Illinois (1984). **Associate Director, Communications (Baseball Contact):** Greg Mette. **2018 Tournament:** Four teams, double-elimination. May 23-26 at J.L. Johnson Stadium, Tulsa, Okla.

SUN BELT CONFERENCE

Mailing Address: 1500 Sugar Bowl Dr., New Orleans, LA 70112. **Telephone:** (504) 556-0884. **Fax:** (504) 299-9068.
E-Mail Address: nunez@sunbeltsports.org.
Website: www.sunbeltsports.org.
Baseball Members (First Year): East Division—Appalachian State (2015), Coastal Carolina (2017), Georgia Southern, (2015), Georgia State (2014), South Alabama (1976), Troy (2006). **West Division**—Arkansas-Little Rock (1991), Arkansas State (1991), Louisiana-Lafayette (1991), Louisiana-Monroe (2007), Texas-Arlington (2014), Texas State (2014). **Assistant Director, Communications:** Keith Nunez. **2018 Tournament:** Eight teams, double-elimination. May 22-27 at Lafayette, La.

WESTERN ATHLETIC CONFERENCE

Mailing Address: 9250 East Costilla Ave., Suite 300, Englewood, CO 80112. **Telephone:** (303) 799-9221.
Fax: (303) 799-3888.
E-Mail Address: cthompson@wac.org.
Website: www.wacsports.com.
Baseball Members (First Year): Cal State Bakersfield (2013), Chicago State (2014), Grand Canyon (2014), New Mexico State (2006), Northern Colorado (2014), Sacramento State (2006), Seattle (2013), Texas-Rio Grande Valley (2014), Utah Valley (2014). **Commissioner:** Jeff Hurd. **Associate Commissioner:** Dave Chaffin. **Director, Media Relations:** Chris Thompson. **2018 Tournament:** Six teams, double-elimination, May 23-26/27 at Hohokam Stadium, Mesa, Ariz.

WEST COAST CONFERENCE

Mailing Address: 1111 Bayhill Dr., Suite 405, San Bruno, CA 94066. **Telephone:** (650) 873-8622. **Fax:** (650) 873-7846. **E-Mail Addresses:** rmccrary@westcoast.org (primary), jtourial@westcoast.org (secondary).
Website: www.wccsports.com.
Baseball Members (First Year): Brigham Young (2012), Gonzaga (1996), Loyola Marymount (1968), Pacific (2014), Pepperdine (1968), Portland (1996), Saint Mary's (1968), San Diego (1979), San Francisco (1968), Santa Clara (1968). **Senior Director, Communications:** Ryan McCrary. **Associate Commissioner, Broadcast Administration/Strategic Communications:** Jeff Tourial. **2018 Tournament:** Four teams, May 24-26 at Banner Island Ballpark, Stockton, Calif.

NCAA DIVISION I TEAMS
* Denotes recruiting coordinator

ABILENE CHRISTIAN WILDCATS

Conference: Southland.
Mailing Address: ACU Box 27916 Abilene, TX 79699.
Website: www.acusports.com.
Head Coach: Britt Bonneau. **Telephone:** (325) 674-2325. **Baseball SID:** Lance Fleming. **Telephone:** (325) 674-2693. **Fax:** (325) 674-6798.
Assistant Coaches: *Greg Evans, Brad Flanders.
Telephone: (325) 674-2817.
Home Field: Crutcher Scott Field. **Seating Capacity:** 4,000. **Outfield Dimension: LF**—334, **CF**—400, **RF**—334.

AIR FORCE FALCONS

Conference: Mountain West.
Mailing Address: 2169 Field House Drive, USAF Academy, CO 80840. **Website:** www.goairforcefalcons.com.

Head Coach: Mike Kazlausky (Maj. retired).
Telephone: (719-333-0835). **Baseball SID:** Nick Arseniak.
Telephone: (719) 333-8286.
Assistant Coaches: Blake Miller, C.J. Gillman.
Telephone: (719) 333-7539.
Home Field: Falcon Field . **Seating Capacity:** 1,000.
Outfield Dimension: LF—349 , **CF**—400, **RF**—315.

ALABAMA CRIMSON TIDE

Conference: Southeastern.
Mailing Address: 1201 Coliseum Drive, Tuscaloosa, AL 35401. **Website:** www.RollTide.com.
Head Coach: Brad Bohannon. **Telephone:** (205) 348-2427. **Baseball SID:** Alex Thompson. **Telephone:** (205) 348-6084.
Assistant Coaches: Jason Jackson, *Jerry Zulli .
Telephone: (205) 348-4029.
Home Field: Sewell Thomas Stadium. **Seating Capacity:** 8,500. **Outfield Dimension: LF**—325, **CF**—390, **RF**—320.

ALABAMA A&M BULLDOGS

Conference: Southwestern Athletic.
Mailing Address: 4900 Meridian Street, PO Box 1597, Normal, AL 35762. **Website:** www.aamusports.com.
Head Coach: Mitch Hill. **Telephone:** (256) 372-4004.
Baseball SID: Bud McLaughlin . **Telephone:** (256) 372-4005.
Assistant Coaches: Manny Lora. **Telephone:** 256-372-7213.
Home Field: Bulldog Baseball Field. **Seating Capacity:** 500. **Outfield Dimension: LF**—330, **CF**—402, **RF**—318.

ALABAMA STATE HORNETS

Conference: Southwestern Athletic
Mailing Address: 915 Jackson Street, Montgomery, AL, 36104 . **Website:** www.bamastatesports.com.
Head Coach: Jose Vazquez. **Telephone:** (334) 229-5600 . **Baseball SID:** Brian Howard . **Telephone:** (334) 229-5217.
Assistant Coaches: Drew Clark*, Matt Crane.
Telephone: 334-229-5607.
Home Field: Wheeler-Watkins Complex. **Seating Capacity:** 1,000. **Outfield Dimension: LF**—330, **CF**—400, **RF**—330.

ALABAMA-BIRMINGHAM BLAZERS

Conference: Conference USA.
Mailing Address: 617 13th Street South Birmingham, AL, 35294. **Website:** www.uabsports.com.
Head Coach: Brian Shoop. **Telephone:** (205) 934-5181. **Baseball SID:** Abby Vinson. **Telephone:** (205) 934-0722.
Assistant Coaches: Josh Hopper, *Perry Roth.
Telephone: (205) 934-5182.
Home Field: Young Memorial Field. **Seating Capacity:** 1000. **Outfield Dimension: LF**—330, **CF**—400, **RF**—330.

ALBANY GREAT DANES

Conference: America East.
Mailing Address: 1400 Washington Avenue Albany, NY 12222. **Website:** www.ualbanysports.com.
Head Coach: Jon Mueller. **Baseball SID:** John Reilly.
Telephone: (518) 442-5733.
Assistant Coaches: *Jeff Kaier, Paul Panik.
Home Field: Varsity Field. **Outfield Dimension: LF**—330, **CF**—400, **RF**—330.

ALCORN STATE BRAVES

Conference: Southwestern Athletic.
Mailing Address: 1000 ASU Drive #510, Lorman, MS 39096. **Website:** www.alcornsports.com.
Head Coach: Bretton Richardson. **Telephone:** (601) 877-4090. **Baseball SID:** Robbie Kleinmuntz. **Telephone:** (601) 877-2322.
Assistant Coaches: David Duncan.
Home Field: McGowan Stadium.

APPALACHIAN STATE MOUNTAINEERS

Conference: Sun Belt.
Mailing Address: 425 Jack Branch Dr. Boone, N.C., 28608. **Website:** www.appstatesports.com.
Head Coach: Kermit Smith. **Baseball SID:** Bret Strelow. **Telephone:** (828) 262-7162.
Assistant Coaches: Justin Aspegren, *Britt Johnson. **Telephone:** 828-262-8664.
Home Field: Beaver Field at Jim and Bettie Smith. **Seating Capacity:** 827. **Outfield Dimension: LF**—330, **CF**—400, **RF**—330.

ARIZONA WILDCATS

Conference: Pac-12.
Mailing Address: 1 National Championship Dr. Tucson, AZ, 85721. **Website:** www.arizonaathletics.com.
Head Coach: Jay Johnson. **Telephone:** (520) 621-8808. **Baseball SID:** Daniel Berk. **Telephone:** (520) 621-1814.
Assistant Coaches: *Sergio Brown, Dave Lawn. **Telephone:** (520) 621-5793.
Home Field: Hi Corbett Field. **Seating Capacity:** 9,500. **Outfield Dimension: LF**—366, **CF**—410, **RF**—349.

ARIZONA STATE SUN DEVILS

Conference: Pac-12.
Mailing Address: 5999 E. Van Buren Phoenix AZ. **Website:** www.thesundevils.com.
Head Coach: Tracy Smith. **Telephone:** (480) 965-1904. **Baseball SID:** Jeremy Hawkes. **Telephone:** (520) 403-0121.
Assistant Coaches: Mike Cather, *Ben Greenspan. **Telephone:** (480) 965-5060.
Home Field: Phoenix Municipal Stadium. **Seating Capacity:** 8,775. **Outfield Dimension: LF**—345, **CF**—410, **RF**—345.

ARKANSAS RAZORBACKS

Conference: Southeastern.
Mailing Address: 1240 W. Leroy Pond Drive, Fayetteville, AR, 72701. **Website:** www.arkansasrazorbacks.com.
Head Coach: Dave Van Horn. **Telephone:** (479) 575-3655. **Baseball SID:** John Thomas. **Telephone:** (479) 575-7430. **Fax:** (479) 575-4781.
Assistant Coaches: Wes Johnson, *Nate Thompson. **Telephone:** (479) 575-3552.
Home Field: Baum Stadium. **Seating Capacity:** 10,737. **Outfield Dimension: LF**—320, **CF**—400, **RF**—320.

ARKANSAS STATE RED WOLVES

Conference: Sun Belt.
Mailing Address: 228 Broyles Center, PO Box 7777, Fayetteville, AR 72701. **Website:** www.astateredwolves.com.
Head Coach: Tommy Raffo. **Telephone:** (870) 972-

2700 . **Baseball SID:**.Dennen Cuthbertson. **Telephone:** (870) 972-3383.
Assistant Coaches: *Rick Guarno, Rowdy Hardy. **Telephone:** (972) 680-4338.
Home Field: Tomlinson Stadium. **Seating Capacity:** 1,200. **Outfield Dimension: LF**—335, **CF**—400, **RF**—335.

ARKANSAS-LITTLE ROCK TROJANS

Conference: Sun Belt.
Mailing Address: 2801 south university drive, Little Rock Arkansas 72204. **Website:** www.ualrtrojans.com.
Head Coach: Chris Curry. **Telephone:** (501) 663-8095. **Baseball SID:** Tyler Morrison. **Telephone:** (501) 683-7003.
Assistant Coaches: Noah Sanders, *Mike Silva. **Telephone:** (501) 280-0759.
Home Field: Gary Hogan Field. **Seating Capacity:** 1,000. **Outfield Dimension: LF**—325, **CF**—390, **RF**—305.

ARKANSAS-PINE BLUFF GOLDEN LIONS

Conference: Southwestern Athletic.
Website: www.uapblionsroar.com.
Head Coach: Carlos James. **Telephone:** (870) 575-8995. Baseball SID: Habtom Keleta. Telephone: (870) 575-7949.
Assistant Coaches: Trennis Grant, *Roger Mallison. **Telephone:** (870) 575-8995.
Home Field: Torii Hunter Baseball Complex. **Seating Capacity:** 1,500. **Outfield Dimension: LF**—330, **CF**—400, **RF**—330.

ARMY BLACK KNIGHTS

Conference: Patriot.
Mailing Address: 639 Howard Road, West Point, N.Y., 10996. **Website:** www.goarmysports.com.
Head Coach: Jim Foster. **Telephone:** (845) 938-5877. **Baseball SID:** Kat Castner. **Telephone:** (845) 938-7197. **Fax:** (845) 938-1725.
Assistant Coaches: *John Murphy, Jamie Pinzino. **Telephone:** (845) 938-5877.
Home Field: Johnson Stadium at Doubleday Field. **Seating Capacity:** 880. **Outfield Dimension: LF**—327, **CF**—400, **RF**—327.

AUBURN TIGERS

Conference: Southeastern.
Mailing Address: 351 South Donahue Drive Auburn, Ala. 36830. **Website:** www.auburntigers.com.
Head Coach: Butch Thompson. **Telephone:** (334) 844-4990. **Baseball SID:** George Nunnelley. **Telephone:** (334) 844-9656.
Assistant Coaches: Gabe Gross, *Karl Nonemaker. **Telephone:** (334) 844-4990.
Home Field: Samford Stadium-Hitchcock Field at Plainsman Park at. **Seating Capacity:** 4096. **Outfield Dimension: LF**—315, **CF**—385, **RF**—330.

AUSTIN PEAY STATE GOVERNORS

Conference: Ohio Valley.
Mailing Address: 601 College Street, Clarksville, TN 37044. **Website:** www.letsgopeay.com.
Head Coach: Travis Janssen. **Telephone:** (931) 221-6266. Baseball SID: Cody Bush. **Telephone:** (931) 221-7561.
Assistant Coaches: Greg Byron, *David Weber. **Telephone:** (931) 221-6392.
Home Field: Raymond C. Hand Park. **Seating Capacity:** 777. **Outfield Dimension: LF**—319, **CF**—392, **RF**—327.

BALL STATE CARDINALS

Conference: Mid-American.
Mailing Address: 2000 W. University Ave., Muncie, IN 47306. **Website:** www.ballstatesports.com.
Head Coach: Rich Maloney. **Telephone:** (765) 285-8911. **Baseball SID:** Michael Clark. **Telephone:** (765) 285-8904.
Assistant Coaches: *Scott French, Dustin Glant. **Telephone:** (765) 285-2862.
Home Field: First Merchants Ballpark Complex.
Seating Capacity: 1,500. **Outfield Dimension: LF**—325, **CF**—394, **RF**—325.

BAYLOR BEARS

Conference: Big 12.
Mailing Address: 1500 S. University Parks Dr., Waco, TX 76706. **Website:** www.baylorbears.com.
Head Coach: Steve Rodriguez. **Telephone:** (254) 710-3029. **Baseball SID:** Zach Peters. **Telephone:** (254) 710-3784. **Fax:** (254) 710-1369.
Assistant Coaches: Jon Strauss, *Mike Taylor. **Telephone:** (254) 710-3044.
Home Field: Baylor Ballpark. **Seating Capacity:** 5000.
Outfield Dimension: LF—330, **CF**—400, **RF**—330.

BELMONT BRUINS

Conference: Ohio Valley.
Mailing Address: 1900 Belmont Boulevard, Nashville, TN 37212. **Website:** www.belmontbruins.com.
Head Coach: Dave Jarvis. **Telephone:** (615) 460-6166. **Baseball SID:** Hannah Jo Riley. **Telephone:** (615) 460-8023. **Fax:** (615) 460-5584.
Assistant Coaches: Matt Barnett, *Aaron Smith. **Telephone:** (615) 460-5586.
Home Field: E.S. Rose Park. **Seating Capacity:** 500.
Outfield Dimension: LF—330, **CF**—400, **RF**—330.

BETHUNE-COOKMAN WILDCATS

Conference: Mid-Eastern.
Mailing Address: 640 Dr Mary McLeod Bethune Blvd, Daytona Beach, FL 32114. **Website:** www.bcuathletics.com
Head Coach: Barrett Shaft. **Telephone:** (386) 481-2241. **Baseball SID:** Bryan Harvey. **Telephone:** (386) 481-2206.
Assistant Coaches: Jason Bell. **Telephone:** (386) 481-2242.
Home Field: Jackie Robinson Ballpark. **Seating Capacity:** 6,000. **Outfield Dimension: LF**—318, **CF**—405, **RF**—325.

BINGHAMTON BEARCATS

Conference: America East.
Mailing Address: Binghamton University, PO Box 6000, Binghamton, NY, 13902. **Website:** www.bubearcats.com.
Head Coach: Tim Sinicki. **Telephone:** (607) 777-2525. **Baseball SID:** John Hartrick. **Telephone:** (607) 777-6800.
Assistant Coaches: Mike Folli, *Ryan Hurba. **Telephone:** (607) 777-4552.
Home Field: Bearcats Baseball Complex. **Seating Capacity:** 700. **Outfield Dimension: LF**—325, **CF**—390, **RF**—325.

BOSTON COLLEGE EAGLES

Conference: Atlantic Coast.
Mailing Address: 140 Commonwealth Ave. **Website:** www.bceagles.cstv.com.
Head Coach: Mike Gambino. **Telephone:** (617) 552-2674. **Baseball SID:** Zanna Ollove. **Telephone:** (617) 552-2004.
Assistant Coaches: *Greg Sullivan, Alex Trezza. **Telephone:** (617) 552-1131.
Home Field: Brighton Field. **Seating Capacity:** 2,500.
Outfield Dimension: LF—330, **CF**—400, **RF**—330.

BOWLING GREEN STATE FALCONS

Conference: Mid-American.
Mailing Address: 1610 Stadium Drive, Bowling Green Ohio 43403. **Website:** www.bgsufalcons.com.
Head Coach: Danny Schmitz. **Telephone:** (419) 372-7065. **Baseball SID:** James Nahikian. **Telephone:** (419) 372-7105.
Assistant Coaches: *Rick Blanc, Ryan Shay. **Telephone:** (419) 372-7641.
Home Field: Warren E. Steller. **Seating Capacity:** 1,100. **Outfield Dimension: LF**—345, **CF**—400, **RF**—345.

BRADLEY BRAVES

Conference: Missouri Valley.
Mailing Address: 1501 W. Bradley Avenue, Peoria, IL 61625. **Website:** www.bradleybraves.com.
Head Coach: Elvis Dominguez. **Telephone:** (309) 677-2671. **Baseball SID:** Bobby Parker. **Telephone:** (309) 677-2624. **Fax:** (309) 677-2626.
Assistant Coaches: *Larry Scully, Kyle Trewyn. **Telephone:** (309) 677-4583.
Home Field: Dozer Park. **Seating Capacity:** 7,500.
Outfield Dimension: LF—310, **CF**—400, **RF**—310.

BRIGHAM YOUNG COUGARS

Conference: West Coast.
Mailing Address: 111 Miller Park, Provo UT 84602. **Website:** www.byucougars.com.
Head Coach: Mike Littlewood. **Telephone:** (801) 422-5049. **Baseball SID:** Ralph Zobell. **Telephone:** (801) 422-9769.
Assistant Coaches: *Brent Haring, Trent Pratt. **Telephone:** (801) 422-5064.
Home Field: Miller Park. **Seating Capacity:** 2,500.
Outfield Dimension: LF—330, **CF**—400, **RF**—330.

BROWN BEARS

Conference: Ivy League.
Mailing Address: 235 Hope St. Box 1932, Providence, RI 02912. **Website:** www.brownbears.com.
Head Coach: Grant Achilles. **Telephone:** (401) 863-3090. **Baseball SID:** Eric Peterson. **Telephone:** (401) 863-7014.
Assistant Coaches: Jonathan Grosse, *Mike McCormack. **Telephone:** (401) 863-1310.
Home Field: Murray Stadium. **Seating Capacity:** 1,500. **Outfield Dimension: LF**—330, **CF**—415, **RF**—320.

BRYANT BULLDOGS

Conference: Northeast.
Mailing Address: 1150 Douglas Pike Smithfield, RI 02917. **Website:** www.bryantbulldogs.com.
Head Coach: Steve Owens. **Telephone:** (401) 232-6397. **Baseball SID:** Tristan Hobbes.

Telephone: (401) 232-6558.
Assistant Coaches: *Brendan Monaghan, Kyle Pettoruto. **Telephone:** (401) 232-6967.
Home Field: Conaty Park. **Seating Capacity:** 300.
Outfield Dimension: LF—330, **CF**—400, **RF**—330.

BUCKNELL BISON

Conference: Patriot.
Mailing Address: 1 Dent Drive Drive, Lewisburg, PA 17837. **Website:** www.bucknellbison.com.
Head Coach: Scott Heather. **Telephone:** (570) 577-3593. **Baseball SID:** Christian Rauch. **Telephone:** (570) 577-1227.
Assistant Coaches: C.J. Baker, *Jason Neitz. **Telephone:** (570) 577-1059.
Home Field: Depew Field. **Seating Capacity:** 300.
Outfield Dimension: LF— 330, **CF**— 400, **RF**— 330.

BUTLER BULLDOGS

Conference: Big East.
Mailing Address: 4600 Sunset Avenue, Indianapolis, IN 46208. **Website:** www.butlersports.com.
Head Coach: Dave Schrage. **Telephone:** (317) 940-9721. **Baseball SID:** Kit Stetzel. **Telephone:** (317) 940-9994.
Assistant Coaches: Ben Norton, *Andy Pascoe. **Telephone:** (317) 940-6536.
Home Field: Bulldog Park. **Seating Capacity:** 500.
Outfield Dimension: LF—330. **CF**—400. **RF**—300.

CAL POLY MUSTANGS

Conference: Big West.
Mailing Address: 1 Grand Avenue, San Luis Obispo, CA 93407-0388. **Website:** www.gopoly.com.
Head Coach: Larry Lee. **Telephone:** (805) 756-6367.
Baseball SID: Eric Burdick. **Telephone:** (805) 756-6550.
Fax: (805) 756-7255.
Assistant Coaches: Chal Fanning, *Teddy Warrecker. **Telephone:** (805) 756-1201.
Home Field: Baggett Stadium. **Seating Capacity:** 2800. **Outfield Dimension: LF**—335, **CF**—405, **RF**—335.

CAL STATE BAKERSFIELD ROADRUNNERS

Conference: Western Athletic.
Mailing Address: 9001 Stockdale Highway, Bakersfield, CA 93311. **Website:** www.gorunners.com.
Head Coach: Jeremy Beard. **Telephone:** (661) 654-2678. **Baseball SID:** Isaac Comelli. **Telephone:** (661) 654-3071. **Fax:** (661) 654-6978.
Assistant Coaches: Ryan Cisterna, Jonathan Johnson. **Telephone:** (661) 654-2678.
Home Field: Hardt Field. **Seating Capacity:** 2,000.
Outfield Dimension: LF—325, **CF**—390, **RF**—325.

CAL STATE FULLERTON TITANS

Conference: Big West.
Mailing Address: 800 N. State College Blvd., Fullerton, CA 92834. **Website:** www.fullertontitans.com.
Head Coach: Rick Vanderhook. **Telephone:** (657) 278-3780. **Baseball SID:** Derrick Fazendin. **Telephone:** (657) 278-3970.
Assistant Coaches: *Chad Baum, Steven Rousey. **Telephone:** (657) 278-2492.
Home Field: Goodwin Field. **Seating Capacity:** 3,500.
Outfield Dimension: LF—330, **CF**—400, **RF**—330.

CAL STATE NORTHRIDGE MATADORS

Conference: Big West.
Mailing Address: 18111 Nordhoff St., Northridge, CA 91330. **Website:** www.gomatadors.cstv.com.
Head Coach: Greg Moore. **Telephone:** (818) 677-7055.
Baseball SID: Nick Bocanegra. **Telephone:** (818) 677-7188. **Fax:** (818) 677-2661.
Assistant Coaches: Tony Asaro, *Chris Hom. **Telephone:** (818) 677-3218.
Home Field: Matador Field. **Seating Capacity:** 1,000.
Outfield Dimension: LF—325, **CF**—390, **RF**—325.

CALIFORNIA GOLDEN BEARS

Conference: Pac-12.
Mailing Address: Haas Pavilion #4422, Berkeley, CA 94720-4422. **Website:** www.calbears.com.
Head Coach: Mike Neu. **Telephone:** (510) 643-6006.
Baseball SID: Ben Enos. **Telephone:** (510) 643-1741. **Fax:** (510) 642-6807.
Assistant Coaches: *Noah Jackson, Pat Shine. **Telephone:** (510) 643-6006.
Home Field: Evans Diamond. **Seating Capacity:** 2,500. **Outfield Dimension: LF**—320, **CF**—395, **RF**—320.

CAMPBELL CAMELS

Conference: Big South.
Mailing Address: 79 Upchurch Ln, Buies Creek, NC 27506. **Website:** www.gocamels.com.
Head Coach: Justin Haire. **Telephone:** (910) 893-1338.
Baseball SID: None at this time.
Assistant Coaches: *Chris Marx, Jake Wells. **Telephone:** (910) 893-1354.
Home Field: Jim Perry Stadium. **Seating Capacity:** 1,500. **Outfield Dimension: LF**—337, **CF**—395, **RF**—328.

CANISIUS GOLDEN GRIFFINS

Conference: Metro Atlantic.
Mailing Address: 1829 Main St, Buffalo, NY 14208. **Website:** www.gogriffs.com.
Head Coach: Matt Mazurek. **Telephone:** (716) 888-8479. **Baseball SID:** Tyler DeGiacomo. **Telephone:** (716) 888-8473.
Assistant Coaches: Brandon Bielecki. **Telephone:** (716) 888-8485.
Home Field: Demske Sports Complex. **Seating Capacity:** 2,000. **Outfield Dimension: LF**—327, **CF**—378, **RF**—315.

CENTRAL ARKANSAS BEARS

Conference: Southland.
Mailing Address: 201 Donaghey Ave, Conway, AR 72035. **Website:** www.ucasports.com.
Head Coach: Allen Gum. **Telephone:** (501) 499-1707.
Baseball SID: Steve East. **Telephone:** (501) 450-5743.
Fax: (501) 450-3151.
Assistant Coaches: Nick Harlan, *Jon Ubbenga. **Telephone:** (501) 450-3407.
Home Field: Bear Stadium. **Seating Capacity:** 1,500.
Outfield Dimension: LF—330, **CF**—400, **RF**—330.

CENTRAL CONNECTICUT STATE BLUE DEVILS

Conference: Northeast.
Mailing Address: 1615 Stanley Street, New Britain, CT 06050. **Website:** www.ccsubluedevils.com.
Head Coach: Charlie Hickey. **Telephone:** (860) 832-3074. **Baseball SID:** Jeff Mead. **Telephone:** (860) 832-3057.

Assistant Coaches: *Pat Hall, Jim Ziogas. Telephone: (860) 832-3579.
Home Field: CCSU Baseball Field. Seating Capacity: 500. Outfield Dimension: LF—330, CF—400, RF—315.

CENTRAL FLORIDA KNIGHTS

Conference: American Athletic.
Mailing Address: UCF Athletics UCF Spectrum Stadium 4465 Knights Victory Way Orlando, FL 32816.
Website: www.ucfathletics.com.
Head Coach: Greg Lovelady. Telephone: (407) 823-4869. Baseball SID: Ian MacDougall. Telephone: (407) 823-5395. Fax: (407) 823-5293.
Assistant Coaches: *Ryan Klosterman, Justin Parker.
Home Field: John Euliano Park. Seating Capacity: 3,700. Outfield Dimension: LF—320, CF—390, RF—320.

CENTRAL MICHIGAN CHIPPEWAS

Conference: Mid-American.
Mailing Address: Rose 120, Mt. Pleasant, MI 48859. www.cmuchippewas.com.
Head Coach: Steve Jaksa. Telephone: (989) 774-4392. Baseball SID: Andy Sneddon. Telephone: (989) 774-3277. Fax: (989) 774-5391.
Assistant Coaches: *Jeff Opalewski, Doug Sanders. Telephone: (989) 774-2123.
Home Field: Theunissen Stadium. Seating Capacity: 2,046. Outfield Dimension: LF—330, CF—400, RF—330.

CHARLESTON SOUTHERN BUCCANEERS

Conference: Big South.
Mailing Address: 9200 University Blvd, North Charleston, S.C 29406. Website: www.csusports.com.
Head Coach: Adam Ward. Telephone: (843) 863-7591. Baseball SID: Seth Montgomery. Telephone: (843) 863-7853.
Assistant Coaches: Zack Hagaman, *George Schaefer. Telephone: (843) 863-7832.
Home Field: CSU Ballpark. Seating Capacity: 1,500. Outfield Dimension: LF—320, CF—395, RF—325.

CHARLOTTE 49ERS

Conference: Conference USA.
Mailing Address: 9201 University City Blvd., Charlotte, NC 28223. Website: www.charlotte49ers.com.
Head Coach: Loren Hibbs. Telephone: (704) 687-0726. Baseball SID: Sean Fox. Telephone: (704) 687-1023. Fax: (704) 687-4918.
Assistant Coaches: Shohn Doty, *Bo Robinson. Telephone: (704) 687-0727.
Home Field: Hayes Stadium. Seating Capacity: 1,200.

CHICAGO STATE COUGARS

Conference: Western Athletic.
Mailing Address: JCC 1502, 9501 South King Drive, Chicago, IL 60628. Website: www.gocsucougars.com.
Head Coach: Steve Joslyn. Telephone: (773) 995-3637. Baseball SID: Corey Miggins. Telephone: (773) 995-2217.
Assistant Coaches: David Harden, Kellon McFarlin.
Home Field: Cougar Stadium. Seating Capacity: 200. Outfield Dimension: LF—330, CF—400, RF—330.

CINCINNATI BEARCATS

Conference: American Athletic.
Mailing Address: 2751 O'Varsity Way, Cincinnati, OH 45221. Website: www.gobearcats.com.
Head Coach: Scott Googins. Telephone: (513) 556-0566. Baseball SID: Mollie Radzinski. Telephone: (513) 556-0667.
Assistant Coaches: *JD Heilmann, Kyle Sprague. Telephone: (513) 556-0565.
Home Field: Marge Schott Stadium. Seating Capacity: 3,085. Outfield Dimension: LF—325, CF—400, RF—325.

CITADEL BULLDOGS

Conference: Southern.
Mailing Address: 171 Moultrie St., Charleston, SC, 29409. Website: www.citadelsports.com.
Head Coach: Tony Skole. Baseball SID: Zeke Beam. Telephone: (843) 953-6795.
Assistant Coaches: Blake Cooper, *Aaron Gershenfeld.
Home Field: Joseph. P Riley Park. Seating Capacity: 6,000. Outfield Dimension: LF—337, CF—398, RF—337.

CLEMSON TIGERS

Conference: Atlantic Coast.
Mailing Address: 100 Perimeter Road, Clemson, SC 29633. Website: www.clemsontigers.com.
Head Coach: Monte Lee. Telephone: (864) 656-1947. Baseball SID: Brian Hennessy. Telephone: (864) 656-1921.
Assistant Coaches: *Bradley LeCroy, Andrew See. Telephone: (864) 656-1948.
Home Field: Doug Kingsmore Stadium. Seating Capacity: 6,272. Outfield Dimension: LF—310, CF—390, RF—320.

COASTAL CAROLINA CHANTICLEERS

Conference: Sun Belt.
Mailing Address: PO Box 261954, Conway, SC 29528. Website: .
Head Coach: Gary Gilmore. Telephone: (843) 349-2816. Baseball SID: Mike Cawood. Telephone: (843) 349-2822. Fax: (843) 349-2819.
Assistant Coaches: *Kevin Schnall, Drew Thomas.
Home Field: Spring Brooks Stadium. Seating Capacity: 5,400. Outfield Dimension: LF—320, CF—390, RF—320.

COLLEGE OF CHARLESTON COUGARS

Conference: Colonial Athletic.
Mailing Address: 66 George Street, Charleston, SC 29424. Website: www.cofcsports.com.
Head Coach: Chad Holbrook. Telephone: (843) 953-5961. Baseball SID: Whitney Noble. Telephone: (843) 953-3683.
Assistant Coaches: Kevin Nichols, *Jim Toman. Telephone: (843) 953-7013.
Home Field: The Ball Park at Patriots Point. Seating Capacity: 2,000. Outfield Dimension: LF—300, CF—400, RF—330.

COLUMBIA LIONS

Conference: Ivy League.
Mailing Address: The Campbell Sports Center/Baker Athletics Complex 505 West 218th Street New York, N.Y. 10034. Website: www.gocolumbialions.com.
Head Coach: Brett Boretti. Telephone: (212) 854-8448. Baseball SID: Mike Kowalsky. Telephone: (212) 854-7064.
Assistant Coaches: Erik Supplee, *Dan Tischler. Telephone: (212) 854-7772.

Home Field: Robertson Field at Satow Stadium. **Seating Capacity:** 600.

CONNECTICUT HUSKIES

Conference: American Athletic.
Mailing Address: 2095 Hillside Rd Unit 1173, Storrs, CT 06269. **Website:** www.uconnhuskies.com.
Head Coach: Jim Penders. **Telephone:** (860) 208-9140. **Baseball SID:** Chris Jones. **Telephone:** (860) 486-3531.
Assistant Coaches: Jeff Hourigan, *Joshua McDonald. **Telephone:** (860) 465-6088.
Home Field: J.O. Christian Field. **Seating Capacity:** 2,000. **Outfield Dimension: LF**—337, **CF**—400, **RF**—325.

COPPIN STATE EAGLES

Conference: Mid-Eastern.
Mailing Address: 2500 W. North Avenue Baltimore, MD 21216. **Website:** www.coppinstatesports.com.
Head Coach: Sherman Reed. **Telephone:** (410) 951-3723. **Baseball SID:** Steve Kramer. **Telephone:** (410) 951-3729. **Fax:** (410) 951-3717.
Assistant Coaches: *Matthew Greely, Lyndon Watkins. **Telephone:** (410) 951-6941.
Home Field: Joe Cannon Stadium. **Seating Capacity:** 1500. **Outfield Dimension: LF**—310, **CF**—410, **RF**—310.

CORNELL BIG RED

Conference: Ivy League.
Mailing Address: Teagle Hall, Campus Rd. Ithaca, NY 14853. **Website:** www.cornellbigred.com.
Head Coach: Dan Pepicelli. **Telephone:** (607) 255-3812. **Baseball SID:** Brandon Thomas. **Telephone:** (607) 255-5627.
Assistant Coaches: Tom Ford, *Frank Hager. **Telephone:** (607) 255-6604.
Home Field: Hoy Field. **Seating Capacity:** 1,000. **Outfield Dimension: LF**—315, **CF**—400, **RF**—325.

CREIGHTON BLUEJAYS

Conference: Big East.
Mailing Address: 2500 California Plaza, Athletic Department, Omaha, NE 68178. **Website:** www.go creighton.com.
Head Coach: Ed Servais. **Telephone:** (402) 280-2483. **Baseball SID:** Glen Sisk. **Telephone:** (402) 280-2433.
Assistant Coaches: *Connor Gandossy, Eric Wordekemper. **Telephone:** (402) 280-5545.
Home Field: TD Ameritrade Park Omaha. **Seating Capacity:** 24,000. **Outfield Dimension: LF**—335, **CF**—408, **RF**—335.

DALLAS BAPTIST PATRIOTS

Conference: Missouri Valley.
Mailing Address: 3000 Mountain Creek Pkwy. Dallas, TX 75231. **Website:** www.dbupatriots.com.
Head Coach: Dan Heefner. **Telephone:** (214) 333-5324. **Baseball SID:** Reagan Ratcliff. **Telephone:** (214) 333-5942.
Assistant Coaches: *Dan Fitzgerald, Rick McCarty. **Telephone:** (214) 333-5324.
Home Field: Horner Ballpark. **Seating Capacity:** 2,000. **Outfield Dimension: LF**—330, **CF**—390, **RF**—330.

DARTMOUTH BIG GREEN

Conference: Ivy League.
Mailing Address: 6083 Alumni Gym, Hanover, NH 03755. **Website:** www.dartmouthsports.com.

Head Coach: Bob Whalen. **Telephone:** (603) 646-2477. **Baseball SID:** Rick Bender. **Telephone:** (603) 646-1030. **Fax:** (603) 646-3348.
Assistant Coaches: *Jonathan Anderson, Andy Revell. **Telephone:** (603) 646-9775.
Home Field: Red Rolfe Field at Biondi Park. **Seating Capacity:** 2,000. **Outfield Dimension: LF**—324, **CF**—403, **RF**—342.

DAVIDSON WILDCATS

Conference: Atlantic 10.
Mailing Address: Box 7158, Davidson, NC 28035. **Website:** www.davidsonwildcats.com.
Head Coach: Dick Cooke. **Telephone:** (937) 229-2368. **Baseball SID:** Caitie Smith. **Telephone:** (704) 894-2931.
Assistant Coaches: Rucker Taylor. **Telephone:** (937) 229-2772.
Home Field: Wilson Field. **Seating Capacity:** 700. **Outfield Dimension: LF**—320, **CF**—385, **RF**—320.

DAYTON FLYERS

Conference: Atlantic 10.
Mailing Address: 300 College Park, Dayton, OH 45469. **Website:** www.daytonflyers.com.
Head Coach: Jayson King. **Telephone:** (937) 229-4456. **Baseball SID:** Ross Bagienski. **Telephone:** (937) 229-4431. **Fax:** (937) 229-4461.
Assistant Coaches: *Tommy Chase, Travis Ferrick. **Telephone:** (937) 229-4465.
Home Field: Woerner Field. **Seating Capacity:** 2,000. **Outfield Dimension: LF**—330, **CF**—400, **RF**—330.

DELAWARE BLUE HENS

Conference: Colonial.
Mailing Address: 621 S. College Ave, Newark, Del. 19711. **Website:** www.bluehens.com.
Head Coach: Jim Sherman. **Telephone:** (302) 831-8596. **Baseball SID:** Andrew Stern. **Telephone:** (302) 831-6519. **Fax:** (302) 831-7206.
Assistant Coaches: Dan Hammer, *Troy O'Neal. **Telephone:** (302) 831-2723.
Home Field: Bob Hannah Stadium. **Seating Capacity:** 1300. **Outfield Dimension: LF**—320, **CF**—400, **RF**—330.

DELAWARE STATE HORNETS

Conference: Mid-Eastern Athletic.
Mailing Address: 1200 North DuPont Highway, Dover, DE. **Website:** www.dsuhornets.com.
Head Coach: J.P. Blandin. **Telephone:** (302) 857-6035. **Baseball SID:** Derrick Slayton. **Telephone:** (302) 857-6239.
Assistant Coaches: Sam Barber. **Telephone:** (302) 857-7809.
Home Field: Soldier Field. **Seating Capacity:** 500. **Outfield Dimension:** LF-320-, **CF**—380, **RF**—320.

DUKE BLUE DEVILS

Conference: Atlantic Coast.
Mailing Address: Duke University Athletics, PO Box 90555, Durham, NC 27708. **Website:** www.goduke.com.
Head Coach: Chris Pollard. **Telephone:** (919) 384-6172. **Baseball SID:** Ashley Wolf. **Telephone:** (919) 668-4393.
Assistant Coaches: *Josh Jordan, Jason Stein. **Home Field:** Durham Bulls Athletic Park. **Seating Capacity:** 10,000. **Outfield Dimension: LF**—305, **CF**—400, **RF**—325.

EAST CAROLINA PIRATES

Conference: American Athletic.
Mailing Address: E 5th St., Greenville, NC 27858.
Website: www.ecupirates.com.
Head Coach: Cliff Godwin. **Telephone:** (252) 737-1982. **Baseball SID:** Malcolm Gray. **Telephone:** (252) 737-4523.
Assistant Coaches: *Jeff Palumbo, Dan Roszel.
Telephone: (252) 737-1467.
Home Field: Lewis Field at Clark-LeClair Stadium.
Seating Capacity: 6,000. **Outfield Dimension:** LF—320, CF—400, RF—320.

EAST TENNESSEE STATE BUCCANEERS

Conference: Southern.
Mailing Address: 1081 John Robert Bell Dr., PO Box 70707, Johnson City, TN 37614.
Head Coach: Joe Pennucci. **Telephone:** (423) 439-4496. **Baseball SID:** Mike Ezekiel. **Telephone:** (423) 439-8212.
Assistant Coaches: *Ross Oeder, Micah Posey.
Telephone: (423) 439-4485.
Home Field: Thomas Stadium. **Seating Capacity:** 1,000. **Outfield Dimension:** LF—325, CF—400, RF—325.

EASTERN ILLINOIS PANTHERS

Conference: Ohio Valley.
Mailing Address: 600 Lincoln Ave., Charleston, IL 61920. **Website:** www.eiupanthers.com.
Head Coach: Jason Anderson. **Telephone:** (217) 581-7283. **Baseball SID:** Thomas Manzello. **Telephone:** (217) 581-6408.
Assistant Coaches: *Blake Beemer, Julio Godinez.
Telephone: (217) 581-7283.
Home Field: Coaches Stadium. **Seating Capacity:** 550. **Outfield Dimension:** LF—340, CF—390, RF—340.

EASTERN KENTUCKY COLONELS

Conference: Ohio Valley.
Mailing Address: 115 Alumni Coliseum, 521 Lancaster Ave., Richmond, KY 40475. **Website:** www.ekusports.com.
Head Coach: Edwin Thompson. **Telephone:** (859) 622-2128. **Baseball SID:** Kevin Britton. **Telephone:** (859) 622-2006.
Assistant Coaches: *Tyler Hanson, Adam Revelette.
Telephone: (859) 622-4996.
Home Field: Turkey Hughes Field at Earle Combs Stadium. **Seating Capacity:** 1,000. **Outfield Dimension:** LF—340, CF—410, RF—330.

EASTERN MICHIGAN EAGLES

Conference: Mid-American.
Mailing Address: 206 Bowen Field House, Ypsilanti MI 48197. **Website:** www.emueagles.com.
Head Coach: Eric Roof. **Telephone:** (734) 487-1985.
Baseball SID: Dan Whitaker. **Telephone:** (734) 487-0317.
Assistant Coaches: A.J. Achter, Spencer Schmitz.
Telephone: (734) 487-8660.
Home Field: Oestrike Stadium. **Seating Capacity:** 1,200. **Outfield Dimension:** LF—325 FT, CF—390 FT, RF—325

ELON PHOENIX

Conference: Colonial Athletic.
Mailing Address: 2500 Campus Box, 104 E. Haggard Ave., Elon NC 27244. **Website:** www.elonphoenix.com.

Head Coach: Mike Kennedy. **Telephone:** (336) 278-6741. **Baseball SID:** Chris Rash. **Telephone:** (336) 278-6710. **Fax:** (336) 278-6767.
Assistant Coaches: *Robbie Huffstetler, Sean McGrath. **Telephone:** (336) 278-6708.
Home Field: Latham Park. **Seating Capacity:** 2,000.
Outfield Dimension: LF—325, CF—385, RF—328.

EVANSVILLE PURPLE ACES

Conference: Missouri Valley.
Mailing Address: 1800 Lincoln Ave., Evansville, IN 47222. **Website:** www.gopurpleaces.com.
Head Coach: Wes Carroll. **Telephone:** (812) 488-2059.
Baseball SID: Clay Trainum. **Telephone:** (812) 488-2394.
Assistant Coaches: *Cody Fick, Jake Mahon.
Telephone: (812) 488-2764 .
Home Field: Charles H. Braun Stadium. **Seating Capacity:** 1,200. **Outfield Dimension:** LF—330, CF—400, RF—330.

FAIRFIELD STAGS

Conference: Metro Atlantic.
Mailing Address: 1073 North Benson Rd., Fairfield, CT 06824. **Website:** www.fairfieldstags.com.
Head Coach: Bill Currier. **Telephone:** (203) 254-4000.
Baseball SID: Ivey Speight. **Telephone:** (203) 254-4000.
Assistant Coaches: *Ted Hurvul, Kyle Nisson.
Home Field: Alumni Diamond. **Seating Capacity:** 400. **Outfield Dimension:** LF—320, CF—400, RF—325.

FAIRLEIGH DICKINSON

Conference: Northeast.
Mailing Address: 1000 River Road, Athletic Department, Teaneck, NJ 007666. **Website:** www.fdu knights.com.
Head Coach: Gary Puccio. **Telephone:** (201) 692-2245.
Baseball SID: Bryan Jackson. **Telephone:** (201) 692-2149.
Assistant Coaches: Eric Anderson, *Justin McKay.
Home Field: Naimoli Family Baseball Complex.
Seating Capacity: 1,000. **Outfield Dimension:** LF— 320, CF— 365, RF— 320.

FLORIDA GATORS

Conference: Southeastern.
Mailing Address: University Athletic Association, PO Box 14485, Gainesville, FL 32604. **Website:** www.gatorzone.com.
Head Coach: Kevin O'Sullivan. **Telephone:** (352) 375-4457. **Baseball SID:** Dan Apple. **Telephone:** (352) 692-6008.
Assistant Coaches: *Craig Bell, Brad Weitzel.
Home Field: McKethan Stadium. **Seating Capacity:** 5,500. **Outfield Dimension:** LF—326, CF—404, RF—321.

FLORIDA A&M RATTLERS

Conference: Mid-Eastern.
Mailing Address: 1800 Wahnish Way Tallahassee, FL. 32307. **Website:** www.famuathletics.com.
Head Coach: Jamey Shouppe. **Telephone:** (850) 599-3202. **Baseball SID:** Mike Morrell. **Telephone:** (850) 599-3200.
Assistant Coaches: Bryan Henry. **Telephone:** (850) 556-0769.
Home Field: Moore-Kittles Field. **Seating Capacity:** 500. **Outfield Dimension:** LF—330, CF—410, RF—330.

FLORIDA ATLANTIC OWLS.

Conference: Conference USA.
Mailing Address: 777 Glades Road, Boca Raton, FL, 33431. **Website:** www.fausports.com.
Head Coach: John McCormack. **Telephone:** (561) 297-1055. **Baseball SID:** Jonathan Fraysure. **Telephone:** (561) 430-7148. **Fax:** (561) 297-3963.
Assistant Coaches: *Greg Mamula, Brett Schneider. **Telephone:** (561) 297-3956.
Home Field: FAU Baseball Stadium. **Seating Capacity:** 1,718. **Outfield Dimension:** LF—330, CF—400, RF—330.

FLORIDA GULF COAST EAGLES.

Conference: Atlantic Sun.
Mailing Address: 10501 FGCU Blvd. South, Fort Myers, FL 33965. **Website:** www.fgcuathletics.com.
Head Coach: Dave Tollett. **Telephone:** (239) 590-7051. **Baseball SID:** Matt Fischer. **Telephone:** (239) 590-1327.
Assistant Coaches: Matt Reid, *Brandon Romans. **Telephone:** (239) 590-7058.
Home Field: Swanson Stadium. **Seating Capacity:** 1,500. **Outfield Dimension:** LF—325, CF—400, RF—325.

FLORIDA INTERNATIONAL PANTHERS.

Conference: Conference USA.
Mailing Address: 11200 SW 8th St., Miami, FL 33199. **Website:** www.fiusports.com.
Head Coach: Mervyl Melendez. **Telephone:** (305) 348-3166. **Baseball SID:** Pete Pelegrin. **Telephone:** (305) 348-1357. **Fax:** (305) 348-1357.
Assistant Coaches: *Jered Goodwin, Dax Norris. **Telephone:** (305) 348-3168.
Home Field: Panther Stadium. **Seating Capacity:** 2,000. **Outfield Dimension:** LF—325, CF—405, RF—325.

FLORIDA STATE SEMINOLES

Conference: Atlantic Coast.
Mailing Address: 403 W. Stadium Dr. **Website:** www.seminoles.com.
Head Coach: Mike Martin. **Telephone:** (850) 644-1073. **Baseball SID:** Steven McCartney. **Telephone:** (850) 644-3920. **Fax:** (850) 644-3820.
Assistant Coaches: Mike Bell, *Mike Martin. **Telephone:** (850) 644-1072.
Home Field: Mike Martin Field at Dick Howser Stadium. **Seating Capacity:** 6,700. **Outfield Dimension:** LF—340, CF—400, RF—320.

FORDHAM RAMS

Conference: Atlantic 10.
Mailing Address: 441 East Fordham Rd., Bronx, NY 10458. **Website:** www.fordhamsports.com.
Head Coach: Kevin Leighton. **Telephone:** (718) 817-4292. **Baseball SID:** Scott Kwiatkowski. **Telephone:** (718) 817-4219. **Fax:** (718) 817-4244.
Assistant Coaches: *Rob Ditoma, Pete Larson. **Telephone:** (718) 817-4290.
Home Field: Houlihan Park. **Seating Capacity:** 500. **Outfield Dimension:** LF—339, CF—390, RF—325.

FRESNO STATE BULLDOGS

Conference: Mountain West.
Mailing Address: 1620 E. Bulldog Lane OF 87, Fresno, CA 93740. **Website:** www.gobulldogs.com.
Head Coach: Mike Batesole. **Telephone:** (559) 278-2178. **Baseball SID:** Travis Blanshan. **Telephone:** (559)

278-4647.
Assistant Coaches: Jermaine Clark, *Ryan Overland. **Telephone:** (559) 278-2178.
Home Field: Beiden Field. **Seating Capacity:** 3,575. **Outfield Dimension:** LF—330, **CF—400, RF—330.**

FURMAN PALADINS

Conference: Southern.
Mailing Address: 3300 Pointsett Highway, Greenville, SC 29613. **Website:** www.furmanpaladins.com.
Head Coach: Brett Harker. **Telephone:** (864) 294-2243. **Baseball SID:** Hunter Reid. **Telephone:** (864) 294-2061.
Assistant Coaches: Kaleb Davis, *Taylor Harbin. **Telephone:** (864) 294-3052.
Home Field: Latham Stadium. **Seating Capacity:** 2,000. **Outfield Dimension:** LF— 330, CF— 393, RF— 330.

GARDNER-WEBB RUNNIN' BULLDOGS

Conference: Big South.
Mailing Address: 110 S. Main St., Boiling Springs, N.C. 28017. **Website:** www.gwusports.com.
Head Coach: Rusty Stroupe. **Telephone:** (704) 406-4421. **Baseball SID:** Ryan Bridges. **Telephone:** (704) 406-3523. **Fax:** (704) 406-4739.
Assistant Coaches: Conner Scarborough, *Ross Steedley. **Telephone:** (704) 406-3557.
Home Field: John Henry Moss Stadium. **Seating Capacity:** 550. **Outfield Dimension:** LF—335, CF—385, RF—335.

GEORGE MASON PATRIOTS

Conference: Atlantic 10.
Mailing Address: 4400 University Drive Fairfax, Va. 22030. **Website:** www.gomason.com.
Head Coach: Bill Brown. **Telephone:** (703) 993-3282. **Baseball SID:** Steve Kolbe. **Telephone:** (703) 993-3268. **Fax:** (703) 993-3259.
Assistant Coaches: *Tag Montague, Brian Pugh. **Telephone:** (703) 993-3328.
Home Field: Spuhler Field. **Seating Capacity:** 900. **Outfield Dimension:** LF—320, CF—400, RF—320.

GEORGE WASHINGTON COLONIALS

Conference: Atlantic 10.
Mailing Address: 600 22nd Street, NW, Washington, DC 20052. **Website:** www.gwsports.cstv.com.
Head Coach: Gregg Ritchie. **Telephone:** (202) 994-7399. **Baseball SID:** Dan DiVeglio. **Telephone:** (202) 994-5666.
Assistant Coaches: *Dave Lorber, Rick Oliveri. **Telephone:** (202) 994-5933.
Home Field: Tucker Field at Barcroft Park. **Seating Capacity:** 500. **Outfield Dimension:** LF—330, CF—380, RF—330.

GEORGETOWN HOYAS

Conference: Big East.
Mailing Address: 3700 O St. NW, Washington, DC 20057. **Website:** www.guhoyas.com.
Head Coach: Pete Wilk. **Telephone:** (202) 687-2462. **Baseball SID:** Brendan Thomas. **Telephone:** (202) 687-6783.
Assistant Coaches: Eric Niesen, *Ryan Wood. **Telephone:** (202) 687-6406.
Home Field: Shirley Povich Field. **Seating Capacity:** 1,500. **Outfield Dimension:** LF—330, CF—375, RF—330.

GEORGIA BULLDOGS

Conference: Southeastern.
Mailing Address: P.O. Box 1472, Athens, Ga. 30603.
Website: www.georgiadogs.com.
Head Coach: Scott Stricklin. **Telephone:** (706) 542-7971. **Baseball SID:** Christopher Lakos. **Telephone:** (706) 542-7994. **Fax:** (706) 542-9339.
Assistant Coaches: *Scott Daeley, Sean Kenny. **Telephone:** (706) 542-7971.
Home Field: Foley Field. **Seating Capacity:** 2,760.
Outfield Dimension: LF—350, CF—404, RF—314.

GEORGIA SOUTHERN EAGLES

Conference: Sun Belt.
Mailing Address: P.O. Box 8086, Statesboro, GA 30460. **Website:** www.georgiasoutherneagles.com.
Head Coach: Rodney Hennon. **Baseball SID:** A.J. Henderson. **Telephone:** (912) 478-5071.
Assistant Coaches: Alan Beck, *B.J. Green. **Telephone:** (912) 478-1331.
Home Field: J.J. Clements Stadium. **Seating Capacity:** 3,000. **Outfield Dimension:** LF—325, CF—390, RF—325.

GEORGIA STATE PANTHERS

Conference: Sun Belt.
Mailing Address: 755 Hank Aaron Drive, Atlanta, GA 30315. **Website:** www.georgiastatesports.com.
Head Coach: Greg Frady. **Telephone:** (404) 413-4153. **Baseball SID:** Allison George. **Telephone:** (404) 413-4032.
Assistant Coaches: Josh Davis, *Adam Pavkovich. **Telephone:** (404) 413-4077.
Home Field: GSU Baseball Complex. **Seating Capacity:** 1,000. **Outfield Dimension:** LF—334, CF—385, RF—338.

GEORGIA TECH YELLOW JACKETS

Conference: Atlantic Coast.
Mailing Address: 255 5th St. NW, Atlanta, GA 30332. **Website:** www.ramblinwreck.com.
Head Coach: Danny Hall. **Telephone:** (404) 894-5471. **Baseball SID:** Kevin Davis. **Telephone:** (404) 894-5445.
Assistant Coaches: *Jason Howell, Mike Nickeas. **Telephone:** (404) 894-5081.
Home Field: Russ Chandler Stadium. **Seating Capacity:** 4,157. **Outfield Dimension:** LF—329, CF—390, RF—334.

GONZAGA BULLDOGS

Conference: West Coast.
Mailing Address: Gonzaga University 502 E Boone Ave., Spokane, WA 99258-0066. **Website:** www.gozags.com.
Head Coach: Mark Machtolf. **Telephone:** (509) 313-4209. **Baseball SID:** Kyle Scholzen. **Telephone:** (509) 313-4227.
Assistant Coaches: *Danny Evans, Brandon Harmon. **Telephone:** (509) 313-3597.
Home Field: Patterson Baseball Complex & Washington Trust Field. **Seating Capacity:** 1,500. **Outfield Dimension:** LF—328, CF—398, RF—328.

GRAMBLING STATE

Conference: Southwestern Athletic.
Mailing Address: PO Box 4252, Grambling, LA 71245. **Website:** www.gsutigers.com.
Head Coach: James Cooper. **Telephone:** (318) 274-6466. **Baseball SID:** Brian Howard. **Telephone:** (318) 274-6414.
Assistant Coaches: *Davin Pierre. **Telephone:** (318) 274-2416.
Home Field: Jones Park Ellis Field. **Seating Capacity:** 2,500. **Outfield Dimension:** LF—315, CF—400, RF—350.

GRAND CANYON LOPES

Conference: Western Athletic.
Mailing Address: 3300 W Camelback Road, Phoenix, AZ 85017. **Website:** www.gculops.com.
Head Coach: Andy Stankiewicz. **Telephone:** (602) 639-6042. **Baseball SID:** Josh Hauser. **Telephone:** (602) 639-8328.
Assistant Coaches: Rich Dorman, *Gregg Wallis. **Telephone:** (602) 639-8416.
Home Field: Brazell Field at GCU Ballpark. **Seating Capacity:** 3,500. **Outfield Dimension:** LF—320, CF—375, RF—330.

HARTFORD HAWKS

Conference: America East.
Mailing Address: 200 Bloomfield Ave., West Hartford, CT 06117. **Website:** www.hartfordhawks.com.
Head Coach: Justin Blood. **Telephone:** (860) 768-5760. **Baseball SID:** Patrick Reilly.
Assistant Coaches: Elliot Glynn, *Steve Malinowski. **Telephone:** (860) 768-4972.
Home Field: Fiondella Field. **Seating Capacity:** 1,500. **Outfield Dimension:** LF—325, CF—400, RF—325.

HARVARD CRIMSON TIDE

Conference: Ivy League.
Mailing Address: 65 North Harvard Street, Boston, MA 02163. **Website:** www.gocrimson.com.
Head Coach: Bill Decker. **Telephone:** (617) 495-2629. **Baseball SID:** Devan Horahan. **Telephone:** (617) 495-2206.
Assistant Coaches: Ron Rakowski, *Bryan Stark. **Telephone:** (617) 495-3465.
Home Field: O'Donnell Field. **Seating Capacity:** 1,600. **Outfield Dimension:** LF—340, CF—415, RF—340.

HAWAII RAINBOW WARRIORS

Conference: Big West.
Mailing Address: 1337 Lower Campus Rd., Honolulu, HI 96822. **Website:** www.hawaiiathletics.com.
Head Coach: Mike Trapasso. **Telephone:** (808) 956-6247. **Baseball SID:** Michael Stambaugh. **Telephone:** (808) 956-7506.
Assistant Coaches: Carl Fraticelli, *Rusty McNamara. **Telephone:** (808) 956-6247.
Home Field: Les Murakami Stadium. **Seating Capacity:** 4,312. **Outfield Dimension:** LF—325, CF—385, RF—325.

HIGH POINT PANTHERS

Conference: Big South.
Mailing Address: 1 University Parkway, High Point, NC 27268. **Website:** www.highpointpanthers.com.
Head Coach: Craig Cozart. **Telephone:** (336) 841-9190. **Baseball SID:** Kevin Burke. **Telephone:** (336) 841-4638.
Assistant Coaches: *Jason Laws, Rick Marlin. **Telephone:** (336) 841-4614.
Home Field: Williard Stadium. **Seating Capacity:** 550. **Outfield Dimension:** LF—325, CF—400, RF—330.

HOFSTRA PRIDE

Conference: Colonial Athletic.
Mailing Address: 230 Hofstra University, PEC Room 233, Hempstead, NY 11549. **Website:** www.gohofstra.com.
Head Coach: John Russo. **Telephone:** (516) 463-3759.
Baseball SID: Len Skoros. **Telephone:** (516) 463-4602.
Assistant Coaches: John Hayban, Matt Wessinger.
Telephone: (516) 463-5065.
Home Field: University Field. **Outfield Dimension:** LF—322, CF—382, RF—337.

HOLY CROSS CRUSADERS

Conference: Patriot.
Mailing Address: 1 College Street, Worcester, MA 01610. **Website:** www.goholycross.com.
Head Coach: Greg DiCenzo. **Baseball SID:** Greg Celona. **Telephone:** (508) 793-2583.
Assistant Coaches: Jason Falcon, *Ed Kahovec.
Telephone: (508) 793-2753.
Home Field: Fitton Field. **Seating Capacity:** 3,000.
Outfield Dimension: LF— 332, **CF—**400, **RF—**330.

HOUSTON COUGARS

Conference: American Athletic.
Mailing Address: 3204 Cullen Blvd., Houston, TX 77204. **Website:** www.uhcougars.com.
Head Coach: Todd Whitting. **Telephone:** (713) 743-9396. **Baseball SID:** Allison McClain. **Telephone:** (713) 743-9406.
Assistant Coaches: *Terry Rooney, Ryan Shotzberger.
Telephone: (713) 743-9396.
Home Field: Schroeder Park. **Seating Capacity:** 3,500.
Outfield Dimension: LF—330, **CF—**390, **RF—**330.

HOUSTON BAPTIST HUSKIES

Conference: Southland.
Mailing Address: 7502 Fondren Rd., Houston, TX 77074. **Website:** www.hbuhuskies.com.
Head Coach: Jared Moon. **Telephone:** (281) 649-3332.
Baseball SID: Russ Reneau. **Telephone:** (281) 649-3098.
Fax: (281) 649-3496.
Assistant Coaches: *Xavier Hernandez, Russell Stockton. **Telephone:** (281) 649-3264.
Home Field: Husky Field. **Seating Capacity:** 500.
Outfield Dimension: LF—330, **CF—**405, **RF—**330.

ILLINOIS

Conference: Big Ten.
Mailing Address: 1800 S. First St., Champaign, IL 61820. **Website:** www.fightingillini.com.
Head Coach: Dan Hartleb. **Telephone:** (217) 244-8144.
Baseball SID: Brett Moore. **Telephone:** (309) 212-6367.
Assistant Coaches: Adam Christ, *Drew Dickinson.
Telephone: (217) 300-2220.
Home Field: Illinois Field. **Seating Capacity:** 1,500.
Outfield Dimension: LF—330, **CF—**400, **RF—**330.

ILLINOIS STATE REDBIRDS

Conference: Missouri Valley.
Mailing Address: Campus Box 7130; Normal, IL 61790. **Website:** www.goredbirds.com.
Head Coach: Bo Durkac. **Telephone:** (309) 438-3249.
Baseball SID: Matt Wing. **Telephone:** (309) 438-3249.
Assistant Coaches: Michael Kellar, *Mike Stalowy.
Telephone: (309) 438-5151.
Home Field: Duffy Bass Field. **Seating Capacity:** 1,500. **Outfield Dimension: LF—**330, **CF—**400, **RF—**330.

ILLINOIS-CHICAGO FLAMES

Conference: Horizon.
Mailing Address: 839 West Roosevelt Road, Chicago, IL 60608. **Website:** www.uicflames.cstv.com.
Head Coach: Mike Dee. **Telephone:** (312) 996-8645.
Baseball SID: Dan Yopchick. **Telephone:** (312) 413-9340.
Fax: (312) 996-8349.
Assistant Coaches: *John Flood, Sean McDermott.
Telephone: (312) 355-1757.
Home Field: Curtis Granderson Stadium. **Seating Capacity:** 2000. **Outfield Dimension: LF—**325, **CF—**400, **RF—**325.

INCARNATE WORD CARDINALS

Conference: Southland.
Mailing Address: 4301 Broadway, San Antonio, TX 78209. **Website:** www.uiwcardinals.com.
Head Coach: Patrick Hallmark. **Baseball SID:** Zachary Carlton. **Telephone:** (210) 805-3071.
Assistant Coaches: *Ryan Aguayo, Scott Shepperd.
Telephone: (210) 805-3025.
Home Field: Sullivan Field. **Seating Capacity:** 1,000.
Outfield Dimension: LF—335, **CF—**405, **RF—**335

INDIANA HOOSIERS

Conference: Big Ten.
Mailing Address: 1001 E. 17th Street, Bloomington, IN 47408. **Website:** www.iuhoosiers.com.
Head Coach: Chris Lemonis. **Telephone:** (812) 855-4770. **Baseball SID:** Greg Kincaid. **Telephone:** (812) 855-4770.
Assistant Coaches: Kyle Bunn, *Kyle Cheesebrough.
Telephone: (812) 855-9155.
Home Field: Bart Kaufman Field. **Seating Capacity:** 4,000. **Outfield Dimension: LF—**330, **CF—**400, **RF—**340.

INDIANA STATE SYCAMORES

Conference: Missouri Valley.
Mailing Address: 401 N. 4th St., Terre Haute, IN 47809.
Website: www.gosycamores.com.
Head Coach: Mitch Hannahs. **Baseball SID:** Tim McCaughan. **Telephone:** (812) 237-4159.
Assistant Coaches: *Brian Smiley, Jordan Tiegs.
Telephone: (812) 237-4090.
Home Field: Bob Warn Field. **Seating Capacity:** 2,500.
Outfield Dimension: LF—330, **CF—**395, **RF—**330.

IONA GAELS

Conference: Metro Atlantic Athletic.
Mailing Address: Hynes Center, 715 North Ave., New Rochelle, NY 10801. **Website:** www.icgaels.com.
Head Coach: Pat Carey. **Telephone:** (914) 633-2319.
Baseball SID: Pat McWalters. **Telephone:** (914) 633-2334.
Assistant Coaches: Lou Bernardi, John Galanoudis.
Home Field: City Park.

IOWA HAWKEYES

Conference: Big Ten.
Mailing Address: N411 Carver-Hawkeye Arena, Iowa City, IA 52242. **Website:** www.hawkeyesports.com.
Head Coach: Rick Heller. **Telephone:** (319) 335-9259.
Baseball SID: James Allan. **Telephone:** (319) 335-6439.
Assistant Coaches: Desi Druschel, *Marty Sutherland.
Telephone: (319) 335-9259.
Home Field: Duane Banks Field. **Seating Capacity:** 3,000. **Outfield Dimension: LF—**329, **CF—**395, **RF—**329.

IPFW FORT WAYNE

Conference: Summit.
Mailing Address: 2101 E. Coliseum Blvd., Fort Wayne, IN 46805. **Website:** www.gomastodons.com.
Head Coach: Bobby Pierce. **Telephone:** (260) 481-5480. **Baseball SID:** Derrick Sloboda. **Telephone:** (260) 481-0729.
Assistant Coaches: *Grant Birely, Connor Lawhead. **Telephone:** (260) 481-0710.
Home Field: Mastodon Field. **Seating Capacity:** 500. **Outfield Dimension:** LF—330, CF—405, RF—330.

JACKSON STATE

Conference: Southwestern Athletic.
Mailing Address: 1400 JR Lynch St., Jackson, MS 39127. **Website:** www.jsutigers.com.
Head Coach: Omar Johnson. **Telephone:** (601) 979-3930. **Baseball SID:** Wesley Peterson. **Telephone:** (601) 979-5899.
Assistant Coaches: Christopher Crenshaw. **Telephone:** (601) 979-2316.
Home Field: Bob Braddy Field. **Seating Capacity:** 800. **Outfield Dimension:** LF—325, CF—401, RF—325.

JACKSONVILLE DOLPHINS

Conference: Atlantic Sun.
Mailing Address: 2800 University Blvd. N., Jacksonville, FL 32211. **Website:** www.judolphins.com.
Head Coach: Chris Hayes. **Telephone:** (904) 256-7476.
Baseball SID: Cooper Welch. **Telephone:** (904) 256-7761.
Assistant Coaches: Mark Guerra, *Rich Wallace. **Telephone:** (904) 256-7367.
Home Field: Sessions Stadium. **Seating Capacity:** 3,000. **Outfield Dimension:** LF—340, CF—405, RF—340.

JACKSONVILLE STATE GAMECOCKS

Conference: Ohio Valley.
Mailing Address: 700 Pelham Rd., N., Jacksonville, AL 36265. **Website:** www.jsugamecocksports.com.
Head Coach: Jim Case. **Telephone:** (256) 782-5367.
Baseball SID: Tony Schmidt. **Telephone:** (256) 782-5377.
Assistant Coaches: Evan Bush, Mike Murphree. **Telephone:** (256) 782-8141.
Home Field: Rudy Abbott Field. **Seating Capacity:** 1,000. **Outfield Dimension:** LF—330, CF—400, RF—335.

JAMES MADISON DUKES

Conference: Colonial.
Mailing Address: 395 S. High St., Harrisonburg, VA 22807. **Website:** www.jmusports.com.
Head Coach: Marlin Ikenberry. **Telephone:** (540) 460-0000. **Baseball SID:** Eric Evans. **Telephone:** (540) 568-6155.
Assistant Coaches: *Alex Guerra, Jimmy Jackson. **Telephone:** (540) 568-6516.
Home Field: Eagle Field at Veterans Memorial Park. **Seating Capacity:** 3,500. **Outfield Dimension:** LF—330, CF—400, RF—320.

KANSAS JAYHAWKS

Conference: Big 12.
Mailing Address: 1651 Naismith Dr., Lawrence, KS 66045. **Website:** www.kuathletics.com.
Head Coach: Ritch Price. **Telephone:** (785) 864-4196.
Baseball SID: D.J. Haurin. **Telephone:** (785) 864-3575.
Assistant Coaches: Ryan Graves, *Ritch Price.

Telephone: (785) 864-7908.
Home Field: Hoglund Ball Park. **Seating Capacity:** 2,300. **Outfield Dimension:** LF—330, CF—395, RF—330.

KANSAS STATE WILDCATS

Conference: Big 12.
Mailing Address: Tointon Family Stadium, 1700 College Ave., Manhatan, KS 66503. **Website:** www.kstate sports.com.
Head Coach: Brad Hill. **Telephone:** (785) 532-5723.
Baseball SID: Chris Brown. **Telephone:** (785) 532-6735.
Assistant Coaches: Mitch Gaspard, *Tyler Kincaid. **Telephone:** (785) 532-7976.
Home Field: Tointon Family Stadium. **Seating Capacity:** 1,200. **Outfield Dimension:** LF—340, CF—400, RF—330.

KENNESAW STATE OWLS

Conference: Atlantic Sun.
Mailing Address: 590 Cobb Ave., Mailbox 0201, Kennesaw, GA 30144. **Website:** www.ksuowls.com.
Head Coach: Mike Sansing. **Telephone:** (470) 578-6264. **Baseball SID:** Jake Dorow. **Telephone:** (470) 578-2562.
Assistant Coaches: Kevin Erminio, *Trey Fowler. **Telephone:** (470) 578-2099.
Home Field: Stillwell Stadium. **Seating Capacity:** 1,500. **Outfield Dimension:** LF—330, CF—400, RF—330.

KENT STATE GOLDEN FLASHES

Conference: Mid-American.
Mailing Address: MAC Center, P.O. Box 5190, Kent, OH 44242. **Website:** www.kentstatesports.com.
Head Coach: Jeff Duncan. **Telephone:** (330) 672-8432.
Assistant Coaches: Mike Birkbeck, *Derek Simmons. **Telephone:** (330) 672-8433.
Home Field: Schoonover Stadium. **Seating Capacity:** 2,000. **Outfield Dimension:** LF—330, CF—415, RF—320.

KENTUCKY WILDCATS

Conference: Southeastern.
Mailing Address: Joe Craft Center, 338 Lexington Ave., Lexington, KY 40506. **Website:** www.ukathletics .com.
Head Coach: Nick Mingione. **Telephone:** (859) 257-8052. **Baseball SID:** Matt May. **Telephone:** (859) 257-8504. **Fax:** (859) 323-4310.
Assistant Coaches: Jim Belanger, *Roland Fanning. **Telephone:** (859) 257-8052.
Home Field: Cliff Hagan Stadium. **Seating Capacity:** 3,000. **Outfield Dimension:** LF—340, CF—390, RF—310.

LA SALLE EXPLORERS

Conference: Atlantic 10.
Mailing Address: 1900 West Olney Ave., Philadelphia, PA 19141. **Website:** www.goexplorers.com.
Head Coach: David Miller. **Telephone:** (215) 991-5157.
Baseball SID: Joe Scarpano. **Telephone:** (215) 991-2886. .
Assistant Coaches: Andrew Amaro, *jim Gulden. **Telephone:** (215) 991-5157.
Home Field: DaVincent Field. **Seating Capacity:** 1,000. **Outfield Dimension:** LF—305, CF—458, RF—305.

LAFAYETTE LEOPARDS

Conference: Patriot.
Mailing Address: Kirby Sports Center, Easton, PA 18042. **Website:** www.goleopards.com.

Head Coach: Joseph Kinney. Telephone: (610) 330-5476. Baseball SID: Steve Kline. Telephone: (610) 330-5518.
Assistant Coaches: Greg Durrah, *Tim Reilly. Telephone: (610) 330-5476.
Home Field: Hilton Rahn Field at Kamine Stadium. Seating Capacity: 500. Outfield Dimension: LF—332, CF—403, RF—335.

LAMAR CARDINALS

Conference: Southland.
Mailing Address: Jim Gilligan Way, Beaumont, TX 77705. Website: www.lamarcardinals.com.
Head Coach: Will Davis. Telephone: (409) 880-8974.
Baseball SID: Cooper Welch. Telephone: (409) 880-7845.
Assistant Coaches: Scott Hatten, Sean Snedeker. Telephone: (409) 880-8135.
Home Field: Vincent-Beck Stadium. Seating Capacity: 3,500. Outfield Dimension: LF—325, CF—380, RF—325.

LEHIGH MOUNTAIN HAWKS

Conference: Patriot.
Mailing Address: 641 Taylor St., Bethlehem, PA 18015. Website: www.lehighsports.com.
Head Coach: Sean Leary. Telephone: (610) 758-2948.
Baseball SID: Derek Behrenshausen. Telephone: (610) 758-5101. Fax: (610) 758-6629.
Assistant Coaches: John Bisco, *John Fugett. Telephone: (610) 758-2948.
Home Field: J. David Walker Field at Legacy Park. Seating Capacity: 370. Outfield Dimension: LF—320, CF—400, RF—320.

LIBERTY FLAMES

Conference: Big South.
Mailing Address: 1971 University Blvd., Lynchburg, VA 24515. Website: www.libertyflames.com.
Head Coach: Scott Jackson. Telephone: (434) 582-2305. Baseball SID: Ryan Bomberger. Telephone: (434) 582-2292. Fax: (434) 582-2706.
Assistant Coaches: *Tyler Cannon, Bryant Gaines. Telephone: (434) 582-2103.
Home Field: Liberty Baseball Stadium. Seating Capacity: 2,500. Outfield Dimension: LF—375, CF—395, RF—375.

LIPSCOMB BISONS

Conference: Atlantic Sun.
Mailing Address: 1 University Park Dr., Nashville, TN 37204. Website: www.lipscombsports.com.
Head Coach: Jeff Forehand. Telephone: (615) 966-5716. Baseball SID: Kirk Downs. Telephone: (615) 966-5457. Fax: (615) 966-1806.
Assistant Coaches: Brad Coon, *Brian Ryman. Telephone: (615) 966-5149.
Home Field: Ken Dugan Field at Stephen L. Marsh Stadium. Seating Capacity: 750. Outfield Dimension: LF—330, CF—405, RF—330.

LONG BEACH STATE DIRTBAGS

Conference: Big West.
Mailing Address: 1250 Bellflower Blvd., Long Beach, CA 90840. Website: www.longbeachstate.com.
Head Coach: Troy Buckley. Telephone: (562) 985-4661. Baseball SID: Tyler Hendrickson. Telephone: (562) 985-7797.

Assistant Coaches: *Greg Bergeron, Danny Ricabal. Telephone: (562) 985-7548.
Home Field: Blair Field. Seating Capacity: 3,000. Outfield Dimension: LF—335, CF—393, RF—330.

LONG ISLAND-BROOKLYN BLACKBIRDS

Conference: Northeast.
Mailing Address: 1 University Plaza, Brooklyn, NY 11201. Website: www.liuathletics.com.
Head Coach: Dan Pirillo. Telephone: (718) 488-1538.
Baseball SID: Casey Snedecor. Telephone: (718) 488-1307.
Assistant Coaches: *Tom Carty, John Ziznewski. Telephone: (718) 780-6059.
Home Field: "The Birdcage". Seating Capacity: 200. Outfield Dimension: LF—300, CF—390, RF—285.

LONGWOOD LANCERS

Conference: Big South.
Mailing Address: 201 High St., Farmville, VA 23909. Website: www.longwoodlancers.com.
Head Coach: Ryan Mau. Telephone: (434) 395-2843.
Baseball SID: Darius Thigpen. Telephone: (434) 395-2345.
Assistant Coaches: Evan Wells, *Daniel Wood. Telephone: (434) 395-2351.
Home Field: Buddy Bolding Stadium. Seating Capacity: 500. Outfield Dimension: LF—335, CF—400, RF—335.

LOUISIANA STATE FIGHTING TIGERS

Conference: Southeastern.
Mailing Address: N. Stadium Drive @ Nicholson Drive, Baton Rouge, LA 70803. Website: www.lsusports.net.
Head Coach: Paul Mainieri. Telephone: (225) 578-4148. Baseball SID: Bill Franques. Telephone: (225) 578-8226. Fax: (225) 578-1861.
Assistant Coaches: *Nolan Cain, Alan Dunn. Telephone: (225) 578-4148.
Home Field: Alex Box Stadium. Seating Capacity: 10,326. Outfield Dimension: LF—330 line, CF—405, RF—330

LOUISIANA TECH BULLDOGS

Conference: Conference USA.
Mailing Address: 1650 W. Alabama Ave., Ruston, LA 71270. Website: www.latechsports.com.
Head Coach: Lane Burroughs. Telephone: (318) 257-5318. Baseball SID: Brock McKee. Telephone: (318) 257-5305. Fax: (318) 257-3757.
Assistant Coaches: Cory Barton, *Travis Creel. Telephone: (318) 257-5220.
Home Field: J.C. Love Field at Pat Patterson Park. Seating Capacity: 2,000. Outfield Dimension: LF—315, CF—385, RF—325.

LOUISIANA-LAFAYETTE RAGIN' CAJUNS

Conference: Sun Belt.
Mailing Address: 201 Reinhardt Dr., Lafayette, LA 70506. Website: www.ragincajuns.com.
Head Coach: Tony Robichaux. Telephone: (337) 262-5189. Baseball SID: Jeff Schneider. Telephone: (337) 482-6332.
Assistant Coaches: Anthony Babineaux, *Jeremy Talbot. Telephone: (337) 262-5193.
Home Field: M.L. "Tigue" Moore Field at Russo Park. Seating Capacity: 4,650. Outfield Dimension: LF—330, CF—400, RF—330.

LOUISIANA-MONROE WARHAWKS

Conference: Sun Belt.
Mailing Address: 308 Warhawk Way, Monroe, LA 71209. **Website:** www.ulmwarhawks.com.
Head Coach: Michael Federico. **Telephone:** (318) 342-3591. **Baseball SID:** John Lewandowski. **Telephone:** (318) 342-5378.
Assistant Coaches: Matt Collins, *Joel Mangrum. **Telephone:** (318) 342-3589.
Home Field: Warhawks Stadium. **Seating Capacity:** 1,500. **Outfield Dimension: LF**—330, **CF**—400, **RF**—330.

LOUISVILLE CARDINALS

Conference: Atlantic Coast.
Mailing Address: 215 Cardinal Station, Louisville, KY 40292. **Website:** www.uoflsports.com.
Head Coach: Dan McDonnell. **Telephone:** (502) 852-0103. **Baseball SID:** Garett Wall. **Telephone:** (502) 852-3088. **Fax:** (502) 852-6581.
Assistant Coaches: *Eric Snider, Roger Williams. **Telephone:** (502) 852-3929.
Home Field: Jim Patterson Stadium. **Seating Capacity:** 4,000. **Outfield Dimension: LF**—330, **CF**—402, **RF**—330.

LOYOLA MARYMOUNT LIONS

Conference: West Coast.
Mailing Address: 1 LMU Dr., Los Angees, CA 90045. **Website:** www.lmulions.com.
Head Coach: Jason Gill. **Telephone:** (310) 338-2949. **Baseball SID:** Tyler Geivett. **Telephone:** (310) 338-7638.
Assistant Coaches: Bobby Andrews, *Ronnie Prettyman. **Telephone:** (310) 338-4511.
Home Field: Page Stadium. **Seating Capacity:** 600. **Outfield Dimension: LF**—326, **CF**—406, **RF**—321.

MAINE BLACK BEARS

Conference: America East.
Mailing Address: 5745 Mahaney Clubhouse, Orono, ME 04469. **Website:** www.goblackbears.com.
Head Coach: Nick Derba. **Telephone:** (207) 581-1096. **Baseball SID:** Katie Peverada. **Telephone:** (207) 581-4158.
Assistant Coaches: *Conor Burke, John Schiffner. **Telephone:** (207) 581-1097.
Home Field: Mahaney Diamond. **Seating Capacity:** 4,400. **Outfield Dimension: LF**—330, **CF**—400, **RF**—300.

MANHATTAN JASPERS

Conference: Metro Atlantic.
Mailing Address: 4513 Manhattan College Parkway, Riverdale, NY 10471. **Website:** www.gojaspers.com.
Head Coach: Mike Cole. **Telephone:** (718) 862-7821. **Baseball SID:** Kevin Ross. **Telephone:** (718) 862-7228.
Assistant Coaches: *Chris Cody, Vincent Redmond. **Telephone:** (718) 862-7218.
Home Field: Dutchess Stadium. **Seating Capacity:** 4,494. **Outfield Dimension: LF**—325, **CF**—400, **RF**—325.

MARIST RED FOXES

Conference: Metro Atlantic.
Mailing Address: 3399 North Rd., Poughkeepsie, NY 12601. **Website:** www.goredfoxes.com.
Head Coach: Chris Tracz. **Telephone:** (845) 575-2570. **Baseball SID:** Sam Rathbun. **Telephone:** (845) 575-2441.
Assistant Coaches: *Eric Pelletier, Lance Ratchford.

Telephone: (845) 575-7583.
Home Field: McCann Field. **Outfield Dimension: LF**—320, **CF**—390, **RF**—320.

MARSHALL THUNDERING HERD

Conference: Conference USA.
Mailing Address: 1801 Third Ave., Huntington, WV 25703. **Website:** www.herdzone.com.
Head Coach: Jeff Waggoner. **Telephone:** (304) 696-7146.
Assistant Coaches: *Joe Renner, Victor Gomez. **Telephone:** (304) 696-7146.
Home Field: Appalachian Power Park. **Seating Capacity:** 4,500. **Outfield Dimension: LF**—330, **CF**—400, **RF**—320.

MARYLAND TERRAPINS

Conference: Big Ten.
Mailing Address: University of Maryland, College Park, MD 20742. **Website:** www.umterps.com.
Head Coach: Rob Vaughn. **Telephone:** (301) 314-1845. **Baseball SID:** Taylor Smyth. **Telephone:** (301) 314-8052.
Assistant Coaches: Corey Muscara, *Matt Swope. **Telephone:** (301) 314-9772.
Home Field: Bob "Turtle" Smith Stadium. **Seating Capacity:** 2,500. **Outfield Dimension: LF**—320, **CF**—380, **RF**—325.

MARYLAND-BALTIMORE COUNTY RETRIEVERS.

Conference: America East.
Mailing Address: 1000 Hilltop Circle, Baltimore, MD 21250. **Website:** www.umbcretrievers.com.
Head Coach: Bob Mumma. **Telephone:** (410) 455-2239. **Baseball SID:** David Castellanos. **Telephone:** (410) 455-2639.
Assistant Coaches: *Liam Bowen, Larry Williams.
Home Field: Alumni Field. **Seating Capacity:** 1,000. **Outfield Dimension: LF**—330, **CF**—360, **RF**—340.

MARYLAND-EASTERN SHORE

Conference: Mid-Eastern.
Mailing Address: 1 Backbone Rd., Princess Anne, MD, 21853. **Website:** www.umeshawks.com.
Head Coach: Brian Hollamon. **Telephone:** (410) 651-7864. **Baseball SID:** Matt McCann. **Telephone:** (410) 621-2354.
Assistant Coaches: Ben Kirk. **Telephone:** (410) 621-7014.
Home Field: Hawks Stadium. **Seating Capacity:** 500. **Outfield Dimension: LF**—340, **CF**—400, **RF**—340.

MASSACHUSETTS MINUTEMEN

Conference: Atlantic 10.
Mailing Address: 131 Commonwealth Ave., Amherst, MA 01003. **Website:** www.umassathletics.com.
Head Coach: Matt Reynolds. **Telephone:** (413) 545-3120. **Baseball SID:** Ryan Gallant. **Telephone:** (413) 687-3793.
Assistant Coaches: *Nathan Cole, Mark Royer. **Telephone:** (413) 545-3766.
Home Field: Earl Lorden Field. **Seating Capacity:** 1,500. **Outfield Dimension: LF**—330, **CF**—400, **RF**—330.

MASSACHUSETTS-LOWELL RIVER HAWKS

Conference: America East.
Mailing Address: 1 University Avenue Lowell, Mass.

01854. **Website:** www.goriverhawks.com.
Head Coach: Ken Harring. **Telephone:** (978) 943-2344.
Baseball SID: Tommy Coyle. **Telephone:** (978) 934-6748.
Fax: (978) 934-4001.
Assistant Coaches: *Jerod Edmondson, Matt Perper.
Telephone: (978) 934-2564.
Home Field: LeLacheur Park. **Seating Capacity:** 5,030.
Outfield Dimension: LF—337, **CF**—400, **RF**—301.

McNEESE STATE COWBOYS

Conference: Southland.
Mailing Address: 700 E. McNeese St., Lake Charles, LA
70609. **Website:** www.mcneesesports.com.
Head Coach: Justin Hill. **Telephone:** (337) 475-5484.
Baseball SID: Matthew Bonnette. **Telephone:** (337)
475-5207.
Assistant Coaches: Jimmy Ricklefsen, *Nick Zaleski.
Telephone: (337) 475-5903.
Home Field: Joe Miller Ballpark. **Seating Capacity:**
2,000. **Outfield Dimension: LF**—330, **CF**—400, **RF**—330.

MEMPHIS TIGERS

Conference: American Athletic.
Mailing Address: 3720 Alumni Ave., Memphis, TN
38152. **Website:** www.gotigersgo.com.
Head Coach: Daron Schoenrock. **Telephone:** (901)
678-4137. **Baseball SID:** Kevin Rodriguez. **Telephone:**
(901) 678-4137.
Assistant Coaches: *Clay Greene, Russ Mcnickle.
Telephone: (901) 678-4139.
Home Field: Fed Ex Park. **Seating Capacity:** 2,500.
Outfield Dimension: LF—319, **CF**—380, **RF**—319.

MERCER BEARS

Conference: Southern.
Mailing Address: 1501 Mercer University Drive,
University Center, Macon, GA 31207. **Website:** www.
mercerbears.com.
Head Coach: Craig Gibson. **Telephone:** (478) 301-
2396. **Baseball SID:** Gerrit Van Genderen. **Telephone:**
(478) 301-5209.
Assistant Coaches: *Brent Shade, Willie Stewart.
Telephone: (478) 301-2738.
Home Field: OrthoGeorgia Park at Claude Smith Field.
Seating Capacity: 1,500. **Outfield Dimension: LF**—330,
CF—400, **RF**—320.

MIAMI HURRICANES

Conference: Atlantic Coast.
Mailing Address: 6201 San Amaro Dr., Coral Gables,
FL 33146. **Website:** www.hurricanesports.com.
Head Coach: Jim Morris. **Telephone:** (305) 284-4171.
Baseball SID: Camron Ghorbi. **Telephone:** (305) 284-
3230.
Assistant Coaches: J.D. Arteaga, *Gino DiMare.
Telephone: (305) 284-4171.
Home Field: Mark Light Field at Alex Rodriguez Park.
Seating Capacity: 5,000. **Outfield Dimension: LF**—330,
CF—400, **RF**—330.

MIAMI (OHIO) REDHAWKS

Conference: Mid-American.
Mailing Address: 550 E. Withrow St., Oxford, OH
45056. **Website:** www.miamiredhawks.com.
Head Coach: Danny Hayden. **Telephone:** (513) 529-
6631. **Baseball SID:** Caleb Saunders. **Telephone:** (513)
529-4651.

Assistant Coaches: Matt Davis, Justin Dedman.
Telephone: (513) 529-6746.
Home Field: McKie Field at Hayden Park. **Seating
Capacity:** 2,000. **Outfield Dimension: LF**—332,
CF—400, **RF**—343.

MICHIGAN WOLVERINES

Conference: Big Ten.
Mailing Address: 1000 S. State St., Ann Arbor, MI
48109. **Website:** www.mgoblue.com.
Head Coach: Erik Bakich. **Telephone:** (734) 647-4550.
Baseball SID: Katie Hewitt. **Telephone:** (813) 748-5293.
Assistant Coaches: Chris Fetter, *Nick Schnabel.
Home Field: Ray Fisher Stadium. **Seating Capacity:**
4,000. **Outfield Dimension: LF**—312, **CF**—395, **RF**—320.

MICHIGAN STATE SPARTANS

Conference: Big Ten.
Mailing Address: 223 Kalamazoo St., East Lansing, MI
48824 . **Website:** www.msuspartans.com.
Head Coach: Jake Boss. **Telephone:** (517) 355-4486.
Baseball SID: Zach Fisher. **Telephone:** (517) 355-2271.
Assistant Coaches: *Graham Sikes, Mark Van Ameyde.
Telephone: (517) 355-0259.
Home Field: McLane Stadium at Kobs Field. **Seating
Capacity:** 2,500. **Outfield Dimension: LF**—340,
CF—402, **RF**—302.

MIDDLE TENNESSEE STATE BLUE RAIDERS

Conference: Conference USA.
Mailing Address: MTSU Box 90, 1500 Greenland Dr.,
Murfreesboro, TN 37132. **Website:** www.goblueraiders.
com.
Head Coach: Jim McGuire. **Telephone:** (615) 898-
2961. **Baseball SID:** Dominic LoBianco. **Telephone:** (901)
569-8539.
Assistant Coaches: *Tim Donnelly, Caleb Longshore.
Telephone: (615) 494-8796.
Home Field: Reese Smith Jr. Field. **Seating Capacity:**
2,100. **Outfield Dimension: LF**—330, **CF**—390, **RF**—330.

MINNESOTA GOLDEN GOPHERS

Conference: Big Ten.
Mailing Address: 516 15th Ave. SE, Minneapolis, MN
55455. **Website:** www.gophersports.com.
Head Coach: John Anderson. **Telephone:** (612) 625-
4057. **Baseball SID:** Joe Hansen. **Telephone:** (612) 625-
4090. **Fax:** (612) 625-0359.
Assistant Coaches: Patrick Casey, *Rob Fornasiere.
Telephone: (612) 625-1060.
Home Field: Siebert Field. **Seating Capacity:** 2,500.
Outfield Dimension: LF—330, **CF**—390, **RF**—330.

MISSISSIPPI REBELS

Conference: Southeastern.
Mailing Address: 400 University Place, Oxford, MS
38677. **Website:** www.olemisssports.com.
Head Coach: Mike Bianco. **Telephone:** (662) 915-
6643. **Baseball SID:** Brandon Lee. **Telephone:** (662)
915-1083.
Assistant Coaches: Mike Clement, *Carl Lafferty.
Telephone: (662) 915-7556.
Home Field: Swayze Field. **Seating Capacity:** 10,323.
Outfield Dimension: LF—330, **CF**—390, **RF**—330.

MISSISSIPPI STATE BULLDOGS

Conference: Southeastern.
Mailing Address: P.O. Box 5327, Mississippi State, Starkville, MS 39762. **Website:** www.mstateathletics.com.
Head Coach: Andy Cannizaro. **Telephone:** (662) 325-3597. **Baseball SID:** Andrew Piper. **Telephone:** (662) 325-0972.
Assistant Coaches: *Jake Gautreau, Gary Henderson. **Telephone:** (662) 325-3597.
Home Field: Dudy Noble Field. **Seating Capacity:** 9,000. **Outfield Dimension: LF**—330, **CF**—390, **RF**—326.

MISSISSIPPI VALLEY STATE DELTA DEVILS

Conference: Southwestern Athletic.
Mailing Address: 14000 Hwy. 82 W. #7246, Itta Bena, MS 38941. **Website:** www.mvsusports.com.
Head Coach: Aaron Stevens. **Telephone:** (662) 254-3834. **Baseball SID:** LaMonica Scott. **Telephone:** (662) 254-8378.
Assistant Coaches: Terrance Steele.
Home Field: Magnolia Field. **Seating Capacity:** 3,006. **Outfield Dimension: LF**—315, **CF**—395, **RF**—315.

MISSOURI TIGERS

Conference: Southeastern.
Mailing Address: 100 MATC, Columbia, MO 65201. **Website:** www.mutigers.com.
Head Coach: Steve Bieser. **Telephone:** (573) 884-9486. **Baseball SID:** Shawn Davis. **Telephone:** (573) 882-0711.
Assistant Coaches: Fred Corral, *Lance Rhodes. **Telephone:** (573) 884-4783.
Home Field: Taylor Stadium. **Seating Capacity:** 3,031. **Outfield Dimension: LF**—330, **CF**—400, **RF**—340.

MISSOURI STATE BEARS

Conference: Missouri Valley.
Mailing Address: 901 S. National, Springfield, MO 65897. **Website:** www.missouristatebears.com.
Head Coach: Keith Guttin. **Telephone:** (417) 836-4497. **Baseball SID:** Eric Doennig. **Telephone:** (417) 836-4586.
Assistant Coaches: Paul Evans, *Matt Lawson. **Telephone:** (417) 836-4496.
Home Field: Hammons Field. **Seating Capacity:** 8,000. **Outfield Dimension: LF**—315, **CF**—400, **RF**—330.

MONMOUTH HAWKS

Conference: .Metro Atlantic
Mailing Address: 400 Cedar Ave., West Long Branch, NJ 07764. **Website:** www.monmouthhawks.com.
Head Coach: Dean Ehehalt. **Telephone:** (732) 263-5186. **Baseball SID:** Gary Kowal. **Telephone:** (732) 263-5557.
Assistant Coaches: *Chris Collazo, Brady Kirkpatrick. **Telephone:** (732) 263-5347.
Home Field: MU Baseball Field. **Seating Capacity:** 2,100. **Outfield Dimension: LF**—325, **CF**—395, **RF**—320.

MOREHEAD STATE EAGLES

Conference: Ohio Valley.
Mailing Address: 195 Academic-Athletic Center, Morehead, KY 40351. **Website:** www.msueagles.com.
Head Coach: Mike McGuire. **Telephone:** (606) 783-2882. **Baseball SID:** Ryan Frye. **Telephone:** (606) 783-2500.
Assistant Coaches: *Adam Brown, Kane Sweeney.

Telephone: (606) 783-2881.
Home Field: Allen Field. **Seating Capacity:** 1,000.
Outfield Dimension: LF—320, **CF**—380, **RF**—320.

MOUNT ST. MARY'S

Conference: Northeast.
Mailing Address: 16300 Old Emmitsburg Rd., Emmitsburg, MD 21727. **Website:** www.mountathletics.com.
Head Coach: Scott Thompson. **Telephone:** (301) 447-3806. **Baseball SID:** Zach Kenworthy. **Telephone:** (301) 447-5384.
Assistant Coaches: Ivor Hodgson, Kyle Kane.
Home Field: E.T. Straw Family Stadium.

MURRAY STATE RACERS

Conference: Ohio Valley.
Mailing Address: 207 Stewart Stadium, Murray, KY, 42071. **Website:** www.goracers.com.
Head Coach: Kevin Moulder. **Telephone:** (270) 809-4892. **Baseball SID:** Kevin DeVries. **Telephone:** (270) 809-7044.
Assistant Coaches: *Grayson Crawford, Joe Migliaccio. **Telephone:** (270) 809-3869.
Home Field: Johnny Reagan Field. **Seating Capacity:** 800. **Outfield Dimension: LF**—330, **CF**—400, **RF**—330.

NAVY MIDSHIPMEN

Conference: Patriot.
Mailing Address: 566 Brownson Rd., Annapolis, MD 21402. **Website:** www.navysports.com.
Head Coach: Paul Kostacopoulos. **Telephone:** (410) 293-5571. **Baseball SID:** Alex Lumb. **Telephone:** (410) 293-8771. **Fax:** (410) 293-8954.
Assistant Coaches: Bobby Applegate, *Jeff Kane. **Telephone:** (410) 293-8946.
Home Field: Terwilliger Brothers Field at Max Bishop Stadium. **Seating Capacity:** 1,500. **Outfield Dimension: LF**—318, **CF**—390, **RF**—300.

NEBRASKA CORNHUSKERS

Conference: Big Ten.
Mailing Address: 1 Memorial Stadium, Lincoln, NE 68588. **Website:** www.huskers.com.
Head Coach: Darin Erstad. **Telephone:** (402) 472-2269. **Baseball SID:** Connor Stange. **Telephone:** (402) 472-6684.
Assistant Coaches: Mike Kirby, *Ted Silva. **Telephone:** (402) 472-2269.
Home Field: Hawks Field at Haymarket Park. **Seating Capacity:** 8,486. **Outfield Dimension: LF**—335, **CF**—395, **RF**—325.

NEBRASKA-OMAHA MAVERICKS

Conference: Summit.
Mailing Address: Sapp Fieldhouse, 6001 Dodge St., Omaha, NE 68182. **Website:** www.omavs.com.
Head Coach: Evan Porter. **Telephone:** (402) 554-2141. **Baseball SID:** Bonnie Ryan. **Telephone:** (402) 554-3267.
Assistant Coaches: Chris Gadsden, Brian Strawn.
Home Field: Ballpark at Boys Town. **Outfield Dimension: LF**—335, **CF**—410, **RF**—335.

NEVADA WOLF PACK

Conference: Mountain West.
Mailing Address: University of Nevada, 1664 North Virginia, Reno, NV 89557. **Website:** www.nevadawolfpack.com.

Head Coach: T.J. Bruce. Telephone: (775) 682-6978. Baseball SID: Jack Kuestermeyer. Telephone: (775) 682-6984.
Assistant Coaches: Steven Bennett, *Jake Silverman. Home Field: Don Weir Field at Peccole Park. Seating Capacity: 3,000. Outfield Dimension: LF—340, CF—401, RF—340.

NEVADA-LAS VEGAS REBELS

Conference: Mountain West.
Mailing Address: 4505 S. Maryland Parkway, Las Vegas, NV 89154-0009. Website: www.unlvrebels.com.
Head Coach: Stan Stolte. Telephone: (702) 895-3499. Baseball SID: Jeff Seals. Telephone: (702) 895-3134.
Assistant Coaches: Patrick Armstrong, *Kevin Higgins. Telephone: (702) 895-3835.
Home Field: Earl E. Wilson Stadium. Seating Capacity: 3,000. Outfield Dimension: LF—335, CF—400, RF—335.

NEW JERSEY TECH HIGHLANDERS

Conference: Atlantic Sun.
Mailing Address: 323 Martin Luther King Blvd., Newark, NJ 07102. Website: www.njithighlanders.com.
Head Coach: Brian Guiliana. Telephone: (973) 985-6434. Baseball SID: Stephanie Pillari. Telephone: (973) 596-8324.
Assistant Coaches: *Robert McClellan, Grant Neary. Telephone: (973) 596-8396.
Home Field: Riverfront Stadium. Seating Capacity: 6,500. Outfield Dimension: LF—305, CF—396, RF—315.

NEW MEXICO LOBOS

Conference: Mountain West.
Mailing Address: The University of New Mexico Lobos, Colleen J. Maloof Administration Building, 1 University of New Mexico, MSC04 2680, Albuquerque, NM 87131. Website: www.golobos.com.
Head Coach: Ray Birmingham. Telephone: (505) 925-5721. Baseball SID: Clayton Jones.
Assistant Coaches: *Buddy Gouldsmith, Ken Jacome. Telephone: (505) 925-5721.
Home Field: Santa Ana Star Field. Seating Capacity: 1,000. Outfield Dimension: LF—338, CF—413, RF—338.

NEW MEXICO STATE AGGIES

Conference: Western Athletic.
Mailing Address: PO Box 30001, Las Cruces, NM 88003. Website: www.nmstatesports.com.
Head Coach: Brian Green. Telephone: (575) 646-7693. Baseball SID: Chris Kennedy. Telephone: (575) 646-3269.
Assistant Coaches: Anthony Claggett, *Terry Davis. Telephone: (575) 646-5813.
Home Field: Presley Askew Stadium. Seating Capacity: 1,000. Outfield Dimension: LF—345, CF—400, RF—345.

NEW ORLEANS PRIVATEEERS

Conference: Southland.
Mailing Address: 2000 Lakeshore Dr., New Orleans, LA 70148. Website: www.unoprivateers.com.
Head Coach: Blake Dean. Telephone: (504) 280-3879. Baseball SID: Emmanuel Pepis. Telephone: (504) 280-6284.
Assistant Coaches: *Brett Stewart, Rudy Darrow. Telephone: (504) 280-3879.
Home Field: Maestri Field at First NBC Ballpark.

Seating Capacity: 2,900. Outfield Dimension: LF—330, CF—405, RF—330.

NIAGARA PURPLE EAGLES

Conference: Metro Atlantic Athletic.
Mailing Address: Upper Level Gallagher Center, P.O. Box 2009, Niagara University, NY 14109. Website: www.purpleeagles.com.
Head Coach: Rob McCoy. Telephone: (716) 286-7361. Baseball SID: Breanna Jacobs. Telephone: (716) 286-8586.
Assistant Coaches: *Matt Spatafora. Telephone: (716) 286-8624.
Home Field: Bobo Field.

NICHOLLS STATE COLONELS

Conference: Southland.
Mailing Address: 906 East 1st St., Thibodaux, LA 70301. Website: www.geauxcolonels.com.
Head Coach: Seth Thibodeaux. Telephone: (985) 449-7149. Baseball SID: Jordan Bergeron. Telephone: (985) 448-4282. Fax: (985) 448-4814.
Assistant Coaches: Zach Butler, *Walt Jones. Telephone: (985) 448-4882.
Home Field: Ray E. Didier Field at Ben Meyer Diamond. Seating Capacity: 2,000. Outfield Dimension: LF—330, CF—400, RF—315.

NORFOLK STATE SPARTANS

Conference: Mid-Eastern Athletic.
Mailing Address: 700 Park Ave., Norfolk, VA 23504. Website: www.nsuspartans.com.
Head Coach: Keith Shumate. Telephone: (757) 823-8196. Baseball SID: Matt Michalec. Telephone: (757) 823-2628.
Assistant Coaches: Matt Mitchell.
Home Field: Marty L. Miller Field. Seating Capacity: 1,500. Outfield Dimension: LF—330, CF—404, RF—318.

NORTH CAROLINA TAR HEELS

Conference: Atlantic Coast.
Mailing Address: 101 Ridge Road Chapel Hill, NC 27514. Website: www.tarheelblue.com.
Head Coach: Mike Fox. Telephone: (919) 962-2351. Baseball SID: T.J. Scholl. Telephone: (919) 962-8916.
Assistant Coaches: *Scott Forbes, Robert Woodard. Telephone: (919) 962-5451.
Home Field: Boshamer Stadium. Seating Capacity: 5,000. Outfield Dimension: LF—335, CF—400, RF—340.

NORTH CAROLINA A&T AGGIES

Conference: Mid-Eastern Athletic.
Mailing Address: 1601 E. Market St., Greensboro, NC 27411. Website: www.ncataggies.com.
Head Coach: Ben Hall. Telephone: (336) 285-4272. Baseball SID: Brian Holloway. Telephone: (336) 285-3608.
Assistant Coaches: *Tyrone Dawson, Jamie Serber. Telephone: (336) 285-4273.
Home Field: War Memorial Stadium. Seating Capacity: 2,000. Outfield Dimension: LF—370, CF—401, RF—336.

NORTH CAROLINA CENTRAL EAGLES

Conference: Mid-Eastern Athletic.
Mailing Address: McDougald-McLendon Arena, 1801 Fayetteville St., Durham, NC 27707. Website: www.

nccueaglepride.com.

Head Coach: Jim Koerner. **Telephone:** (919) 530-6273. **Baseball SID:** Jonathan Duren. **Telephone:** (919) 530-6892.

Assistant Coaches: A.J. Battisto, Neal Henry. **Telephone:** (919) 530-5439.

Home Field: Durham Athletic Park. **Seating Capacity:** 2,000. **Outfield Dimension: LF**—327, **CF**—398, **RF**—290.

NORTH CAROLINA STATE WOLFPACK

Conference: Atlantic Coast.
Mailing Address: 1081 Varsity Dr., Raleigh, NC 27606. **Website:** www.gopack.com.
Head Coach: Elliott Avent. **Telephone:** (919) 515-3613. **Baseball SID:** Justin Wilson. **Telephone:** (919) 746-8438.
Assistant Coaches: Scott Foxhall, *Chris Hart. **Telephone:** (919) 515-3613.
Home Field: Doak Field at Dail Park. **Seating Capacity:** 3,100. **Outfield Dimension: LF**—325, **CF**—400, **RF**—330.

NORTH DAKOTA STATE BISON

Conference: Summit.
Mailing Address: 1600 University Dr. N., Fargo, ND 58102. **Website:** www.gobison.com.
Head Coach: Tod Brown. **Telephone:** (701) 231-8853. **Baseball SID:** Ryan Anderson. **Telephone:** (701) 231-5591.
Assistant Coaches: Jeff Ditch, *Tyler Oakes. **Telephone:** (701) 231-8739.
Home Field: Newman Outdoor Field. **Seating Capacity:** 4,172. **Outfield Dimension: LF**—318, **CF**—408, **RF**—314.

NORTH FLORIDA OSPREY

Conference: Atlantic Sun.
Mailing Address: 1 UNF Dr. Jacksonville, Fla. 32224. **Website:** www.unfospreys.com.
Head Coach: Tim Parenton. **Telephone:** (904) 620-1556. **Baseball SID:** Tanner Ives. **Telephone:** (904) 620-4029. **Fax:** (904) 620-2836.
Assistant Coaches: Tommy Boss, *Andrew Hannon. **Telephone:** (904) 620-2586.
Home Field: Harmon Stadium. **Seating Capacity:** 1,000. **Outfield Dimension: LF**—325, **CF**—400, **RF**—325.

NORTHEASTERN HUSKIES

Conference: Colonial.
Mailing Address: 360 Huntington Ave Boston, MA. **Website:** www.gonu.com.
Head Coach: Mike Glavine. **Telephone:** (617) 373-3657. **Baseball SID:** Mike Skovan. **Telephone:** (617) 373-7931.
Assistant Coaches: Kevin Casey, *Kevin Cobb. **Telephone:** (617) 373-5256.
Home Field: Friedman Diamond. **Seating Capacity:** 5,000. **Outfield Dimension: LF**—326, **CF**—415, **RF**—346.

NORTHERN COLORADO BEARS

Conference: Western Athletic.
Mailing Address: 270 D Butler-Hancock Athletic Center, Greeley, CO 80639. **Website:** www.uncbears.com.
Head Coach: Carl Iwasaki. **Telephone:** (970) 351-1714. **Baseball SID:** Ryan Pfeifer. **Telephone:** (970) 351-3645.
Assistant Coaches: R.D. Spiehs, Nate Rasmussen. **Telephone:** (970) 351-1203.

Home Field: Jackson Field. **Seating Capacity:** 1,500. **Outfield Dimension: LF**—345, **CF**—407, **RF**—356.

NORTHERN ILLINOIS HUSKIES

Conference: Mid-American.
Mailing Address: Convocation Center, DeKalb, IL 60115. **Website:** www.niuhuskies.com.
Head Coach: Mike Kunigonis. **Telephone:** (815) 753-0147.
Assistant Coaches: *Andrew Maki, Luke Stewart. **Telephone:** (815) 753-0149.
Home Field: Ralph McKinzie Field. **Seating Capacity:** 1,500. **Outfield Dimension: LF**—312, **CF**—395, **RF**—322.

NORTHERN KENTUCKY NORSE

Conference: Horizon.
Mailing Address: 133 BB&T Arena at Northern Kentucky University, 500 Nunn Dr., Highland Heights, KY 41099. **Website:** www.nkunorse.com.
Head Coach: Todd Asalon. **Telephone:** (859) 572-6474. **Baseball SID:** Ryan Wilker. **Telephone:** (859) 572-7850.
Assistant Coaches: Dizzy Peyton. **Telephone:** (859) 572-5940.
Home Field: Bill Aker Baseball Complex. **Seating Capacity:** 500. **Outfield Dimension: LF**—320, **CF**—365, **RF**—320.

NORTHWESTERN WILDCATS

Conference: Big Ten.
Mailing Address: 2750 Ashland Ave., Evanston, IL 60201. **Website:** www.nusports.com.
Head Coach: Spencer Allen. **Telephone:** (847) 491-4652. **Baseball SID:** Ray O'Connell. **Telephone:** (847) 467-3418.
Assistant Coaches: Dusty Napoleon, *Josh Reynolds. **Telephone:** (847) 491-1211.
Home Field: Rocky and Berenice Miller Park. **Seating Capacity:** 2,500. **Outfield Dimension: LF**—325, **CF**—402, **RF**—318.

NORTHWESTERN STATE DEMONS

Conference: Southland.
Mailing Address: 220 S. Jefferson, Natchitoches, LA 71497. **Website:** www.nsudemons.com.
Head Coach: Bobby Barbier. **Telephone:** (318) 357-4139. **Baseball SID:** Jason Pugh. **Telephone:** (318) 357-6469. **Fax:** (318) 357-4515.
Assistant Coaches: *Chris Bertrand, Taylor Dugas. **Telephone:** (318) 357-4134.
Home Field: Brown-Stroud Field. **Seating Capacity:** 1,200. **Outfield Dimension: LF**—320, **CF**—405, **RF**—340.

NOTRE DAME FIGHTING IRISH

Conference: Atlantic Coast.
Mailing Address: University of Notre Dame, Notre Dame, IN 46556. **Website:** www.und.com.
Head Coach: Mik Aoki. **Telephone:** (574) 631-4840. **Baseball SID:** Megan Golden. **Telephone:** (574) 631-2664.
Assistant Coaches: Chuck Ristano, Jesse Woods. **Telephone:** (574) 631-4840.
Home Field: Frank Eck Field. **Seating Capacity:** 2,500. **Outfield Dimension: LF**—330, **CF**—400, **RF**—330.

OAKLAND

Conference: Horizon.
Mailing Address: 569 Pioneer Dr., Rochester, MI 48309. **Website:** www.goldengrizzlies.com.
Co-Head Coaches: Jacke Healey, Colin Kaline. **Telephone:** (248) 370-4059. **Baseball SID:** Mekye Phelps. **Telephone:** (248) 370-2933.
Assistant Coaches: Hayden Fox. **Telephone:** (248) 370-4228.
Home Field: Oakland Baseball Field. **Seating Capacity:** 500. **Outfield Dimension: LF**—333, **CF**—380, **RF**—320.

OHIO BOBCATS

Conference: Mid-American.
Mailing Address: 140 S. Shafer St., Athens, OH 45701. **Website:** www.ohiobobcats.com.
Head Coach: Rob Smith. **Telephone:** (740) 593-1180. **Baseball SID:** Mike Ashcraft. **Telephone:** (740) 593-1299. **Fax:** (740) 593-2420.
Assistant Coaches: Craig Moore, *C.J. Wamsley. **Telephone:** (740) 593-1954.
Home Field: Bob Wren Stadium. **Seating Capacity:** 4,000. **Outfield Dimension: LF**—340, **CF**—380, **RF**—400.

OHIO STATE BUCKEYES

Conference: Big Ten.
Mailing Address: 250 Bill Davis Stadium, 650 Borror Dr., Columbus, OH 43210. **Website:** www.ohiostatebuckeyes.com.
Head Coach: Greg Beals. **Telephone:** (614) 292-1075. **Baseball SID:** Alex Morando. **Telephone:** (614) 292-1389.
Assistant Coaches: *Chris Holick, Mike Stafford. **Telephone:** (614) 292-1075.
Home Field: Bill Davis Stadium. **Seating Capacity:** 4,450. **Outfield Dimension: LF**—330, **CF**—400, **RF**—330.

OKLAHOMA SOONERS

Conference: Big 12.
Mailing Address: 401 W. Imhoff Rd., Norman, OK, 73072. **Website:** www.soonersports.com.
Head Coach: Skip Johnson. **Telephone:** (405) 325-8354. **Baseball SID:** Brendan Flynn. **Telephone:** (405) 325-6449. **Fax:** (405) 325-7623.
Assistant Coaches: Clay Overcash, *Clay Van. **Telephone:** (405) 325-8354.
Home Field: L. Dale Mitchell Park. **Seating Capacity:** 3,180. **Outfield Dimension: LF**—330, **CF**—410, **RF**—330.

OKLAHOMA STATE COWBOYS

Conference: Big 12.
Mailing Address: Allie P. Reynolds Stadium, Stillwater, OK 74078. **Website:** www.okstate.com.
Head Coach: Josh Holliday. **Telephone:** (405) 744-7141. **Baseball SID:** Wade McWhorter. **Telephone:** (405) 744-7853. **Fax:** (405) 744-7754.
Assistant Coaches: *James Vilade, Rob Walton. **Telephone:** (405) 744-7141.
Home Field: Allie P. Reynolds Stadium. **Seating Capacity:** 4,000. **Outfield Dimension: LF**—330, **CF**—398, **RF**—330.

OLD DOMINION MONARCHS

Conference: Conference USA.
Mailing Address: Jim Jarrett Athletic Admin. Building, Norfolk, VA 23529. **Website:** www.odusports.com.

Head Coach: Chris Finwood. **Telephone:** (757) 683-4230. **Baseball SID:** Tim Wentz. **Telephone:** (757) 683-5581.
Assistant Coaches: Mike Marron, *Logan Robbins. **Telephone:** (757) 683-4331.
Home Field: Bud Metheny Baseball Complex. **Seating Capacity:** 2,500. **Outfield Dimension: LF**—325, **CF**—395, **RF**—325.

ORAL ROBERTS GOLDEN EAGLES

Conference: Summit.
Mailing Address: 7777 S. Lewis Ave., Tulsa, OK 74171. **Website:** www.oruathletics.com.
Head Coach: Ryan Folmar. **Telephone:** (918) 495-7639. **Baseball SID:** Scott Slarks. **Telephone:** (918) 495-6646.
Assistant Coaches: Wes Davis, *Ryan Neill. **Telephone:** (918) 495-7206.
Home Field: JL Johnson. **Seating Capacity:** 2,418. **Outfield Dimension: LF**—330, **CF**—400, **RF**—330.

OREGON DUCKS

Conference: Pac-12.
Mailing Address: Len Casanova Center, 2727 Leo Harris Parkway, Eugene, OR 97401. **Website:** www.goducks.com.
Head Coach: George Horton. **Telephone:** (541) 646-5235. **Baseball SID:** Todd Miles. **Telephone:** (541) 346-0962.
Assistant Coaches: Jason Dietrich, Jay Uhlman. **Telephone:** (541) 346-5229.
Home Field: PK Park. **Seating Capacity:** 4,000. **Outfield Dimension: LF**—335, **CF**—400, **RF**—325.

OREGON STATE BEAVERS

Conference: Pac-12.
Mailing Address: 114 Gill Coliseum, Corvallis, OR 97331. **Website:** www.osubeavers.com.
Head Coach: Pat Casey. **Baseball SID:** Hank Hager. **Telephone:** (541) 737-7472.
Assistant Coaches: Pat Bailey, *Nate Yeskie. **Telephone:** (541) 737-0598.
Home Field: Goss Stadium at Coleman Field. **Seating Capacity:** 3,315. **Outfield Dimension: LF**—330, **CF**—400, **RF**—330.

PACIFIC TIGERS

Conference: West Coast.
Mailing Address: 3601 Pacific Ave., Stockton, CA 95211. **Website:** www.pacifictigers.com.
Head Coach: Ryan Garko. **Telephone:** (209) 946-2709.
Assistant Coaches: Joey Centanni, Michael Reuvekamp. **Telephone:** (209) 946-2386.
Home Field: Klein Family Field. **Seating Capacity:** 2,800. **Outfield Dimension: LF**—317, **CF**—405, **RF**—325.

PENN STATE NITTANY LIONS

Conference: Big Ten.
Mailing Address: 701 Porter Rd., State College, PA 16801. **Website:** www.gopsusports.com.
Head Coach: Rob Cooper. **Telephone:** (814) 863-0239. **Baseball SID:** Mark Brumbaugh. **Telephone:** (814) 863-1377.
Assistant Coaches: Andre Butler, *Josh Newman. **Telephone:** (814) 865-8607.
Home Field: Medlar Field at Lubrano Park. **Seating Capacity:** 5,406. **Outfield Dimension: LF**—325, **CF**—399, **RF**—320.

PENNSYLVANIA QUAKERS

Conference: Ivy League.
Mailing Address: 233 S. 33rd St., Philadelphia, PA 19104. **Website:** www.pennathletics.com.
Head Coach: John Yurkow. **Telephone:** (215) 898-6282.
Assistant Coaches: *Mike Santello, Josh Schwartz. **Telephone:** (215) 746-2325.
Home Field: Meiklejohn Stadium. **Seating Capacity:** 1,000. **Outfield Dimension: LF**—325, **CF**—390, **RF**—325.

PEPPERDINE WAVES

Conference: West Coast.
Mailing Address: 24255 Pacific Coast Hwy., Malibu, CA 90263. **Website:** www.pepperdinesports.com.
Head Coach: Rick Hirtensteiner. **Telephone:** (310) 506-4404. **Baseball SID:** Jacob Breems. **Telephone:** (310) 506-4333.
Assistant Coaches: *Cooper Fouts, Rolando Garza. **Telephone:** (310) 506-4371.
Home Field: Eddy D. Field Stadium. **Seating Capacity:** 1,800. **Outfield Dimension: LF**—330, **CF**—400, **RF**—330.

PITTSBURGH PANTHERS

Conference: Atlantic Coast.
Mailing Address: Fitzgerald Field House, Allequippa St., Pittsburgh, PA 15261. **Website:** www.pittsburghpanthers.com.
Head Coach: Joe Jordano. **Telephone:** (412) 648-8208. **Baseball SID:** Kely Dumrauf. **Telephone:** (412) 648-8240.
Assistant Coaches: Billy Alvino, *Jerry Oakes. **Telephone:** (412) 680-8556.
Home Field: Cost Field. **Seating Capacity:** 2,500. **Outfield Dimension: LF**—315, **CF**—405, **RF**—330.

PORTLAND PILOTS

Conference: West Coast.
Mailing Address: 5000 N. Willamette Blvd., Portland, Oregon. 97203. **Website:** www.portlandpilots.com.
Head Coach: Geoff Loomis. **Telephone:** (503) 943-7707. **Baseball SID:** Adam Linnman. **Telephone:** (503) 943-7731.
Assistant Coaches: Connor Lambert, *Jake Valentine. **Telephone:** (503) 943-7745.
Home Field: Joe Etzel Field. **Seating Capacity:** 1,300. **Outfield Dimension: LF**—325, **CF**—390, **RF**—325.

PRAIRIE VIEW A&M PANTHERS

Conference: Southwestern Athletic.
Mailing Address: PVAMU Athletics Department, P.O. Box 519, MS 1500, Prairie View, TX 77446. **Website:** www.pvpanthers.com.
Head Coach: Auntwan Riggins. **Telephone:** (936) 261-3955. **Baseball SID:** Duane Lewis. **Telephone:** (936) 261-3950.
Assistant Coaches: Terry Burrel, Brian White. **Telephone:** (936) 261-9115.
Home Field: Tankersley Field. **Seating Capacity:** 512.

PRESBYTERIAN BLUE HOSE

Conference: Big South.
Mailing Address: 105 Ashland Ave., Clinton, SC 29325. **Website:** www.gobluehose.com.
Head Coach: Elton Pollock. **Telephone:** (864) 833-8236. **Baseball SID:** Davis Simpson.
Telephone: (864) 833-7095.
Assistant Coaches: Parker Bangs. **Telephone:** (864) 833-7093.
Home Field: Presbyterian College Baseball Complex. **Seating Capacity:** 500. **Outfield Dimension: LF**—325, **CF**—400, **RF**—325.

PRINCETON TIGERS

Conference: Ivy League.
Mailing Address: Princeton University, Jadwin Gym, Princeton, NJ 08544. **Website:** www.goprincetontigers.com.
Head Coach: Scott Bradley. **Telephone:** (609) 258-5059. **Baseball SID:** Warren Croxton. **Telephone:** (609) 258-2630.
Assistant Coaches: Lloyd Brewer. **Telephone:** (609) 258-5684.
Home Field: Clarke Field. **Seating Capacity:** 1,000. **Outfield Dimension: LF**—335, **CF**—400, **RF**—320.

PURDUE BOILERMAKERS

Conference: Big Ten.
Mailing Address: 900 John R. Wooden Drive, West Lafayette, IN 47907. **Website:** www.purduesports.com.
Head Coach: Mark Wasikowski. **Telephone:** (765) 494-3998. **Baseball SID:** Ben Turner. **Telephone:** (765) 494-3198.
Assistant Coaches: Wally Crancer, *Steve Holm. **Telephone:** (765) 494-9360.
Home Field: Alexander Field. **Seating Capacity:** 2,000. **Outfield Dimension: LF**—340, **CF**—408, **RF**—330.

QUINNIPIAC BOBCATS

Conference: Metro Atlantic Athletic.
Mailing Address: 275 Mount Carmel Ave., Hamden, CT 06518. **Website:** www.quinnipiacbobcats.com.
Head Coach: John Delaney. **Telephone:** (203) 582-6546. **Baseball SID:** Andrew Carlson.
Assistant Coaches: Pat Egan. **Telephone:** (203) 582-7774.
Home Field: QU Baseball Field. **Seating Capacity:** 1,000. **Outfield Dimension: LF**—340, **CF**—400, **RF**—325.

RADFORD HIGHLANDERS

Conference: Big South.
Mailing Address: 501 Stockton St., Radford, VA 24142. **Website:** www.ruhighlanders.com.
Head Coach: Joe Raccuia. **Telephone:** (540) 831-5881. **Baseball SID:** Jordan Childress. **Telephone:** (540) 831-5211. **Fax:** (540) 831-6095.
Assistant Coaches: Jeff Kemp. **Telephone:** (540) 831-6513.
Home Field: Williams Field at Carter Memorial Stadium. **Seating Capacity:** 4,500. **Outfield Dimension: LF**—330, **CF**—400, **RF**—330.

RHODE ISLAND RAMS

Conference: Atlantic 10.
Mailing Address: 3 Keaney Rd. Suite 1, Kingston RI 02881. **Website:** www.gorhody.com.
Head Coach: Raphael Cerrato. **Telephone:** (401) 874-4550. **Baseball SID:** Jodi Pontbriand. **Telephone:** (401) 874-5356.
Assistant Coaches: *Sean Obrien, Kevin Vance. **Telephone:** (401) 874-4888.
Home Field: Bill Beck. **Seating Capacity:** 500. **Outfield Dimension: LF**—330, **CF**—400, **RF**—330.

RICE OWLS

Conference: Conference USA.
Mailing Address: 6100 Main St., Houston, TX 77005.
Website: www.riceowls.com.
Head Coach: Wayne Graham. **Telephone:** (713) 348-8864. **Baseball SID:** John Sullivan. **Telephone:** (713) 348-5636.
Assistant Coaches: Paul Janish, John Pope.
Telephone: (713) 348-8859.
Home Field: Reckling Park. **Seating Capacity:** 6,193.
Outfield Dimension: LF—335, **CF**—400, **RF**—335.

RICHMOND SPIDERS

Conference: Atlantic 10.
Mailing Address: 28 Westhampton Way, Robins Center, Richmond, VA 23173. **Website:** www.richmond spiders.com.
Head Coach: Tracy Woodson. **Telephone:** (804) 289-8391. **Baseball SID:** Kristen Litchfield. **Telephone:** (804) 289-8365.
Assistant Coaches: Nate Mulberg, *R.J. Thomas.
Telephone: (804) 289-8391.
Home Field: Pitt Field. **Seating Capacity:** 3,000.
Outfield Dimension: LF—330, **CF**—390, **RF**—330.

RIDER BRONCS

Conference: Metro Atlantic.
Mailing Address: 2083 Lawrenceville Rd., Lawrenceville, NJ 08648. **Website:** www.gobroncs.com.
Head Coach: Barry Davis. **Telephone:** (609) 896-5055.
Baseball SID: Steve Cunha. **Telephone:** (609) 896-5135.
Fax: (609) 896-0341.
Assistant Coaches: *John Crane, Lee Lipinski.
Telephone: (609) 896-5055.
Home Field: Sonny Pittaro Field. **Seating Capacity:** 400. **Outfield Dimension: LF**—330, **CF**—405, **RF**—330.

RUTGERS SCARLET KNIGHTS

Conference: Big Ten.
Mailing Address: 83 Rockafeller Rd., Piscataway, NJ 08854. **Website:** www.scarletknights.com.
Head Coach: Joe Litterio. **Baseball SID:** Jimmy Gill.
Telephone: (732) 445-8103.
Assistant Coaches: *Phil Cundari, Jim Duffy.
Telephone: (732) 445-7834.
Home Field: Bainton Field. **Seating Capacity:** 1,500.
Outfield Dimension: LF—330, **CF**—410, **RF**—320.

SACRAMENTO STATE HORNETS

Conference: Western Athletic.
Mailing Address: 6000 J St., Sacramento, CA 95819.
Website: www.hornetsports.com.
Head Coach: Reggie Christiansen. **Telephone:** (916) 278-4036. **Baseball SID:** Robert Barsanti. **Telephone:** (916) 278-6896.
Assistant Coaches: Jake Angier, Tim Wheeler.
Telephone: (916) 278-2017.
Home Field: John Smith Field. **Seating Capacity:** 1,200. **Outfield Dimension: LF**—333, **CF**—400, **RF**—333.

SACRED HEART PIONEERS

Conference: Northeast.
Mailing Address: 5151 Park Ave., Fairfield, CT 06825.
Website: www.sacredheartpioneers.com.
Head Coach: Nick Restaino. **Telephone:** (203) 365-7632. **Baseball SID:** Brian Duane. **Telephone:** (203)

396-8127.
Assistant Coaches: T.K. Kiernan, * Wayne Mazzoni.
Telephone: (203) 365-4469.
Home Field: The Ballpark at Harbor Yard. **Seating Capacity:** 5,300. **Outfield Dimension: LF**—325, **CF**—405, **RF**—325.

SAINT LOUIS BILLIKENS

Conference: Atlantic 10.
Mailing Address: 3330 Laclede Ave., St Louis, MO 63103. **Website:** www.slubillikens.com.
Head Coach: Darin Hendrickson. **Telephone:** (314) 977-3172. **Baseball SID:** Brian Kunderman. **Telephone:** (314) 808-4868.
Assistant Coaches: *Will Bradley, Joey Hawkins.
Telephone: (314) 977-3260.
Home Field: The Billiken Sports Center. **Seating Capacity:** 500. **Outfield Dimension: LF**—330, **CF**—408, **RF**—330.

SAM HOUSTON STATE BEARKATS

Conference: Southland.
Mailing Address: 620 Bowers Blvd Huntsville, TX 77341. **Website:** www.gobearkats.com.
Head Coach: Matt Deggs. **Telephone:** (936) 294-1731.
Baseball SID: Andrew Pate. **Telephone:** (936) 294-2692.
Assistant Coaches: *Lance Harvell, Jay Sirianni.
Telephone: (936) 294-2580.
Home Field: Don Sanders Stadium. **Seating Capacity:** 1,163. **Outfield Dimension: LF**—330, **CF**—400, **RF**—330.

SAMFORD BULLDOGS

Conference: Southern.
Mailing Address: 800 Lakeshore Dr., Birmingham, AL 35229. **Website:** www.samfordsports.com.
Head Coach: Casey Dunn. **Telephone:** (205) 726-2134.
Baseball SID: Zac Schrieber. **Telephone:** (205) 726-2802.
Assistant Coaches: Tony David, * Tyler Shrout.
Telephone: (205) 726-4294.
Home Field: Joe Lee Griffin Field. **Seating Capacity:** 1,000. **Outfield Dimension: LF**—330, **CF**—390, **RF**—335.

SAN DIEGO TOREROS

Conference: West Coast.
Mailing Address: 5998 Alcala Park, San Diego, CA 92110. **Website:** www.usdtoreros.cstv.com.
Head Coach: Rich Hill. **Telephone:** (619) 260-5953.
Baseball SID: Ben Pearson. **Telephone:** (619) 260-2323.
Assistant Coaches: Nathan Choate, *Brad Marcelino.
Telephone: (619) 260-5989.
Home Field: Fowler Park. **Seating Capacity:** 1,700.
Outfield Dimension: LF—312, **CF**—391, **RF**—327.

SAN DIEGO STATE AZTECS

Conference: Mountain West.
Mailing Address: 5500 Campanile Rd., San Diego, CA 92182. **Website:** www.goaztecs.com.
Head Coach: Mark Martinez. **Telephone:** (619) 594-3357. **Baseball SID:** Martin Foley. **Telephone:** (619) 594-5242.
Assistant Coaches: *Joe Oliveira, Sam Peraza.
Telephone: (619) 594-3357.
Home Field: Tony Gwynn Stadium. **Seating Capacity:** 3,500. **Outfield Dimension: LF**—340, **CF**—410, **RF**—340.

COLLEGE

SAN FRANCISCO DONS

Conference: West Coast.
Mailing Address: 2130 Fulton St., San Francisco, CA 94117. **Website:** www.usfdons.com.
Head Coach: Nino Giarratano. **Telephone:** (415) 422-2934. **Baseball SID:** Kevin Boyle. **Telephone:** (415) 422-8222.
Assistant Coaches: Aritz Garcia, *Troy Nakamura. **Telephone:** (415) 422-6881.
Home Field: Benedetti Diamond. **Seating Capacity:** 1,000. **Outfield Dimension: LF**—330, **CF**—405, **RF**—300

SAN JOSE STATE SPARTANS

Conference: Mountain West.
Mailing Address: 1 Washington Square, San Jose, CA 95192. **Website:** www.sjsuspartans.com.
Head Coach: Jason Hawkins. **Telephone:** (408) 924-1255.
Assistant Coaches: Tyler LaTorre. **Telephone:** (408) 924-1262.
Home Field: Municipal Stadium. **Seating Capacity:** 5,200. **Outfield Dimension: LF**—320, **CF**—390, **RF**—320.

SANTA CLARA BRONCOS

Conference: West Coast.
Mailing Address: 500 El Camino Real, Santa Clara, CA 95053. **Website:** www.santaclarabroncos.com.
Head Coach: Rusty Filter. **Telephone:** (408) 554-4882. **Baseball SID:** Dean Obara. **Telephone:** (408) 554-4690.
Assistant Coaches: *Jon Karcich, B.K. Santy. **Telephone:** (408) 554-4151.
Home Field: Stephen Schott Stadium. **Seating Capacity:** 1,500. **Outfield Dimension: LF**—340, **CF**—402, RF 335.

SAVANNAH STATE TIGERS

Conference: Mid-Eastern Athletic.
Mailing Address: 3219 College St., Savannah, GA 31404. **Website:** www.ssuathletics.com.
Head Coach: Carlton Hardy. **Telephone:** (912) 358-3082. **Baseball SID:** Opio Mashariki. **Telephone:** (912) 358-3430. **Fax:** (912) 358-3682.
Assistant Coaches: *Eric McCombie, Nick Tracy. **Telephone:** (912) 358-3093.
Home Field: Tigers Field. **Seating Capacity:** 800. **Outfield Dimension: LF**—330, **CF**—400, **RF**—330

SEATTLE REDHAWKS

Conference: Western Athletic.
Mailing Address: 901 12th Ave., Seattle, WA 98203. **Website:** www.goseattleu.com.
Head Coach: Donny Harrel. **Telephone:** (206) 398-4399. **Baseball SID:** Sarah Finney. **Telephone:** (206) 296-5915.
Assistant Coaches: *Elliott Cribby, Greg Goetz. **Telephone:** (206) 398-4396.
Home Field: Bannerwood Park. **Seating Capacity:** 1,500. **Outfield Dimension: LF**—325, **CF**—405, **RF**—325.

SETON HALL PIRATES

Conference: Big East.
Mailing Address: 400 South Orange Ave., South Orange, NJ 07079. **Website:** www.shupirates.com.
Head Coach: Rob Sheppard. **Telephone:** (973) 761-9557. **Baseball SID:** Matt Sweeney. **Telephone:** (973) 761-9493.
Assistant Coaches: *Mark Pappas, Pat Pinkman. **Telephone:** (973) 761-9557.
Home Field: Owen T. Carroll Field. **Seating Capacity:** 1,000. **Outfield Dimension: LF**—318, **CF**—400, **RF**—325.

SIENA SAINTS

Conference: Metro Atlantic.
Mailing Address: 515 Loudon Rd., Loudonville, NY 12211. **Website:** www.sienasaints.com.
Head Coach: Tony Rossi. **Telephone:** (518) 786-5044. **Baseball SID:** Mike Demos. **Telephone:** (518) 783-2377. **Fax:** (518) 783-2992.
Assistant Coaches: *Steve Adkins, Dave Yamane. **Telephone:** (518) 782-6875.
Home Field: Siena Field. **Seating Capacity:** 1,000. **Outfield Dimension: LF**—300, **CF**—400, **RF**—325.

SOUTH ALABAMA JAGUARS

Conference: Sun Belt.
Mailing Address: 70 Stadium Blvd., Mobile, AL 36608. **Website:** www.usajaguars.com.
Head Coach: Mark Calvi. **Telephone:** (251) 414-8243. **Baseball SID:** Charlie Nichols. **Telephone:** (251) 414-8017.
Assistant Coaches: Bob Keller, *Chris Prothro. **Telephone:** (251) 414-8209.
Home Field: Stanky Field. **Seating Capacity:** 4,000. **Outfield Dimension: LF**—330, **CF**—400, **RF**—330.

SOUTH CAROLINA GAMECOCKS

Conference: Southeastern.
Mailing Address: 431 Williams St., Columbia, SC 29201. **Website:** www.gamecocksonline.com.
Head Coach: Mark Kingston. **Telephone:** (803) 777-7808. **Baseball SID:** Kent Reichert. **Telephone:** (803) 777-5257.
Assistant Coaches: *Mike Current, Stuart Lake. **Telephone:** (803) 777-7808.
Home Field: Founders Park. **Seating Capacity:** 8,242. **Outfield Dimension: LF**—325, **CF**—400, **RF**—325.

SOUTH CAROLINA-UPSTATE

Conference: Atlantic Sun.
Mailing Address: 800 University Way, Spartanburg, SC 29303. **Website:** www.upstatespartans.com.
Head Coach: Matt Fincher. **Telephone:** (864) 503-5135. **Baseball SID:** Steven Grandy. **Telephone:** (864) 503-5129.
Assistant Coaches: Tim Brown, *Tyler Cook. **Telephone:** (864) 503-5164.
Home Field: Cleveland S. Harley Park. **Seating Capacity:** 500. **Outfield Dimension: LF**—330, **CF**—402, **RF**—330.

SOUTH DAKOTA STATE JACKRABBITS

Conference: Summit.
Mailing Address: 2820 Marshall Center, Brookings, SD 57007. **Website:** www.gojacks.com.
Head Coach: Rob Bishop. **Telephone:** (605) 688-5742. **Baseball SID:** Jason Hove. **Telephone:** (605) 688-4623. **Fax:** (605) 688-5999.
Assistant Coaches: *Brian Grunzke, Mitch Mormann. **Telephone:** (605) 592-6007.
Home Field: Erv Huether Field. **Seating Capacity:** 500. **Outfield Dimension: LF**—325, **CF**—390, **RF**—320.

SOUTH FLORIDA BULLS

Conference: American Athletic.
Mailing Address: 4202 E. Fowler Ave., Tampa, FL 33620. **Website:** www.gousfbulls.com.
Head Coach: Billy Mohl. **Telephone:** (813) 974-2504.
Baseball SID: Patrick Puzzo. **Telephone:** (813) 974-4087.
Assistant Coaches: Chris Cates, *Chuck Jeroloman. **Telephone:** (813) 974-2995.
Home Field: USF Baseball Stadium. **Seating Capacity:** 3,211. **Outfield Dimension: LF**—325, **CF**—400, **RF**—330.

SOUTHEAST MISSOURI STATE

Conference: Ohio Valley.
Mailing Address: 1 University Plaza, Cape Girardeau, MO 63701. **Website:** www.gosoutheast.com.
Head Coach: Andy Sawyers. **Telephone:** (573) 986-6002.
Assistant Coaches: *Curt Dixon, Craig Ringe.
Home Field: Alumni Field. **Seating Capacity:** 2,000.
Outfield Dimension: LF—330, **CF**—400, **RF**—330.

SOUTHEASTERN LOUISIANA LIONS

Conference: Southland.
Mailing Address: SLU Athletics, 800 Galloway Dr., Hammond, LA 70402. **Website:** www.lionsports.net.
Head Coach: Matt Riser. **Telephone:** (985) 549-5130.
Baseball SID: Damon Sunde. **Telephone:** (985) 549-3774.
Assistant Coaches: *Andrew Gipson, Daniel Latham. **Telephone:** (985) 549-5130.
Home Field: Pat Kenelly Diamond at Alumni Field. **Seating Capacity:** 2,000. **Outfield Dimension: LF**—330, **CF**—400, **RF**—330.

SOUTHERN JAGUARS

Conference: Southwestern Athletic.
Mailing Address: 801 Harding Blvd., Baton Rouge, LA 70813. **Website:** www.gojagsports.com.
Head Coach: Kerrick Jackson. **Telephone:** (225) 771-2513. **Baseball SID:** Christopher Jones. **Telephone:** (225) 771-3495.
Assistant Coaches: Elliott Jones, *Stephanos Stroop. **Telephone:** (225) 771-3882.
Home Field: Lee-Hines Stadium. **Seating Capacity:** 2,500. **Outfield Dimension: LF**—360, **CF**—400, **RF**—325.

SOUTHERN CALIFORNIA TROJANS

Conference: Pac-12.
Mailing Address: 1021 Childs Way, Los Angeles, CA 90089. **Website:** www.usctrojans.com.
Head Coach: Dan Hubbs. **Telephone:** (213) 740-8446.
Baseball SID: Jacob Breems. **Telephone:** (213) 740-3809.
Assistant Coaches: *Gabe Alvarez, Matt Curtis. **Telephone:** (213) 740-8447.
Home Field: Dedeaux Field. **Seating Capacity:** 2,500.
Outfield Dimension: LF—328, **CF**—400, **RF**—330.

SOUTHERN ILLINOIS SALUKIS

Conference: Missouri Valley.
Mailing Address: 425 Saluki Dr., Carbondale, IL 62901. **Website:** www.siusalukis.com.
Head Coach: Ken Henderson. **Telephone:** (618) 453-3794. **Baseball SID:** John Lock. **Telephone:** (618) 453-7102.
Assistant Coaches: P.J. Finigan, Seth LaRue. **Telephone:** (618) 453-2802.
Home Field: Itchy Jones Stadium. **Seating Capacity:** 2,000. **Outfield Dimension: LF**—330, **CF**—390, **RF**—330.

SOUTHERN ILLINOIS-EDWARDSVILLE COUGARS

Conference: Ohio Valley.
Mailing Address: 35 Circle Dr., Edwardsville, IL 62026. **Website:** www.siuecougars.com.
Head Coach: Sean Lyons. **Telephone:** (618) 650-2032.
Baseball SID: Joe Pott. **Telephone:** (618) 650-3608.
Assistant Coaches: Tyler Hancock, Brandon Scott.
Home Field: Simmons Complex. **Seating Capacity:** 1,300. **Outfield Dimension: LF**—330, **CF**—390, **RF**—330.

SOUTHERN MISSISSIPPI GOLDEN EAGLES

Conference: Conference USA.
Mailing Address: 118 College Dr., Box 5017, Hattiesburg, MS 39406. **Website:** www.southernmiss.com.
Head Coach: Scott Berry. **Telephone:** (601) 266-6542.
Baseball SID: Jack Duggan. **Telephone:** (601) 266-5947. **Fax:** (601) 266-4507.
Assistant Coaches: *Chad Caillet, Christian Ostrander. **Telephone:** (601) 266-6542.
Home Field: Pete Taylor Park at Hill Denson Field.
Seating Capacity: 4,200. **Outfield Dimension: LF**—340, **CF**—400, **RF**—340.

ST. BONAVENTURE BONNIES

Conference: Atlantic 10.
Mailing Address: P.O. Box G, Reilly Center, St. Bonaventure, NY 14778. **Website:** www.gobonnies.sbu.edu.
Head Coach: Larry Sudbrook. **Telephone:** (716) 375-2641. **Baseball SID:** Scott Eddy. **Telephone:** (716) 375-4019.
Assistant Coaches: B.J. Salerno. **Telephone:** (716) 375-2699.
Home Field: Fred Handler Park. **Seating Capacity:** 500. **Outfield Dimension: LF**—330, **CF**—403, **RF**—330.

ST. JOHN'S RED STORM

Conference: Big East.
Mailing Address: 8000 Utopia Pkwy., Queens, NY 11439. **Website:** www.redstormsports.com.
Head Coach: Ed Blankmeyer. **Telephone:** (718) 990-6148. **Baseball SID:** Andrew O'Connell. **Telephone:** (718) 990-1522.
Assistant Coaches: George Brown, Mike Hampton. **Telephone:** (718) 990-7523.
Home Field: Jack Kaiser Stadium. **Seating Capacity:** 3,500. **Outfield Dimension: LF**—325, **CF**—400, **RF**—325.

ST. JOSEPH'S HAWKS

Conference: Atlantic 10.
Mailing Address: 5600 City Ave., Philadelphia, PA 19131. **Website:** www.sjuhawks.com.
Head Coach: Fritz Hamburg. **Telephone:** (610) 660-1718. **Baseball SID:** Joe Greenwich. **Telephone:** (610) 660-1738. **Fax:** (610) 660-1724.
Assistant Coaches: Matt Allison, *Ryan Wheeler. **Telephone:** (610) 660-1704.
Home Field: Smithson Field. **Seating Capacity:** 400.
Outfield Dimension: LF—327, **CF**—400, **RF**—330.

ST. MARY'S GAELS

Conference: West Coast.
Mailing Address: 1928 St. Mary's Rd., Moraga, CA 94575. **Website:** www.smcgaels.com.
Head Coach: Eric Valenzuela. **Telephone:** (925) 631-4637. **Baseball SID:** Mark Rivera. **Telephone:** (925) 631-4950.

Assistant Coaches: Daniel Costanza, *Matt Fonteno. **Telephone:** (925) 631-4658. **Home Field:** Louis Guisto Field. **Seating Capacity:** 1,500. **Outfield Dimension: LF**—330, **CF**—400, **RF**—330.

SAINT PETER'S PEACOCKS

Conference: Metro Atlantic. **Mailing Address:** 2641 Kennedy Blvd., Jersey City, NJ 07306. **Website:** www.saintpeterspeacocks.com. **Head Coach:** Danny Ramirez. **Telephone:** (201) 761-7319. **Baseball SID:** Hamilton Cook. **Telephone:** (201) 761-7316. **Assistant Coaches:** Ron Hayward. **Home Field:** Jaroshack Field. **Outfield Dimension: LF**—318, **CF**—405, **RF**—310.

STANFORD CARDINAL

Conference: Pac-12. **Mailing Address:** 450 Serra Mall, Stanford, CA 94305. **Website:** www.gostanford.com. **Head Coach:** David Esquer. **Telephone:** (650) 723.4528. **Baseball SID:** Nick Sako. **Telephone:** (650) 224.0979. **Assistant Coaches:** Thomas Eager, Tommy Nicholson. **Telephone:** (650) 725.2373. **Home Field:** Klein Field at Sunken Diamond. **Seating Capacity:** 4,000. **Outfield Dimension: LF**—335, **CF**—400, **RF**—335.

STEPHEN F. AUSTIN STATE LUMBERJACKS

Conference: Southland. **Mailing Address:** SFA Athletics, P.O. Box 13010, SFA Station, Nacogdoches, TX 75962. **Website:** www.sfajacks.com. **Head Coach:** Johnny Cardenas. **Telephone:** (936) 468-5982. **Baseball SID:** Charlie Hurley. **Telephone:** (936) 468-2606. **Assistant Coaches:** Caleb Clowers, * Mike Haynes. **Telephone:** (936) 468-7796. **Home Field:** Jaycees Field. **Seating Capacity:** 500. **Outfield Dimension: LF**—320, **CF**—390, **RF**—320.

STETSON HATTERS

Conference: Atlantic Sun. **Mailing Address:** 421 N. Woodland Blvd., DeLand, FL 32723. **Website:** www.gohatters.com. **Head Coach:** Steve Trimper. **Telephone:** (386) 822-8100. **Baseball SID:** Ricky Hazel. **Telephone:** (386) 822-8130. **Fax:** (386) 822-7486. **Assistant Coaches:** *Joe Mercadante, Dave Therneau. **Telephone:** (386) 822-8733. **Home Field:** Melching Field at Conrad Park. **Seating Capacity:** 2,500. **Outfield Dimension: LF**—335, **CF**—403, **RF**—335.

STONY BROOK SEAWOLVES

Conference: America East. **Mailing Address:** Indoor Sports Complex. **Website:** www.stonybrookathletics.com. **Head Coach:** Matt Senk. **Telephone:** (631) 632-9226. **Baseball SID:** Brian Miller. **Telephone:** (631) 632-4318. **Assistant Coaches:** Tyler Kavanaugh, *Jim Martin. **Telephone:** (631) 632-4755. **Home Field:** Joe Nathan Field. **Seating Capacity:** 1,000. **Outfield Dimension: LF**—330, **CF**—390, **RF**—330.

TENNESSEE VOLUNTEERS

Conference: Southeastern. **Mailing Address:** Brenda Lawson Athletic Center, 1551 Lake Loudoun Blvd., Knoxville, TN 37996. **Website:** www.utsports.com. **Head Coach:** Tony Vitello. **Telephone:** (865) 974-2057. **Baseball SID:** Sean Barows. **Telephone:** (865) 974-7478. **Assistant Coaches:** Frank Anderson, *Josh Elander. **Home Field:** Lindsey Nelson Stadium. **Seating Capacity:** 4,283. **Outfield Dimension: LF**—320, **CF**—404, **RF**—320.

TENNESSEE TECH GOLDEN EAGLES

Conference: Ohio Valley. **Mailing Address:** 110 McGee Ave., Cookeville, TN 38505. **Website:** www.ttusports.com. **Head Coach:** Matt Bragga. **Telephone:** (931) 372-3925. **Baseball SID:** Mike Lehman. **Telephone:** (931) 372-3088. **Assistant Coaches:** *Justin Holmes, Mitchell Wright. **Telephone:** (931) 372-6546. **Home Field:** Quillen Field. **Seating Capacity:** 500. **Outfield Dimension: LF**—330, **CF**—405, **RF**—330.

TENNESSEE-MARTIN SKYHAWKS

Conference: Ohio Valley. **Mailing Address:** 1022 Elam Center, 15 Mt. Pelia Rd., Martin, TN 38238. **Website:** www.utmsports.com. **Head Coach:** Ryan Jenkins. **Telephone:** (731) 881-3691. **Baseball SID:** Jake Rogers. **Telephone:** (731) 881-7694. **Assistant Coaches:** Geoff Murphy, John O'Neil. **Home Field:** Skyhawk Park. **Seating Capacity:** 1,000. **Outfield Dimension: LF**—325, **CF**—394, **RF**—325.

TEXAS LONGHORNS

Conference: Big 12. **Mailing Address:** 403 E. 23rd St., Austin, TX 78712. **Website:** www.texassports.com. **Head Coach:** David Pierce. **Telephone:** (512) 471-5732. **Baseball SID:** Carli Todd. **Telephone:** (732) 606-3915. **Assistant Coaches:** *Sean Allen, Philip Miller. **Telephone:** (512) 471-5732. **Home Field:** UFCU Disch-Falk Field. **Seating Capacity:** 7,373. **Outfield Dimension: LF**—340, **CF**—400, **RF**—325.

TEXAS A&M AGGIES.

Conference: Southeastern. **Mailing Address:** 756 Houston St., College Station, TX 77840. **Website:** www.aggieathletics.com. **Head Coach:** Rob Childress. **Telephone:** (979) 845-4810. **Baseball SID:** Thomas Dick. **Telephone:** (979) 845-4810. **Assistant Coaches:** Wil Bolt, *Justin Seely. **Telephone:** (979) 845-4810. **Home Field:** Olsen Field at Blue Bell Park. **Seating Capacity:** 6100. **Outfield Dimension: LF**—330-375, **CF**—400, **RF**—375-330.

TEXAS A&M-CORPUS CHRISTI ISLANDERS

Conference: Southland. **Mailing Address:** 6300 Ocean Dr., Unit 5719, Corpus Christi, TX 78412. **Website:** www.goislanders.com. **Head Coach:** Scott Malone. **Telephone:** (361) 825-3413. **Baseball SID:** Mark Pinkerton.

Assistant Coaches: Nick Magnifico, Marty Smith. Telephone: (361) 825-3720.
Home Field: Chapman Field. Seating Capacity: 700.
Outfield Dimension: LF—330, CF—404, RF—330.

TEXAS CHRISTIAN HORNED FROGS

Conference: Big 12.
Mailing Address: 2900 Stadium Dr., Fort Worth, TX 76129. Website: www.gofrogs.com.
Head Coach: Jim Schlossnagle. Telephone: (817) 257-5354. Baseball SID: Brandie Davidson. Telephone: (817) 257-7479.
Assistant Coaches: Bill Mosiello, *Kirk Saarloos. Telephone: (817) 257-5588.
Home Field: Lupton Stadium. Seating Capacity: 4,500. Outfield Dimension: LF—330, CF—395, RF—330.

TEXAS SOUTHERN TIGERS

Conference: Southwestern Athletic.
Mailing Address: 3100 Cleburne St., Houston, TX 77004. Website: www.tsusports.com.
Head Coach: Michael Robertson. Telephone: (713) 313-4315. Baseball SID: Alan Wiederhold. Telephone: (713) 313-7271.
Assistant Coaches: Aaron Garza, Ehren Moreno. Telephone: (713) 313-7993.
Home Field: MacGregor Park. Outfield Dimension: LF—315, CF—395, RF—315.

TEXAS STATE BOBCATS

Conference: Sun Belt.
Mailing Address: 601 University Dr., San Marcos, TX 78666. Website: www.txstatebobcats.com.
Head Coach: Ty Harrington. Telephone: (512) 245-3383. Baseball SID: Cedrique Flemming. Telephone: (512) 245-4387.
Assistant Coaches: Chad Massengale, *Steven Trout. Telephone: (918) 245-3383.
Home Field: Bobcat Ballpark. Seating Capacity: 2,000. Outfield Dimension: LF—330, CF—404, RF—330.

TEXAS TECH RED RAIDERS

Conference: Big 12.
Mailing Address: 2526 6th St., Lubbock, TX 79409. Website: www.texastech.com.
Head Coach: Tim Tadlock. Telephone: (806) 834-4836. Baseball SID: Michael Minshew. Telephone: (806) 742-2770.
Assistant Coaches: Matt Gardner, *J-Bob Thomas. Telephone: (806) 834-4836.
Home Field: Dan Law Field at Rip Griffin Park. Seating Capacity: 4,432. Outfield Dimension: LF—330, CF—404, RF—330.

TEXAS-ARLINGTON MAVERICKS

Conference: Sun Belt.
Mailing Address: 601 Spaniolo Dr., Arlington, TX 76019. Website: www.utamavs.com.
Head Coach: Darin Thomas. Telephone: (817) 272-2542. Baseball SID: Brent Ingram. Telephone: (817) 272-2212.
Assistant Coaches: *Fuller Smith, Jon Wente.
Home Field: Clay Gould Ballpark. Seating Capacity: 3,000. Outfield Dimension: LF—340, CF—400, RF—340.

TEXAS-RIO GRANDE VALLEY VAQUEROS

Conference: Western Athletic.
Mailing Address: UTRGV Department of Intercollegiate Athletics, 1201 W. University Dr., Edinburg, TX 78539. Website: www.goutrgv.com.
Head Coach: Derek Matlock. Telephone: (956) 665-2235. Baseball SID: Jonah Goldberg. Telephone: (956) 665-2240.
Assistant Coaches: Cody Atkinson, Russell Raley. Telephone: (956) 665-2891.
Home Field: Edinburg Baseball Stadium. Seating Capacity: 4,000. Outfield Dimension: LF—325, CF—410, RF—325.

TEXAS-SAN ANTONIO ROADRUNNERS

Conference: Conference USA.
Mailing Address: 1 UTSA Circle, San Antonio, TX 78249. Website: www.goutsa.com.
Head Coach: Jason Marshall. Telephone: (210) 458-4811. Baseball SID: Tony Baldwin. Telephone: (210) 302-2536.
Assistant Coaches: Jim Blair, Jake Carlson. Telephone: (210) 458-4805.
Home Field: Roadrunner Field. Seating Capacity: 800. Outfield Dimension: LF—335, CF—405, RF—340.

TOLEDO ROCKETS

Conference: Mid-American.
Mailing Address: 2801 West Bancroft St., Toledo, OH, 43606. Website: www.utrockets.com.
Head Coach: Cory Mee. Telephone: (419) 530-6263. Baseball SID: Chris Cullum. Telephone: (419) 530-4913. Fax: (419) 530-4428.
Assistant Coaches: *Josh Bradford, Nick McIntyre. Telephone: (419) 530-3097.
Home Field: Scott Park. Seating Capacity: 1,000. Outfield Dimension: LF—330, CF—400, RF—330.

TOWSON TIGERS

Conference: Colonial Athletic.
Mailing Address: 8000 York Rd., Towson, MD 21252. Website: www.towsontigers.com.
Head Coach: Matt Tyner. Telephone: (410) 704-3775. Baseball SID: John Brush. Telephone: (410) 704-3102.
Assistant Coaches: Tanner Biagini, Miles Miller. Telephone: (410) 704-2646.
Home Field: Schuerholz Park. Seating Capacity: 500. Outfield Dimension: LF—312, CF—424, RF—301.

TROY TROJANS

Conference: Sun Belt.
Mailing Address: Troy University Athletics, Tine Davis Field House, Troy, AL 36082. Website: www.troytrojans.com.
Head Coach: Mark Smartt. Telephone: (334) 670-5945. Baseball SID: Jace Sanders. Telephone: (334) 670-5654.
Assistant Coaches: *Shane Gierke, Brad Phillips. Telephone: (334) 670-5705.
Home Field: Riddle Pace Field. Seating Capacity: 2,000. Outfield Dimension: LF—312, CF—404, RF—301.

TULANE GREEN WAVE

Conference: American Athletic.
Mailing Address: James W. Wilson Jr. Intercollegiate Athletics Center, 2950 Ben Weiner Dr., New Orleans, LA 70118. Website: www.tulanegreenwave.com.

Head Coach: Travis Jewett. **Telephone:** (504) 862-8216. **Baseball SID:** Eric Hollier. **Telephone:** (504) 314-7271.

Assistant Coaches: Tighe Dickinson, *Eddie Smith. **Telephone:** (504) 314-7203.

Home Field: Greer Field at Turchin Stadium. **Seating Capacity:** 5,000. **Outfield Dimension: LF**—325, **CF**—400, **RF**—325.

UC DAVIS AGGIES.

Conference: Big West.
Mailing Address: One Shields Avenue, Davis, CA, 95616. **Website:** www.ucdavisaggies.com.
Head Coach: Matt Vaughn. **Telephone:** (530) 752-7513. **Baseball SID:** Bryn Lutz. **Telephone:** (530) 752-3680.

Assistant Coaches: *Lloyd Acosta, Brett Lindgren.
Home Field: Dobbins Stadium. **Seating Capacity:** 3,500. **Outfield Dimension: LF**—385, **CF**—410, **RF**—385.

UC IRVINE ANTEATERS

Conference: Big West.
Mailing Address: 625 Humanities Quad, Irvine, CA 92697. **Website:** www.ucirvinesports.com.
Head Coach: Mike Gillespie. **Telephone:** (949) 824-4292. **Baseball SID:** Alex Croteau. **Telephone:** (949) 824-7350.

Assistant Coaches: Danny Bibona, *Ben Orloff. **Telephone:** (949) 824-1154.
Home Field: Cicerone Field at Anteater Ballpark. **Seating Capacity:** 1,500. **Outfield Dimension: LF**—335, **CF**—408, **RF**—335.

UC RIVERSIDE HIGHLANDERS

Conference: Big West.
Mailing Address: 900 University Ave. Riverside CA 92521. **Website:** www.gohighlanders.com.
Head Coach: Troy Percival. **Telephone:** (951) 827-5441. **Baseball SID:** John Maxwell. **Telephone:** (951) 827-5438.

Assistant Coaches: *Bryson LeBlanc, Curt Smith. **Telephone:** (951) 827-5441.
Home Field: The Plex. **Seating Capacity:** 2,500. **Outfield Dimension: LF**—330, **CF**—400, **RF**—330.

UC SANTA BARBARA GAUCHOS

Conference: Big West.
Mailing Address: UCSB Intercollegiate Athletics Department, ICA Building, Santa Barbara, CA 93106. **Website:** www.ucsbgauchos.com.
Head Coach: Andrew Checketts. **Telephone:** (805) 893-3690. **Baseball SID:** Andrew Wagner. **Telephone:** (805) 893-8603. **Fax:** (805) 893-5477.
Assistant Coaches: *Eddie Cornejo, Casey Harms. **Telephone:** (805) 893-2021.
Home Field: Caesar Uyesaka Stadium. **Seating Capacity:** 1,000. **Outfield Dimension: LF**—335, **CF**—400, **RF**—335.

UCLA BRUINS

Conference: Pac-12.
Mailing Address: J.D. Morgan Center, P.O. Box 24044, Los Angeles, CA 93106. **Website:** www.uclabruins.com.
Head Coach: John Savage. **Telephone:** (310) 794-8210. **Baseball SID:** Dan Gliot. **Telephone:** (310) 206-7873.
Assistant Coaches: Rex Peters, *Bryant Ward.

Telephone: (310) 794-2473.
Home Field: Jackie Robinson Stadium. **Seating Capacity:** 1,250. **Outfield Dimension: LF**—330, **CF**—395, **RF**—330.

UNC-ASHEVILLE BULLDOGS

Conference: Big South.
Mailing Address: 1 University Heights, CPO #2600, Asheville, NC 28804. **Website:** www.uncabulldogs.com.
Head Coach: Scott Friedholm. **Telephone:** (828) 251-6920. **Baseball SID:** Mitchell Miegel. **Telephone:** (828) 251-6931.
Assistant Coaches: Chris Bresnahan, Jonathan Johnston. **Telephone:** (828) 250-2309.
Home Field: Greenwood Field. **Seating Capacity:** 750. **Outfield Dimension: LF**—324, **CF**—395, **RF**—335.

UNC GREENSBORO SPARTANS

Conference: Southern.
Mailing Address: 1400 Spring Garden St., Greensboro, NC 27412. **Website:** www.uncgspartans.com.
Head Coach: Link Jarrett. **Baseball SID:** Dan Wacker. **Telephone:** (608) 487-3858.
Assistant Coaches: Jerry Edwards, *Joey Holcomb. **Telephone:** (336) 334-3247.
Home Field: UNCG Baseball Stadium. **Seating Capacity:** 3,500. **Outfield Dimension: LF**—340, **CF**—410, **RF**—340.

UNC WILMINGTON SEAHAWKS

Conference: Colonial.
Mailing Address: 601 South College Rd., Wilmington, NC 28403. **Website:** www.uncwsports.com.
Head Coach: Mark Scalf. **Telephone:** (910) 962-3570.
Baseball SID: Tom Riorda. **Telephone:** (910) 962-4099.
Assistant Coaches: *Randy Hood, Matt Williams. **Telephone:** (910) 962-7471.
Home Field: Brooks Field. **Seating Capacity:** 3,500.
Outfield Dimension: LF—340, **CF**—380, **RF**—340.

UTAH UTES

Conference: Pac-12.
Mailing Address: 1825 E. South Campus Dr., Salt Lake City, UT 84112. **Website:** www.utahutes.com.
Head Coach: Bill Kinneberg. **Telephone:** (801) 581-3526. **Baseball SID:** Brooke Frederickson. **Telephone:** (801) 581-8302.
Assistant Coaches: Jay Brossman, *Michael Crawford. **Telephone:** (801) 581-3024.
Home Field: Smith's Ballpark. **Seating Capacity:** 14,511. **Outfield Dimension: LF**—345, **CF**—420, **RF**—345.

UTAH VALLEY WOLVERINES.

Conference: Western Athletic.
Mailing Address: 800 W University Parkway, Orem, UT 84058. **Website:** www.wolverinegreen.com.
Head Coach: Eric Madsen. **Telephone:** (801) 863-6509. **Baseball SID:** Clint Burgi. **Telephone:** (801) 863-8644. **Fax:** (801) 863-8813.
Assistant Coaches: *Derek Amicone, David Carter. **Telephone:** (801) 863-8647.
Home Field: UCCU Ballpark. **Seating Capacity:** 5,000. **Outfield Dimension: LF**—312, **CF**—408, **RF**—315.

VALPARAISO CRUSADERS

Conference: Missouri Valley.
Mailing Address: 1700 Chapel Drive Valparaiso, IN 46383. **Website:** www.valpoathletics.com.
Head Coach: Brian Schmack. **Telephone:** (219) 464-6117. **Baseball SID:** Brandon Vickrey. **Telephone:** (219) 464-5396.
Assistant Coaches: Nic Mishler, *Ben Wolgamot. **Telephone:** (219) 465-7961.
Home Field: Emory G. Bauer Field. **Seating Capacity:** 500. **Outfield Dimension:** LF—330, CF—400, RF—330.

VANDERBILT COMMODORES

Conference: Southeastern.
Mailing Address: 2601 Jess Neely Dr., Nashville, TN 37212. **Website:** www.vucommodores.com.
Head Coach: Tim Corbin. **Telephone:** (615) 322-3716. **Baseball SID:** Andrew Pate. **Telephone:** (615) 322-4121.
Assistant Coaches: *Mike Baxter, Scott Brown. **Telephone:** (615) 322-3716.
Home Field: Hawkins Field. **Seating Capacity:** 3,700. **Outfield Dimension:** LF—310, CF—400, RF—330.

VILLANOVA WILDCATS

Conference: Big East.
Mailing Address: 800 Lancaster Ave., Villanova, PA 19085. **Website:** www.villanova.com.
Head Coach: Kevin Mulvey. **Telephone:** (610) 519-4529. **Baseball SID:** David Berman. **Telephone:** (610) 519-4122.
Assistant Coaches: Eddie Brown, Rob Delaney. **Telephone:** (610) 519-5520.
Home Field: Villanova Ballpark at Plymouth. **Seating Capacity:** 750. **Outfield Dimension:** LF—330, CF—410, RF—330.

VIRGINIA CAVALIERS

Conference: Atlantic Coast.
Mailing Address: University Hall, P.O. Box 400839, Charlottesville, VA 22904. **Website:** www.virginiasports.com.
Head Coach: Brian O'Connor. **Telephone:** (434) 982-4932. **Baseball SID:** Scott Fitzgerald. **Telephone:** (434) 924-9878.
Assistant Coaches: Karl Kuhn, *Kevin McMullan.
Home Field: Davenport Field. **Seating Capacity:** 5,025. **Outfield Dimension:** LF—332, CF—404, RF—332.

VIRGINIA COMMONWEALTH RAMS

Conference: Atlantic 10.
Mailing Address: 1300 W. Broad St., Richmond, VA 23284. **Website:** www.vcuathletics.com.
Head Coach: Shawn Stiffler. **Telephone:** (804) 828-4822. **Baseball SID:** Brett Bosley. **Telephone:** (804) 828-8496.
Assistant Coaches: Mike McRae, Rich Witten. **Telephone:** (804) 828-4821.
Home Field: The Diamond. **Seating Capacity:** 9,560. **Outfield Dimension:** LF—330, CF—402, RF—330.

VIRGINIA MILITARY INSTITUTE KEYDETS

Conference: Southern.
Mailing Address: Cameron Hall, Lexington, VA 24450. **Website:** www.vmikeydets.com.
Head Coach: Jonathan Hadra. **Telephone:** (540) 464-7601. **Baseball SID:** Brad Salois. **Telephone:** (540)

464-7015.
Assistant Coaches: *Casey Dykes, Sam Roberts. **Telephone:** (540) 464-7605.
Home Field: Gray-Minor Stadium. **Seating Capacity:** 1,000. **Outfield Dimension:** LF—330, CF—395, RF—330.

VIRGINIA TECH HOKIES

Conference: Atlantic Coast.
Mailing Address: 25 Beamer Way, Virginia Tech, Blacksburg, Va 24061. **Website:** www.hokiesports.com.
Head Coach: John Szefc. **Telephone:** (540) 231-5906. **Baseball SID:** Marc Mullen. **Telephone:** (540) 231-1894. **Fax:** (540) 231-6984.
Assistant Coaches: *Kurt Elbin, Ryan Fecteau. **Telephone:** (540) 231-5906.
Home Field: English Field at Union Park. **Seating Capacity:** 4,000. **Outfield Dimension:** LF—330, CF—400, RF—330.

WAGNER SEAHAWKS

Conference: Northeast.
Mailing Address: 1 Campus Rd., Staten Island, NY 10301. **Website:** www.wagnerathletics.com.
Head Coach: Jim Carone. **Telephone:** (718) 390-3154. **Baseball SID:** Brian Morales. **Telephone:** (718) 390-3215.
Assistant Coaches: Chris Greco, *Craig Noto. **Telephone:** (718) 420-4121.
Home Field: Richmond County Bank Ballpark. **Seating Capacity:** 7,171. **Outfield Dimension:** LF—320, CF—390, RF—318.

WAKE FOREST DEMON DEACONS

Conference: Atlantic Coast.
Mailing Address: 401 Deacon Blvd., Winston-Salem, NC 27106. **Website:** www.wakeforestsports.com.
Head Coach: Tom Walter. **Telephone:** (336) 758-5570. **Baseball SID:** Jay Garneau. **Telephone:** (336) 758-3229.
Assistant Coaches: *Bill Cilento, Matt Hobbs. **Telephone:** (336) 758-4208.
Home Field: David F. Couch Ballpark. **Seating Capacity:** 3,823. **Outfield Dimension:** LF—310, CF—400, RF—300.

WASHINGTON HUSKIES

Conference: Pac-12.
Mailing Address: Box 354070, Graves Building, Seattle, WA 98195. **Website:** www.gohuskies.com.
Head Coach: Lindsay Meggs. **Telephone:** (206) 616-4335. **Baseball SID:** Brian Tom. **Telephone:** (206) 897-1742.
Assistant Coaches: *Donegal Fergus, Jason Kelly. **Telephone:** (206) 543-2919.
Home Field: Husky Ballpark. **Seating Capacity:** 2,995. **Outfield Dimension:** LF—327, CF—395, RF—317.

WASHINGTON STATE COUGARS

Conference: Pac-12.
Mailing Address: Bohler Addition 195, Pullman, WA, 99164. **Website:** www.wsucougars.com.
Head Coach: Marty Lees. **Telephone:** (509) 335-0368. **Baseball SID:** Bobby Alworth. **Telephone:** (509) 355-5785.
Assistant Coaches: Dan Spencer. **Telephone:** (509) 335-0216.
Home Field: Bailey-Brayton Field. **Seating Capacity:** 3,500. **Outfield Dimension:** LF—335, CF—400, RF—335.

WEST VIRGINIA MOUNTAINEERS

Conference: Big 12.
Mailing Address: P.O. Box 0877, Morgantown, WV 26507. **Website:** www.wvusports.com.
Head Coach: Randy Mazey. **Telephone:** (304) 293-2821. **Baseball SID:** Charlie Healy. **Telephone:** (304) 293-2821.
Assistant Coaches: Steve Sabins, Dave Serrano.
Home Field: Monongalia County Ballpark. **Seating Capacity:** 2,500. **Outfield Dimension:** LF—325, CF—400, RF—325.

WESTERN CAROLINA CATAMOUNTS

Conference: Southern.
Mailing Address: Ramsey Center – Athletics, 92 Catamount Rd., Cullowhee, NC 28723. **Website:** www.catamountsports.com.
Head Coach: Bobby Moranda. **Telephone:** (828) 227-7338. **Baseball SID:** Daniel Hooker. **Telephone:** (828) 227-2339.
Assistant Coaches: *Nate Cocolin, Brock Doud. **Telephone:** (828) 227-7338.
Home Field: Childress Field at Hennon Stadium. **Seating Capacity:** 1,500. **Outfield Dimension:** LF—325, CF—395, RF—325.

WESTERN ILLINOIS LEATHERNECKS

Conference: Summit.
Mailing Address: 1 University Circle, Macomb, IL 61455. **Website:** www.goleathernecks.com.
Head Coach: Ryan Brownlee. **Telephone:** (309) 298-1521. **Baseball SID:** Monyae Williamson. **Telephone:** (309) 298-1133.
Assistant Coaches: Shane Davis, Matt Risdon.
Home Field: Alfred D. Boyer Stadium. **Seating Capacity:** 502. **Outfield Dimension:** LF—325, CF—395, RF—330.

WESTERN KENTUCKY HILLTOPPERS

Conference: Conference USA.
Mailing Address: 1605 Avenue of Champions, Bolwing Green, KY 42101. **Website:** www.wkusports.com.
Head Coach: John Pawlowski. **Telephone:** (270) 745-2277. **Baseball SID:** Bryan Fyalkowski. **Telephone:** (270) 745-5388.
Assistant Coaches: *Ty Megahee, Rob Reinstetle. **Telephone:** (270) 745-2274.
Home Field: Nick Dennis Field. **Seating Capacity:** 1,500. **Outfield Dimension:** LF—330, CF—400, RF—330.

WESTERN MICHIGAN BRONCOS

Conference: Mid-American.
Mailing Address: 1903 W. Michigan Ave., Kalamazoo, MI 49008. **Website:** www.wmubroncos.com.
Head Coach: Billy Gernon. **Telephone:** (269) 276-3205. **Baseball SID:** Nathan Palcowski. **Telephone:** (269) 387-4138.
Assistant Coaches: Blaine McFerrin, Adam Piotrowicz. **Telephone:** (269) 276-3208.
Home Field: Robert J. Bobb Stadium at Hyames Field. **Seating Capacity:** 1,500. **Outfield Dimension:** LF—310, CF—395, RF—335.

WICHITA STATE SHOCKERS

Conference: American Athletic.
Mailing Address: 1845 Fairmont Dr., Wichita, KS 67260. **Website:** www.goshockers.com.
Head Coach: Todd Butler. **Telephone:** (316) 978-3636.
Baseball SID: Tami Cutler.
Assistant Coaches: *Sammy Esposito, Mike Steele.
Home Field: Eck Stadium. **Seating Capacity:** 7,851.
Outfield Dimension: LF—330, CF—390, RF—330.

WILLIAM & MARY TRIBE

Conference: Colonial.
Mailing Address: 751 Ukrop Way, Williamsburg, VA 23185. **Website:** www.tribeathletics.com.
Head Coach: Brian Murphy. **Telephone:** (757) 221-3492. **Baseball SID:** Jordan Williams. **Telephone:** (757) 221-3368.
Assistant Coaches: *Brian Casey, Pat McKenna. **Telephone:** (757) 221-3399.
Home Field: Plumeri Park. **Seating Capacity:** 1,400.
Outfield Dimension: LF—325, CF—410, RF—325.

WINTHROP EAGLES

Conference: Big South.
Mailing Address: 1162 Eden Terrace, Rock Hill, SC 29733. **Website:** www.winthropeagles.com.
Head Coach: Tom Riginos. **Telephone:** (864) 903-9796. **Baseball SID:** Brittany Lane.
Assistant Coaches: *Clint Chrylser, Robbie Monday.
Home Field: The Winthrop Ballpark. **Seating Capacity:** 1,800. **Outfield Dimension:** LF—325, CF—390, RF—325.

WISCONSIN-MILWAUKEE PANTHERS

Conference: Horizon.
Mailing Address: 3409 N. Downer Ave., Milwaukee, WI 53211. **Website:** www.mkepanthers.com.
Head Coach: Scott Doffek. **Telephone:** (414) 750-4738. **Baseball SID:** Ashley Steltenpohl. **Telephone:** 414) 435-8118.
Assistant Coaches: Cory Bigler, Shaun Wegner. **Telephone:** (414) 750-0629.
Home Field: Henry Aaron Field. **Seating Capacity:** 500. **Outfield Dimension:** LF—320, CF—390, RF—320.

WOFFORD TERRIERS

Conference: Southern.
Mailing Address: 429 N. Church St., Spartanburg, SC 29303. **Website:** www.athletics.wofford.edu.
Head Coach: Todd Interdonato. **Telephone:** (864) 597-4497. **Baseball SID:** Brent Williamson. **Telephone:** (864) 597-4093. **Fax:** (864) 597-4129.
Assistant Coaches: Seth Cutler-Voltz, *JJ Edwards. **Telephone:** (864) 597-4126.
Home Field: King Field. **Seating Capacity:** 2,500.
Outfield Dimension: LF—325, CF—395, RF—325.

WRIGHT STATE RAIDERS

Conference: Horizon.
Mailing Address: 3640 Colonel Glenn Hwy., Dayton, OH 45435. **Website:** www.wsuraiders.com.
Head Coach: Jeff Mercer. **Telephone:** (937) 775-3668.
Baseball SID: Bob Noss. **Telephone:** (937) 775-2816.
Assistant Coaches: Nate Metzger, Alex Sogard. **Telephone:** (937) 775-4188.
Home Field: Nischwitz Stadium. **Seating Capacity:** 750. **Outfield Dimension:** LF—330, CF—400, RF—330.

XAVIER MUSKETEERS

Conference: Big East.
Mailing Address: 3800 Victory Parkway, Cincinnati, OH 45207. **Website:** www.goxavier.com
Head Coach: Billy O'Conner. **Telephone:** (513) 745-2890. **Baseball SID:** Brendan Bergen. **Telephone:** (513) 745-3388. **Fax:** (513) 745-2825.
Assistant Coaches: *Nick Otte, Matt Reida. **Telephone:** (513) 745-2891.
Home Field: Hayden Field. **Seating Capacity:** 500.
Outfield Dimension: LF—310, **CF**—385, **RF**—355.

YALE BULLDOGS

Conference: Ivy League.
Mailing Address: P.O. Box 208216, New Haven, CT 06520. **Website:** www.yalebulldogs.com.
Head Coach: John Stuper. **Telephone:** (203) 432-1466. **Baseball SID:** Ernie Bertothy.
Assistant Coaches: Craig Driver, *Tucker Frawley. **Telephone:** (203) 432-1467.
Home Field: Yale Field. **Seating Capacity:** 5,000.
Outfield Dimension: LF—330, **CF**—405, **RF**—315.

YOUNGSTOWN STATE PENGUINS

Conference: Horizon.
Mailing Address: 1 University Plaza, Youngstown, OH 44555. **Website:** www.ysusports.com.
Head Coach: Dan Bertolini. **Baseball SID:** Drae Smith. **Telephone:** (330) 941-1480.
Assistant Coaches: Josh Merrigan, *Eric Smith.
Home Field: Eastwood Field. **Seating Capacity:** 6,300.
Outfield Dimension: LF—335, **CF**—405, **RF**—335.

XAVIER MUSKETEERS

Conference: Big East.
Mailing Address: 3800 Victory Parkway, Cincinnati, OH 45207. **Website:** www.goxavier.com.
Head Coach: Scott Googins. **Telephone:** (513) 745-2891. **Baseball SID:** Brendan Bergen. **Telephone:** (513) 745-3388.
Assistant Coaches: Billy O'Conner, *Nick Otte. **Telephone:** (513) 745-2890.
Home Field: Hayden Field. **Outfield Dimension: LF**—310, **CF**—380, **RF**—310.

YALE BULLDOGS

Conference: Ivy League.
Mailing Address: PO Box 208216, New Haven, CT 06520. **Website:** www.yalebulldogs.com.
Head Coach: John Stuper. **Telephone:** (203) 432-1466. **Baseball SID:** Steve Conn. **Telephone:** (203) 432-1455. **Fax:** (203) 432-1454.
Assistant Coaches: *Tucker Frawley, Ray Guario. **Telephone:** (203) 432-1467.
Home Field: Yale Field. **Seating Capacity:** 5,000.
Outfield Dimension: LF—330, **CF**—405, **RF**—315.

YOUNGSTOWN STATE PENGUINS

Conference: Horizon.
Mailing Address: 1 University Plaza, Youngstown, OH 44555. **Website:** www.ysusports.com.
Head Coach: Dan Bertolini. **Baseball SID:** John Vogel. **Telephone:** (330) 941-1480. **Fax:** (330) 941-3191.
Assistant Coaches: Josh Merrigan, *Eric Smith. **Telephone:** N/A.
Home Field: Eastwood Field. **Seating Capacity:** 6300.
Outfield Dimension: LF—335, **CF**—405, **RF**—335.

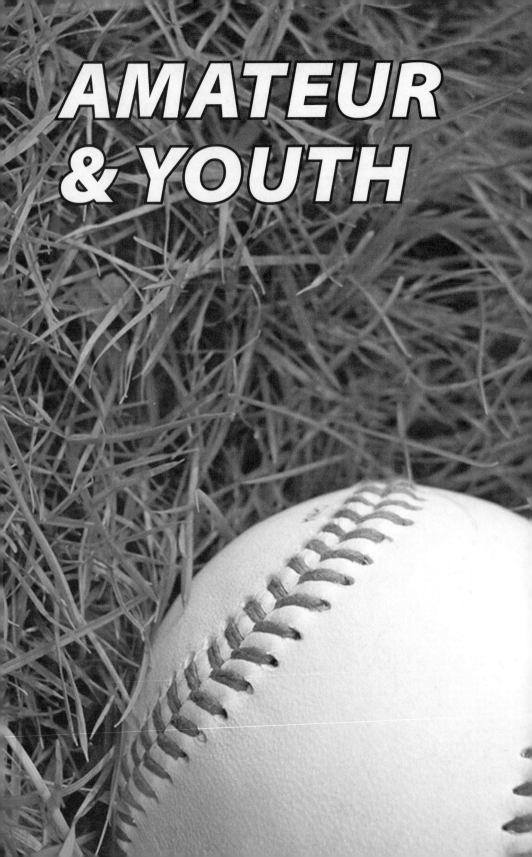

AMATEUR & YOUTH

INTERNATIONAL ORGANIZATIONS

WORLD BASEBALL SOFTBALL CONFEDERATION

Headquarters: Maison du Sport International—54, Avenue de Rhodanie, 1007 Lausanne, Switzerland. **Telephone:** (+41-21) 318-82-40. **Fax:** (41-21) 318-82-41.
Website: www.wbsc.org. **E-Mail:** office@wbsc.org.
Year Founded: 1938.
President: Riccardo Fraccari (Italy). **Secretary General:** Beng Choo Low (Japan). **Vice President Baseball:** Willi Kaltschmitt Luján (Guam). **Vice President Softball:** Beatrice Allen (Gambia). **Softball Executive VP:** Craig Cress (USA). **Baseball Executive VP:** Tom Peng (Taiwan). **Treasurer:** Angelo Vicini (San Marino). **Membesr At-Large:** Ron Finlay (Australia), Paul Seiler (USA). Taeki Utsugi (Japan), Tommy Velázquez (Puerto Rico). **Athlete Representative For Baseball:** Justin Huber (Australia). **Athlete Representative For Softball:** María José Soto Gil (Venezuela). **Global Ambassador:** Antonio Castro Soto del Valle (Cuba), Meliton Sanchez Rivas (Panama). **Executive Director:** Michael Schmidt. **Softball Director:** Ron Radigonda. **Assistant to the President:** Giovanni Pantaleoni. **Marketing/Tournament Manager:** Masaru Yokoo, Laurie Gouthro. **Public Relations Officer:** Oscar Lopez, Lori Nolan. **National Federation Relations:** Francesca Fabretto, Brian Glauser, Aki Huang, Amy Park. **Antidoping Officer:** Victor Isola. **Administration/Finance:** Sandrine Pennone, Laetitia Barbey.

CONTINENTAL ASSOCIATIONS

CONFEDERATION PAN AMERICANA DE BEISBOL (COPABE)

Mailing Address: Calle 3, Francisco Filos, Vista Hermosa, Edificio 74, Planta Baja Local No. 1, Panama City, Panama. **Telephone:** (507) 229-8684. **Website:** www.cop-abe.net. **E-Mail:** copabe@sinfo.net.
Chairman: Eduardo De Bello (Panama). **Secretary General:** Hector Pereyra (Dominican Republic).

AFRICA BASEBALL SOFTBALL ASSOCIATION (ABSA)

Office Address: Paiko Road, Chanchaga, Minna, Niger State, Nigeria.
Mailing Address: P.M.B. 150, Minna, Niger State, Nigeria.
Telephone: (234) 8037188491. **E-mail:** absasecretariat@yahoo.com.
President: Sabeur Jlajla. **Vice President Baseball:** Etienne N'Guessan. **Vice President Softball:** Fridah Shiroya. **Secretary General:** Ibrahim N'Diaye. **Treasurer:** Moira Dempsey. **Executive Director:** Lieutenant Colonel (rtd) Friday Ichide. **Deputy Executive Director:** Francoise Kameni-Lele.

BASEBALL FEDERATION OF ASIA

Mailing Address: 9F. -3, No. 288, Sec 6 Civic Blvd.,Xinyi Dist., Taipei City, Taiwan (R.O.C.). **Telephone:** 886-2-27473368. **E-Mail Address:** bfa@baseballasia.org
President: Tom Peng. **Vice Presidents:** Suzuki Yoshinobu, Chen Xu, Hae Young Yang. **Secretary General:** Hua-Wei Lin. **Executive Director:** Richard Lin. **Members At Large:** Allan Mak, Alfonso Martin Eizmendi, Syed Khawar Shah. **Senior Advisor:** Kazuhiro Tawa. **China Baseball Development Executive Director:** Tian Yuan. **West Asia Baseball Development Executive Director:** Syed Khawar Shah.

EUROPEAN BASEBALL CONFEDERATION

Mailing Address: Savska cesta 137, 10 000 Zagreb, Croatia. **Telephone/Fax:** +385 1 561 5227. **E-Mail Address:** office@baseballeurope.com. **Website:** baseball europe.com.
President: Didier Seminet (France). **1st Vice President:** Petr Ditrich (Czech Republic). **2nd Vice President:** Jürgen Elsishans (Germany). **3rd Vice President:** Rainer Husty (Austria). **Secretary General:** Krunoslav Karin (Croatia) **Treasurer:** Rene Laforce (Belgium). **Vocals:** Roderick Balk (Netherlands), Marco Mannucci (Italy), Oleg Boyko (Ukraine).

BASEBALL CONFEDERATION OF OCEANIA

Mailing Address: 48 Partridge Way, Mooroolbark, Victoria 3138, Australia. **Telephone:** +613 9727 1779. **Fax:** 613 9727 5959. **E-Mail Address:** bcosecgeneral@baseball oceania.com. **Website:** www.baseballoceania.com.
President: Bob Steffy (Guam). **1st Vice President:** Laurent Cassier (New Caledonia). **2nd Vice President:** Victor Langkilde (American Samoa). **Secretary General:** Chet Gray (Australia). **Executive Committee:** Rose Igitol (CNMI), Temmy Shmull (Palau), Innoke Niubalavu (Fiji).

INTERNATIONAL GOODWILL SERIES, INC.

Mailing Address: 981 Slate Drive, Santa Rosa, CA 95405. **Telephone:** (707) 538-0777. **E-Mail Address:** goodwillseries24@gmail.com.
Website: www.goodwillseries.org.
President, Goodwill Series, Inc.: Bob Williams.

INTERNATIONAL SPORTS GROUP

Mailing Address: 3829 S Oakbrook Dr. Greenfield, WI 53228. **Telephone:** 414-704-5467. **E-Mail Address:** isgbaseball14@gmail.com. **Website:** www.isgbaseball.com. **President:** Tom O'Connell. **Vice President:** Peter Caliendo. **Secretary/Treasurer:** Randy Town. **Board Members:** Jim Jones, Rick Steen, Bill Mathews, Pat Doyle, John Vodenlich.

NATIONAL ORGANIZATIONS

USA BASEBALL

Mailing Address, Corporate Headquarters: 1030 Swabia Court Suite 201, Durham, NC 27703
Telephone: (919) 474-8721.
Fax: (855) 420-5910.
E-mail Address: info@usabaseball.com.
Website: www.usabaseball.com.
President: Mike Gaski.
Treasurer: Jason Dobis.
Board of Directors: Mike Gaski (President), Jason Dobis (Treasurer), Jenny Dalton-Hill (Secretary); Members: Charles M. Blackburn Jr., Willie Bloomquist, John Gall, George Grande, Steve Keener, Abraham Key, Chris Marinak, John McHale Jr., Davis Whitfield
National Members Organizations: Amateur Athletic Union (AAU); American Amateur Baseball Congress (AABC); American Baseball Coaches Association (ABCA); American Legion Baseball, Babe Ruth Baseball, Dixie Baseball, Little League Baseball, National Amateur Baseball Federation (NABF); National Association of Intercollegiate Athletics (NAIA); National Baseball Congress (NBC); National Collegiate Athletic Association (NCAA); National Federation of State High School Athletic Associations, National High School Baseball Coaches Association (BCA); National Junior College Athletic Association (NJCAA); Police Athletic League (PAL); PONY Baseball, T-Ball USA, United States Specialty Sports Association (USSSA).
Events: www.usabaseball.com/events/schedule.jsp.

STAFF
Executive Director/Chief Executive Officer: Paul Seiler. **Assistant Director, Marketing**: Brittany Allen. **Senior Director, Retail**: Carrington Austin. **Director, 18U National Team Program**: Matt Blood. **Senior Director, Baseball Operations**: Ashley Bratcher. **General Manager, National Teams**: Eric Campbell. **Senior Director, Sport Development**: Sean Campbell. **Director, Youth Programs**: Tyler Collins. **Chief Financial Officer**: Ray Darwin. **Assistant Director, Media Relations**: Emily Fedewa. **Director, Travel Services**: Monica Garza. **Assistant Director, Travel Services**: Allison Gupton. **Director, USABat Program**: Russell Hartford. **Director, Prospect Development Pipeline**: Jules Johnson.

Director, Digital Media: Kevin Jones. **Director, Retail Operations**: Megan Kane. **Assistant Director, Baseball Operations**: Ben Kelley. **Director, Marketing**: Kristen Krebs. **Assistant Director, Educational Resources**: Emma Lingan. **Director, Accounting & Finance**: Cicely Mclaughlin. **Assistant Director, Operations**: Wiley McLeod. **Assistant Director, Prospect Development Pipeline**: Matt Pajak. **Chief Operating Officer**: David Perkins. **Director, Educational Resources**: Lauren Rhyne. **Chief Development Officer**: Rick Riccobono. **Director, NTC Operations**: James Vick. **Director, Media Relations**: Brad Young.

BASEBALL CANADA

Mailing Address: 2212 Gladwin Cres., Suite A7, Ottawa, Ontario K1B 5N1. **Telephone**: (613) 748-5606. **Fax**: (613) 748-5767. **E-mail Address**: info@baseball.ca. **Website**: www.baseball.ca.
Director General: Jim Baba. **Head Coach/Director, National Teams**: Greg Hamilton. **Business/Sport Development Director/Women's National Team Manager**: Andre Lachance. **Program Coordinator**: Kelsey McIntosh. **Media/PR Coordinator**: Adam Morissette. **Administrative Coordinator**: June Sterling. **Administrative Assistant**: Penny Baba.

NATIONAL BASEBALL CONGRESS

Mailing Address: 111 S. Main, Suite 600, Wichita, KS 67202. **Telephone**: (316) 977-9400. **Fax**: (316) 462-4506. **Website**: www.nbcbaseball.com.
Year Founded: 1931.

ATHLETES IN ACTION

Mailing Address: 651 Taylor Dr., Xenia, OH 45385. **Telephone**: (937) 352-1000. **Fax**: (937) 352-1245. **E-mail Address**: baseball@athletesinaction.org. **Website**: www.aiabaseball.org.
Director, AIA Baseball: Chris Beck. **General Manager, Alaska**: Chris Beck. **General Manager, Great Lakes**: Dave Gnau. **General Manager, New York Collegiate League**: Justin Dillard. **International Teams Director**: John McLaughlin. **Youth Baseball Director**: Dave Gnau.

SUMMER COLLEGE LEAGUES

NATIONAL ALLIANCE OF COLLEGE SUMMER BASEBALL

Telephone: (321) 206-9714 **E-Mail Address**: RSitz@FloridaLeague.com. **Website**: www.nacsb.org
Executive Director: Rob Sitz (Florida League) **Assistant Executive Director**: Bobby Bennett (Sunbelt Baseball League), Jeff Carter (Southern Collegiate Baseball League). **Treasurer**: Jason Woodward (Cal Ripken Collegiate Baseball League). **Director, Public Relations/Secretary**: Stefano Foggi (Florida Collegiate Summer League). **Compliance Officer**: Paul Galop (Cape Cod Baseball League).

Member Leagues: Atlantic Collegiate Baseball League, California Collegiate League, Cal Ripken Collegiate Baseball League, Cape Cod Baseball League, Florida Collegiate Summer League, Great Lakes Summer Collegiate League, New England Collegiate Baseball League, New York Collegiate Baseball League, Southern Collegiate Baseball League, Sunbelt Baseball League, Valley Baseball League, Hamptons Collegiate Baseball League.

ALASKA BASEBALL LEAGUE

League Mailling Address: 435 W. 10th Avenue, Ste. B, Anchorage, AK, 99501. 5 teams, 44 league games and approximately 5 non league games. Season begins play June 5 and ends Aug. 1. **Commissioner:** Jim Posey.

MAT-SU MINERS

General Manager: Pete Christopher.
Mailing Address: P.O. Box 2690 Palmer, AK 99645.
Telephone: 907-746-4914/907-745-6401. **Fax:** 907-746-5068. **E-Mail:** gmminers@gci.net. **Fax:** 907-561-2920. **Website:** www.matsuminers.org.
Head Coach: Ben Taylor, Chandler-Gilbert (Ariz.) CC.
Field: Hermon Brothers, Grass, No Lights.

ANCHORAGE BUCS

General Manager: Shawn Maltby
Baseball Operations: Gary Lichtenstein
Mailing Address: PO Box 240061, Anchorage, AK 99524-0061. **Office:** 907-561-2827. **Fax:** 907-561-2920.
E-Mail: gm@anchoragebucs.com. **Website:** www.anchoragebucs.com
Head Coach: Anthony Hutting, Cypress (Calif.) JC
Field: Mulcahy Field -Turf Infield, Grass Outfield, Lights

ANCHORAGE GLACIER PILOTS

General Manager: Mike Hinshaw
Mailing Address: 435 W. 10th Avenue, Suite A, Anchorage, Alaska 99501. **Office:** 907-274-3627. **Fax:** 907-274-3628. **E-Mail:** gpilots@alaska.net. **Website:** www.glacierpilots.com.
Head Coach: Kevin Smallcomb.
Field: Mulcahy Field -Turf Infield, Grass Outfield, Lights

CHUGIAK-EAGLE RIVER CHINOOKS

General Manager: Chris Beck
Mailing Address: 651 Taylor Drive, Xenia, Ohio 45385. **Office:** 937-352-1237. Fax 937-352-1001. **E-Mail:** Chris.beck@athletesinaction.org. **Website:** www.cerchinooks.com.
Head Coach: Jon Groth, Tyler (Texas) CC
Field: Lee Jordan Field -Turf Infield, Grass Outfield, No Lights

PENINSULA OILERS

General Manager: Tory Smith.
Mailing Address: 601 S. Main St., Kenai, Alaska 99611. **Office:** 907-283-7133. **Fax:** 907-283-3390. **E-Mail:** gm@oilersbaseball.com. **Website:** www.oilersbaseball.com
Head Coach: Jim Dietz, San Diego State, retired
Field: Coral Seymour Memorial Park -Grass , No Lights

ATLANTIC COLLEGIATE BASEBALL LEAGUE

Mailing Address: 1760 Joanne Drive, Quakertown, PA 18951. **Telephone:** (215) 536-5777. **Fax:** (215) 536-5777. **E-Mail:** tbonekemper@verizon.net. **Website:** www.acbl-online.com.
Year Founded: 1967.
Commissioner: Ralph Addonizio. **President/Acting Secretary:** Tom Bonekemper. **Vice President:** Angelo Fiore, Doug Cinella. **Treasurer:** Bob Hoffman.
Regular Season: 40 games. **Opening date:** June 1. **Closing date:** August 6. **All-Star Game:** July 9 Onondaga CC. **Roster Limit:** 26.

ALLENTOWN RAILERS

Mailing Address: Suite 202, 1801 Union Blvd, Allentown, PA 18109. **E-Mail Address:** ddando@lehigh valleybaseballacademy.com. **Field Manager:** Dylan Dando.

JERSEY PILOTS

Mailing Address: 11 Danemar Drive, Middletown, NJ 07748. **Telephone:** (732) 939-0627. **E-Mail Address:** baseball@jerseypilots.com. **General Manager:** Mike Kalb. **Field Manager:** Zac Dreher.

NORTH JERSEY EAGLES

Mailing Address: 12 Wright Way, Oakland NJ 07436. **General Manager:** Brian Casey. **Field Manager:** Chris Buser.

OCEAN GULLS

General Manager: Angelo Fiore, afiore@fioreservice group.com. **Field Manager:** Rich Gawlak

QUAKERTOWN BLAZERS

Telephone: (215) 679-5072. **E-Mail Address:** gbonekemper@yahoo.com.
Website: www.quakertownblazers.com. **General Manager:** George Bonekemper. **Field Manager:** Chris Ray.

TRENTON GENERALS

E-Mail Address: coachbillrogers19@gmail.com. **General Manager:** Bill Rogers. **Field Manager:** Matt Facendo.

CALIFORNIA COLLEGIATE LEAGUE

Mailing Address: 806 W Pedregosa St, Santa Barbara, CA 93101. **Telephone:** (805) 680-1047. **Fax:** (805) 684-8596. **E-Mail Address:** burns@calsummerball.com. **Website:** www.calsummerball.com.
Founded: 1993.
Commissioner: Pat Burns.
Division Structure: North Division—Healdsburg Prune Packers, Menlo Park Legends, Neptune Beach Pearl, Walnut Creek Crawdads. **Central**—Conejo Oaks, San Luis Obispo Blues, Santa Barbara Foresters, Ventura Halos. **South**—Academy Barons, Long Beach Legends, Orange County Riptide, Southern California Catch.
Regular Season: 36 games (24 divisional games, 12 inter-divisional games). **2016 Opening Date:** June 1. **Closing Date:** July 31. **Playoff Format:** Divisional champions and wild card team play double-elimination championship tournament. **Roster Limit:** 33.

ACADEMY BARONS

Address: 901 E. Artesia Blvd, Compton, CA 90221. **Telephone:** (310) 635-2967. **Website:** www.academy barons.org. **E-Mail Address:** darrell.miller@mlb.com. **Contact:** Darrell Miller, director. **Field manager:** Kenny Landreaux.

ARROYO SECO SAINTS

Telephone: (626) 695-6903. **E-mail Address:** amilam @arroyosecobaseball.com. **General Manager:** Aaron Milam.

CONEJO OAKS

Address: 1710 N. Moorpark Rd., #106, Thousand Oaks, CA91360. **Telephone:** 805-304-0126. **Website:** www. oaksbaseball.org. **E-Mail Address:** oaksbaseball@yahoo .com. **Field Manager:** David Soliz. **General Manager:** Randy Riley.

HEALDSBURG PRUNE PACKERS

Telephone: (707) 280-6693. **E-mail Address:** jgg21@ aol.com. **Field Manager:** Joey Gomes.

NEPTUNE BEACH PEARL

Address: PO Box 2602, Alameda, CA 94501. **Telephone:** (510) 590-3139. **Website:** www.neptune beachpearl.com. **E-Mail Address:** bcummings@neptune beachpearl.com. **Field Manager:** Brant Cummings. **General Manager:** Pearl Scott Tully. **Telephone:** (510) 612-0402. **E-mail Address:** info@neptunebeachpearl.com

ORANGE COUNTY RIPTIDE

Address: 14 Calendula Rancho, Santa Margarita, CA 92688. **Telephone:** (949) 228-7676. **Website:** ocriptide. com. **E-Mail Address:** ocriptidebaseball@gmail.com. **Field Manager:** Tyger Pederson. **General Manager:** Moe Geohagen.

SAN LUIS OBISPO BLUES

Address: 241-B Prado Rd., San Luis Obispo, CA 93401. **Telephone:** (805) 704-4388. **Website:** www.bluesbase ball.com. **E-Mail Address:** adam@bluesbaseball.com. **General Manager:** Adam Stowe. **Field Manager:** Dan Marple. **Telephone:** (805) 710-6900. **E-mail Address:** drmarple@hotmail.com.

SANTA BARBARA FORESTERS

Address: 4299 Carpinteria Ave., Suite 201, Carpinteria, CA 93013. **Telephone:** (805) 684-0657. **Website:** www. sbforesters.org. **E-Mail Address:** pintard@earthlink.net. **Field Manager:** Bill Pintard.

SOUTHERN CALIFORNIA CATCH

Telephone (GM): (562) 686-8262. **E-mail Address (GM):** BOrr@fca.org. **Telephone (Asst. GM):** (303) 483-8328. **E-mail Address (Asst. GM):** catchgm@fca.org. **General Manager:** Ben Orr. **Assistant General Manager:** Hunter Bingham.

CAL RIPKEN COLLEGIATE LEAGUE

Address: 4006 Broadstone St, Frederick, MD 21704. **Telephone:** (301) 693-2577. **E-Mail:** jwoodward@cal ripkenleague.org or brifkin@calripkenleague.org. **Website:** www.calripkenleague.org.

Year Founded: 2005.

Commissioner: Jason Woodward. **League President:** Brad Rifkin. **Deputy Commissioner:** Jerry Wargo.

Regular Season: 40 games. **Playoff Format:** Top two teams from each division plus two remaining teams with best records qualify. Teams play best of three series, winners advance to best of three series for league championship. **Roster Limit:** 30 (college-eligible players 22 and under).

ALEXANDRIA ACES

Address: 221 9th Street, S.E. Washington, DC 20003. **Telephone:** (202) 255-1683. **E-Mail:** cberset21@gmail. com. **Website:** www.alexandriaaces.org. **Chairman/CEO:** Donald Dinan. **General Manager:** TBD. **Ballpark:** Frank Mann Field at Four Mile Run Park.

BALTIMORE DODGERS

Address: 17 Sunrise Court Randallstown, MD 21133. **Telephone:** (443) 834-3500. **Email:** juan.waters@verizon. net. **Website:** www.baltimoredodgers.org. **President:** Juan Waters. **Head Coach:** Derek Brown. **Ballpark:** Joe Cannon Stadium at Harmans Park.

BALTIMORE REDBIRDS

Address: 2208 Pine Hill Farms Lane, Cockeysville, MD 21030. **Telephone:** (410) 802-2220. **Fax:** (410) 785-6138. **E-Mail:** johntcarey@hotmail.com.

Website: baltimoreredbirds.org. **President:** John Carey. **Head Coach:** Tom Eller. **Ballpark:** Carlo Crispino Stadium at Calvert Hall High School.

BETHESDA BIG TRAIN

Address: 6400 Goldsboro Road Suite 220 Bethesda, MD 20817. **Telephone:** 301-983-1006. **Fax:** 301- 229-8362. **E-Mail:** faninfo@bigtrain.org. **Website:** www. bigtrain.org. **General Manager:** David Schneider. **Head Coach:** Sal Colangelo. **Ballpark:** Shirley Povich Field.

D.C. GRAYS

Address: 1800 M Street NW, 500 South Tower, Washington, DC 20036. **Telephone:** (202) 492-6226. **Website:** www.dcgrays.com. **E-Mail Address:** barbera@ acg-consultants.com. **President:** Michael Barbera. **General Manager:** Antonio Scott. **Head Coach:** Reggie Terry. **Ballpark:** Washington Nationals Youth Academy.

GAITHERSBURG GIANTS

Address: 10 Brookes Avenue, Gaithersburg, MD 20877. **Telephone:** (240) 888-6810. **E-Mail:** alriley13@ gmail.com. **Website:** www.gaithers burggiants.org. **General Manager:** Alfie Riley. **Head Coach:** Jeff Rabberman. **Ballpark:** Criswell Automotive Field.

FCA HERNDON BRAVES

Address: 1305 Kelly Court, Herndon, VA 20170-2605. **Telephone:** (702) 909-2750. **Fax:** (703) 783-1319. **E-Mail:** fcaherndonbraves@yahoo.com. **Website:** www.herndon braves.com. **President/General Manager:** Todd Burger. **Head Coach:** Chris Warren. **Ballpark:** Alan McCullock Field at Herndon High School.

ROCKVILLE EXPRESS

Address: PO Box 10188, Rockville, MD 20849. **Telephone:** 301-367-9435. **E-Mail:** info@rockvilleexpress .org. **Website:** www.rockvilleexpress.org. **President/General Manager:** Jim Kazunas. **Email:** jameskazunas@ rockvilleexpress.org. **Head Coach:** Rick Price. **Ballpark:** Knights Field at Montgomery College-Rockville.

SILVER SPRING-TAKOMA T-BOLTS

Address: 906 Glaizewood Court, Takoma Park, MD 20912. **Telephone:** 301-983-1358. **E-Mail:** tboltsbaseball @gmail.com. **Website:** www.tbolts.org. **General Manager:** David Stinson. **Head Coach:** Doug Remer. **Ballpark:** Blair Stadium at Montgomery Blair High School.

LOUDOUN RIVER DOGS

Address: 43460 Loudoun Reserve Dr, Ashburn, VA 20148. **Telephone:** (703) 615-4396. **E-Mail Address:** tickets@brucehallsports.com. **Website:** www.viennariver dogs.org. **President/General Manager/Head Coach:** Bruce Hall. **Ballpark:** Rock Ridge High School.

CAPE COD BASEBALL LEAGUE

Mailing Address: PO Box 266, Harwich Port, MA 02646. **Telephone:** (508) 432-6909. **E-Mail:** info@capecod baseball.org. **Website:** www.capecodbaseball.org. **Year Founded:** 1885.

Commissioner: Paul Galop. **President:** Chuck Sturtevant. **Treasurer/Webmaster:** Steven Wilson. **Secretary:** Kim Wolfe. **Senior VP/Deputy Commissioner:** Bill Bussiere. **VP:** Tom Gay, Mary Henderson. **Senior Deputy Commissioner/Umpire-In-Chief:** Sol Yas. **Deputy Commissioner, West:** Mike Carrier. **Deputy Commissioner, East:** Peter Hall. Director Public Relations Kyla Costa. **Director Broadcasting:** John Garner Jr. **Director, Communications:** Jim McGonigle. Director, **Publications:** Sean Sullivan. **Division Structure: East**—Brewster, Chatham, Harwich, Orleans, Yarmouth-Dennis. **West**—Bourne, Cotuit, Falmouth, Hyannis, Wareham.

Regular Season: 44 games. **2018 Opening Date:** June 12. **Closing Date:** August 12. **All-Star Game:** July 22. **Playoff Format:** Top four teams in each division qualify for three rounds of best-of-three series.

Roster Limit: 30 (college-eligible players only).

BOURNE BRAVES

Mailing Address: PO Box 895, Monument Beach, MA 02553. **Telephone:** (508) 868-8378. **E-Mail Address:** nnor kevicius@yahoo.com. **Website:** www.bournebraves.org. **President:** Nicole Norkevicius. **General Manager:** Darin Weeks. **Head Coach:** Harvey Shapiro.

BREWSTER WHITECAPS

Mailing Address: PO Box 2349, Brewster, MA 02631. **Telephone:** (508) 896-8500, ext. 147. **Fax:** (508) 896-9845. **E-Mail Address: ckenney@brewsterwhitecaps.com. Website:** www.brewsterwhitecaps.com. **President:** Chris Kenney. **General Manager:** Ned Monthie. **Head Coach:** Jamie Shevchick.

CHATHAM ANGLERS

Mailing Address: PO Box 428, Chatham, MA 02633. **Telephone:** (508) 348-1607. **Website:** www.chathamas. com. **President:** Steve West. **General Manager:** Mike Geylin. **Head Coach:** Tom Holliday.

COTUIT KETTLEERS

Mailing Address: PO Box 411, Cotuit, MA 02635. **Telephone:** (508) 428-3358. **Fax:** (508) 420-5584. **E-Mail Address:** info@kettleers.org. **Website:** www.kettleers. org. **President:** Andy Bonacker. **General Manager:** Bruce Murphy. **Head Coach:** Mike Roberts.

FALMOUTH COMMODORES

Mailing Address: PO Box 808 Falmouth, MA 02541. **Telephone:** (508) 566-4988. **Website:** www.falmouth commodores.org. **President:** Mark Kasprzyk. **General Manager:** Eric Zmuda. **Head Coach:** Jeff Trundy.

HARWICH MARINERS

Mailing Address: PO Box 201, Harwich Port, MA 02646. **Telephone:** (508) 432-2000. **Fax:** (508) 432-5357. **E-Mail Address:** mehendy@comcast.net. **Website:** www. harwichmariners.org.

President: Mary Henderson. **General Manager:** Ben Layton. **Head Coach:** Steve Englert.

HYANNIS HARBOR HAWKS

Mailing Address: PO Box 852, Hyannis, MA 02601. **Telephone:** (508) 737-5890. **Fax:** (877) 822-2703. **E-Mail Address:** brpfeifer@aol.com. **Website:** www. harborhawks.org.

President: Brad Pfeifer. **General Manager:** Tino DiGiovanni. **Head Coach:** Chad Gassman.

ORLEANS FIREBIRDS

Mailing Address: PO Box 504, Orleans, MA 02653. **Telephone:** (508) 255-0793. **Fax:** (508) 255-2237. **E-Mail Address:** gene.hornsby@outlook.com. **Website:** www. orleansfirebirds.com.

President: Gene Hornsby. **General Manager:** Sue Horton. **Head Coach:** Kelly Nicholson.

WAREHAM GATEMEN

Mailing Address: PO Box 287, Wareham, MA 02571. **Telephone:** (508) 748-0287. **Fax:** (508) 880-2602. **E-Mail Address:** paulatufts4gatemen@@gmail.com . **Website:** www.gatemen.org. **President:** Tom Gay. **General Manager:** Andrew Lang. **Head Coach:** Don Sneddon .

YARMOUTH-DENNIS RED SOX

Mailing Address: PO Box 78 Yarmouth Port, MA 02675. **Telephone:** (508) 889-8721. **Fax:** **E-Mail Address:** sfaucher64@gmail.com. **Website:** www.ydredsox.org. **President:** Ed Pereira. **General Manager:** Steve Faucher. **Head Coach:** Scott Pickler.

CENTRAL VALLEY COLLEGIATE LEAGUE

Mailing Address: P.O. Box 561, Fowler, CA 93625. **E-mail:** j_scot25@hotmail.com, jcederquist@aol.com. **Website:** www.cvclbaseball.webs.com. **Twitter:** @CVCL1.

Year Founded: 2013. **President:** Jon Scott. **Regular Season:** 30 games. **2018 Opening Date:** Mat 31. **Closing Date:** July 26. **All-Star Game:** July 15, Fresno, Calif. **Roster Limit:** 30

BAKERSFIELD BRAVES

Mailing Address: PO Box 20760, Bakersfield, CA, 93390. **Website:** eteamz.com/bakersfieldbraves. **Field Manager:** Bobby Maitia.

CALIFORNIA EXPOS

Mailing Address: P.O. Box 561, Fowler, CA 93625. **E-mail:** exposcv@aol.com. **Website:** www.calibaseball. com. **Twitter:** @cvexpos. **Field Manager:** Thomas Raymundo.

CALIFORNIA PILOTS

Mailing Address: PO Box 561 Fowler, CA 93625. **E-mail:** valleystormbaseball@aol.com. **Website:** www.calibaseball.com. **Twitter:** @calistorm1. **Field Manager:** Kenny Corona.

CALIFORNIA STORM

Mailing Address: PO Box 561 Fowler, CA 93625. **E-mail:** valleystormbaseball@aol.com. **Website:** www.calibaseball.com. **Twitter:** @calistorm1. **Field Manager:** Kolton Cabral.

SANTA MARIA PACKERS

Mailing Address: P.O Box 144, Kingsburg, CA 93631. **E-mail:** j_scot25@hotmail.com. **Website:** www.cvipers.webs.com. **Twitter:** @SouthcountryV. **Field Manager:** Jon Scott.

SOUTH COUNTY VIPERS

Mailing Address: P.O Box 144, Kingsburg, CA 93631. **E-mail:** j_scot25@hotmail.com. **Website:** www.cvipers.webs.com. **Twitter:** @SouthcountryV. **Field Manager:** Jon Scott.

COASTAL PLAIN LEAGUE

Mailing Address: 112 N. Main St., Holly Springs, NC 27540. **Telephone:** (919) 852-1960. **Fax:** (919) 516-0852. **Email Address:** justins@coastalplain.com. **Website:** www.coastalplain.com.

Year Founded: 1997.

Chairman/CEO: Jerry Petitt. **COO/Commissioner:** Justin Sellers. **Director of Media Relations:** Shelby Hilliard. Director of Operations & **Sponsorships:** Catherine Roth.

Division Structure: East— Fayetteville, Holly Springs, Morehead City, Wilmington. **West—**Asheboro, Gastonia, High Point-Thomasville, Forest City. **North—**Edenton, Martinsville, Peninsula, Wilson. **South—**Florence, Lexington County, Macon, Savannah

Regular Season: 52 games (split schedule). **2018 Opening Date:** May 31. **Closing Date:** August 4. **All-Star Game:** July 9. **Playoff Format:** Three rounds. **Rd 1/2:** One game, **Rd 3:** Best of three.

Roster Limit: 32 (college-eligible players and graduated seniors only).

ASHEBORO COPPERHEADS

Mailing Address: PO Box 4006, Asheboro, NC 27204. **Telephone:** (336) 460-7018. **Fax:** (336) 629-2651. **E-Mail Address:** info@teamcopperhead.com. **Website:** www.teamcopperhead.com. **Owners:** Ronnie Pugh, Steve Pugh, Doug Pugh, Mike Pugh. **General Manager:** Max Kaufmann. **Head Coach:** Keith Ritsche

EDENTON STEAMERS

Mailing Address: PO Box 86, Edenton, NC 27932. **Telephone:** (252) 482-4080. **Fax:** (252) 482-1717. **E-Mail Address:** edentonsteamers@hotmail.com. **Website:** www.edentonsteamers.com. **Owner:** Frank Burke. **General Manager:** Tyler Russell. **Head Coach:** Russ Burroughs.

FAYETTEVILLE SWAMPDOGS

Mailing Address: PO Box 64691, Fayetteville, NC 28306.**Telephone:** (910) 426-5900. **Fax:** (910) 426-3544. **E-Mail Address:** info@goswampdogs.com. **Website:** www.goswampdogs.com. **Owner:** Lew Handelsman. **General Manager:** Jeremy Aagard. **Head Coach:** Matt Hollod

FLORENCE REDWOLVES

Mailing Address: PO Box 809, Florence, SC 29503. **Telephone:** (843) 629-0700. **Fax:** (843) 629-0703. **E-Mail Address:** barbara@florenceredwolves.com. **Website:** www.florenceredwolves.com. **Owners:** Kevin Barth, Donna Barth. **General Manager:** Barbara Osborne. **Head Coach:** Cory Brownsten

FOREST CITY OWLS

Mailing Address: PO Box 1062, Forest City, NC 28043. **Telephone:** (828) 245-0000. **Fax:** (828) 245-6666. **E-Mail Address:** info@forestcitybaseball.com. **Website:** www.forestcitybaseball.com. **Owners:** Phil & Becky Dangel. **General Manager:** Kiva Fuller. **Head Coach:** Matt Reed.

GASTONIA GRIZZLIES

Mailing Address: PO Box 177, Gastonia, NC 28053. **Telephone:** (704) 866-8622. **Fax:** (704) 864-6122. **E-Mail Address:** jesse@gastoniagrizzlies.com. **Website:** www.gastoniagrizzlies.com. **Owners:** Fans First Entertainment (Jesse & Emily Cole). **General Manager:** David McDonald. **Head Coach:** Charles Bradley.

HIGH POINT-THOMASVILLE HI-TOMS

Mailing Address: PO Box 3035, Thomasville, NC 27361. **Telephone:** (336) 472-8667. **Fax:** (336) 472-7198. **E-Mail Address:** info@hitoms.com. **Website:** www.hitoms.com. **Owner:** Richard Holland. **President:** Greg Suire. **Head Coach:** Brian Rountree.

HOLLY SPRINGS SALAMANDERS

Mailing Address: PO Box 1208, Holly Springs, NC 27540. **Telephone:** 919-249-7322. **Email Address:** tommya@salamandersbaseball.com. **Website:** www.salamandersbaseball.com. **Owner:** Jerry Petitt. **General Manager:** Tommy Atkinson. **Head Coach:** Dustin Coffman.

LEXINGTON COUNTY BLOWFISH

Mailing Address: PO Box 2018, Lexington, SC. **Telephone:** (803) 254-3474. **Fax:** (803) 254-4482. **E-Mail Address:** info@blowfishbaseball.com. **Website:** www.blowfishbaseball.com. **Owner:** Bill & Vicki Shanahan. **Vice President:** Brian Larkin. **General Manager:** Theo Bacot. **Head Coach:** Marshall McDonald.

MACON BACON

Mailing Address: 225 Willie Smokey Glover Drive, Macon, GA. **Telephone:** 478-803-1795. **E-Mail Address:** info@**maconbacon**.com **Website:** www.maconbacon-baseball.com. **Owner:** SRO Partners (Jon Spoelstra & Steve DeLay). **General Manager:** Todd Pund. **Head Coach:** Danny Higginbotham.

MARTINSVILLE MUSTANGS

Mailing Address: PO Box 1112, Martinsville, VA 24114. **Telephone:** (276) 403-5250. **Fax:** (276) 403-5387. **E-Mail Address:** brian@martinsvillemustangs.com. **Website:** www.martinsvillemustangs.com. **Owner:** City of Martinsville. **General Manager:** Brian McConnell. **Head Coach:** Kevin Soine.

MOREHEAD CITY MARLINS

Mailing Address: 1921 Oglesby Road, Morehead City, NC 28557. **Telephone:** (252) 269-9767. **Fax:** (252) 727-9402. **E-Mail Address:** croth@mhcmarlins.com. **Website:** www.mhcmarlins.com. **President:** Buddy Bengel. **Head Coach:** Jesse Lancaster.

PENINSULA PILOTS

Mailing Address: PO Box 7376, Hampton, VA 23666. **Telephone:** (757) 245-2222. **Fax:** (757) 245-8030. **E-Mail Address:** jeffscott@peninsulapilots.com. **Website:** www.peninsulapilots.com. **Owner:** Henry Morgan. **General Manager:** Jason Cantone. **Head Coach/Vice President:** Hank Morgan.

SAVANNAH BANANAS

Mailing Address: PO Box 5267, Savannah, Ga. **31414** **Telephone:** 912-712-2482. **E-Mail Address:** jared@thesavannahbananas.com. **Website:** www.thesavannahbananas.com. **Owner:** Fans First Entertainment (Jesse & Emily Cole). **President:** Jared Orton. **Head Coach:** Tyler Gillum

WILMINGTON SHARKS

Mailing Address: PO Box 15233, Wilmington, NC 28412. **Telephone:** (910) 343-5621. **Fax:** (910) 343-8932. **E-Mail Address:** info@wilmingtonsharks.com. **Website:** www.wilmingtonsharks.com. **Owners:** Smith Family Baseball Wilmington, LLC. **General Manager:** Pat Hutchins. **Head Coach:** Tyler Jackson

WILSON TOBS

Mailing Address: PO Box 633, Wilson, NC 27894. **Telephone:** (252) 291-8627. **Fax:** (252) 291-1224. **E-Mail Address:** wilsontobs@gmail.com. **Website:** www.wilsontobs.com. **Owner:** Richard Holland. **President:** Greg Suire. **General Manager:** Mike Bell. **Head Coach:** Bryan Hill.

FLORIDA COLLEGIATE SUMMER LEAGUE

Mailing Address: 250 National Place, Unit #152, Longwood, FL 32750. **Telephone:** (321) 206-9174. **Fax:** (407) 574-7926. **E-Mail Address:** info@floridaleague.com. **Website:** www.floridaleague.com.
Year Founded: 2004.
President: Rob Sitz. **Vice President:** Stefano Foggi. **League Operations Director:** Phil Chinnery.
Regular Season: 45 games. **2018 Opening Date:** May 31. **All-Star Game:** July 7. **Playoffs begin:** July 31. **Playoff Format:** Five teams qualify; No. 4 and No. 5 seeds meet in one-game playoff. Remaining four teams play best-of-three series. Winners play best-of-three series for league championship.
Roster Limit: 28 (college-eligible players only). High school grads allowed with MLB approval.

DELAND SUNS

Operated by the league office. **E-Mail Address:** suns@floridaleague.com. **Head Coach:** Rick Hall. **General Manager:** Trevor Stultz.

LEESBURG LIGHTNING

E-Mail Address: lightning@floridaleague.com. **Head Coach:** Rich Billings.

SANFORD RIVER RATS

Operated by the league office. **E-Mail Address:** rats@floridaleague.com. **Head Coach:** Scotty Makarewicz. **General Manager:** Kenne Brown

SEMINOLE COUNTY SCORPIONS

Operated by the league office. **E-Mail Address:** rats@floridaleague.com. **Head Coach:** TBA. **General Manager:** Kenne Brown

WINTER GARDEN SQUEEZE

Operated by the league office.
Email Address: squeeze@floridaleague.com. **Head Coach:** Jay Welsh. **General Manager:** Adam Bates.

WINTER PARK DIAMOND DAWGS

E-Mail Address: dawgs@floridaleague.com. **Head Coach:** Chuck Schall. **General Manager:** Phil Chinnery.

FUTURES COLLEGIATE LEAGUE OF NEW ENGLAND

Mailing Address: 46 Chestnut Hill Rd, Chelmsford, MA 01824. **Telephone:** (617) 593-2112. **E-Mail Address:** futuresleague@yahoo.com
Website: www.thefuturesleague.com.
Year Founded: 2010.
Commissioner: Chris Hall.
Teams (Contact): Bristol Blues (www.bristolbluesbaseball.com) (**Brian Rooney:** gm@bristolblues.com); Brockton Rox (**Todd Marlin:** tmarlin@brocktonrox.com); Martha's Vineyard Sharks (**Russ Curran:** russ.curran@mvsharks.com); Nashua Silver Knights (**Rick Muntean:** rick@nashuasilverknights.com); North Shore Navigators (**Bill Terlecky:** navigatorsgm@gmail.com); Pittsfield Suns (**Kristen Huss:** kristen@pittsfieldsuns.com); Worcester Bravehearts (**Dave Peterson:** dave@worcesterbravehearts.com)
Regular Season: 56 games; 28 home, 28 away.
Playoff Format: Six teams qualify. First round consists of two single elimination play-in games (3 seed vs. 6 seed and 4 seed vs 5 seed), two remaining teams play a best of three semi-final round followed by a best of three championship round to determine league champion. Extra-inning Games are determined by Homerun Derby!!
Roster Limit: 35. 10 must be from New England or play collegiately at a New England college.

GREAT LAKES SUMMER COLLEGIATE LEAGUE

Mailing Address: PO Box 666, Troy, OH 45373. **Telephone:** (937) 308-1536. **Fax:** none.
Website: www.greatlakesleague.org.
Year Founded: 1986.
President: Jim DeSana. **Commissioner:** Deron Brown. **Regular Season:** 42 games. **Playoff Format:** Top six

teams meet in playoffs. **Roster Limit:** 30 (college-eligible players only).

Teams: (15 Teams)—Cincinnati Steam (Cincinnati, OH); Galion Graders (Galion, OH); Grand Lake Mariners (Celina, OH); Grand River Loggers (Grand Haven, MI); Hamilton Joes (Hamilton, OH); Irish Hills Leprechauns (Adrian, MI); Lake Erie Monarchs (Flat Rock, MI); Licking County Settlers (Newark, OH); Lima Locos (Lima, OH); Lorain County Ironmen (Lorain, OH); Muskegon Clippers (Muskegon, MI); Richmond Jazz (Richmond, IN); Saint Clair Green Giants (Tecumseh, ON); Southern Ohio Copperheads (Athens, OH); Xenia Scouts (Xenia, OH).

GREAT WEST LEAGUE

League Office
Mailing Address: 1915 S.W. Elizabeth Street, Portland, Oregon 97201. **Telephone:** 503-946-1122 **E-Mail Address:** greatwestleague@comcast.net **Website:** www.greatwestleague.com
Year Founded: 2016
Commissioner: Ken Wilson
Teams: Chico Heat, Klamath Falls Gems, Lincoln Potters, Medford Rogues, San Francisco Seals, Yuba Sutter Gold Sox
Regular Season: 60 games. **2018 Opening Date:** May 29. **Closing Date:** August 4. **All-Star Game:** July 23 at Klamath Falls. **Playoff Format:** Top four teams play two best-of-three series with winners moving to the best-of-three Championship Series.
Roster Limit: 25 (college-eligible players only)
Supervisor of Umpires: Bill Speck
Telephone: 209-614-2321 **E-Mail Address:** nobangers@aol.com

CHICO HEAT

Mailing Address: 1722 Mangrove, Suite 24, Chico, California 95973. **Telephone:** 530-725-5444. **E-Mail Address:** chicoheatgm@gmail.com. **Website:** www.chi-coheat.com. **Owners:** CSH International, Pat Gillick and Steve Nettleton. **General Manager:** Hunter Hampton. **Manager:** Fred Ludwig. **Stadium:** Nettleton Stadium.

KLAMATH FALLS GEMS

Mailing Address: 2001 Crest Street, Klamath Falls, Oregon 97603. **Telephone:** 541-883-4367. **E-Mail Address:** oconnjos@gmail.com. **Website:** www.klamath-fallsgems.com. **Owner/General Manager:** Joe O'Connor. **Manager:** Nick Gauna. **Stadium:** Kiger Stadium.

LINCOLN POTTERS

Mailing Address: 436 Lincoln Blvd., Suite 184, Lincoln, California 95648. **Telephone:** 520-850-0829. **E-Mail Address:** lundgrenmt@gmail.com. **Website:** www.lincol-npotters.com. **Owner:** Clifton Taylor. **General Manager:** Matt Lundgren. **Manager:** Ryan Stevens. **Stadium:** McBean Stadium.

MEDFORD ROGUES

Mailing Address: Harry & David Field, 2929 S. Pacific Highway, Medford, Oregon 97501. **Telephone:** 541-973-2883. **E-Mail Address:** dave@medfordrogues.com. **Website:** www.medfordrogues.com. **Owner:** CSH International. **Chief Operating Officer:** Dave May. **Manager:** Tyler Graham. **Stadium:** Harry & David Field.

SAN FRANCISCO SEALS

Mailing Address: 555 Ralph Appezzato Memorial Parkway, Alameda, California 94501. **Telephone:** 510-545-9618. **E-Mail Address:** info@sealsbaseball.com. **Website:** www.sfsealsbaseball.com. **Owner/General Manager:** Abel Alcantar. **Manager:** Eric Vasquez. **Stadium:** Alameda Field.

YUBA SUTTER GOLD SOX:

Mailing Address: 429 10th Street, Marysville, California 95901. **Telephone:** 530-741-3600. **E-Mail Address:** team@goldsox.com. **Website:** www.goldsox.com. **Owner:** CSH International. **General Manager:** Michael Mink. **Manager:** Jeramy Gillen. **Stadium:** Colusa Casino Stadium.

JAYHAWK LEAGUE

Mailing Address: 865 Fabrique, Wichita, KS 67218. **Telephone:** (316) 687-2309. **Website:** www.jayhawkbaseballleague.org. **Year Founded:** 1976.
Regular Season: 42 games. **Playoff Format:** Top three teams qualify for National Baseball Congress World Series. **Roster Limit:** Unlimited.
Teams: Derby Twins, Dodge City A's, El Dorado Broncos, Great Bend Bat Cats, Hays Larks, Haysville Aviators, Liberal Bee Jays, Oklahoma City Indians.

METROPOLITAN COLLEGIATE BASEBALL LEAGUE

Mailing Address: 78 Knollwood Drive, Paramus NJ 07652
President: Brian Casey 374-545-1991
Website: www.metropolitanbaseball.com
Email: mcbl@metropolitanbaseball.com

MIDWEST COLLEGIATE LEAGUE

Mailing Address: PO Box 172, Flossmoor, IL 60422. **E-Mail Address:** commissioner@midwestcollegiateleague.com. **Website:** www.midwestcollegiateleague.com.
Year Founded: 2010.
President/Commissioner: Don Popravak.
Regular Season: 52 games. **2018 Opening Date:** May 26. **Closing Date:** Aug. 7. **All-Star Game:** July 11. **Playoff Format:** Top four teams meet in best of three series. Winners meet in best of three championship series.
Roster Limit: 30
Teams: Bloomington Bobcats, Crestwood Panthers, DuPage County Hounds, Joliet Admirals, NWI Oilmen, Southland Vikings.

M.I.N.K. LEAGUE

(Missouri, Iowa, Nebraska, Kansas)
Mailing Address: PO Box 367, Nevada, MO 64772. **Telephone:** (417) 667-6159. **Fax:** (417) 667-4210. **E-mail Address:** jpost@morrisonpost.com. **Website:** www.minkleaguebaseball.com.
Year Founded: 1995.
Commissioner: Bob Steinkamp. **President:** Jeff Post. **Vice President:** Jud Kindle. **Secretary:** Edwina Rains.
Regular Season: 44 games. **Playoff Format:** MINK League officials also voted for a new playoff format. For the 2018 season, the top three teams from each division will qualify for the playoffs. The second and third place finishers in each division will play a "Wild Card" one game playoff. The winner of those games will play the regular season division winner from each division in a one

game playoff. The winner of each division will then play a two out three series to determine the MINK League Champion. **All-Star Game:** July 6 at Chilicothe, MO.

CHILLICOTHE MUDCATS

Mailing Address: 426 E Jackson, Chillicothe, MO 64601. **Telephone:** (660) 247-1504. **Fax:** (660) 646-6933. **E-Mail Address:** doughty@greenhills.net. **Website:** www.chilli cothemudcats.com. **General Manager:** Doug Doughty.

CLARINDA A'S

Mailing Address: 225 East Lincoln, Clarinda, IA 51632. **Telephone:** (712) 542-4272. **E-Mail Address:** m.everly@ mchsi.com. **Website:** www.clarindaiowa-as-baseball.org. **General Manager:** Ryan Eberly. **Head Coach:** Ryan Eberly.

JOPLIN OUTLAWS

Mailing Address: 5860 North Pearl, Joplin, MO 64801. **Telephone:** (417) 825-4218. **E-Mail Address:** merains@mchsi.com. **Website:** www.joplinoutlaws.com. **President/General Manager:** Mark Rains.

NEVADA GRIFFONS

Mailing Address: PO Box 601, Nevada, MO 64772. **Telephone:** (417) 667-6159. **E-Mail Address:** Ryan. Mansfield@mcckc.edu . **Website:** www.nevadagriffons. org. **President:** Dan Keller. **General Manager:** Ryan Mansfield. **Head Coach:** Ryan Mansfield.

OZARK GENERALS

Mailing Address: 1336 W Farm Road 182, Springfield, MO 65810. **Telephone:** (417) 832-8830. **Fax:** (417) 877-4625. **E-Mail Address:**rda160@yahoo.com. **Website:** www.generalsbaseballclub.com. **General Manager/ Head Coach:** Rusty Aton.

ST. JOSEPH MUSTANGS

Mailing Address: 2600 SW Parkway, St. Joseph, MO 64503. **Telephone:** (816) 279-7856. **Fax:** (816) 749-4082. **E-Mail Address:**kyturner@stjoemustangs.com. **Website:** www.stjoemustangs.com. **President:** Dan Gerson. **General Manager:** Ky Turner. **Manager/Director,** **Player Personnel:** TBA.

SEDALIA BOMBERS

Mailing Address: 2205 S Grand, Sedalia, MO 65301. **Telephone:** (660) 287-4722. **E-Mail Address:** eric@ sedaliabombers.com. **Website:** www.sedaliabombers. com. President/**General Manager/Head Coach:** Jud Kindle. **Vice President:** Ross Dey.

JEFFERSON CITY RENEGADES

Mailing Address: **Telephone:** 630-781-7247 **E-Mail Address:** jcrenegades@gmail.com. **Website:** www. jcrenegades.com. **President/General Manager:** Steve Dullard. **Head Coach:** Mike DeMilia.

NEW ENGLAND COLLEGIATE LEAGUE

Mailing Address: 122 Mass Moca Way, North Adams, MA 01247. **Telephone:** (413) 652-1031. **Fax:** (413) 473-0012. **E-Mail Address:** smcgrath@necbl.com. **Website:** www.necbl.com.
 Year founded: 1993.

President: John DeRosa. **Commissioner:** Sean McGrath. **Deputy Commissioner:** Gregg Hunt. **Secretary:** Max Pinto. **Treasurer:** Tim Porter.
 Regular Season: 44 games. **2018 Opening Date:** June 5. **Closing Date:** Aug. 10. **All-Star Game:** July 29 in Holyoke, MA (home of Valley Blue Sox.
 Roster Limit: 33 (college-eligible players only).

DANBURY WESTERNERS

Mailing Address: PO Box 3828, Danbury, CT 06813. **Telephone:** (203) 502-9167. **E-Mail Address:** jspit-ser@msn.com. **Website:** www.danburywesterners. com. **President:** Jon Pitser. **General Manager:** Chris Nathanson. **Field Manager:** Josh Parrow.

VALLEY BLUE SOX

Mailing Address: 100 Congress St, Springfield, MA 01104. **Telephone:** 860-305-1684. **E-Mail Address:** hunter@valleybluesox.com. **Website:** www.valley-bluesox.com
 President: Clark Eckhoff. **General Manager:** Hunter Golden. **Field Manager:** John Raiola.

KEENE SWAMP BATS

Mailing Address: 303 Park Ave., Keene, NH 03431. **Telephone:** 603-731-5240. **Fax:** (603) 357-5090. **E-Mail Address:** kwatterson@ghousen.com.
 Website: www.swampbats.com. **President:** Kevin Watterson. **VP/General Manager:** Walter Kilburn. **Field Manager:** Lyndon Coleman.

WINNIPESAUKEE MUSKRATS

Mailing Address: 65 Water Street, Laconia, NH 03246. **Telephone:** 603-303-7806. **E-Mail Address:** kristian@ muskratsbaseball.com. **Website:** www.winnipesau-keemuskrats.com. **President:** Mike Smith. **General Manager:** Kristian Svindland. **Field Manager:** tbd.

MYSTIC SCHOONERS

Mailing Address: PO Box 432, Mystic, CT 06355. **Telephone:** (860) 608-3287. **E-Mail Address:** dlong@ mysticbaseball.org. **Website:** www.mysticbaseball.org. **Executive Director:** Don Benoit. **General Manager:** Dennis Long. **Field Manager:** Rob Bono.

BAY STATE BAY SOX

Mailing Address: 427 John St, New Bedford, MA 02740. **Telephone:** 508-985-3052. **E-Mail Address:** tsilveira17@gmail.com. **Website:** www.nbbaysox.com. **President:** Stephen King. **General Manager:** Tammy Silveira. **Field Manager:** Chris Cabe.

NEWPORT GULLS

Mailing Address: PO Box 777, Newport, RI 02840. **Telephone:** (401) 845-6832. **E-Mail Address:** gm@ newportgulls.com. **Website:** www.newportgulls.com. **President/General Manager:** Chuck Paiva. **Field Manager:** Mike Coombs.

NORTH ADAMS STEEPLECATS

Mailing Address: PO Box 540, North Adams, MA 01247. **Telephone:** 413-896-3153. **E-Mail Address:** andrew.agostini@steeplecats.org. **Website:** www. steeplecats.org. **President:** Allen Hall. **General Manager:** Andrew Agostini. **Field Manager:** Justin Sumner

OCEAN STATE WAVES

Mailing Address: 1174 Kingstown Rd, Wakefield, RI 02879. **Telephone:** (401) 360-2977. **E-Mail Address:** matt@oceanstatewaves.com. **Website:** www. oceanstatewaves.com. **President/General Manager:** Matt Finlayson. **Field Manager:** Jim Sauro.

PLYMOUTH PILGRIMS

Mailing Address: 111 Camelot Drive, Plymouth, MA 02360. **Telephone:** 617-694-2658.. **E-Mail Address:** KPlant@pilgrimsbaseball.com **Website:** www.pilgrimsbaseball.com. **President:** Peter Plant. **General Manager:** Kevin Plant. **Field Manager:** Greg Zackrison.

VERMONT MOUNTAINEERS

Mailing Address: PO Box 57, East Montpelier, VT 05651. **Telephone:** (802) 223-5224. **E-Mail Address:** gmvtm@comcast.net. **Website:** www.thevermontmountaineers.com. **General Manager:** Brian Gallagher. **Field Manager:** Blake Nation.

UPPER VALLEY NIGHTHAWKS

Mailing Address: 134 Stevens Road Lebanon, NH 03766. **Telephone:** 864-380-2873 **E-Mail Address:** noah@uppervalleynighthawks.com **Website: http://**uppervalleybaseball.pointstreaksites. com. **President: Jonathan Crane General Manager:** Noah Crane. **Field Manager:** Jason Szafarski.

NEW YORK COLLEGIATE BASEBALL LEAGUE

Mailing Address: 398 East Dyke St. Wellsville, NY 14895. **Telephone:** (585) 455-2345. **Website:** www.nycbl. com.

Year founded: 1978.

President: Bill McConnell. **Commissioner:** Joe Brown. **Vice President:** Brian McConnell Jr. **Senior Marketing Director:** Dave Meluni. **Treasurer:** Dennis Duffy. **Secretary:** Steven Ackley.

Franchises: Eastern Division: Cortland Crush, Onondaga Flames, Rome Generals, Sherrill Silversmiths, Syracuse Spartans, Saratoga Revolution. **Western Division:** Genesee Rapids, Hornell Dodgers, Niagara Power, Olean Oilers, Rochester Ridgemen, Wellsville Nitros.

2018 Opening Date: June 1. **Season Ends:** July 23. **Playoff Format:** six teams qualify and play a 1 game playoff and then two rounds of best of three series.

Roster Limit: Unlimited (college-eligible players only).

CORTLAND CRUSH

Mailing Address: 2745 Summer Ridge Rd, LaFayette, NY 13084. **Telephone:** 315-391-8167. **Email Address:** wmmac4@aol.com. **Website:** www.cortlandcrush. com. **President:** Gary VanGorder. **Field Manager:** Bill McConnell.

GENESEE RAPIDS

Mailing Address: 9726 Rt. 19 Houghton, NY 14474. **Telephone:** 716-969-0688. **Email Address:** rkerr@frontiernet.net. **President:** Ralph Kerr. **Field Manager:** Joe Mesa.

HORNELL DODGERS

Mailing Address: PO Box 235, Hornell, NY 14843. **Telephone:** (607) 661-4173. **Fax:** (607) 661-4173. **E-Mail Address:** gm@hornelldodgers.com. **Website:** hornelldodgers.com. **General Manager:** Paul Welker. **Field Manager:** Unavailable.

NIAGARA POWER

Mailing Address: P.O. Box 2012, Niagara University, NY 14109. **Telephone:** (716) 286-8653. **E-Mail Address:** ptutka@niagara.edu. **Website:** www.niagarapowerball.com. **President:** Dr. Patrick Tutka. **Field Manager:** Unavailable.

OLEAN OILERS

Mailing Address: 126 N 10th, Olean, NY 14760. **Telephone:** 716-378-0641. **E-Mail Address:** Brian@oconnelllaw.net. **President:** Brian O'Connell. **Field Manager:** Unavailable

ONONDAGA FLAMES

Mailing Address: 4877 Onondaga Road, Syracuse, NY 13215. **Telephone:** (315) 728-9688. **E-Mail Address:** gm@cnybaseball.org. **Website:** www.onondagaflames. com. **General Manager:** Wayne Walker. **Field Manager:** Mike Cordero.

ROCHESTER RIDGEMEN

Mailing Address: 651 Taylor Dr, Xenia, OH 45385. **Telephone:** (937) 352-1225. **E-Mail Addresses:** baseball @athletesinaction.org. **Website:** www.rochesterridgemen.org. **President:** Jason Jipson. **Field Manager:** Unavailable.

ROME GENERALS

Email Address: Romegenerals@gmail.com. **Website:** www.romegenerals.com. **Baseball Director:** Ray DiBrango. **Field Manager:** Unavailable.

SHERRILL SILVERSMITHS

Mailing Address: PO Box 111, Sherrill, NY 13440. **Telephone:** (315) 264-4334. **E-Mail Address:** Djduffy316@gmail.com. **Website:** www.leaguelineup. com/silversmiths. **President:** Dennis Duffy & Mike Sherlock. **Field Manager:** Unavailable.

SYRACUSE SALT CATS

Mailing Address: 208 Lakeland Ave, Syracuse, NY 13209. **Telephone:** (315) 727-9220. **Fax:** (315) 488-1750. **E-Mail Address:** mmarti6044@yahoo.com. **Website:** www.leaguelineup.com/saltcats. **President:** Mike Martinez. **Field Manager:** Unavailable

SYRACUSE SPARTANS

Website: www.syracusespartans.com. **General Manager:** JJ Potrikus. **Field Manager:** Unavailable.

WELLSVILLE NITROS

Mailing Address: 2848 O'Donnell Rd, Wellsville, NY 14895. **Telephone:** 585-596-9523. **Fax:** 585-593-5260. **E-Mail Address:** nitros04@gmail.com. **Website:** www. nitrosbaseball.com. **President:** Steven J. Ackley. **Field Manager:** Tucker Hughes.

NORTHWOODS LEAGUE

Office Address: 2900 4th St SW, Rochester, MN 55902. **Telephone:** (507) 536-4579. **Fax:** (507) 536-4597. **E-Mail Address:** info@northwoodsleague.com.
Website: www.northwoodsleague.com.
Year Founded: 1994.
Chairman: Dick Radatz, Jr. **President:** Gary Hoover. **Vice President, Business Development:** Matt Bomberg. **Vice President, Operations:** Glen Showalter. **Vice President, Licensing/Technology:** Tina Coil. **Vice President, Technology Development:** Greg Goodwin. **Division Structure:** North-Bismarck, Duluth, Eau Claire, La Crosse, Mankato, Rochester, St. Cloud, Thunder Bay, Waterloo, Willmar. South-Battle Creek, Fond du Lac, Green Bay, Kalamazoo, Kenosha, Lakeshore, Madison, Rockford, Wisconsin, Wisconsin Rapids.
Regular Season: 72 games (split schedule).
2018 Opening Date: May 29. **Closing Date:** August 12. **All-Star Game:** July 24
Playoff Format: 8 teams, 4 from each division, meet in single elimination games. Winners meet in best of three series for league championship.
Roster Limit: 30 (college-eligible players only).

BATTLE CREEK BOMBERS

Mailing Address: 189 Bridge Street, Battle Creek, MI 49017. **Telephone:** (269) 962-0735. **Fax:** (269) 962-0741. **Email Address:** info@battlecreekbombers.com.
Website: www.battlecreekbombers.com. **General Manager:** Tyler Shore. **Field Manager:** Josh Rebandt. **Field:** C.O. **Brown Stadium.**

BISMARCK LARKS

Mailing Address: 121 E. Rosser Ave, Bismarck, ND 58501. **Telephone:** (701) 557-7600. **Email Address:** info@larksbaseball.com.
Website: www.larksbaseball.com. **General Manager:** John Bollinger. **Field Manager:** Sean Repay. **Field:** Dakota Community Bank & Trust Field

DULUTH HUSKIES

Mailing Address: PO Box 16231, Duluth, MN 55816. **Telephone:** (218) 786-9909.
Fax: (218) 786-9001. **E-Mail Address:** huskies@duluthhuskies.com. **Website:** www.duluthhuskies.com. **Owner:** Michael Rosenzweig. **General Manager:** Greg Culver. **Field Manager:** Tyger Pederson. **Field:** Wade Stadium.

EAU CLAIRE EXPRESS

Mailing Address: 108 E Grand Ave, Eau Claire, WI 54701. **Telephone:** (715) 839-7788. **Fax:** (715) 839-7676. **E-Mail Address:** info@eauclaireexpress.com.
Website: www.eauclaireexpress.com. **Owner:** Bill Rowlett. **Assistant Managing Director:** Andy Neborak. **General Manager:** Spencer Larson. **Director of Operations/Field Manager:** Dale Varsho. **Field:** Carson Park.

FOND DU LAC DOCK SPIDERS

Mailing Address: 254 Winnebago Dr., Fond du Lac, WI 54935. **Telephone:** (920) 907-9833. **Email Address:** info@dockspiders.com
Website: www.dockspiders.com. **President:** Rob Zerjav. **General Manager:** Ryan Moede
Field Manager: Zac Charbonneau. **Field:** Herr-Baker Field

GREEN BAY BULLFROGS

Mailing Address: 1306 Main Street, Green Bay, WI 54302. **Telephone:** (920) 497-7225. **Fax:** (920) 437-3551. **Email Address:** info@greenbaybullfrogs.com.
Website: www.greenbaybullfrogs.com. **General Manager:** Sieeria Vieaux. **Field Manager:** Chris Sabo. **Field:** Joannes Stadium.

KALAMAZOO GROWLERS

Mailing Address: 251 Mills St, Kalamazoo, MI 49048. **Telephone:** (555) 555-1212.
Website: www.growlersbaseball.com. **General Manager:** Brian Colopy. **Field Manager:** Cody Piechocki. **Field:** Homer Stryker Field.

KENOSHA KINGFISH

Mailing Address: 7817 Sheridan Rd, Kenosha, WI 53143. **Telephone:** (262) 653-0900. **Website:** www.king fishbaseball.com. **General Manager:** Scott Preimesberger. **Field Manager:** Duffy Dyer. **Field:** Simmons Field.

LA CROSSE LOGGERS

Mailing Address: 1223 Caledonia St, La Crosse, WI 54603. **Telephone:** (608) 796-9553. **Fax:** (608) 796-9032. **E-Mail Address:** info@lacrosseloggers.com.
Website: www.lacrosseloggers.com. **Owner:** Dan Kapanke. **General Manager:** Chris Goodell. **Assistant General Manager:** Ben Kapanke. **Field Manager:** Brian Lewis. **Field:** Copeland Park.

LAKESHORE CHINOOKS

Mailing Address: 995 Badger Circle, Grafton, WI 53024. **Telephone:** (262) 618-4659. **Fax:** (262) 618-4362. **E-Mail Address:** info@lakeshorechinooks.com.
Website: www.lakeshorechinooks.com. **Owner:** Jim Kacmarcik. **General Manager:** Shawn Kison. **Field Manager:** TBD. **Field:** Kapco Park.

MADISON MALLARDS

Mailing Address: 2920 N Sherman Ave, Madison, WI 53704. **Telephone:** (608) 246-4277. **Fax:** (608) 246-4163. **E-Mail Address:** conor@mallardsbaseball.com.
Website: www.mallardsbaseball.com. **Owner:** Steve Schmitt. **President:** Vern Stenman. **General Manager:** Tyler Isham. **Field Manager:** Donnie Scott. **Field:** Warner Park.

MANKATO MOONDOGS

Mailing Address: 1221 Caledonia Street, Mankato, MN 56001. **Telephone:** (507) 625-7047. **Fax:** (507) 625-7059. **E-Mail Address:** office@mankatomoondogs.com.
Website: www.mankatomoondogs.com. **General Manager:** Austin Link. **Field Manager:** Ryan Kragh. **Field:** Franklin Rogers Park.

ROCHESTER HONKERS

Mailing Address: 307 E Center St, Rochester, MN 55904. **Telephone:** (507) 289-1170. **Fax:** (507) 289-1866. **E-Mail Address:** honkers@rochesterhonkers.com.
Website: www.rochesterhonkers.com. **Owner General Manager:** Dan Litzinger.
Field Manager: Thomas Walker. **Field:** Mayo Field.

ROCKFORD RIVETS

Mailing Address: 4503 Interstate Blvd., Loves Park, IL 61111. **Telephone:** 815-240-4159. **E-Mail Address:** info@rockfordrivets.com

Website: www.rockfordrivets.com. **General Manager:** Chad Bauer

Field Manager: Brian Smith. **Field:** Rivets Stadium

ST. CLOUD ROX

Mailing Address: 5001 8th St N, St. Cloud, MN 56303. **Telephone:** (320) 240-9798. **Fax:** (320) 255-5228. **E-Mail Address:** info@stcloudrox.com. **Website:** www.stcloud rox.com. **President:** Gary Posch. **Vice President:** Scott Schreiner. **General Manager:** Mike Johnson. **Field Manager:** Al Newman. **Field:** Joe Faber Field.

THUNDER BAY BORDER CATS

Mailing Address: PO Box 29105 Thunder Bay, Ontario P7B 6P9. **Telephone:** (807) 766-2287. **General Manager:** Dan Grant. **Field Manager:** Mitchell Feller. **Field:** Port Arthur Stadium.

WATERLOO BUCKS

Mailing Address: PO Box 4124, Waterloo, IA 50704. **Telephone:** (319) 232-0500.

Fax: (319) 232-0700. **E-Mail Address:** waterloobucks@waterloobucks.com. **Website:** www.waterloobucks.com. **General Manager:** Dan Corbin. **Field Manager:** Scott Douglas. **Field:** Riverfront Stadium.

WILLMAR STINGERS

Mailing Address: PO Box 201, Willmar, MN, 56201. **Telephone:** (320) 222-2010.

E-Mail Address: ryan@willmarstingers.com. **Website:** www.willmarstingers.com. **Owners:** Marc Jerzak, Ryan Voz. **General Manager:** Nick McCallum. **Field Manager:** Bo Henning. **Field:** Bill Taunton Stadium.

WISCONSIN RAPIDS RAFTERS

Mailing Address: 521 Lincoln St, Wisconsin Rapids, WI 54494. **Telephone:** (715) 424-5400. **E-Mail Address:** info@raftersbaseball.com. **Website:** www.raftersbaseball.com. **Owner/President:** Vern Stenman. **General Manager:** John Fanta. **Field Manager:** Craig Noto. **Field:** Witter Field.

WISCONSIN WOODCHUCKS

Mailing Address: PO Box 6157, Wausau, WI 54402. **Telephone:** (715) 845-5055.

Fax: (715) 845-5015. **E-Mail Address:** info@woodchucks.com. **Website:** www.woodchucks.com. **Owner:** Mark Macdonald. **General Manager:** Ryan Treu. **Field Manager:** TBD

PACIFIC INTERNATIONAL LEAGUE

Mailing Address: 4400 26th Ave W, Seattle, WA 98199. **Telephone:** (206) 623-8844. **Fax:** (206) 623-8361. **E-Mail Address:** spotter@potterprinting.com. **Website:** www.pacificinternationalleague.com.

Year Founded: 1992.

President: Al Oremus. **Vice President:** Martin Lawrence. **Commissioner:** Terry Howard. **Secretary:** Steve Potter. **Treasurer:** Mark Dow. **Member Clubs:** Northwest Honkers, Everett Merchants, Seattle Studs,

Highline Bears, Redmond Dudes, North Sound Emeralds Regular Season: 20 league games. **2018 Opening Date:** June 1. **Playoff Format:** Top team is invited to National Baseball Congress World Series.

Roster Limit: 30; 25 eligible for games (players must be at least 18 years old).

PERFECT GAME COLLEGIATE LEAGUE

Mailing Address: 8 Michaels Lane, Old Brookville, NY 11545. **Telephone:** (516) 521-0206. **Fax:** (516) 801-0818.

E-Mail Address: valkun@aol.com.

Website: www.pgcbl.com.

Year Founded: 2010.

President: Jeffrey Kunion.

Director of Communications: Travis Larner

Executive Committee: Bob Ohmann (Newark Pilots), Paul Samulski (Albany Dutchmen). Robbie Nichols (Elmira Pioneers), George Deak (Utica Blue Sox), Kevin Hinchey (Saugerties Stallions)

Teams: East—Albany Dutchmen, Amsterdam Mohawks, Glens Falls Dragons, Mohawk Valley DiamondDawgs, Oneonta Outlaws, Saugerties Stallions. **Utica Blue Sox West**—Adirondack Trail Blazers, Elmira Pioneers, Geneva Red Wings, Jamestown Jammers, Newark Pilots, Onondaga Flames

Regular Season: 50. **2018 Opening Date:** June 1. **Closing Date:** July 30. **All-Star Game:** July 18. **Playoff Format:** Top four teams in each division qualify for one-game playoff; next two series are best of three. **Roster Limit:** 35 (maximum of two graduated high school players per team).

PROSPECT LEAGUE

Mailing Address: 200 Line Drive Lane, Elkville, IL 62932. **Telephone:** (618) 559-1343. **E-Mail Address:** commissioner@prospectleague.com. **Website:** www.prospectleague.com.

Year Founded: 1963 as Central Illinois Collegiate League; known as Prospect League since 2009.

Commissioner: Dennis Bastien.

Regular Season: 60 games. **2018 Opening Date:** May 30. **Closing Date:** Aug. 5. **Championship Series:** Aug 10-13. **Roster Limit:** 28.

BUTLER BLUESOX

Mailing Address: 6 West Diamond Street, Butler, PA 16001. **Telephone:** (724) 256-9994. **Fax:** (724) 282-6565. **E-Mail Address:** frontoffice@butlerbluesox.net.

Website: www.butlerbluesox.com. **Team President:** Larry Sassone. **General Manager:** Patrick Reddick. **Field Manager:** Cody Herald.

CHAMPION CITY KINGS

Mailing Address: 1301 Mitchell Blvd., Springfield, OH 45503. **Telephone:** (937) 342-0320. **Fax:** (937) 342-0320. **E-Mail Address:** rwhite@championcitykings.com. **Website:** www.championcitykings.com. **General Manager/League Director:** Rick White. **Field Manager:** Arthur Ted Stenberg.

CHILLICOTHE PAINTS

Mailing Address: 59 North Paint Street, Chillicothe, OH 45601.

Telephone: (740) 773-8326. **Fax:** (740) 773-8338. **E-Mail Address:** paints@bright.net. **Website:** www.

chillicothepaints.com. **League Director:** Brian Mannino. **Field Manager:** Brian Bigam.

DANVILLE DANS

Mailing Address: 4 Maywood, Danville, IL 61832. **Telephone:** (217) 918-3401. **Fax:** (217) 446-9995. **E-Mail Address:** danvilledans@comcast.net. **Website:** www.danvilledans.com. **League Director:** Jeanie Cooke. **Co-General Managers:** Jeanie Cooke. **Field Manager:** Eric Coleman.

HANNIBAL HOOTS

Contact: 573-629-2018. **Team President:** Rick DeStefane. **GM:** Matt Stembridge. **Field Manager:** Clayton Hicks.

KOKOMO JACKRABBITS

Mailing Address: 319 S Union St, Kokomo, IN 46901. **Telephone:** (414)-224-9283. **Fax:** (414) 224-9290. **E-Mail Address:** no-reply@mkesports.com. **Website:** www.kokomojackrabbits.com. **League Director:** Dan Kuenzi. **Field Manager:** Gary McClure.

LAFAYETTE AVIATORS

Mailing Address: Loeb Stadium, 1915 Scott St., Lafayette, IN 47904. **Telephone:** (414) 224-9283. **Fax:** (414) 224-9290. **E-Mail Address:** no-reply@mkesports.com. **Website:** www.lafayettebaseball.com. **League Director:** Dan Kuenzi. **Field Manager:** Will Arnold.

QUINCY GEMS

Mailing Address: 1400 N. 30th St., Suite 1, Quincy, IL 62301. **Telephone:** (217) 214-7436. **Fax:** (217) 214-7436. **E-Mail Address:** quincygems@yahoo.com. **Website:** www.quincygems.com. **League Director/General Manager:** Jimmie Louthan. **Field Manager:** Rick Fraire.

SPRINGFIELD SLIDERS

Mailing Address: 1415 North Grand Avenue East, Suite B, Springfield, IL 62702. **Telephone:** (217) 679-3511. **Fax:** (217) 679-3512. **E-Mail Address:**slidersfun@springfieldsliders.com. **Website:** www.springfieldsliders.com. **League Director:** Todd Miller.
General Manager: Todd Miller. **Field Manager:** Steve Leonetti.

TERRE HAUTE REX

Mailing Address:111 North 3rd St, Terre Haute, IN 47807. **Telephone:** (812) 478-3817. **Fax:** (812) 232-5353. **E-mail Address:** frontoffice@rexbaseball.com. **Website:** www.rexbaseball.com.**League Director/General Manager:** BruceRosselli. **Field Manager:**Tyler Wampler.

WEST VIRGINIA MINERS

Mailing Address: 476 Ragland Road, Suite 2, Beckley, WV 25801. **Telephone:** (304) 252-7233. **Fax:** (304) 253-1998. **E-mail Address:** wvminers@wvminersbaseball.com. **Website:** www.wvminersbaseball.com. **President:** Doug Epling. **League Director/General Manager:** Tim Epling. **Field Manager:** Tim Epling

SOUTHERN COLLEGIATE BASEBALL LEAGUE

Mailing Address: 9723 Northcross Center Court, Huntersville, NC 28078. **Telephone:** (704) 635-7126. **Cell:** (704) 906-7776. **E-Mail Address:** hhampton@scbl.org. **Website:** www.scbl.org.
Year Founded: 1999.
Chairman: Bill Capps, **Commissioner:** Harold Hampton. **President:** Jeff Carter. **Treasurer:** Brenda Templin.. **Umpire in Chief:** Gary Swanson.
Regular Season: 42 games. **Playoff Format:** Six-team single-elimination tournament with best of three championship series between final two teams.
Roster Limit: 35 (College-eligible players only).

GALAXY

Mailing Address: 7209 East WT Harris Blvd, Suite J #245, Charlotte, NC 28227. **Telephone:** (704) 668-9167. **Email Address:** baseballnbeyond@aol.com. **General Manager:** David "Doc" Booth. **Head Coach:** Jaylen Benjamin.

CONCORD ATHLETICS

Mailing Address: 366 George Lyles Parkway, Suite 125, Concord, NC 28027. **Telephone:** (704) 786-2255. **Email Address:** playconcordathletics@gmail.com. **General Manager:** David Darwin. **Head Coach:** Charles Weber

LAKE NORMAN COPPERHEADS

Mailing Address: 16405 Northcross Drive, Suite A Huntersville, NC 28078. **Telephone:** (704) 305-3649. **Email Address:** jcarter@copperheadsports.org. **General Manager:** Jeff Carter. **Head Coach:** TBA

PIEDMONT PRIDE

Mailing Address: 1524 Summit View Drive, Rock Hill, SC 29732. **Telephone:** (803) 412-7982. **E-Mail Address:** joe@pridebaseball.net. **General Manager:** Joe Hudak. **Head Coach:** Joe Hudak.

CAROLINA VIPERS

Mailing Address: 12104 Copper Way, Suite 200, Charlotte NC 28277. **Telephone:** 980-256-5346. **E-Mail Address:** bnichols@goviperbaseball.com. **General Manager:** Blaine Nichols. **Head Coach:** Aaron Bray

MOORSVILLE SPINNERS

Mailing Address: 2643 N Hwy 16 Denver, NC 28037. **Telephone:** (704) 491-4112. **E-Mail Address:** ploftin@mooresvillespinners.com. General Manager Phillip Loftin. **Head Coach:** David Newcomer

LINOIRE OILERS

Mailing Address: PO Box 1113 Icard NC 28666. Telephone 828-455-1289. **E-Mail Address:** LenoirOilers@gmail.com. General Manager Sara Wert. **Head Coach:** Ivan Acuna.

TEXAS COLLEGIATE LEAGUE

Mailing Address: 735 Plaza Blvd, Suite 200, Coppell, TX 75019. **Telephone:** (979) 985-5198. **Fax:** (979) 779-2398. **E-Mail Address:** info@tclbaseball.com. **Website:** www.texascollegiateleague.com. **Year Founded:** 2004. **President:** Uri Geva. **Roster Limit:** 30 (College-eligible players only)

ACADIANA CANE CUTTERS

Mailing Address: 221 La Neuville, Youngsville, LA 70592. **Telephone:** (337) 451-6582. **E-Mail Address:** info@cane cuttersbaseball.com. **Website:** www.canecuttersbaseball.com. **Owners:** Richard Chalmers, Sandi Chalmers. **General Manager:** Richard Haifley.

BRAZOS VALLEY BOMBERS

Mailing Address: 405 Mitchell St, Bryan, TX 77801. **Telephone:** (979) 799-7529. **Fax:** (440) 425-8592. **E-Mail Address:** info@bvbombers.com. **Website:** www.bv bombers.com. **Owners:** Uri Geva. **Managing Partner:** Chris Clark.

TEXAS MARSHALS

Mailing Address: 7920 Beltline Rd, Suite 1005 Dallas, TX 75254. **Telephone:** (214) 578-4388. **E-Mail Address:** info@texasmarshals.com. **Website:** www.texasmarshals.com. **Owner:** Marc Landry.

TEXARKANA TWINS

Ballpark: George Dobson Field, 4303 N Park Rd, Texarkana, TX 75503. **Telephone:** (903) 294-7529.

VICTORIA GENERALS

Mailing Address: 1307 E Airline Road, Suite H, Victoria, TX 77901. **Telephone:** (361) 485-9522. **Fax:** (361) 485-0936. **E-Mail Address:** info@baseballinvictoria.com, tkyoung@victoriagenerals.com. **Website:** www.victoria generals.com. **President:** Tracy Young. **VP/General Manager:** Mike Yokum.

VALLEY BASEBALL LEAGUE

Mailing Address: Valley Baseball League, PO Box 1127, New Market, VA 22844. **Telephone:** (540) 810-9194. **Fax:** (540) 435-8453. **E-Mail Addresses:** cbalger@shentel.net. **Website:** www.valleyleaguebaseball.com. **Year Founded:** 1897. **President:** C. Bruce Alger. **Assistant to the President:** Steve Shifflett. **Executive Vice President:** Jay Neal. **Media Relations Director:** Jimmy McCumber. **Secretary:** Stacy Locke. **Treasurer:** Ed Yoder. **Regular Season:** 42 games. **2018 Opening Date:** June 1. **Closing Date:** July 26. **All-Star Game:** North vs South, July 8 at Harrisonburg. **Playoff Format:** Eight teams qualify; play three rounds of best of three series. **Roster Limit:** 30 (college eligible players only)

COVINGTON LUMBERJACKS

Mailing Address: PO Box 30, Covington, VA 24426. **Telephone:** (540) 969-9923, (540) 962-1155. **Fax:** (540) 962-7153. **E-Mail Address:** covingtonlumberjacks@valley leaguebaseball.com. **Website:** www.lumberjacksbase ball.com. **President:** Dizzy Garten. **Head Coach:** Alex Kotheimer.

PURCELLVILLE CANNONS

Mailing Address: P.O. Box 114, Purcellville, VA 20132. **Telephone:** (540) 303-9673, (540) 327-9714. **Fax:** (304) 856-1619. **E-Mail Address:** bigdaddy432@verizon.net. **Website:** www.purcellvillecannons.com. **President:** Brett Fuller. **Recruiting Coordinator:** Brett Fuller. **General Manager:** Ridge Fuller. **Head Coach:** Brett Fuller.

CHARLOTTESVILLE TOM SOX

Mailing Address: P. O. Box 166, Ivy, Virginia 22945-0166. **Telephone:** (703)282-4425. **E-Mail:** contact@tom-sox.com. **Website:** www.TomSox.com. **President:** Greg Allen. **General Manager:** Mike Paduano. **Head Coach:** Cory Hunt.

FRONT ROYAL CARDINALS

Mailing Address: 382 Morgans Ridge Road, Front Royal, VA 22630. **Telephone:** (703) 244-6662, (540) 905-0152. **E-Mail Address:** DonnaSettle@centurylink.net. frontroyalcardinals@valleyleaguebaseball.com. **Website:** www.valleyleaguebaseball.com. **President:** Donna Settle. **Head Coach:** Zeke Mitchem.

HARRISONBURG TURKS

Mailing Address: 1489 S Main St, Harrisonburg, VA 22801. **Telephone:** (540) 434-5919. **Fax:** (540) 434-5919. **E-Mail Address:** turksbaseball@hotmail.com. **Website:** www.harrisonburgturks.com. **Operations Manager:** Teresa Wease. **General Manager/Head Coach:** Bob Wease.

NEW MARKET REBELS

Mailing Address: PO Box 902, New Market, VA 22844. **Telephone:** (540) 435-8453. **Fax:** (540) 740-9486. **E-Mail Address:** nmrebels@shentel.net. **Website:** www.new-marketrebels.com. **President/General Manager:** Bruce Alger. **Head Coach:** Zac Cole.

STAUNTON BRAVES

Mailing Address: PO Box 428, Stuarts Draft, VA 24447. **Telephone:** (443) 250-2657. **Fax:** (540) 886-0905. **E-Mail Address:** sbraves@hotmail.com. **Website:** www.stauntonbravesbaseball.com. **General Manager:** Steve Cox. **Head Coach:** Nolan Neiman.

STRASBURG EXPRESS

Mailing Address: PO Box 417, Strasburg, VA 22657. **Telephone:** (540) 325-5677, (540) 459-4041. **Fax:** (540) 459-3398. **E-Mail Address:** neallaw@shentel.net. **Website:** www.strasburgexpress.com. **General Manager:** Jay Neal. **Head coach:** Anthony Goncalves.

WAYNESBORO GENERALS

Mailing Address: 3144 Village Drive, Waynesboro, VA 22980. **Telephone:** (540) 241-0065. **Fax:** (540) 932-2322. **E-Mail Address:** waynesborogenerals@valleyleaguebase-ball.com. **Website:** www.waynesboro generals.com. **Chairman:** Brent Ward. **Head Coach:** John Jeanes.

WINCHESTER ROYALS

Mailing Address: PO Box 2485, Winchester, VA 22604. **Telephone:** (540) 539-8888, (540) 664-3978. **Fax:** (540) 662-1434. **E-Mail Addresses:** winchesterroyals@valley leaguebaseball.com, jimphill@shentel.net. **Website:** www.winchesterroyals.com. **President:** Donna Turrill. **Operations Director:** Jimmie Shipp. **Coach:** Jacob Mays.

WOODSTOCK RIVER BANDITS

Mailing Address: P.O. Box 227, Woodstock, VA 22664. **Telephone:** (540) 481-0525. **Fax:** (540) 459-8227. **E-Mail Address:** woodstockriverbandits@valleyleaguebaseball. com. **Website:** www.woodstockriverbandits.org. **General Manager:** R.W. Bowman Jr. **Head Coach:** Greg Keaton.

WEST COAST LEAGUE

Mailing Address: PO Box 794 Bellevue, WA 98009. **Telephone:** 425-238-4660. **E-Mail Address:** info@west coastleague.com. **Website:** www.westcoastleague.com.

Year Founded: 2005.

President: Tony Bonacci. **Vice President:** Glenn Kirkpatrick. **Secretary:** Jim Corcoran. **Treasurer:** Dan Segel. Supervisor, **Umpires:** Dave Perez.

Division Structure: South—Bend Elks, Corvallis Knights, Cowlitz Black Bears, Portland Pickles, Walla Walla Sweets. **North**—Bellingham Bells, Kelowna Falcons, Port Angeles Lefties, Victoria Harbourcats, Wenatchee Applesox, Yakima Valley Pippins.

2018 Opening Date: June 1. **Closing Date:** August 8. **Playoff Format:** Four-team tournament.

Roster Limit: 35 (college-eligible players only).

BELLINGHAM BELLS

Mailing Address: 1221 Potter Street, Bellingham, WA 98229. **Telephone:** (360) 527-1035. **E-Mail Address:** stephanie@bellinghambells.com. **Website:** www.bell-inghambells.com. **Owner:** Glenn Kirkpatrick. **General Manager:** Stephanie Morrell. **Head Coach:** Bob Miller. **Assistant Coaches:** Jim Clem, Jake Whisler, Darrien Moran.

BEND ELKS

Mailing Address: 70 SW Century Dr Suite 100-373 Bend, Oregon 97702. **Telephone:** (541) 312-9259. **Website:** www.bendelks.com. **Owners:** John and Tami Marick. **Marketing and Sales:** Kelsie Hirko. **General Manager:** Michael Hirko.

Head Coach: Alan Embree.

CORVALLIS KNIGHTS

Mailing Address: PO Box 1356, Corvallis, OR 97339. **Telephone:** (541) 752-5656. **E-Mail Address:** dan.segel@ corvallisknights.com. **Website:** www.corvallisknights. com. **President:** Dan Segel. **General Manager:** Bre Miller.

Head Coach: Brooke Knight. **Associate Head Coach/ Pitching Coach:** Ed Knaggs. **Assistant Coach:** Youngjin Yoon, Kellen Camus..COWLITZ BLACK BEARS

Mailing Address: PO Box 1255, Longview, WA 98632. **Telephone:** (360) 703-3195.

Website: www.cowlitzblackbears.com. **Owner/ President:** Tony Bonacci. **General Manager:** Jim Appleby.

Head Coach: Grady Tweit. **Assistant Coaches:** Jason Mackey, Michael Forgione.

KELOWNA FALCONS

Mailing Address: 201-1014 Glenmore Dr, Kelowna, BC, V1Y 4P2. **Telephone:** (250) **763-4100.Website:** www.kelownafalcons.com. **Owner:** Dan Nonis. **General Manager:** Mark Nonis.

Head Coach: Bryan Donohue.

PORT ANGELES LEFTIES

Mailing Address: PO Box 2204, Port Angeles, WA 98362. **Phone:** (360) 797-1151. **Website:** www.lefties-baseball.com. **Owners:** Matt Acker, Jacob Oppelt.

General Manager: Ryan Hickey.

Head Coach: Darren Westergard.

PORTLAND PICKLES

Address: 5308 SE 92nd Ave. Portland, OR 97266. **Phone:** (503) 390-2225. **Owners:** Alan Miller, Bill Stewart, Jon Ryan, Scott Barchus. **Director of Baseball Operations:** Gregg Swenson.

Head Coach: Justin Barchus. **Assistant Coach:** Mark Magdaleno.

VICTORIA HARBOURCATS

Mailing Address: 101-1814 Vancouver Street, Victoria, BC, Canada, V8T 5E3. **Telephone:** (778) 265-0327. **Website:** www.harbourcats.com. **Owners:** Rich Harder, Jim Swanson, Ken Swanson, John Wilson.

Managing Partner: Jim Swanson. **General Manager:** Brad Norris-Jones.

Head Coach: Brian McRae. **Assistant Coaches:** Ian Sanderson, Todd Haney, Troy Birtwistle, Jason Leone.

WALLA WALLA SWEETS

Mailing Address: 109 E Main Street, Walla Walla, WA 99362. **Telephone:** (509) 522-2255. **E-Mail Address:** info@wallawallasweets.com. **Website:** www.wallawalla sweets.com. **Owner:** Pacific Baseball Ventures, LLC.

President/COO: Zachary Fraser. **General Manager:** Dan Ferguson.

Head Coach: Frank Mutz. **Assistant Coaches:** Raul Camacho, Kyle Wilkerson.

WENATCHEE APPLESOX

Mailing Address: 610 N. Mission St. #204, Wenatchee, WA 98801. **Telephone:** (509) 665-6900. **E-Mail Address:** info@applesox.com. **Website:** www.applesox.com. **Owner/General Manager:** Jim Corcoran. **Owner/ Assistant General Manager:** Ken Osborne.

Head Coach: Kyle Krustangel.

YAKIMA VALLEY PIPPINS

Mailing Address: 1301, S. Fair Avenue, Shattuck Bldg., Yakima, WA 98908. **Telephone:** (509) 575-4487. **E-Mail Address:** info@pippinsbaseball.com. **Website:** www. pippinsbaseball.com. **Owner:** Pacific Baseball Ventures, LLC.

President/COO: Zachary Fraser. **General Manager:** Jeff Garretson.

Head Coach: Marcus McKimmy. **Assistant Coaches:** Bob Wells, Eric Hull, Jaime Cortes

HIGH SCHOOL BASEBALL

NATIONAL FEDERATION OF STATE HIGH SCHOOL ASSOCIATIONS

Mailing Address: PO Box 690, Indianapolis, IN 46206. **Telephone:** (317) 972-6900. **Fax:** (317) 822-5700. **E-Mail Address:** baseball@nfhs.org. **Website:** www.nfhs.org.

Executive Director: Bob Gardner. **Chief Operating Officer:** Davis Whitfield. **Director of Sports, Sanctioning and Student Services:** B. Elliot Hopkins. **Director, Publications/Communications:** Bruce Howard.

NATIONAL HIGH SCHOOL BASEBALL COACHES ASSOCIATION

Mailing Address: PO Box 12843, Tempe, AZ 85284. **Telephone:** (602) 615-0571. **Fax:** (480) 838-7133. **E-Mail Address:** rdavini@cox.net. **Website:** www.baseball coaches.org. **Executive Director:** Tim Saunders. **Executive Secretary:** Robert Colburn (St. Andrews's School, New Castle, DE. **President:** Mel Gardner (Delaware BCA President, New Castle, DE). **First Vice President:** Tony Perkins, (Howell HS MO). **Second Vice President:** Tim Bordenet, (Central Catholic Jr.-Sr. High, Ind.).

2018 National Convention: Nov. 29-Dec. 2 in St. Louis, Ill.

NATIONAL TOURNAMENTS

IN-SEASON

HORIZON NATIONAL INVITATIONAL

Mailing Address: Horizon High School, 5653 Sandra Terrace, Scottsdale, AZ 85254. **Telephone:** (602) 291-1952. **E-mail:** huskycoach2@gmail.com. **Website:** www.hori-zonbaseball.com.

Tournament Director: Eric Kibler.
2018 Tournament: March 12-15.

INTERNATIONAL PAPER CLASSIC

Mailing Address: 4775 Johnson Rd., Georgetown, SC 29440. **Telephone:** (843) 527-9606. **Fax:** (843) 546-8521. **Website:** www.ipclassic.com.

Tournament Director: Alicia Johnson.
2018 Tournament: March 1-4.

44TH ANNUAL ANAHEIM LIONS CLUB BASEBALL TOURNAMENT

Mailing Address: 8281 Walker Street, La Palma, CA 90623. **Telephone:** (714) 220-4101x27502. **Fax:** (714) 995-1833. **Email:** Pascal_C@AUHSD.US. **Website:** www.anaheimlionstourney.com.

Tournament Director: Chris Pascal.
2018 Tournament: March 24-28 (86 teams).

NATIONAL CLASSIC BASEBALL TOURNAMENT

Mailing Address: 1651 Valencia Ave, Placentia, CA 92870. **Telephone:** (714) 993-2838. **Fax:** (714) 993-5350. **E-Mail Address:** mlucas@pylusd.org. **Website:** www.national-classic.com.

Tournament Director: Matt Lucas.
2018 Tournament: April 2-5.

USA BASEBALL NATIONAL HIGH SCHOOL INVITATIONAL

Mailing Address: 1030 Swabia Ct., Suite 201; Durham, NC 27703. **Telephone:** (919) 474-8721. **Fax:** (919) 474-8822. **Email:** mattblood@usabaseball.com. **Website:** www.usabaseball.com.

Tournament Director: Matt Blood.
2018 Tournament: March 28-31 at USA Baseball National Training Complex, Cary, NC (16 teams).

POSTSEASON

ALL-STAR GAMES/AWARDS
PERFECT GAME ALL-AMERICAN CLASSIC

Mailing Address: 850 Twixt Town Rd. NE, Cedar Rapids, IA 52402. **Telephone:** (319) 298-2923. Fax (319) 298-2924. **Event Organizer:** Blue Ridge Sports & Entertainment. **VP, Showcases/Scouting:** Greg Sabers.

2018 Game: Aug. 12 at Petco Park, San Diego.

UNDER ARMOUR ALL-AMERICA GAME, POWERED BY BASEBALL FACTORY

Mailing Address: 9212 Berger Rd., Suite 200, Columbia, MD 21046. **Telephone:** (410) 715-5080. **E-mail Address:** jason@factoryathletics.com. **Website:** baseball factory.com/AllAmerica. **Event Organizers:** Baseball Factory, Team One Baseball.

2018 Game: Summer, TBD.

GATORADE CIRCLE OF CHAMPIONS

(National HS Player of the Year Award)

Mailing Address: The Gatorade Company, 321 N. Clark St., Suite 24-3, Chicago, IL, 60610. **Telephone:** (312) 821-1000. **Website:** www.gatorade.com.

SHOWCASE EVENTS

AREA CODE BASEBALL GAMES PRESENTED BY NEW BALANCE
Mailing Address: 23954 Madison Street, Torrance, CA 90505. **Telephone:** (310) 791-1142 x 4426. **E-Mail:** baseball@studentsports.com. **Website:** AreaCodeBaseball.com.
Event Organizer: Kirsten Leetch.
2018 Area Code Games: Aug. 6-10 at Blair Field in Long Beach, Calif.

AREA CODE BASEBALL UNDERCLASS GAMES PRESENTED BY NEW BALANCE
Event Organizer: Kirsten Leetch.
2018 Area Code Games: Aug. 10-12 at MLB Youth Academy in Compton, Calif.

ARIZONA FALL CLASSIC
Mailing Address: 9962 W. Villa Hermosa, Peoria, AZ 85383. **Telephone:** (602) 228-1592.
E-mail Address: azfallclassic@gmail.com.
Website: www.azfallclassic.com.
President: Tracy Heid
Event Director: Trevor Heid,
Information Directors: Tiffini Robinson, Tiana Eves

2018 EVENTS

Four Corner Classic............ Peoria, AZ, May 31-June 3

California Classic Qualifiers:

Freshman.................................August 10-12
Sophomore.................................. August 3-5
Junior .... July 20-22
Senior ....June 8-10
SoCal Locations TBA

AZ Freshman
Fall Classic (class of 2022) .... Peoria, AZ, Sept. 27-30

AZ Sophomore
Fall Classic (class of 2021) .... Peoria, AZ, Oct. 4-7

AZ Senior
Fall Classic (class of 2019) .... Peoria, AZ, Oct. 10-14

Senior All Academic Tryout & Game .... Oct. 11

Junior College All Star Series .... Oct. 11-13

AZ Junior
Fall Classic (class of 2020) .... Peoria, AZ , Oct. 18-21

Junior All Academic Tryout & Game............... Oct. 18

Universal Fall Classic .... Peoria, AZ, Oct. 25-28

BASEBALL FACTORY
Office Address: 9212 Berger Rd., Suite 200, Columbia, MD 21046. **Telephone:** (800) 641-4487, (410) 715-5080. **Fax:** (410) 715-1975. **E-mail Address:** info@baseballfactory.com. **Website:** www.baseballfactory.com.
Chief Executive Officer/Founder: Steve Sclafani. **President:** Rob Naddelman. **Chief Program Officer:** Jim Gemler. **Executive VP, Baseball Operations/Chairman, Under Armour All-America Game Selection Committee:** Steve Bernhardt. **Senior VP, Player Development:** Dan Forester. **VP, Tournament Division:** Justin Roswell. **VP, Business Development:** Dave Packer. **VP, Marketing/Brand:** Dave Lax. **Executive Director, College Recruiting:** Dan Mooney. **Senior Multimedia Producer:** Brian Johnson. **Senior Director, Web Development:** Wei Xue. **Senior Director, Event Experience:** Ryan Liddle. **Senior Director, Baseball Player Development Events:** Nolan Fuller. **Senior Director, Under Armour Baseball Factory National Tryouts:** Geoff Lang.
Executive Player Development Coordinator: Steve Nagler. **Senior Player Development Coordinators:** Adam Darvick, John Perko. **Senior Regional Player Development Coordinators:** Chris Brown, Rob Onolfi. **Regional Player Development Coordinators:** Robert Appleby, Ed Bach, Chris Brown, Josh Eldridge, Corson Fidler, Josh Hippensteel, Jane Lukas, David O'Neil, Julia Rice, Jesse Tome, Patrick Wuebben. **Director of College Recruiting:** Matt Richter.
Director, Athlete & Family Experience: Danielle Lawson. **Director, Social Media/Web Content:** Matt Lund. **Director of Player Development at FDI:** Mike Landis. **Director, Retail & Team Sales:** Lindsey Gutridge & Kevin Heinrich. **Director, Factory Athletics Foundation:** Emma Connor.

Under Armour All-America
Pre-Season Tournament...........Jan. 12-14, Mesa, Ariz.
(Sloan Park, Spring Training Home of the Chicago Cubs).

Under Armour
All-America Game.........................Summer, TBD

2018 Under Armour Baseball Factory National Tryouts/College PREP Recruiting Program: Year round at various locations across the country. Open to high school players, ages 14–18, with a separate division for middle school players, ages 12–14. **Full schedule:** www.baseballfactory.com/tryouts.

EAST COAST PROFESSIONAL SHOWCASE
Website: www.eastcoastpro.org. **Mailing Address:** Hoover Met Complex, 100 Ben Chapman Dr, Hoover, AL 25244. **E-mail Address:** info@eastcoastpro.org
Tournament Directors: John Castleberry, Rich Sparks, Sean Gibbs, Arthur McConnehead, Lori Bridges.
2018 Showcase: Aug. 1-4, Hoover Met Complex, 100 Ben Chapman Dr., Hoover, AL 35244.

IMPACT BASEBALL
Mailing Address: P.O. Box 47, Sedalia, NC 27342. **E-mail Address:** impactbaseballstaff@gmail.com. **Website:** impactbaseball.com. **Founder/CEO:** Andy Partin. **2018 Events:** Various dates, May-Aug. 2018.

NORTHWEST CHAMPIONSHIPS
Mailing Address: 9849 Fox Street, Aumsville, OR 97325. **Telephone:** (503) 302-7117. **E-mail Address:** joshuapwarner@gmail.com. **Website:** www.baseballnorthwest.com. **Tournament Organizer:** Josh Warner.

2018 EVENTS

Senior Northwest
Championship Tournament
(2019-2021 grads) in Centralia, WA ....Aug. 9-12

Junior Northwest
Championship Tournament
(2022-2023 grads) in Centralia, WA ....Aug. 16-19

PERFECT GAME USA

(A Division of Perfect Game USA)

Mailing Address: 850 Twixt Town Rd. NE, Cedar Rapids, IA 52402. **Telephone:** (319) 298-2923. **Fax:** (319) 298-2924. **E-mail Address:** pgba@perfectgame.org. **Website:** www.perfectgame.org.

Year Founded: 1997.

President: Jerry Ford. **VP, Operations:** Taylor McCollough. **VP, Showcases/Scouting:** Greg Sabers.

PROFESSIONAL BASEBALL INSTRUCTION—BATTERY INVITATIONAL

(for top high school pitchers and catchers)

Mailing Address: 12 Wright Way, Oakland NJ 07436. **Telephone:** (800) 282-4638. **Fax:** (201) 760-8820. **E-mail Address:** info@baseballclinics.com. **Website:** www.baseballclinics.com/battery-invitational/

President: Doug Cinnella.

Director of PR/Marketing/Social Media: Jim Monaghan.

Event Date: Nov. 3, 2018.

SELECTFEST BASEBALL

Mailing Address: P.O. Box 852, Morris Plains, NJ 07950. **E-mail Address:** selectfest@optonline.net. **Web site:** www.selectfestbaseball.org. **Camp Directors:** Bruce Shatel, Robert Maida.

2018 Showcase: June 23-25.

TEAM ONE BASEBALL

(A division of Baseball Factory)

Office Address: 220 Newport Center Drive, 11418, Newport Beach, CA 92660. **Telephone:** (800) 621-5452, (805) 451-8203. **Fax:** (949) 209-1829. **E-Mail Address:** jroswell@teamonebaseball.com. **Website:** www.teamonebaseball.com.

Executive Director: Justin Roswell. **Chief Program Officer:** Jim Gemler. **Executive VP:** Steve Bernhardt. **Senior VP, Player Development:** Dan Forester.

2018 Under Armour Showcases:

UA West Showcase . . . . June 2-3, Southern California

UA South Showcase . . . . June 5-6, Atlanta, GA

UA Texas Showcase . . . . June 9-10, Houston, TX

UA Florida Showcase . . . . June 12-13, Florida

For a full listing of showcases visit www.teamonebaseball.com/showcases.

2018 Under Armour Tournaments:

Under Armour Memorial Day Classic . . . . May 25-28
Jupiter, FL (Roger Dean Sports Complex)

Under Armour Father's Day Classic . . . . June 15–18
La Verne, CA (University of La Verne)

Under Armour 4th of July Classic . . . . June 29 –July 3
La Verne, CA (University of La Verne)

Under Armour Firecracker Classic . . . . July 6-10

Jupiter, FL (Roger Dean Sports Complex)

Under Armour
Southwest Championships 16U . . . . July 13-17
in La Verne, CA (University of La Verne)

Under Armour
Southwest Championships 17U . . . . July 20 – July 24
La Verne, CA (University of La Verne)

Under Armour Fall Classic . . . . September 15–16
Jupiter, FL (Roger Dean Sports Complex)

Under Armour Invitational . . . . October 14–15
St. Petersburg, FL (Walter Fuller Complex)

Under Armour SoCal Classic Underclass . . .October 19–21
La Verne, CA (University of La Verne)

Under Armour SoCal Classic Upperclass . . .October 26-28
La Verne, CA (University of La Verne).

For a full listing of tournaments visit www.teamonebaseball.com/tournaments.

TOP 96 COLLEGE COACHES CLINICS

Mailing Address: 6 Foley Dr. Southboro, MA 01772. **Telephone:** (508) 481-5935.

E-mail Address: doug.henson@top96.com. **Website:** www.top96.com. **Directors:** Doug Henson, Dave Callum.

YOUTH BASEBALL

ALL AMERICAN AMATEUR BASEBALL ASSOCIATION

Mailing Address: 607 East 25th Ave, Altoona, PA 16601. **Cell:** (814) 931-8698.
E-Mail Address: aaabaprez@atlanticbb.net.
Website: aaabajohnstown.org
President: John Austin
Executive Director: John Austin
2018 Events: AAABA National Tournament August 6-11 in Johnstown PA.

AMATEUR ATHLETIC UNION OF THE UNITED STATES, INC.

Mailing Address: P.O. Box 22409, Lake Buena Vista, FL 32830. **Telephone:** (407) 828-3459. **Fax:** (407) 934-7242.
E-mail Address: tmeyer@aausports.org. **Website:** www.aaubaseball.org.
Year Founded: 1982. **Senior Sport Manager, Baseball:** Tim Meyer.

AMERICAN AMATEUR BASEBALL CONGRESS

National Headquarters: 100 West Broadway, Farmington, NM 87401. **Telephone:** (505) 327-3120. **Fax:** (505) 327-3132. **E-mail Address:** aabc@aabc.us. **Website:** www.aabc.us.
Year Founded: 1935.
President: Richard Neely.

AMERICAN AMATEUR YOUTH BASEBALL ALLIANCE

Mailing Address: 3851 Iris Lane, Bonne Terre, MO 63628. **Telephone:** (314) 650-0028. **E-mail Address:** info@aayba.com. **Website:** www.aayba.com.
President, Baseball Operations: Carroll Wood.
President, Business Operations: Greg Moore.

AMERICAN LEGION BASEBALL

National Headquarters: American Legion Baseball, 700 N Pennsylvania St., Indianapolis, IN 46204.
Telephone: (317) 630-1213. **Fax:** (317) 630-1369. **E-mail Address:** baseball@legion.org. **Website:** www.legion.org/baseball.
Year Founded: 1925.
Program Coordinator: Steve Cloud.
2018 World Series (19 and under): Aug. 10-15 at Keeter Stadium, Shelby, N.C. 2018 Regional Tournaments (Aug. 8-12): **Northeast**—Shrewsbury, Mass.; Mid-**Atlantic**—Leesburg, Va.; **Southeast**—Asheboro, N.C.; Mid-**South**—New Orleans, La.; **Great Lakes**—Napoleon, Ohio.; **Central Plains**—Dickinson, N.D.; **Northwest**—Missoula, Mont.; **West**—Denver, Col.

BABE RUTH BASEBALL

International Headquarters: 1670 Whitehorse-Mercerville Rd., Hamilton, NJ 08619. **Telephone:** (609) 695-1434. **Fax:** (609) 695-2505. **E-mail Address:** info@baberuthleague.org. **Website:** www.baberuthleague.org.
Year Founded: 1951.
President/Chief Executive Officer: Steven Tellefsen.

BASEBALL FOR ALL

Mailing Address: 30745 Pacific Coast Hwy #328 Los Angeles, CA 90265. **E-mail Address:** girlsbaseball@baseballforall.com. **Website:** BaseballForAll.com
Providing baseball programming for girls.

BASEBALL USA

Mailing Address: 2626 West Sam Houston Pkwy. N., Houston, TX 77043. **Telephone:** (713) 690-5564. **E-mail Address:** info@baseballusa.com. **Website:** www.baseballusa.com.
President: Jason Krug.

CALIFORNIA COMPETITIVE YOUTH BASEBALL

Mailing Address: P.O. Box 338, Placentia, CA 92870. **Telephone:** (714) 993-2838. **E-mail Address:** ccybnet@gmail.com. **Website:** www.ccyb.net.
Tournament Director: Todd Rogers.

COCOA EXPO SPORTS CENTER

Mailing Address: 500 Friday Road, Cocoa, FL 32926. **Telephone:** (321) 639-3976. **Fax:** (407) 390-9435.
E-mail Address: brad@cocoaexpo.com. **Website:** www.cocoaexpo.com.
Activities: Spring training program, spring & fall leagues, instructional camps, team training camps, youth tournaments.

CONTINENTAL AMATEUR BASEBALL ASSOCIATION

Mailing Address: P.O. Box 1684 Mt. Pleasant, SC 29465. **Telephone:** (843) 860-1568. Fax: (843) 856-7791.
E-mail Address: Diamonddevils@aol.com. **Website:** www.cababaseball.com.
Year Founded: 1984.
Chief Executive Officer: Larry Redwine. **President/COO:** John Rhodes. **Executive Vice President:** Fran Pell.

COOPERSTOWN BASEBALL WORLD

Mailing Address: P.O. Box 646, Allenwood, NJ 08720. **Telephone:** (888) CBW-8750. **Fax:** (888) CBW-8720.
E-mail: cbw@cooperstownbaseballworld.com. **Website:** www.cooperstownbaseballworld.com.
Complex Address: Cooperstown Baseball World, SUNY-Oneonta, Ravine Parkway, Oneonta, NY 13820.
President: Debra Sirianni.
2018 Tournaments (15 Teams Per Week): Open to 12U, 13U, 14U, 15U, 16U

COOPERSTOWN DREAMS PARK

Mailing Address: 330 S. Main St., Salisbury, NC 28144. **Telephone:** (704) 630-0050. **Fax:** (704) 630-0737. **E-mail Address:** info@cooperstowndreamspark.com. **Website:** www.cooperstowndreamspark.com.
Complex Address: 4550 State Highway 28, Milford, NY 13807.
Chief Executive Officer: Louis Presutti. **Director, Baseball Operations:** Geoff Davis.
2018 Tournaments: June 2-Aug. 18.

COOPERSTOWN ALL STAR VILLAGE

Mailing Address: P.O. Box 670, Cooperstown, NY 13326. **Telephone:** (800) 327-6790. **Fax:** (607) 432-1076. **E-mail Address:** info@cooperstownallstarvillage.com. **Website:** www.cooperstownallstarvillage.com.

Team Registrations: Hunter Grace. Hotel Room **Reservations:** Tracie Jones & Virginia Perez. **Presidents:** Martin and Brenda Patton.

DIXIE YOUTH BASEBALL

Mailing Address: P.O. Box 877, Marshall, TX 75671. **Telephone:** (903) 927-2255. **Fax:** (903) 927-1846. **E-mail Address:** dyb@dixie.org. **Website:** youth.dixie.org.

Year Founded: 1955.
Commissioner: Wes Skelton.

DIXIE BOYS BASEBALL

Mailing Address: P.O. Box 8263, Dothan, AL 36304. **Telephone:** (334) 793-3331. **E-mail Address:** jjones29@sw.rr.com. **Website:** http://baseball.dixie.org.

Commissioner/Chief Executive Officer: Sandy Jones.

DIZZY DEAN BASEBALL

Mailing Address: P.O. Box 856, Hernando, MS 38632. **Telephone:** (662) 429-4365. **E-mail Address:** danny phillips637@gmail.com. **Website:** www.dizzydeanbbinc.org.

Year Founded: 1962.
Commissioner: Danny Phillips. **President:** Chris Landry. **VP:** Bobby Dunn. **Secretary:** Joe Chandler. **Treasurer:** Jim Dunn.

HAP DUMONT YOUTH BASEBALL

(A Division of the National Baseball Congress)
E-mail Address: bruce@prattrecreation.com, gbclev@hapdumontbaseball.com. **Website:** www.hapdumont baseball.com.

Year Founded: 1974.
President: Bruce Pinkall

KC SPORTS TOURNAMENTS

Mailing Address: KC Sports, 6324 N. Chatham Ave., No. 136, Kansas City, MO 64151. **Telephone:** (816) 587-4545. **Fax:** (816) 587-4549. **E-mail Address:** info@kcsports.org. **Website:** www.kcsports.org. **Activities:** USSSA Youth tournaments (ages 6-18).

LITTLE LEAGUE BASEBALL

International Headquarters: 539 US Route 15 Hwy, P.O. Box 3485, Williamsport, PA 17701-0485. **Telephone:** (570) 326-1921. **Fax:** (570) 326-1074. **Website:** www. littleleague.org.

Year Founded: 1939.
Chairman: Hugh E. Tanner.
President/Chief Executive Officer: Stephen D. Keener. **Chief Financial Officer:** David Houseknecht. **Vice President, Operations:** Patrick Wilson. **Treasurer:** Melissa Singer. **Vice President, Marketing and Communications:** Liz Brown.

NATIONS BASEBALL-ARIZONA

Mailing Address: 5160 W Glenview Pl, Chandler, AZ 85226. **Telephone:** (602) 793-8940. **Website:** new. nationsbaseballaz.com. **E-Mail:** Nationsbaseballarizona@gmail.com.

NATIONAL AMATEUR BASEBALL FEDERATION

Mailing Address: P.O. Box 705, Bowie, MD 20718. **Telephone:** (410) 721-4727. **Fax:** (410) 721-4940.

E-mail Address: nabf1914@aol.com.
Website: www.nabf.com.
Year Founded: 1914.
Executive Director: Charles Blackburn.

INSTRUCTIONAL SCHOOLS/ PRIVATE CAMPS

ALL-STAR BASEBALL ACADEMY

Mailing Address: 1475 Phoenixville Pike Suite 12, West Chester, PA 19380. **Telephone:** (484) 770-8325. **Fax:** (484) 770-8336. **E-mail Address:** basba@allstarbaseball academy.com. **Website:** www.allstarbaseballacademy. com. **President/CEO :** Jim Freeman. **Executive Director:** Mike Manning.

AMERICAN BASEBALL FOUNDATION

Mailing Address: 833 Saint Vincent's Drive Suite 205A, Birmingham, AL 35205. **Telephone:** (205) 558-4235. **Fax:** (205) 918-0800. **E-mail Address:** abf@asmi.org. **Website:** www.americanbaseballfoundation.com. **Executive Director:** David Osinski.

AMERICA'S BASEBALL CAMPS

Mailing Address: 3020 ISSQ Pine Lake Road #12, Sammamish, WA 98075. **Telephone:** (800) 222-8152. **Fax:** (888) 751-8989. **E-mail Address:** info@baseballcamps. com. **Website:** www.baseballcamps.com.

CHAMPIONS BASEBALL ACADEMY

Mailing Address: 5994 Linneman Street Cincinnati, OH 45230. **Telephone:** (513) 831-8873. **Fax:** (513) 247-0040. **E-mail Address:** information@ChampionsBaseball. net. **Website:** www.championsbaseball.net. **Director:** Mike Bricker.

DOYLE BASEBALL ACADEMY

Mailing Address: P.O. Box 9156, Winter Haven, FL 33883. **Telephone:** (863) 439-1000. **Fax:** (863) 294-8607. **E-mail Address:** info@doylebaseball.com.

Website: www.doylebaseball.com. **President:** Denny Doyle. **CEO:** Blake Doyle.

ELEV8 SPORTS INSTITUTE

Mailing Address: 490 Dotterel Road, Delray Beach, FL 33444. **Telephone:** (800) 970-5896. **Fax:** (561) 865-7358. **E-mail Address:** info@elev8si.com. **Website:** http:// elev8sportsinstitute.com/

FROZEN ROPES TRAINING CENTERS

Mailing Address: 24 Old Black Meadow Rd., Chester, NY 10918. **Telephone:** (845) 469-7331. **Fax:** (845) 469-6742. **E-mail Address:** info@frozenropes.com. **Website:** www.frozenropes.com.

IMG ACADEMY

Mailing Address: IMG Academy, 5500 34th St. W., Bradenton, FL 34210. **Telephone:** (941) 749-8627. **Fax:** 941-739-7484. **E-mail Address:** colbe.herr@img.com **Website:** www.imgacademy.com

MARK CRESSE BASEBALL SCHOOL

Mailing Address: P.O. Box 1596 Newport Beach, CA 92659. **Telephone:** (714) 892-6145. **Fax:** (714) 890-7017. **E-mail Address:** info@markcresse.com. **Website:** www. markcresse.com.

Owner/Founder: Mark Cresse.

US SPORTS CAMPS/NIKE BASEBALL CAMPS

Mailing Address: 1010 B Street Suite 450, San Rafael, CA 94901. **Telephone:** (415) 479-6060. **Fax:** (415) 479-6061. **E-mail Address:** baseball@ussportscamps.com. **Website:** www.ussportscamps.com/baseball/.

MOUNTAIN WEST BASEBALL ACADEMY

Mailing Address: 389 West 10000 South, South Jordan, UT 84095. **Telephone:** (801) 561-1700. **E-mail Address:** kent@utahbaseballacademy.com. **Website:** www.mountainwestbaseball.com. **Director:** Bob Keyes

NORTH CAROLINA BASEBALL ACADEMY

Mailing Address: 1137 Pleasant Ridge Road, Greensboro, NC 27409. **Telephone:** (336) 931-1118. **E-mail Address:** info@ncbaseball.com. **Website:** www. ncbaseball.com.

Owner/Director: Scott Bankhead.

PENNSYLVANIA DIAMOND BUCKS

Mailing Address: 2320 Whitetail Court, Hellertown, PA 18055. **Telephone:** (610) 838-1219, (610) 442-6998. **E-mail Address:** janciganick@yahoo.com. **Camp Director:** Jan Ciganick. **Head of Instruction:** Chuck Ciganick.

PROFESSIONAL BASEBALL INSTRUCTION

Mailing Address: 12 Wright Way, Oakland, NJ 07436. **Telephone:** (800) 282-4638. **Fax:** (201) 760-8820. **E-mail Address:** info@baseballclinics.com. **Website:** www.baseballclinics.com. **President:** Doug Cinnella.

RIPKEN BASEBALL CAMPS

Mailing Address: 1427 Clarkview Rd., Suite 100, Baltimore, MD 21209. **Telephone:** (410) 297-9292. **Fax:** (410) 823-0850. **E-mail Address:** information@ripken baseball.com. **Website:** www.ripkenbaseball.com.

SHO-ME BASEBALL CAMP

Mailing Address: P.O. Box 2270, Branson West, MO 65737. **Telephone:** (417) 338-5838. **Fax:** (417) 338-2610. **E-mail Address:** info@shomebaseball.com. **Website:** www.shomebaseball.com.

COLLEGE CAMPS

Almost all of the elite college baseball programs have summer/holiday instructional camps. Please consult the college section for listings.

SENIOR BASEBALL

MEN'S SENIOR BASEBALL LEAGUE

(18+, 25+, 35+, 45+, 55+, 65+)

Mailing Address: One Huntington Quadrangle, Suite 3N07, Melville, NY 11747. **Telephone:** (631) 753-6725. **Fax:** (631) 753-4031.

President: Steve Sigler. **Vice President:** Gary D'Ambrisi.

E-Mail Address: info@msblnational.com.
Website: www.msblnational.com.

MEN'S ADULT BASEBALL LEAGUE

(18 and Over)

Mailing Address: One Huntington Quadrangle, Suite 3N07, Melville, NY 11747. **Telephone:** (631) 753-6725. **Fax:** (631) 753-4031.

E-Mail Address: info@msblnational.com. **Website:** www.msblnational.com.

President: Steve Sigler. **Vice President:** Gary D'Ambrisi.

NATIONAL ADULT BASEBALL ASSOCIATION

Mailing Address: 5944 S. Kipling St., Suite 200, Littleton, CO 80127. **Telephone:** (800) 621-6479. **Fax:** (303) 639-6605. **E-Mail:** nabanational@aol.com. **Website:** www.dugout.org.

President: Shane Fugita.

NATIONAL AMATEUR BASEBALL FEDERATION

Mailing Address: P.O. Box 705, Bowie, MD 20718. **Telephone:** (410) 721-4727. **Fax:** (410) 721-4940.

Email Address: nabf1914@aol.com.
Website: www.nabf.com.
Year Founded: 1914.
Executive Director: Charles Blackburn.

ROY HOBBS BASEBALL

Veterans (30 or 35 and Over), Masters (45 and Over), Legends (53 and Over); Classics (60 and Over), Vintage (65 and Over), Timeless (70 and Over), Forever Young (75 and Over).

Mailing Address: 4301-A Edison Ave., Fort Myers, FL 33916. **Telephone:** (330) 923-3400. **Fax:** (330) 923-1967. **E-Mail Address:** rhbb@royhobbs.com. **Website:** www.royhobbs.com.

CEO: Tom Giffen. **President:** Rob Giffen.

DIRECTORIES

- **AGENT**
- **SERVICE**

AGENT DIRECTORY

ACES, INC.
188 Montague St.
Brooklyn, NY 11201
Phone: (718) 237-2900
Fax: (718) 522-3906
Web: www.acesincbaseball.com
E-mail: aces@acesinc1.com

PRO STAR MANAGEMENT INC.
1600 Scripps Center
Cincinatti, OH 45202
Phone: (513) 762-7676
Fax: (513) 721-4628
Web: www.prostarmanagement.com
E-mail: prostar@fuse.net
President: Joe Bick;
Executive Vice President: Brett Bick

SOSNICK COBBE & KARON
712 Bancroft Rd. #510
Walnut Creek, CA 94598
Phone: (925) 890-5283
Fax: (925) 476-0130
Web: www.SosnickCobbeKaron.com
E-mail: Info@SosnickCobbeKaron.com
Matt Sosnick, Paul Cobbe, Adam Karon, Jon
Einalhori, Matt Hofer, Jon Pridie, Tripper
Johnson, John Furmaniak

THE L. WARNER COMPANIES
9690 Deereco Road Ste 650
Timonium, MD 21093
Phone: (410) 252-0808
Fax: (443) 281-5554
Web: www.lwarner.com/baseball
E-mail: roliver@lwarner.com
Chairman and CEO: Lee Warner; President:
Rick Oliver

TLA WORLDWIDE
1500 Broadway, Ste 2501
New York, NY 10036
Phone: (212) 334-6880
Fax: (212) 334-6895
Web: www.tlaworldwide.com
E-mail: info@tlaworldwide.com
Peter E. Greenberg, Esq; Edward L.
Greenberg; Chris Leible; Eric Izen; Stephen
Veltman; Ed Cerulo

TLA WORLDWIDE
500 Newport Center Drive Ste 800
Newport Beach, CA 92660
Phone: (949) 720-8700
Fax: (949) 720-1331
Web: www.tlaworldwide.com
E-mail: info@tlaworldwide.com
Greg Genske, Brian Peters, Brodie Scoffield,
RJ Hernandez, Kenny Felder, Joe Brennan,
Joe Mizzo, Mike Maulini, Scott Parker

VERRILL DANA
SPORTS LAW GROUP
One Portland Square
Portland, ME 04101
Phone: (207) 774-4000
Web: www.verrilldana.com
E-mail: dabramson@verrilldana.com
David S. Abramson, Esq

SERVICE DIRECTORY

BASES

BEAM CLAY
One Kelsey Park
Great Meadows, NJ 07838
See our ad on the inside front cover!
Phone: (800) 247-BEAM (2326)
Fax: (908) 637-8421
Web: www.beamclay.com
E-mail: sales@beamclay.com

C&H BASEBALL, INC
10615 Technology Terrace #100
Lakewood Ranch, FL 34211
Phone: (941) 727-1533
Fax: (941) 462-3076
Web: www.chbaseball.com
E-mail: sales@chbaseball.com

BATTING CAGES

BALL FABRICS
510 West Arizona Ave.
Deland, FL 32720
Phone: (866) 360-1008
Fax: (386) 740-7206
Web: www.ballfabrics.com
E-mail: info@ballfabrics.com

BEAM CLAY
One Kelsey Park
Great Meadows, NJ 07838
See our ad on the inside front cover!
Phone: (800) 247-BEAM (2326)
Fax: (908) 637-8421
Web: www.beamclay.com
E-mail: sales@beamclay.com

C&H BASEBALL, INC
10615 Technology Terrace #100
Lakewood Ranch, FL 34211
Phone: (941) 727-1533
Fax: (941) 462-3076
Web: www.chbaseball.com
E-mail: sales@chbaseball.com

PROFESSIONAL BASEBALL INSTRUCTION
12 Wright Way
Oakland, NJ 7436
Phone: (201) 760-8720
Fax: (201)760-8820
Web: www.baseballclinics.com
E-mail: info@baseballclinics.com

WEST COAST NETTING, INC.
5075 Flightline Drive
Kingman, AZ 86401
Phone: (928) 692-1144
Fax: (928) 692-1501
Web: www.westcoastnetting.com

BATS

B45 BASEBALL
2200 Leon-Harmel Unit 4
Quebec City, QC G1N 4L2
Phone: (888) 669-0145
Web: www.b45baseball.com
E-mail: info@b45baseball.com

OLD HICKORY BAT COMPANY
P.O. Box 588
White House, TN 37188
Phone: (866) PRO-BATS
Fax: (615) 285-0512
Web: www.oldhickory.com
E-mail: mail@oldhickory.com

TRINITY BAT COMPANY
2493 E. Orangethorpe
Fullerton, CA 92831
Phone: (714) 449-1275
Fax: (714) 449 1285
Web: www.trinitybatco.com
E-mail: steve@trinitybatco.com

VIPER BATS INC
4807 Ivan Ln.
Sedro Woolley, WA 98284
Phone: (360) 630-5168
Web: www.viperbats.com
E-mail: sales@viperbats.com

BUNTING/PLEATED FANS/FLAGS

INDEPENDENCE BUNTING & FLAG CORP
44 West Jefryn Blvd. Ste T
Deer Park, NY 11729
Phone: (631) 761-6007
Fax: (888) 824-1060
Web: www.independence-bunting.com
E-mail: independencebunting@gmail.com

CAMPS/SCHOOLS

PROFESSIONAL BASEBALL INSTRUCTION
12 Wright Way
Oakland, NJ 7436
Phone: (201) 760-8720
Fax: (201)760-8820
Web: www.baseballclinics.com
E-mail: info@baseballclinics.com

CONCESSION OPERATIONS

BUSH BROTHERS & COMPANY
1016 E Weisgarber Rd.
Knoxville, TN 37909
Phone: (865) 450-4142
Fax: (865) 909-8670
Web: www.bushbeansfoodservice.com
E-mail: ehenry@bushbros.com

STADIUM1 SOFTWARE, LLC
13479 Polo Trace Drv.
Delray Beach, FL 33446
Phone: (561) 779-4040
Fax: (561) 498-8358
Web: www.stadium1.com
E-mail: tim.mcdulin@stadium1.com

CUP HOLDERS

CADDY PRODUCTS, INC.
73850 Dinah Shore Dr. # 115
Palm Desert, CA 92211
See our ad on the insert!
Phone: (800) 845-0591
Fax: (760) 770-1799
Web: www.caddyproducts.com
E-mail: info@caddyproducts.com

ENGINEERED BACKSTOP DESIGN BUILD

C&H BASEBALL, INC
10615 Technology Terrace #100
Lakewood Ranch, FL 34211
Phone: (941) 727-1533
Fax: (941) 462-3076
Web: www.chbaseball.com
E-mail: sales@chbaseball.com

ENTERTAINMENT

THE SKILLVILLE GROUP
P.O. Box 36061
Louisville, KY 40233
Phone: (800) 219-0899
Fax: (502) 458-0867
Web: www.theskillvillegroup.com
E-mail: info@theskillvillegroup.com

EMBROIDED SOURCE

THE EMBLEM SOURCE
4575 Westgrove #500
Addison, TX 75001
Phone: (972) 248-1909
Fax: (972) 248-1615
Web: www.theemblemsource.com
E-mail: larry@theemblemsource.com

FIELD COVERS/TARPS

BEAM CLAY
One Kelsey Park
Great Meadows, NJ 07838
See our ad on the inside front cover!
Phone: (800) 247-BEAM (2326)
Fax: (908) 637-8421
Web: www.beamclay.com
E-mail: sales@beamclay.com

C&H BASEBALL, INC
10615 Technology Terrace #100
Lakewood Ranch, FL 34211
Phone: (941) 727-1533
Fax: (941) 462-3076
Web: www.chbaseball.com
E-mail: sales@chbaseball.com

FIELD WALL PADDING

BEAM CLAY
One Kelsey Park
Great Meadows, NJ 07838
See our ad on the inside front cover!
Phone: (800) 247-BEAM (2326)
Fax: (908) 637-8421
Web: www.beamclay.com
E-mail: sales@beamclay.com

C&H BASEBALL, INC
10615 Technology Terrace #100
Lakewood Ranch, FL 34211
Phone: (941) 727-1533
Fax: (941) 462-3076
Web: www.chbaseball.com
E-mail: sales@chbaseball.com

WEST COAST NETTING, INC.
5075 Flightline Drive
Kingman, AZ 86401
Phone: (928) 692-1144
Fax: (928) 692-1501
Web: www.westcoastnetting.com

GLOVES

B45 BASEBALL
2200 Leon-Harmel Unit 4
Quebec City, QC G1N 4L2
Phone: (888) 669-0145
Web: www.b45baseball.com
E-mail: info@b45baseball.com

FORCE3 PRO GEAR
155 New Haven Ave.
Derby, CT 06418
Phone: (315) 367-2331
Fax: (866) 332-3492
Web: www.force3progear.com
E-mail: info@force3progear.com

INFLATABLES

HYPEFAN
3560 Morning Ivy Way
Suwanee, GA 30024
Phone: (404) 217-7933
Web: www.hypefan.com
E-mail: info@hypefan.com

LOCKERS

SUMMIT LOCKERS
138 McLeod Rd.
Columbia, SC 29203
Phone: (949) 795-0552
Web: summitlockers.com
E-mail: steve@summitlockers.com
Durable, Low Maintenance, Rust Proof,
Designer Stadium Lockers

MEMORABILIA

STEINER SPORTS
145 Huguenot St.
New Rochelle, NY 10801
Phone: (914) 307-1000
Fax: (914) 365-6428
Web: steinersports.com
E-mail: accountspayable@steinersports.com

MUSIC/SOUND EFFECTS

SOUND DIRECTOR INC.
2918 SW Royal Way
Gresham, OR 97080
Phone: (888) 276-0078
Fax: (503) 914-1812
Web: www.sounddirector.com
E-mail: info@sounddirector.com

NETTING/POSTS

BALL FABRICS
510 West Arizona Ave.
Deland, FL 32720
Phone: (866) 360-1008
Fax: (386) 740-7206
Web: www.ballfabrics.com
E-mail: info@ballfabrics.com

BEAM CLAY
One Kelsey Park
Great Meadows, NJ 07838
Phone: (800) 247-BEAM (2326)
Fax: (908) 637-8421
Web: www.beamclay.com
E-mail: sales@beamclay.com

See our ad on the inside front cover!

C&H BASEBALL, INC
10615 Technology Terrace #100
Lakewood Ranch, FL 34211
Phone: (941) 727-1533
Fax: (941) 462-3076
Web: www.chbaseball.com
E-mail: sales@chbaseball.com

COVERMASTER INC.
100 Westmore Dr. #11-D
Rexdale, ON M9V 5C3
Phone: (800) 387-5808
Fax: (800) 691-1181
Web: www.covermaster.com
E-mail: info@covermaster.com

WEST COAST NETTING, INC.
5075 Flightline Drive
Kingman, AZ 86401
Phone: (928) 692-1144
Fax: (928) 692-1501
Web: www.westcoastnetting.com

PLAYING FIELD PRODUCTS

BEAM CLAY
One Kelsey Park
Great Meadows, NJ 07838
Phone: (800) 247-BEAM (2326)
Fax: (908) 637-8421
Web: www.beamclay.com
E-mail: sales@beamclay.com

See our ad on the inside front cover!

C&H BASEBALL, INC
10615 Technology Terrace #100
Lakewood Ranch, FL 34211
Phone: (941) 727-1533
Fax: (941) 462-3076
Web: www.chbaseball.com
E-mail: sales@chbaseball.com

WEST COAST NETTING, INC.
5075 Flightline Drive
Kingman, AZ 86401
Phone: (928) 692-1144
Fax: (928) 692-1501
Web: www.westcoastnetting.com

PROFESSIONAL SERVICES

DONNA COHEN STRATEGIES
20 Willett Pond Dr.
Westwood, MA 02090
Phone: (617) 407-1755
E-mail: donnacohenstrategies@gmail.com

PROMOTIONAL ITEMS

HYPEFAN
3560 Morning Ivy Way
Suwanee, GA 30024
Phone: (404) 217-7933
Web: www.hypefan.com
E-mail: info@hypefan.com

PROTECTIVE EQUIPMENT

BEAM CLAY
One Kelsey Park
Great Meadows, NJ 07838
Phone: (800) 247-BEAM (2326)
Fax: (908) 637-8421
Web: www.beamclay.com
E-mail: sales@beamclay.com

See our ad on the inside front cover!

C&H BASEBALL, INC
10615 Technology Terrace #100
Lakewood Ranch, FL 34211
Phone: (941) 727-1533
Fax: (941) 462-3076
Web: www.chbaseball.com
E-mail: sales@chbaseball.com

FORCE3 PRO GEAR
155 New Haven Ave.
Derby, CT 06418
Phone: (315) 367-2331
Fax: (866) 332-3492
Web: www.force3progear.com
E-mail: info@force3progear.com

RADAR EQUIPMENT

POCKET RADAR
3535 Industrial Drive Ste A4
Santa Rosa, CA 95403
Phone: (888) 381-2672
Fax: (888) 381-2672
Web: www.pocketradar.com
E-mail: tscaturro@pocketradar.com

STALKER RADAR
855 E Collins Blvd.
Richardson, TX 75081
Phone: (800) STALKER
Fax: (972) 398-3871
Web: www.stalkersportsradar.com
E-mail: paul@stalkerradar.com

SEATING

SERIES SEATING
20900 NE 30th Ave. Ste 901
Miami, FL 33180
Phone: (305) 932-4626
Web: www.seriesseating.com
E-mail: sburgess@seriesseating.com

STADIUM SERVICES

ARENAS, PARKS & STADIUMS SOLUTIONS, INC.
45 Nicole Ln.
Wingdale, NY 12594
Phone: (917) 330-7630
Web: www.apssolutionsinc.com
E-mail: jessica@apssolutionsinc.com

TRAINING EQUIPMENT

WEST COAST NETTING, INC.
5075 Flightline Drive
Kingman, AZ 86401
Phone: (928) 692-1144
Fax: (928) 692-1501
Web: www.westcoastnetting.com

WINDSCREENS

BALL FABRICS
510 West Arizona Ave.
Deland, FL 32720
Phone: (866) 360-1008
Fax: (386) 740-7206
Web: www.ballfabrics.com
E-mail: info@ballfabrics.com

BEAM CLAY
One Kelsey Park
Great Meadows, NJ 07838
Phone: (800) 247-BEAM (2326)
Fax: (908) 637-8421
Web: www.beamclay.com
E-mail: sales@beamclay.com

See our ad on the inside front cover!

C&H BASEBALL, INC
10615 Technology Terrace #100
Lakewood Ranch, FL 34211
Phone: (941) 727-1533
Fax: (941) 462-3076
Web: www.chbaseball.com
E-mail: sales@chbaseball.com

COVERMASTER INC.
100 Westmore Dr. #11-D
Rexdale, ON M9V 5C3
Phone: (800) 387-5808
Fax: (800) 691-1181
Web: www.covermaster.com
E-mail: info@covermaster.com

YOUR NAME HERE. Make sure the baseball community can find you in 2019
Call 919-213-7924 or e-mail advertising@baseballamerica.com

MAJOR LEAGUE TEAMS

ANDREW WOOLLEY

MINOR LEAGUE TEAMS

ANDREW WOOLLEY

MINOR LEAGUE TEAMS, CONT.

INDEPENDENT TEAMS

ANDREW WOOLLEY

DIAMOND IMAGES

OTHER ORGANIZATIONS